COMPREHENSIVE
Graphic Arts

Third Edition

Ervin A. Dennis, Ed.D.
Professor
Department of Industrial Technology
University of Northern Iowa
Cedar Falls, Iowa

John D. Jenkins, Ed.D.
Professor
Department of Industrial Education and
Technology
Eastern Kentucky University
Richmond, Kentucky

GLENCOE

Macmillan/McGraw-Hill

Lake Forest, Illinois
Columbus, Ohio
Mission Hills, California
Peoria, Illinois

Send all inquiries to:
GLENCOE DIVISION
Macmillan/McGraw-Hill
3008 W. Willow Knolls Drive
Peoria, IL 61614-1083

ISBN 0-02-681251-7 (Student Text)
ISBN 0-02-681252-5 (Instructor's Guide)
ISBN 0-02-681253-3 (Student Workbook)

Printed in the United States of America.

2 3 4 5 6 7 8 9 10   AGK   99 98 97 96 95 94 93 92

Cover photo: Image Bank

PREFACE

This third edition of *Comprehensive Graphic Arts* has been extensively revised. The entire text of the second edition and all of its illustrations were reviewed in light of recent changes in graphic arts technology. Every effort has been made to produce a textbook that reflects the technologies currently used in the graphic arts industry. The popular short-unit format has been retained, for it provides an excellent organizational structure for the users of the text.

This new edition is divided into twenty-three sections. Each section contains four to sixteen units. Each unit explains in specific detail one aspect of the general area covered by the section. Within each section, the first unit provides a brief introduction to the section topic, and the final unit presents key terms, discussion topics, and meaningful activities. The units between discuss graphic arts technologies and procedures. This information will help the reader understand the major technological processes involved in the production of printed products.

Section 1 defines the graphic arts and surveys this increasingly important industry. Sections 2 and 3 show how to solve problems at the design and layout stage for efficient graphic reproduction. Sections 4, 5, and 6 explain and illustrate the techniques, including typesetting and imagesetting, used in copy preparation. Within these sections, important topic areas include proofing procedures and techniques for preparing camera-ready paste-ups. Photoconversion techniques are emphasized in Section 7. Here, process cameras and the use of high-contrast light-sensitive materials (including a discussion of photographic chemistry) are covered in detail.

Sections 8 through 15 describe the preparation of image carriers and the operation of the image transfer equipment used in the four major methods of printing: letterpress, lithography, gravure, and screen. Several units within these sections highlight safety practices and procedures concerning the proper handling of chemicals and operation of equip-ment. Imaging methods and equipment are also discussed in Section 16, which covers continuous-tone photography, and in Section 17, which covers duplicating and special printing processes.

Section 18 covers finishing and binding. Here a full unit again accents safety. The major product-finishing methods, including paper cutting methods and the common soft- and hardcover binding methods, are presented in step-by-step detail. The two most important materials necessary for graphic arts printed products—paper and ink—are featured in Sections 19 and 20. A study of graphic arts technology would not be complete without a detailed look at these two critical components of visual communications.

Section 21 presents important material concerning legal, moral, and ethical considerations for the printer. Section 22—which is new—discusses a major content area, *desktop composition*. Desktop composition has become a standard procedure in the graphic arts industry. Thus it is appropriate that it be covered in a separate section, which contains four complete units of information and learning experiences. Section 23 details the career opportunities available in the vast graphic arts and graphic communications industries. Two new units have been added to this concluding section. One discusses how to be a successful employee. The other discusses the excitement of entrepreneurship in the graphic arts industry.

The book is heavily illustrated and contains a second-emphasis color throughout its entirety. Several pages of four-color process printing help communicate essential information about selected graphic arts topics. Detailed instructions should promote readers' successful learning of graphic arts procedures from prepress through postpress operations. Equipment manuals and company literature should always be used to supplement and to provide up-to-date technological information about the rapidly changing graphic arts field.

Graphic arts technology is an exciting and

expanding field of knowledge. It offers many opportunities for interesting and rewarding careers. As authors and educators with more than sixty years of combined experience in graphic arts educational technology, we hope the readers of this book will become as fasci-

nated and excited about making it a lifelong career as we continue to be.

Ervin A. Dennis
John D. Jenkins

About the Authors

Dr. Ervin A. Dennis is a professor in the Department of Industrial Technology, University of Northern Iowa, Cedar Falls, Iowa. He has had a long and varied career in education, including over thirty years of teaching at the high school, college, and university levels. Dennis has authored and contributed to several other textbooks and publications about communications, graphic arts, and photography. He is an active member of several education and industry organizations.

Dr. John D. Jenkins is professor and Coordinator of Industrial Technology Programs, Department of Industrial Education and Technology, Eastern Kentucky University, Richmond, Kentucky. He has had graphic arts teaching experience for over thirty years at the high school and university levels. In addition to his contributions to several publications, he has been active in several local and national technology education associations.

ACKNOWLEDGMENTS

A book of this size and complexity would not be possible without the direct and indirect assistance of many people, companies, corporations, and associations. The authors especially wish to express appreciation to their immediate family members who provided considerable moral support throughout the lengthy revision process. Their wives, Mrs. B. LaVada Dennis and Mrs. Jerry Ann Jenkins, deserve a significant word of thanks for their assistance in making this and the previous two editions possible. Without their direct aid and understanding, this third edition would never have been completed.

During the preparation of the first and second editions, several people gave considerable effort to assist the authors. Among them were Dr. Chris H. Groneman, Mrs. Virginia Groneman, Dr. Darrel L. Smith, Dr. Claude Rieth, and Ms. Jean Michaelsen. Graphic arts industry personnel extending their valuable assistance were Mr. Alan Haley, Mr. Donald Marsden, Mr. David J. Barton, and Mr. George Dalente. A number of university graphic arts students, colleagues, and friends assisted with selected photographs used throughout the book. Our thanks to all of them.

Because graphic arts technology is advancing so rapidly, several industry personnel were asked to review selected sections and units for this third edition, and to recommend content for them. Their input greatly assisted the authors and lends considerable credibility to the entire book. These people, their companies, and the content involved are listed for the benefit of the users of this book: Ms. Cynthia J. D. Hollandsworth, Typographic Advisor, and Mr. Glen Rippel, Software Section Manager, both of AGFA Compugraphic Division, and Mr. Curits E. Leszczynski, Governmental/Education Specialist, Linotype Company, all reviewed and suggested content for the several composition and typesetting units. Mr. William E. Seaman, Vice President, Cameron Press Division of Somerset Technologies, Inc., contributed his expertise for the book production system unit.

Appreciation is also extended to these people for their valuable assistance: Mr. Alan R. Hunter, Vice President of Operations at J. W. Fergusson & Sons, Inc., and Mr. David A. Smith, Executive Vice President of Gravure Association of America, Inc., and Mr. Walter J. Zwarg, Gravure Consultant, for their critical review of the gravure-related content: Mr. Donald Marsden of Ulano Corporation, and Miss Anne T. Slamka, Pre-Press Product Manager at Advance Process Supply Co., for their extensive assistance with the screen printing units; Ms. Rose Marie Kenny, Publicity and Promotional Coordinator at Hammermill Papers, and Mr. John F. Westhoff, Manager of Advertising and Sales Promotion at Nekoosa Papers, Inc., for their noteworthy assistance with the pulp and paper manufacturing units.

Figure and text content was obtained from many sources. The authors and the publisher's editorial personnel are indebted to the following companies, corporations, and organizations for their valuable contributions:

A. B. Dick Company
AGFA Compugraphic
AM Multigraphics, division of AM International, Inc.
AM Varityper
Advance Process Supply
American Equipment, division of Advance Process Supply
American Paper Institute
American Printer and Lithographer
Apex Machine Company
Atlas Screen Printing Supply Company
BASF Systems
Baumfolder Corporation
Bedford Computer Corporation
Berkey Marketing Companies, Gossen and Omega Divisions
Berthold of North America
Bestifo, Inc.
Bobst Champlain, Incorporated
Brandtjen & Kluge, Incorporated
Brown and Bigelow
Brown Camera Company, Incorporated

Bruning
Bunting Magnetics Company
By Chrome Company, Inc.
Calumet Manufacturing Company
Carint Graphic Equipment
Challenge Machinery
Chandler & Price Company
Chesley F. Carlson Company
Cincinnati Printing & Drying Systems, Inc.
Coherent/Laser Division
Colight, Incorporated
Collins Avionics Group, Rockwell International
Colonial Williamsburg
Consar Corporation
Consolidated International Corporation
The Craftool Company
Max Daetwyler Corporation
The Denver Press
Des Moines Register and Tribune
Dick Blick
Didde Graphic Systems Corporation
Digital Equipment Corporation
Dimco-Gray Company
R.R. Donnelley & Sons, Company
Dow Jones & Company, Inc.
E. I. du Pont de Nemours & Company
Du Pont Imaging Systems
Dynamic Graphics, Incorporated
Eastman Kodak Company
Evatype/division of Eva-Tone Soundsheets, Inc.
Falcon Safety Products, Inc.
Foster Manufacturing Company
Frederick Post Company
General Binding Corporation
General Research, Incorporated
Gestetner Corporation
Goerz Optical Company, Inc.
Gotaverken Energy Systems, Ltd.
Graflex, Incorporated
Graphic Arts Monthly
Gravure Association of America
Alan Haley and *Graphic Arts Today*
Halvorford-Kwikprint Company
Harris Corporation
HCM Graphic Systems, Incorporated
Heidelberg USA
Hendrix Electronics, Incorporated
L. B. Holliday and Company, Ltd.
Honeywell Photographic

Hopkins Screen Printing Machinery
Horan Engraving Company, Inc.
Hunt Manufacturing Company
Dard Hunter Paper Museum
IBM Corporation
Industrial Timer Corporation/Gilbert, Whitney, & Johns, Inc.
Information International, Incorporated
Interlake Packaging Corporation
Interleaf, Inc.
International Association of Electrotypers & Stereotypers, Inc.
Itek Corporation, Graphic Products Division
Jomac Incorporated
Josten's Scholastic Division
Konica Business, Machines, Inc.
Koh-I-Noor Rapidograph Incorporated
Kroy, Inc.
Leedal, Incorporated
Leslie Paper Company
The E. G. Lindner Company, Ltd.
LogEtronics, Incorporated
Lud Company, Inc.
Ludlow Typograph Company
Mable Tainter Literary Library and Educational Society
3M Company
3M Company, Industrial Graphics Division
McCain Manufacturing Company
M & M Research Engineering Company
Master Sales and Service Corporation
The Mead Corporation
Meredith/Burda Corporation
Mergenthaler Linotype Company
Methods Research Corporation
Midland-Ross Corporation
Michael Business Machines Corporation
Minolta Corporation
Mohawk Industries
Monotype Graphic Systems, Incorporated
M. P. Goodkin Company
Mosstype Corporation
Motter Printing Press Company
Muller-Martini Corporation
National Association of Printing Ink Manufacturers, Inc.
National Machine Company
Nekoosa Paper Incorporated
Nikon
North American Color, Inc.
nuArc Company, Inc.

Olivetti Corporation
Omnitrade Industrial Co., Ltd.
Paasche Airbrush Company
Paillard, Incorporated
Pako Corporation
Pasadena Hydraulics, Incorporated
Pitney Bowes, Incorporated
Photo Materials Company
QWIP Systems
Regar World Corporation
Remington Office Machines
Rockwell International, Graphics Systems Division, Goss Products
Rockwell International, Graphics Systems Division, Miehle Products
Rockwell International, Graphics Systems Division, Sta-Hi Products
F. P. Rosback, Company
Rotaprint Company
Roto Cylinders
H. B. Rouse & Company
Royal Zenith Corporation
Schuler Sales and Service Company
Scitex America Corporation
Seal, Incorporated
Shelburne, Vermont, Museum

Smyth Manufacturing Company
Solna Corporation
Spiral Binding Company, Inc.
Standard Duplicating Machines Corporation
Standard Process Corporation
StripPrinter Incorporated
The Swingline Company
TAB
Tameran, Inc.
Thompson Cabinet Company
Turco Manufacturing Company
Ulano
U. S. Forest Service
Varigraph Incorporated
Varitrmic Systems, Inc.
Virkotype Corporation
K. Walter Service Corporation
Wang Laboratories, Incorporated
S. D. Warren Company
Webtron Corporation
Westvaco
Wolverine Flexographic Manufacturing Company
World Color Press
Xerox Corporation
Yashica, Incorporated

CONTENTS

Most food packaging is produced by the graphic arts industry.

GRAPHIC ARTS INDUSTRY

INTRODUCTION TO GRAPHIC ARTS

Graphic arts is a means of communication. It includes all arts and processes that give information by means of images printed on surfaces. Graphic arts is an essential part of visual communication. It uses a wide range of methods and tools. Craftsmanship, mechanical aptitude, and a sense of the possibilities for using materials are needed to produce professional graphic arts products.

THE PURPOSE OF GRAPHIC ARTS

The main purpose of the graphic arts industry is to create products that communicate visually. Not all graphic arts products communicate by words or pictures, however. The industry also makes non-communicating products such as paper bags, towels, dinner napkins, and plain paper.

Most graphic arts communication materials, such as sheets of paper, have two dimensions (length and width). Many others, such as bottles and packages, have three-dimensions (depth) as well.

Examples of common image-using products are books, magazines, newspapers, and packages (Fig. 1-1). Photographs, illustrations, and words are used on countless printed products that fill newsstands and stores everywhere (Fig. 1-2).

THE INFLUENCE OF GRAPHIC ARTS

Studies reveal that people learn 80 percent of what they know through their eyes. An industry that produces visual images is one that has a strong effect on society.

Our culture relies greatly on graphic arts products. The information explosion has increased the output of both hardcover and paperback books (Fig. 1-3). There are more magazines and technical journals. The communication revolution has also expanded markets for

Fig. 1-1. Just a few samples of the many products of today's graphics arts industry.

Fig. 1-2. Magazines are a graphic arts product that entertains and informs.

Fig. 1-3. Books are among the most essential products of the graphic arts.

advertising and promotional copy, brochures, catalogs, and dictionaries. The printed page (graphic reproduction) has never been more prominent in society than it is today.

EARLY GRAPHIC ARTS

Graphic arts has grown along with human civilization. Printed playing cards were among

Fig. 1-4. Playing cards were one of the first printed products of the graphic arts.

the first graphic arts products (Fig. 1-4). One of the earliest forms of graphic arts was branding (Fig. 1-5). This means of identification was used as early as 2000 B.C. Tombs in Egypt show ancient brands and the process of branding. The book of Genesis tells how Jacob, the great herdsman, branded his stock. The Romans, Greeks, and Chinese marked their animals, and even their human slaves, by branding. The first branding of cattle in America was done by Hernando Cortes, conqueror of Mexico.

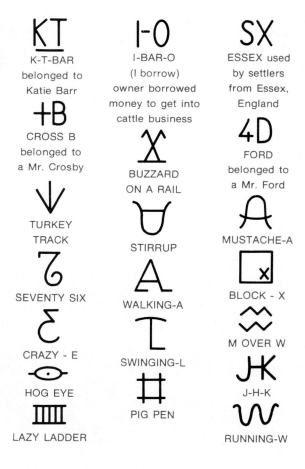

Fig. 1-5. Brands were among the first trademarks produced by a graphic arts process.

UNIT 2 THE SCOPE OF GRAPHIC ARTS

Graphic arts exists wherever there is civilization. People use graphic materials to communicate in their daily lives. Newspapers, books, magazines, advertisements, clothes labels, letters, and other printed products are everywhere. Who can go through a day without seeing some kind of printed material?

People find more and more uses for graphic arts as new technologies develop. The computer, for example, has had a great impact on business, industry, and everyday life. People in the graphic arts industry quickly recognized the value of this new tool. Today the computer plays a major role in all phases of the graphic arts industry (Fig. 2-1). In fact, this book was manufactured with equipment controlled by computers. Typesetting machines use computers, as do graphic arts cameras, film processors, platemakers, printing presses, and bindery equipment.

A BUSINESS ENTERPRISE

Several types of businesses make up the graphic arts industry. *Commercial printing plants* and *newspapers* are the most common graphic arts businesses. Commercial printing plants produce all kinds of printed materials, from simple letterheads and business forms to complicated advertising materials and books. Newspaper publishers print millions of copies daily. Everywhere materials are printed to inform and entertain us.

Most printing is done on paper. Paper manufacturers all over the world make the millions of tons of paper used each year (Fig. 2-2).

Graphic arts also uses large amounts of *ink*. Without ink, there would be no way to put information on paper and many other surfaces.

Equipment and *chemical* manufacturing also are important parts of the graphic arts indus-

BEDFORD COMPUTER CORPORATION

Fig. 2-1. As do other industries, the graphic arts relies more and more on computers like these.

MEAD CORPORATION

Fig. 2-2. Millions of tons of paper in sheets and rolls are used each year.

try. They make the machines and raw materials needed to produce printed materials.

GRAPHIC ARTS PRODUCTION

Graphic arts products usually go through six production phases (Fig. 2-3), each carried out by specialists skilled in that particular area. Printing plant personnel may call them different names, but these are the six steps most printed jobs pass through.

New technology has enabled some steps to merge. Some copy preparation equipment can be used to create visual images (type, artwork, and halftone photographs), film negatives and positives, and printing plates. As technology advances, the distinctions be-

tween the six basic production areas may lessen further. They remain an excellent model to understand the manufacture of most printed products.

1. Design and layout. Planning the *design* and preparing the *layout* are the first and most important steps. The design and layout artist must be creative, have skilled hands, and know the basic reproduction methods. (Fig. 2-4). To master these skills, it is important to know the principles of design and color, the characteristics of type, and the way to prepare a basic layout.

2. Copy preparation. Putting copy into printable form is the second production phase. There are many methods of typesetting, and a wide choice of type sizes and styles. Sophisticated equipment allows the typesetter or *compositor* to set type and even to prepare artwork and photographs for printing (Fig. 2-5).

Fig. 2-4. When planning a company brochure, a design and layout artist must understand the customer's needs.

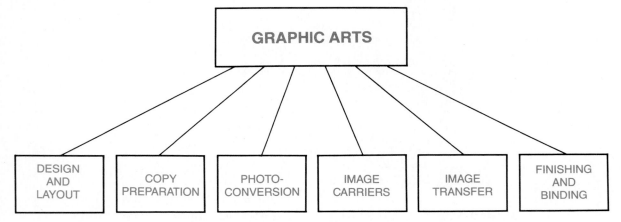

Fig. 2-3. The six production phases of graphic arts.

AM VARITYPER

Fig. 2-5. Compositors prepare type composition on versatile photographic typesetting machines.

3. Photoconversion. *Photoconversion* includes the processes by which light-sensitive materials capture images on paper or film.

WORLD COLOR PRESS

Fig. 2-6. A photographic technician readies the process camera to make a film negative.

BUNTING MAGNETICS COMPANY

Fig. 2-7. A research specialist tests a new image carrier (often called a printing plate).

Cameras, lights, film processors, light-sensitive film and paper, and chemicals are used in this production phase. The darkroom is where photoconversion is done by a *photographic technician* (Fig. 2-6).

SOLNA CORPORATION

Fig. 2-8. A skilled press operator using a computer-assisted management system. This helps control the production of printed products from inception through distribution.

NORTH AMERICAN COLOR, INC.

Fig. 2-9. Skilled operators are needed to operate a paper-folding machine safely and accurately.

4. **Image carriers.** *Image carriers* are devices that are used to carry the images or graphics from which printed copies are made. *Plates, cuts, stencils,* and *printing screens* are common types of image carriers. Researchers are constantly experimenting to find new processes, methods, and equipment. Several new printing plates have been developed in recent years (Fig. 2-7).

5. **Image Transfer.** The actual printing is done in this phase. Machines holding image carriers transfer images to many kinds of materials such as paper, cloth, metal, glass, and wood (Fig. 2-8). Skilled personnel operate the printing presses and other image transfer machines.

6. **Finishing and binding.** Some printing jobs are completed when they have been printed. Others must be finished. During this phase, paper may be folded, cut, perforated, drilled, punched with holes, gathered, or whatever is necessary to prepare a finished product (Fig. 2-9). If the printed product is to be a book or pamphlet, it must be bound, after which, it is ready for the customer. This book itself has gone through all six production phases.

Specialties

Graphic arts companies may often have different phases of a project done by specialized companies. These *specialty houses* may deal only with one phase of production—either design and layout, copy preparation, or photo-conversion. For example, a commercial printer may not have a means of composing type and will subcontract this to an outside typesetter. Specialty houses play a major role in the graphic arts industry as it becomes more complex.

UNIT 3 CULTURAL CONTRIBUTIONS OF GRAPHIC ARTS

For centuries, the graphic arts have helped to develop human culture. In their desire to communicate, prehistoric people used gestures and sounds. However, these forms of communication could be used only over a short distance. People had to discover ways to share knowledge with others who were not present before they could advance their way of life. Graphic forms evolved slowly. By about 1500 B.C., the first simple alphabet was used (see Unit 8). Writing became the link between places and between the past, present, and future.

HISTORICAL EVENTS

Many specific events in the history of graphic arts have contributed to cultural development. In A.D. 105 in China, Ts'ai Lun invented paper. Wood blocks were first used for printing by the Japanese in A.D. 770. About a hundred years later, the Chinese produced the first book, entitled *The Diamond Sutra*. The first movable type was cast in A.D. 1100 by the Chinese. This type consisted of reusable symbols or characters made of baked clay.

News of these early developments travelled slowly. It was not until about 1450 that Johann Gutenberg of Germany developed reusable, movable *metal* type. His type characters were cast individually and could be put together in any order. Gutenberg's invention brought about a cultural revolution over the next centuries. Other events helped people to record their thoughts and desires, but none had an impact like Gutenberg's invention. His work made possible the development of mass communication.

EARLY PRINTING IN THE UNITED STATES

The first printing press in the United States was set up near Boston, Massachusetts, in 1638. Here materials were printed for Harvard University (then in its third year). The printer was Matthew Daye. He produced the first book printed in the colonies, called *The Whole Book of Psalms*.

Fifty years later, William Bradford started the second printing shop in America. He was a Quaker and lived in Philadelphia, Pennsylvania. In 1690, Bradford also helped start America's first paper mill. It was called the Rittenhouse Mill and was also in Philadelphia. Soon other printing shops were established, most of them in seaport cities.

THE BEGINNING OF NEWSPAPERS

By the early 1700s, printers had begun to print newspapers. These soon became the major source of information for the colonists. The British authorities did not like the newspapers because much of the news concerned problems of British control of the American colonies.

Among the earliest of the controversial printer-journalists was James Franklin. His paper was called the *New England Courant*. In 1721 he upset the British so much that he spent a month in a Boston prison. He served his time, then started another controversial paper. Within a year he was banned from publishing. He then decided to publish the paper under the name of a sixteen-year-old apprentice, his brother Benjamin.

Because it would not have looked right for a publisher to be a lowly apprentice, James tore up Benjamin's apprenticeship agreement, which had five more years to run. In its place they signed a private agreement to continue Benjamin's apprenticeship. However, James could not get along with his brother and soon Ben Franklin left for New York. After he resettled in Philadelphia, he became a famous printer and political figure.

PEOPLE AND MACHINES

Type was composed by hand in early Colonial days (Fig. 3-1). In the 1880s a German-born American named Ottmar Mergenthaler introduced the first successful typesetting machine. It was called the Linotype. The editorial page of the *New York Tribune* of July 3, 1886, was composed on Mergenthaler's machine. The Linotype changed the graphic arts

DIDEROT'S ENCYCLOPEDIA/COLONIAL WILLIAMSBURG

Fig. 3-1. A composing room in the 1700s.

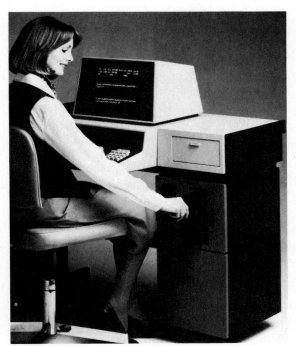

ITEK CORPORATION

Fig. 3-2. A high-speed phototypesetting system that uses flexible magnetic discs to store information and control machine functions.

industry. Today, machines using computers can produce hundreds of type characters per second (Fig. 3-2).

One of the better early metal printing presses was made in London, England, in 1838 (Fig. 3-3). It was used in the first printing of the *Kent Times* in Southeast England in 1860. Since then, research, engineering,

Fig. 3-3. The Clymer Columbian Press, manufactured in England in 1838.

and technology have made printing machines much faster and better. Today giant printing presses produce thousands of high-quality copies per hour (Fig. 3-4).

The first papermaking machine was invented by Nicolas Louis Robert in 1798 (Fig.3-5). A commercial model was developed in the early 1880s by the Fourdrinier brothers of England. The continuous-wire principle, or wire belt, used in the first machine is still basic to today's modern papermaking machines.

The quality and speed of graphic communication devices have constantly improved. On

Fig. 3-5. A model of the first papermaking machine. It was invented in 1798 by Nicolas-Louis Robert of France and developed by the Fourdrinier Brothers of England.

October 17, 1967, a full-size newspaper front page was sent by satellite, telephone wire, and underground cable. It travelled nearly 5,000 miles in less than fifteen minutes, from London, England, to San Juan, Puerto Rico. The information was sent as electronic signals that were recorded on photographic film at the receiving end. The film was then used to prepare the printing plate for the newspaper press. The newspaper front page appeared at the same time in London and San Juan. Events like this are common today.

Fig. 3-4. High levels of productivity and quality are possible with multistory lithography printing presses.

UNIT 4 SIZE OF THE INDUSTRY

The graphic arts industry is growing because of its central role in spreading knowledge (Fig. 4-1). New products are constantly being introduced. New methods of production are being developed. Speed and quality of production are increasing. New jobs are being created for people of many different backgrounds and talents.

R. R. DONNELLEY & SONS

Fig. 4-1. Graphic designers must be able to combine artwork, photographs, and type creatively. Thousands of useful printed products are designed and printed every working day.

The industry has many small companies in addition to a number of large ones. These companies are found in every country in the world. For example, in the United States, about 50,000 individual commercial graphic arts facilities are spread over the fifty states. Major printing plants are concentrated in areas with large populations and some industrial development, but most counties have some sort of newspaper or a commercial printing plant. Commercial printing plants do printing jobs for large numbers of outside customers. There are also thousands of *in-plant* shops. These are small departments in a non-printing firm. They do the printing and duplicating only for that firm.

EMPLOYMENT

The graphic arts industry has very stable employment. All told, the industry employs over one million employees (Fig. 4-2). In the past, total employment has shown a growth of 1.5 percent per year. There is still a shortage of qualified management personnel and skilled production workers. The industry needs talented students to seek new careers in all phases of the graphic arts.

The wages and salaries of graphic arts employees tend to be equal to or higher than those in most manufacturing industries. This is because of the shortage of skilled workers and because of the high level of skill needed to work in this technical industry.

INDUSTRY GROWTH

The graphic arts industry is highly competitive. Individual production plants compete with

COLLINS AVIONICS GROUP/ROCKWELL INTERNATIONAL

Fig. 4-2. Skilled workers operate a machine that collates sheets of paper at high speed.

others in their own geographical areas. They also compete with those in other parts of the United States and foreign countries. Experts predict a continued rapid rise in the production and use of printed materials. Because of this, the graphic arts industry is considered a growth industry.

Compared to all United States industries, graphic arts ranks high both in payroll (dollars paid to employees) and in product value. No industry has more manufacturing facilities. Graphic arts is ranked within the top ten major manufacturing industries in the United States.

GOVERNMENT PRINTING OFFICE

The United States Government Printing Office (GPO) in Washington, D.C., is the largest single printing plant in the world. It also has smaller plants in New York City, Chicago, and other cities. It operates around-the-clock and employs about 7,500 people. The GPO handles about 204,000 separate printing orders per year.

The GPO prints materials for Congress. It also prints for the Executive Office and the federal courts (other than the Supreme Court). Because every executive department and independent office of the government can ask the GPO to do printing, it is impossible for the GPO to print all materials requested. Over 60 percent of its work is completed outside by private commercial graphic arts plants. All work sent outside is competitively bid and contracts are awarded by the GPO.

UNIT 5 GRAPHIC ARTS PRINTING PROCESSES

Printing transfers images from one surface to another. There are six basic printing processes: (1) letterpress, (2) lithography, (3) gravure, (4) screen, (5) photographic, (6) electrostatic. The first four methods have been used for years. The last two processes, photographic and electrostatic, are relatively new. Research and experience are making them more widely used. Printing processes can be further grouped according to the type of printing surface that does the printing.

Other methods of applying images are now being used. These include *ink jet* printing and *heat transfer* printing. Now these two methods are being used for special purposes, but in the future they may become useful for general purpose printing. More information about these two imaging methods is presented in Unit 149.

LETTERPRESS

The letterpress image transfer concept is shown in Figure 5-1. It uses a raised or *relief* surface

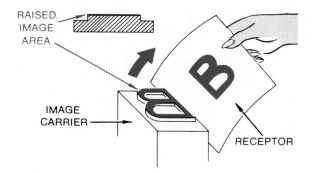

Fig. 5-1. The principle of the letterpress (relief) image-transfer method.

that is inked and pressed against paper or other material. The area without image is cut or etched below the area with image. Thus, ink does not come in contact with areas where no image is wanted. Details of the letterpress or relief printing method are covered in Sections 8, 9, and 10.

The letterpress image transfer method is centuries years old. The Japanese are credited with first using this principle in approximately A.D.

770. Their printing was done mainly from relief-carved wooden blocks.

Johann Gutenberg's invention, movable metal type, is an example of letterpress image transfer (see Unit 3). The images on his movable metal characters were cast in relief. The same principle is still in use today. Calendars, books, magazines, and tickets, are often produced by means of letterpress printing.

Flexography is a major form of letterpress printing. It uses flexible printing plates and special inks. Common products printed by flexography are packaging and pressure-sensitive labels such as those found on products in retail stores. See Units 70 and 81 for more about this important image transfer method.

LITHOGRAPHY

The lithographic image transfer concept is shown in Figure 5-2. It produces an image from a smooth surface rather than a raised surface. This is possible because oil and water do not mix. On a lithographic plate, an image is created with a substance that accepts oil but repels water. A thin coating of water is then placed

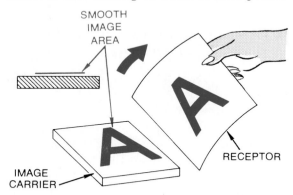

Fig. 5-2. The principle of the lithographic (planographic) image-transfer method.

over the entire image-carrier area. The water stays only on the non-image area. Oil-based ink is applied to the entire image-carrier area. It sticks only where there is no water. The ink is then transferred to paper by means of a rubber blanket which receives the inked image from the image carrier. Sections 11, 12, and 13 cover this process in detail. Historically, the term *planographic* has been used to identify the lithographic printing method. The term *offset* by

itself is often used in referring to lithographic image-transfer, although it is not strictly correct. Offset is a mechanical process that uses a rubber blanket between plate and paper. Offsetting simply lets plates be made "right reading" instead of backward. It can be used with other image-transfer methods, not just lithography (see Unit 103). Still, many people say "offset" as a short form of "offset lithography."

Alois Senefelder of Germany is said to have discovered the lithographic printing method in 1796. He applied an image to a flat limestone surface with a greased pencil. Then he wet the stone, inked the image, and pressed paper to the stone surface causing the image to be transferred. The mechanical offset lithography press was invented near the beginning of the twentieth century. Modern-day offset lithography presses are used to print many products, including newspapers, books, and magazines. Much general commercial printing uses this process. Catalogs, directories, and brochures are common products of offset lithography. The process is very versatile and allows the designer to be creative.

GRAVURE

The gravure image-transfer method is shown in Figure 5-3 and described in detail in Section 14. In gravure, the image is cut into the non-image area of the image carrier. Ink is applied to the entire surface of the image carrier. The ink fills in the recessed (below surface) image areas. It is removed from the non-image areas by either scraping or wiping. When paper is pressed

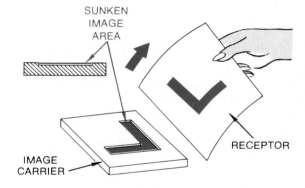

Fig. 5-3. The principle of the gravure (intaglio) image-transfer method.

against the image carrier, the ink in the recessed areas transfers to the paper.

Gravure is a variation of *intaglio* printing (say inTALyo). The term *intaglio* generally refers to hand-prepared below-surface image carriers. Engraving is an example of intaglio, and a common product of intaglio printing is paper money.

Gravure uses the principles of photography, chemistry, and electronics, rather than hand carving, to prepare the below-surface image carrier for printing. The gravure image-transfer method was probably invented by Karl Kleitsch of Austria in 1879. The process developed rapidly. By 1905, there was a gravure printing plant in New York City. A few years later the *New York Times* started its own gravure facility to produce parts of its newspaper. Gravure is used for calendars, magazines, Sunday newspaper supplements, and many kinds of product packagings.

SCREEN

The *screen* image-transfer concept is shown in Figure 5-4. In screen printing, the ink is forced through open image areas and blocked out in the non-image areas. Section 15 describes this process in detail.

Other names for this printing method are *stencil, screen process*, and *silk-screen printing*. The term "screen" is the most accurate and is commonly used throughout the graphic arts industry. The process has been called silk screening, because originally silk was the only material that could be stretched over the printing frame to hold the image carrier. Today other fabric screen materials are used, such as nylon, polyester, and stainless steel mesh.

The screen printing process is an ancient image transfer method. The early Chinese and Egyptians experimented with stenciling. The Japanese used stenciling and screen printing methods similar to those of today. The modern version of this process developed in the United States between 1900 and 1910.

Screen printing can be used to produce images on nearly any surface or shape. Felt sports pennants were among the first items produced by this method. Common screen-printed

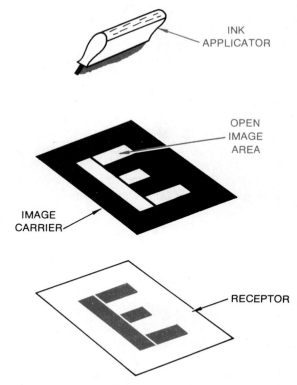

Fig. 5-4. The principle of the screen (stencil) image-transfer method.

products are posters, bumper stickers, and glass food containers. Children's toys, electrical circuits, plastic products, and textiles are also screen printed.

PHOTOGRAPHIC

The *photographic* image-transfer method is shown in Figure 5-5 and described in Section 16. It involves light, a film negative, light-sensitive paper, and photographic developing chemicals. After light has struck the light-sensitive paper through the film negative, the chemicals make the image visible.

The photographic method is not used for reproductions as much as the other methods because light-sensitive paper is very expensive. A job becomes very costly if more than a few copies must be made. Perhaps research will find a way to make photography a high production printing method.

The first attempt at photography took place about 1802. The picture showed only a silhou-

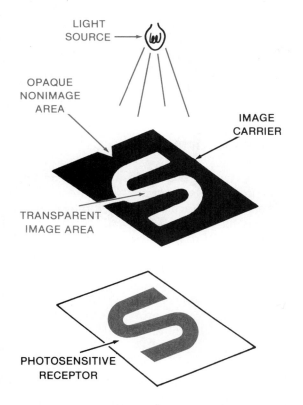

Fig. 5-5. The principle of the photographic image-transfer method.

ette of the photographed subject. Over the years, photographic methods improved. For a long time, the light-sensitive coating was put on glass, which needed careful handling. In 1884, the first flexible light-sensitive film was patented. Space-age materials and techniques have

made photographic printing more convenient and today it is a valuable imaging method. Photographs of all types are important to the communication process.

ELECTROSTATIC

The *electrostatic* concept of image transfer is shown in Figure 5-6. It works on the principle that *like* electrical charges repel and *unlike* charges attract. When light is projected onto a charged material, the material changes polarity (electrical charge). When positive-charged powder is sprinkled over the sheet being printed, it sticks only to the negative-charged areas. After the powder is attracted to the image areas, it is heated and fused permanently onto the sheet. This process is covered in Section 17.

The electrostatic process is still rather new. The first patent for electrostatic printing was issued in 1940. Many office copying machines use this principle. Most business offices have an electrostatic copier so that copies (also called *photocopies*) can be made as needed. Some machines can reproduce photocopies in multiple colors. This reproduction method is used more every year.

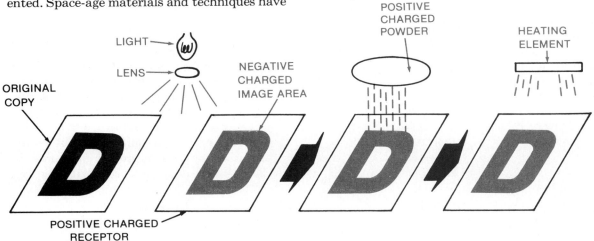

Fig. 5-6. The principle of the electrostatic image-transfer method.

UNIT 6 LEARNING EXPERIENCES: GRAPHIC ARTS INDUSTRY

KEY TERMS

Unit 1

Graphic Arts
Graphic
  communications

Mass Communication

Unit 2

Commercial printing
Compositor
Copy preparation
Design and layout
Finishing and binding
Image carrier
Image transfer

Photoconversion
Photographic
  technician
Plate
Press operator
Specialty house

Unit 3

Linotype

Unit 4

GPO

In-plant shop

Unit 5

Electrostatic
Engraving
Flexography
Gravure
Intaglio
Letterpress
Lithography
Offset

Photographic
Planographic
Polarity
Recessed
Relief
Screen
Stencil

DISCUSSION TOPICS

1. In what ways does civilization depend on the graphic arts industry?
2. What trends have been seen in the graphic arts industry in recent years?
3. Describe the part that each of its divisions plays in the overall graphic arts industry.
4. What are some of the major events in graphic arts that have contributed to our cultural development?
5. Why is the graphic arts industry a growth industry?

ACTIVITIES

Unit 1

1. Without moving from where you are seated, look around and carefully list all products and materials that are produced by the graphic arts industry. Group these items to show whether they are reading materials, packaging materials, or paper products.

Unit 2

2. Visit a commercial graphic arts printing plant. Attempt to locate the six production phases of the graphic arts—design and layout, copy preparation, photoconversion, image carriers, image transfer, and finishing and binding. Ask the printing plant representative why each production phase is placed where it is. Has it changed recently?

Unit 3

3. Conduct some library research into the cultural growth of the people of the United

States and throughout the world. Determine what role the graphic arts has had in this growth. Discuss these factors with a history teacher. Prepare your findings as a written report.

Unit 4

4. Find a recent copy of the *U. S. Industrial Outlook*. Look under the headings for printing and publishing. Compare the current size rankings of the graphic arts industry with those of other manufacturing indus-

tries. Find current industry reports that give the status of the manufacturing industry. Compare the graphic arts with the manufacturing industry in general. Why does it have the position that it does?

Unit 5

5. Sketch the basic concept underlying each of the six image transfer methods. Try not to use the drawings shown in Unit 5. Instead, use your imagination and other resource materials.

Selecting a typeface for a typesetting job.
TYPE HOUSE OF IOWA

TYPE STYLES

INTRODUCTION TO TYPEFACES

A *typeface* is a single style of type, including all the letters, numbers, and punctuation marks. We begin learning about typefaces very early, even before kindergarten. We notice the shapes of letters and we relate them to words we have already learned to speak. Later, we notice that there are different typeface designs and that different typefaces have different jobs to do. Some are meant to attract our attention. Others are meant to inform. Still others are meant to express a mood or feeling.

Typefaces provide a link between the author and the reader. They take the place of the human voice, with its many expressive tones. Without the wide variety of typefaces, there would be a wide gap in our communication.

The twenty-six letters of our alphabet are the chief raw materials for typefaces. Although the basic shape of each letter stays the same, parts of the letter can be changed slightly to make a specific typeface. The development of our alphabet is described in Unit 8.

PSYCHOLOGY OF A TYPEFACE

A typeface is like the human voice. It can express many moods and tones. Some typefaces talk; others shout. Those that talk are used to explain things to us. These typefaces are designed to make words as easy to read as possible. Those that shout are used to gain our attention. Some typefaces have an old-fashioned look that reminds us of the past. Others have a modern look with a bold feeling and a smooth flow.

Some typeface designs create a gay, happy feeling. Others create a formal mood. The designs may aim to entertain the reader or they may suggest a feeling of closeness or distance.

Typefaces have texture. They create a look or feeling in the same way that threads in a cloth give texture. Without the wide variety of typefaces, printed communication would be very monotonous.

KINDS OF LETTERS

Most typefaces have two distinct kinds of letters, *lowercase* and *uppercase*. At this moment you are reading both kinds of letters. Lowercase letters are often called small letters, and uppercase letters are often called capital letters. Both kinds of letters have their purpose.

Uppercase (capital) letters are used to begin sentences. They give special notice to proper nouns, and they draw attention to headlines in books and newspapers. Uppercase letters should be used with care because, in some type styles, they can be difficult to read. The type style used for this book is an open and modern face. When it is printed in all capitals, it is harder to read.

THE PARAGRAPH YOU ARE NOW READING IS SET IN ALL CAPITALS. WHICH IS EASIER TO READ, THIS OR THE PREVIOUS PARAGRAPH? LINES OF TYPE SET IN ALL CAPITALS CAUSE A READER TO SLOW DOWN. THE DESIGN OF THE CAPITALS DOES NOT PERMIT EVEN SPACING OF LETTERS. THERE-FORE, THE WORDS HAVE AN UNEVEN LOOK THAT KEEPS THE EYE FROM FLOWING SMOOTHLY FROM LETTER TO LETTER.

Lowercase letters have been designed in a special way. They blend together very well, so that few gaps ever appear between the letters. This is true in any sequence of the twenty-six small letters. A good guideline to follow is to use capitals very sparingly.

CHOOSING A TYPEFACE

There are five major factors to think about when choosing a typeface: (1) legibility, (2) readability, (3) appropriateness, (4) reproducibility, and (5) practicality.

Legibility. *Legibility* means how easily the letters and numbers of a typeface can be seen and recognized. In choosing a typeface, ask yourself— Can the typeface be seen easily? Can it be recognized at a distance and up close? Does it have a familiar shape and proper design for the use? Lettershapes that are too unusual make for slow reading.

Readability. *Readability* means how easily a typeface can be read for meaning. Ask yourself— Is the typeface easy for the eye to follow? If it is for a book or magazine, can it be read for long periods of time without tiring the eyes? If it is for a special use, such as road signs, can the words be read quickly and easily from a distance?

Appropriateness. The typeface must fit the intended reader. It must also fit the message it is meant to convey. The company sending the message must be well represented by the typeface. The typeface must be chosen with as much care as the paper. The photos and artwork must blend with the typeface.

Reproducibility. The reproducibility of the typeface is vital. Some typefaces do not work well with certain printing methods. For instance, those with very narrow lines do not reproduce well by the gravure process.

Practicality. A basic factor in printing is whether the typeface is available. The firm reproducing the printed product should have it on hand. The cost of using a certain typeface must be given some thought. Since some typefaces need more hand work than others, they are more expensive.

TYPEFACE CLASSIFICATIONS

There are several hundred typefaces, each with its own name. Few graphic arts people ever learn all of the types by their names. But they can place most of them within certain groupings.

Some experts divide typefaces into only two or three classes. Others list a dozen classes or more. But many graphic arts people agree on six major typeface groups: (1) text, (2) Roman, (3) sans-serif, (4) square-serif, (5) script, and (6) novelty. Samples and details of each group are shown in Units 11 through 16. Knowing these classifications will help you be a better graphic designer.

UNIT 8 EVOLUTION OF THE ALPHABET

Spoken language enabled human beings to communicate. But for many years the only way to store knowledge was memory. Memory was not very reliable. Words changed in meaning and facts could easily become distorted after being repeated several times. To make a civilization, people had to be able to write down messages easily and permanently.

VISUAL COMMUNICATION

A written, visible language developed gradually. People began to communicate visually in many ways. They broke twigs to form pointers, made marks on tree trunks, and set up piles of rocks to show that something had happened. But these could not tell *what* had happened.

The most important stage in early written communication came when people learned to draw pictures to show things they had seen and to express their ideas. The first drawings or writings called *pictograms* (Fig. 8-1) were done on walls of caves.

The next important development in the history of writing was to show action in the drawings (Fig. 8-2). American Indians developed a system of picture writings that could describe many activities. One famous picture writing (Fig. 8-3) tells of a person leaving home and tak-

TYPE HOUSE OF IOWA

Fig. 8-1. Early cave drawings showing animals without action (pictograms).

Fig. 8-2. Cave drawings showing animals with action (ideograms).

Fig. 8-3. Picture writing (ideograms) developed by the native Americans.

ing a canoe to travel ten days to a friend's home. Together they travel in their canoe to the hunting area. They stalk their prey with bows and arrows and make a kill. They then travel homeward, taking the amount of time indicated by the number of fingers shown. The picture drawings in Figures 8-2 and 8-3 are called *ideograms* because they show an idea or a happening.

APPROACHING AN ALPHABET

A system of several hundred signs and small pictures was developed by the ancient Egyptians. These picture-signs stood for full words or for syllables, but some also stood for sounds. By combining these signs the Egyptians could communicate messages. Study the example of Egyptian hieroglyphics (picture script) shown in Figure 8-4. You can see that this form of written communication is precise and permanent. But it is also clumsy and time consuming.

In Figure 8-4, the name Cleopatra (Kleopatra) is spelled phonetically (by sounds). Idea pictures are used for the concept words, *divine* and *queen*. These symbols are called *phonograms* because they represent full words. To spell out these two words, the Egyptians would have had to use a true alphabet, but they never reached this stage of development.

A TRUE ALPHABET

Most scholars give the Phoenicians credit for taking the final step toward creating a true alphabet. This is a writing system without pictures in which the symbols (letters) stand for sounds rather than ideas. It is not clear where the Phoenicians got their ideas for each alpha-

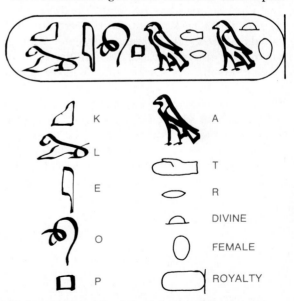

Fig. 8-4. A sample of Egyptian hieroglyphics. Symbols, called *phonograms*, represent both sounds and ideas.

betical character. They leaned heavily on partial alphabets used by the other peoples around them. Gradually a twenty-two character alphabet was developed. This greatly helped the Phoenicians in their energetic trade and travel. By about 1000 B.C., their alphabet was in full use.

The Phoenicians' alphabet, like those of their Semitic neighbors, had only consonants. The reader had to decide where vowel sounds were to be added. It was as if "horse" was written "HRS" and the reader had to tell from the context that it was not "hares," or "hours," or "hers." When the Greeks adapted the Phoenician alphabet, they made some of the letters stand for vowels. The Greek alphabet was complete by about 600 B.C.

The Romans also needed a sophisticated system of writing. They borrowed much of the Grecian alphabet and adapted it to their own needs. They learned the Greek alphabet from the Etruscans, who lived in central Italy before the rise of the Roman empire. The Roman alphabet of twenty-three characters was perfected around A.D. 114.

It is interesting to study and compare the Phoenician, Greek, and Roman alphabets. Their versions of the first three letters of our alphabet are shown in Figure 8-5. The letter *A* originally was a picture of the head of an ox. The Phoenicians used the symbol as their letter *Aleph*. The Greeks changed the symbol and called it *Alpha*. The Romans redesigned the letter to look and sound like our familiar *A*.

The Phoenicians' symbol for the letter *B* was the shape of a shelter. This letter was called *Beth*; the Greeks called it *Beta*. The Romans borrowed the character, gave it round and graceful strokes, and called it *B*.

The third letter originally represented the camel, an important means of travel for the

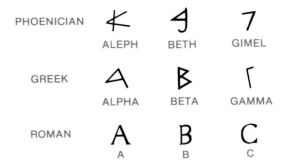

Fig. 8-5. Development of the letters *A*, *B*, and *C*.

Phoenicians. The symbol was shaped like the head and neck of a camel and was named *Gimel*. The Greeks turned the character around and called it *Gamma*. The Romans borrowed it, gave it a graceful curve, and called it *C*.

Each letter of our present-day alphabet of twenty-six characters has a similar interesting history. It took several hundred years to develop each symbol.

THE TWENTY-SIX LETTERS

The word *alphabet* comes from the first two letters of the Greek alphabet, *Alpha* and *Beta*. The capital, or uppercase, letters were the only forms used for centuries. The lowercase or small letters were developed in the Middle Ages by scribes, writers, and scholars as they copied manuscripts and books. As they copied the capital letters, they rounded them, made them easier to write, and smaller, so that they did not use so much room. They kept the original letters for the beginnings of sentences and important words. The alphabet used today is far from perfect, but it has served well in helping people to communicate with their fellow human beings.

UNIT 9 DEVELOPMENT OF A TYPEFACE

There are many typefaces. Some are used over and over in publications, while others gather dust on the shelves of commercial graphic arts plants. Even though these typefaces already exist, new ones are created each year. Some manufacturers of typesetting equipment sponsor annual type-styling contests. These encourage professional designers and novices to create new type designs. Some manufacturers of typesetting equipment employ type designers full time.

TYPEFACE DESIGN

A purpose or reason must be established for a new typeface before it is designed. As we noted in Unit 7, a type must be legible and readable. Designers must put these two requirements first as they work. If type cannot be seen and read, it has no value.

Typefaces are designed to meet the needs of specific typesetting systems. Not all typefaces are available on every typesetting system, and many typefaces with the same names are not quite the same when set on different systems.

Printing methods also affect type design. For example, letterpress prints letters a little thicker than the type is, because the ink spreads as the type is pressed against the paper. When letterpress type is redesigned for lithographic printing, the lines are made a little wider, because they will print exactly as they are on the printing plate. Typefaces for gravure and screen printing need to be more open in their design. This means more space is needed between each character stroke. A *stroke* is a line that forms all or part of the letter. For example, the letter *t* is made with two strokes, a vertical one and a horizontal one.

There must also be *continuity* among the twenty-six letters and other characters. Letters, numbers, and punctuation marks must look as

Championed
Championed Home 8

ALAN HALEY / *Graphics Today*

Fig. 9-1. Letters for three key words are often created in the early design stages. These key words help the designer see if all characters are designed well.

if they belong together. Without such continuity, type matter would be difficult to read.

CREATING A FACE

A type designer begins by setting up basic design requirements. Such things as stroke weights, letter heights, and letter widths must be decided. With these basic data, the designer can start to shape individual characters.

Designers often begin by creating four basic characters. These are the lowercase *n* and *o* and the uppercase *H* and *O*. These characters contain nearly all the strokes present in the letters in the rest of the alphabet. The other letters are created after the designer is satisfied with these four prototype letters. After the basic look has been created, it can be developed in full.

Often the letters for a key word are designed first. The key word is often *Championed* or, sometimes, *Championed Home 8* (Fig. 9-1). The key word allows the designer to see relationships among the characters. After these main characters are designed, the rest should go smoothly.

The technology of typeface design has changed substantially. Formerly the procedure was, in effect, a manual design process for phototypesetting systems. The letters were drawn in black ink. Sometimes, they were cut from *stripping film.*

The type letters were then placed on mechanically registered cards and unitized.

AGFA COMPUGRAPHIC DIVISION

Fig. 9-2. A type designer unitizing a letter on a 54-unit grid.

Fig. 9-3. A typeface designer creating a type character on a CAD terminal.

Unitizing means figuring out the amount of space each character will occupy when typeset. This is done by using a very accurate grid system (Fig. 9-2). The lettercard is then photographed by a precision process camera (see Unit 51). The letters are made much larger than the size they will be when printed. They are then reduced and placed on photographic film to make the acetate or glass font matrix.

Type designed for the CRT and laser imagesetters (typesetters) must be translated into a digital format. The two most common digital formats used in computer typesetters are vector and line-and-arc. Vector data for CRT composition can be derived from high-resolution scanning of the lettercards produced for phototypesetters.

Laser imagesetters require more complete digital descriptions of the characters. These sophisticated electronic graphic shapes are produced on *computer-aided design* (CAD) terminals. These require the designer to manipulate and correct the outlines to conform exactly to the shapes of the letters (Fig. 9-3). The digital-type letters are then compiled into a typeface that will function in an electronic typesetter.

TYPE PRODUCTION METHODS

Today most type is produced by photographic or electronic means, as described in Units 32 and 33. These are both non-mechanical methods. Older, mechanical methods are still in use, however.

The design and making of movable metal type, called *foundry type,* is the oldest of the mechanical type production methods (see Unit 28). A special engraving machine called a *pantograph* is used to produce a brass matrix for foundry type (Fig. 9-4). The matrix is a mold or die for forming type characters from hot metal. The metal type characters may be formed on a casting machine. Modern, automatic typecasters have been developed that cast hundreds of type characters in minutes. An early hand-operated typecasting machine is shown in Figure 9-5. It was developed in the United States.

Other mechanical type producing methods include *hot type,* a variation of foundry type, (see Unit 29) and *impact composition,* such as

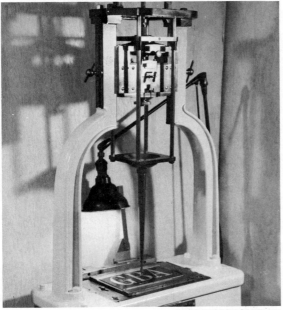

ATF-DAVIDSON COMPANY

Fig. 9-4. A Pantograph, an engraving machine used to produce the type matrix.

typewriting (see Unit 30). There are also hand-mechanical methods, such as dry transfer and hand lettering (see Unit 31).

TYPOGRAPHY

Typography is the process of arranging type in a form that both conveys a message and pleases the eye. A person who is skilled in arranging type images is a *typographer*. A typographer

DARD HUNTER PAPER MUSEUM

Fig. 9-5. An early hand cranked typecasting machine designed and built in the United States.

must be familiar with all the typefaces, how they are used, and how they are produced for printing. A typographer must also know how to select a type size that will fit into the space allowed for type material in the graphic design of a printed product (a procedure called *copyfitting*, described in Unit 25). These are highly specialized skills that require training and experience.

UNIT **10** CHARACTERISTICS OF TYPEFACES

To know the different typefaces, you must know the parts of letters. Study the typeface parts shown in Figure 10-1.

Thick strokes are the wide parts of a letter. They are either vertical, diagonal, or horizontal.

Thin strokes are the narrow parts of a letter. They are either vertical, diagonal or horizontal.

Serifs are the little extra strokes used in many kinds of type. They occur at the end of the main character strokes. They finish the stroke. Not all type has serifs.

The *ascender* occurs in such letters as *b, d, f, h,* and *k.* It is the part of the vertical stroke that extends above the body of the letter. (The

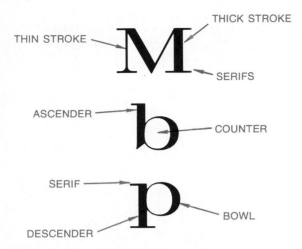

Fig. 10-1. The typeface parts.

height of the body of the letter is called the *x-height*.)

The *counter* is the open space within a letter. This space can be fully enclosed, as in the letter *b*. Or it may be only partly closed, as in the letter *n*.

The *bowl* is the loop or rounded portion of a letter. A bowl is seen in the letters *p* and *c*.

The *descender* occurs in letters like *p* and *g*. It is the part of the vertical stroke that extends below the base line.

DISTINGUISHING FEATURES

As a student of graphic arts, you should know the six basic classes of type and be able to clas-

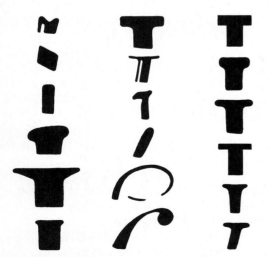

Fig. 10-2. Examples of the many kinds of serifs.

sify any certain kind of type. The most important feature for identifying different classes and kinds of type is the serif. Some types contain serifs and others do not. Those that do not are called *sans serif* types. The word *sans* means "without." Thus *sans serif* means without serifs. Within the types that do have serifs, there are serifs of all sizes, shapes, and forms (Fig. 10-2). These help further classify the types.

Serifs first appeared on Roman letters carved into stone. The stone carvers followed the patterns of letters written on the stone with flat-tipped reed pens. The pens gave the thick and thin lines of the classic Roman letter. But the carvers found it hard to end the lines neatly. So they added the finishing strokes that we call serifs at the ends of lines. Early scribes and monks made serifs by using quills and pens. Other serif designs came from brushes that left distinct ending strokes. Today, serifs are a major part of the designs of letters. Horizontal serifs help the eye to see type as lines that are easy to follow.

The weight of the lines in a typeface also helps to distinguish certain kinds of type (Fig. 10-3). There are five common weights. They are (1) light, (2) medium, (3) bold, (4) extra-bold, and (5) ultra-bold. The first two weights are for normal reading. The last three are used for emphasis, headlines and poster work. They are used to attract attention.

The thickness, or *stroke weight*, of a letter varies from one typeface to another. This is also a major means of distinguishing between types. The length of ascenders and descenders also varies and identifies type styles.

Look for these special characteristics of type when you read a newspaper or a magazine. See how they affect the readability of the type. Does the ease of reading vary because of the serif? Does it vary because of the weight of the stroke? Does the thickness within a letter or the length of ascenders and descenders make a difference?

TYPE FONTS

A *font* is an assortment of any kind style (Fig. 10-4). "Kind" refers to the name of the type, like "Bodoni," and "style" refers to the look of

aa bb cc dd ee

LIGHT   MEDIUM   BOLD   EXTRABOLD   ULTRABOLD
(Regular)

Fig. 10-3. Five common face weights of typeset letters.

CAPITALS	*ABCDEFGHIJKLMNOPQRSTUVWXYZ*
LOWERCASE	*abcdefghijklmnopqrstuvwxyzffffffiflffflfl*
PUNCTUATION	*$$¢£%.:,;·--–-·.()?![]'‘"”"* &*
FIGURES	*1234567890*

Fig. 10-4. A traditional font of type containing 96 characters. Fonts for photographic and digital typesetting equipment now often include over 300 characters.

the face. Examples of type styles include light, condensed, bold, and italic. With modern typesetting equipment, type fonts can be set in point and half-point sizes from 4 to 900 points. A point is approximately ¹⁄₇₂ of an inch. The type you are reading is 10-point type. See Unit 19 to learn about typeface measurement.

Complete type fonts are divided into four groups of characters: (1) upper case letters, or capitals, (2) lower case letters, (3) punctuation, and (4) figures. Many type fonts contain all these characters, but some fonts have only part of them. For example, some display fonts have only capitals, punctuation, and figures, leaving out the lowercase letters.

This is the Spartan Book typeface.

This is the Spartan Medium Condensed typeface.

This is the Spartan Heavy typeface.

This is the Spartan Black typeface.

This is the Spartan Black Condensed typeface.

This is Spartan Extra Black typeface.

Fig. 10-6. A type series, 10 point through 72 point.

Various typefonts are shown in Section 4. Different fonts are available for different methods of typesetting.

TYPE SERIES

A *type series* consists of several sizes of one kind and style of type (Fig. 10-5). The Times Roman typeface, for example, is shown in twelve different sizes, or in a series that ranges from 6 point through 72 point. Some metal typefaces are available only in 18 through 36 point, or in some other specific range. Type sizes can be as small as 4 point, or as large as 120 point. In computer-assisted typesetting, the font is sized electronically or photographically (see Units 32 and 33).

TYPE FAMILY

A family of type includes several different styles of type under the same basic name. Six styles of

72 POINT # Graphic Arts

60 POINT ## Graphic Arts Te

48 POINT ### Graphic Arts Technol

36 POINT Graphic Arts Technology Gr

30 POINT Graphic Arts Technology Graphic

24 POINT Graphic Arts Technology Graphic Arts Tec

18 POINT Graphic Arts Technology Graphic Arts Technology Graph

14 POINT Graphic Arts Technology Graphic Arts Technology Graphic Arts Techn

12 POINT Graphic Arts Technology Graphic Arts Technology Graphic Arts Technology Graphi

10 POINT Graphic Arts Technology Graphic Arts Technology Graphic Arts Technology Graphic Arts Technolog

8 POINT Graphic Arts Technology Graphic Arts Technology Graphic Arts Technology Graphic Arts Technology Graphic Arts

6 POINT Graphic Arts Technology Graphic Arts Technology Graphic Arts Technology Graphic Arts Technology Graphic Arts Technology Graphic Arts Technology Graphic Arts

H.B. ROUSE & COMPANY

Fig. 10-5. The traditional type series used for metal type. With current computer-assisted typesetting equipment, a type series is anything between 4 and 900 point in half-point increments.

the Spartan family are shown in Figure 10-6. These styles range from the standard book face to the extra black face, but each face shows the same basic design except for the weight, angle, or space given to each character. Type families have been designed so that different face styles can be used together and keep a harmonious design.

Italic typefaces

Italic typefaces slant forward in the reading direction, as shown in this sentence. Italic type is used mostly when the printed material is to be emphasized. Italics should be used sparingly. Of the six typeface classifications (Units 11–16), only Roman, sans serif, and square serif include an italic style.

UNIT 11 TEXT TYPE STYLE

Text typefaces (Fig. 11-1) are marked by heavy vertical and angular strokes. They are usually decorated with extra strokes and thin lines.

Text type is somewhat hard to read (Fig. 11-2) and is not often seen in modern publications. It is sometimes used to suggest great age. It may also suggest a religious or reverent mood, because it is based on a style of writing developed in monasteries.

This style of type is sometimes called Blackletter, because its heavy design makes a dark block on the page. It is also called Old English. This typeface should never be composed in all capitals because its capital letters are not designed to fit together. Combinations of text capitals are almost unreadable.

Wedding Text

Pack My Box With Five Do 123

Cloister Black

Pack My Box With F 123

Engravers Text

Pack My Box With Five Doz 1234

Engravers Old English

Pack My Box With Fiv 123

Fig. 11-1. Samples of text typefaces.

WEST VIRGINIA PULP AND PAPER COMPANY

This kind of type would have been considered the most legible to any person who lived in the fifteenth and early sixteenth centuries anywhere in western Europe north of the Alps. In fact, it was only near the end of the sixteenth century that this letter disappeared from English printing, and yielded to the form called roman. Today, it survives only as a quaint type which we use discreetly to set a few words for a greeting card or a formal invitation. Nobody expects the reader to read continuous prose set in this type—are you still with us?—because it is considered to be illegible in the mass. Illegibility does not mean that it cannot be read, but rather that it cannot be read easily; the eye and the mind become fatigued with the effort involved in trying to identify the letters whose forms are unfamiliar to us today.

Fig. 11-2. A paragraph composed in a text typeface.

USES

Text typefaces are commonly used by churches and for formal announcements and invitations to weddings, graduations, and receptions. Greeting cards often use text typefaces, particularly those for religious holidays like Christmas and Easter.

HISTORICAL HIGHLIGHTS

Text type originated as ancient scribes copied religious works by hand. The flat shape of their pens, held at an angle and moved vertically, made the thick and thin lines and angular strokes. The Gothic style of architecture also influenced the design of this type.

Examples of text style lettering have been found as early as A.D. 700. Gutenberg, originator of movable metal type, used this style for his first characters, making text style the oldest cast-metal type in the world. Almost without exception, the early typeset Bibles used this style of type. Today, text style is most often seen in the work of calligraphers (people who practice the art of beautiful handwriting). Pens and brushes with broad tips easily produce this style of lettering.

UNIT 12 ROMAN TYPE STYLE

Roman typefaces have many shapes of serifs and thick and thin strokes (Fig. 12-1). Roman typefaces can easily be told from the other five classifications by their serifs. Serifs may be angular, rounded, rectangular, or a combination of all three shapes. On the basis of serif shape and stroke contrast, Roman is divided into three classifications: (1) oldstyle faces, (2) modern faces, and (3) transitional faces.

Oldstyle faces have serifs that are rounded at the ends. The contrast between the thick and thin strokes is only moderate, giving an even face weight.

Modern Roman type (Fig. 12-2) has the most

Caslon No.

PACK MY BOX WITH
Pack my box with five d 123

Century Schoolbook

PACK MY BOX WITH FI
Pack my box with five 123

Cooper Black Italic

PACK MY BOX WITH
Pack my box with 123

Goudy Bold Italic

PACK MY BOX WITH
Pack my box with five 123

Fig. 12-1. Old Style Roman typefaces.

Craw Modern Bold

PACK MY BOX
Pack my bo 123

Onyx

PACK MY BOX WITH FIVE DOZEN JUG
Pack my box with five dozen jugs 12345

Bodoni Bold

PACK MY BOX WITH FIV
Pack my box with five   123

Bernhard Modern Italic

PACK MY BOX WITH FIVE
Pack my box with five dozen 123

Fig. 12-2. Modern Roman typefaces.

extreme contrast between the thin and thick strokes. This gives a bright and shadowed effect. The serifs are generally straight and thin. They are also somewhat rectangular except for some rounding at the corners. The ascenders and descenders of the modern style are often quite long. The counters of the letters are large, which makes for easy reading.

Transitional Roman style (Fig. 12-3) is a combination of the old and modern styles. The contrast between the thin and thick strokes is

Whitin Black Condensed

PACK MY BOX WITH F
Pack my box with fiv 123

Baskerville Roman

PACK MY BOX WITH FI
Pack my box with five d   123

Whitehall

PACK MY BOX WITH FIV
Pack my box with five d   123

Bulmer Roman

PACK MY BOX WITH FIVE
Pack my box with five doze   123

Fig. 12-3. Transitional Roman typefaces.

not as great as in modern Roman type. The serifs are fairly long and have smooth, rounded curves.

Most Roman type styles are very legible and can be used for long passages. Many are dignified and easy to read. The serifs tend to lead the eye from one letter to another and from word to word. Some people think this reduces eye strain when reading. The shapes of the capital letters combine well. Because of this, Roman typefaces can be typeset in all capital letters, as in headlines.

USES

The bulk of reading material contained in newspapers, books, and magazines is composed with Roman typefaces because of its high readability. Few other type styles have challenged Roman faces in these media.

HISTORICAL HIGHLIGHTS

Roman type was first created in the fifteenth century by a Frenchman named Nicholas Jenson. Jenson became interested in the art of producing graphic images. He travelled to Germany to learn the new art of printing. He then settled in Venice, Italy, where he created his distinctive typeface in about 1470. He printed nearly a hundred books in this face. Because of his work, Jenson is considered the world's first great type designer.

Many other type designers developed their variations of the Roman typefaces. These type designers were Claude Garamond of France, William Caslon of England, and Giambattista Bodoni of Italy. Their typefaces are still in use.

Caslon typefaces were popular in the early United States. The Declaration of Independence was first typeset in Caslon type, and so was Benjamin Franklin's *Pennsylvania Gazette*. Roman typefaces have been adopted for machine use. No new machine face has become as useful and well liked as the hand-made faces that were designed during the fifteenth through the eighteenth centuries.

UNIT 13 SANS-SERIF TYPE STYLE

Sans-serif type has no serifs, and the strokes of the letters all have the same weight or thickness (Fig. 13-1). In some styles, the strokes contain a light variation, but the pure sans-serif has none.

Sans-serif letters are the simplest and most primitive of all styles. Very direct and abrupt strokes are used. Because the letters have a simple design, the capitals are easy to read. This allows sans-serif typefaces to be set in all capitals, which gives headlines of great power.

Univers
PACK MY BOX WITH FIVE
Pack my box with five 123

News Gothic
PACK MY BOX WITH FIVE D
Pack my box with five   123

Headline Gothic
PACK MY BOX WI 123

Huxley Vertical
PACK MY BOX WITH FIVE DOZEN JUGS   12345

Spartan Heavy Italic
PACK MY BOX WITH FIVE
Pack my box with five d 123

Lydian Bold Italic
PACK MY BOX WITH FIVE D
Pack my box with five do 123

Fig. 13-1. A sample of sans-serif typefaces.

Several sans-serif faces have italic styles, as shown in Figure 13-1. As in the Roman faces, italic sans-serif is used for emphasis and variety.

Sans-serif types are also used a great deal with advertising material. Business cards and personal and business stationery are often set in sans-serif. The clear-cut design of the letters gives a modern appearance which is important for these kinds of printed products.

Optima is a sans-serif face with thick and thin lines. It combines Roman and sans-serif features. It is often used for setting text in books.

USES

Sans-serif types are coming to be used instead of Roman typefaces in books, magazines, and newspapers. With proper spacing this type style can be used where there is a great amount of copy.

There has been much research to discover whether sans-serif or Roman typefaces are more readable. The issue is far from settled. Some experts say Roman typefaces are more readable because the serifs lead the eye from one character to another. Others argue that sans-serif types are easier to read because of their clean look. In this textbook, the captions under the illustrations are typeset in a modern sans-serif type called Helvetica. The text is set in an old-style Roman typeface called Century Schoolbook. Do you think that one is more readable than the other?

The name Gothic is sometimes used for letters whose lines are all of the same weight. "Gothic," however, makes most people think of a very ornamental appearance. *Gothic* seems better as another name for the text typeface classification.

HISTORICAL HIGHLIGHTS

The Greeks first used even line weight letters when carving their words into stone after 4 B.C.

Sans-serif for printed matter is a product of the twentieth century. In 1927, Paul Renner, a German type designer, created a sans-serif typeface that has become very popular.

UNIT 14 SQUARE-SERIF TYPE STYLE

Square-serif typefaces (Fig. 14-1) are a cross between Roman and sans-serif types. Like Roman typefaces, they have many serifs, but these are rectangular rather than curved and

Tower

PACK MY BOX WITH FIVE DOZEN JU

Pack my box with five dozen jugs 1234

Stymie Medium

PACK MY BOX WITH F

Pack my box with f 123

Stymie Bold Italic

PACK MY BOX WIT

Pack my box with 123

Hellenic Wide

PACK MY B

Pack my 123

Barnum

PACK MY BOX WITH FIVE DOZE

Pack my box with five dozen 123

Trylon

PACK MY BOX WITH FIVE DOZEN JUG

Pack my box with five dozen jugs 1234

Fig. 14-1. A sample of square-serif typefaces.

pointed. The uniform strokes of the letters resemble the sans-serif types.

Square-serif types have a geometric look. For example, in some square-serif types, the letter *O* can be constructed with a compass, because it is a perfect circle. All of the letters can be constructed using three instruments: the T-square, triangle, and compass. The typefaces are open and very legible.

There are only a few square-serif typefaces, in contrast to the many Roman types. Most square-serif types have a companion italic style, to be used for emphasis.

USES

Square-serif types are not suited for newspapers, books, and magazines, where large amounts of copy must be read. The geometric structure of the letters slows reading. However, the type is good for advertisements, newspaper headlines, letterheads, and some invitational items. It tends to draw attention and in some cases seems to shout at the reader.

HISTORICAL HIGHLIGHTS

The square-serif type style first appeared in sample type books in the early 1800s. It did not become popular until it was made more modern by Heinrich Jost of Germany in 1931. Since that time the typefaces with rectangular serifs have proved quite useful.

UNIT 15 SCRIPT TYPE STYLE

Script type resembles handwriting or hand lettering. It has both thin and thick strokes. These are like the natural differences in line width that occur in handwriting with a pen.

There are two classes of script types: (1) those with letters that join and (2) those whose letters do not join. In the letters that join, all the lower case letters touch one another (Fig. 15-1). This demands special care by the type designer. The letters that do not join are sometimes called *cursive* letters (Fig. 15-2).

Some script faces look fragile and graceful. Others look strong and bold. Most of the faces slant forward about 22 degrees. The design of the capital letters is complex. Obviously, lines should never be composed all in script capitals, as they would be nearly impossible to read.

USES

Script types are very popular for advertisements, announcements, and invitations. Greeting cards are sometimes designed with script to give a personal, handwritten feeling.

HISTORICAL HIGHLIGHTS

The script type style developed as scribes and monks copied books by hand. To save time in producing individual text style letters, they began connecting the letters. This script style came into use in European printing during the Georgian period (1740–1830).

Bank Script
Pack My Box With Five 123

Brush
Pack My Box With Five 123

Kaufmann Script
Pack My Box With Five Doz 123

Typo Script
Pack My Box With Five Dozen Ju 1234

Commercial Script
Pack My Box With Five 123

Bernhard Tango
PACK MY BOX WITH FIV
Pack my box with five dozen j 123

Keynote
Pack My Box With Five D 123

Grayda
Pack My Box With Five Dozen Ju 123

Liberty
Pack My Box With Five Doze 123

Park Avenue
Pack My Box With Five Do 123

Fig. 15-1. Samples of joining script typefaces.

Fig. 15-2. Samples of non-joining script typefaces.

UNIT 16 NOVELTY TYPE STYLE

The novelty type classification is a catch-all. It includes those types that do not fit into the other five classifications. Novelty types can be divided into conservative novelty faces and contemporary novelty faces.

Conservative faces (Fig. 16-1) include slightly altered versions of one of the other type styles. Shading, outlining, uneven letters, and unique serif designs are a few of the variations. It is often difficult to tell a conservative novelty face

Copperplate Gothic Bold

PACK MY BO 123

Balloon Extrabold

PACK MY BOX WITH F 123

Engravers Shaded

PACK   M 123

Cheltenham Bold Outline

PACK MY BOX WITH FI

Dom Casual

PACK MY BOX WITH FIVE DOZEN JU

Fig. 16-1. Some conservative novelty typefaces.

from another typeface. Look closely at the samples in Figure 16-1. Some of these faces look very much like sans-serif types.

Contemporary faces (Fig. 16-2) may use expressive drawing or exaggeration to carry out a theme or mood. Almost any look can be given to this typeface. The designer can be very creative.

Each novelty typeface has individuality and can be very eye catching. There is no hard-and-fast rule about composing novelty type in all capitals, because each face is different. The decision depends on the taste and creativity of the typographer or the layout artist.

USES

The ability of the novelty typeface type style to be very expressive makes it especially useful for trade names of companies. When asked to design a name treatment or identification symbol, a graphic artist can create a new type style that fits the situation. Many typographic trademarks have gone on to become new novelty typefaces.

Some standard novelty typefaces are shown in Figures 16-1 and 16-2. These faces are used for advertising material. They demand attention, making people notice the products or services that they tell about.

HISTORICAL HIGHLIGHTS

Typefaces in the novelty classification are the only ones developed in the United States of America. Their development began right after the First World War. At that time, American business and industry were geared up to produce large quantities of products. The new, modern typefaces were designed to help sell these products.

Novelty typefaces were made to get people's attention through visual means. Novelty types helped advertisements sell products and services. Today, novelty typefaces are still very effective.

ABCDEFGHIJKLMN
ABCDEFGHI
ABCDEFGHIJKL
ABCDE   ABCDE

Fig. 16-2. Some contemporary novelty typefaces.

UNIT 17 LEARNING EXPERIENCES: TYPE STYLES

Unit 7

Appropriateness	Readability
Italic	Reproducibility
Legibility	Typeface
Lowercase	Typographer,
Practicality	Typography
	Uppercase

Unit 8

Hieroglyphics	Phonogram
Ideogram	Pictogram
	(Pictograph)

Unit 9

Continuity	Stripping film
Foundry type	Stroke
Light table	Type casting
Pantograph	Unitize

Unit 10

Ascender	Font
Bowl	Sans-serif
Counter	Serif
Descender	Series
Family	Square-serif

Unit 11

Blackletter	Text type
Old English	

Unit 12

Modern Roman	Transitional Roman
Oldstyle Roman	

Unit 13

Gothic types

Unit 15

Cursive script	Script

Unit 16

Conservative novelty	Contemporary novelty

DISCUSSION TOPICS

1. Why is it important to learn to recognize and understand typefaces?
2. What were some forms of non-verbal communication used before the development of the alphabet?
3. Why was there a need for a written form of visual communication?
4. Why is there a need for new typefaces to be designed?
5. What is the difference between a *type font*, a *type series*, and a *type family*?

ACTIVITIES

Unit 7

1. Obtain printed examples of several different type styles. Group the printed examples according to the main features of the typefaces. Have several of your friends and instructors study the type styles and give their impressions of how the typeface makes them feel. Note the reactions of each person and analyze the comments. Note whether or not there are similarities in their reactions to each typeface.

Unit 8

2. From your school or city library obtain several books dealing with the development of the alphabet. Read how each of our twenty-six letters was developed. Prepare an oral report on the development of the alphabet.

Unit 9

3. Sketch an original typeface design. Begin by identifying a purpose for the typeface and keep continuity among all the letters. Have your new typeface critiqued by your friends and teachers. Make refinements based upon their evaluations. Reproduce several copies of your alphabet, using the offset-lithography printing process.

Unit 10

4. Obtain a type catalog and review it thoroughly. Does it show an example of a type font? If so, name the kind and style of type. Also, locate a family of type. Write down the name of each specific kind of type in the family. Make sure the list is complete.

Units 11-16

5. Locate printed examples of each of the six typeface classifications. Clip these samples from outdated or unwanted publications and glue them to sheets of paper—one for each type classification. Obtain different sizes and specific typefaces within each classification. Compare each specific type style with each basic type classification.

A design and layout artist at work.

SECTION 3 PLANNING, DESIGN, AND LAYOUT

UNIT 18 THE VALUE OF PLANNING, DESIGN, AND LAYOUT

A printed product or job must be well planned. The combination of ideas used in planning and designing the product is called a *layout*. A layout is the arrangement of all the units or elements into a printed usable format. These units or elements include the heading, subheading, body matter, illustrations, and photographs (Fig. 18-1). The preparation of a complete set of layouts requires pre-layout planning, thumbnail sketches, a rough layout, and a com-

Graphic Arts Careers

Your Life Long working career could be in the graphic arts

Contact
Tri-County Vocational-Technical College

Fig. 18-1. The steps in preparing graphic layouts. If you find and fix all your problems in doing the layouts, the actual printing will be trouble-free.

prehensive layout. These are described in this and the following units.

THE VALUE OF GOOD PLANNING

Graphic planning lets the designer review and revise ideas while changes are still easy to make. When all the people involved in a project know what they are to do, the work can be done more quickly.

Good planning and a complete layout will make sure that spelling, spacing, sizes, and placement of material are right. The specifications of the client must be accurately met. When a high-quality final printed product is delivered, everyone—the buyer, the graphic arts commercial printing plant management, and the skilled workers—will be satisfied with a job well done.

PRE-LAYOUT PLANNING

Completing the pre-layout planning form is the first step. Doing this will help shape the ideas of the person who is originating the printed job. Each of the following twelve items should be listed on the form. Answers should be well thought out. Write down the answers so that they can be used as the layout is prepared.

1. Purpose of the product. What is the finished product to do? Is it supposed to attract attention, inform, entertain? A good design carries out the objective.

2. Users of the product. Will the printed material be for business or personal use? Should it appeal to students, parents, or some other group? The design should appeal to the intended users.

3. Personality of the product. Should it be sophisticated, gaudy, dignified, humorous, or sentimental? Choice of paper, typography, and illustration may depend on this item.

4. Content of the finished product. Will it be typographic (all type)? Will it have photographs, drawings, illustrations, or a combination of these?

5. Layout format. Will the product be a booklet, folder, bulletin, brochure, single sheet, or a book? Will it be a label, package, or bumper sticker?

6. Dimensions. What will be the physical size of the printed product?

7. Number of pages. Will there be one sheet printed on only one side or on both sides? Will a sheet be printed on both sides and folded? Will there be several pages?

8. Number of copies. The printing process used often depends on the number of copies wanted.

9. Finishing and binding. Will the printed sheets from the press or duplicator need to be trimmed, folded, scored, or bound together? Which method should be used?

10. Layouts required. Does the customer want to see thumbnail sketches, a rough layout, and a comprehensive layout before the final layout is prepared?

11. Estimated hours for completion. How long will the entire job take? The answer to this question will depend on the answers to the ten previous questions, and will help in making a cost estimate.

12. Completion date. How many hours work will be needed? How many working days will that take?

LAYOUT PROCEDURE

The sequence for preparing graphic layout materials is shown in Figure 18-2. Several thumbnail sketches are usually proposed, as indicated in step 2 of this figure. The selection of one of the thumbnail sketches may be made by the person ordering the product or by the designer.

After the thumbnail sketch is chosen, the *rough layout* is made (step 3, Fig. 18-2). This rough layout is generally the same size as the final product and contains all of the copy and illustrations. Changes can be easily made between the thumbnail sketch and the rough layout, and again between the rough and the comprehensive layout.

The *comprehensive layout* in step 4 is based on the thumbnail sketch and the rough layout. This is a precision layout that lets the customer see how the final product will look. The overlay sheet, attached to the base sheet, indicates how the final product should be produced. The procedures for preparing these layouts are described in Units 22-24.

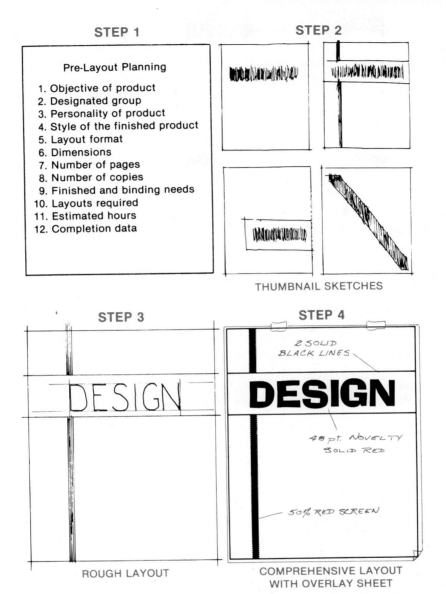

Fig. 18-2. A well-planned layout helps to insure high quality in the printed product.

TOOLS AND SUPPLIES

The work of the layout artist is made easier by having the right tools, supplies, and materials. To do layouts, you need paper, pencil, a straightedge, and a table top. Not necessary but helpful are a drawing board, a triangle, and a T-square.

Other useful items are a line gauge or measuring device of some kind, an eraser, several pencils of various colors, rubber cement, and pads of drawing, tracing, and grid paper. Additional useful items are type sample catalogs, an illus-

trator's art book, samples of papers, and an ink sample catalog.

DESIGN AND LAYOUT CONSIDERATIONS

1. Planning is important.
2. Design and layout are essential to a quality finished product. Know the elements in each layout stage.
3. Make it readable. A printed product is designed to give information.

4. A comprehensive layout is a blueprint, a master plan.
5. Prepare the final product in pencil; then compose the final product with type, illustrations, and photographs.
6. Keep it simple.

7. Know type styles and principles of typography.
8. Understand the point measurement system.
9. Understand basic design principles.
10. Know about color and how it affects people.

UNIT 19 The Point and Metric Measurement Systems

The measurement system for type composition uses *points* and *picas*. *Points* are used to measure type sizes, and *picas* are used to measure line lengths. It is important to become very familiar with these basic units of measure. They are listed in Figure 19-1. The inch divides into approximately 72 points. Twelve points equal one pica and six picas equal about one inch. Points and picas are not always used for measuring. Use the table in Figure 19-2 in converting from picas to inches.

The *line gauge* is used to make point and pica measurements. Several styles are shown in Figure 19-3. The standard gauge is marked with

picas on the left side and inches on the right side. It is a useful tool for the graphic arts production worker. Estimators and designers also use it.

Graphic arts basic units of measure

1 inch	=	72 points (approximate)
12 points	=	1 pica (exactly)
6 picas	=	1 inch (approximate)

Fig. 19-1. The basic units of measure in the graphic arts are points and picas. They are used to measure type sizes and line lengths.

Conversion of picas to inches

Picas	Inches	Picas	Inches	Picas	Inches	Picas	Inches
1	.166	26	4.316	51	8.466	76	12.616
2	.332	27	4.482	52	8.632	77	12.782
3	.498	28	4.648	53	8.798	78	12.948
4	.664	29	4.814	54	8.964	79	13.114
5	.830	30	4.980	55	9.130	80	13.280
6	.996	31	5.146	56	9.296	81	13.446
7	1.162	32	5.312	57	9.462	82	13.612
8	1.328	33	5.478	58	9.628	83	13.778
9	1.494	34	5.644	59	9.794	84	13.944
10	1.660	35	5.810	60	9.960	85	14.110
11	1.826	36	5.976	61	10.126	86	14.276
12	1.992	37	6.142	62	10.292	87	14.442
13	2.158	38	6.308	63	10.458	88	14.608
14	2.324	39	6.474	64	10.624	89	14.774
15	2.490	40	6.640	65	10.790	90	14.940
16	2.656	41	6.806	66	10.956	91	15.106
17	2.822	42	6.972	67	11.122	92	15.272
18	2.988	43	7.138	68	11.288	93	15.438
19	3.154	44	7.304	69	11.454	94	15.604
20	3.320	45	7.470	70	11.620	95	15.770
21	3.486	46	7.636	71	11.786	96	15.936
22	3.652	47	7.802	72	11.952	97	16.102
23	3.818	48	7.968	73	12.118	98	16.268
24	3.984	49	8.134	74	12.284	99	16.434
25	4.150	50	8.300	75	12.450	100	16.600

Fig. 19-2. Use this table to convert picas to inches. Sometimes you need to do this when positioning lines of type in

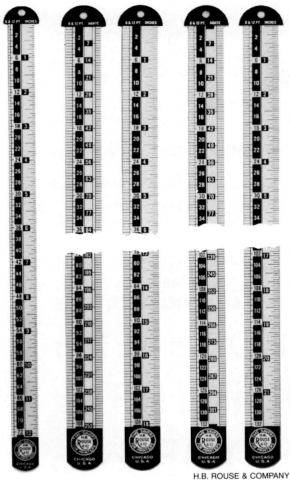

H.B. ROUSE & COMPANY

Fig. 19-3. Styles of line gauges used in graphic arts (the one at left is shown full-length; the others are enlarged to show detail).

HISTORICAL HIGHLIGHTS

In about 1737 Simon-Pierre Fournier of France developed a system for measuring type sizes and for other graphic arts purposes. In about 1770 two men, Franois and Firman Didot, amended the Fournier point system. In 1879 the Europe Type Founders Congress adopted their system.

The Anglo-American Point System was adopted in 1886 by the United States Type Founders Association. Despite much criticism, it kept the value of 1 point as 0.01384 inch. The European system has a slightly larger point value: 1 point equals 0.01483 inch. Some equipment made in the United States for use in Europe must therefore have certain different specifications to be used with the European measurement system.

MEASURING TYPE

Type that is used in books, magazines, newspapers, and other materials is measured in points. The typeface that you are reading at this moment is 10 point. Type size is measured from the top of the ascender to the bottom of the decender (Fig. 19-4). Tall letters such as capitals or *f, b, d,* and *l* touch the *ascender line.* Letters like *y, p, q,* and *g* touch the *descender line.*

All letters rest on the *base line.* The *body height,* or *x-height, line* position varies with the type style. The x-height is the height of letters such as *x* and *z.* Some letters are more open than others, that is, the x-height is greater and the counter is larger. The type designer uses these four lines as a basis for forming the letters.

In type that is cast in metal (foundry type), the size refers to the type-body size (Fig. 19-5). The actual letters as printed are smaller than the point size. This makes it hard to measure a printed typeface correctly.

The common sizes of type range from 6 point through 72 point. Larger sizes are available for

ASCENDER LINE

X-HEIGHT LINE

Fig. 19-4. Typefaces are measured from the ascender line to the descender line.

x HEIGHT Abeg

TYPEFACE HEIGHT

BASE LINE

DESCENDER LINE

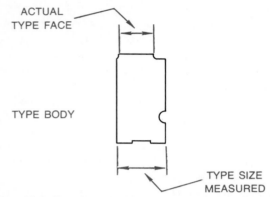

Fig. 19-5. The method of measuring foundry type.

headlines and posters. The various mechanical and photographic methods of producing type, discussed in Section 4, make it possible to obtain any size of type. Examples of the traditional type sizes are shown in Figure 19-6.

THE METRIC SYSTEM

In the metric system, the units are all multiples of ten. This is a great convenience. It conforms to our familiar numbering system (decimal notation), which is also a base ten system. You do not need to multiply or divide to convert between units and their multiples and sub-multiples. Simply shift the decimal point where it is needed.

For example, multiplying 1 foot, 9 inches by 10 means reducing the two units of measurement to one—21 inches. Multiplying 21 inches by 10 results in 210 inches. This is then reconverted to 17 feet 6 inches. By contrast, to multiply 1.9 centimeters by 10, you move the decimal point one place to the right, and the product of 19 centimeters is obtained easily. This is almost instant computation.

Metric measure should be learned by itself, without thinking what it means in feet and inches. Thinking metric is difficult for people who have learned the U. S. Standard system. When it is necessary to convert from one system to the other, use a table like the one in Figure 19-7. It shows the basic metric measures of volume, length, weight, and temperature. Use the metric measurement system whenever possible.

6 PT.
THE EARLY PRINTERS CAST THEIR OWN TYPES, MADE INK
They instructed some local blacksmith to make the iron frames

8 PT.
THE EARLY PRINTERS CAST THEIR OWN TYPES AND
They instructed some local blacksmith to make the iron

10 PT.
THE EARLY PRINTERS CAST THEIR TYPES
They instructed the local blacksmith to make

12 PT.
THE EARLY PRINTER CAST blacksmith

14 PT.
THE EARLY PRINTERS instructed

16 PT.
THE EARLY printers cast their

18 PT.
THE EARLY printers came

24 PT.
BRAZIL and countries

30 PT.
JADE varies into

36 PT.
KNIGHTS us

42 PT.
SOME xylo

48 PT.
FINE quali

60 PT.
WHILE a

72 PT.
THE pri

Fig. 19-6. The traditional type sizes.

Approximate conversions

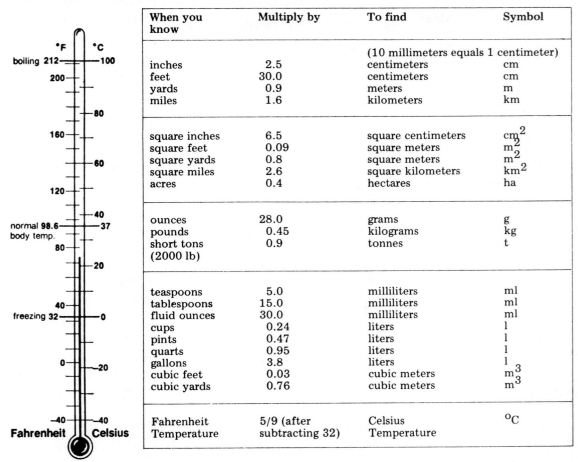

When you know	Multiply by	To find	Symbol
		(10 millimeters equals 1 centimeter)	
inches	2.5	centimeters	cm
feet	30.0	centimeters	cm
yards	0.9	meters	m
miles	1.6	kilometers	km
square inches	6.5	square centimeters	cm^2
square feet	0.09	square meters	m^2
square yards	0.8	square meters	m^2
square miles	2.6	square kilometers	km^2
acres	0.4	hectares	ha
ounces	28.0	grams	g
pounds	0.45	kilograms	kg
short tons (2000 lb)	0.9	tonnes	t
teaspoons	5.0	milliliters	ml
tablespoons	15.0	milliliters	ml
fluid ounces	30.0	milliliters	ml
cups	0.24	liters	l
pints	0.47	liters	l
quarts	0.95	liters	l
gallons	3.8	liters	l
cubic feet	0.03	cubic meters	m^3
cubic yards	0.76	cubic meters	m^3
Fahrenheit Temperature	5/9 (after subtracting 32)	Celsius Temperature	$^{\circ}C$

Fig. 19-7. This metric conversion table gives information on the basic units of volume, length, weight, and temperature.

Metrics and the graphic arts

The graphic arts industry, like all industry, has been slowly changing to metrics. Some equipment and smaller tools are available that use metric measure. Much equipment now has dual measurements listed. A typical example is shown in Figure 19-8. These press specifications show sizes in both inches and millimeters.

The point system will likely stay in use for years to come. The table in Figure 19-9 shows conversions of picas and points to fractions, decimals, and millimeters. This table may be useful for various kinds of work in the graphic arts.

New paper dimensions based on metric sizes have been proposed (Fig. 19-10). Some use has been made of these sizes, but they will require many changes in the industry. The paper mills will need to make paper in these sizes, and equipment manufacturers will also need to change their standards. Finished product sizes like newspapers, books, and magazines will need to be adjusted in their sizes too.

All of these changes will take time and money. The graphic arts industry will very probably go metric, but the process will not be finished for another fifteen or twenty years.

Specifications
Heidelberg SORSZ 28 x 40″ (71 x 102 cm)

Technical Data

Maximum sheet	28 x 40^5/$_{32}$″	710 x 1020 mm
Maximum sheet	14^1/$_2$″ 20^1/$_2$″	360 x 520 mm
Maximum image area	27^5/$_{32}$″ x 40^5/$_{32}$″	690 x 1020 mm
Maximum speed	10.000 sheets p.h.	
Maximum speed	2.000 sheets p.h.	
Cylinder diameter	10^5/$_8$″	270 mm

Plates

Length	30^5/$_{36}$″	770 mm
Width	40^5/$_8$″	1030 mm
Cylinder undercut	.020″	0,5 mm
Distance from front edge plate to front line of image	1^{11}/$_{16}$	48 mm

Blanket

Length	31^1/$_8$″	790 mm
Width	41^1/$_8$″	1045 mm
Thickness	.065″	1,65 mm
Cylinder undercut	.126″ (.091″)	3,2 mm (2,3 mm)

Inking unit

Forme inking rollers	4	4
Diameter of forme Inking rollers	2^{15}/$_{32}$″, 2^1/$_4$″ 2^3/$_8$″, 2^9/$_{16}$″	62,5, 57, 60, 65 mm

Pile heights

(distance from palette frame to top of pile)		
Feeder	42^{15}/$_{16}$″	1090 mm
Delivery	23^{19}/$_{32}$″	600 mm

HEIDELBERG USA

Fig. 19-8. A printing press specification listing. Dimensions are given in both inches and millimeters so that people in nonmetric countries can fully understand the measurements.

PRINTER'S UNIT CUSTOMARY & METRIC EQUIVALENTS

| PRINTER'S | | CUSTOMARY | | METRIC |
| | | Inches | | |
Picas	Points	Fraction	Decimal	Millimeters
	1	1/64	.014	.35
	2	1/32	.028	.70
	3	3/64	.042	1.05
	4	7/128	.055	1.40
	5	1/16	.069	1.75
	6	5/64	.083	2.10
	7	3/32	.097	2.45
	8	7/64	.111	2.80
	9	1/8	.125	3.15
	10	9/64	.138	3.50
1	12	21/128	.166	4.20
	14	25/128	.194	4.90
	18	1/4	.249	6.30
2	24	21/64	.332	8.40
	30	53/128	.414	10.50
3	36	1/2	.498	12.60
	42	37/64	.581	14.70
4	48	85/128	.664	16.80
5	60	53/64	.828	21.00
6	72	1	.996	25.20

Fig. 19-9. Use this table to convert picas and points to fractions, decimals, and millimeters.

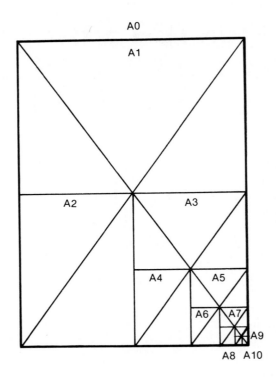

ISO -sizes	METRIC millimeters	CUSTOMARY inches
A0	841 x 1189	33.11 x 46.81
A1	591 x 841	23.39 x 33.11
A2	420 x 594	16.54 x 23.39
A3	297 x 420	11.69 x 16.54
A4	210 x 297	8.27 x 11.69
A5	148 x 210	5.83 x 8.27
A6	105 x 148	4.13 x 5.83
A7	74 x 105	2.91 x 4.13
A8	52 x 74	2.05 x 2.91
A9	37 x 52	1.46 x 2.05
A10	26 x 37	1.02 x 1.46

Fig. 19-10. Metric A paper sizes. The basic A0 sheet of paper measures 841 by 1189 mm (33.1 by 46.8 inches). Each time the sheet is cut in half, a new identification number is given.

UNIT 20 DESIGN PRINCIPLES

You need to understand some basic design principles before you prepare a set of layouts. Five important principles are reviewed in this unit: (1) page proportion, (2) balance, (3) contrast, (4) unity and (5) rhythm. Space is also discussed, because without it there would be no place to use the five principles.

SPACE

Space is not interesting until something is done with it. A designer in graphic arts works mostly with the two dimensions of length and width. A blank space—whether it is a billboard, a poster, a page of a newspaper, a book, or even a small display space on a page—is always ready to take graphic elements. Before placing these elements in a given space, the artist must think about the elements using content and then arrange the five basic design principles. A well-designed space will be noticed and do what it was meant to do.

Open or unused space, called *white space*, around and within type, artwork, and photographs is as important as the printed area. White space lets the printed contents be seen and clearly understood. Correct use of white space adds to the readability of a printed page. For example, large type needs more white space between lines than small type does. In a book like this one, white space helps to separate the different subjects.

PAGE PROPORTION

One of the first things that a designer does is to select a functional and attractive plan for the page. The decision depends on the amount of copy to be placed on the page and also on the purpose of the material being prepared.

A well-known system of proportion discovered by the ancient Greeks is called the *Golden Section*. This involves dividing a line into two sections so that the short part has the same relationship to the long part that the long part has to the whole line. There are several ways of constructing the Golden Section. The parts are approximately 3 by 5. A Golden Rectangle, one whose sides have the Golden Section relationship, is very pleasing to the human eye. Golden Rectangles are often used by architects in designing buildings and by artists in composing drawings.

Several standard page proportions used in education, business, and industry are shown in Figure 20-1. Index file cards have proportions of 3 by 5, 4 by 6, and 5 by 8 inches. Photographic

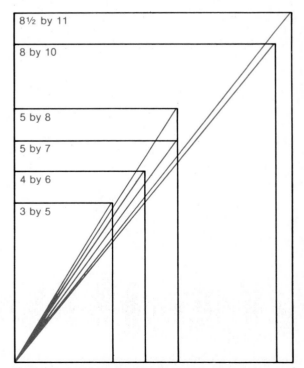

Fig. 20-1. Common page sizes. The diagonal lines show the relationships among the proportions.

enlargements are usually 5 by 7 or 8 by 10 inches. The proportion most used by the business world is 8½ by 11 inches. By placing all of these sizes of pages with their left edges and bottom edges together, it is possible to see their relationship. Diagonal lines drawn through the bottom left and top right corners of each size of page show how their proportions vary. (Refer to Figure 19-10 in the previous unit for page proportions in metric measure.)

If these different sizes of paper had the same shape (proportions), a diagonal line beginning in their common corner (lower left) would pass through all their opposite corners (upper right). You can use this principle when working on art that must be reduced or enlaged to fit a certain space. In Figure 20-2, the artist wanted to prepare artwork in a different size to fit a 3 by 5 inch space. The artist marked off a 3 by 5 shape in one corner of the paper and drew a diagonal line through the opposite corner of the shape. Notice the rectangles drawn with dashes. One is larger than the original 3 by 5 area and one is smaller, but both are exactly the same shape. You know this because all three shapes have two sides in common and their opposite corners are on the same diagonal line. You can put a dot at any point on the line, draw two new sides that meet there, and have a new rectangle with the same proportions as the original one.

The square, or a page with equal width and height, is not usually used for two-dimensional graphic materials. It is uninteresting to the eye because it does not suggest movement or change.

DYNAMIC GRAPHICS/PEORIA

Fig. 20-3. Formal balance, with graphic elements equally balanced on either side of a center line.

BALANCE

There are two kinds of balance: *formal* and *informal*. With formal balance the elements of the page are centered horizontally and an equal amount of each major unit is placed on either side of the imaginary center line (Fig. 20-3). With informal balance, there is no obvious center line (Fig. 20-4). Note in Figure 20-4 that the page is balanced by placing the graphic elements in relationship to each other. The caption, white space, and lighter part of the

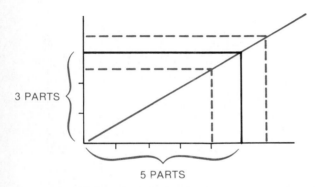

Fig. 20-2. The diagonal line method of enlarging or reducing, using a 3 by 5 sheet.

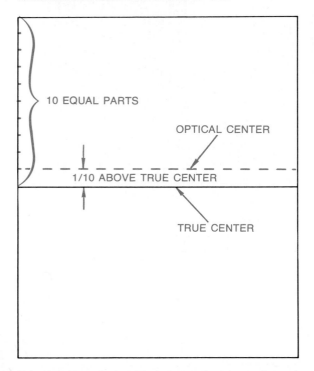

Fig. 20-4. Informal balance, with graphic elements counterbalanced on either side of a center line.

Fig. 20-5. The relationship between the true center and the optical center of a page.

drawing in the upper left balance the heavy drawing in the lower right. This style is more modern and is used extensively in advertising.

Balance also means that the elements of a page must be in the proper vertical position. They should be arranged according to the *optical center*, which is the imaginary center line slightly above the true vertical center of a page. It is normally $^1/_{10}$ of the distance from the true center to the top of the page (Fig. 20-5). If elements are placed at the true center, they will look low on the page. When dividing the page or deciding where to put the center of interest, use the optical center (Fig. 20-6).

CONTRAST

Contrast is a useful way to make copy elements stand out. When a copy element contrasts with others, it is different from them in some way.

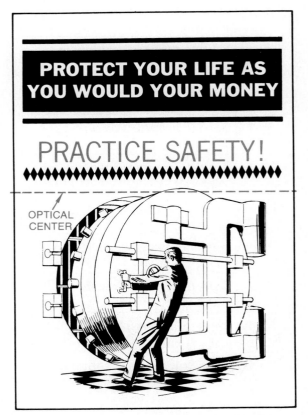

Fig. 20-6. Graphic elements placed according to the optical center.

Several ways of using contrast to emphasize words are shown in Figure 20-7.

As a general rule, "All display is no display." If all elements of the page are large, bold, underlined, or in color, none of them will stand out from the others. No one item will be noticed.

UNITY

The graphic elements of a two-dimensional layout should have unity. That is, without seeming crowded, elements should look as if they belong together. Illustrations and type must be complementary and arranged so that each single element has its place (Fig. 20-8). Normally the eye enters a page at the upper left-hand corner, goes across the page and down to the lower left-hand corner, and leaves the page at the lower right-hand corner. Figure 20-9 illustrates typical eye movement on the layout shown in Figure 20-8. Eye movement should be built into every layout. Otherwise, parts of the page might not be noticed at all.

RHYTHM

The principle of rhythm is hard to define. Rhythm is a feeling of visual movement. See the layout shown in Figure 20-10. The large headline gets attention. The people pointing quickly direct the reader's eyes to the central theme of the ad. Repeating elements also helps to create rhythm.

The principles of unity and rhythm are much the same. See how rhythm creates unity in Figures 20-8 and 20-9.

Twelve ways to emphasize with type.   1. Change the size.
Twelve ways to EMPHASIZE with type.   2. Use capital letters.
Twelve ways to EMPHASIZE with type.   3. Use small capital letters.
Twelve ways to *emphasize* with type.   4. Use italic type.
Twelve ways to **emphasize** with type.   5. Use a different kind of type.
Twelve ways to **emphasize** with type.   6. Change the face.
Twelve ways to emphasize with type.   7. Underline the word or words.
Twelve ways to → emphasize with type.   8. Use eye directing symbols.
Twelve ways to emphasize with type.   9. Alter the position
Twelve ways to emphasize with type.   10. Enclose the word(s) with lines.
Twelve ways to emphasize with type.   11. Use color when possible.
Twelve ways to emphasize with type.   12. Create reverse type.

Fig. 20-7. Twelve ways to emphasize words with type.

DYNAMIC GRAPHICS/PEORIA

Fig. 20-8. A layout showing the design principle of rhythm. There are repetitious elements and a clear direction for eye movement.

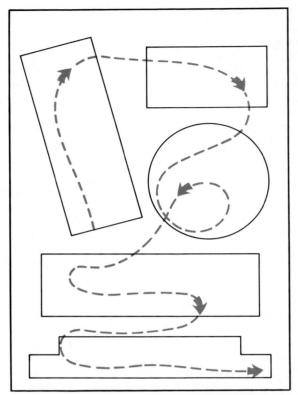

DYNAMIC GRAPHICS/PEORIA

Fig. 20-9. A layout showing unity among the elements.

Fig. 20-10. Eye movement is directed when a design such as Figure 20-9 has unity.

UNIT 21 COLOR PRINCIPLES

Color in the graphic arts makes the products interesting. A designer of two-dimensional graphic materials must be familiar with the principles of color.

THE COLOR WHEEL

The color wheel (Fig. 21-1) is a useful tool for the graphic arts designer. It shows the relationship between the several basic pigment colors. Experienced designers use more complicated color wheels, but a wheel like the one shown is adequate for normal design work.

In dealing with pigments, three *primary colors* can produce all colors. These are yellow, red, and blue (Fig. 21-2). These three cannot be formed by mixing other colors, but other colors result when these three are mixed.

Secondary colors (Fig. 21-3) are made by mixing equal amounts of primary ones. They are

green, made by mixing yellow and blue; violet, made by mixing red and blue; and orange, made by mixing red and yellow.

Intermediate colors (Fig. 21-4) are made by mixing equal amounts of one primary color and a secondary color next to it on the wheel. These are yellow-green, blue-green, blue-violet, red-violet, red-orange, and yellow-orange. Note that the primary color is named first.

You may have heard that black and white are not colors. Strictly speaking, white is a mixture of all colors and black is the lack of all colors. However, this is seen most clearly when dealing directly with light (See Unit 60). Here we are talking about light reflected from pigments. In printing, white is usually made by leaving the paper blank, and black is made by printing a black pigment. Thus, in printing, black is considered a color. In four-color printing, the colors are magenta (process red), yellow, cyan (process blue), and black.

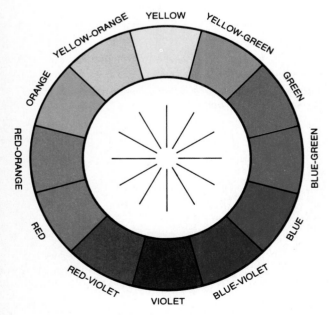

Fig. 21-1. Colors of the pigment color wheel.

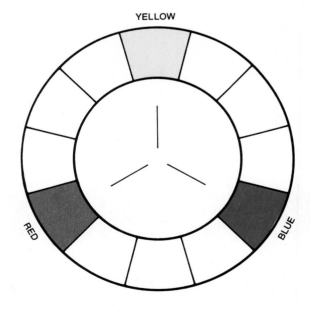

Fig. 21-2. Primary pigment colors.

Fig. 21-3. Secondary pigment colors.

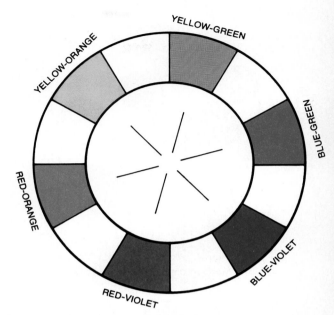

Fig. 21-4. Intermediate pigment colors.

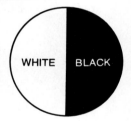

Fig. 21-5. White and black are not considered colors by some people. Both, however, are very important when producing printed products.

COLOR HARMONY

There are four color harmonies obtained by combining colors from a color wheel: monochromatic, analogous, complementary, and triadic.

Monochromatic color harmony is obtained by placing color next to a shade or tint of the same color (Fig. 21-6). A *shade* results when black is added; a *tint* is obtained when color is added to white. (When preparing a tint, always add the color to the white—never add the white to the color.)

Analogous color harmony uses two adjacent colors on the color wheel (Fig. 21-7). A primary and an intermediate or a secondary and an intermediate color combination can be used. Analogous differs from monochromatic in that two colors are used instead of only one.

Complementary color harmony results when two colors exactly opposite each other are used together. This color harmony is a combination of primary and secondary, or two intermediate colors (Fig. 21-8).

Triadic color harmony involves three colors. Any three colors which form the points of an equilateral triangle on the color wheel may be used. The three primary colors on the color wheel form this harmony. So do the secondary colors and two combinations of intermediate ones (Fig. 21-9).

Note that in making the four color harmonies, one color should stand out, either in strength or amount used. One color should dominate the combination used in any two-dimensional graphic layout. Study examples of the four harmonies and note the relationships.

PSYCHOLOGY OF COLOR

Colors are described as warm or cool. Yellow, orange, and red are considered *warm*. They make people think of heat. Green, blue, and violet are *cool*: green, the color of grass; blue, the color of water; and violet, the color of night or darkness. Human emotions are often affected by the selection of colors in a graphic arts design. Warm colors excite. Cool ones tend to be quieting.

Fig. 21-6. Monochromatic color harmony.

Fig. 21-8. Complementary color harmony.

Fig. 21-7. Analogous color harmony.

Fig. 21-9. Triadic color harmony.

MODERN USE OF COLOR

Color can be used to identify objects, as some cans of soft drinks are known by a certain color. Situations also can be controlled with color. In traffic lights, red means danger; green means proceed. The effect of color in graphic arts cannot be overemphasized. To use color effectively in two-dimensional graphic material, study what advertisers and packagers are doing. A few years ago, psychedelic colors were popular—strong blues, purples, and pinks. Later, earth tones were popular—browns, reds, and oranges. Combinations of colors speak their own language. Choose them with care.

UNIT 22 THUMBNAIL SKETCHES

Thumbnail sketches are simple idea sketches which help the designer quickly think through a number of possible ways of presenting the product. The designer and the buyer can then select the ideas that they would like to develop further.

Thumbnail sketches serve three main purposes: (1) They record ideas that might be forgotten. (2) They let you—and others—see how an idea looks. (3) They let you compare ideas.

Thumbnail sketches should be made as soon as the information is available and the pre-layout planning sheet has been done (Fig. 18-1). The copy should be written before thumbnail sketches are made so that all elements are planned for. The designer of a printed product should have all copy and specifications in hand when beginning work.

METHOD OF PREPARATION

1. Prepare the prelayout planning sheet (See Unit 18) and list the copy.
2. Mark the area of the printed product in one-quarter final size on grid paper (printed in light blue ink).
3. Select the copy elements that need emphasis. Using block shapes and shading, show in the thumbnail sketch where you want the main elements to be.
4. Use straight lines to represent type that is 12 points or smaller in size. For larger type you may shade in areas approximately the size you want. Do not use actual lettering for either the large or small type.
5. Outline the space for illustrations or photographs. Within this space, sketch the illustrations or content of the photograph. Just show outlines or shapes—enough for another person to get the idea. Thumbnail sketches of illustrations or photographs do not need much detail.

Prepare as many thumbnail sketches as you have ideas. Skilled designers prepare at least four of any copy given to them. Beginners sometimes have trouble in trying to think of several possibilities. You will need several sketches to give your customer a selection to choose from.

Figures 22-1 and 22-2 are examples of thumbnail sketches. Here is the copy for Figure 22-1:

Baseball
Support Little League
Every Saturday 9:00 A.M. Valley Park
Sponsored by the City Council

Study the copy. Note various positions in which copy elements could be placed for four different thumbnail sketches.

Copy for Figure 22-2 includes:

Summer Clothes Drive
April 8
We Need Clothes
Please Contribute
Bring Clothes to Main Lounges of the Dorms
7:00 to 9:00 P.M.

Note that only the word content is listed. The designer usually selects an illustration, if one is needed to help get the message to the reader. Each of the four thumbnail sketches uses a different illustration.

Thumbnail sketches are very important. They serve as the basis for the final printed material.

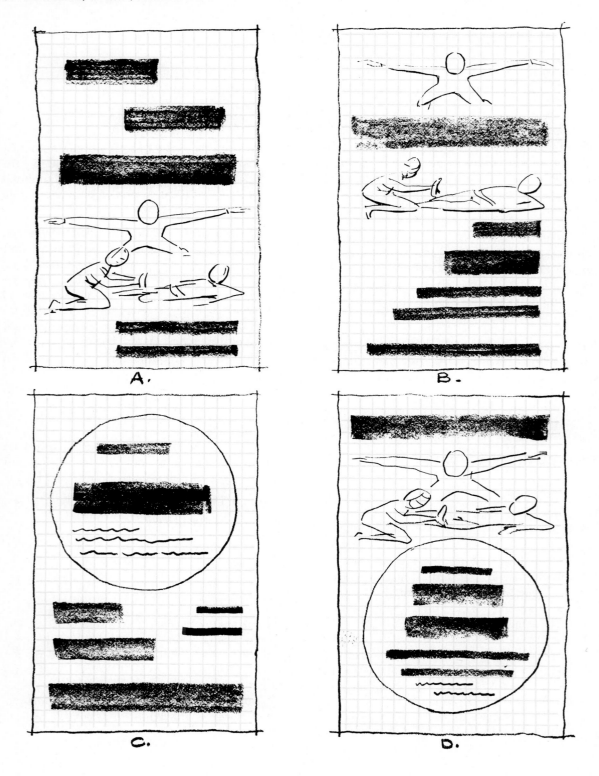

Fig. 22-1. A set of thumbnail sketches based on the customer's copy.

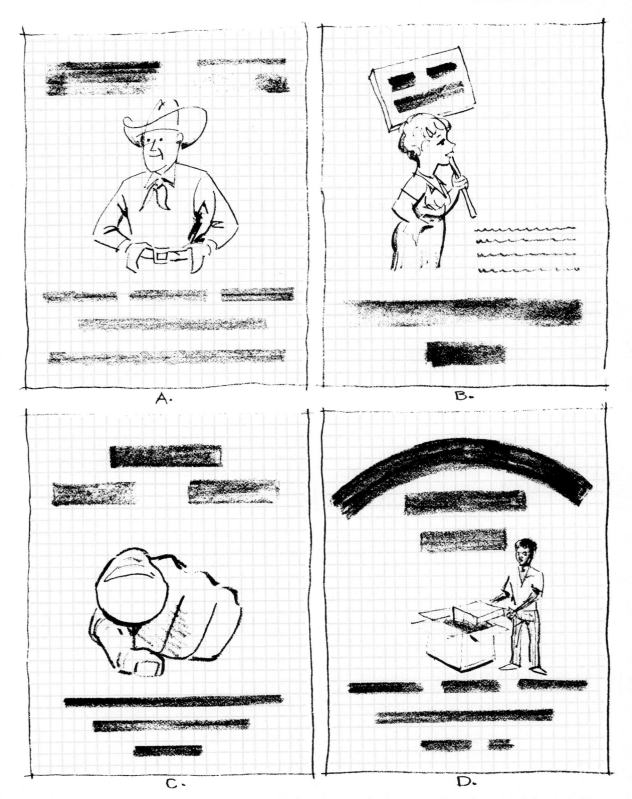

Fig. 22-2. A set of thumbnail sketches. Note that each sketch has a different illustration but uses the same copy.

UNIT 23 THE ROUGH LAYOUT

The second major step in the layout stage is preparing a rough layout, or *rough*. The rough is an improvement or refinement of a thumbnail sketch.

A rough layout has three main purposes. (1) It makes the client and designer choose one of the several sketched ideas. They may also decide to combine elements of two or more of the sketches. Whatever they do, the rough will represent their final decision. (2) It gives everyone concerned something to look at that can be studied and changed. (3) It lets the designer refine the final ideas.

In some cases, the rough layout is the only one prepared. If the material is simple or time is short, you may skip the thumbnail sketch and the comprehensive layout stages.

METHOD OF PREPARATION

1. Study the several thumbnail sketches that have been made.
2. Select the one that best presents the content. The selection can be made by the designer or customer or both.
3. Get a sheet of paper with a ¼-inch (6.35 mm) grid. The paper should be large enough for the layout to be drawn full size. The grid will help you to place design elements from the thumbnail sketch without guesswork.
4. Block in or outline the areas where the type and the illustrations are to go (Fig. 23-1).
5. Refer to the copy and add type to the type areas. When the type is larger than 12 point, sketch in the actual words or numbers. When it is smaller, show the lines of type with straight lines.
6. Sketch in the illustrations (Fig. 23-2). They should show more care and detail than the thumbnail-sketch illustration. The rough should give a good idea of what the finished product will look like.

7. Study the rough layout. Make additions or changes. Apply the five design principles from Unit 20. Let the customer comment on the rough. Changes are easiest to make at this stage.

As we said at the start of this unit, two or more thumbnail sketches can be combined in one rough layout. An example of such a combination is shown in Figure 23-3. This rough is based upon two thumbnail sketches (A and B) in Figure 22-2. Study these two figures to see how the combined rough layout was made.

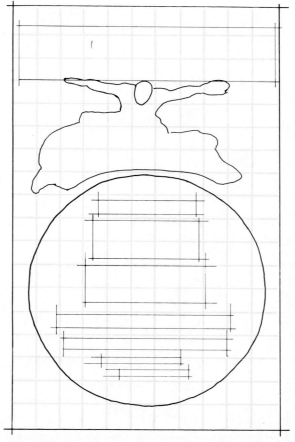

Fig. 23-1. Beginning a rough layout based on thumbnail sketch D in Figure 22-1.

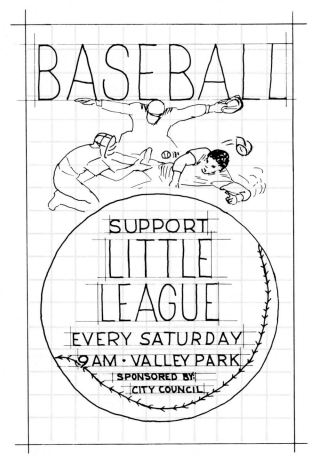

Fig. 23-2. Words and illustration sketched within the outlined areas.

Fig. 23-3. A rough layout based on two thumbnail sketches—Figure 22-2 A and B.

UNIT 24 THE COMPREHENSIVE LAYOUT

The comprehensive layout is the most important step in the production of a printed work. It is the master plan or blueprint of the finished product. It lets the designer and the purchaser see the finished product and change it if necessary.

After the designer and purchaser have made all the necessary decisions, the comprehensive layout will be marked with all information needed to complete the printed product. It will guide specialists who will produce the final product.

STEPS OF PREPARATION

1. Study the rough layout (Unit 23). This will give you the information for the comprehensive layout.
2. If the finished job is to have two or more colors, choose the colors where they will appear. Use colored pencils or felt-tip markers to show the color of each element.
3. Letter all display type in the exact position desired. *Display type* is type that is 14 points and larger. Make the letters look like

Fig. 24-1. The first three steps of a comprehensive layout have been completed, based on the rough layout in Figure 23-2.

the actual type as much as possible. Figure 24-1 shows the first three procedural steps completed.

4. Lines should be used to show the correct position of body type. Body type is type that will be 12 points or smaller. The actual copy should also be attached and identified with labels (for example, copy A, copy B). Notes on the layout should show where copy A, copy B, etc., are to go.
5. Sketch the illustrations carefully in the correct positions.
6. Block the space for the photographs, if they are used, and attach the glossy print if it is available. If the photographs have not yet been taken, describe their content and tell where the photographs can be obtained.
7. After all content has been placed on the layout, make the overlay sheet.

8. Thoroughly review the layout. Be sure you have included all copy and given full production information on the overlay sheet. For detailed instructions on how to make an overlay sheet, study the following seven steps.

CONTENT OF THE OVERLAY SHEET

The overlay sheet should contain all information the production personnel need to put together the finished product. The overlay sheet lets the designer keep the layout itself free of instructions.

1. Give the kind, size, and style of type for each group or element of the layout.
2. Show the type position if specific margins or line lengths are wanted. The compositor should be able to measure the position of the words or lines from the layout.
3. Give specific information about the illustrations and photographs. Tell where the camera-ready illustration copy is available or where the photograph can be obtained. *Camera-ready* material (copy or illustrations) requires no further preparation. It is ready to be photographed with the process camera.
4. List the color or colors of ink. If the entire product is printed in one color mention this only once. If several colors are used, show the color to be used by each colored element (See Fig. 24-2).
5. Indicate the kind, finish, weight, color, and size of paper.
6. Tell the number of finished copies wanted.
7. If possible, give the reproduction process to be used. Sometimes this decision is not the responsibility of the design specialist but is made by the foreman for the production department.

The importance of the overlay sheet cannot be stressed too much. The quality of the entire comprehensive layout is very important, but if the overlay sheet is not correct the final product will not be right. Study the overlay sheet shown in Figure 24-2. It contains the information that should be listed. Note how and where these data are listed.

Fig. 24-2. A completed comprehensive layout, based on the rough layout in Figure 23-3. This illustration is reduced. Production information is on an overlay sheet.

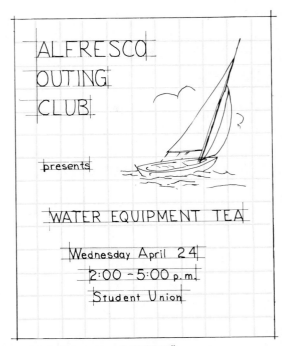

Fig. 24-4. Rough layout (reduced).

Fig. 24-3. Thumbnail sketches.

Fig. 24-5. Comprehensive layout (reduced).

Normally the thumbnail sketches, rough layout, and comprehensive layout make up a complete set of layouts. However, sometimes the purchaser of the printed product also desires to see a finished or *final layout*. This layout is sometimes called a *mechanical* and can be used as a camera-ready paste-up. It contains quality

ALFRESCO OUTING CLUB

presents

WATER EQUIPMENT TEA

Wednesday, April 24
2:00–5:00 p.m.
Student Union

Fig. 24-6. A finished, or final, layout (reduced). It is also called a *mechanical* and can be used for camera-ready copy.

reproductions of the original illustrations or copies of the photographs used. It also has reproduction proofs of the type that has already been typeset. The customer can then see exactly how the final product will look. This is the final opportunity for changes before the manufacture of the printed product begins.

Study the complete sets of layouts, from the thumbnail sketches, to the rough layout, to the comprehensive, to the finished or final one (Figs. 24-3 through 24-6). See how the theme or basic idea was carried from the thumbnail sketches to the final layout.

DESIGN PRINCIPLES REVIEWED

While making the layout, it is important to keep in mind the five basic design principles discussed in Unit 20: page proportion, balance, contrast, unity, and rhythm. Persons who have not worked on the layouts may be asked for their frank comments. During the process of preparing the series of layouts needed for a finished printed product, changes may constantly be made to improve the final product.

The designer and the customer should closely study the layouts before the mechanical operations start. The customer can see what the product will look like. Changes and corrections can be made without delays and undue production costs. Planning cannot be overemphasized; it can be only underdone.

_{UNIT} 25 PAGE AND SIGNATURE LAYOUT

A page for a book, magazine, newspaper, or other printed material should be designed for easy reading. The eye should enter the page at the upper left-hand corner and follow the lines of the text and illustrations without difficulty. Pages of printed matter should look interesting. Design principles must be applied when preparing page and signature layouts.

MARGINS

Margins need careful planning. The amount of white space around printed material affects both the beauty and the readability of the page.

Single page margins. To choose margins for a single page, first see how much type and other material must be fitted in. Then choose the margins for the left and right sides of the page. The top margin will usually be about 25 percent larger than the side margin. The bottom margin is usually about 75 percent larger than the side

margin (Fig. 25-1). Remember that the visual center of the page is above the actual center. The larger bottom margin keeps the proper vertical balance. Remember also that larger type needs larger margins than smaller type.

Double page margins. When two pages open next to each other, as in a book or magazine, the margins must help the pages look as though they belong together. The size of the outside margin is based, generally, on the type size and the length of lines. The inside margin, called the *gutter*, is half the width of the outside one. The two inside margins combined should be as wide as one outside one. Thus, the three vertical margins are equal and look balanced (Fig. 25-2).

Figure 25-3 shows how to establish the top and bottom margins. Draw diagonal lines from the upper inside corner to the lower outside corner of each page. Where the diagonal line crosses the vertical side margins, mark the top and bottom margins. Draw solid marginal lines

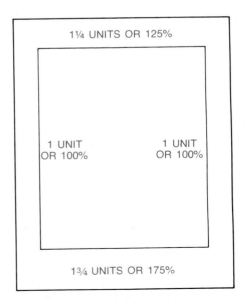

Fig. 25-1. Single page margins.

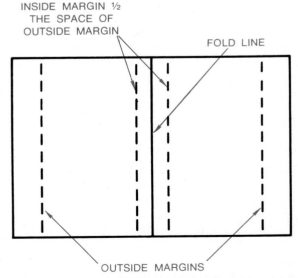

Fig. 25-2. Book margins. Fix outside margins, then inside ones.

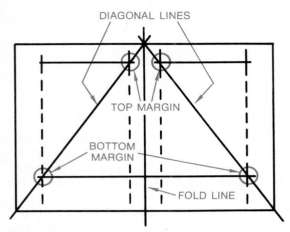

Fig. 25-3. Book margins. Fix top margins, then bottom ones.

for each page. Note how the two areas in Figure 25-4 that are to contain reading material appear to belong together. Also note that they seem balanced.

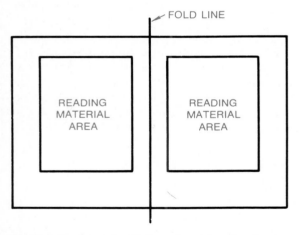

Fig. 25-4. Book margins. Balanced margins give pleasing and readable pages.

DUMMY LAYOUT

When books are printed, groups of pages are printed on the front and back of one large sheet of paper. This large sheet is then folded so that each panel of the folded paper is about the size of the final book page. The printed, folded sheet is called a *signature*. A signature is trimmed to the exact page size by cutting off the three outside edges. The pages will then turn and appear in the proper order.

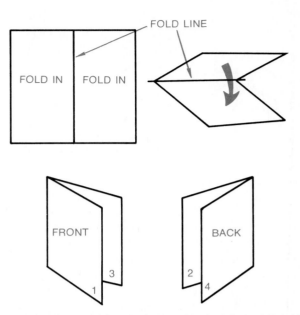

Fig. 25-5. A four-page signature printed on both sides.

Normally, signatures contain four, eight, sixteen, thirty-two, or sixty-four pages. How do you know how to place the pages so that, when they are printed on the large sheet, they will be in the right relationship to one another when the sheet is folded? Easy. You make a dummy layout.

A *dummy layout* is simply a piece of paper folded so that it has the same number of panels as there will be pages in the signature. You then go through the dummy layout and number the pages in the lower outside corner. When you unfold it, you have each page marked at the bottom. Figure 25-5 shows how to make a four-page signature. Figure 25-6 shows an eight-page signature.

Note that most greeting cards are eight-page signatures, untrimmed and printed on only one side. To make a book, several signatures may be bound together. Signatures of different lengths may be combined. For example, if you want a forty-page booklet, it may be printed in two signatures—one of thirty-two pages and one of eight pages.

In addition to page numbers, the dummy should have headings, illustrations, and key pages marked. It is good practice to make up a separate list showing page numbers and what content will appear on each page. This will help

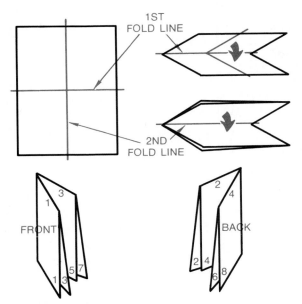

Fig. 25-6. An eight-page signature printed on both sides, or a four-page greeting card printed on one side.

to identify the pages during the several mechanical functions needed to complete the final product.

COPYFITTING PROCEDURE

The word *copyfitting* means exactly what it says—fitting copy to a given space. It is also true that the space needed may be determined by the amount of copy. The design and layout artist must be able to copyfit accurately to do a good job.

The design and layout artist will be faced with the following situations:

1. The layout has been prepared and the copy has been written. The job is to decide the best kind of type, the correct size, and the correct line spacing (leading).
2. The layout has been prepared and the type and leading have been selected. The job is to decide the correct amount of copy.
3. The copy has been written and the type and leading have been chosen. The job is to prepare a layout that will present it attractively. Layout people who know copyfitting thoroughly should be able to handle all these situations.

METHODS AVAILABLE

Copyfitting may be done in several different ways. Among them are the square-inch, the character count, and the character-space methods. The first is based on the number of words that will fit in a square inch.

The character-count method is based on the actual type characters in a line. This includes numbers, punctuation marks, and word spaces. It is very accurate, and is used by many copyfitters. Details of this method are given in this unit.

The character-space method gives each character a specific number of units. It is very accurate but very time consuming. It is used mostly when fitting headings or headlines.

CHARACTER COUNT METHOD

This method is fairly simple. However, it does involve using large tables of numbers and some basic arithmetic. A hand-held calculator is useful. In this method, the main task is to count accurately and read the type charts properly. Here are the basic steps to use on prepared copy.

1. Count the characters, including spaces between words. There are several ways to do this. The most common is to review the typed page, select the average length line, and draw a vertical line (Fig. 25-7). Count the number of characters in the average line. Then, multiply by the number of lines. This will give an approximate amount. If greater accuracy is desired, add the characters beyond the vertical line. Then subtract the characters short of this vertical line. This will provide the exact number of characters on a page of copy (manuscript).
2. Decide on the line length (column width) to be used for the typeset matter. This length is always measured in picas.
3. Select the type—kind, style, and size. Choose the amount of leading. Refer to a type specimen book, and choose a type that suits the job.

TASTE

What is taste? To me, taste is the ladder by which we mount toward greater perceptions of beauty, by exchanging, progressively, the thing which we recognize most instinctively as not altogether good, for something we recognize as less gross, and in turn, exchanging that thing for something more pleasing, until, finally, we become more and more capable of distinguishing between mere personal opinion and the opinion of those whose taste is accepted as fine; our taste has now become a discriminating faculty which we exercise almost intuitively.

Taste in printing determines the form typography is to take; the selection of a congruous type; the quality and suitability for its purpose of the paper to be used; the care, and labor, and time, and cost of materials devoted to its production, and all in direct ratio to its ultimate worth and destination. Taste determines, too, whether the work shall bear decoration or not, how much, and where it is to be introduced; in short, what is admissible and what is becoming.

The quality of taste revealed in the great printing of the past is, usually, the outcome of simple thinking, simplicity in form and in execution. Quaintness in an old piece of printing may be admired because of its sincerity; to revive or imitate it in a piece of modern work is distasteful, hateful even, because of its affectation.

Fig. 25-7. In the character count method of copyfitting, a vertical line is drawn to mark the average line length. (The copy is from a talk by typographer Frederic W. Goudy.)

4. Find the number of characters that will fit into the selected line length. See Figure 25-8. It shows the characters per pica for the different kinds, styles, and sizes of type. Figure 25-10 gives the number of characters for various line lengths. Typesetting equipment firms and commercial type houses provide character count tables for their customers.

5. Decide the number of typeset lines needed for the manuscript copy. To do this, divide the total number of manuscript characters by the number of characters that can be typeset in one line.

6. Find the column depth. Do this by multiplying the number of needed typeset lines by the point size. Include the leading. To convert this figure (points) into picas, divide by 12 (number of points in a pica).

8.0		8.5		9.0		9.5		10.0		10.5		11.0		11.5		12.0	
set	c/p	set	c/p	set	c/p	set	c/p	set	c/p	set	c/p	set	c/p	set	c/p	set	c/p
8.0	3.34			9.0	2.97			10.0	2.67			11.0	2.43			12.0	2.23
8.0	3.34			9.0	2.97			10.0	2.67			11.0	2.43			12.0	2.23
8.0	3.27			9.0	2.90			10.0	2.61			11.0	2.38			12.0	2.18
8.0	3.27			9.0	2.90			10.0	2.61			11.0	2.38			12.0	2.18
8.0	3.27			9.0	2.90			10.0	2.61			11.0	2.38			12.0	2.18
8.0	3.27			9.0	2.90			10.0	2.61			11.0	2.38			12.0	2.18
8.0	2.95			9.0	2.61			10.0	2.36			11.0	2.15			12.0	1.97
8.0	2.95			9.0	2.61			10.0	2.36			11.0	2.15			12.0	1.97
8.0	3.99			9.0	3.54			10.0	3.19			11.0	2.90			12.0	2.65
8.0	3.99			9.0	3.54			10.0	3.19			11.0	2.90			12.0	2.65
8.0	3.99			9.0	3.54			10.0	3.19			11.0	2.90			12.0	2.65
8.0	3.99			9.0	3.54			10.0	3.19			11.0	2.90			12.0	2.65
8.0	3.53			9.0	3.14			10.0	2.82			11.0	2.57			12.0	2.35
8.0	3.53			9.0	3.14			10.0	2.82			11.0	2.57			12.0	2.35
8.0	3.53			9.0	3.14			10.0	2.82			11.0	2.57			12.0	2.35
8.0	3.53			9.0	3.14			10.0	2.82			11.0	2.57			12.0	2.35
7.5	3.35	8.5	2.96	9.0	2.80	9.5	2.65					10.0	2.51			11.0	2.28
7.5	3.35	8.5	2.96	9.0	2.80	9.5	2.65					10.0	2.51			11.0	2.28

AGFA–COMPUGRAPHIC

Fig. 25-8. Manufacturers of composing equipment supply tables like this one to help in copyfitting. The table shows the number of characters per pica for various faces and point sizes. Futura Book, for instance, has 2.97 characters per pica when set in 9 point.

Fig. 25-9. A textbook production editor determining the amount of page space needed for the manuscript copy.

Characters Per Multiple Picas

1	8	9	10	11	12	13	14	15	16	17	18	19	20	21	22	23	24	25	26	27	28	29	30
1.0	8.0	9.0	10	11	12	13	14	15	16	17	18	19	20	21	22	23	24	25	26	27	28	29	30
1.1	8.8	9.9	11	12	13	14	15	17	18	19	20	21	22	23	24	25	26	28	29	30	31	32	33
1.2	9.6	11	12	13	14	16	17	18	19	20	22	23	24	25	26	28	29	30	31	32	34	35	36
1.3	10	12	13	14	16	17	18	20	21	22	23	25	26	27	29	30	31	33	34	35	36	38	39
1.4	11	13	14	15	17	18	20	21	22	24	25	27	28	29	31	32	34	35	36	38	39	41	42
1.5	12	14	15	17	18	20	21	23	24	26	27	29	30	32	33	35	36	38	39	41	42	44	45
1.6	13	14	16	18	19	21	22	24	26	27	29	30	32	34	35	37	38	40	42	43	45	46	48
1.7	14	15	17	19	20	22	24	26	27	29	31	32	34	36	37	39	41	43	44	46	48	49	51
1.8	14	16	18	20	22	23	25	27	29	31	32	34	36	38	40	41	43	45	47	49	50	52	54
1.9	15	17	19	21	23	25	27	29	30	32	34	36	38	40	42	44	46	48	49	51	53	55	57
2.0	16	18	20	22	24	26	28	30	32	34	36	38	40	42	44	46	48	50	52	54	56	58	60
2.1	17	19	21	23	25	27	29	32	34	36	38	40	42	44	46	48	50	53	55	57	59	61	63
2.2	18	20	22	24	26	29	31	33	35	37	40	42	44	46	48	51	53	55	57	59	62	64	66
2.3	18	21	23	25	28	30	32	35	37	39	41	44	46	48	51	53	55	58	60	62	64	67	69
2.4	19	22	24	26	29	31	34	36	38	41	43	46	48	50	53	55	58	60	62	65	67	70	72
2.5	20	23	25	28	30	33	35	38	40	43	45	48	50	53	55	58	60	63	65	68	70	73	75
2.6	21	23	26	29	31	34	36	39	42	44	47	49	52	55	57	60	62	65	68	70	73	75	78
2.7	22	24	27	30	32	35	38	41	43	46	49	51	54	57	59	62	65	68	70	73	76	78	81
2.8	22	25	28	31	34	36	39	42	45	48	50	53	56	59	62	64	67	70	73	76	78	81	84
2.9	23	26	29	32	35	38	41	44	46	49	52	55	58	61	64	67	70	73	75	78	81	84	87
3.0	24	27	30	33	36	39	42	45	48	51	54	57	60	63	66	69	72	75	78	81	84	87	90
3.1	25	28	31	34	37	40	43	47	50	53	56	59	62	65	68	71	74	78	81	84	87	90	93
3.2	26	29	32	35	38	42	45	48	51	54	58	61	64	67	70	74	77	80	83	86	90	93	96
3.3	26	30	33	36	40	43	46	50	53	56	59	63	66	69	73	76	79	83	86	89	92	96	99
3.4	27	31	34	37	41	44	48	51	54	58	61	65	68	71	75	78	82	85	88	92	95	99	102
3.5	28	32	35	39	42	46	49	53	56	60	63	67	70	74	77	81	84	88	91	95	98	102	105
3.6	29	32	36	40	43	47	50	54	58	61	65	68	72	76	79	83	86	90	94	97	101	104	108
3.7	30	33	37	41	44	48	52	56	59	63	67	70	74	78	81	85	89	93	96	100	104	107	111
3.8	30	34	38	42	46	49	53	57	61	65	68	72	76	80	84	87	91	95	99	103	106	110	114
3.9	31	35	39	43	47	51	55	59	62	66	70	74	78	82	86	90	94	98	101	105	109	113	117
4.0	32	36	40	44	48	52	56	60	64	68	72	76	80	84	88	92	96	100	104	108	112	116	120
4.1	33	37	41	45	49	53	57	62	66	70	74	78	82	86	90	94	98	103	107	111	115	119	123
4.2	34	38	42	46	50	55	59	63	67	71	76	80	84	88	92	97	101	105	109	113	118	122	126
4.3	34	39	43	47	52	56	60	65	69	73	77	82	86	90	95	99	103	108	112	116	120	125	129
4.4	35	40	44	48	53	57	62	66	70	75	79	84	88	92	97	101	106	110	114	119	123	128	132
4.5	36	41	45	50	54	59	63	68	72	77	81	86	90	95	99	104	108	113	117	122	126	131	135
4.6	37	41	46	51	55	60	64	69	74	78	83	87	92	97	101	106	110	115	120	124	129	133	138
4.7	38	42	47	52	56	61	66	71	75	80	85	89	94	99	103	108	113	118	122	127	132	136	141
4.8	38	43	48	53	58	62	67	72	77	82	86	91	96	101	106	110	115	120	125	130	134	139	144
4.9	39	44	49	54	59	64	69	74	78	83	88	93	98	103	108	113	118	123	127	132	137	142	147
5.0	40	45	50	55	60	65	70	75	80	85	90	95	100	105	110	115	120	125	130	135	140	145	150

Fig. 25-10. Characters per pica. This table tells the number of characters in a line of a given pica length. For example, if a face has 3 characters per pica, a 16-pica line will have 48 characters.

UNIT 26 LEARNING EXPERIENCES: PLANNING, DESIGNING, AND LAYOUT

KEY TERMS

Unit 18

Layout

Pre-layout planning

Unit 19

Line gauge
Pica

Point

Unit 20

Balance (formal and
  informal)
Center
Contrast
Golden proportion

Optical
Page proportion
Rhythm
Unity
White space

Unit 21

Analogous
Color harmony
Color wheel
Complementary
Cool colors
Intermediate colors

Monochromatic
Primary colors
Shade
Tint
Triadic
Warm colors

Unit 22

Grid paper

Thumbnail sketch

Unit 23

Rough layout

Unit 24

Body matter (body
  copy)
Camera-ready
Comprehensive
  layout
Display type

Heading
Line gauge
Mechanical layout
Overlay sheet
Subheading

DISCUSSION TOPICS

1. Why is a layout for a printed product valuable?
2. What is the value of using the metric system instead of the linear-inch system?
3. How does color affect us? How is this put to use in the graphic arts?
4. What is the purpose of preparing thumbnail sketches?
5. Why must the margins be chosen carefully when preparing layouts for a book, magazine, newspaper, or other printed matter?

ACTIVITIES

Units 18, 19, 22, 23, & 24

1. Make a complete set of layouts for a poster advertising a future sporting event in your school. Prepare the pre-layout planning form, four thumbnail sketches, one rough layout, and one comprehensive layout. Be sure to include the overlay sheet on the comprehensive layout.

Unit 20

2. Obtain several printed samples of advertising brochures. Examine them closely. Was the space used as effectively as possible? Were the five principles of design—page proportion, balance, contrast, unity, and rhythm—considered in the brochures? What areas of the layout in the brochures could have been improved?

Unit 21

3. Prepare a color wheel. Use water paints and mix them to match the proper primary, secondary, and intermediate colors. Also, show examples of the four common color harmonies.

Unit 25

4. Prepare a dummy for a sixteen-page booklet. Identify each page by number. Locate and rule in the margins for pages 1, 8, 9, and 16.

A N
INQUIRY
INTO THE
RIGHTS of the BRITISH Colonies,

Intended as an Anſwer to

The Regulations lately made concerning the Colonies, and the Taxes impoſed upon them conſidered.

In a Letter addreſſed to the Author of that Pamphlet.

By *RICHARD BLAND*, of VIRGINIA.

Dedit omnibus Deus pro virili portione ſapientiam, ut et inaudita inveſtigare poſſent et audita perpendere.
LACTANTIUS.

WILLIAMSBURG:
Printed by ALEXANDER PURDIE, & C°.
MDCCLXVI.

Charts and graphs are produced in minutes on electronic composition equipment.
INTERLEAF

4 TYPE COMPOSITION METHODS

27 INTRODUCTION TO TYPE AND IMAGE COMPOSITION

Type composition and *typesetting* are names for the processes of setting, preparing, and arranging type. They refer to the act of generating characters and symbols and arranging them to communicate thoughts and ideas to someone else. The letters, words, sentences, and paragraphs that you are reading now have been composed or set by one of several methods.

METHODS OF TYPE COMPOSITION

There are two basic typesetting classifications: hot and cold. In *hot* type composition, molten metal is cast to form the letter (symbol) or the entire line of type. From type composed in hot metal, printed copies can be produced directly on a printing press.

Cold type composition is non-hot metal typesetting. It is done in several ways. Some of these methods are: impact, dry transfer, photographic, and electronic or digital composition. Machines that place an image on paper using pressure action are called *impact devices*. A second method is *dry transfer*. In the dry transfer method, the preprinted letters are put in place by hand. Machines designed to place images on paper photographically or by means of a CRT or laser light beam are called *photocomposers*. They make up the third cold composition method.

Systems have now been designed to assemble and produce type characters, illustrations, and halftone photographs by electronic/digital means. Both the electronic/digital and the photographic typesetting methods have been made possible by the computer. This fourth category of cold typesetting is often referred to as *imagesetting*. Such equipment systems permit all types of images to be collected, sized, positioned, and collectively assembled into a single document. This technique is sometimes called "electronic paste-up," as compared to hand paste-up (see Unit 46).

QUALITY AND SPEED

The need for quality and speed has led the graphic arts industry to develop sophisticated machinery for type and image composition. This book, for example, was typeset using a fully automatic computer-controlled, high speed, photocomposition system (Fig. 27-1).

HISTORICAL NOTES

In about 1450 Johann Gutenberg of Germany first invented a practical method for using individual letters in composition. He devoted his entire life to perfecting movable metal type. Before his invention, pages were cut by hand, in reverse, on blocks of wood. By casting individual letters Gutenberg was able to compose a page, print it, and reuse the type, which, unlike

Fig. 27-1. An electronic typesetting machine like this one was used to create the type for this book.

MABLE TAINTER LITERARY LIBRARY AND EDUCATIONAL SOCIETY.

Fig. 27-2 A ticket printer set manufactured before the U.S. Civil War.

the wood block, did not have to be thrown away.

An early ticket printer is shown in Figure 27-2. the small box of type characters and the printing palet (which held the type while printing) could be carried easily from place to place.

Mechanical composition was not developed until four centuries after Gutenberg's invention. In 1884 Ottmar Mergenthaler, who came to the United States from Germany as a young man, introduced a machine called a *slug caster* that could cast a complete line of type. This machine, under the trade name of Linotype, was put into practical use about 1886.

Figure 27-3 shows an early model of a slug casting machine in operation. Some machines like this and others shown in Unit 29 are still in use in the United States and throughout the world. Mechanical hot metal composition was the dominant method of typesetting until the 1960s. Today, these machines are no longer manufactured in the western world. Hot type machines are still being manufactured in the Soviet Union.

At the close of the Second World War another major development took place in type composition. A machine was developed that produced type photographically. Today, most type is set by machines that combine not only photographic, but also electronic and computer technology.

HARRIS CORPORATION

Fig. 27-3. An early model typesetting machine that made entire lines of type in single pieces of metal called *slugs*.

WORD AND INFORMATION PROCESSING

Word processing was created as a business office function. Word processing means the handling of words used in letters, memorandums, and business records. Businesses and manufacturing companies large and small must move great amounts of information among individuals and groups of people. To do this, they are now using information processing equipment and systems.

A modern word processing and office information system is shown in Figure 27-4. Each person has a workstation, or a terminal, where information can be entered, or input, into the total processing system. All of the workstations are networked, or joined, together. This permits access to common information and output devices.

Word processing equipment becomes involved in graphic arts when it is interfaced (linked) with photographic and digital image-setting equipment. Once the type characters and artwork have been entered into the system, they can, with the proper coding instructions to the machine, be transmitted to imagesetting devices. The material goes straight from the word processor storage into type. It no longer must be rekeyboarded on a typesetting machine. This saves time and expense.

New technologies called *Page Description Languages* (PDLs) have brought word processing and typesetting closer than ever. The most popular PDL today is the PostScript language created by Adobe Systems, Inc., which enables the user to create text in composition programs such as Ventura, PageMaker, and Microsoft Word. PostScript also allows the integration of text with graphics. Thus, it treats all graphic images—text and illustrations—

COURTESY OF KONICA BUSINESS MACHINES U.S.A., INC.

Fig. 27-5. Facsimile (Fax) machines are frequently used to transmit graphic information anywhere in the world over standard telephone lines.

in the same way. Images can be scanned and positioned on pages in a WYSIWYG (What You See Is What You Get) display on the screen. Type and images can also be rotated, enlarged, cropped, and enhanced.

A similar, though somewhat less powerful PDL is the Printer Command Language (PCL) used by most office printers, such as Hewlett Packard laser printers. Type is scaled and composed very much as it would be by a typesetter.

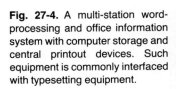

Fig. 27-4. A multi-station word-processing and office information system with computer storage and central printout devices. Such equipment is commonly interfaced with typesetting equipment.

WANG LABORATORIES

Many businesses today depend on the *facsimile* (fax) machine. This transmits a document as digital data over telephone lines to another fax machine, which reproduces the document at low to medium resolution (less than 300 dpi). Earlier fax machines were slow—eight minutes per page. Transmission time is now as low as 10 seconds per page. In addition, the machines themselves have become less expensive as they have become more popular. (Fig. 27-5).

DESKTOP COMPOSITION

Desktop composition, or desktop publishing, has become common in business. Special software makes it possible to assemble type, artwork, and photographs by using personal computers. See Section 22 for detailed information.

UNIT 28 FOUNDRY TYPE COMPOSITION

Foundry type composition is a fundamental method of reproduction. It was the basic method from the fifteenth through the nineteenth centuries, and some specialty jobs are still done with hand-set type. While it is not much used today, learning to set foundry type will help you understand other kinds of typesetting much better. Many of the words used in all types of composition come from the days of foundry type.

FOUNDRY TYPE

Foundry type is made of lead, tin, and antimony. Foundry type characters are available in the point sizes as shown in Figure 19-6. The parts of foundry type are shown in Figure 28-1. Knowing these parts will help you understand foundry type composition. Foundry type is .918 of an inch from foot to face. Rules, leaders, and cuts are the same height. *Rules* are strips of metal that will print straight lines. *Leaders* are strips of metal that print dotted or dashed lines. *Cuts* are illustrations from either artwork or photographs. "Cuts" is short for woodcuts,

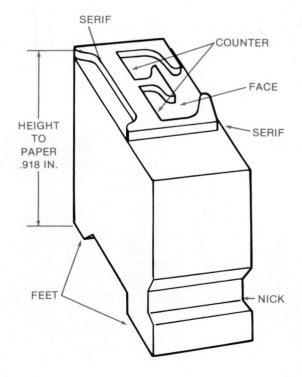

Fig. 28-1. A foundry type character, showing the important parts and the height.

reminding us of the time when most illustrations were made in that way.

Here are the main parts of a piece of foundry type.

Face. The printing surface of the relief character.

Serif. The finishing lines of the strokes forming the character.

Counter. The center areas of letters that are lower than the letter surface.

Nick. The indentation in the base of the character, which guides the person setting type.

Feet. The bottom of the type character.

CALIFORNIA JOB CASE

The California job case, shown in Figure 28-2, is a basic storage and retrieval system for foundry type. The typecase or drawer measures about 1 by 16 by 32 inches. It has 89 individual compartments. It has storage for small or lowercase letters, capital or uppercase letters, numbers, punctuation marks, and word-spacing materials. Special characters, called *ligatures*, are also stored in the typecase. Ligatures are two or more letters formed on one piece of metal, such as *ff*, *fl*, *fi*, *ffi*, and *ffl*. This is done to save space and keep the letters from being broken.

Typecases are stored in cabinets called *banks* (Fig. 28-3). They are placed on top of the bank while composing or making up type. The lay or arrangement of type in the case should be studied and learned before beginning to compose.

THOMPSON CABINET COMPANY

Fig. 28-3. Typecase storage and work area, called a *bank*.

SPACING MATERIALS

There are seven spacing materials used to put space between and around words (Fig. 28-4). The size of these word-spacing materials matches the type sizes. The unit, or *em quad,* is the basic spacing; it is always the square of the particular type size being used. For example: with 12-point type, the em quad is 12 points by 12

Fig. 28-2. The lay (arrangement) of the California job case.

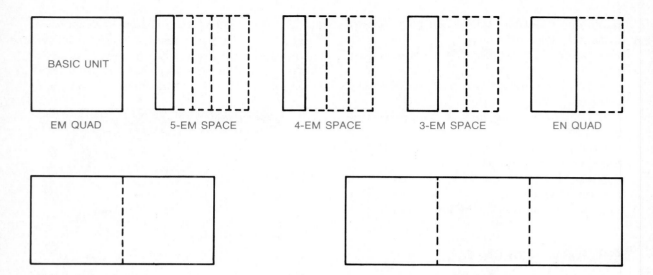

EM QUAD   5-EM SPACE   4-EM SPACE   3-EM SPACE   EN QUAD

BASIC UNIT

Fig. 28-4. The seven basic sizes of word-spacing materials.

points. All other spaces and quads have a direct size relationship to the em quad.

The en quad is ½ the width of an em quad. A 3-em space is ⅓ the width of an em quad, a 4-em space is ¼ of the width and a 5-em space is ⅕ of the width. The 2-em quad is twice the width of the em quad: the 3-em quad is three times as wide.

Hair spaces or *thin spaces* are used for word spacing when a very small amount of additional space is required. A brass hair space is 1 point in thickness; a copper hair space is ½ point.

Material for line spacing (putting spaces between lines) comes in two major thicknesses (Fig. 28-5). The *slug* is commonly 6 points thick and can be cut to any pica length. A *lead* is generally 2 points thick and can also be cut to any pica length.

COMPOSING STICK AND GALLEY

The *composing stick* (Fig. 28-6) is a hand-held device that is used while composing, or setting up, foundry type. The stick is about 2 inches wide and is adjustable in pica and half-pica lengths. A common maximum length for a composing stick is 34 picas.

A *galley* is a three-sided metal tray used for type storage and typeform make-up (Fig. 28-7). A *typeform* is a set of lines of type arranged to

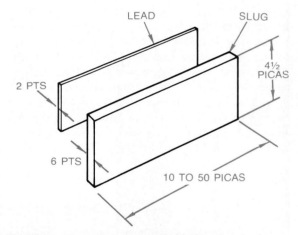

Fig. 28-5. Line-spacing materials and their measures.

form paragraphs and pages. Several galleys can be stored in a galley cabinet, shown in Figure 28-8.

COMPOSING TYPE

Foundry type composition is not difficult, but it must be done carefully. Knowledge of the lay of the typecase and the point system of measurement, discussed in Unit 19, are needed for good composition. Follow these steps closely for successful foundry type composition:

1. Place the typecase on top of a bank. Be sure

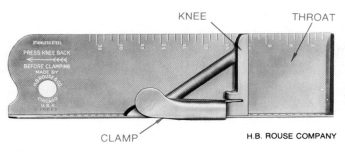

Fig. 28-6. A composing stick.

THOMPSON CABINET COMPANY

Fig. 28-7. A galley, used for typeform storage and make-up.

THOMPSON CABINET COMPANY

Fig. 28-8. A galley storage cabinet.

Fig. 28-9. The correct way to hold a composing stick.

Fig. 28-10. Composing lines of foundry type.

the case is caught by the lip of the slanting top so it will not slide to the floor.

2. Select a composing stick and adjust it to the desired length of line. Hold the composing stick in the palm of the left hand, with the thumb extending into the open throat (Fig. 28-9).

3. Place a slug in the stick. Slugs and leads should be slightly shorter than the line length to avoid binding in the stick.

4. Insert the first letter of the first word in the lower left corner of the stick as shown in Figure 28-10. Be sure that the nick on the type is toward the open side or scale of the composing stick. Type in the stick is always upside down but you can read it from left to right.

5. Continue composing the remaining letters of the first word.

6. Insert a 3-em space, which is the usual word

spacing between words composed in small letters (Fig. 28-4). An en quad should be used between words composed in all capital letters. Continue composing until there is no space left to compose another word.

7. *Justify* (space the line to the correct length) by placing equal spaces and quads between words to make the line snug. When the line of type can be pushed away from the back of the stick and stand alone, it is properly justified.

8. Insert a lead or slug into the stick. The one chosen depends on the amount of space wanted between the lines. Sometimes two leads or a lead-slug combination are used.

9. Continue composing lines in the same way. Carefully justify each line. All lines must be the same length to be held properly in the printing press.

DUMPING AND TYING

When the composing stick is full or when the needed lines have been composed, the type must be removed (dumped) from the stick and tied with string. The operations should be done so that you don't make pi. Making *pi* (pronounced like *pie*) is what printers call spilling the type.

1. Insert a slug against the last line that was composed in the stick. This supports the line and the entire typeform.
2. Place a galley on top of the bank.
3. Position the composing stick inside the galley.
4. Grasp the lines of type (typeform) as shown in Figure 28-11 and push from the stick.
5. Slide the typeform against the corner of the galley, as shown in Figure 28-12.

Fig. 28-11. Removing lines of type from the composing stick.

6. Tie the typeform. (Fig. 28-12). Wrap the string clockwise around the form six or seven times and tie it with a printer's knot, as illustrated in Figure 28-13.

7. Proofing, or taking an impression of the type, is the next step. It is discussed in Section 5, Unit 36.

Fig. 28-12. Tying a typeform.

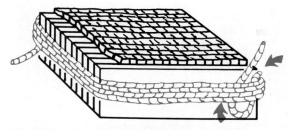

Fig. 28-13. A tied typeform. Note the printer's knot.

DISTRIBUTING TYPE

After the typeform has been proofed or printed, the individual letters and spaces must be put back where they belong. All materials—type characters, spaces, quads, leads, and slugs—must be put away so they can be found the next time.

1. Place the galley, with the typeform and the typecase on top of the bank.
2. Position the typeform with the nicks away from you and untie it. Be careful not to pi the form while removing the string.
3. Put two or three lines of type in your left hand as in Figure 28-14. Squeeze the lines

Fig. 28-14. Distributing type—putting it back into the type-case.

tightly on all four sides and lift carefully. Place the lines in your left hand between the thumb and middle finger, with the index finger supporting the bottom slug.

4. Remove the top slug and begin on the right side by grasping a complete word between your right thumb and index finger, also as in Fig. 28-14.
5. Distribute the letters and spacing to their proper locations in the case by carefully dropping one character at a time. Doing this takes practice; do not become discouraged if you have trouble dropping only one character.
6. Put all other materials back where they belong—leads, slugs, galley, string, and typecase.

∪ᴺᴵᵀ 29 HOT-METAL TYPE COMPOSITION

Hot-metal typesetting machines were the backbone of the graphic arts industry from the latter part of the nineteenth century until photographic and electronic typesetting became more common in the 1970s. Hot metal typesetting machines are those that use molten metal to cast letters. Some cast complete lines of type, called *slugs*; others cast individual characters of type. Foundry type, a hand composition method presented in Unit 28, belongs in the hot-metal category. In this unit, we discuss several mechanical hot-metal composition methods.

LINE CASTING

Line- or slug-casting machines can be controlled by either a punched tape or a keyboard (Fig. 29-1). Because many controls are needed, an operator must practice for several years to become skilled.

MERGENTHALER LINOTYPE COMPANY

Fig. 29-1. A slug-casting machine with dual keyboard and tape control.

Slug-casting machines work on the principle of a circulating matrix or mold. Character molds are used over and over (Fig. 29-2). At the

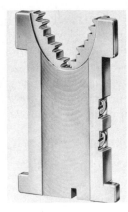

Fig. 29-2. A matrix (mold) used in a circulating matrix line-casting machine.

touch of a key or at the direction of a control tape, matrices are released from a *magazine* (matrix storage case). When the matrices for one line have dropped into place, the line is automatically justified and an entire slug of type is cast (Fig. 29-3). Many slugs of type are

Fig. 29-3. A slug from a circulating matrix line-casting machine.

needed to make up a page of type like the one shown in Figure 29-4.

After the casting has been done, matrices are returned automatically to the magazine for reuse. Each size, kind, and style of type has its own magazine. Keyboard- and tape-controlled slug casters can produce fourteen newspaper lines per minute.

The two line-casting machines available are the *Linotype* and the *Intertype*. New line-

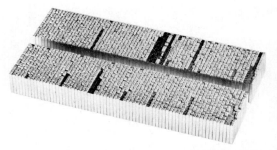

Fig. 29-4. A book page or newspaper column is made up of many slugs.

casting machines are no longer manufactured, except in Russia. However, many of the old Linotype and Intertype machines still exist and are being used by typesetters and commercial printers. Re-built machines are for sale with a three-year guarantee. These machines still have a valuable job to do for the graphic arts industry.

SEMI-AUTOMATIC SLUG CASTER

Another slug-casting machine, the *Ludlow*, uses a semi-automatic method that combines both hand and machine functions. This method is used mainly for display composition with large letters. The machine has a casting device and matrix storage cases, shown in Figure 29-5. It

Fig. 29-5. A slug-casting machine used for display composition, shown with storage cases.

uses special brass molds or matrices to form the display letters. These matrices are gathered by hand, placed into the casting device, and a slug

Fig. 29-6. Matrices (molds) and a slug of display type.

is cast, like those in Figure 29-6. Type sizes range from 4 to 96 points.

Here are the basic steps for using a Ludlow machine:

1. Gather the matrices from the matrix case and place the matrices in the specially designed composing stick.
2. Tighten the matrices in the composing stick and place them in the casting position.
3. Cast as many slugs as needed from the one assemblage of matrices.
4. Assemble the slugs into a form for proofing or printing on a press.

Fig. 29-7. A casting machine (Elrod) that produces leads and slugs.

LINE SPACING CASTING

Unit 28 showed how leads and slugs are used for line spacing with foundry type. These leads and slugs are made by an *Elrod* machine, pictured in Figure 29-7. This machine produces a continuous strip of metal from 1 through 36 points in thickness.

Molten metal is fed into the mold, where it is cast, solidified under pressure, and pushed from the machine in a continuous strip. This is the principle of *extrusion*. Most commercial graphic arts companies that use hot-composition methods have a stripmaking machine of this kind.

UNIT 30 IMPACT, THERMAL, AND LASER IMAGING SYSTEMS

Impact (or strike-on) imaging machines are commonly operated through a computer. Two types of computer printout devices are classified as impact printers. These are the *dot matrix* and *daisy wheel* units.

Some machines, like typewriters, have fixed type styles. Most, however, have a rather wide selection of typefaces. These image-producing systems are used to make original copy suitable for printing. The quality, however, does not equal that of type produced on the photographic and digital equipment discussed in Units 32 and 33.

Thermal and laser computer printers are excellent image-producing machines (Fig. 30-1). They quickly produce copy with dense im-

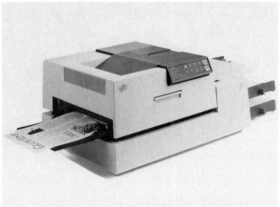

COURTESY OF KONICA BUSINESS MACHINES U.S.A., INC.

Fig. 30-1. Laser printers are capable of producing dense images on plain bond paper in 45 or more type styles.

ages. Because they have fewer moving parts than impact printers, they are reliable. All four types of computer printers are used to produce proof copy for high-quality imagesetters. See Unit 184 for an in-depth look at the printers used in desktop composition.

REGULAR TYPEWRITERS

The first crude typewriters were made during the first half of the nineteenth century. In 1867 the first practical typewriter (Fig. 30-2) was designed and built by Christopher L. Sholes, Carlos Glidden, and S. W. Soulé of Milwaukee, Wisconsin. These inventors pat-

REMINGTON OFFICE MACHINES

Fig. 30-2. One of the first typewriters to be built and demonstrated to the public.

```
    The guidelines for printed communica-
tions of the future seem to be very well
drawn.  At one point in history, people worked
from sun to sun; there was no time to think of
self-improvement or even of the operation they
were part of.  Automation has freed us from
humdrum, repetitious, backbreaking chores, and
people are free to spend more time in learning
and improving.
```

Fig. 30-3. Typewritten copy reduced to 75 percent of original size.

ented the machine in 1868 and placed it on the market in 1874.

As an imaging device, the typewriter has been and continues to be useful. In today's

```
    The guidelines for printed communica-
tions of the future seem to be very well
drawn.  At one point in history, people worked
from sun to sun; there was no time to think of
self-improvement or even of the operation they
were part of.  Automation has freed us from
humdrum, repetitious, backbreaking chores, and
people are free to spend more time in learning
and improving.
```

Fig. 30-4. Typewritten copy enlarged to 125 percent of original size.

computerized business world, many typewriters have been replaced by computers. However, because of their convenience, typewriters are still commonly used to prepare forms, short letters, and envelopes. Computer printers are often too cumbersome for these types of imaging requirements.

Before the advent of the computer and impact computer printers, typewriters were used for producing original copy. The copy was printed using the lithography process. For example, when typed copy is reduced to 75 percent of its original size, its readability is improved considerably (Fig. 30-3). At this smaller size, typewriter and impact computer printer copy take on a "typeset" look. This is economical for creating original copy for printed products such as one-page flyers and multiple-page newsletters. Enlarged to 125 percent of its original size, the copy loses some quality. Nonetheless, it is still very usable (Fig. 30-4).

INTERCHANGEABLE TYPEFACE TYPEWRITERS

James B. Hammone, a news correspondent during the U.S. Civil War, is credited with developing the first typewriter-like machine with interchangeable typefaces. In 1881 he produced the first commercial model, shown in Figure 30-5. Woodrow Wilson was one of the first persons to use this machine. While President of the United States, he prepared his historic document, "Fourteen Points," on this new invention.

Sophisticated interchangeable typeface typewriters are available today that come very near to being typesetting machines because they have excellent copy quality. Electronic typewriters like the one shown in Figure 30-6 have a built-in memory that can

IBM CORPORATION

Fig. 30-6. An electronic typewriter with memory and interchangeable typefaces that can produce nearly typeset quality.

store approximately 7,000 characters, which is about three to five 8½-by-11-inch pages of typed copy. There is a character display near the keyboard which shows the operator up to 24 characters before they are typed on paper. The operator can correct errors almost immediately.

Anyone who types can quickly learn to use these machines. Nearly all type styles and sizes up to 12 point are available. Letters of foreign language alphabets, including ancient Greek, are available, as are mathematical symbols.

Typewriters can be used as computer printers. This makes using a typewriter for normal office purposes possible, as well as connecting it to a personal computer. With its expanded memory, large screen monitor, and software options, the computer makes typewriters more valuable than ever.

VARITYPER, INC.

Fig. 30-5. The first impact machine with interchangeable typefaces.

The guidelines for printed communications of the future seem to be very well drawn. At one time in history, people worked from sun to sun; there was no time to think of self-improvement or even the operation they were part of. Automation has freed us from humdrum, repetitious, backbreaking chores, and people may now spend more time learning and improving. I have been told that 75 percent of all the scientists who have lived in the history of the world are alive and working today. A new generation is coming along and they are extremely smart. They are not going to be content with tradition. They are being trained to study problems and meet new objectives, to find better systems and not copy what has been done.

Fig. 30-7. Lines of type composed uneven at the right margin are called "ragged right." This means the lines are typeset flush left.

The guidelines for printed communications of the future seem to be very well drawn. At one time in history, people worked from sun to sun; there was no time to think of self-improvement or even the operation they were part of. Automation has freed us from humdrum, repetitious, backbreaking chores, and people may now spend more time learning and improving. I have been told that 75 percent of all the scientists who have lived in the history of the world are alive and working today. A new generation is coming along and they ate extremely smart. They are not going to be content with tradition. They are being trained to study problems and meet new objectives, to find better systems and not copy what has been done.

Fig. 30-8. Lines of type composed uneven at the left margin are called "ragged left." This means the lines are typeset flush right.

JUSTIFYING LEFT AND RIGHT MARGINS

Typesetting equipment and office computers can be used to prepare lines of copy with flush left and flush right margins. Flush left means that all lines start even on the left side and end unevenly at the right margin. Flush right means just the opposite. The lines are even at the right margin and are uneven at the left margin.

In justified lines, the letters and words are both flush left and flush right, as are the lines and columns of this book. To make all lines of type equal length, varying amounts of space are placed between the words. Generally the differences in word spacing among the lines of type are so small that readers seldom notice.

Sometimes the specifications call for lines to be set ragged right (Fig. 30-7). This means that the lines are flush left but are uneven on the right. In this arrangement, all word spaces are equal. The computer is programmed to begin a new line when no additional full or hyphenated words can be added to the previous line. Typographers use this design technique in newsletters and newspapers to create an informal appearance.

Lines of type can also be typeset so they are ragged left (Fig. 30-8). Typographers seldom use this technique because it reduces the readability of the printed page. In most languages, reading is done from left-to-right, as with English. For high readability, the lines of type should all begin at the left margin. Paragraph indentations are an exception, but readers have learned the meaning of this variance in the line beginning. Ragged left composition is sometimes used in advertising literature because it tends to attract the readers' attention.

KROY INCORPORATED

Fig. 30-9. An impact lettering machine that prints type characters on strips of pressure-sensitive paper or transparent film.

VARITRONICS SYSTEMS, INC.

Fig. 30-10. A lettering machine that uses thermal (heat) technology to produce the visual images.

LETTERING MACHINES

Impact lettering machines are used to produce type characters on strips of pressure-sensitive paper or transparent film (Fig. 30-9). The type character is made when the relief image on the font disc is struck sharply against the paper or film strip. A carbon ribbon, similar to ones used in typewriters, creates the visible image. Letter and word spacing are completely automatic and many type styles are available from 8 to 60 point. These machines are useful and economical when limited amounts of typesetting are needed.

On other lettering machines, dot matrix, thermal, and laser technology are used to produce images. Thermal imaging is becoming widely used for lettering machines (Fig. 30-10) and computer printers. The image-receiving paper is specially formulated so the letters are formed quickly. The lettering strip or sheet can be used immediately. Some lettering machines have been designed to print in several languages.

UNIT 31 DRY-TRANSFER AND HAND-MECHANICAL TYPE COMPOSITION

Dry-transfer and hand-mechanical type composition methods are not designed for a high rate of production. They are used by specialty job printers and in-plant reproduction departments of manufacturing industries and business establishments.

Dry-transfer type and symbols are preprinted and attached to a clear plastic or translucent paper carrier. The back side of the type and symbols has a wax-like adhesive. Engineering drawings, maps, charts, newsletter headlines, and advertising brochures can be prepared with dry-transfer type and symbols.

Hand-mechanical type composition creates type by using stencils, templates, pens, and brushes. These devices assist in producing type of many sizes and styles, at small cost, compared with impact and photographic type-setting machines. Hand-mechanical type composition is mainly used for display material, such as headlines and advertisements.

Fig. 31-1. A blunt pencil is being used to rub the carrier sheet to transfer a character from a special dry transfer material called *Image 'N Transfer*.

DRY-TRANSFER MATERIALS

Several dry-transfer materials offer complete alphabets and punctuation marks of many sizes and styles. Symbols, borders, and background textures are also available.

Another type of dry transfer material on the market permits users to create their own type characters and symbols (Fig. 31-1). This material is used in the same way as the prepared dry transfer materials. Rubbing, or *burnishing*, the image area with a blunt instrument, or *stylus*, releases the image from the *carrier sheet* and lets it stick tightly to a new surface. These self-prepared dry transfer sheets are made by exposing the light-sensitive transfer material through a regular high contrast film negative. The exposed material is then processed with developing chemistry (Fig. 31-2). This kind of material is highly flexible because the user is not limited to certain type sizes and styles as in prepared dry transfer material. The user can create unique designs and still get good quality production.

USING DRY-TRANSFER MATERIALS

Quality type composition by this method can be achieved with little or no previous experience. For quality results, take the following steps.

1. Draw light blue guidelines on the copy sheet. Light blue lines will not photograph and make unwanted lines on the film negative (see Sections 6 and 7).

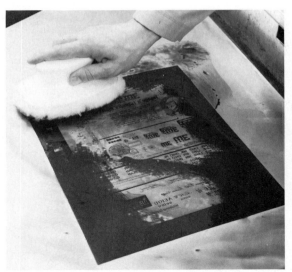

3M COMPANY/INDUSTRIAL GRAPHICS DIVISION

Fig. 31-2. Processing a sheet of Image 'N Transfer material with the special developing chemistry.

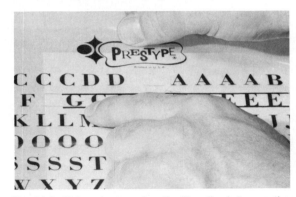

Fig. 31-3. Using dry transfer. Position the letter on the copy sheet.

Fig. 31-4. Extra burnishing makes lettering adhere better.

Fig. 31-5. Guidelines for adding a pattern.

Fig. 31-6. Pattern completed.

2. Remove the protective backing sheet of an alphabet sheet. It is best to remove the backing sheet only from the area of the selected letters. The adhesive behind the other areas will stay cleaner when protected.

3. Position the selected letters on the guidelines of the copy sheet (Fig. 31-3).

4. Rub the area to be transferred with a blunt stylus. The end of a dowel, a ball-point pen, or a pencil, will work as a rubbing instrument. Be careful to rub only the area that you wish transferred.

5. Lift the carrier sheet from the copy sheet. If burnished correctly, the entire letter will stick to the copy sheet.

6. For longer lasting results, place a plastic sheet over the transferred symbols as a shield and burnish the entire copy area again (Fig. 31-4). Give more protection to the image face by applying a clear plastic spray. This technique can be used when the dry-transfer materials are used directly on a poster.

7. Special effects can be created by using a background pattern. Draw guidelines to outline area to be covered (Fig. 31-5).

8. Lay the background pattern down and burnish only the area to be textured.

9. Cut on guidelines and lift the unwanted pattern from the copy sheet (Fig. 31-6).

HAND-MECHANICAL TYPE

Images of all shapes can be created by hand-mechanical means. A versatile tool for making creative letters and symbols is a *technical inking pen* (Fig. 31-7). Pens like this carefully meter the ink to the pen point, thus there is a

KOH-I-NOOR RAPIDOGRAPH

Fig. 31-7. A technical inking pen for creating type characters, symbols, and illustrations.

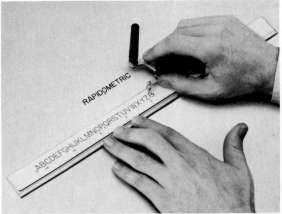

KOH-I-NOOR RAPIDOGRAPH

Fig. 31-8. A technical pen and template lettering system.

high degree of control when using these instruments. Various pen point sizes are available to create different line widths.

Lettering template systems let a skillful person create some very accurate lettering (Fig. 31-8). Letter sizes and styles are determined by the lettering template and pen point selection. A more complex template lettering device creates many different letter styles and sizes (Fig. 31-9). This kind of device lets an artist make specialty typefaces of high quality without elaborate equipment.

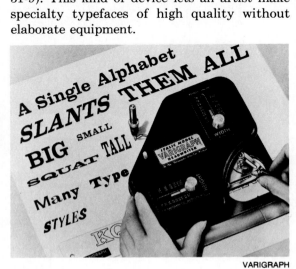

VARIGRAPH

Fig. 31-9. A lettering device which creates several letter styles from one template.

UNIT 32 PHOTOGRAPHIC TYPE COMPOSITION

In phototypesetting, a beam of light is sent through a transparent image in an opaque background. This projects a positive image onto light-sensitive paper or film (Fig. 32-1). Photographic images have very sharp line edges, and never have the voids or broken type effects that sometimes occur with hot metal composition.

During the early 1940s the first phototypesetting device was designed in the cellar of a French home during the Nazi occupation. The first practical photographic typesetting machine was introduced in 1950—the Intertype Fotosetter (Fig. 32-2). This first-generation machine operated with a keyboard, in much the same way as the slug-casting machine described in Unit 29. It used the circulating-matrix principle, but instead of having a character mold on the edge, each matrix had a character on the negative film embedded in its side (Fig. 32-3). Characters were photographed one at a time.

There have been four generations of photographic-electronic–based typesetting machines (Fig. 32-4). The first-generation typesetters, based on the mechanical principles of hot typesetting machines, were not very efficient. The second-generation phototypesetters

HARRIS CORPORATION

Fig. 32-2. A first-generation phototypesetting machine with a keyboard.

used electromechanical principles. Third-generation phototypesetting machines create the characters electronically and transfer them to photographic paper or film. Fourth-generation machines use the laser to create images including type, illustrations, and halftone photographs.

This unit describes the electromechanical (second-generation) typesetter principles. Electronic and digital typesetting (generations three and four) are presented in Unit 33. The machines using this technology should be referred to as *imagesetters*. They have been designed to produce high-quality type along with all other images on the printed page—including charts, artwork, black-and-white halftones, and four-color separations. Fully dedicated typesetting machines will continue to be used in the graphic arts industry. Both imagesetters and typesetters produce quality type and images on phototypesetting paper and film. The choice of equipment depends on the needs of printers and publishers.

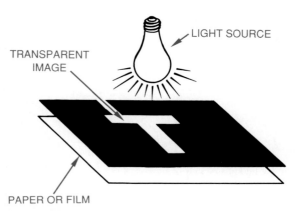

Fig. 32-1. The basic principle of phototypesetting.

CATEGORIES OF PHOTOTYPESETTERS

Generally speaking, phototypesetting machines are of two kinds: *display* and *body*. Display machines are specifically designed to set large face type, from 18 point to 360 point. Some of these machines have keyboards; others do not.

Body phototypesetting machines are specifically designed to compose type for normal reading: 7 to 12 point. Most contemporary body typesetting machines can set type from 4½ point to 84 point in one-half point increments. Some machines can set type up to 999 point.

DISPLAY PHOTOTYPESETTERS

Display phototypesetters are sometimes called photolettering machines. They vary widely in size, speed, design, and flexibility. Some of the machines are operated by hand and produce the image by *contact*. In other words, a film font is held in contact with light-sensitive paper, which is exposed to light to create the image (Fig. 32-5).

Another style of machine uses the *projection* method of making an image (Fig. 32-6).

HARRIS CORPORATION

Fig. 32-3. A matrix (pattern) used by the phototypesetter in Figure 32-2.

That is, the light passes through a film font and then through a lens, which projects the image onto the photographic paper. It gives the operator a great deal of flexibility because it allows the image to be reduced or enlarged. It also allows quality typography to be produced easily in different sizes, kinds, and styles. Many creative options are available: line printed over line, letters that appear to

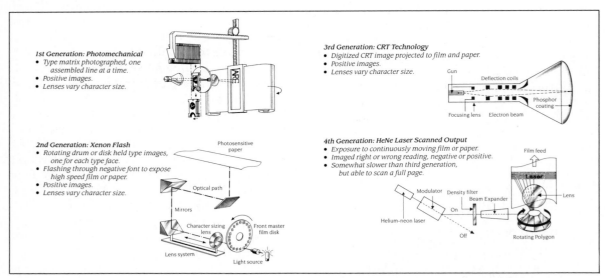

STRIPPRINTER, INC.

Fig. 32-4. A comparison of the four generations of typesetting and imagesetting systems. With all four generations, the final output is created on photosensitive paper or film.

STRIPPRINTER

Fig. 32-5. A small display phototypesetting machine that uses a font in strip form.

bounce, interlocking letters, and perspective effects in which letters increase in size when forming a single word.

Some projection photolettering machines have type sizes ranging from 36 to 400 point. They may have special lenses, automatic letter fitting and spacing, precise line-advance control, and even photographic processing of the paper or film.

All phototypesetting machines use a type font of some kind, as presented in Unit 10. A type font, you remember, is a complete assortment of uppercase and lowercase letters, numbers, and punctuation marks. Some typefonts contain other special characters. A typical typefont for a display phototypesetter is shown in the display phototypesetting machine in Figure 32-5. The font is actually a film negative strip that is moved back and forth to select a letter or other character. There are few dedicated display phototypesetting machines. Most photographic and digital typesetters are capable of setting type from very small sizes to extremely large sizes in one or one-half point increments.

TYPESETTING SYSTEMS

Historically, first-generation phototypesetting machines were in use for only a short time. When second-generation machines be-

came available, they quickly became the backbone of the typesetting industry. *Direct entry* phototypesetting machines became very popular in the late 1960s and early 1970s, and were widely used in smaller daily and most weekly newspapers. They were designed for typesetting the columns of type that are characteristic of newspapers. This type of machine was limited by its lack of memory storage. It lacked, for example, the flexible discs or hard discs now common in typesetting equipment.

The next major innovation involved the development of an *input system* consisting of a keyboard, special function keys, and a video screen; development of a memory-storage system comprising single- and dual-head flexible discs was introduced with this new input technology. The phototypesetting system was then attached to this apparatus. The only item missing was the processor for the photographic paper and film. This was a separate unit.

This equipment was excellent for commercial typesetting because several kinds and

STRIPPRINTER, INC.

Fig. 32-6. A projection-type photolettering machine designed to use the same film fonts as the machine in Figure 32-5.

styles of type were available online within the machine. Also, with several lenses, it was possible to set type in a range of sizes from 6 through 48 point. This typesetting equipment served the graphic arts industry through the 1970s and into the early 1980s.

The next major revolution besides cathode-ray tube (CRT) technology was the introduction of *modular composition equipment*. These systems were made up of three basic parts: (1) the input device (keyboard, screen, and floppy disc storage), (2) the typesetting equipment (type fonts, exposure source, and photosensitive paper and film), and (3) the processing unit (Figure 32-7).

This arrangement provided more flexibility in the typesetting process. The usual arrangement was to hardwire the input and typesetting units together, although it was possible to have several keyboard units connected to only one typesetting unit and one processing unit. This provided excellent utilization of equipment with a higher degree of productivity.

The *desktop composition* revolution followed this wave of new development. This is discussed in detail in Section 22. It became possible to keyboard book manuscripts, newspaper stories, and advertising copy directly into personal computers using special soft-

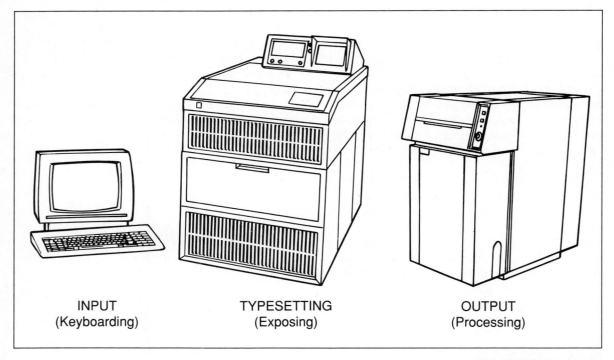

INPUT
(Keyboarding)

TYPESETTING
(Exposing)

OUTPUT
(Processing)

AGFA COMPUGRAPHIC DIVISION

Fig. 32-7. Modular-type composition systems became popular in the 1980s. They remain the format for the 1990s.

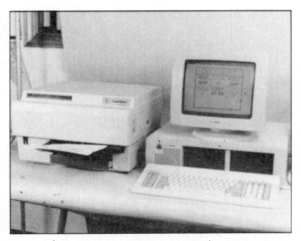

Fig. 32-8. Personal computers are frequently used as input devices for photographic and digital typesetters. Laser printers serve as accurate proofing devices and save on the cost of phototypesetting paper.

ware programs specially written for that purpose. Flexible discs were used to transfer the captured keystrokes from input directly to typesetting equipment. Current technology is shown in Figure 32-8. Desktop computers are widely used as input devices. There are, however, many dedicated input systems, often called front-end systems, still being manufactured for use in the graphic arts industry.

OPERATING PHOTOTYPESETTERS

Operators must become familiar with typesetting equipment before being able to produce type accurately. The best place to get information about a specific machine is in the operator's manual. These manuals give nearly all of the details needed to use a typesetting machine. Maintenance and diagnosing problems are also covered.

It is critical that all typesetting parameters

(specifications) be included by the keyboard operator. Such parameters include kind, size, and style of type; line length; word, line, and letter spacing; type position; and other special data. In addition, the keyboard operator must be familiar with and use good typography. The operator must check that widows do not occur. (A *widow* is a single word or part of a word on a line by itself.) A *widow line* is a very short last line in a paragraph that begins a new column or page.

Quality typography means using typesetting functions such as kerning, letterspacing, and appropriate word spacing. *Kerning* means the reduction of space between selected letters, such as the *AW* combination. The sloping sides of these and other letters often leave too much space. The terms *letterspacing* and *wordspacing* mean just what they say: the addition or reduction of space between letters or words to improve the appearance of the typeset page.

Once the parameters have been entered, typesetting can be done. If the information has been properly entered in the machine, it will perform as the operator expects.

PROCESSING IMAGE COMPOSITION

After the phototypesetting paper or film has been exposed in the type/imagesetter, it must be processed to make the images visible. Most phototypesetting papers are of the resin-coated (RC) type. They are designed for three-stage processing (Fig. 32-9). Typesetting film is processed using the same procedure as that for paper.

A stand-alone photoprocessor can be either a table model or a floor model. These machines are not hooked to water and plumbing systems. When the developer and fixer are ex-

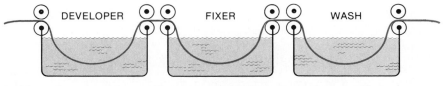

Fig. 32-9. Standard three-stage processing used for resin-coated (RC) photosensitive typesetting paper.

hausted, the containers are removed from the processor, and the used solutions are discarded. It is important that provisions have been made to discard these chemicals properly. They should not be poured down a sanitary sewer system. The same is true with the water used to wash the chemical solutions from the paper and film.

For high production, processors can be attached directly to the type/imagesetter (Fig. 32-10). These processors contain replenishment systems to keep the developer and fixer at their proper strength levels. These units are attached to a fresh water supply and an approved sewer system. Temperature control of the developing and fixing chemicals, and the speed of the paper or film through the processor, are critical to proper processing.

After processing, the type/imageset material is ready to be laid out and pasted up as described in Unit 46. More and more imageset material is ready to go directly to the photoconversion stage because the copy can be entirely produced, sized, and positioned with type/imagesetting equipment. Registration

marks, as needed, can also be added. These will aid the image carrier workers as they prepare the printing plates for the presses.

TYPOGRAPHIC COMMUNICATION

The advantages of phototypesetting over type produced on dot-matrix and daisy-wheel computer printers and typewriters is its typographic quality. There is the copy compaction factor. Typeset copy occupies approximately one-half the space required for typewriter-style material. This factor alone saves paper, postage, and handling costs.

To designate phototypesetting quality, a special symbol was created by Hermann Zapf (Fig. 32-11), the foremost typographic designer of this generation. The symbol, when used with typeset material, certifies that the typeset matter on which it appears was produced by genuine photocomposition. This is the only process among present technologies capable of yielding the highest quality typographic image.

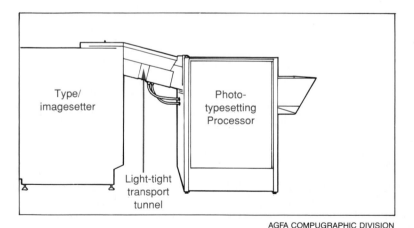

AGFA COMPUGRAPHIC DIVISION

Fig. 32-10. Phototypesetting processors can be attached directly to type/imagesetters for increased production.

PHOTOTYPESET ℺ FOR QUALITY

TYPOGRAPHER'S INTERNATIONAL ASSOCIATION

Fig. 32-11. This symbol, when properly used, certifies that the typeset material is genuine photocomposition.

UNIT 33 ELECTRONIC IMAGESETTING

Imagesetting is the process of creating visible images that include type, line art, and halftones. Imagesetting emerged with the development of cathode-ray tube (CRT) technology. However, the technological breakthrough that made full imagesetting possible was the use of the laser to form controlled images on photosensitive paper, film, and printing plates. CRT technology has been categorized as third generation, and laser technology as fourth generation. Both are discussed in this unit.

Electron-image generation has become an important method of creating visual images. Various types of computer hardware (machine) and software (program) configurations have been developed. These permit electronic imagesetting to be easily accomplished. Such imagesetting can be done with desktop composition systems (see Section 22) and with dedicated imagesetting input hardware (Fig.

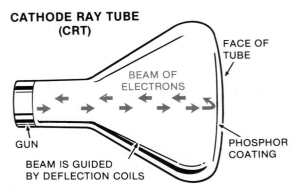

CATHODE RAY TUBE (CRT)

Fig. 33-2. Phosphors on the face of a cathode ray tube (CRT) glow when they are struck by an electronic beam coming from the back of the tube.

33-1). The key element in electronic imagesetting is the variety of software programs available for use with computer front-end hardware.

Fig. 33-1. A dedicated computer workstation for use in inputting and editing imageset copy.

THIRD GENERATION EQUIPMENT

Electromechanical equipment used for regular phototypesetting reached its maximum speed in the late 1960s. Ultra-high-speed typesetting was needed to deal with the millions of words being generated in an information explosion. Engineers and technicians found the solution in a third generation of machines that used the *cathode ray tube* (CRT) to create letter images.

Images are drawn on the face of the CRT by the scanning of an electronic beam (Fig. 33-2). Standard home television screens in North America are made up of 525 horizontal lines, regardless of screen size. CRT screens in typesetters have many more lines for greater detail—typically 2,600 lines per inch. The lines are formed by a raster scan—a pattern in which an electronic beam moves back and forth across the screen one line at a time. The raster scan is so fast that a complete image is drawn 30 times a second.

Computerized typesetting machines using this scanning principle were very popular in the early- and mid-1980s. In this technology, images are divided into many thousands of parts (digitized) and each part is given an electronic value. When the input system calls for a given letter or image, the computer forms the image by scanning the surface of the cathode ray tube with the electronic beam (Fig. 33-3). The image is then exposed on a sheet of photographic paper or film which can be positioned directly against the face of the CRT. A typesetting machine that used this principle is shown in Figure 33-4.

FOURTH GENERATION EQUIPMENT

Lasers play an important part in creating images for printing. The word *laser* is an acronym formed from the phrase, "light

MERGENTHALER LINOTYPE COMPANY

Fig. 33-4. A digital CRT typesetter that could store 60 typefaces in 136 sizes. This machine could set 450 lines a minute in 8-point size and 11-pica length.

amplification by stimulated emission of radiation." A laser creates a single sharp narrow beam of light in one color wavelength that can be precisely controlled. Type characters, artwork, and halftones are generated dot-by-dot. The laser beam scans the full width of the

MERGENTHALER LINOTYPE COMPANY

Fig. 33-3. The electronic beam painted characters stroke by stroke in lines of light on the CRT. The character's outline, stored in the front memory, directed the computer-controlled beam where to begin and end each stroke.

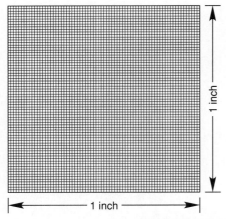

DUPONT PRINTING SYSTEMS

Fig. 33-5. A 200 percent enlargement of a square inch of space. Pixels are the small areas of space between the horizontal and vertical lines. Computer technology identifies each of these pixels as an individual area of space.

image area and makes the exposures dot-by-dot and line-by-line.

Each square inch of a page is divided into *pixels* of space (Fig. 33-5). These pixels are created by the laser light beam, which is used to form a series of horizontal and vertical lines (also called dots). A typical plain-paper laser printer is designed to print at 300 lines per inch (lpi), [or dots per inch (dpi)]. An imagesetter, however, prints over 2,500 lpi (or dpi) to make the visible images. The quality of these images can easily be compared (Fig. 33-6). A 300 dpi laser printer creates 90,000 pixels per inch. Because imagesetters form images with more pixels, the image edges are much smoother and more complete.

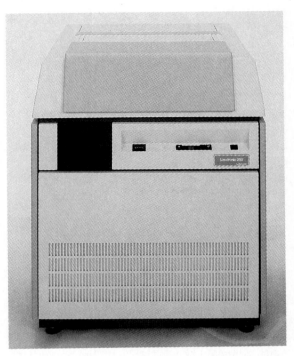

Fig. 33-7. A laser forms the images in this fourth generation typesetting machine.

300 DPI   2540 DPI
DUPONT PRINTING SYSTEMS

Fig. 33-6. A comparison of enlarged letters created by a 300 dpi laser printer and a 2,540 dpi laser imagesetter.

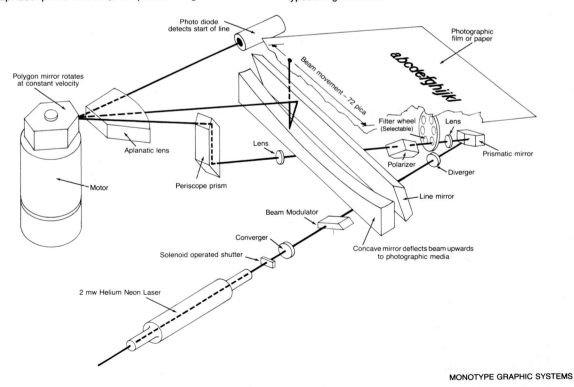

MONOTYPE GRAPHIC SYSTEMS

Fig. 33-8. A diagram of the laser optical system used in the typesetter shown in Figure 33.7.

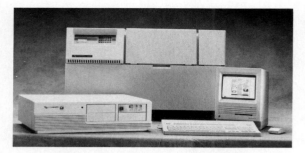

Fig. 33.9. A typesetting system that goes from original copy input to finished type composition. Images on paper and film are created electrostatically and not photographically.

Equipment manufacturers have used the laser in very high-level equipment (Fig. 33-7). Laser equipment having PostScript® software capability can produce sizes from 2 point to 999 point and offer hundreds of kinds of type at one time on a single machine. A schematic diagram shows the basic components of such a system (Fig. 33-8). Such systems can be used to imageset difficult material like the Chinese language. Ideographic languages have been hard to typeset in years past, but they are now being set speedily and effectively in several places in China.

Laser imagesetting systems do not look different from other phototypesetting systems (Fig. 33-9). The difference is in the software and electronics inside the units. The workings of these machines draw on years of research and engineering by many companies and their employees.

ELECTRONIC PUBLISHING

Total automated prepress preparation of type, artwork, and halftone photographs became a reality early in the 1980s. By digitizing, it became possible to merge and convert the three kinds of copy into electronic signals. The diagram in Figure 33-10 shows how original material is taken electronically through various stages to platemaking. At this point, the printing plates are put on the press and thousands of copies can be produced.

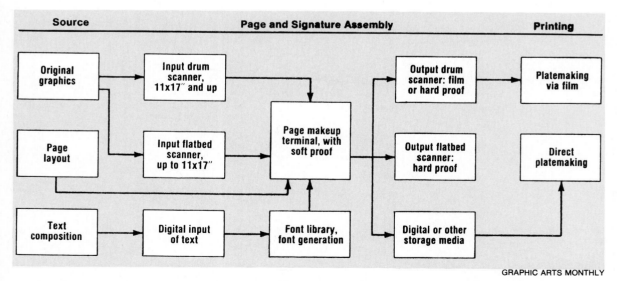

GRAPHIC ARTS MONTHLY

Fig. 33-11. An electronic-publishing model, showing how original copy—type, artwork, and photographs—can be taken through the various production stages to platemaking.

Total systems must include equipment such as that shown and illustrated in Figure 33-11. Other pieces of equipment are also needed in a complete system. Typical publications created with such equipment include technical manuals, magazines, catalogs, and directories. These publications include hundreds of type styles and sizes, a variety of page formats, and several kinds of halftones, line art, and logos. People involved in electronic publishing must be able to handle a large volume of revisions and tight deadlines. This sophisticated equipment gives them the tools to complete their work with a high level of quality.

SCITEX AMERICA CORPORATION

Fig. 33-11. A primary design workstation used to bring together full-color design operations including text, line art, and 4-color halftones.

UNIT 34 LEARNING EXPERIENCES: TYPE AND IMAGE COMPOSITION

KEY TERMS

Unit 27
Casting
Cold type composition
Desktop composition
Desktop publishing
Digital composition
Facsimile
Fax
Hot type composition
Imagesetting
Page description
 languages
Pixel
Slug caster
Type composition
Typesetting
Word processing

Unit 28
California job case
Composing stick
Cuts
Dumping
Em quad
3-em space
En quad
Foundry type
Galley
Hair space
Justify
Lead
Leaders
Manuscript
Pi
Rules
Type bank
Typecase
Typeform

Unit 29

Elrod	Ludlow
Extrusion	Magazine
Intertype	Matrix (matrices)
Linotype	Slugs

Unit 30

Impact composer	Flush left
Impact or strike-on composition	Flush right

Unit 31

Burnish	Lettering template
Carrier sheet	Stylus
Dry transfer type	Technical lettering pen
Hand mechanical type	

Unit 32

Body type	Photo paper
Direct entry	Photoprocessor
Display type	Phototypesetting
Floppy disc	Q Symbol
Imagesetter	Regular (RC) photopaper
Input	
Kerning	Typesetter
Keyboarding	Widow
Letterspacing	Widow line
Output	Word spacing
Photolettering	

Unit 33

CRT	Laser
Digitizing	Laser printer
DPI	PostScript®
Electronic publishing	Scanner
Imagesetting	

DISCUSSION TOPICS

1. Briefly describe the two general classifications of type composition.
2. Why do you think that foundry type composition is still taught in many schools offering graphic arts courses?
3. Briefly describe the four generations of phototypesetting machines.
4. What makes a laser imagesetting machine valuable to the graphic arts industry?
5. Briefly describe the concept of *electronic publishing*.

ACTIVITIES

Unit 27

1. Find several printed materials and look at each of them closely. Which method of type composition was used to typeset each printed item? Compare the quality and readability of each method and discuss the cost of producing type by each method.

Unit 28

2. Compose several lines of foundry type from any given copy. Use various sizes of type and carefully justify each line. Have your work critiqued and then carefully distribute the type back into the type cases.

Unit 29

3. Visit several commercial graphic arts plants and study their composing departments. Carefully record the kinds of typesetting machines that each company has and categorize these machines according to the information presented in this section. Also study the operating principle of each machine so that you can better understand how the several machines work. Choose one machine and write a complete description of its operation.

Unit 30

4. Using a computer equipped with word-processing software, keyboard three to four double-spaced paragraphs with line lengths of 25 to 35 picas. Create one printout with all lines flush left, ragged right. Create a second printout with the

lines justified. Compare the results of the two formats. In addition, use a photocopier to reduce either or both printouts to 75 percent of original size. Compare the original printout with reduced copy. Is there a visual difference? Enlarge the original printout to 125 percent. Compare this enlarged copy with the original. Report your findings either orally or in a brief written report.

Unit 31

5. Compose some headlines using the dry-transfer, hand-mechanical and photographic type composition methods. Compare the results and quality of each method.

Unit 32

6. Using a phototypesetting machine, typeset one to two pages of typewritten manu-script. Determine the parameters before beginning to keyboard the type characters. Carefully prepare the typesetter so it will produce the results you want. Inspect the type after you have processed it.

Unit 33

7. Prepare or obtain some copy produced with a laser computer printer and an imagesetter. Use a photocopier or a process camera to enlarge the laser printer and imagesetter copy 150 to 200 percent. Inspect the original and enlarged output without magnification. Then inspect it using a seven- to ten-power magnifying glass. Compare the output quality of the two systems. Report your findings either orally or in a short written report.

Proofreading is an essential job in the graphic arts.
DOW JONES & COMPANY

PROOFING TYPE COMPOSITION

35 INTRODUCTION TO PROOFING

Proofing and proofreading are two important steps in preparing type composition. Before the work of typesetters can be used to reproduce multiple copies of graphic images, the output must be proofed and *proofread* with utmost care. Nothing is more annoying to a publisher and a reader than to discover several misspelled words in a newspaper, magazine, or book.

A proof is a copy of typeset material. It is a checking copy that can be corrected before the final version is printed. Proofs are made either with special proof presses (in the case of hot type methods) or they are simple readouts of photocomposition or electronic typesetting machines.

Proofing is often done in two stages. First is the typesetter's proof. On this proof, the typesetter corrects any gross errors in composition (positioning of type, spelling, etc.). Then a second proof is made for the customer. The customer corrects the proof, and this copy serves as the master set as the typesetter makes the final corrections. Nowadays the proof is usually copied electrostatically and corrections are marked on the copy rather than on the proof itself.

There are two types of proofs: *reading proofs* and *reproduction proofs*. Reading proofs can be rough copies. They just have to be readable for corrections. The reproduction proof is a fully corrected proof suitable for paste-up, photographing, and final printing. With hot metal composition methods, reproduction proofs must be pulled on proof presses that give high quality reproduction. In photo and electrocomposition the reproduction proof is simply the fully corrected version printed on a paper that will photograph well.

Proofing and proofreading require the skills of many people. Proofreaders catch keyboarding errors, mark corrections on the proof copy

(Fig. 35-1). The original copy from the customer is the *master copy* that proofreaders follow. In Figure 35-1, notice three important graphic items that the proofreader is using: the original customer copy, the rough layout, and a proof of the typeset copy. With these three important items, proofreaders can do their job.

Proofreading is the closest link between the composing room and the customer. Educated and skilled proofreaders are needed to be sure that the final printed product is correct. Large graphic arts companies employ full-time proofreaders to correct and improve daily newspapers, monthly magazines, or school textbooks.

DES MOINES REGISTER

Fig. 35-1. Proofreading copy for a newspaper advertisement.

VALUE OF PROOFING

The basic proofing job has changed very little over the years. The need to produce error-free printed products is the same as it has always been. The methods of doing it have changed. Now, operators can call the manuscript to the video screens of electronic editing terminals and make needed changes at the keyboard before printing (Fig. 35-2). This procedure saves time and greatly improves the overall efficiency of writers and editors.

The importance of proofing typeset material cannot be over-emphasized. Printed errors stand out for everyone to see, not once but many times over. Proofreaders face great challenges as they work. If they do their work well, no one will notice. If their work is less than perfect, everyone will notice.

HARRIS CORPORATION

Fig. 35-2. A composition keyboard specialist is responsible for proofreading "on-screen" and after hard-copy proof has been made.

UNIT 36 PROOFING RELIEF TYPE

There are several styles of relief proof presses, each with its own uses and capabilities. Some are hand operated and others are power operated. Some proof presses give press-like quality. This makes it possible to judge the quality of relief type and printing plates.

LETTERPRESS PROOF PRESSES

Hand-operated proof presses are small and inexpensive (Fig. 36-1). They are designed to make reading proofs. Their use is limited because they cannot be adjusted for different thicknesses and qualities of paper. A letterpress proof press with adjustable packing on the impression cylinder is more versatile. This feature allows the operator to vary the distance between the impression cylinder and the carrier bed in order to get just the right pressure on the paper. These presses also have the advantage of *grippers* or finger-like devices that hold the paper securely to the

impression cylinder while the proof is being taken. The quality of the proof is much better than with non-adjustable relief proof presses.

Power-operated proof presses like the one shown in Figure 36-2 contain a power operated

BRAYER OR INK ROLLER   IMAGE CARRIER BED   IMPRESSION CYLINDER

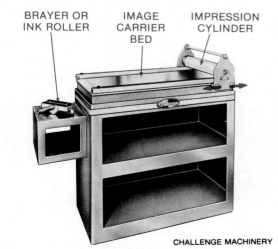

CHALLENGE MACHINERY

Fig. 36-1. A small, inexpensive proof press.

ink distribution system that inks the type before taking the proof. Grippers on the cylinder hold the paper securely while the cylinder is rolled over the type by turning the hand crank. These presses are known as reproduction proof presses because they give proofs of very high quality for photographic purposes.

Another kind of proof press is one that proofs image carriers or plates before they are put on a press for high-speed reproduction. A four-color proof press (Fig. 36-3) can pull proofs for four-color reproduction. The operator places four image carriers on the press, one for each color. In one pass of the press a sheet of paper receives ink from each printing plate to make proofs of the four-color reproduction. Usually the first image carrier contains the yellow copy; the second, magenta; the third, cyan; and the fourth,

black. The four-color proofs are taken so that the quality of the image carriers can be inspected and the necessary **corrections** made.

MAKING READING PROOFS

Reading proofs are used for proofreading the copy and to find errors in spelling and grammar. Proper spacing of lines, paragraphs, and full pages are also checked. The following is the procedure for pulling a proof on a letterpress proof press.

1. Position the typeform on the proof press bed (Fig. 36-4). Be sure the typeform is tied securely and slid into the corner of a galley.
2. Spread proofing ink on the ink plate of the proof press with an *ink brayer* as shown in

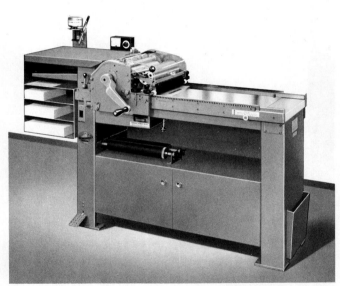

Fig. 36-2. This hand-operated proof press features power ink distribution and automatic washup.

VANDERSONS CORPORATION

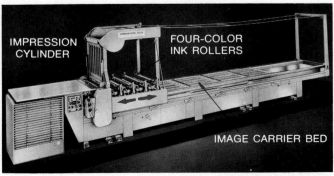

IMPRESSION CYLINDER

FOUR-COLOR INK ROLLERS

IMAGE CARRIER BED

Fig. 36-3. A power-operated proof press for four-color proofing.

VANDERSONS CORPORATION

Fig. 36-4. The typeform in proper position.

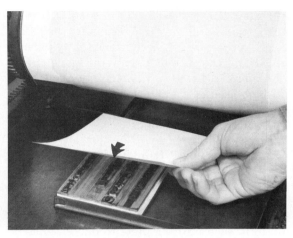

Fig. 36-7. Placing the proofing paper on the typeform.

Fig. 36-5. Spreading ink on the ink plate.

Fig. 36-8. Taking the proof.

Fig. 36-6. Inking the typeform with the brayer.

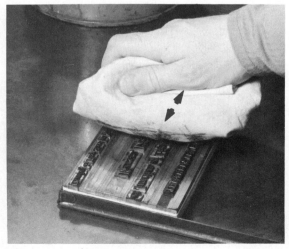

Fig. 36-9. Washing the typeform.

Figure 36-5.

3. Ink the typeform (Fig. 36-6). Roll the brayer over the form two or three times, but do not over-ink the form. Too much ink makes a poor proof.

4. Lay proofing paper carefully on the typeform (Fig. 36-7).

5. Roll the cylinder gently over the paper and the typeform (Fig. 36-8). Pressure causes the ink to transfer from the typeform to the paper.

6. Strip (remove) the paper from the typeform.

7. Remove the galley and typeform from the proof press.

8. Wash the face of the type (Fig. 36-9).

9. Proofread the proof as outlined in Unit 38. If corrections are needed, make the typeform changes by following instructions in Unit 39.

UNIT 37 PROOFING PHOTOGRAPHIC AND DIGITAL TYPE COMPOSITION

Sophisticated imagesetting equipment makes it relatively easy to create visual images. The final copy generated by such equipment can be either correct or incorrect (Fig. 37-1); therefore, it is important that all copy be proofread. In spite of new imagesetting techniques, proofreading is still essential.

COPY INPUT AND CONTINUOUS PROOFING

Front-end typesetting equipment uses a television-type screen that shows each character entered. In addition, scanned line art and halftone photographs are displayed. Illustrations containing only blacks and whites, with no shading, are known as *line art*. Illustrations that contain shading, such as photographs, are known as *halftones*.

Standard personal computers, as well as specially designed front-end systems, are used to input type and images for output on digital imagesetters. Most of the software used for this contains the WYSIWYG feature (Fig. 37-2).

Fig. 37-1. A composition management system using PC equipment and sophisticated software that gives operators considerable flexibility and control.

Fig. 37-2. A front-end typesetting/imagesetting system that permits the operator to create a complete newspaper page on screen.

The acronym WYSIWYG stands for "what you see is what you get." This feature allows the computer operator to check the copy for correct spelling, as well as correct type size and font. Image positioning, word spacing, and line spacing can also be checked. It also is possible to position type and graphics accurately within a designated space. This is especially useful when laying out magazines and newspapers.

Spell-check software ensures that all words are spelled correctly. This does eliminate the need for accuracy in keyboarding. Also, such spell-checking programs identify only those words that are misspelled, not misused. For example, if the operator meant to type the word *too,* but typed instead the word *to,* the spell-checking program would not catch the error.

Once the type has been set photographically or electronically, the copy must be separately proofed again. This is true with other methods of cold type composition too. The normal steps to take are these:

1. The typesetter does the typesetting, following the original copy as accurately as possible.
2. Proof copies are made from the photographic type with an electrostatic copier or with a laser printer. These proofs are often called *galleys,* or *galley proofs,* terms carried over from hot metal typesetting. In hot metal typesetting, slugs of

Fig. 37-3. Laser printers are designed to produce high-density images on plain paper. This unit has 73 installed type fonts and can produce 12 8½″ × 11″ imaged pages per minute at 400 dpi.

type making up a typeform are placed in a metal galley (see Unit 28) and proofed (see Unit 36).

3. A proofreader or two proofreaders will closely read the proof copy and mark keyboarding, image spacing, and positioning errors. This proofreading step should always be done inside the typesetting company. The commercial customer should never see this proof. Special proofreading marks and procedures are used to ensure proper communication between the proofreader and the typesetter. (See Unit 38).
4. Errors are corrected, using the input terminal. With magnetic storage and retrieval systems, the floppy disc or hard disc is corrected electronically.
5. Corrected phototype is made with the typesetter or imagesetter.
6. Electrostatic copies are then made from these second-stage proofs.
7. The customer is shown copies of the corrected proofs and asked to review them. The customer should mark errors and note suggested changes in the overall layout of the imageset matter.
8. With the customer's corrected proofs, the typesetter should be able to make all final corrections and changes.

The process takes much time and effort, but following these steps will give quality results.

HARD COPY PROOFS

Laser printers are frequently interfaced with microcomputers and front-end typesetting input units to produce hard copy proofs (Fig. 37-3). *Hard copy proofs* are on plain paper, are easier to read and correct than the electronic images on video screens, and are more economical than proofs made on light-sensitive photographic paper with a typesetter/imagesetter.

Printed proofs allow the proofreader greater accuracy in comparing the keyboarded copy with the original copy. The proofreader can also study the proofs longer without needing to use the computer or front-end input terminals.

Laser printers produce finished copy of lesser quality than more sophisticated typesetting/imagesetting equipment. However, the quality is appropriate for proofing purposes. Typically, laser printers produce images at 300 to 400 dpi (dots per inch), whereas digital imagesetters typically produce copy at 2,400 to 2,500 dpi. In the future, laser printers will very likely be manufactured to produce image quality even closer to that of imagesetters. See Unit 32 for additional information on laser printers and digital imagesetters.

UNIT 38 PROOFREADING PROCEDURES

If possible, proofreading should be done by two people: a copyholder and a proofreader. The copyholder does just what the name says—holds the manuscript or marked-up original copy and reads aloud to the proofreader. The proofreader closely watches the proof and marks necessary corrections.

PROOFREADERS AND COPYHOLDERS

The proofreader's job is to find errors and mark them for correction. These errors are often called *typos,* an abbreviation for "typographical error." The proofreader does not read the proof for pleasure or for information. He or she must see every letter, number, and punctuation mark on the proof, and must also check word, line, and paragraph spacings.

The copyholder's job is to read the original manuscript to the proofreader. The copyholder must learn to read clearly and without error, and at a speed matched to the proofreader's work. Accuracy is a must; speed is only a bonus.

Many commercial firms do not use copyholders. Their proofreaders check the manuscript copy carefully against the proof. This takes more time, but avoids the cost of using two persons.

Proofreaders must be able to read, hear, and spell well; they must react quickly, concentrate well, and know the rules of grammar. Copyholders should also be able to read accurately, distinctly, and rapidly; they should be patient and follow directions.

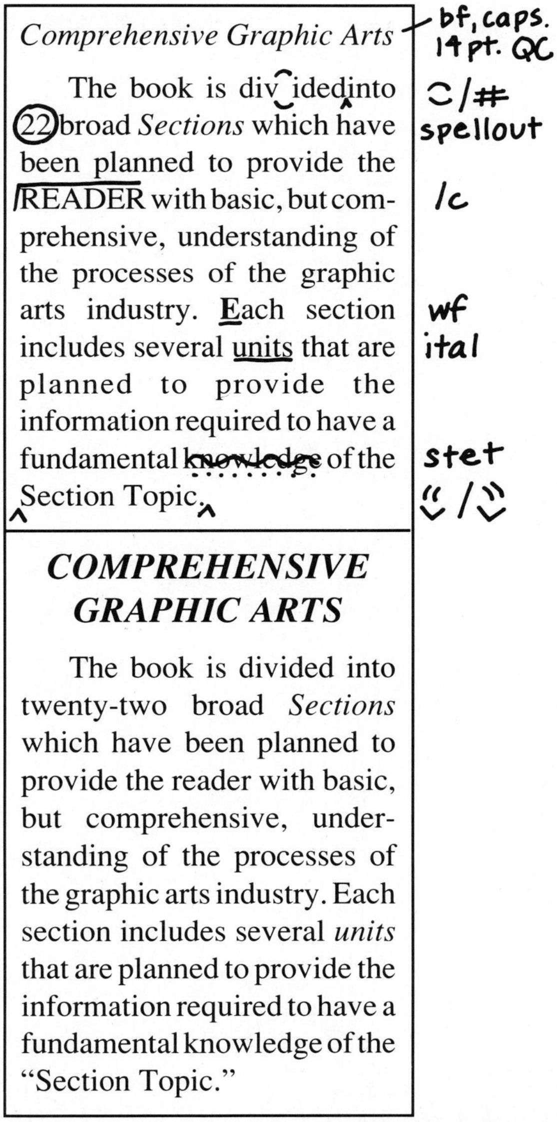

Comprehensive Graphic Arts — bf, caps.
14 pt. QC

The book is diṽidedᵢnto ㉒broad *Sections* which have C/# spellout
been planned to provide the
READER with basic, but com- lc
prehensive, understanding of
the processes of the graphic
arts industry. Each section wf
includes several <u>units</u> that are ital
planned to provide the
information required to have a
fundamental knowledge of the stet
Section Topic. "/"

COMPREHENSIVE GRAPHIC ARTS

The book is divided into twenty-two broad *Sections* which have been planned to provide the reader with basic, but comprehensive, understanding of the processes of the graphic arts industry. Each section includes several *units* that are planned to provide the information required to have a fundamental knowledge of the "Section Topic."

Fig. 38-1. Proofreading marks or symbols serve as a shorthand for proofreaders. Knowing and using these symbols correctly serve as an excellent communication system among personnel involved in copy preparation.

PROOFREADERS' MARKS

Proofreaders' marks are the shorthand used by the person reading proofs to mark changes (Fig. 38-1). With proofreaders' marks, changes can be notated without long explanations. All marks made by the proofreader must be legible so that the compositor can see clearly what to do. The correct use of standard marks will make proofreading more efficient.

The marks are used in pairs. One set of marks is put in the margin to tell the keyboard operator what changes to make. The other set of marks is written directly in the text to show the typesetter exactly where to make corrections. Fast and effective proofreading reduces costs and makes a graphic arts business more competitive (Fig. 38-2).

PROOFREADING SYMBOLS

Meaning	Margin	Text
Dele, or delete, take out		People macke things happen.
Insert space	#	People makethings happen.
Close up, no space		People make things hap pen
Insert apostrophe		People make childrens things.
Character of wrong size or style, wrong font	wf	People make things happen.
Put in lower case	lc	PEOPLE make things happen.
Reset in bold face	bf	People make things happen.
Reset in italic type	ital	People make things happen.
Let it stand; ignore marks above dots	stet	People make things happen.
Make paragraph.	¶	People make Things happen.
No paragraph	no ¶	happen. People make things happen.
Insert period	⊙	People make things happen.
Carry to the left	L	People make things happen.
Carry to the right	⏌	People make things happen.
Center the line (quad center)	QC	People make things happen.
Even left margin (quad left)	QL	People make things happen.
Even right margin (quad right)	QR	People make things happen. People make things happen.
Lower as indicated		
Raise as indicated		People make things happen. People make things happen.
Transpose	tr	People make things happen.
Insert hyphen	/=/	People make things hip hop.
Reset in small capitals	sc	People make things happen.
Insert comma	∧	Yes people make things happen.
Query to author	make?	People things happen.
Spell out circled matter	sp	People make 4 things happen.
Space evenly	eq #	People make things happen.
Indent 1 em	□	People make things happen.
Indent 2 ems	□□	People make things happen.
1-em dash	/em/	People make things happen.
2-em dash	/2em/	People make things happen.
En dash	/n/	People make things 9-5.
Align	=	People make things happen.
Insert quotation marks	""	People make things happen.
Reset in Roman type	rom	People make things happen.
Words omitted	out see copy	People happen.
Reset in capitals	caps	people make things happen.

Fig. 38-1. Proofreading marks or symbols serve as a shorthand for proofreaders. Knowing and using these symbols correctly serve as an excellent communication system among personnel involved in copy preparation.

UNIT 39 CORRECTING TYPE COMPOSITION

Correcting type composition costs money. The composition must be made free of errors after the proofs are read by the proofreader and copyholder. This takes up much of the time needed for the original manuscript to go from typesetting to final printing. There are special techniques for correcting each of the type composition methods presented in Section 4. They are used to shorten the time needed to correct the type and graphics set by each method.

FOUNDRY TYPE COMPOSITION

Individual characters: If letters are the same width (*set width*), change character for character. If letters are a different width, place the entire line in the composing stick. Spacing material must be removed, the character changed (Fig. 39-1), and the line rejustified. Complete words: Follow the same steps used to correct individual characters. Complete lines: Compose the correct line the same length as the incorrect one. Exchange the correct line for the incorrect one in the typeform (Fig. 39-2). Complete paragraphs: Follow the steps used to correct complete lines. Space: To change word spacing, place the line in the composing stick. Remove a quad from the end of the line. Make the spacing change, and then rejustify the line.

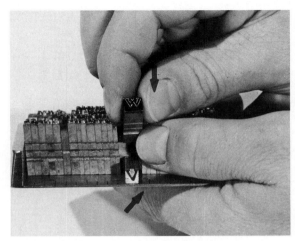

Fig. 39-1. Making a correction with foundry type.

To change line spacing, insert or remove leads and slugs as needed while the form is in the galley.

HOT-METAL TYPE COMPOSITION

Individual characters: To change one character, a complete new line is made on a slug-casting machine. Complete words: Follow the same procedure as in correcting individual characters. Complete lines: With slugs, cast a correct slug and exchange it for the incorrect one (Fig. 39-3).

Fig. 39-2. Changing a corrected line of type for an incorrect one in a typeform. (1) Slide the incorrect line to the left, then (2) slide down the correct line.

Fig. 39-3. Changing a corrected slug of type for an incorrect one.

Complete paragraphs: With slugs of type, the necessary lines are cast and exchanged for the incorrect paragraph. Space: To change word spacing, cast a new line to replace the incorrect one. To change line spacing, insert or remove leads and slugs as necessary while the form is in a galley. The leads and slugs are the same ones used with foundry type.

IMPACT TYPE COMPOSITION

As discussed in Unit 30, most impact-imaging machines are computer assisted. Because of this, errors in text entry are corrected by the keyboard operator. After the corrections have been made, they are placed into magnetic memory on a floppy disc or hard disc. A new printout is then made.

DRY-TRANSFER AND HAND-MECHANICAL TYPE COMPOSITION

Dry-transfer letters can be removed with a soft rubber eraser or with the adhesive on masking tape. Once removed, the letter cannot be reused. A new letter must be selected.

Hand-mechanically produced letters can be removed using standard erasure techniques, but this damages the surface of the paper. The roughened surface makes it hard to ink in the same area again. Therefore, if an error has been made, the entire word or line should be done over.

PHOTOGRAPHIC AND DIGITAL TYPE COMPOSITION

With display phototypesetters, it is often easier and quicker to reset the display type than to correct it. Corrections made by hand with scissors, art knives, and tape do not have the quality of original printouts.

In both photographic and digital typesetting, the computer terminal is the best place to correct errors. Time can be saved if a clean (error-free) floppy disc or hard disc is created. When the type is created on the photographic paper or film, it will be complete and without errors. This makes the typesetting and proofing steps more cost-effective.

UNIT 40 LEARNING EXPERIENCES: PROOFING TYPE AND IMAGE COMPOSITION

KEY TERMS

Unit 35
Proof
Proofing
Proofreading

Unit 36
Ink brayer
Grippers
Proof
Proof press
Reading
Reproduction (repro) proof

Unit 37
Galley proofs
Hard copy printer
Hard copy proofs
Spell-check software

Unit 38
Copyholder
Proofreader
Proofreaders' marks
Typo

Unit 39
"Clean" floppy disc   Rejustify
Light table   Set width

DISCUSSION TOPICS

1. Why are proofing and proofreading important in preparing type composition?
2. What is meant by the statement, "Many unsung heros are involved in proofreading?"
3. Explain the difference between *reading proofs* and *reproduction proofs*.
4. Briefly describe the value and caution of using spell-check software when keyboarding copy for typesetting.
5. What is the primary purpose of proofreaders' marks?

ACTIVITIES

Units 35 and 38

1. Get the current issue of your daily newspaper and read each article on the front page. Indicate the type composition errors according to the proofreader's marks listed in Unit 38. List the errors on a separate sheet of paper under the headings *punctuation, delete, insert, paragraphing, position, spacing, style of type*, and *miscellaneous*. Repeat this for an entire week and then carefully compare the total number of errors found during the week. On what days were there more errors and fewer errors? Repeat this procedure with another newspaper or one of your favorite journals. One week later, compare the two tabulations and report on your analysis.

Unit 36

2. Get a galley of foundry type composition or hot-type machine-set type composition. Prepare a reading proof. Select a fellow classmate and proofread the reading proof, using the original hand-written or typed copy. Take turns being the proofreader and copyholder. Be sure to use the proper proofreading marks when you discover errors in the type composition. Use a red- or blue-leaded pencil for marking the errors.

Unit 37

3. Ask your instructor to give you a floppy disc that contains several hundred words of keyboarded manuscript for phototypesetting or digital typesetting. Place the disc in the input terminal and make the needed corrections. If a corrected reading proof has not been provided, your first step should be to prepare one with a laser printer.

Unit 38

4. Visit a daily newspaper plant. If possible, arrange to spend some time with the proofreaders. If it is permitted, sit down and observe them at work. Note how the copyholder and proofreader word together, and also how the proofreader marks errors that he or she has found. Also observe how the proofs reach the proofreader and what happens to the proofs once the proofreader has finished with them. Prepare a written report on your visit.

Units 37 and 39

5. Obtain one page of photo or digital type composition. Make a reading proof with an electrostatic copying machine, or create another hard copy with a laser printer. Proofread this page very carefully, using the standard proofreading procedures and marks. After finishing this important step, correct the composition using the methods as described in Unit 39.

This artist is completing an ink drawing illustration.

COPY PREPARATION FOR PROCESS PHOTOGRAPHY

INTRODUCTION TO COPY PREPARATION

Much of today's visual material is printed from image carriers (Sections 8, 12, 14, and 15) prepared by photographic techniques. Image carriers are made from *copy*. Copy is the material to be printed. Each element must be exactly where it should be when printed. The placing of the elements is usually guided by the layout (discussed in Section 3). Two kinds of elements found in copy are type matter and illustrations.

Type Matter. Letters that form the words are the type matter in a piece of copy. As explained in Section 4, type matter can be prepared by several different methods. You should know about each way of preparing type matter.

Illustrations. Illustrations are the elements of copy that are not type matter. Some common types of illustrations are photographs, drawings, charts, and diagrams. Several examples of illustrations are shown in Unit 43.

This section shows how to prepare material to be photographed for printing, starting from a layout. This is often done by an artist in a printing plant. Some companies do nothing but prepare artwork (copy) to be printed. Printers often buy artwork from these companies.

When preparing copy, the artist must know how the customer wants the copy to look when it is printed. The artist also must know how the printed item will be used. The color of paper and ink to be used is important. Different treatments will give different feelings—happy, quiet, bold, or funny. The artist must also think about

when the artwork is due. Figure 41-1 shows a piece of copy with illustrations and type matter in place.

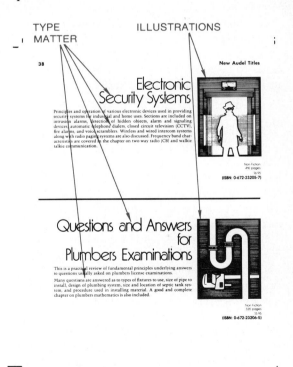

Fig. 41-1. A piece of copy ready to be photographed for printing. This piece of copy has both type matter and illustrations.

UNIT 42 EQUIPMENT AND MATERIALS FOR COPY PREPARATION

Only the skill of the artist is more important than equipment and materials used for copy preparation. Artists express their creative ideas through their materials and equipment.

Good quality materials should be used for the best results. The artist should know what materials will do and which are available. Equipment and tools should be kept clean and in good working condition.

Copy is prepared by placing either black or red on a white background. Either color will produce an image on a negative when photographed. Black is most commonly used.

Until recently, type matter and illustrations had to be prepared separately. These items were combined in the paste-up process or after photography had been done. Computer technology permits type and illustrations to be combined without making a paste-up. This saves time and is more accurate.

BACKGROUND FOR THE COPY

White paper or board is used most often as a background for copy. Not all papers or boards are suitable for all kinds of copy preparation. The artist must select material for a background carefully.

Color. Dyes are often blended into paper to make it look whiter. But dyes sometimes make the paper or board unsuitable for copy preparation. Only papers tested and recommended for copy preparation should be used.

Weight. Many different weights of paper and board are used for copy preparation. It is usually best to use the heaviest possible paper or board because it is easier to handle and is not so affected by moisture. Copy is sometimes prepared on lightweight paper and then attached to heavier paper or board.

Surface. The effect desired by the artist should determine the type of paper surface selected. Striking effects can be obtained on papers with unusual textured surfaces. The artist should know how different drawing mediums, such as inks or pencils, will act on various surfaces.

Layout sheets. Layout sheets are preprinted sheets used to prepare copy. Layout sheets have measurements printed on the borders. They are useful for making rapid measurements without using a ruler, T-square, or triangle. They come in a variety of sizes and weights.

DRAWING EQUIPMENT AND INSTRUMENTS

Drawing instruments are used for drawing guide lines and actual lines to be reproduced. The artist should have a complete set of drawing instruments to use in copy preparation.

Drawing boards. A good drawing board or drawing table is needed for copy preparation. The surface should be large enough for most projects.

T-squares and triangles. When a drawing board is used, a T-square is needed (Fig. 42-1).

FREDERIC POST COMPANY

Fig. 42-1. A typical T-square.

You should be careful to protect the drawing edges of the T-square and the alignment of the head and blade. Triangles are used to draw accurate vertical and diagonal lines (Fig. 42-2, 42-3).

Copy for this method can be prepared in reverse (white). As shown in Figure 43-4, white letters can be placed over a black background. Here, the black truck was drawn on illustration board with ink.

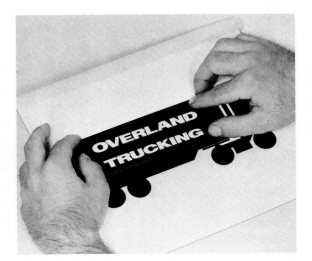

Fig. 43-4. White lettering being applied directly to the black artwork.

A more common method of preparing reversal copy is the overlay method. Figure 43-5 shows a piece of copy prepared in this manner.

1. Make a drawing of everything to be printed (Fig. 43-6).

2. Attach a piece of clear acetate (the overlay sheet) to one edge of the illustration board.
3. Attach the letters to be reversed in the proper location on the overlay sheet (Fig. 43-7).
4. Make register marks on both the illustration board and the overlay sheet. The register marks must be aligned (See Unit 45). The actual reversal will then be done photographically in the darkroom. The register marks will be removed before printing.

Screened tints. An example of various screened tints is shown in Figure 43-8. Screened tints come in dry-transfer material (discussed in Unit 31) and on acetate film base. Dry-transfer material is applied directly to the copy before it is photographed. Acetate film tints are placed underneath the negatives before making the printing plates.

As shown in Figure 43-8, tints come in several densities (5 to 90 percent) and in many screen sizes (65 to 150 lines per inch). Other densities and screen sizes are also available. *Density* is a measure of the light that passes through the screen—the less light, the bigger the dots formed, and the higher the density. Figure 43-9 shows a print with and without a tint. Figure 43-10 shows how tints can be used to emphasize parts of a printed form. Use only enough tint to be noticed. Too much tint makes the print unreadable.

Fig. 43-5. A reversal prepared by the overlay method.

Fig. 43-6. Display type and artwork for each part of the reversal copy.

Fig. 43-7. The overlay positioned over the part of the copy that will be printed in black.

CONTINUOUS-TONE COPY

Continuous-tone copy has middle tones of gray between black to white. To be printed, it is broken up into a dot formation to produce a *halftone* (Fig. 43-11). Each of the following examples of continuous-tone copy will be printed as a halftone.

Photographs. The most common kind of continuous-tone copy is a photograph. Photographs with glossy finishes make the best reproductions. Photographs are printed in many different ways. Figure 43-12 is an example of a *rectangular* photograph.

Figure 43-13 shows an *outline* photograph. Parts of the original photograph were eliminated in the darkroom or by an artist. Using a red masking film is one way to produce printed outline photographs. Figure 43-14 shows a photograph with a mask attached.

Pencil or charcoal drawings. Pencil or charcoal drawings are treated as continuous-tone copy. Variation in shades should be reproduced faithfully. Figure 43-15 is a pencil sketch. Figure 43-16 is a sketch done with charcoal. Chalk is sometimes used in drawings.

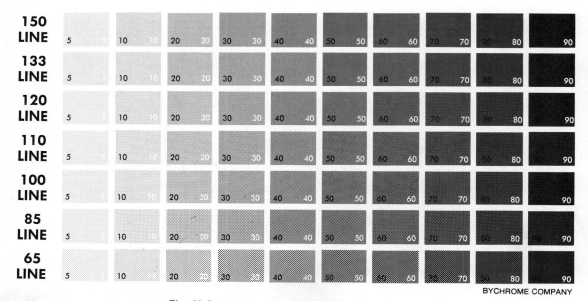

BYCHROME COMPANY

Fig. 43-8. An example of screened tints.

TINTS ADD "VALUE" TO YOUR PRINTING

normal line copy

An acetate overlay was prepared to add a tint block to this illustration, then screened with a 150 line—20 percent tint and double-exposed onto the plate (shown at right).

LITHOGRAPHY

... with screen tints added

The "shadow" effect on the word "lithography" was easily prepared by stripping a second line negative (screened with a 150 line—20 percent tint) slightly out of register with the solid type.

LITHOGRAPHY

Fig. 43-9. Screened tints used to point out a part of the copy.

STOCK REQUEST

No. of Sheets_____SIZE:_____

KIND_____

WT._____COLOR_____

CUT_____OUT, TO PRESS SIZE_____

NEEDED: DAY_____HOUR_____

SPECIAL STOCK: FROM_____

PO# _____ DAY NEEDED_____

SPECIAL INK REQUEST

Fig. 43-10. Tints used to separate elements of a typeform.

Fig. 43-11. Part of a halftone enlarged to show the dot formation.

Fig. 43-12. A rectangular photograph.

Airbrush renderings. The illustration in Figure 43-17 was done with an airbrush. Airbrush artwork often looks like a photograph. Airbrush techniques are often used to touch up photographs. In an outdoor scene, for example, telephone wires can be taken out and clouds added.

Wash drawings. A wash drawing is one made with a *wash*—a thin application of water-

Fig. 43-13. An outline photograph.

Fig. 43-15. A pencil sketch of an artist using an airbrush.

ORIGINAL PHOTOGRAPH

MASKING FILM

Fig. 43-14. The background in the photograph in Figure 43-13 was removed by means of a masking sheet, shown above. The masking film was cut to show only the part of the image that was wanted.

NEKOOSA PAPERS

Fig. 43-16. A charcoal sketch.

color paint or ink, usually in black. Ink wash or lamp black solution is sometimes used in place of water colors. The solution is applied to the paper with a brush. A more diluted solution produces lighter grays (See Fig. 43-18).

Combinations. These combine line and continuous-tone copy in one printed image. Such techniques can add variety to printed items. Figure 43-19 shows a combination. The wash forms the continuous-tone background.

The examples given are the ones most commonly used to produce continuous-tone copy. This list, however, is not complete. All copy should be examined to see whether it should be treated as continuous-tone or line copy.

NEKOOSA PAPERS

Fig. 43-17. An airbrush rendering.

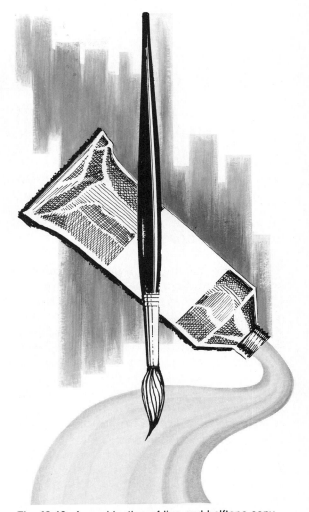

Fig. 43-19. A combination of line and halftone copy.

KIMBERLY-CLARK CORPORATION

Fig. 43-18. A wash drawing.

UNIT 44 COPY CONSIDERATIONS

Producing and handling copy are of great concern to the customer and the printer. The condition of the copy often affects the quality of the printed item. Printing costs can be kept low if care is given to preparing and handling copy.

SIZE OF THE COPY

Copy should usually be prepared the same size or larger than the printed product. Rarely is it wise to prepare copy smaller than the size of the printed item.

When copy is made larger than the finished size, it is made smaller photographically before printing. The reduction in size makes errors or poor line quality less noticeable. However, large reductions are not good ideas because the copy elements may be distorted. Thin lines may become too thin for quality printing.

When possible, reductions should be no more than a third smaller than the original. If the final copy is to be 8 or 9 inches (20.3 by 22.9 cm), the original should be no more than 12 inches (30.5 cm).

If reducing copy hides errors, enlarging copy magnifies them. Figure 44-1 shows some of the effects of enlargement and reduction on typewritten copy.

Length and width change equally when copy is enlarged or reduced. If you reduce a piece of 8-inch by 10-inch (20.3 by 25.4 cm) copy by 50 percent, the final printed material will be 4 inches by 5 inches (10.16 by 12.7 cm). Thus the printed copy is actually $1/4$ the size of the original copy (Fig. 44-2). The person preparing copy should be aware of this change in both dimensions. It is important when copyfitting.

PROTECTING COPY

Protecting copy is almost as important as preparing copy. Time, effort, and expense are wasted when copy is damaged, soiled, or destroyed before it is used.

All copy should have a protective *overlay sheet* attached to one edge (Fig. 44-3). It can be either tissue (tracing) paper or bond paper. The overlay sheet is attached with either tape or rubber cement. Notes to the process photographer or printer are often written on the overlay sheet.

Copy should be packaged and stored so that it will not curl, fold, or tear. One technique is to place the copy in an envelope for storage and mailing. The envelope should be clearly marked with the customer's name, the artist's name,

25% This copy was prepared by a typewriter.

50% This copy was prepared by a typewriter.

75% This copy was prepared by a typewriter.

100% This copy was prepared by a typewriter.

125% This copy was prepared by a typewriter.

150% This copy was prepared by a typewriter.

175% This copy was prepared by a typewri

Fig. 44-1. A typewritten line enlarged and reduced.

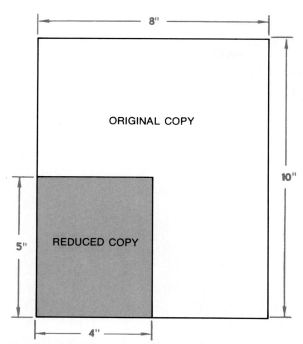

Fig. 44-2. The size of a 50 percent reduction.

Fig. 44-3. Illustration with an overlay sheet.

and notes that describe the piece of copy. Some people put a piece of cardboard in the envelope to keep it from bending.

Special attention should be given to handling photographs. They should be mounted on heavy board when possible. Never make marks on either the front or back of a photograph. Brief notes and marks can be made in photograph margins. It is best to put notes about photographs on a separate sheet of paper. This sheet of paper can be taped to the back of the photograph. Paper clips should never be used on photographs.

Always handle copy so that dirt or smudges will not get onto it. Handle copy by the edges to keep fingerprints off the image areas. Keep your hands very clean when working with copy. Never have food or drinks near the places where copy is being prepared or used. Many companies have extremely strict rules of cleanliness for employees who are working with copy.

CHECKING THE FINAL COPY

Final printed material can be no better than the original copy. It is very important that copy be thoroughly checked before it is sent to the photographer. Many companies have a regular procedure for making final checks on copy. Usually, the procedure has copy examined by someone other than the person who prepared it.

The copy should be carefully checked for accuracy. Type matter should be proofread. It should be examined for image damage and for completeness. Both type matter and illustrations should be straight and parallel when appropriate. It is important to check the accuracy of paste-up copy. It is quite easy to paste up elements so that they are not straight.

All of the elements of the copy must be located in proper relation to the other elements. The artist should compare the layout with the final copy. If photographs or large drawings are not attached to the copy, be sure that they are included and that their position is properly noted on the copy.

Be sure that all notes and instructions are on the copy. The printer will have questions unless the notes tell exactly what must be done. Notes to the printer should be included even though they may not be needed.

All smudges and unwanted marks should be removed from the copy. Use a clean cloth to wipe off wax and an eraser to rub out smudges. Be careful with the copy elements because they could be moved or damaged.

UNIT 45 CROPPING, SCALING, AND REGISTER MARKS

Illustrations should be cropped and scaled before the copy is sent to the photographer or printer. *Cropping* is selecting the area to be printed. *Scaling* is giving the finished printed size of the illustrations. Register marks are also often attached to the copy. These align sheets that must correspond exactly. These procedures help the photographer and printer know exactly what must be done to the copy.

CROPPING

The artist should select carefully the area of a photograph to be printed. Only the part that illustrates the main idea should be used. In Figure 45-1, only the area containing the action has been selected to be used. Unless the cropping is shown, the printer will reproduce the entire photograph.

AREA TO BE PRINTED

CATERPILLAR TRACTOR COMPANY

Fig. 45-1. A photograph may be more effective if only the area showing action is printed.

Making crop marks. Crop marks can be made on the borders of the photograph. They should be placed on all four sides (Fig. 45-2). Either ink or a grease pencil is used to make the marks. Never mark on the image area of a photograph.

Fig. 45-2. Crop marks on the borders of a photograph.

Fig. 45-3. Crop marks on an overlay sheet.

Crop marks can also be made on an overlay sheet (Fig. 45-3). In both Figures 45-1 and 45-2 the finished size of one of the two dimensions has been clearly marked. The photographer determines the exact reduction or enlargement.

SCALING COPY

Copy must be prepared to fit the space where it will be printed. The artist prepares the copy in proportion to the final printed size. Any of the following methods can be used to determine the size.

Fig. 45-4. A typical proportional scale.

Proportional scale method. Proportional scales are tools that determine the reduction or enlargement of copy. Using a proportional scale is probably the simplest and most accurate method.

Figure 45-4 shows a proportional scale. Notice that it has two scales. The outside scale is for the reproduction size. The inside scale is for the original size. Here is the procedure for using this tool:

1. Determine the actual length (height) of the copy. (Width could be used instead of the length.)
2. Find this number on the inside scale.
3. Determine the length that the copy will be when it is printed. (Width would be used when width is used in step 1.)
4. Find this number on the outside scale.
5. Rotate the two wheels until the numbers are next to each other.
6. Read the number in the opening marked *percentage* on the proportional scale.

The number in the window is the reproduction percentage used for photographing the copy. The other dimension can also be read at this time. This is done by finding the other dimension on the *original size* wheel. The reproduction size can be read from the mark next to it on the *reproduction* size scale.

Mathematical formula technique. The following formula can be used when you have no proportional scale. The formula can be used to determine enlargements and reductions:

$$\frac{WO}{HO} = \frac{we}{he}$$

In this formula:

WO = width of the original copy
HO = height of the original copy
we = width of the enlargement or reduction
he = height of the enlargement or reduction

The formula can be used to solve a problem like this: An 8-inch by 10-inch (20.3 by 25.4 cm) photograph is to be reduced to fit a space 3½ inches (8.9 cm) wide. By substituting into the formula the height of the reproduction size, calculate:

Customary			Metric	
$\frac{8}{10}$	=	$\frac{3.5}{he}$	$\frac{20.3}{25.4}$	$= \frac{8.9}{he}$
8he	=	35	20.3he	= 226.1
he	=	$\frac{35}{8}$	he	$= \frac{226.1}{20.3}$
he	=	4.375 inches	he	$= \frac{11.14}{cm}$

Diagonal line technique. A third method is sometimes used to determine copy size. It takes more time and gives only an approximate answer. First, draw a rectangle exactly the same size as the original copy (Fig. 45-5). Draw a diagonal line from the bottom corner (W) out through the opposite corner (Y). Now any rectangle with the same bottom corner (W) and its opposite corner on the diagonal line will have the same proportions as the original. Say that you have to fill a copy space that is 9 by 12 inches (22.9 by 30.5 cm) and you want to make your original copy 15 inches (38.1 cm) high. You measure the vertical 15 inches on your diagram (WB), draw a line over to the diagonal line (BA). Measure this horizontal line (BA) and that is the approximate width for your original copy—11.25 inches (28.6 cm).

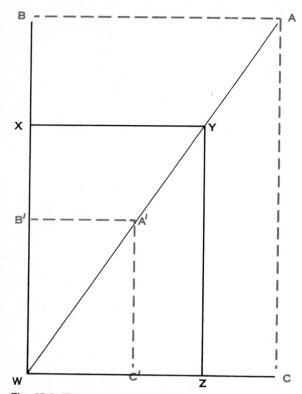

Fig. 45-5. The diagonal method of scaling copy.

SPECIFYING REDUCTION AND ENLARGEMENT SIZE

Reduction or enlargement sizes can be given in many ways. It is very important that the artist and printer understand each other so that errors will not be made.

The most common way is to mark either the height or width of the reproduction size. The marks should be made in the margins or on an overlay sheet. Enlargements and reductions are specified in inches, picas, or centimeters.

Another way is to give the specifications as a percentage. Say that the width of the original copy is 8 inches (20.3 cm). It is to be reproduced so that it is 6 inches wide (15.2 cm). The correct percentage to indicate on the copy is 75%. Copy that is to be reproduced the same size as the original should be marked *same size*, or 100%. If the copy were to be reproduced at 10 inches (25.4 cm), the percentage notation would be 125%.

Marking the exact reproduction size on copy causes less confusion than using percentages. To avoid errors, many artists use both methods.

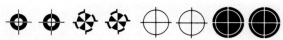

Fig. 45-6. Register marks.

AMOS AIRLINES

Fig. 45-7. Base element with register marks in place.

TIMELINE FIELD
LIGHTHOUSE, KENTUCKY, 44391

Fig. 45-8. Overlay for the base element in Figure 45-7 with register marks in place.

AMOS AIRLINES
TIMELINE FIELD
LIGHTHOUSE, KENTUCKY, 44391

Fig. 45-9. Base element and overlay printed in register.

AMOS AIRLINES
TIMELINE FIELD
LIGHTHOUSE, KENTUCKY, 44391

Fig. 45-10. Base element and overlay printed out of register.

USING REGISTER MARKS

Register marks are marks used to identify the correct position of two or more copy elements that are to be photographed separately and printed together. Register marks are frequently used in multicolor printing. They make it possible to print the different color images directly on top of one another—in register.

Figure 45-6 shows several kinds of pre-printed register marks. They can be attached directly to the elements of copy. Register marks can also be drawn on the copy by the artist.

Register marks should be placed at two to four points on the copy as shown in Figure 45-7. They are also placed on the overlay so that the register marks on the overlay sheet line up with the register marks on the base (Fig. 45-8).

Register marks will print on top of each other when the printing is *in register* (Fig. 45-9). The register marks will not line up if the printing is *out of register* (Fig. 45-10).

UNIT 46 MAKING THE PASTE-UP

Copy for photographic reproduction is prepared in several ways. Each element can be prepared and photographed separately and the negatives later brought together in a process called *stripping* (see Units 91-94). However, it is less expensive to place as many elements as possible on a single base. Everything can then be photographed at the same time. This is done by using the *paste-up* technique. Computer technology allows the combination of several copy elements without the need for a paste-up. For a complete discussion of electronic composition, see Section 22.

To make the paste-up, the artist attaches copy elements to the base. It is important that all elements are at the proper location. The paste-up is then used as the copy to make the photographic negative. This unit explains the procedure for making a paste-up.

DETERMINING THE SIZE OF THE BASE

The person who makes the paste-up usually works from a comprehensive layout or a sketch. The layout or sketch should show the location of each element and give the size of the final reproduction. The artist decides whether the copy will be prepared *smaller,* the *same size,* or *larger* than the final reproduction size. Copy is most often prepared the same size or larger than the reproduction size.

SECURING THE ELEMENTS FOR THE PASTE-UP

The next step in preparing a paste-up is to obtain the copy elements. These consist of typeset and display material, drawings, and sometimes prescreened photographs. Each element must also be proportionate to the final reproduction size. For example, if the copy is supposed to be reduced to 66 percent, the original type must be 18 point so that it will be 12 point in the printed product.

Drawings should be prepared so they are proportionate to the space they will use on the paste-up. Drawings can be made directly on the base material, or they can be prepared on another material and then attached to the base.

Drawings are frequently prepared larger than can be used on the paste-up. The drawing must then be marked so that it will be put in the correct place. The artist also must mark the exact location on the base where the drawing should go. This requires making two negatives that must be combined at a later time.

A drawing can be reduced or enlarged to the desired size by using the *diffusion transfer process.* The process gives a positive print from a drawing in one photographic step (see Unit 58). The print is then attached in the proper position on the base. It is much more efficient than trying to combine two separate negatives.

TREATMENT OF PHOTOGRAPHS

Photographs and other continuous-tone copy must be photographed separately from line copy. Because of this, glossy or original photographs are not put directly on the paste-up. Three methods are usually used to locate photographs on copy or paste-ups: (1) The block method, (2) the outline method, and (3) the halftone positive print method. Photographs should be cropped and scaled before using any of these methods.

Block method. In the *block method*, a piece of black or red material is placed on the paste-up. The block should be exactly the shape and size of the photograph when printed. Or if the paste-up is larger, it should be proportionate to the final reproduction size (Fig. 46-1). If a paste-up is prepared the same size as the final reproduction (100%), a 2- by 3-inch (5.1 by 7.6 cm) block would be placed in the exact location where the 2- by 3-inch photograph will be positioned.

Separate negatives are made of the paste-up (line copy) and the photograph (continuous-tone copy). The block is often called a *window*. It will be a clean, clear spot on the negative of the paste-up. The halftone negative of the photograph is then taped behind the clear block. This method is economical because it saves time in combining the halftone negative with the line negative.

Outline method. The outline method is similar to the block method. The location of the photograph is marked by four lines, instead of the solid block (Fig. 46-2). When the two negatives are prepared—one of the line copy and one of the photograph—a hole is cut into the negative where the lines were drawn. The halftone negative is then taped into the hole. This method takes more time than the block method but sometimes it works better.

Halftone positive print method. In this method, the *diffusion transfer* process is used to make a halftone positive print (see Unit 58), sometimes called a *screened print*. A halftone positive is made to the exact size needed for the space on the paste-up. It is then attached in the correct place on the base with the line elements. This method saves time because the paste-up can be photographed as a single piece of line copy. (The block and outline methods require separate line and halftone negatives.)

The halftone positive method should be used only when the paste-up will be photographed at 100 percent. Dot formation of the halftone positive will be changed if enlarged or reduced. Halftone screens with more than 100 lines per inch should not be used with the halftone positive method. Each photographic step may lose a small amount of detail. The final print could be of lower quality than ones made by the other two methods.

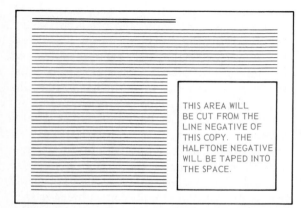

Fig. 46-1. A solid red or black image placed on the paste-up where the photograph will appear.

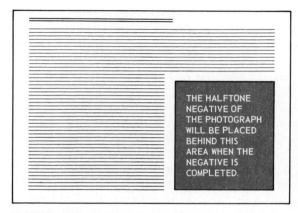

Fig. 46-2. An outline drawn on the paste-up where the halftone will be attached on the negative.

ATTACHING THE IMAGE ELEMENTS

Several techniques are used to paste up or attach elements to the base of a piece of copy. Three basic methods are (1) waxing, (2) taping, and (3) cementing.

Waxing. A waxing machine is needed for this method. It is desirable because the finished paste-up can be made faster and cleaner than with tape or cement. Another feature is that each element is removable. This allows the elements to be used later on another paste-up.

Attaching elements to the paste-up with wax is quite simple. First, elements are fed into the waxing machine rollers (see Fig. 42-9). Here, wax is applied to the *back* of the elements. The elements are then placed into the proper position on the base. Finally, they are pressed with a *burnisher*. A burnisher is a tool used to apply pressure. Be sure that the elements are properly located on the base when burnishing.

Taping. Double-surface tape has adhesive on both sides of the tape material. The tape is applied to the back of the element and the element is put in the correct position on the base (Fig. 42-8). The element must be put in the exact location the first time because it is difficult to remove without damage. Small marks or corners put on the base can help you to position the element.

Cementing. Rubber cement is applied to both the back of the element and to the area on the base where the element will be located (Fig. 42-10). When the cement is dry on both the element and the base, carefully place the element in position. (After the element touches the base, it cannot be moved.) Then rub off excess rubber cement around the element.

UNIT 47 COPY DIVISION FOR MULTI-COLOR REPRODUCTION

Multi-color printing has become very popular. (Multi-color printing means using more than one color of ink on the same printed sheet.) The use of color adds interest to the printed items. Important parts of the printing can be emphasized. To prepare copy for multi-color printing, more skill and attention to detail is required. Copy must be prepared so each printing operation will be done properly and accurately.

Copy for multi-color printing is classified as either *process-color* or *mechanical-color*. Sometimes both kinds of copy are used to produce a single printed product.

PROCESS-COLOR COPY

Process-color printing is used to reproduce continuous tone copy in full color. Examples are color photographs, transparencies (such as 35 mm slides), and color paintings. The full-color copy is photographed three or four times, using filters on the process camera. Separate halftone negatives or positives of each color are made. Each single-color negative or positive is referred to as a *color printer* (yellow printer, cyan printer, etc.). The process of making these color printers is called *color separation*.

Each of the three or four negatives or positives is used to produce an image carrier that will print a single but different primary color *yellow, magenta* (process red), or *cyan* (process blue) or black ink. The colors blend with each other when printed to produce a product that looks like the original copy. Examples of process-color prints are shown in the color pages of this book.

Process-color copy may be further classified as either reflection copy or transmission copy. *Reflection copy* is photographed by reflecting light from the surface of the continuous-tone copy to the camera (Fig. 47-1). Examples are reproductions of oil paintings, watercolors, and color photographs. *Transmission copy* is photo-

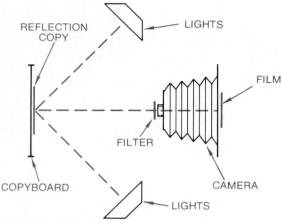

Fig. 47-1. With reflection copy, light is reflected from the surface of the copy through a filter and into the camera where it exposes the film.

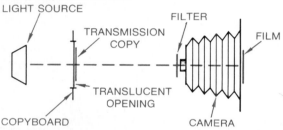

Fig. 47-2. With transmission copy, light passes through the copy and a filter and into the camera to expose the film.

Fig. 47-3. Copy that can be used to make a multicolor print, using the masking technique.

Fig. 47-4. The part of Figure 47-3 that will be on the first image carrier.

Fig. 47-5. The part of Figure 47-3 that will be on the second image carrier.

Fig. 47-6. A print of Figure 47-3 with two colors in register.

graphed by passing light through the copy (Fig. 47-2). Transparencies like 35mm slides are typical.

MECHANICAL-COLOR COPY

Mechanical-color copy is copy prepared so that two or more colors will print on the same sheet. The artist prepares a paste-up of all of the elements. The images might require the colors to butt (touch) or overlap each other. In other cases they may be separate.

The effect wanted in a printed item determines the technique used. The details for preparing the copy vary with the artist and are often determined by the needs of the printer. Whatever technique is used, all of the images must be either black-and-white or red-and-white.

There are three methods for preparing mechanical-color copy: (1) masking, (2) overlay method, and (3) key line method.

Masking. The masking technique is used when none of the colors overlap or butt. Copy is prepared as though the item will be printed in a single color (Fig. 47-3). Notes are attached to the copy to indicate which parts are to be printed in a particular color. The copy is photographed only once. On the negative, all of the areas to be printed in one color are *masked off—* that is, the images are covered to prevent light from exposing the image carrier. Masking is usually done with lithographic tape or a lithographic masking sheet (goldenrod). This leaves all of the areas to be printed in the second color uncovered. (See Unit 94.)

The masked negative is used to prepare the first image carrier (plate). An example of the first image carrier after printing is shown in Figure 47-4. After the first image carrier is made, the areas that were exposed for the first image carrier are masked-off for the second. Images that were blocked off for the first image carrier are exposed for the second. A print of the second image carrier is shown in Figure 47-5. A copy of both image carriers printed in register is shown in Figure 47-6.

Overlays. This technique is used when one color must overlap the other color. The image for each color is put on a different sheet of paper. One color (usually the black image) is put on a piece of heavy illustration board.

For each additional color, a piece of acetate or polyester film is attached to the base. The artwork for the overlays must be perfectly matched with each other and with the base. Register marks are placed on the base and the overlays to insure accurate printing of the images. All images on the base and overlays must be prepared in either black or red so that they will photograph.

Key line. The key line preparation technique is often used when two colors are to butt or touch. It produces a very accurate print. The colors should overlap slightly to avoid spaces between the images. Many artists prefer the key line method because small and precise overlaps are difficult to draw when using the overlay technique.

A single drawing of all images to be printed is prepared in black and white. A narrow line is drawn where the colors touch. This line is the *key line*. The line will be the width of the overlap. The areas to be printed are not completely filled with ink (Fig. 47-7). Fuzzy edges are made to show the printer that the illustration is not complete. Notes are placed on the copy or an overlay to indicate which images will be printed in each color.

The same number of negatives as colors to be printed are made. If two colors are required, there will be two negatives. Each will be used to prepare the image carrier for one color.

Each negative will need additional work before the image carrier can be made from it. The following procedure is used to prepare the negatives for making image carriers.

1. Obtain the negative to be used to print the first color.
2. Opaque the area to be used to print the second color. See Units 90 and 93.
3. Permit the opaqued negative to dry.
4. Turn the negative over so the emulsion side is up.
5. Scratch away the emulsion carefully to the key line separation.
6. Follow the same procedure to prepare the negative for the second color. The areas that were clear in the first negative will be opaqued in the second one.

A print of Figure 47-7 is shown in Figure 47-8. When the two colors are black and a second color, they are not always butted. The second color is often prepared so that it is overlapped by the black.

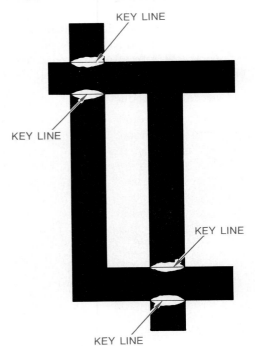

Fig. 47-7. An example of key-line copy.

Fig. 47-8. A two-color print of the key-line copy in Figure 47-7.

UNIT 48 NOTES AND INSTRUCTIONS TO THE PRINTER

Notes and instructions should accompany each piece of copy. The instructions should be complete but as brief as possible. They must include all of the information needed by the copy preparation personnel and the printer. The notes can be made by the artist, the customer, the photographer, the printer, or anyone else concerned with the printed material. The customer must say how the material should look when printed. The printer must be sure that the notes and instructions are complete enough for all the people who will handle the copy. Much of the information can be obtained when the printer first meets with the customer or artist. There are no standard procedures that are followed throughout the graphic arts industry, but similar information is required by all printers. Two kinds of information usually go with copy: personal data and technical production data.

PERSONAL DATA

Personal data is information about the persons involved in the printing. The following items are necessary:

1. Name of the customer.
2. Address and telephone number of the customer.
3. Name, address, and telephone number of the person who will answer questions about the copy.
4. Place to deliver the final printed material.

Many customers, artists, or advertising agencies include the information mentioned for items 3 and 4 as standard procedure. The printer can often save time by obtaining complete information for each job in the printing plant.

TECHNICAL PRODUCTION DATA

Technical production data include information necessary to change the copy into printed material. The amount and kind of information for copy is different for each job. Different instructions must be written for nearly every piece of copy. Following are examples of items that should be included on the copy.

1. Size of the final reproduction.

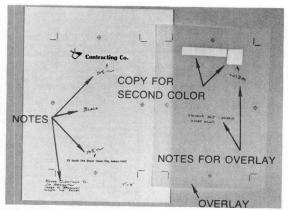

Fig. 48-1. Notes made directly on the copy in light blue pencil. The overlay sheet has additional copy for the second color.

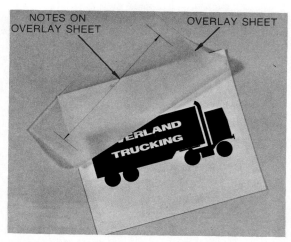

Fig. 48-2. Notes made on an overlay sheet.

THE WALDEMAR PRESS, INC.

	Last Job No.	**Job No.**	
			Customer No.

Date

Job Promised Proof To

Salesman

Customer

Job Description

Quantity Ordered Quantity Delivered

Finished Size: Width × **Height**

Comp.

Copy / Art

Camera

Stripping Plate

Paper

No. of Sheets	Size	Sub	Kind of Stock	Ordered From	Date Due
	×				
	×				
	×				
	×				
	×				
	×				

Pressroom

Start No. Sheets	Press No.	Press Sheet Size & Method of Run	No. of Plates	Final Count

Ink

Bindery

☐ Cut
☐ Fold   ☐ Gather
Style of Binding: ☐ Saddle Stitch   ☐ Sidewire   ☐ Sewed   ☐ Plastic   ☐ Cover
☐ Punching   ☐ Perforate
☐ Trim
Special Instructions:

Packing Delivery

NOTE: Keep 25 samples of each job—Deliver to Production Dept.

Fig. 48-3. A typical job ticket.

2. Special photographic treatment (reversals, drop-outs, etc).
3. Location of photographs and drawings (when separate from the composed type matter).
4. Kind of paper stock to be used.
5. Color(s) of ink.
6. Finishing operations (padding, collating, packaging, etc.).

Items other than the ones listed above are often needed. Any information required to produce the material should be listed.

METHODS OF MAKING NOTES AND INSTRUCTIONS

Three methods are used to make sure that notes stay with copy throughout the printing processes. In actual practice these methods are often combined.

1. Notes are made directly on the copy.
2. Notes are attached to the copy.
3. Notes are made on the envelope in which the copy is placed.

Notes made directly on the copy are usually the most explanatory because they cannot be separated from the copy. This procedure is used most often when the notes are brief and do not get in the way of the images to be photographed (Fig. 48-1). Notes placed directly on the copy should be done with a *light blue* pencil. Light blue lines, you remember, will not photograph.

Attaching notes to the copy is used when several items must be attached or when there is no room on the copy for comments. The overlay method (Fig. 48-2) is often used. With an overlay, the notes are close to the copy and the copy is protected. Instructions are also often attached to the back of the copy.

Some companies prefer to keep copy in large envelopes. The envelope protects the copy and gives space for notes. All items required (negatives, flats, and plates) can be placed in the envelope when finished. Figure 48-3 shows the information included on an envelope or a job ticket. Since more information can be placed on the job ticket than is needed for a single job, a job ticket can be used for all types of printing jobs. Notes may be written on the back of the job ticket. Notes also can be put inside the envelope when there is not enough space on the outside.

UNIT 49 LEARNING EXPERIENCES: PREPARING COPY FOR PROCESS PHOTOGRAPHY

KEY TERMS

Unit 41

Copy elements	Type matter
Illustrations	

Unit 42

Air brush	Ruling pen
Copy support or basis	T-square
French curve	

Unit 43

Combination copy	Reversal
Continuous-tone copy	Scratch board
Line copy	Silverpoint
Photograph	Wash drawing

Unit 44

Overlay

Unit 45

Cropping   Register marks
Proportional scale   Scaling

Unit 46

Paste-up   Window

Unit 47

Cyan   Mechanical color
Duotone   Moire
Key line   Process color
Magenta   Reflection copy
Masking   Transmission copy

DISCUSSION TOPICS

1. What are some factors to think about when choosing the base materials for copy?
2. What is the difference between *line copy* and *continuous-tone copy*?
3. Why should copy be prepared the same size as or larger than the desired printed size?
4. Explain how and where register marks are used.
5. Name two kinds of process-color copy and explain the difference between them.

ACTIVITIES

Units 43 and 44

1. Collect printed material that shows various kinds of copy preparation. Tell how the copy was prepared for printing.

Unit 45

2. Use a proportion scale to solve this problem: Assume that the copy is to be printed on $8\frac{1}{2}$- by 11-inch (21.6 by 27.9 cm) paper. The paper has a one-inch (2.54 cm) border around the copy. What size should the image be if it will be reduced by 25 percent? (Copy will be printed at 75% of the original size.)

Unit 46

3. Prepare four different paste-ups. Try to use many kinds of elements, including display type, typeset copy, line drawings, and continuous-tone copy. Also include the many methods used to attach elements to the base.

Unit 47

4. Use the key line method of multiple color to prepare a piece of copy.
5. Obtain two halftone screens, two halftone negatives, or two screen tints. Place one on top of the other. Turn them from side to side. Observe the pattern that is produced. Describe it on paper. Where is the pattern seen the most? Where is it seen the least?

Adjusting the lens to make an exposure on the process camera.

PROCESS CAMERAS AND DARKROOM PROCEDURE

50 INTRODUCTION TO PROCESS CAMERAS AND DARKROOM PROCEDURES

It is difficult to find a printed article that has not, in part, been produced by using a process camera. While photography dates from the early 1800s, its use in graphic arts is a twentieth-century development. The photographic process has made printing much more flexible than it was years ago.

Process cameras are those used to reproduce two-dimensional copy. They make precise enlargements, reductions, and same-size reproductions. Cameras have several precision parts that must be protected and handled with extreme care.

PARTS OF A CAMERA

Process cameras, regardless of the kind or manufacturer, have the same basic parts: (1) lens, (2) bellows (lens extension), (3) camera back (film holder), (4) copyboard (copy holder), and (5) lights. There are many other parts and attachments, some of which will be mentioned later. Figure 50-1 and Figure 50-2 show typical process cameras with some of the parts identified. These are horizontal cameras, the kind that will be discussed throughout this unit. They will also be compared with other kinds of cameras later.

Lens. The lens is the most precise and costly part of a process camera. The quality of reproduction depends largely on the quality of the lens. It consists of several glass elements (Fig.

50-3) and a diaphragm or iris. These are enclosed in a case called a *lens barrel*. Two typical lenses used are illustrated in Figure 50-4.

The *diaphragm*, or *iris*, regulates the amount of light entering the camera. An arrangement of metal leaves or blades mesh to make a circular opening called the aperture for light to pass through (Fig. 50-5). The diaphragm is opened or closed by turning a ring or collar on the outside of the lens barrel (Fig. 50-4).

The numbers on the collar refer to the size of the diaphragm opening. They are called f-stops (see Fig. 50-4). Some common diaphragm f-stop numbers are f/8, f/11, f/16, f/22, and f/32. The larger the f-stop number, the smaller the diaphragm opening: f/16 is smaller than f/11. Each larger f-stop number reduces the size of the aperture by half. The number f/16 has twice the aperture as f/22, letting in twice the amount of light.

To enlarge or reduce copy, the lens and copyboard must be moved either closer or farther apart. When this is done, the aperture must be adjusted by changing the diaphragm setting. Many cameras have a manual diaphragm control that in turn, adjusts the aperture. This maintains constant exposure light.

The lens unit is attached to a lensboard, which in turn, is fastened to the front case (Fig. 50-2). The front case can be moved either forward or backward to make adjustments for enlargements or reductions.

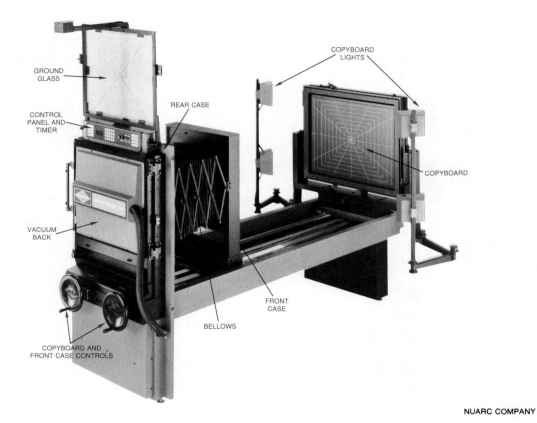

NUARC COMPANY

Fig. 50-1. Rear view of a typical process camera.

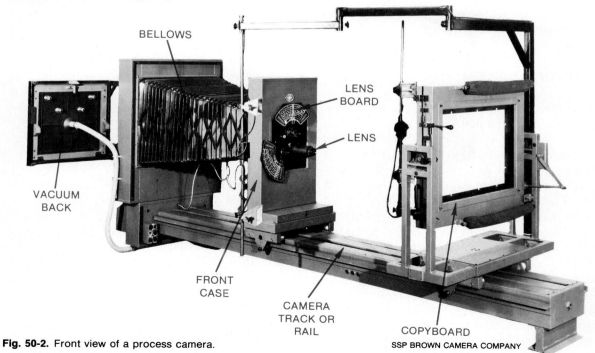

Fig. 50-2. Front view of a process camera.

SSP BROWN CAMERA COMPANY

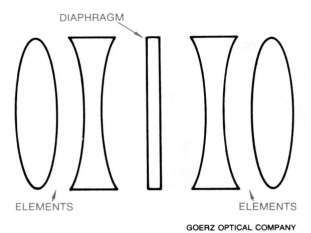

GOERZ OPTICAL COMPANY

Fig. 50-3. The elements and diaphragm of a lens.

GOERZ OPTICAL COMPANY

Fig. 50-4. Two typical lenses for process cameras.

Fig. 50-5. A lens diaphragm.

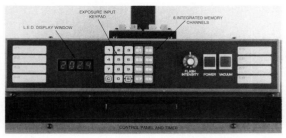

DAINIPPON SCREEN MFG. CO. LTD.

Fig. 50-6. Computer control panel for a camera.

The lens should be protected at all times. A lens cap should be placed over the lens when the camera is not in use to prevent dust from settling on it. Examine the lens frequently for dust or dirt because it can cause flaws on the negative. Fan the lens with a sheet of paper to remove dust. If this does not work, use lens cleaner and a piece of commercial lens tissue. Never use plain household tissue or cloth because they contain abrasive matter that will scratch the lens. Never touch the lens surface with your fingers, because acid in perspiration can eat away the lens surface. Always check with the person in charge before cleaning a lens.

Control Panel. The *camera control panel* is used to adjust the camera exposure and to turn the lights on and off. The control panel shown in Figure 50-6 has a computer that stores information and permits more precise adjustments.

Shutter. A *shutter* is included on the front case of most cameras. It is behind the lens and inside the bellows.

Bellows. The *bellows* provides a light-tight closure between the front case and the camera back where the film is held. The bellows is made of cloth or similar material, which stretches or compresses when adjustments are made to the camera for enlargements or reductions. A bellows is easy to puncture. It should be protected from sharp objects and inspected every six months to be sure it is light-tight. If light enters the camera through the bellows, film will be exposed and ruined.

Camera back. The *camera back,* which holds the film in the camera, is behind the lens and bellows. The kind most in use is the vacuum back. This is actually a swinging door with holes on the plate surface that holds the film (Fig. 50-1). There is a vacuum chamber behind the plate, and a vacuum pump is attached to the vacuum chamber. The film is placed in the correct position and held by the vacuum. The vacuum back opens for putting film on the camera back and closes to make the exposure.

Most cameras also have a ground-glass back to check the focus of the camera (Fig. 50-1). The ground glass is put in position exactly where the film will be located. When the camera lights are turned on and the lens is opened, the image from the copy can be seen on the ground glass. The photographer can check for focus, sharpness of image, and proper placement of the copy on the copyboard.

Copyboard. Copy is held in place in the *copyboard*, which is attached to the same rail or track as the front case (Fig. 50-1). Most copyboards consist of a frame with a spring-loaded back or foam cushion. The pad is covered with a glass lid that covers the copy and locks into place. The center of the copyboard is in line with the center of the camera back. It

moves either forward or backward on the rail or track to make adjustments.

Lights. Three kinds of lights are often used on process cameras. They are *incandescent, quartz,* and *pulsed xenon.* Each has advantages and disadvantages. Incandescent lamps are the least expensive and work well with black-and-white copy. But the light from incandescent lights is not as bright as some of the other lights and the bulbs dim with age. Quartz lights are much brighter and do not dim with age. Quartz lights are used for black-and-white work. Pulsed xenon lights are much brighter than quartz lights and are used for both black-and-white and color work. This makes it possible to have much shorter exposures.

Lights are usually held on the copyboard frame. They can be adjusted to different angles (Fig. 50-1).

Darkroom. The *darkroom* is a room that can be made completely dark and is used to process photographic materials. Because of the nature of the work done in the darkroom, special tools, equipment, procedures, and layout will be discussed in the following units.

UNIT 51 CLASSIFICATIONS OF PROCESS CAMERAS

Process cameras can be classified in many ways. The two most common ways are discussed in this unit. The first concerns where the cameras are placed in the printing plant. The second defines cameras according to their construction.

GALLERY AND DARKROOM CAMERAS

Some cameras are made to use in a room with normal lighting; some are designed to use in a darkroom; others can be used in either area. Parts of cameras differ, depending on where the camera is used. Each camera has advantages and disadvantages.

Gallery cameras. Process cameras used or located entirely in normally lighted rooms are

called *gallery cameras.* They are not used very often because it is not easy to make negatives with them. Film must be loaded into the film holder in the darkroom and then transported to the camera in the lighted room. After the exposure, the film holder is removed from the camera and brought back to the darkroom for processing. This process takes up time. A gallery camera usually has a shutter to control the amount of light that enters it, and most of the other features of any quality camera. The chief advantage of a gallery camera is that it takes up no valuable darkroom space.

Darkroom cameras. Sometimes the entire camera is placed in the darkroom. In most situations, however, only the rear case is in the darkroom, and the rest is put in the lighted

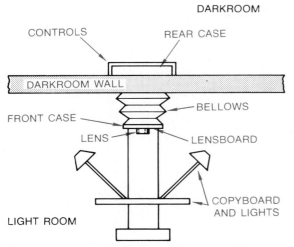

Fig. 51-1. A darkroom camera with the rear case in the darkroom.

room. Figure 51-1 shows the camera installed through the wall. The darkroom camera is popular because film can be loaded and unloaded directly in the darkroom.

When the whole camera is placed in the darkroom, exposures cannot be made while the film is being processed, because light would ruin it. Sometimes a camera is placed in a separate, next-door darkroom and used only for making exposures.

The best arrangement is to have only the rear case of the camera in the darkroom. The film is loaded into the camera in the darkroom and exposures are made while film processing is being done. The exposure lights are located in the lighted room. The main problem in this method is that the camera operator must leave the darkroom to change the copy in the copyboard. This problem can be overcome if one person changes the copy in the lighted room while another makes the exposure in the darkroom.

HORIZONTAL AND VERTICAL CAMERAS

Cameras are also classified by the direction in which the exposure is made. There are both horizontal and vertical cameras. Most photographic departments have the horizontal darkroom type. Both cameras have essentially the same basic parts.

Horizontal cameras. With this camera, a line drawn through the center of the copyboard, lens, and film holder will be horizontal (Fig. 51-2). The horizontal camera in Figure 51-2 is much larger than the camera in Figure 50-1. It is large enough for the photographer to walk under the overhead camera track. This camera is used to make exposures on very large materials.

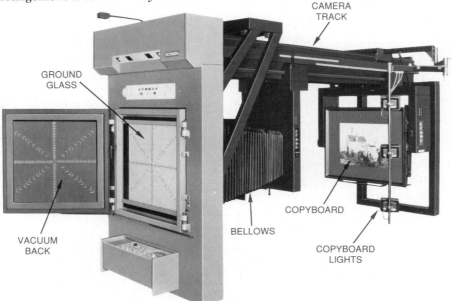

DAINIPPON SCREEN MFG. CO. LTD.

Fig. 51-2. A large horizontal camera.

Vertical cameras. The photographic film is in a horizontal position on a vertical process camera. The parts of a vertical camera are shown in Figure 51-3. The copyboard is at the bottom of the camera and the film holder is at the top. This type of camera must be used entirely in the darkroom or entirely in a lighted room. Most are used in the darkroom because this makes film loading easier. When the vertical camera is used in the darkroom, it is not necessary to use a shutter. The camera lights are connected to the timer. The time the lights are on serves the same purpose as the shutter. The copyboard lights prevent film from being processed when the vertical camera is used in a darkroom.

An advantage of the vertical camera is that it requires less floor space. However, its physical size limits the size of copy, enlargements, and reductions. Another disadvantage is that the photographer must bend over each time when changing copy.

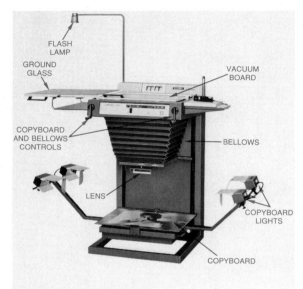

DAINIPPON SCREEN MFG. CO. LTD.

Fig. 51-3. The parts of a vertical camera.

UNIT

52 FILMS AND CHEMICALS FOR PROCESS PHOTOGRAPHY

In most printing processes, copy must be photographed before it can be reproduced or printed. With cameras, film is exposed while it is held in a camera or contact frame. After the exposure is made, the film must be processed in certain chemicals.

There are many films and chemicals available for photographic reproduction. This unit is concerned only with films and chemicals that are commonly used for process photography. For answers to specific questions, you should also consult film manufacturers' literature and representatives.

STRUCTURE OF FILM

The basic parts of a piece of film are the base (support), and the emulsion (the light-sensitive

coating). The other parts or elements of a film are shown in Figure 52-1.

Base. The *base* supports the light-sensitive emulsion. The material may be translucent, permitting some light to pass through. Most film bases, however, are transparent, or clear, like

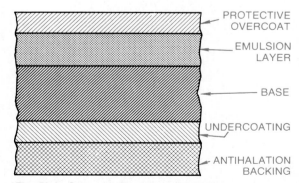

Fig. 52-1. Cross section of a piece of film.

glass. Film is made with many kinds of base materials—polyester, acetate, glass, and paper. Until recently, acetate was the most frequently used, but polyester has become popular because it has more dimensional stability. In other words, it does not expand and contract with changes in temperature and humidity.

Bases come in several thicknesses. A standard thickness is about 0.005-inch. Film of 0.0035-inch would be considered thin-base film. Film of approximately 0.007-inch is thick-base film. All film must be able to withstand the effects of chemicals and handling.

Emulsion. The *emulsion* is light-sensitive material suspended in a clear gelatin. It covers one side of the base, as shown in Figure 52-1. The image is formed in the emulsion. The light-sensitive materials most often used in emulsions are silver halides. When silver halides are developed after being exposed to light, they turn black and form the image on the piece of film.

Overcoat. A protective *overcoat* is applied to the emulsion side of the film. It is a thin layer of clear gelatin. This protects the emulsion from abrasion and scratching during handling.

Antihalation. *Antihalation backing* is a dye applied to the base side opposite the emulsion. During exposure, the light reflected from the copy could go completely through the emulsion and bounce back through the base and cause secondary exposures. The dye or antihalation back absorbs all of the light that passes through the emulsion. This stops the light from reflect-

ing back into the emulsion (Fig. 52-2). The dye is removed from the film during processing.

Anticurl. Many films have an *anticurl coating*. Anticurl coatings help to keep the film flat.

KINDS OF FILM

Several kinds of film are used in the graphic arts. Students should be familiar with these films. They should know where they are used and how they are processed. In general most graphic arts films make high-contrast negatives (either black or clear areas).

To understand film better, it is important to understand how film reacts to light. One way to show how film reacts to light is to discuss the way in which the human eye reacts to light. Light is described by wavelengths, measured in millimicrons (1 millimicron equals one billionth of a meter or about 40 millionths of an inch). Infared light has a wavelength of about 700 millimicrons. Ultraviolet light has a wavelength of about 400 millimicrons. The human eye can see wavelengths from about 400 to 700 millimicrons. Figure 52-3 illustrates that the panchromatic film comes closest to "seeing" the same wavelengths as the human eye.

Blue sensitive film. *Blue sensitive films* are sensitive to blue light. They are sometimes used for copying black-and-white photographs and for duplicating halftone negatives. This film can be handled under darkroom safelights.

Panchromatic film. *Panchromatic film* is sensitive to nearly the same light as the human eye. Because of this, it is often said to be sensitive to all visible light. Panchromatic film must be developed in total darkness. It is most frequently used to make color separations and for color photographs.

Orthochromatic film. *Orthochromatic film* is sensitive to blue and green light, but is not sensitive to red light. Thus it may be developed in a darkroom equipped with red lights. Also, blue lines can be drawn on the copy being photographed. These blue lines will not be recorded on the film. These films are widely used to photograph black-and-white copy and for other applications where colors do not have to be recorded.

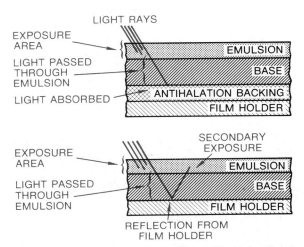

Fig. 52-2. Passage of light in films with and without antihalation backing.

Silverless film. *Silverless film* uses a diazo compound in its light-sensitive emulsion. It can be used in subdued light, but it requires bright light to make effective exposures.

Rapid access film. *Rapid access film* is designed for faster film processing than that of normal films. Early rapid access film was used to make good line negatives, but it did not produce good halftone negatives. More recent developments have resulted in film that can provide adequate halftone negatives.

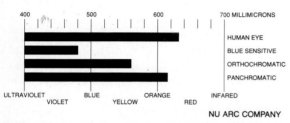

Fig. 52-3. Light sensitivity of film compared to the human eye.

Contacting film. *Contacting film* is used to make contact reproductions of negatives or positives; that is, it is used to make negatives from positives or positives from negatives.

Duplicating film. *Duplicating film* is used to make exact copies of negatives or positives: a positive from a positive or a negative from a negative. Duplicating film is often used when more than one negative or positive is needed.

HANDLING FILM

Film is very delicate and highly sensitive to light. It can be damaged very easily by temperature, humidity, gases, and scratches.

Film should be stored at temperatures ranging from 68 to 75°F (20 to 24°C). The humidity should be from 40 to 50 percent. When film is stored for long periods of time, it can be kept in a refrigerator.

Avoid handling film more than necessary. It can be damaged by fingerprints, so it should be handled only by the edges. Care should also be taken to avoid scratching the film or laying it on surfaces that are not clean and dry.

CHEMICALS

Exposed film has a latent, or invisible, image. The latent image cannot be seen, and the processing chemicals act to make it visible.

The three main solutions for processing film to produce a negative or film positive are developer, stop bath, and fixer. Manufacturers recommend specific chemicals to be used with particular films. Follow the directions of the film manufacturer.

Developer. Exposed film is first placed into the *developer solution*. This solution penetrates the gelatin and changes the latent image or exposed areas from silver halides to black metallic silver. Developer is an alkaline, or basic, chemical solution.

Developer is made up of several chemical agents, each with a specific purpose. The main reducing or developing agent is *hydroquinone*. This chemical is what turns the exposed silver salts to black metallic silver.

Chemicals such as accelerators speed up developing, buffers control activity of the accelerator, restrainers retard the speed of developing, and preservatives lengthen the life of the developer. These chemicals are included in many developer solutions.

Most developers for orthochromatic process film are made in two parts—Part A and Part B. These parts are prepared and stored separately, but they are mixed to make one solution just before developing the film. The developer lasts only a short time after mixing—thirty minutes to an hour.

Stop bath. The *stop bath* stops the developing action of the developer. A very weak *acetic acid* and water solution is used. Plain water will work, but the action is slower. The stop bath also removes the developer from the film and protects the fixing solution from contamination.

Fixer. The *fixer* (sometimes called *hypo*) removes the undeveloped silver halides and clears the film. The main ingredient is *sodium thiosulfate*. Acetic acid is also added to the fixer to remove any remaining alkaline developer. Most fixers contain a chemical to harden the emulsion that remains after developing. After the film has been fixed, it is no longer sensitive to light. White lights can then be turned on in the darkroom. The fixer must be thoroughly washed from the photographic film with clean water before it is dried.

_{UNIT} 53 DARKROOMS

A darkroom holds the equipment and materials used in processing photographs. A darkroom must be arranged so that it can be kept clean, neat, and safe. Very costly and sophisticated equipment is available for darkrooms, but often simpler equipment will do the job well enough. If high quality results are needed, however, the photographer must use high quality equipment.

DARKROOM EQUIPMENT

Darkroom sinks provide fresh running water. They also provide space for trays. Many sinks have a place for the photographer to dispose of used chemicals. Sinks are made of fiberglass or stainless steel. A fiberglass sink is shown in Figure 53-1. Stainless steel sinks are more rigid than fiberglass sinks. Stains from water and chemicals can be easily cleaned from stainless steel sinks. A temperature-controlled sink is shown in Figure 53-2. The temperature controlled unit below the sink circulates a constant temperature water. Such sinks also have areas to wash photographic materials and view negatives.

Water mixers are often used to provide a constant supply of circulating water around processing trays. The mixer shown in Figure 53-3 is accurate to within $\pm 1/4°$ F.

Rigid *trays* hold the chemicals during processing. At least three trays are required: (1) for the developer solution, (2) for the stop bath, and (3) for the fixer solution. The tray should be slightly larger than the material being processed. If the tray is too large, expensive chemicals will be wasted. Trays are made from plastic, hard rubber, fiberglass, and stainless steel (Fig. 53-4).

Thermometers are precise, delicate instruments used when processing photographic materials. They come in many sizes and shapes. Photographers often keep two thermometers in

NUARC COMPANY

Fig. 53-1. A fiberglass processing sink.

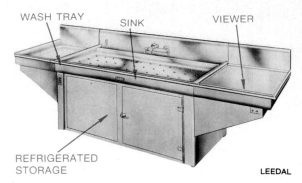

WASH TRAY SINK VIEWER

REFRIGERATED STORAGE LEEDAL

Fig. 53-2. A temperature controlled sink.

Fig. 53-3. Water mixer accurate to $\pm 1/4°$F.

Fig. 53-4. Stainless steel processing tray.   LEEDAL

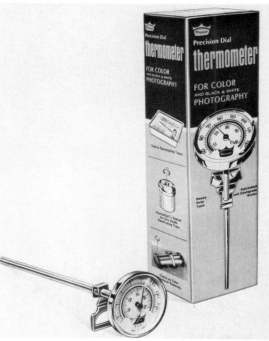

PHOTO MATERIALS COMPANY

Fig. 53-5. A typical thermometer.

Fig. 53-6. Safelights.   NUARC COMPANY

the darkroom and check one against the other for accuracy. A typical thermometer is shown in Figure 53-5.

Safelights provide light for the darkroom worker but will not expose film. They are usually red, because orthochromatic film can be handled under a red safelight. (Safelights are sometimes called *ortho-safe* lights.) Safelights are located where film processing occurs, such as over the sink or near the film storage areas. They are built to be plugged directly into a wall receptacle, attached to a wall, or hung from the ceiling (Fig. 53-6). Some darkroom workers use ordinary red light bulbs, but this practice is risky. Only safelights that do not give off blue or green light should be used in the darkroom.

Utensils are needed for mixing, pouring, and measuring. The utensils commonly found in a darkroom are graduates, beakers, pails, and funnels. The material used to make the utensils should not contaminate the chemicals. Glass, plastic, and stainless steel are satisfactory.

Graduates are commonly used to measure quantities of chemicals. They are usually calibrated in both ounces and cubic centimeters (Fig. 53-7).

Beakers and *pails* are used mainly for mixing chemicals. Beakers have a smaller capacity (usually one gallon or less) than pails (Fig. 53-8). Pails are used to mix large quantities—three to five gallons of chemicals (Fig. 53-9).

Funnels make it easier to pour chemicals into storage bottles with small openings (Fig. 53-10). Funnels come in several useful sizes.

Chemicals are kept in liquid form in *storage containers* until they are needed. Liquid chemicals are bought in containers; others are in powder form and must be mixed with water before they are placed in containers. The kind and size of container used depends on the quantity of chemicals used in the darkroom. If large quantities of chemicals are needed, a storage tank should be used.

Smaller quantities of one gallon or less are usually stored in glass or plastic bottles. All containers should be clearly labeled to describe the contents. Some darkroom workers even like to place additional instructions on the bottles or containers. It is also wise to keep full duplicate containers of each chemical to prevent running out at a crucial time. Containers should keep air

Fig. 53-7. A stainless steel graduate.

Fig. 53-8. A stainless steel beaker.

Fig. 53-9. A stainless steel pail.

Fig. 53-10. A stainless steel funnel.

Fig. 53-11. A contact printer.

Fig. 53-12. Light source for contact printing.

from reaching the chemicals. It is also important that direct light does not come into contact with the chemicals. If you use glass containers, be careful not to break them.

Timers are essential in the darkroom. They can be used to time exposures, but are mainly used when processing film. Some equipment has built-in timers. Appropriate timers should be used to control equipment. Typical timers are shown in Figures 143-19 and 143-20.

Contact printers are used to make reproductions the same size as the negatives or positives. These prints can be made on either film or photographic paper. The negative or film positive is placed on the glass (Fig. 53-11). The photographic material (paper or film) is placed on the negative, emulsion to emulsion, and the lid is closed. The vacuum blanket forces the negative and the material on which the reproduction is being made into tight contact. The lights, located in the lower part of the printer, are turned on for a specific amount of time. The photographic material is then removed and processed.

A *point source light* is used to expose contact prints (Fig. 53-12). This light source is often used with a vacuum printing frame like the one

shown in Figure 53-13. The lamp is located above the frame. A transformer in the control box lets the intensity of the light be changed as needed.

Inspection lights are needed in all darkrooms (Fig. 53-14). The lights are used to examine negatives and film positives during and after processing. They are equipped with ortho-safe (red) and white lights.

A *film dryer* speeds the drying time of processed film. After the film has been properly washed, it is run through a dryer. The film is dried in a few seconds and is ready to be used.

Many other pieces of equipment and utensils

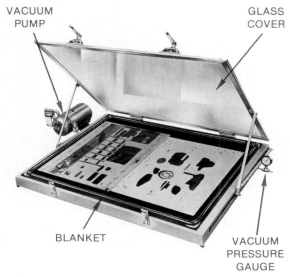

VACUUM PUMP

GLASS COVER

BLANKET

VACUUM PRESSURE GAUGE

NUARC COMPANY

Fig. 53-13. Vacuum printing frame.

NUARC COMPANY

Fig. 53-14. Inspection lights.

can be used in darkrooms, but most are for special purposes and are not absolutely essential. The darkroom worker must decide what equipment and utensils are needed to get the desired results. Equipment has little value unless it can be used properly.

DARKROOM ARRANGEMENTS

Darkrooms are usually set up according to the preference of the camera operator, but there are some features common to all arrangements. A well-planned darkroom should have the following features.

1. It should be completely light-tight.
2. The size and shape should hold the equipment and provide work space without being overcrowded.
3. There should be a door or light trap arrangement so that people can enter and leave without disturbing work in progress.
4. There should be a sink with fresh running water, preferably hot and cold with a temperature control.
5. A system of supplying fresh, clean air is essential. An air conditioner that maintains a constant temperature and humidity is ideal.
6. There should be enough electrical outlets to operate the darkroom equipment safely.
7. There should be ample space for storage.
8. There should be a white-light source for use when cleaning up or preparing the darkroom.

Darkroom light controls. A darkroom must be dark. If even a small amount of light enters the room, the photographic film or paper will be ruined.

There must be constant inspection for possible light leaks. Some darkroom workers do this daily. Inspection includes looking for cracks in walls, space around doors, and places where objects or utilities pass through the walls. These all are potential trouble areas.

Darkroom plans. There are nearly as many darkroom plans and arrangements as there are darkrooms. Many times, the darkroom worker has no control over them. Reasons for a particular plan may include the size and space available, equipment needed, placement and design of the entrances, and location of electrical outlets and water supply.

Work flow. As a darkroom worker, you should try to arrange an efficient work-flow pattern. You should be able to move through the steps of a job smoothly, without hopping from place to place (Fig. 53-15).

Storage and work space. Not all space in the darkroom should be taken up with equipment. Space is also needed for storage of film, chemicals, utensils, and other required materi-

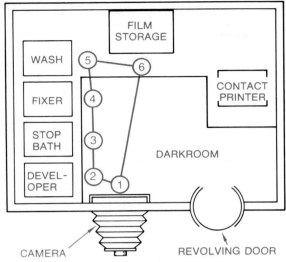

Fig. 53-15. A darkroom, showing workflow.

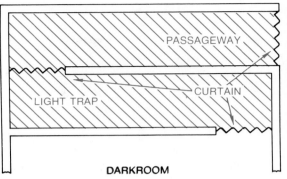

Fig. 53-16. A light trap.

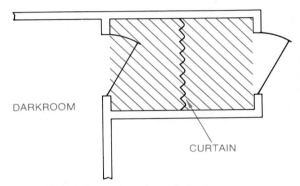

Fig. 53-17. Double doors for a darkroom.

als. A flat work space is needed for cutting paper or film, organizing copy, and placing equipment.

Electrical outlets. Electrical outlets should be placed about every five feet around the darkroom. There should also be several circuits to prevent overloading of any single circuit.

Darkroom doors. Darkroom doors must prevent light from entering when work is in progress. The most desirable types permit persons to enter and leave the darkroom while work is being done. Each has advantages and limitations.

The light trap is a common method of providing for entrance and exit from a darkroom. The light trap must be passed through in order to get from the lighted room into the darkroom (Fig. 53-16). Walls of the light trap are painted black to absorb as much light as possible. Curtains are sometimes placed in the light trap to reduce the amount of light further. The disadvantges of this type of darkroom access are that it takes considerable space and requires more time to enter and leave. Moreover, the passageways are often quite narrow, making it difficult to move equipment in and out.

Double doors are used for some darkrooms. The effect is much like that of the common light trap, but takes up less space (Fig. 53-17).

Revolving doors are quite effective for darkrooms (Fig. 53-18). They consist of two cylinders, the smaller one fitting into the larger (Fig.

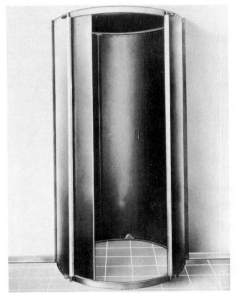

CONSOLIDATED INTERNATIONAL CORPORATION

Fig. 53-18. Revolving door for a darkroom.

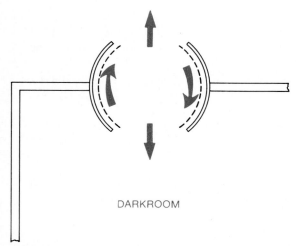

Fig. 53-19. Plan of a two-opening revolving darkroom door.

53-19). The outside cylinder has two openings and the inside cylinder has only one opening. You enter with the inside cylinder's opening aligned with the outside opening toward the lighted room. You then turn the inside cylinder to align with the outside opening into the darkroom.

MULTIPLE DARKROOMS

There are at least three kinds of activities performed in darkrooms. They are: (1) processing photographic materials in total darkness, (2) processing photographic materials in red light, and (3) exposing photographic materials with white light. If there is only one darkroom, it is impossible for all three things to be done at the same time. Many printing plants have divided their darkroom space into several darkrooms so that all activities can be done at the same time. These darkrooms are usually placed next to one another.

DARKROOM CLEANLINESS

Dirt and dust cause some of the biggest problems in the darkroom. You should constantly try to eliminate dirt in the darkroom. Dirt and dust can enter from the outside or be formed by dried chemicals in the darkroom.

Keeping a darkroom clean is a never-ending process. To make cleaning easier, keep as much equipment off the darkroom floor as possible. Mop the floor frequently, because it collects more dirt than any other place in the darkroom. A ventilation system that keeps dust from entering the darkroom will help. Be sure that the filter in the ventilation system is replaced or cleaned frequently. Fill all light leaks in the darkroom, because dirt and dust can enter spaces that are large enough to permit even small amounts of light to enter. All surfaces should be washed before starting any darkroom work and after finishing work. It is often necessary to wash the surfaces several times during the work session. Clean up spilled chemicals immediately even if the spill does not get in your way at that time.

It is good practice to keep to a regular routine for darkroom cleanup. Such a routine means that items get cleaned when they should be cleaned. Your attitude toward cleanliness will pay many benefits in quality photographic work.

UNIT 54 SAFETY IN THE DARKROOM

There are many safety problems when working in a darkroom. Treat the following with care at all times for personal protection and efficiency. Federal law now requires that employers pro-vide effective safety regulations for employees.

Darkness. One of the greatest hazards in the darkroom is the lack of light. It is wise to let the eyes become adjusted to the darkness before starting to work in the darkroom. People working in darkness should be familiar with the location of the equipment and supplies. Activity should be kept to a minimum. Never try to mix chemicals when the main white light is not on.

Chemicals. Chemicals used in the darkroom can irritate some people's skin. Rubber or plastic gloves can be worn to guard against such irritation. Handle chemicals carefully to prevent splashing them into the eyes. Always wash hands thoroughly as soon as possible after working with chemicals. If you get chemicals in or near your eyes, flush them with water or a special eyewash quickly. See a physician as soon as you can.

Moisture. Always clean up moisture from the floors and working surfaces. A wet floor can cause slipping and serious falls. Wetness increases the chance of electrical shock.

Chemical storage. Chemicals should be stored in safe containers where they can be easily reached. Plastic or stainless steel containers will not break so easily as glass ones. Plastic ones are also lighter and easier to handle.

Electrical equipment. All electrical items in the darkroom should be grounded according to the specifications of the manufacturer. Never put electrical equipment near moisture, or where moisture can get into it. Never handle electrical equipment with wet hands.

UNIT 55 EXPOSING AND PROCESSING A LINE NEGATIVE

A line negative is a reproduction of line copy. It is produced on film (usually orthochromatic) and is a reversal of line copy. A negative is black in the areas that are white in the copy (Fig. 55-1).

To make a line negative, you expose the film in a camera and then process it. The major steps are preparing the darkroom, adjusting the camera, placing the copy in the copyboard, locating the film, processing the film, and cleaning up.

PREPARING THE DARKROOM

Before work is done, the camera operator must prepare the darkroom. This should be done with the white light turned on. Many items need attention.

Surfaces. All dust and dirt must be cleaned from the working surfaces and from the darkroom utensils. Dust can cause pinholes (small holes in the emulsion of the negative). Clean the copyboard and the film holder (vacuum back). Examine the lens of the camera to be sure it is clean. When the camera is not being used, keep a lens cap over the lens. Clean the entire dark-

EASTMAN KODAK

Fig. 55-1. A line negative made from line copy.

room and camera with a vacuum cleaner every week if possible.

Sink and chemicals. Put the trays in the sink. They should be slightly larger than the film that will be processed. At least four trays are needed: one for the developer, one for the stop bath, one for the fixer, and one for the water wash. If a sink has a film-washing area, only three trays will be needed. The wash tray should have a supply of fresh running water.

Arrangement of trays. The trays should be arranged so that the film being processed can be moved along without having to move it over another tray. The developer tray should be closest to the camera to eliminate extra movement.

Fig. 55-2. Trays in the right order for film processing.

The tray sequence should be: (1) developer, (2) stop bath, (3) fixer, and (4) wash (Fig. 55-2).

Developer tray. Developer is prepared by mixing equal amounts of part A and part B just before developing the film. As we mentioned in Unit 52, developers have a very short period of usefulness once they have been mixed. Because of this, actual mixing of the two parts should be delayed as long as possible.

The following procedure will give the photographer the most time to use the developer. In a graduate, measure one part of developer A concentrated solution. Add three parts of 68° F water. Stir thoroughly and pour the mixed contents into the developer tray. Rinse out the graduate with water and wipe it out with a lint-free paper towel. Then, in the graduate, measure one part of developer B solution. This amount must be exactly the same as part A. Add three parts water and stir. Do not pour the part B into the tray until you are ready to develop the first piece of film. When you are ready, add the mixture to the developer tray and rock the tray gently a few times to mix parts A and B.

The developer will wear out after a period of time and after several pieces of film have been developed. Follow the manufacturer's recommendations about exhausted developer and throw it away when it wears out. Be sure to wash the tray before mixing more developer.

Stop bath tray. Stop bath solution can be made with 28 percent glacial acetic acid and water, but it is more convenient to use prepared indicator stop bath concentrate. Mix the concentrate carefully with water according to the instructions on the container. Normally, only 5 to 8 ounces of concentrate are needed to make 1 gallon of working solution. When mixed, the

stop bath solution will be a bright yellow. When it becomes exhausted, it will turn purple.

Fixer tray. Fill the fixer tray about half full with fixer. Fixer solution should be pre-mixed in 1- to 5-gallon containers. Follow the instructions on the concentrate container. Fixer lasts much longer than the other chemicals. Throw it away only when it does not clear the film (remove the milky, undeveloped areas) in about 1½ minutes. You also can tell that the fixer is exhausted when it looks dark and dirty.

Water wash. Place a tray siphon in the water tray, attach the hose to a water faucet, and turn on the water. For best results, the water temperature should be 68° F (20° C). If the processing sink has a film washing area, the fourth tray will not be needed.

Fig. 55-3. Photographer's sensitivity guide.

Temperature. Put the overflow standpipe (Fig. 55-3) in the sink. Turn on the water and let it circulate throughout the tray area to keep an even temperature in the processing solutions. Remember, the best temperature for film chemistry is 68° F (20° C).

ADJUSTING THE CAMERA

Basic camera adjustments include the timer, lens, and enlargement or reduction settings. To insure accuracy, all adjustments should be made with the darkroom white light on.

Setting the basic exposure time. Before a line negative can be made, these variables must be controlled: (1) kind of film, (2) developer, (3) temperature, and (4) processing time. Other variables are (5) condition of the copy, (6) camera lens, (7) f-stop, (8) lighting, and (9) enlargement or reduction of the copy. The camera operator should control all of the variables, except possibly the quality of the copy (paste-up). The exposure time must be re-established each time there is a major change in one of the variables, especially the type of film, developer, and light source.

Enlargements and reductions. Often line copy is reduced or enlarged so that the image on the negative is either smaller or larger than the original copy. Most process cameras have gauges for adjusting them to the desired new size. Process cameras are made so that the lens and copyboard can be moved to different positions. The film back is also adjustable on some cameras.

The image produced on the camera back will be the same size (100%) as the copy being photographed when the distance between the copyboard and the center of the lens is equal to the distance between the center of the lens and the film back. The total distance between the copyboard and the camera back for same size copy is four times the focal length of the lens.

Focal length is ¼ the distance from the copyboard of the camera to the camera back (ground glass) when the image on the ground glass is in focus and the same size as the copy being photographed. By placing the copyboard and lens in different positions, the correct enlargement or reduction percentage can be attained. See the manufacturers' instructions to set the camera to make enlargements or reductions.

PLACING THE COPY ON THE COPYBOARD

The exposure will be easier and more accurate if copy is properly placed on the copyboard. Most copyboards have targets (guidelines) to help the camera operator place the copy in the center (Fig. 55-4). The guidelines on the vacuum back should match those on the copyboard. If the piece of film is located in the center of the vacuum back and the copy is in the center of the copyboard, the image will be on the negative after development.

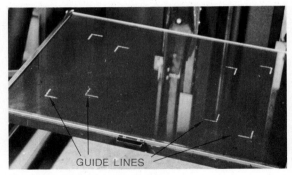

GUIDE LINES

Fig. 55-4. Copyboard guidelines.

The lens inverts the image. The image will therefore be upside down on the ground glass, as compared with the copy on the copyboard. It is wise to put the copy upside down on the copyboard so that the image appears right side up on the ground glass. This makes the image easier to view.

LOCATING THE FILM

The film must be located on the vacuum back of the camera so that it will receive the image during the exposure. Place the film on the vacuum back while the white light is out.

The emulsion side of the film should be toward the lens; the base side toward the vacuum back. Most often, the emulsion side of film is lighter in color than the base side. If orthochromatic film is used, the emulsion side can be identified by holding the film so that the red safelight reflects from it. It is easy to see the lightest (emulsion) side.

PROCESSING THE FILM

After it has been exposed, the film has an invisible latent image of the copy. The structure of the emulsion has been changed where the light struck the film. Development changes the latent image to a visible image. Film can be developed with an automatic processor or by hand.

Film processing is done by passing film through three solutions—developer, stop bath, and fixer. Film must be thoroughly washed after fixing and dried completely before it can be used.

Automatic film processing. Many graphic arts companies use automatic film processors. Processors are used when results must be consistent or when a printer must make many negatives. Fresh chemicals are maintained in a processor at a constant temperature.

Many processors are built into the darkroom wall. The film is placed into the processor in the darkroom where it is processed and dried. The completed negative comes out of the processor in the lighted room. An automatic film processor is shown in Figure 55-5.

Hand film processing. There are several film development methods. The three most common are: (1) time-temperature, (2) visual inspection, and (3) gray scale.

The *time-temperature* method requires the film to be developed for a specific time in a developer of a precise temperature and strength. If developer chemistry temperature and strength cannot be controlled accurately, this method is somewhat unsatisfactory. Still, this method is commonly used to develop half-tone negatives.

The *inspection* method is often used by experienced photographers. In it, the film is observed while it is being developed. Development is completed when both sides of the film are equally dark. This is not a good method for beginners to use.

The *gray scale* method of developing film is probably the most common and satisfactory of the three methods. It is possible to obtain uniform negatives even when there are variations in chemical temperature, chemical contamination, and exposure time. In this method, the gray scale (photographic sensitivity guide) is placed on the copy in the copyboard of the process camera. It should be as near to the center of the copy as possible (Fig. 55-6).

When the film is fully developed, the number 4 step should be black, and the number 5 step should be gray (see Fig. 55-7). It is important to look at the sensitivity guide rather than at the image on the film. When extremely fine line copy is photographed, it is sometimes necessary to develop the negative to the number 3 step to keep the fine lines from closing. A negative developed to a number 3 has a black 3 step and and a gray 4 step. This may cause some extra opaquing during the stripping stage (see Unit 93).

Fig. 55-5. An automatic film processor.

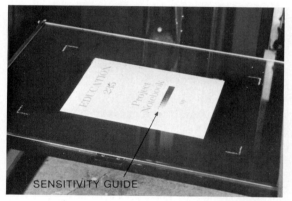

PAKO CORPORATION

Fig. 55-6. Sensitivity guide placed within the copy.

Fig. 55-7. Photographer's sensitivity guide developed to a number 4 step.

The processing procedure. The development technique is a variable that affects the consistency and quality of negatives. It is important to establish a consistent and accurate pattern of film development, so that each piece of film will be developed in exactly the same way.

After the film has been exposed, it should be placed directly into the developer solution as in Figure 55-8. The emulsion side should be up. It is important that the entire piece of film be covered with developer as fast as possible. If one part is not coated with developer, its develop-

Fig. 55-8. Putting exposed film into the developer.

Fig. 55-9. Agitating film during development.

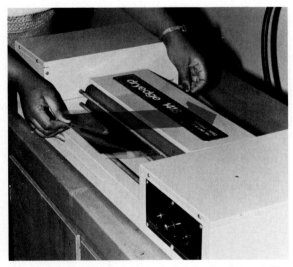

Fig. 55-10. A forced air dryer helps to dry the wet film faster.

ment will be slowed. Follow these steps for consistent results:

1. Grasp the piece of film by the corner.
2. Lift the front of the developer tray until the developer flows to the back of the tray.
3. Place the edge of the film into the developer.
4. Quickly lower the front of the tray as the film is placed into the liquid. This permits the developer to flow quickly over the entire piece of film.
5. Begin immediate *agitation* (movement) of the tray, and continue until the film is developed. Lift the tray corners randomly so that all parts of the negative get fresh developer (Fig. 55-9).
6. When the film is developed, transfer it quickly to the stop bath. Development continues until the film is placed in the stop bath. If too much time elapses between the developer and the stop bath, fine image lines may be lost because of overdevelopment.
7. Let the negative remain in the stop bath for 10 to 30 seconds. The exposed portions will be black; the unexposed ones will appear milky.
8. Remove the negative from the stop bath and let the solution drip from it.
9. Put the film into the fixer for 3 to 5 minutes. The milkiness should leave after about 1 to 2 minutes.
10. Wash the negative in running water for 5 to 10 minutes after it is fully fixed. It is better to wash it too much than not enough. If the film is insufficiently washed, a residue will form on it and cause plate exposure problems.
11. Squeegee the water from the washed film.
12. Dry the film. Use a film dryer if one is available (Fig. 55-10). The film can be hung on a wire line in a dust-free place if necessary. When the film is dry, handle it with care so that the emulsion does not get scratched.

UNIT 56 EXPOSURE CALCULATIONS FOR A HALFTONE NEGATIVE

Halftones are reproductions made from continuous-tone copy. Continuous-tone copy has several shades of gray, from black to white. See Unit 43 for examples.

PRINTING CONTINUOUS-TONE COPY

Printing presses print only one shade of a color at a time. If there is black ink on the press, everything printed will be black. It is impossible to print gray and black with a single printing on a press that has been inked with black ink. The picture in Figure 56-1, however, appears to have black areas and several shades of gray.

This optical illusion is produced by breaking the copy into many small dots. Each dot is printed black; there are no gray dots. In Figure 56-2 there are small black dots with large white areas around them. There are also several small white dots with large black areas around them. When the picture is observed from a distance, the dots blend to form shades of gray. The areas around white dots appear to be darker than those white areas with black dots.

METHODS OF PRODUCING HALFTONE DOTS

Continuous-tone copy is broken into dots by one of three methods: (1) the glass halftone screen, (2) the contact screen, and (3) Autoscreen film. The first two methods use a screen in front of the film in a camera; the third is done directly on a special film labeled Autoscreen Ortho Film.

Glass screens. The first efficient and effective method of making halftone negatives used a glass halftone screen. This consisted of two pieces of glass bonded together with parallel lines etched into each. The lines are filled with an opaque material. The two pieces are

Fig. 56-1. A photograph printed as a halftone.

Fig. 56-2. Haltone dots magnified.

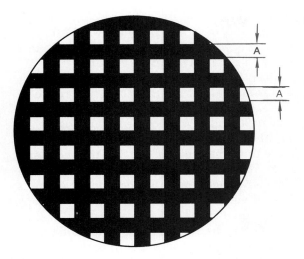

Fig. 56-3. Enlarged pattern of a glass halftone screen.

Fig. 56-4. Enlarged view of a contact screen.

cemented together so that the lines are at right angles to each other. The final screen has many small, clear openings (Fig. 56-3).

The glass screen is held a short, but precise, distance from the film. Each small opening serves as an individual lens. When intense light passes through the openings, it spreads out and produces large dark areas with small, clear dots. When dim light is used, black dots with large clear areas are produced. It is helpful to remember that a negative is a reversal of the final print. Black areas on the negative do not print; clear areas do. Glass screens are expensive and difficult to use. They are rarely used today.

Contact screens. Most halftone negatives today are made by using contact screens. These have vignetted (shaded) dots on a flexible, but stable, base (Fig. 56-4). This type of dot is nearly clear in the center, and becomes progressively darker away from the center.

When weak light strikes the screen, it passes only through the clear areas, or through very little of the darker parts. Strong light penetrates more of the dark area of the dots and makes the negative darker in these areas.

Contact screens are much less expensive than glass ones and are much easier to use. Both magenta (purplish-red) and gray screens are available. They come in several sizes and rulings, ranging from 65 to 200 lines per inch.

In addition to normal dot patterns, halftone screens can be obtained with several different patterns. Some of the patterns are mezzo tint, straight line, wavy line, and others. They are used for special effects.

Autoscreen film. *Autoscreen film* has a screen, or grid, built into the film. Halftone negatives are produced without any screen in front of the film. This film has an emulsion that is not uniform on the entire piece (unlike regular film). There are thousands of small, light-sensitive areas. Weak reflections from the dark areas of the original copy expose only the most sensitive portions of the film. Strong reflections, resulting from the middle tones and highlights (lightest areas of the copy), expose more of the light-sensitive areas and create larger black ones. Autoscreen film is available only in rulings of 133 lines per inch.

NATURE OF CONTINUOUS-TONE COPY

Continuous-tone copy consists of many shades of gray, including white and black. The lightest tones are called *highlights* (Fig. 56-5). The darkest tones are called *shadows*. Gray tones are called *middle tones*.

Densities can be given number values. *The Kodak Reflection Density Guide (24 step)* in Figure 56-6 has numbers next to the different

STEPHEN GRAVES

Fig. 56-5. Continuous-tone copy has highlights, middle tones, and shadows.

densities. This is sometimes called a *calibrated gray scale*. The whitest area has been given the number 0.0. The darkest black has been given the number 2.0.

A piece of continuous-tone copy can be compared to the gray scale in Figure 56-6. It would then be possible to give number values to the various densities on the continuous-tone copy.

Continuous-tone copy used to make halftones will vary widely. Some copy will have bright white highlights. Other copy will have darker highlights. Copy with light highlights will require different exposures than copy with darker highlights.

Tonal range is the difference between high-lights and shadow areas. If a piece of copy has a highlight of .10 and a shadow of 1.60, the tonal range is 1.50. The tonal range of a piece of copy will affect the exposure time.

Most process cameras and photographic materials cannot reproduce a full range of tones. The tonal range will usually be between .90 and 1.30. Because of this, some copy detail will be lost when the tonal range is more than the limits of the camera and materials. For example, suppose that you are using a camera and materials whose tonal range is 1.10. If you make a halftone negative of copy whose tonal range is 1.60, some detail will be lost. If the halftone negative is made with good highlights, the shadow detail will be lost. If the halftone negative is made with good shadows, the highlight detail will be lost. This problem may be overcome by making a *flash exposure*. It compresses the tonal range of the copy. This will cause the halftone negative to have good detail in both the highlights and shadows. The photographer uses a halftone negative computer (described below) to decide how much flash exposure is needed.

USING CONTACT SCREENS

Most halftone negatives are made with contact screens. The screen is placed between the film and the camera lens. Screens should be slightly larger than the film. The vacuum from the camera back holds the screen tightly in contact with the film.

The contact screen has an emulsion side, as does film. It is the dull side of the screen. The emulsion side of the screen should be against the emulsion side of the film (Fig. 56-7).

Most halftone negatives will require two exposures. The first is called the *main exposure*, and the second is called the *flash exposure*. The main exposure is made through the camera lens with the copy in the copyboard

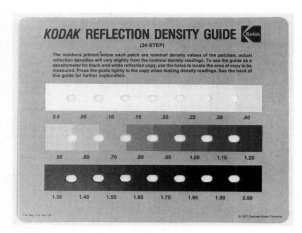

Fig. 56-6. A calibrated gray scale.

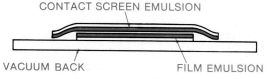

Fig. 56-7. Place the emulsion side of the contact screen against the film emulsion.

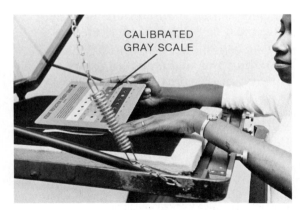

Fig. 56-8. A photographer places a calibrated gray on the camera copyboard to make the main test exposure.

(Fig 56-8). The main exposure forms the highlight and middle tone dots. These are the small clear dots in the dark areas of the negative and the medium-size clear dots in the gray areas of the negative.

The flash exposure is made with a lamp that has a special yellow light. The exposure is made through the screen but not through the camera lens (Fig. 56-9). Flash exposures are used to form the shadow dots in the halftone negative. These are the small clear dots in the dark areas of the negative and the medium-size clear dots in the gray areas of the negative.

The second exposure is called the *flash exposure*. It is made with a lamp that has a special yellow filter. The exposure is made through the screen but not through the camera lens (Fig. 56-9). Flash exposures are used to form the shadow dots in the halftone negative. These are small black dots in the clear areas of a halftone negative. Sometimes a second exposure is needed to increase the highlights. It is called a *bump exposure* and is done with the screen removed. Sometimes this is called a *no screen exposure*.

Contact screens are easily damaged. Scratches, dirt, chemicals, or fingerprints can cause poor halftone negatives. It is best to handle the screen by the edges. It should be stored in a folder.

EXPOSURE COMPUTERS

Camera operators usually use a computer to determine halftone exposures. Electronic computers can be attached to the camera that give

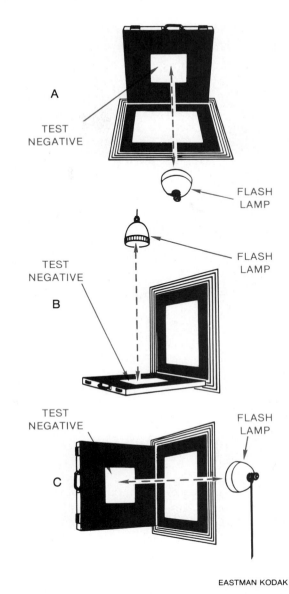

EASTMAN KODAK

Fig. 56-9. Flash lamps are placed in different positions depending on how the camera back opens.

exposure times for halftones automatically, once the computer is adjusted (calibrated). Electronic computers are expensive but they speed the work.

Hand-operated halftone negative computers are also used to determine exposures. The hand model shown in Figure 56-10 is called the *Kodak Halftone Negative Computer*. These computers are very accurate and inexpensive, but they take more time to use.

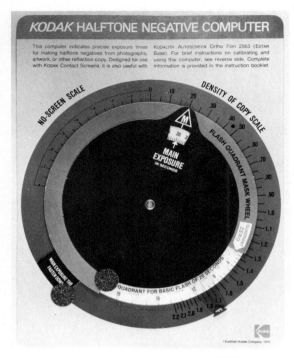

EASTMAN KODAK

Fig. 56-10. A Kodak Halftone Negative Computer.

CALIBRATING THE HAND-OPERATED COMPUTER

The hand-operated computer must be calibrated before it can be used.

The Kodak Halftone Negative Computer is adjusted for use by making two kinds of test exposures. The first is for the main exposure. The second is for the flash exposure.

Test exposures are made with conditions carefully controlled. These same conditions must be used to make the halftone negatives after the computer is calibrated. Some of the conditions that must be controlled are:

1. Kind of process camera.
2. Kind of contact screen.
3. Kind of lighting.
4. Type of film.
5. Kind and strength of developer.
6. Temperature of the developer.
7. Angle and placement of lights.
8. Time of development.
9. Agitation of developer tray.

If any of the conditions change, the computer must be re-calibrated. Even very small changes can cause a poor halftone negative.

Making the main test exposure. A calibrated gray scale (Fig. 56-6) is used to make the main test exposure. This exposure is made through the lens of the process camera with the gray scale in the camera copyboard (Fig. 56-11). Here is the procedure for making the main test exposure:

1. Place the calibrated gray scale in the camera copyboard (Fig. 56-11). Be sure the copyboard glass is clean. Position the gray scale in the center of the copyboard.
2. Set the camera for a 100 percent reproduction.
3. Adjust the lens. It should be set about one or two f-stops smaller than wide open.
4. Place a piece of film on the vacuum back. Turn on the power to the vacuum system. The emulsion side of the film should be toward the camera operator.
5. Place the contact screen over the film with the emulsion side against the film emulsion. Be sure that the contact screen is larger than the film. Smooth out the screen with a film roller so it will be tight over the film.
6. Cover a one-inch (2.54 cm) strip of film with a piece of cardboard or heavy black paper. The vacuum will hold it in position. The cardboard must overlap the screen on three sides (Fig. 56-12).

EASTMAN KODAK

Fig. 56-11. Calibrated gray scale in the camera copyboard.

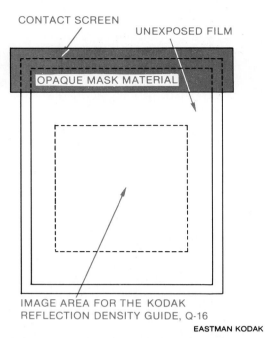

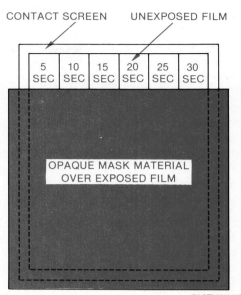

Fig. 56-12. Cover about one inch on the film. This space will be used to make the flash exposure.

Fig. 56-13. Cover the area used to make the main test exposure. Flash exposures are made in this area.

7. Close the camera back.
8. Set the timer. Use a time two to four times as long as used to make line negatives. If this time is not correct on the first test, adjust it.
9. Make the main exposure. *Do not use a flash with this exposure.*

Making the test flash exposure. The second half of the test is a series of flash exposures. These are made in the darkroom with the special flash lamp. Here is the procedure for making the flash test exposure:

1. Open the camera back and leave the vacuum system on.
2. Leave the film and contact screen in place.
3. Place a piece of cardboard or heavy black paper over the area of the film used for the main exposure.
4. Remove the cardboard or black paper that covered the strip of film during the main exposure.
5. Make a series of flash exposures with the flash lamp. The series of flashes can range from 5 to 30 seconds (Fig. 56-13) or from 10 to 25 seconds (Fig. 56-14).
6. Turn off the vacuum and carefully remove the cardboard or black paper covering the film. Be careful to not damage the contact screen.

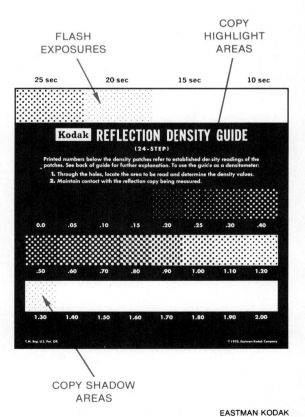

Fig. 56-14. Test negative used to adjust the Kodak Halftone Negative Computer.

7. Remove the screen and place it in the container.
8. Remove the exposed film. Remember to handle all photographic materials by the edges. The film is now ready for processing.

The main test exposure and the flash exposures can be made on separate pieces of film. This makes the procedure less detailed because the film does not have to be covered while making the exposures. However, you should process both pieces of film using exactly the same procedure.

Process the test negative.

1. Set up the chemicals as for making a line negative.
2. Check the developer temperature. It should be 68° F (20° C) if at all possible. *The same temperature used to develop the test negative must be used to develop all halftone negatives.*
3. Develop the test negative for the time recommended by the manufacturer.
4. Finish processing the test negative in the same manner as with a line negative.

Automatic film processors are often used in commercial plants. They help their users to get the same results time after time. You must be very careful when hand-processing halftone negatives. Even the smallest differences in development procedure can ruin the negative. *The procedure for developing a halftone must be exactly the same as for the test exposure.*

Examine the test negative. The test negative should look similar to the one shown in Figure 56-14. The gray scale and flash exposures are important parts of the negative. Use a magnifying glass to examine the negative, because the dots are too small to see with the naked eye.

1. Examine the highlight end of the gray scale.
2. Find the best highlight dots. These should be the smallest printable dots. Often the test negative is printed because dot sizes can vary when printed on several kinds of paper. This makes it easy to find the smallest printable dot. The best dot should be in one of the values between 0.0 and .30. If it is not, this part of the exposure should be made again with new times. In Figure 56-14, the .20 was selected as the best highlight dot.

3. Find the best shadow dots. These will be solid black dots in the clear areas. Dots that look light brown are called *soft dots*. They will not print. A print of the test negative on paper will help find the best shadow dot. The smallest printable black dot should be selected. These are called *hard dots*. The best shadow dot in Figure 56-14 was found to be 1.30.
4. Record the best highlight and best shadow dot. This information will be used to adjust the computer. Sometimes the best dots will appear between density areas. When this happens, estimate the best time.
5. Examine the flash exposures. Find the step where the best flash dot appears. This dot should be the same size as the best shadow dot found in step 3 above. The best flash dot should be in steps 10, 15, 20, or 25 seconds. If there is not a good dot, this part of the test negative should be done again. The lamp distance from the film or the size of the bulb can be changed. The best flash exposure was found in the 20-second area (Fig. 56-14). This time will be called the *Basic Flash Exposure*.

Set the computer. The computer must be adjusted, using information learned from the test exposures. The camera operator will need to know:

1. Density that produced a good highlight dot. In Figure 56-14 the density was .20.
2. Density that produced a good shadow dot. This was 1.30 in Figure 56-14.
3. The Basic Flash Exposure time. The best flash took 20 seconds in Figure 56-14.
4. The exposure time needed to make the main exposure (the exposure of the gray scale). In this example, let it be 30 seconds. This will vary depending on the camera lights.

With this information, you can adjust the *Kodak Halftone Negative Computer* (Fig. 56-10). The following procedure will give a properly adjusted computer:

1. Select the quadrant of the *Basic Flash* dial that is the same as the Basic Flash Exposure. In the example this was 20 seconds.
2. Hold the clear Basic Flash Dial. Cover all but the correct quadrant with the Flash

Quadrant Mask Wheel.

3. Find the large "M" of the Main Exposure Dial. Turn it to the best highlight dot density on the Density of Copy Scale. In the example this was .20.

4. Find the Quadrant Zero on the Flash Quadrant Mask Wheel. Set this next to the density where the best shadow dot was found on the test exposure. The density of 1.30 is used in this example.

5. Fasten the Main Exposure Dial, Flash Quadrant Mask Wheel, and Basic Flash Quadrant together. This can be done with the cork button supplied with the computer. It can also be done with tape. These three dials must remain fastened together.

6. Turn the Main Exposure Tab until the main exposure time lines up with the Main Exposure arrow. This was the time used to expose the gray scale. The time for the example is 30 seconds.

7. Fasten the Main Exposure Tab with a cork button or tape.

8. The computer should look like the one in Figure 56-10.

The computer is now ready for use. The procedure for using the computer will be discussed in Unit 57.

AUTOSCREEN HALFTONES

Halftone negatives can be made with a special kind of film called *Autoscreen Ortho Film*. The screen pattern is built into the film. Procedures for making an Autoscreen halftone are the same as for making a halftone with a screen. The only difference is that no contact screen is used over the film.

UNIT 57 EXPOSING AND PROCESSING A HALFTONE NEGATIVE

The process of exposing and processing halftone negatives is quite different from working with line negatives. You must give much more attention to the details or valuable time and materials will be lost. Photographs add interest to printed material, but poorly produced halftones will reduce the value of the printed item. In this unit, it is assumed that halftone negatives will be produced by using a contact screen.

DETERMINING THE EXPOSURE TIMES

Exposure times, which will be used to photograph the halftones, can be determined in a lighted room. In fact, it is best to determine the essential exposure information for all photographs before entering the darkroom. These calculations should be written on a piece of paper and attached to the photograph. The information needed for making a halftone includes the enlargement or reduction size, main exposure, flash exposure, and lens opening.

Unit 56 told how to adjust the *Kodak Halftone Negative Computer*. This was done so that it can be used to obtain consistent results. Once the computer has been calibrated, it is quite easy to find exposure times for making halftone negatives from continuous-tone copy.

Examine the copy to find the highlight and shadow densities. Remember the lightest areas of the copy are highlights and the darkest areas are shadow areas. These densities are those found on the calibrated gray scale (Fig. 57-1).

An electronic *densitometer* helps to measure densities much more accurately than observa-

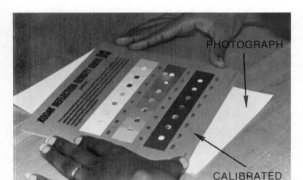

Fig. 57-1. A photographer compares the calibrated gray scale with the photograph, noting highlight and shadow densities.

tion does (Fig. 57-2). An error can be made more easily when using the visual gray scale. When the highlight and shadow densities are known, the halftone negative computer will give the main exposure time and the flash exposure time. These exposures should give a negative with good highlights and good shadows. The highlight dot in the negative should look like the .20 area in Figure 56-14. The shadow dot should look like the 1.30 area in Figure 56-14. All negatives should appear to have the same highlight and shadow densities.

Fig. 57-2. A densitometer measures densities of photographic materials.

A good halftone negative will have a dot formation in all areas of the halftone negative. The only way detail in the copy is shown in a halftone is by different size dots. When there are no highlight dots in the negative, the highlight areas will appear white. The print will be black in the shadow areas when there are no shadow dots.

Finding the densities of the copy to be reproduced. This can be done by comparing the gray scale to the copy. It can also be done with a densitometer. The following procedure should be used when comparing copy to a calibrated gray scale.

1. Obtain the copy to be reproduced.
2. Find the highlight (lightest) area of the copy. Catchlights like those found in eyes or on shiny surfaces should not be used.
3. Place the gray scale over the copy.
4. Use the holes to match the lightest part of the copy with a density value on the gray scale. Be sure this is done where there is good light.
5. Record the density value.
6. Repeat the procedure to find the shadow density of the copy.

The highlight and shadow densities are used to find the main and flash exposures on the computer. The procedure for finding exposure times when using magenta contact screens is different from when using gray contact screens. Both procedures will be given below. For example, assume that a piece of copy has a highlight density of .10 and a shadow density of 1.65.

Determining exposures when using a magenta contact screen.

1. Turn the "M" to the highlight density value on the Density of Copy scale for the copy to be reproduced. For the example, this will be .10 (Fig. 57-3).
2. Read the main exposure time in the Main Exposure window. This will be about 24 seconds for the example (Fig. 57-4).
3. Set the "F" tab on the shadow density of the copy to be reproduced on the Density of Copy scale (1.65).
4. Read the flash exposure time on the Quadrant for Basic Flash of the 20 seconds wheel. It should be about 12 seconds (Fig. 57-5).

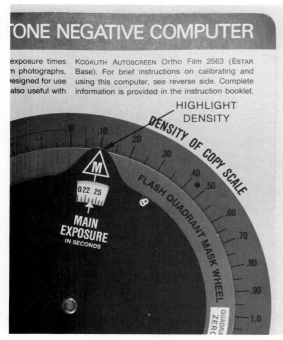

Fig. 57-3. Align the *M* with the copy highlight density.

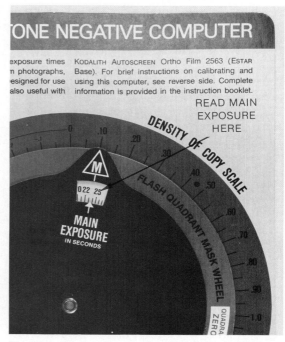

Fig. 57-4. Read main exposure time through window.

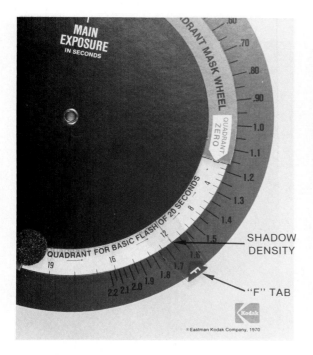

Fig. 57-5. Read the flash exposure time in seconds from the line on the *F* tab.

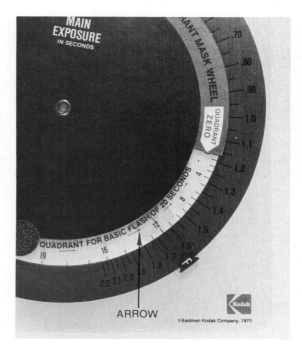

Fig. 57-6. Find the arrow on the Quadrant for Basic Flash that is closest to the *F* pointer line.

5. Record these times and make the exposure.

Determining exposure times when using gray contact screen.

1. Turn the "M" to the highlight density (.10) on the Density of Copy scale (Fig. 57-3).
2. Move the "F" tab to the shadow density (1.65) on the Density of Copy scale (Fig. 57-4).
3. Find the arrow (it will be red) that is closest to the line on the "F" tab (Fig. 57-6).
4. Move the "F" tab to the point of the arrow (Fig. 57-7).
5. Turn the dial counterclockwise the length of the arrow (Fig. 57-8).
6. Reset the "F" tab to the shadow density (1.65) of the copy (Fig. 57-9).
7. Read the main exposure time in the Main Exposure window. In this case it will be about 21 seconds (Fig. 57-10).
8. Read the flash exposure time at the "F" tab. It will be about 13 seconds (Fig. 57-11).
9. Record these times.
10. Make the halftone exposures.

PREPARING THE DARKROOM

The darkroom must be prepared to duplicate precisely the conditions used to calibrate the halftone exposure computer. If some of the conditions are different, the resulting negatives will not be accurate. Arrange the process trays as usual. Prepare the developer so it is exactly the same temperature that was used to make the test negative. Time can be saved by keeping a quantity of developer at the correct temperature, because the developer should be changed more frequently for halftone negatives than for line negatives. The trays for the stop bath, fixer, and wash should also be prepared at this time. Keeping a thermometer in the developer at all times helps you to see whether the temperature is correct.

PREPARING THE CAMERA

Preparing the camera for making halftone negatives is similar to the procedure used for making line negatives. Special attention must be given to cleanliness. Dirt causes pinholes on negatives and pinholes on halftone negatives are much more difficult to work with than those on line negatives. The copyboard, timer, lens opening, and light angles should be checked to be sure that they are properly adjusted. When the camera is clean and properly adjusted, place the copy into the copyboard as you do for a line negative.

SETTING THE FLASH-LAMP

The flash lamp set up must be the same as for the test exposure. The bulb intensity (brightness) should be checked regularly. The bulbs are incandescent bulbs and dim with time. Be sure the lamp has the same filter that was used to make the test exposure. If the lamp is not in a fixed position, check the distance. The flash-lamp timer should be set for the time that was found by using the computer.

MAKING THE MAIN EXPOSURE

The main exposure is made with the darkroom safelight on. Place the piece of film on the vac-

Fig. 57-7. Move the F tab to the head of the closest arrow on the Quadrant for Basic Flash scale.

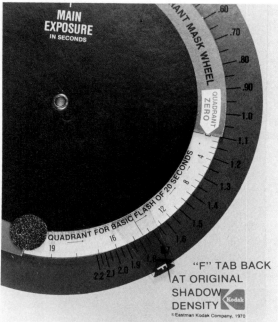

Fig. 57-8. Line up the end of the arrow with the *F* tab line.

Fig. 57-9. Move the *F* tab back to the original shadow density.

Fig. 57-10. Read main exposure time through window.

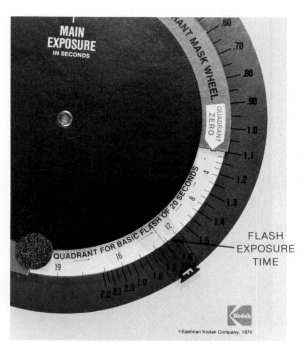

Fig. 57-11. Read the flash exposure at the line on the *F* pointer.

uum back with the base (dark side) side against the vacuum back. The film must be the same kind of film that was used to make the test exposure discussed in Unit 56. When the film is in place, turn on the vacuum. Place the contact screen over the film so that the screen is against the emulsion side of the film. The emulsion side of the screen should be against the film emulsion, too (Fig. 57-12). The screen should be at

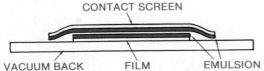

Fig. 57-12. Place the emulsion side of the screen against the emulsion side of the film.

least one inch (2.54 cm) larger than the film on all sides. Be extremely careful as you handle the screen not to get fingerprints on it. Smooth the screen over the film with a roller. Take care not to scratch the screen. When the film and screen are in place, move the vacuum back into place and make the exposure.

MAKING THE FLASH EXPOSURE

Most halftone negatives will need a flash exposure. This is because the copy density range (the difference between the highlight and shadow densities) is greater than the density range that the camera can reproduce.

Open the camera back to the correct position. This should be the same position used for the flash test exposure. Do not disturb the contact screen's position over the film. Make the exposure by turning on the flash lamp timer.

PROCESSING THE NEGATIVE

Development of halftone negatives is extremely critical. The procedure must be *exactly* the same used to make the test exposure. This will help you to get accurate negatives time after time.

Carefully remove the contact screen after the exposure. It should be returned to its protective container. Never put the screen on a surface in the darkroom. It can get dirt or chemicals on it.

Turn off the vacuum and remove the exposed film. Hold the film by the corners to prevent getting fingerprints on the image area of the film. Place the film in the developer for the same time used with the test negative. The temperature must also be the same that was used with the test negative. Even a difference of one degree will change the negative. The same agitation used with the test negative should be used. Too much agitation will cause overdevelopment and close up the highlight dots. Too little agitation will result in underdevelopment and the shadow dots will not form into hard dots.

When development is complete, move the negative to the stop bath. This should be done as fast as possible, because the negative will continue to develop until the developer is removed. The negative should stay in the stop bath for 10 to 15 seconds. Agitation will cut the amount of time needed in the stop bath. Let the stop bath drain from the negative before moving it to the fixer.

Place the negative in the fixer. Watch the negative to see how long it takes the negative to clear (milky appearance will disappear). The negative should remain in the fixer for about twice the time it takes to clear.

Wash the negative thoroughly. It should be in the wash for at least 10 minutes. Beginning photographers often try to cut this time short, but all chemicals must be removed from the negative.

Dry the negative after it has washed with a drier or by hanging it in a dust-free place. When the negative is dry, it is ready for use.

DUOTONES

Duotones add interest to a printed item. A duotone is a halftone printed in two colors. The duotone is made from a single black-and-white continuous-tone photograph. Two halftone negatives are made from the same photograph. When the two negatives are printed, the result is a halftone with a background tint. A duotone is shown in Figure 57-13.

The two negatives must be made with the screen angles at 30° to each other. The two screen angles most commonly used are 45° and 75°. A moiré pattern will result if both negatives are made with the same screen angle (Fig.

Fig. 57-13. A duotone print.

Fig. 57-14. A moiré pattern results when two or more screens are printed over each other at the wrong screen angles.

57-14). Some printers make the black or dark printer at 45° because most black and white halftones are made at 45°. It is very important to mark which negative is to be printed in the dark color.

Halftone negatives for a duotone use a procedure similar to that used for a regular halftone negative. The *Kodak Halftone Negative Computer* can be used as a guide. The first halftone negative is the one that will be printed in the color. Times should be determined as though it was to be printed like a regular halftone. It should have good highlight dots. The shadow exposure should be increased for the computer reading. This will vary from 10 to 20 percent, depending on the photograph and ink color being used. The longer flash exposure will increase the size of the shadow dots (black dots in the clear areas). This will give a halftone negative with lighter shadow areas than normal (Fig. 57-15).

The second halftone negative will be printed in the dark or black color. The main, or highlight, exposure should be longer than for a normal halftone negative, depending on the photograph and the color of ink used for the

Fig. 57-15. One of the halftone negatives is printed in a color.

Fig. 57-16. The second color of a duotone is black or another dark color.

first color. The shadow areas of this negative should be near normal. This negative gives the shadow detail to the duotone. Note that the main exposure should be increased for this negative and the flash exposure time reduced. In some cases no flash exposure will be needed for this negative. Figure 57-16 shows the negative to be printed in black. The negatives from Figures 57-15 and 57-16 are printed together to make the duotone in Figure 57-13.

UNIT 58 CONTACT PRINTING

Contact printing produces a reproduction that is the same size as the original. Copies that are the same as the originals are called *direct* reproductions. Copies that are the opposite of the original are called *indirect* reproductions. There are many materials used for contact printing.

EQUIPMENT

Contact reproductions are made in *vacuum printing frames* (Fig. 58-1). It is used to keep the photographic materials in tight contact while the exposures are made.

A light source is needed to expose the light sensitive materials. Some light sources have adjustments to brighten or dim the light. A

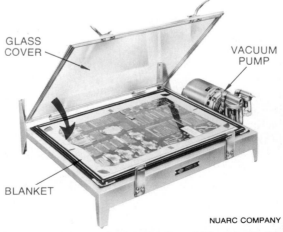

NUARC COMPANY

Fig. 58-1. A vacuum printing frame used for contact printing.

point source light that is connected to a transformer with controls for changing the brightness is best (Fig. 58-2). The light is placed above the vacuum printing frame so that the camera operator can change the distance between the light and the vacuum frame (Fig. 58-3). An open-face contact printing frame with a high intensity point source light is popular in commercial printing firms (Fig. 58-4).

MATERIALS

Both film and paper are used to make contact reproductions. The common kinds of materials are these.

Contact film. These films are used for making indirect reproduction positives from negatives or negatives from positives. Contact films usually have slower emulsions than do regular film used in process cameras.

Duplicating film. These films are used to make direct reproductions that are the same as the original. A positive will yield a positive and a negative will produce a negative. Like contact films, the emulsions are much slower than regular orthochromatic film.

Orthochromatic film. Orthochromatic film is the kind of film usually used in a process camera to make line and halftone negatives. Orthochromatic film is often used to make indirect contact reproduction film positives from negatives.

Contact paper. Contact papers are used to

NUARC COMPANY.

Fig. 58-2. Point source light used for contact printing.

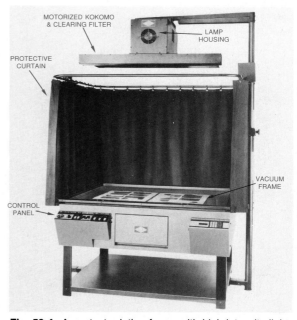

Fig. 58-4. A contact printing frame with high-intensity light source.

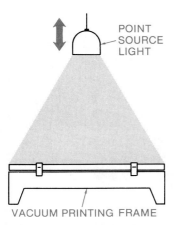

Fig. 58-3. Move the point source light up and down to change the light intensity.

make same-size positive prints from film negatives. The base material for contact paper is opaque paper where the film base is transparent.

Many materials used for contact printing have silver emulsions. However, some materials have diazo emulsion, which can be used in low room light and requires much longer exposures. Film with diazo emulsion is processed and made readable with ammonia fumes. This type of film is popular for contact printing with many graphic arts companies.

MAKING CONTACT REPRODUCTIONS

The procedures for making contact reproductions are similar for all purposes. Equipment, materials, and adjustments will vary in different situations. The following procedures are used for most contact exposures.

1. Clean the vacuum frame glass. Even a little dirt on the glass can ruin the reproduction.
2. Adjust the light source. This can be done by changing the brightness of the light or by changing the distance between the light source and vacuum frame.
3. Place the film or paper on the vacuum printing frame blanket. It is best to place a sheet of heavy black paper or thin plastic between the blanket and the film. Remember to use the correct safelight. The emulsion side of the film or paper should be toward the vacuum frame glass (Fig. 58-5).
4. Place the negative or positive over the contact material. When right-reading images are needed, the emulsion should be toward the vacuum frame glass (Fig. 58-6). When an image reversal is needed the negative or positive emulsion should be against the contacting material emulsion (Fig. 58-7). This same procedure should be used to get right-reading images on contact paper.
5. Close the vacuum frame glass and turn on the vacuum. Be sure that the materials are in tight contact with the vacuum frame glass. This usually takes a few seconds.
6. Make the exposure. You will have to make test exposures on the various materials to find the correct times.

7. Turn off the vacuum pump and remove the materials from the frame.
8. Process the contact material as recommended by the manufacturer.

FILM POSITIVE

A common use for contact printing is to make a film positive. A film positive is the opposite of a film negative. Film positives are used to make reversals.

Film positives are made by first making a line negative of the copy (Fig. 58-8). An indirect contact is made on film. This produces a piece of film with the image exactly like the copy (Fig. 58-9). However, when it is used to make a plate,

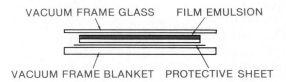

Fig. 58-5. Place the film or paper in the vacuum frame so that the emulsion faces the vacuum frame glass.

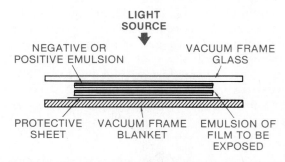

Fig. 58-6. Place the emulsion side of the negative or positive toward the vacuum frame glass to get a right-reading on film.

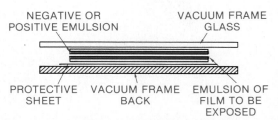

Fig. 58-7. Place the emulsion side of the negative or positive against the emulsion side of the film to get a wrong-reading (image reversal) on film. The same procedure gets a right-reading on photographic paper.

the printed results will be opposite from the copy. Either contacting film or regular orthochromatic film can be used to make a film positive. The film to negative position should be the same as in Figure 58-6. This is also used to produce film for use with positive working lithographic plates.

POSITIVE PRINTS

Positive prints can serve as proofs to check errors. They also can serve as duplicate copies.

Positive prints can be made with either negatives or positives. The emulsion of the negative or positive should be placed against the emulsion of the contact paper (Fig. 58-7). The photographer should use a contact paper that will give a very high contrast image. In recent years, the diffusion transfer process, discussed in detail in Unit 59, has reduced the need for making paper contact prints.

DUPLICATES

A duplicate is a reproduction that is exactly the same as the original. A duplicate of a negative will produce another negative. A duplicate of a

positive will produce a positive. The emulsion on duplicating film is opposite from contacting film. Exposed areas of duplicating film are removed during processing.

Duplicates are made when extra negatives or positives are needed. They are also used to make chokes and spreads (described below). When a right-reading image is needed, the emulsion of the materials should face the vacuum frame glass (Fig. 58-6). The emulsion of the materials should face each other when a wrong-reading image is needed (Fig. 58-7).

SPREADS AND CHOKES

Spreads and chokes are used when two-color line work must have close register. They improve register by causing the two colors to overlap slightly (Fig. 58-10). Spreads and chokes can be used together to form outline letters (Fig. 58-11).

Spreads cause an image to increase in size. *Chokes* reduce the image size. Contact film and duplicating film, along with film negatives and positives, are used to expose spreads and chokes.

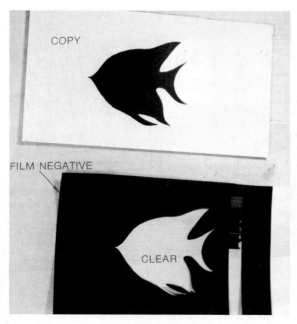

Fig. 58-8. A piece of copy and the negative made from it.

Fig. 58-9. A piece of copy and a film positive. The positive was made from the negative in Figure 58-8.

IMAGES REGISTER BETTER WITH OVERLAP

Fig. 58-10. Use chokes and spreads to make images overlap slightly. This technique is a great help when close color registration is needed.

Fig. 58-11. Use chokes and spreads together to form outline type.

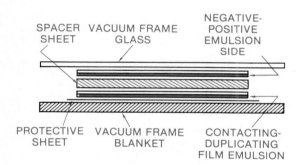

Fig. 58-12. Place the emulsion side of the film and negative or positive toward the vacuum frame blanket when making chokes and spreads.

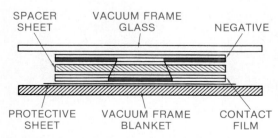

Fig. 58-13. A negative contacted on contact film gives a spread positive image.

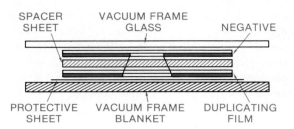

Fig. 58-14. A negative contacted on duplicating film gives a spread negative.

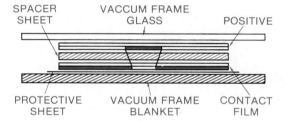

Fig. 58-15. A positive contacted on contact film gives a choked negative.

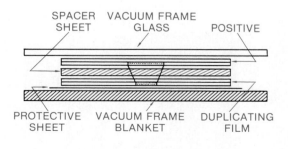

Fig. 58-16. A positive contacted on duplicating film gives a choked positive.

Vacuum printing frames must be used when exposing films for spreads and chokes. Also, a spacer made of diffusion material (clear plastic film) is placed between the unexposed film and the negative or positive. The thicker the spacer, the greater the spread or choke. The emulsion of the unexposed film should face the blanket of the vacuum frame. The emulsion side of the negative or positive should be against the spacer (Fig. 58-12).

You must decide whether to use contact or duplicating film. A negative exposed to contact film will give a spread positive image (Fig. 58-13). A negative exposed to duplicating film will give a spread negative (Fig. 58-14). A film positive exposed to contact with contact film will produce a choked negative (Fig. 58-15). A film positive exposed over duplicating film will give a choked positive (Fig. 58-16).

UNIT 59 DIFFUSION TRANSFER PROCESS

In *diffusion transfer*, images are transferred directly to another carrier. This can be done with a camera or on a contact printer. Diffusion transfer is most often used for preparing copy and making printing plates.

The process permits the printer to get a positive paper print or film positive from a positive without having to make an intermediate negative. Negatives can also be made with the diffusion transfer process. Both line and halftone reproductions can be made using this process.

Two sheets of material are needed to make diffusion transfer copies. The first, called *negative material*, is light sensitive and is handled like orthochromatic film. This material is made for use in a process camera or in a contact printing frame. The material for process cameras is much more sensitive than material for contact printing.

The second material, called the *receiver*, can be paper, transparent film, or printing plates, and is not sensitive to light. Printing plates are discussed in Unit 100 and will not be included in this unit. The receiver material has a special chemical coating that lets the image from the negative material transfer to the receiver sheet when placed in a chemical.

EQUIPMENT FOR DIFFUSION TRANSFER PROCESS

Process camera. A conventional process camera is used in the same way as when making line and halftone negatives. It is specially important when enlargements and reductions are needed.

Contact printing unit. For certain procedures, a contact printing unit is needed (See Unit 58). Only same-size reproductions can be made with contact methods.

Diffusion transfer processor. A typical diffusion transfer processor is shown in Figure 59-1. A drawing of the processor shows how the sheets must be separated as they enter the processor to let the surface of both sheets get

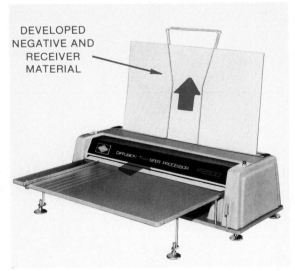

DEVELOPED NEGATIVE AND RECEIVER MATERIAL

NUARC COMPANY

Fig. 59-1. A diffusion transfer processor.

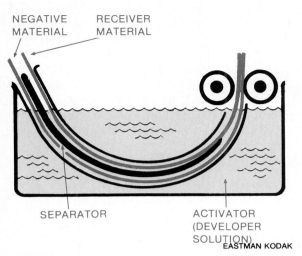

Fig. 59-2. The negative material and receiver paper are separated as material enters the diffusion transfer processor.

Fig. 59-4. Separate diffusion transfer negative and receiver sheets after processing.

LINE PRINTS

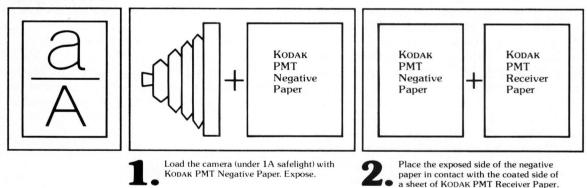

1. Load the camera (under 1A safelight) with KODAK PMT Negative Paper. Expose.

2. Place the exposed side of the negative paper in contact with the coated side of a sheet of KODAK PMT Receiver Paper.

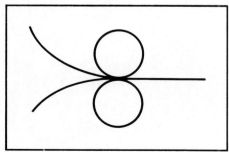

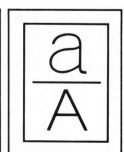

3. Feed both into a diffusion transfer processor filled with KODAK PMT Activator.

4. After about six seconds in the processor, the papers emerge. Wait 30 seconds under safelight conditions and peel apart.

5. The negative paper is discarded, leaving the finished line print.

Fig. 59-3. Procedure for making line paper prints, using the diffusion transfer process.

EASTMAN KODAK

coated with developer (Fig. 59-2). The rollers press the sheets tightly in contact as they leave the processor. The diffusion transfer process was developed by Kodak, whose brand-name negative and receiver materials and processors are labeled *PMT*. As a result, many people call the process "making PMTs," but the correct term is *diffusion transfer*.

MAKING LINE POSITIVES

The procedure for making line paper prints and film positives is nearly the same. After the negative material is exposed, either a paper or film receiver sheet is used. The procedure for making line paper prints is shown in Figure 59-3. The negative sheet and the receiver paper must be separated after development has taken place (Fig. 59-4). The procedure for making a line film positive is shown in Figure 59-5.

Artwork can be enlarged or reduced to fit other copy so that the positive can be placed in the proper location on a paste-up. A single negative can then be made, thus saving time in the stripping procedure. It also helps to make the paste-up more accurate.

Sometimes elements of a paste-up have different densities. This causes difficulties when making negatives. Diffusion transfer positives can be used so that all elements will have the same density. Unwanted background paper color can be eliminated from copy elements and dirty and soiled copy elements can be cleaned

LINE FILM POSITIVES

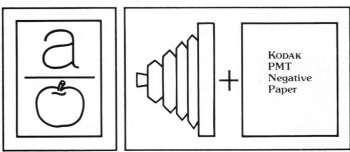

1. Load the camera (under 1A safelight) with PMT Negative Paper. Expose. May require slightly less exposure (try 15% less) than when used with KODAK PMT Receiver Paper.

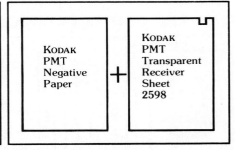

2. Place the exposed side of the negative paper in contact with the coated side of a sheet of KODAK PMT Transparent Receiver Sheet 2598. The notch in the upper right hand corner indicates emulsion up.

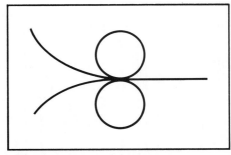

3. Feed both into a diffusion transfer processor filled with KODAK PMT Activator.

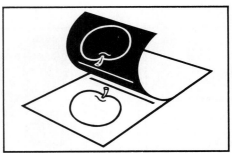

4. After about six seconds in the processor, paper and film emerge. Wait 60 seconds under safelight conditions and peel apart. Image density can be increased by waiting up to 90 seconds longer before peeling. Waiting longer is not recommended.

5. The negative paper is discarded, leaving the finished film positive.

Fig. 59-5. Procedure for making line film positives, using the diffusion transfer process.

EASTMAN KODAK

up. Some printers use the diffusion transfer process to prepare proofs. Film positives can be used for exposing screen printing emulsions, making reversals, and for making overhead transparencies.

Diffusion transfer materials work differently from film. Too much exposure causes too little chemcial action between the negative sheet and the receiver sheet. The result will be an incomplete image. Too little exposure will cause too much chemical action. The image will be very dark and the background will look dirty. You must adjust the exposure times to fit the equipment and material by making a series of test exposures in the camera.

MAKING HALFTONE POSITIVES

Halftone positives are exposed in much the same way as regular halftone negatives. A spe-

cial gray contact screen is placed over the negative material, main and flash exposures are made, and the negative paper is processed with a receiver sheet as was done with line exposures. The procedure used to make halftones is shown in Figure 59-6.

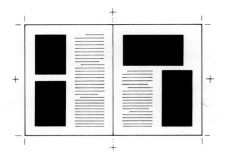

EASTMAN KODAK

Fig. 59-7. A paste-up with space for halftones.

SCREENED PRINTS FROM CONTINUOUS TONE ART

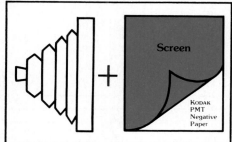

1. Load the camera (under 1A safelight) with PMT Negative Paper. Expose and flash through a KODAK PMT Gray Contact Screen (65, 85, 100, or 133 line). Screens require longer exposure. Try 7–12 × normal.

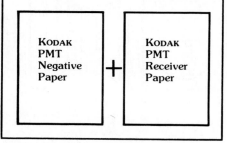

2. Place the exposed side of the negative paper in contact with PMT Receiver Paper.

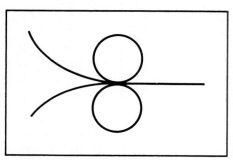

3. Feed both into a diffusion transfer processor filled with KODAK PMT Activator.

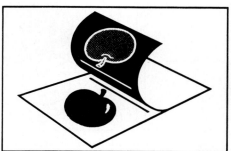

4. After about six seconds in the processor, the papers emerge. Wait 30 seconds under safelight conditions and peel apart.

5. Discard the negative paper, leaving the finished screened print.

Fig. 59-6. Procedure for making screened prints using the diffusion transfer process.

EASTMAN KODAK

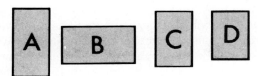

EASTMAN KODAK

Fig. 59-8. A, B, C, and D represent halftone prints made with the diffusion transfer process.

Halftone positives help in copy preparation. The halftone positive can be placed on the paste-up along with line elements. The entire paste-up can then be photographed as line copy. In Figure 59-7 a paste-up is shown with space (windows) where halftones are to appear. The items in Figure 59-8 represent halftone positives made by the diffusion transfer process. The diffusion transfer process halftone positives are

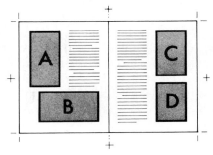

EASTMAN KODAK

Fig. 59-9. Halftone prints are attached to a paste-up so the whole unit can be photographed with one line exposure.

placed on the paste-up and then photographed as a line negative (Fig. 59-9). This saves much lithographic stripping and platemaking time.

REFLEX PROOFS BY CONTACT (In frame, with point-source light or reflex platemaker)

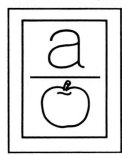

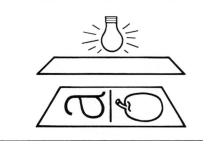

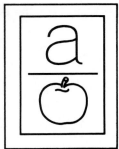

1. Place original paste-up (composed of line work and screened prints) image side up in the contact frame. Then place a sheet of KODAK PMT Reflex Paper emulsion side down on top of the paste-up. Expose through the back of the reflex paper with a high intensity tungsten light source.

2. Place the exposed side of the reflex paper in contact with the coated side of a sheet of KODAK PMT Receiver Paper.

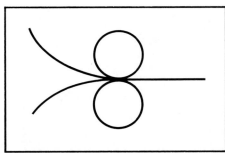

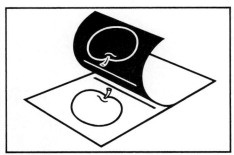

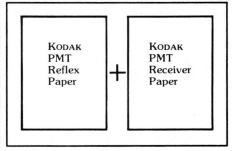

3. Feed both into a diffusion transfer processor filled with KODAK PMT Activator.

4. After about six seconds in the processor, the papers emerge. Wait 30 seconds under safelight conditions and peel apart.

5. The reflex paper is discarded, leaving the finished proof.

Fig. 59-10. Procedure for making reflex proofs, using the diffusion transfer process.

EASTMAN KODAK

MAKING CONTACT PRINTS

Contact prints can be made with the diffusion transfer process, using a special negative paper. This *contact speed* negative material can be used in low room light. It is not as sensitive as the negative paper used for making exposures in a camera.

The exposure is made in a contact printing frame with a high intensity light. The negative material is placed over the original. The original is usually a paste-up and can include both line and halftone images. The procedure for making contact prints is shown in Figure 59-10.

UNIT 60 PROCESS-COLOR REPRODUCTION

Process-color reproduction produces an optical illusion for the viewer. Three or four colors are printed on top of each other to make what appears to be a continuous-tone color print (Fig. 60-1). When a portion of the print in Figure 60-1 is enlarged, many separate colors can be seen (Fig. 60-2). The colors used to make the print are cyan (process blue), magenta (process red), yellow, and black. Nearly any color can be made by combining yellow, cyan, and magenta. Black adds detail to the color print.

Process-color reproduction is much more complicated than black-and-white reproduction. Specialized equipment and materials are required to make color separations. As a beginning graphic arts student, you should try making color separations and should not be discouraged if the quality does not meet the standards of commercial plants.

COLOR

Objects appear to have color because the human eye is sensitive to certain wavelengths of light. White light is said to contain all visible wavelengths of light. It contains the three additive *primary colors* of blue, red, and green.

When white light strikes an object, wavelengths are reflected or absorbed. This is what gives an object color. If all wavelengths of light are reflected, the object looks white.

When all wavelengths are absorbed, the object looks black.

An object looks a certain color because it reflects certain colors and absorbs others. The object in Figure 60-3 is green because it reflects green wavelengths and absorbs red and blue wavelengths. This same principle applies when light passes through an object. For example, a liquid may be red because red wavelengths pass through the liquid while blue and green wavelengths are absorbed.

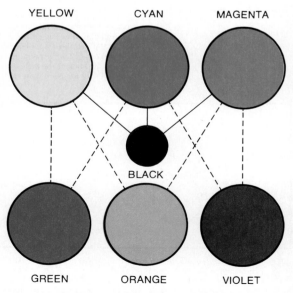

Fig. 60-1. Colors are created by combining yellow, cyan, and magenta. Black adds details.

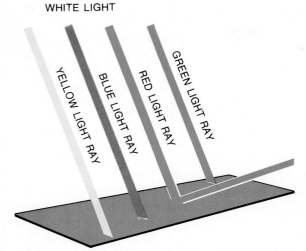

WHITE LIGHT

YELLOW LIGHT RAY

BLUE LIGHT RAY

RED LIGHT RAY

GREEN LIGHT RAY

Fig. 60-2. An enlarged view of Figure 60-1. Notice the dot formation that cannot be seen in Figure 60-1.

Fig. 60-3. A solid object has color because certain light wavelengths are reflected from its surface. The object absorbs other light wavelengths.

Again, red, green, and blue are called additive *primary* colors because white light is produced when they are added together in equal amounts.

Complementary colors are the combination of any two primary colors (Fig. 60-4). Red and blue light will make *magenta*. Red and green light will make *yellow*. Blue and green light make *cyan*.

White light results when a primary color light and its complementary color light are added (Fig. 60-5). This is the same as adding light from the three primary colors. Light from the yellow (green and red) complemen-

tary color can be added to the blue primary color to get white light. Because of this, yellow is said to be the complement of blue, cyan is the complement of red, and magneta is the complement of green.

COLOR SEPARATION COPY

Color separations are made from either *opaque* color copy or *transparent* color copy. Examples of opaque copy are color photographs and paintings. The most common transparent copy is a color slide like the ones taken with a 35mm camera.

Another name for opaque copy is *reflection* copy. Light is reflected from the surface of the copy. Color separation negatives can be made from reflection copy with process cameras or color scanners.

Transparent copy is sometimes called *transmission* copy. Light passes through the copy to make color separation negatives. This can be done with a process camera (Fig. 60-6), a contact printing unit, an enlarger (Fig. 60-7), or a color scanner. Color scanners will be discussed later in this unit.

COLOR SEPARATIONS

The process used to make color separations is known as the *subtractive* method. The separation negatives are produced by using *filters*. The filters are the same as the additive primary col-

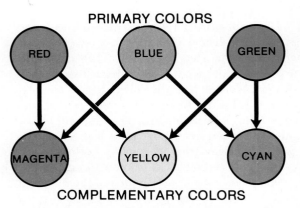

PRIMARY COLORS

RED   BLUE   GREEN

MAGENTA   YELLOW   CYAN

COMPLEMENTARY COLORS

Fig. 60-4. Complementary colors are the result of mixing any two primary colors.

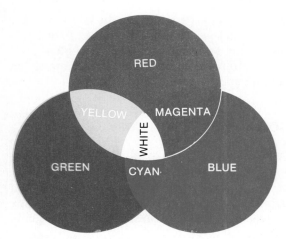

Fig. 60-5. When red, blue, and green light are blended, white light is formed.

ors of red, green, and blue. Filters work like a windowpane. When light passes through a red filter, only red wavelengths pass through the filter. The filter stops blue and green wavelengths from passing through. In this case, green and blue wavelengths are separated from white light. The blue filter permits blue wavelengths to pass through but absorbs green and red wavelengths. The green filter absorbs red and blue wavelengths and permits green light to pass through the filter.

Separations made by using the color separation process are known as *color printers*. For *three-color process* printing, there will be cyan, magenta, and yellow printers. *Four-color process* printing will use cyan, magenta, yellow, and black printers.

The *cyan printer* (color separation negative) is made by placing a red filter between the copy and the film. Red areas from the copy will expose the film when a red filter is used. When the film is developed, the black areas of the negative will be the same as the red areas of the copy. The clear areas of the negative will be the same as the areas that are blue or green on the copy. The clear areas thus will be printed with cyan ink (a combination of blue and green).

The green filter is used to make the *magenta printer*. The green filter permits only green wavelengths to reach the film. Areas of the copy that have green in them will pass through the

filter. The areas that have red and blue are absorbed by the filter. When the negative is developed, the black areas will correspond to the green areas of the copy. The image on a printing plate will be the same as the clear areas of the negative. The process has *subtracted* green from the copy. The plate will print areas that correspond to red and blue areas of the copy (red and blue make magenta). Magenta ink will be used to print this separation.

The *yellow printer* is made with the blue filter. Blue areas of the copy will expose the film. These areas will turn black when the film is developed. The negative will be clear in areas that are red or green on the copy. When red and green light are combined, yellow is formed. This separation negative will be printed with yellow ink.

If the copy has a white area, that area should be black on all color separation negatives. Remember that white light contains all three primary additive colors—red, blue, and green. Because of this, some light passes through all filters.

In theory, the three color printers described above should accurately reproduce the copy, but ink impurities may often cause the gray and black areas to appear brownish. Most printers use a fourth printer to produce a more accurate image: The *black printer* enhances detail. There are several methods that can be used to make the black printer. In the three filter method, a piece of film is exposed three separate times. Each exposure is made through one of the filters. The exposure time can vary from 30 to 100 percent of the time

COPY PLACED
HERE

SSP BROWN CAMERA

Fig. 60-6. A process camera can be used to make process-color separations.

used to produce the printer, but they usually correspond to the proportion of color in the copy.

Figure 60-8 shows some typical copy. Color separations are made from the copy (Fig. 60-9). When the negatives are printed, they appear as shown in Fig. 60-10.

COLOR CORRECTION

Process-color printing is difficult because the ink colors do not faithfully reproduce the colors of the original. Because of impurities in the printing inks, the separation negatives must usually be adjusted. This adjustment is known as *color correction*. Color correction can be done photographically, manually, or electronically. Sometimes both photographic and manual correction is done.

The manual correcting most commonly done is *dot etching* or *re-etching*. Dot etching is done on the negatives and re-etching is done on the printing plates.

Photographic color correction is called *masking*. There are many methods used for masking; the various methods should be studied and the best one be used for your particular situation. Film manufacturers offer masking systems that make this process much simpler. One such system is the *Kodak Tri-Mask System*.

Color correction is often the most difficult part of the color separation process. It often takes large amounts of time and can make process-color separation very expensive. Unfortunately, color correction will be necessary until better inks are available.

SCREENS FOR PROCESS-COLOR

Each process-color separation must be made into a halftone negative or positive. This means it must be screened. Gray contact screens are used to make color separation negatives, because magenta screens would work as filters.

Each color separation negative must be made with a different screen angle. This keeps the undesirable moiré pattern to a min-

imum. For *three-color process* printing, the screen angle for the cyan printer should be 45°, the magenta printer should be 75°, and the yellow printer should be 105°.

The screen angles for *four-color process* printing should be 45° for the black printer, 75° for the magenta printer, 90° for the yellow printer, and 105° for the cyan printer. *Preangled* contact screens can be purchased with appropriate screen angles.

FILM FOR COLOR SEPARATIONS

Panchromatic film must be used to produce color separation negatives. It is sensitive to all colors. The development of panchromatic film, however, causes darkroom problems because it must occur in total darkness. Orthochromatic film is insensitive to red light (it reacts to red as though it were black).

The film should be processed by using the time-temperature method of development. Film can be processed much more accurately with a film processor.

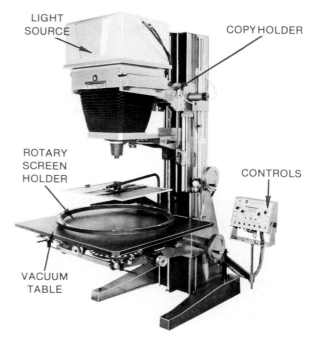

CONSOLIDATED INTERNATIONAL CORPORATION

Fig. 60-7. An enlarger used to make color separations.

COLOR SEPARATION METHODS

There are three methods used to make process-color separations. They are *direct, indirect,* and *color scanning.* Indirect and direct color separations are made with process cameras, enlargers, and contact printers. *Color scanners* are electronic machines that automatically make color separations.

Direct method

Both reflection and transmission (transparent) copy can be used with the direct method. Reflection copy color separations are made on a process camera. Color separations of transmission copy can be made with a process camera, by contact printing, or with an enlarger.

Color separation negatives are screened at the time the negatives are made. The exposures are made with a screen directly in front of the film. Negatives made with the direct method can be used immediately to make plates.

Masks are also used for color correction in the direct screen method. The location of the copy, mask, filter, screen, and film is somewhat different with different equipment.

Making direct separations of reflection copy in a process camera is similar to making regular halftone negatives. The copy is placed on the copyboard with the lights in the correct position. The proper filter is placed in the lens of the camera. Film is placed on the vacuum back of the camera. Register pins are used to locate the film in the proper location. The cor-

rect mask, which was prepared earlier, is placed in register over the film. The contact screen with the proper screen angle is placed over the film and mask. When the materials are in place, the exposure is made. Similar procedures are used to make each printer. A drawing of the set-up for a direct separation of reflection copy in a process camera is shown in Figure 60-11. It is important that the camera be equipped with proper lights and a color-corrected lens.

Direct color separations can be made by contact printing. It should be noted that the separation negatives will be the same size as the original copy. Also, the copy must be transmission copy. These separations are made on a contact printer. The drawing in Figure 60-12 shows the location of the light source, filter, mask, copy (transparency), contact screen, and film. The light source, such as a xenon light, must give the right kind of light.

Process cameras can also be used to make direct color separations of transmission copy. The camera must be equipped with a special copyboard with a hole in it. The copy is placed between two pieces of glass. The light is placed behind the hole so it will pass through the transparency. The mask can be placed in register with the transparency, or it can be used on the camera back. A drawing of the set-up for making separations of transmission copy with a process camera is shown in Figure 60-13. Copy can be reduced or enlarged using the process camera.

An enlarger similar to the one shown in Figure 60-7 can be used to make direct color separations. The enlarger must have the correct kind of light source. The transparency and mask are held in a film holder in the head of the enlarger and the proper filter is placed between the lens and the film. The film and screen are located on the base of the enlarger. The base is usually a vacuum table. Figure 60-14 shows how separations are made on an enlarger.

Indirect method

The indirect method gives better quality color separations than does the direct method. Be-

Fig. 60-8. Typical color copy.

cause it requires more photographic steps, however, it is more expensive. Indirect separations allow greater color correction. The indirect method can be done with a process camera, enlarger, or contact printer.

The first step in making indirect separations is to make masks for each of the four color separations. These are used to correct for impurities in the inks that will be used to print the separations. The second step is to make *continuous-tone color separations* (negatives or positives without dot formations), using the masks. The third step is to make contact-screened halftones of the continuous-tone separations. This step is usually done with a contact printing frame and produces a

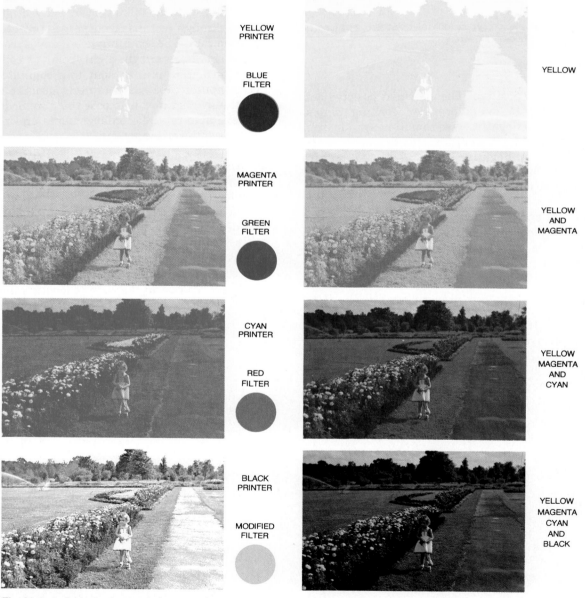

Fig. 60-9. Individual color separations, or printers, printed in the appropriate color.

Fig. 60-10. Progressive reproductions of the four color printers.

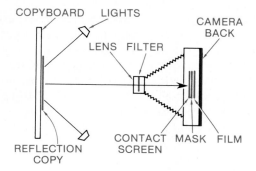

Fig. 60-11. Color separations of reflection copy can be made on process cameras.

screened positive. The screened positive can be used to make positive working plates. Screened negatives are sometimes made from the positives. The negatives are used to make plates on negative working plates. Figure 60-15 shows the steps needed to make indirect separations.

Color scanning

Color scanning is the method most widely used to make color separations. Although very expensive and quite delicate, scanners can produce color separation negatives or positives more rapidly than other color-separation equipment can. To be able to operate color scanners, operators must have extensive training.

There are three kinds of scanners. One type produces continuous-tone separations. Another type of scanner produces halftones by placing a contact screen in contact with the film. The most recent scanners make halftones by creating the dots electronically. These are called *dot-generating scanners*.

Scanners have two drums. One drum holds the copy. The other drum holds the film for making the color separation negatives or positives. Both drums spin very rapidly. Light passes through a transparency or is reflected from the copy. The scanning head moves from side to side to record the light from the copy. The information is then sent to a computer. The computer processes the information and tells the scanner how to expose the film. Scanners are able to make enlargements and reductions of the original copy.

Color scanners interpret the light transmitted from the copy through *photo-multipliers* (PMTs), which filter and transform the light into electrical signals. Three of the PMTs filter red, green, and blue light. The fourth PMT provides unsharp mask information. The PMTs also interpret the intensity or density of the image on the copy. This information is then sent to the computer, which causes the film to be exposed in the correct location and with the correct density. The scanner pro-

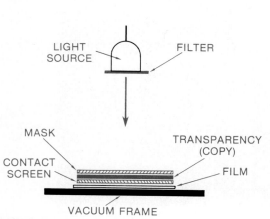

Fig. 60-12. Locations of materials for making color separations with a contact printer.

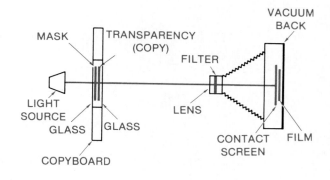

Fig. 60-13. Color separations of transparencies can be made on process cameras.

duces four negatives—magenta, cyan, yellow, and black. Some scanners make one negative (or positive) at a time. Others are able to make all four color separations on a single sheet of film.

Electronic color image systems

Color imaging systems that can electronically change images and do complex page preparation are available. To manipulate data and color images, most systems use a combination of devices such as scanners, powerful computers, and plotters or other output units.

These systems are capable of making color corrections, retouching copy, creating special effects, producing high-resolution line work, combining line art and type with color photographs, and producing color tints—all in a fraction of the time required when using other methods. In fact, some copy could not be prepared by using traditional methods, including scanners. Figure 60-16 shows an operator creating color copy on a color imaging system.

These systems are complex and expensive. However, the cost of the equipment can be justified because of the savings in time, the quality of the work, and the unique kind of work that can be done. Because the process is becoming more common, costs are lowering.

The system scans color images with a conventional scanner. This information is then

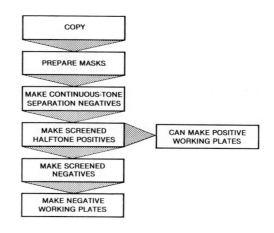

Fig. 60-15. Indirect color separation steps.

sent to interactive color page makeup stations (like computer terminals). The information can be worked on immediately or stored in computers for later use. Once the work has been done, the final product is sent to output equipment such as plotters. Color separations are then prepared. Figure 60-17 shows examples of how images can be manipulated on color imaging systems. All of the images in Fig. 60-17 were produced from the same original.

Good operators are the key to the effective use of these systems. Trained personnel are required to operate the equipment. Also, the operator needs to know about color reproduction and have some artistic talents.

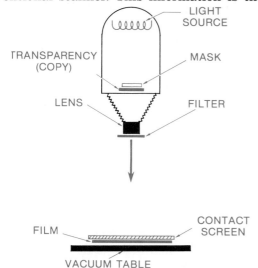

Fig. 60-14. Color separations of transparencies can be made on enlargers.

MAGNA GRAPHIC CORPORATION

Fig. 60-16. Operator working on an electronic color imaging system.

DAINIPPON SCREEN MFG. CO. LTD.

Fig. 60-17.   Electronic color imaging systems can change a copy in several ways. All of these images came from the same original photograph.

UNIT 61 DIFFICULTIES AND ANSWERS IN WORKING WITH NEGATIVES

Completed negatives should be examined after processing to be sure that they do not contain defects. The examination should be done on an illuminator or light table. It is good to use a magnifier for closer examination. Defects in negatives must be found so that poor negatives will not be used to make plates. Also, it is good to find the cause of the defect so that it can be corrected before more negatives are made.

A good quality negative should have black areas that are dense enough to keep light from passing through, and few or no pinholes in the dark areas. The transparent areas should be clean and clear, and image edges should be as sharp as the original copy (proportionate to the original copy when enlargements or reductions are made). Some of the problem areas that should be checked when you find faulty negatives are exposure procedures, film processing procedures, and darkroom cleanliness.

EXPOSURE PROCEDURES

If all procedures are accurate, a negative should give a positive print that looks exactly like the original copy. Figure 61-1 shows a correctly exposed negative and a print of it. The print is the same as the original, and it is proportionate throughout.

Underexposure. Figure 61-2 shows an underexposed negative and a print from the negative. Notice that the printed image is quite different from that in Figure 61-1. The black areas are not as dense (opaque) as those of a normal negative when examined on a light table. The image areas are thicker than those of a normal negative, as can be seen by comparing Figures 61-1 and 61-2. Caution: it is sometimes difficult to distinguish between an underexposed negative and an underdeveloped negative.

Common causes of underexposed negatives are poor lighting (old bulbs or lights aimed incorrectly), low electrical voltage, and inaccurately calculated exposure time. Improper lens adjustment and a change in the film emulsion can also cause problems.

Overexposure. Figure 61-3 shows an overexposed negative and a print of the negative. The negative is very dense, but there is a loss of detail in the image areas. The fine line areas tend to close together on an overexposed negative. Some overexposures have the same causes as underexposure, but the mistakes are made in the opposite direction. (For the causes of underexposure, see above.)

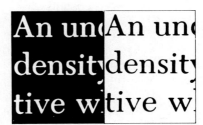

Fig. 61-1. A print of a correctly exposed negative.

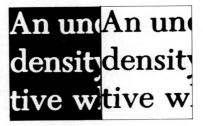

Fig. 61-2. A print of an underexposed negative.

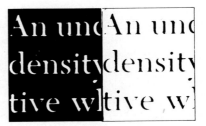

Fig. 61-3. A print of an overexposed negative.

Accurate light placement is critical for properly exposing negatives. This is especially true when large pieces of copy are being photographed. For large negatives, you can easily overexpose one part of the negative and underexpose another.

Image out-of-focus. There are two usual causes for out-of-focus images. The first is improper camera adjustment. The second is vibration in the camera during the exposure. An out-of-focus image is more likely when short exposures are made.

Before exposures are made, make sure that the camera is properly adjusted. Check the camera controls to be sure both the lens and copyboard are set on the same percentage. Also make a visual check on the camera ground glass. If the percentages are the same but the ground glass image is out-of-focus, check the camera.

Vibration can be caused by people merely walking near the camera while the exposure is being made. The camera operator can cause vibration by hitting the camera. It is best to keep movement around the camera to a minimum.

Unfortunately, many photographers consistently produce negatives that are inaccurately exposed. Check your negatives often to be sure that they are accurately exposed. Placement of lights is especially important. If lights are incandescent, they should be checked for brightness on a regular basis.

FILM PROCESSING PROCEDURES

Faulty negatives are often caused by processing problems, because there are so many variables that must be controlled. The four most common problems are underdevelopment, overdevelopment, fogging, and poor fixing.

Underdevelopment. An underdeveloped negative is similar to an underexposed one. The image is thicker; the dark areas are not very dense; excessive pinholes (little clear dots) show in the dense area. Some of the causes of underdevelopment are: developer that is too cool, insufficient development time, inaccurately formulated developer, and exhausted developer. Exhausted developer often causes film to appear brown in color. Be careful not to exceed

the limits of the developer, as recommended by the manufacturer.

Overdevelopment. An overdeveloped negative appears much like an overexposed one. There is loss of detail in the image areas and the dark areas are very dense. Some of the causes of an overdeveloped negative are: developer that is too warm, too much development time, not enough stop bath time, inaccurately formulated developer, and too much agitation.

Fogging. Fogging is a light coating of silver in the clear areas of a negative. It is usually caused by non-image light striking the film or by improper development. The results of fogging often resemble overdevelopment or overexposure. Some causes of fogging are dirty lenses, improper safelights, darkroom light leaks, and poor fixing.

Poor fixing. Fixing solution usually lasts for a long time. It is saved and reused often. However, fixer eventually will become exhausted. Negatives will be slow to clear when placed in the fixer and will scratch more easily.

DARKROOM CLEANLINESS

The darkroom should be vacuumed on a regular schedule. During heavy use, it should be vacuumed at least once a day. It is better not to sweep a darkroom with a broom, because the broom will send more dirt into the air. Wet cleaning should follow the vacuuming. Floors should be mopped to remove dirt and stains. All other surfaces should be wiped with a damp sponge or towel.

All chemical spills should be cleaned immediately. Merely soaking up the chemicals will leave a chemical residue. After the chemicals have been removed, the area should be cleaned with a wet sponge or towel.

Keep the camera clean. The copyboard gets dirty and collects dust quickly. The copyboard should be checked for dirt each time copy is placed in it. The lens should be kept covered when not in use and examined regularly for dirt and fingerprints. The ground glass and vacuum back should be cleaned several times a day. They collect fingerprints each time an exposure is made. Greasy fingerprints collect dust more easily than clean surfaces. The bellows, both inside and out, should be vacuumed. All other parts of the camera should be cleaned weekly. The vacuum pump is another item that easily collects dust.

Darkroom utensils should be another of your concerns. They should be thoroughly washed and wiped when chemicals are removed. Merely rinsing the utensils will leave residues on the utensils that can stain them or contaminate other chemicals. Other things, such as vacuum printing frames, lights, timers, and film cutters, should also be cleaned.

Dust and dirt can be a particular problem when humidity is low. Low humidity means the air is dry. This increases the amount of static electricity and static electricity on film and surfaces attracts dust and dirt. When the air is very dry, you should find some way to increase the humidity in the darkroom.

Most of the dirt and dust in the darkroom is brought in by people. Make sure that your clothes and shoes are clean before entering the darkroom. People, even camera operators, should not go into the darkroom except when necessary. Your hands should be kept clean at all times and should be washed and wiped dry before you handle photographic materials. Photographic materials can be damaged if hands have chemical stains.

The areas around the darkroom should be kept as clean as the darkroom. Dirt on the floors outside can be tracked into the darkroom. The darkroom door should be kept closed at all times to reduce the chance of dirt getting in.

Keeping the darkroom clean is worth the time. You will get better quality work and have less work to do over. It will also reduce the amount of work for the people who use the materials. Further, there will be less waste of valuable photographic materials.

UNIT 62 STANDARDIZING DARKROOM PROCEDURES

It is important to set up precise procedures and to follow them each time you make a negative or positive. Probably the greatest single cause of problems in the darkroom is failure to follow accurate, established procedures. You should be machine-like when handling, exposing, and processing photographic material in the darkroom. Many of these procedures have already been outlined in previous units of this book.

You must be thoroughly familiar with materials and equipment used in each task. Some of the areas that require control are calculating exposure time, preparing materials, preparing the darkroom for exposures, making exposures, processing exposed materials, and cleaning up.

CALCULATING EXPOSURE TIMES

The procedures for calculating various exposure times by means of test exposures have been dis-cussed in previous units. When conditions or materials change, however, the test is no longer useful. You should check your test exposure periodically to insure accurate data. A written record of the test data should be kept where all camera operators and darkroom workers can find it easily and use it when necessary.

PREPARING MATERIALS

Some materials used in the darkroom are prepared by the manufacturer; others are prepared in the commercial plant or graphic arts laboratory. These materials, like the developer, must be mixed in exactly the same way each time.

Materials can be prepared at two different times. First is when they are prepared in bulk form, such as when you mix developer concentrate with water to make developer A and B solutions. The second time is when the two chemicals are mixed for processing an exposure. This is when part A and part B of the developer are mixed together to create the active developer for film processing.

You should also have set procedures for storing and using the materials. Too much heat or humidity can cause light-sensitive products to change structure. Such deterioration may make materials unusable.

PREPARING THE DARKROOM

For efficient and accurate work in the darkroom, you must prepare everything while the room light is on so that no further preparation will be needed after the lights are off. This applies to whatever you are doing in the darkroom—precleaning the darkroom, preparing the chemicals and darkroom sink (this varies with the different types of exposures), adjusting the temperature of the chemicals, locating the equipment for convenient use, and preparing and cleaning the camera and other equipment needed for making the exposure.

MAKING EXPOSURES

When making a regular exposure, one should follow the same steps used when making test exposures. Any change will affect the results in the negatives and positives. The camera operator should establish the most efficient routine that will still retain quality.

PROCESSING EXPOSED MATERIALS

In processing photographic materials, you must follow a set procedure to control the many variables. These variables include developer mixture, development time, temperature, and agitation while developing.

Processing photographic materials is so critical that many commercial plants have installed machines to do part or all of it. The machine shown in Figure 62-1 is used for automatically processing film. After the piece of film is exposed, it is fed into one end of the

processor and in a few minutes it comes out the other end, completely processed and dry. These machines are useful when large amounts of film need to be processed or when more precise finished products are required than can be obtained from tray processing. The machine greatly reduces the chances for human error in processing.

CLEANING UP

Cleaning up consists of putting the darkroom back in order and making the utensils ready

Fig. 62-1. Mechanical tray rocker.

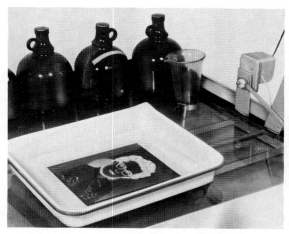

BYCHROME COMPANY

Fig. 62-2. Mechanical tray rocker submerged in water to control the developer temperature.

for the next day of operation. This includes replacing equipment, tools, and materials in the specified storage locations. People sometimes neglect this part of their work when they rush to meet production schedules. But they save no time if exposures are ruined because of an unclean darkroom.

A regular schedule for darkroom cleanup should be set up. It is usually best to pick one specific day each week and set aside one or two hours for this important task. As we have pointed out several times, dust, dirt, chemical stains, and other pollutants can cause great problems in graphic arts photography. A problem-free darkroom makes for efficient work and quality results.

UNIT 63 LEARNING EXPERIENCES: PROCESS CAMERAS AND DARKROOM PROCEDURES

KEY TERMS

Unit 50
Aperture
Bellows
Camera back
Copyboard
Darkroom
Diaphragm
Frontcase
Incandescent light
Iris
Lens
Lensboard
Lens collar
Process camera
Pulsed Xenon light
Quartz light
Shutter

Base (support)
Blue sensitive film
Buffers
Contacting film
Developer
Diazo
Duplicating film
Emulsion
Fixer
Hydroquinone
Latent image
Millimicrons
Orthochromatic
Panchromatic
Preservatives
Restrainers
Silverless film
Sodium thiosulfate
Stop bath
Silver halide

Unit 51
Darkroom camera
Gallery camera
Vertical camera
Horizontal camera

Unit 52
Accelerators
Acetic acid
Antihalation

Unit 53
Contact printer
Graduate
Inspection light
Point source light
Processing trays

Unit 53
Contact printer
Safelight
Water mixer

Unit 55
Agitation
Focal length
Line negative
Pinholes
Sensitivity guide
  (gray scale)

Unit 56
Auto screen
Basic flash exposure
Bump Exposure
Calibrated gray scale
Contact screen
Continuous-tone copy
Flash exposure
Glass screen
Halftone exposure
  computer
Hard dots
Highlights and shadows
Main exposure
Middletones
Soft dots
Tonal range

Unit 57
Densitometer
Duotone

Unit 58
Choke
Contact print
Film positive
Spread
Vacuum printing unit

Unit 59
Diffusion transfer
Negative material
Receiver material

Unit 60
Color correction
Color scanner
Color separation
Continuous-tone separations
Cyan
Dot etching
Magenta
Mask
Photomultiplier (PMT)
Primary colors
Printers
Re-etching

Unit 61
Fogging
Overexposure
Underexposure

DISCUSSION TOPICS

1. What are the advantages and disadvantages of horizontal and vertical cameras?
2. What is the major advantage of orthochromatic film over panchromatic film?
3. Name the three methods of hand developing film and state their advantages or disadvantages.
4. Explain how the dot formation should look on a good halftone negative.
5. Explain what happens when color copy is photographed through a filter.

ACTIVITIES

Units 50 and 51

1. Examine the process camera in your graphic arts laboratory. Identify all of the parts on the camera. Learn how each part works.

Unit 55

2. Cut a piece of orthochromatic film into six small pieces. Perform the following activities. Then process the six pieces of film.
   a. Expose one piece of film to the white light in the room.
   b. Expose one piece of film to only the safelight.
   c. Expose one piece of film to a piece of black-and-white copy with the emulsion side of the film toward the copy.
   d. Expose one piece of film to a piece of black-and-white copy with the base side of the film toward the copy.
   e. Expose one piece of film to red-and-white copy with the emulsion side of the film toward the copy.
   f. Expose one piece of film to copy with blue, green, and yellow images.
      Examine the pieces of processed film on a light table and discuss the results with your fellow students.
3. Determine the basic exposure for making line negatives with your camera. Find the best f-stop to use.

Unit 56

4. Make the test exposures for calibrating the *Kodak Halftone Negative Computer*. Groups of three or four students can do this and compare results after the test exposures are made.
5. Calibrate the computer for making halftone negatives using the data from the test exposures.

Unit 57

6. Obtain several pieces of continuous-tone copy. Calculate the main and flash exposures for each.

Unit 58

7. Typeset two or three words in 24 to 48 point type. Use any available method of typesetting. Make a film negative, 100% size. Using the correct film and procedures, make these words into outline letters. Prepare both a film negative and a film positive. Also, proof them on photographic print paper. Inspect the results with a magnifying glass and determine where improvements can be made.

Unit 59

8. Make test exposures to determine the best time for exposing diffusion transfer process materials.

Units 61 and 62

9. Visit a printing plant that has a process photography department. Discuss with the camera operator the procedures used to produce negatives. Learn what experience and education are necessary to do the work. Prepare a report on your findings and present it orally to your class.

Placing an image carrier on a printing press. (Original Heidelberg)

8 LETTERPRESS IMAGE CARRIERS

SECTION

64 INTRODUCTION TO LETTERPRESS IMAGE CARRIERS

UNIT

The image carriers used on a letterpress printing press are called *plates*. The principle of letterpress is printing from a raised surface; the image on a plate stands out in relief. To give good multiple reproductions on paper or other material, the image carrier must be of high quality. There are several different kinds of letterpress image carriers, each designed for specific purposes.

BASIC KINDS OF IMAGE CARRIERS

There are two major kinds of letterpress image carriers. They are (1) first-generation plates and (2) second-generation plates.

First-generation plates are ones made directly from the film negatives that were made from original copy (Fig. 64-1). Photoengravings and photopolymer image carriers are first generation plates.

However, some first-generation plates do not need film negatives. To make laser engravings, original copy is scanned by a helium neon laser that translates light rays into electronic signals.

This in turn operates a high-powered CO_2 laser that cuts away the non-image area of the image carrier. This method is fast and economical. The graphic arts industry is using it more and more.

Two first-generation original image carriers not shown in Figure 64-1 are the linoleum and wood-block cuts. Before photoengraving, these two hand-cut or hand-carved relief image carriers were important methods of preparing illustrations. Although the modern letterpress has no place for hand-made image carriers, the hobbyist or beginning student of graphic arts will find that these two economical materials offer excellent reproduction qualities. The procedure for preparing a linoleum block is outlined in Unit 72.

Second-generation plates are duplicates (Fig. 64-2) that are made from molds or patterns of first-generation original image carriers. The three common duplicates are (1) stereotype, (2) electrotype, and (3) rubber-flexographic.

Duplicate image carriers are used on presses to save the original image carriers from wear or

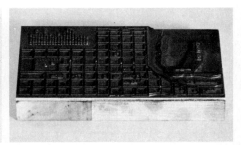

Fig. 64-1. First-generation original letterpress printing plates.

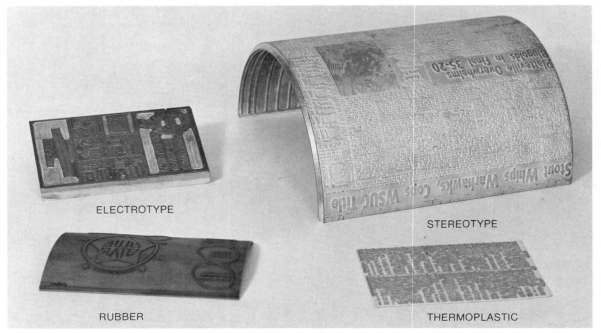

Fig. 64-2. Second-generation duplicate letterpress printing plates.

damage. Several duplicates can be made from an original and used on several presses to complete a production run in less time.

MATERIALS USED

Several different materials, metallic and non-metallic, are used to make letterpress printing plates. The most common metallic materials are copper, zinc, and magnesium. Lead, tin, and antimony are combined to form an alloy for stereotype castings.

Research by several United States and European companies has shown that all-metal image carriers are not necessary. Non-metallic and synthetic materials like plastic and rubber are being used very successfully to make original and duplicate image carriers.

Some of the latest image carriers are made with a combination of metallic and non-metallic materials. A hard plastic reproduction surface can be laminated to a rubber base that provides a cushion for the plate. This combination of materials gives high quality in printing. Photopolymer is being used on a wide variety of relief printing plates.

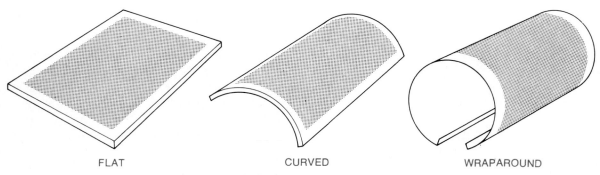

Fig. 64-3. The standard shapes of letterpress image carriers.

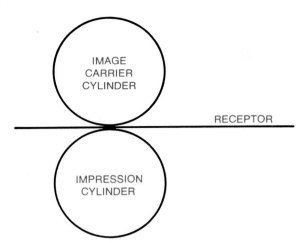

Fig. 64-4. A standard letterpress printing press that uses wraparound image carriers.

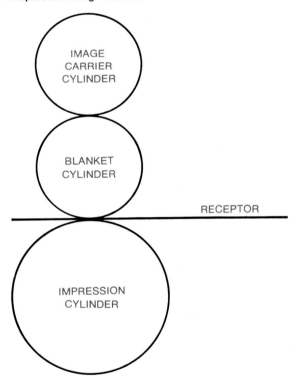

Fig. 64-5. A letterset printing press schematic that uses wraparound image carriers.

SHAPES OF RELIEF IMAGE CARRIERS

Relief image carriers are prepared in three basic forms: (1) flat, (2) curved, and (3) wraparound (Fig. 64-3). Nearly any of the metallic or non-metallic materials can be used to prepare image carriers in these shapes.

BUNTING MAGNETICS COMPANY

Fig. 64-6. Photopolymer and rubber flexible printing plates with thin steel backings.

The flat shape is the oldest and is still being used. Generally, flat image carriers are made type-high (0.918 inch) and are used on platen or cylinder letterpresses (Unit 80). The curved shape is used on rotary letterpresses designed for high-speed reproduction, such as newspaper presses.

The wraparound shape is a more recent development. These flexible carriers are used on both the letterpress and the letterset presses. Wraparound letterpress image carriers print directly on receptors (Fig. 64-4). Letterset

BUNTING MAGNETICS COMPANY

Fig. 64-7. Steel-backed flexible letterpress plates can be fastened to magnetic printing press cylinders.

image carriers print on a blanket, which in turn prints on the receptor (Fig. 64-5). The main difference between them is that the image is wrong-reading on the letterpress image carrier and right-reading on the letterset image carrier.

Some typical flexible relief image carriers are shown in Figure 64-6. All of these plates except one (upper right) are made of photopolymer and have a thin steel backing. The non-polymer plate is made of rubber and also has a thin steel backing. Because of the steel backing and the flexibility of these wraparound plates, they can easily be attached to magnetic printing press cylinders (Fig. 64-7). Flexible plates can be clamped around printing cylinders, using traditional methods.

HISTORICAL HIGHLIGHTS

Relief image carriers made of wood were used in the Orient during the eighth and ninth centuries, but the art of printing was not practiced in Europe until the fifteenth and sixteenth centuries. The first illustration reproduced for the public was in German, in the *Nuremberg Chronical* in 1493.

For over 300 years, it was necessary to hand-cut a wood block or to prepare a metal plate to reproduce an illustration or picture. But in 1880, the photoengraving method of producing relief image carriers was developed. Today, wood blocks are cut only by people interested in original graphic art.

UNIT 65 SAFETY WITH LETTERPRESS CARRIERS

Anyone involved in graphic arts must be safety conscious. Tools and machines with sharp cutting edges must be used with respect and caution. To use them safely, you must know how they operate. Use your best judgment and common sense whenever you are using the machines and equipment.

The National Safety Council has found that most accidents in school and industrial laboratories occur around 10 A.M. More school laboratory accidents happen on Wednesdays than on any other day, with the exception of the day before and the day after a vacation.

SAFETY GUIDELINES

For your own protection, follow these safety suggestions.

Permission. Request permission from your instructor before operating equipment.

Clothing and jewelry. Secure loose clothing and remove jewelry before operating any machine so that they will not get caught in a machine.

Safety guards. Check to see that all guards are in place before turning on the power. Equipment with moving parts should always have protective guards.

Air vents. Start exhaust fans before working with chemicals or toxic metals.

Electrical connections. Be sure that all machines are properly grounded and that all electrical connections are in good repair.

Eye and face protection. Wear safety goggles and face shields when operating cutting machines or using chemical solutions.

Floor drain. There should be floor drains near machines and tanks containing chemical or other solutions. Make sure that all drains are open.

Hand and arm protection. Wear suitable gloves when necessary to protect your hands and arms from cuts, abrasions, heat, and chemical burns.

Body protection. Wear rubber aprons when working with chemicals. The aprons should cover the entire front of your body.

Good housekeeping. Keep good order in any laboratory or work area. Never let waste materials, scrap, or junk collect on the floor. A messy laboratory invites an accident.

Materials storage. Store containers of chemical solutions near the floor. They should all be labeled. Place boxes, tools, and other items on storage shelves so that they are easy to reach and will not vibrate off the shelf.

Illumination. Adequate light is important for safety. An operator who can see everything well is usually able to avoid dangerous situations.

Noise. Too much noise is dangerous. It makes you jumpy and keeps you from hearing what is happening around you. An unusually noisy machine should be repaired, replaced, or operated with special care.

Fire. Fresh fire extinguishers must always be kept where they are easily seen in the laboratory. Be extremely careful when handling flammable materials.

Sharp objects. Handle sharp tools with care. Linoleum block cutting-tools are razor sharp and should be used with special care. Follow all safety rules when cutting a block. Look where you are walking and do not bump into heavy machinery or equipment with sharp corners.

UNIT 66 PHOTOENGRAVINGS

Photoengraving is the art and science of producing original relief image carriers by photographic, chemical, and mechanical means. With the invention of commercial photoengraving about 1880 and the development of the hot-type mechanical composing machine around 1886, the publishing industry was able to increase production and quality of books, newspapers, and all printed material.

Photoengraving changed little from the 1880s until the middle of the twentieth century. It took much tedious and technical hand work to produce a high-quality image carrier. Now, a quality photoengraving can be made in minutes instead of hours. One-step etching has been the key to speed and quality. Before powderless etching, the photoengraver had to etch, or cut away, the metal several times to remove enough material in the non-image areas.

Photoengravings are made from zinc, copper, or magnesium. Zinc is probably the oldest of all photoengraving materials. Magnesium is the latest metal to be used. Copper, because it is fine-grained, is generally used for halftone engravings. Zinc and magnesium are commonly used for line engravings, but halftones with coarse screens can be made with these two metals.

PRODUCING A PHOTOENGRAVING

1. Obtain the illustrations and photographs. Illustrations with solid tones are treated as line copy. Photographs are treated as halftone copy (Unit 43).
2. Photograph the copy with a process camera to obtain high-contrast negatives (Units 56, 57).
3. Strip the negatives in their proper position on a flat (Section 11). NOTE: The negatives are turned over to obtain the necessary wrong-reading image on the photoengraving.
4. Obtain a piece of metal—zinc, copper, or magnesium—with a light-sensitive coating. Using presensitized metal means that you do not need to apply a light-sensitive solution just before making the exposure.
5. Place the high-contrast negatives in contact with the metal. Put both items in an exposure frame and expose them to bright light (Fig. 66-1). The light-sensitive solution hardens as the light rays pass through the transparent areas of the negatives.
6. After exposure, the coated metal is developed. Areas exposed to light keep their coating; the light-sensitive coating on the

Fig. 66-1. Exposing the light-sensitive metal through the negatives, which contain the images.

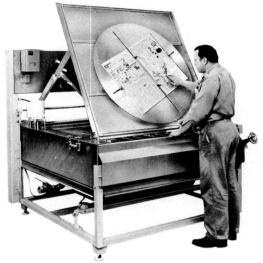

HORAN ENGRAVING COMPANY

Fig. 66-3. An etching machine shown in Figure 66-2, with the top open and two image carriers mounted.

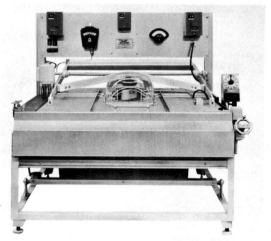

MASTER SALES AND SERVICE CORPORATION

Fig. 66-2. An etching machine used for photoengravings.

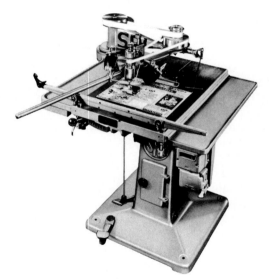

MASTER SALES AND SERVICE CORPORATION

Fig. 66-4. A radial-arm router used to remove large nonimage areas of the photoengraving.

unexposed areas of metal is washed away. The image is further hardened by chemicals or by heat, so that it becomes etch-resistant.

7. The metal is now ready for etching. Put it into an etching machine (Fig. 66-2). Clamp it to a base in a horizontal position (Fig. 66-3).

8. Spray or splash the liquid etching solution against the surface of the metal. The non-image area (the area that is not etch resistant) is washed away, leaving the image to stand out in relief.

9. The next step is to cut away, or rout, the larger non-image areas of the metal. A radial-arm router is used for this (Fig. 66-4).

This step is necessary to keep the larger non-image areas from reproducing when proofing or printing.

10. The last step of the production is called finishing. An engraver inspects the image area and uses hand tooling and spot etching to improve the final reproduction (Fig. 66-5).

11. The metal, now a relief image carrier, is

proofed in a reproduction proof press. Simulated press conditions are used to control quality during the press run to follow.

12. Blocking or mounting is done after the

proofs have been approved. The metal is fastened to a block of wood or metal to make it type-high. It is placed directly on a press or used to prepare duplicate image carriers (Fig. 66-6).

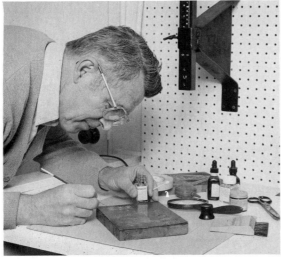

HORAN ENGRAVING COMPANY

Fig. 66-5. A skilled engraver inspecting and spot etching the machine-made photoengraving.

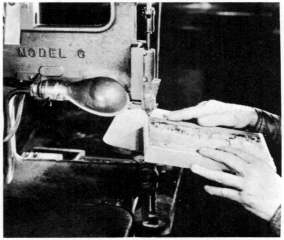

E. I. DU PONT DE NEMOURS

Fig. 66-6. Blocking or mounting the photoengraving to make it type-high.

UNIT 67 RIGID PHOTOPOLYMER RELIEF PLATES

Photopolymer is a light sensitive plastic material. It was developed for use in the manufacture of letterpress printing plates. These plates have a layer of light-sensitive photopolymer bonded to a metal or film support base (Fig. 67-1). These relief plates can be made quickly by exposure to ultraviolet light and automatic processing in a weak alkaline solution.

Photopolymer plates can be made in several thicknesses, ranging from .0172 to .2500 inches (.437 to 6.35 mm). Plate sizes up to 40.5 by 58 inches (102.9 by 142.3 cm) are possible. These plates are used on platen and cylinder relief presses and rotary letterpresses (Fig. 67-2). Photopolymer plates are also used for letterset (see Unit 68). Photopolymer plates are used to print many products, such as folding cartons,

labels, paper bags, and other packaging products.

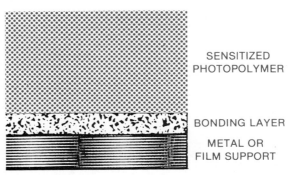

SENSITIZED PHOTOPOLYMER

BONDING LAYER

METAL OR FILM SUPPORT

E.I. DU PONT DE NEMOURS

Fig. 67-1. A cross-section view of a photopolymer printing plate.

E.I. DU PONT DE NEMOURS

Fig. 67-2. Removing ink from the printing surface of rigid photopolymer plates that are attached to the cylinder of a rotary letterpress.

BUNTING MAGNETICS COMPANY

Fig. 67-3. Pre-curving a photopolymer plate to fit a press cylinder. Completed curved plates are shown on the left.

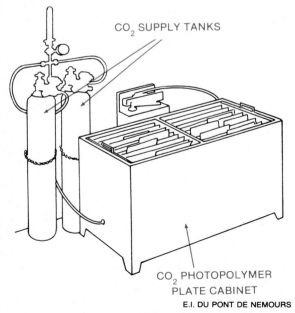

CO₂ SUPPLY TANKS

CO₂ PHOTOPOLYMER PLATE CABINET

E.I. DU PONT DE NEMOURS

Fig. 67-4. A carbon dioxide cabinet is one way to make a photopolymer plate very sensitive to ultraviolet light.

PRODUCING PHOTOPOLYMER PLATES

First the plate material must be cut to size and, if necessary, precurved (Fig. 67-3). A plate to be attached to a cylinder must be precurved. The image would be distorted if it were curved after the image was formed.

The second important step is to make the photopolymer layer very sensitive to ultraviolet light. This step, called *sensitization*, reduces the time needed for the actual plate exposure. It also helps to produce correctly shaped relief image areas during the washout step. A plate can be sensitized in any of three ways.

1. Carbon Dioxide Conditioning. Plates stored in a CO_2 cabinet (Fig. 67-4) are sensitized as carbon dioxide replaces the oxygen in the air.

2. Photosensitizing. A standard ultraviolet exposure unit is used to expose the plate to ultraviolet light through a special filter (Fig. 67-5).

BASF SYSTEMS

Fig. 67-5. An ultraviolet exposure unit, containing the special filter material, is used to photosensitize a photopolymer plate.

3. Heat Sensitizing. A plate oven uses controlled heat to drive out the oxygen within the plate. (Fig. 67-6).

When the plate has been sensitized, it can be exposed. A film negative is placed in contact with the photopolymer coating (Fig. 67-7). For letterpress plates, the negative is positioned so the image is wrong reading. The light rays pass through the non-image transparent areas of the negative (Fig. 67-8). The ultraviolet light penetrates the photopolymer layer and hardens the

E.I. DU PONT DE NEMOURS

Fig. 67-6. Controlled ovens make the plate sensitive to ultraviolet light by driving the oxygen out of a photopolymer plate.

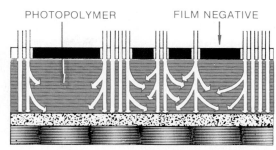

E.I. DU PONT DE NEMOURS

Fig. 67-8. Ultraviolet light passes through the transparent areas of the negative and hardens the photopolymer layer.

E.I. DU PONT DE NEMOURS

Fig. 67-7. A film negative is placed over the photopolymer plate before exposure.

BASF SYSTEMS

Fig. 67-9. An exposure unit for pre-curved photopolymer plates. Notice the large number of special fluorescent tubes that create the ultraviolet light.

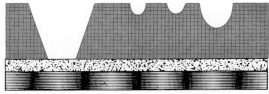

E.I. DU PONT DE NEMOURS

Fig. 67-10. The soluble non-exposed areas of the plate are washed away during the washout stage. Those areas made insoluble by hardening with ultraviolet light remain in relief.

material so that it will not wash away. This is called making the printing image insoluble. Specially designed exposure units are used for precurved plates (Fig. 67-9).

Washout is done right after exposure. The plate is put inside the washout machine and the door is closed. The plate is sprayed with a dilute

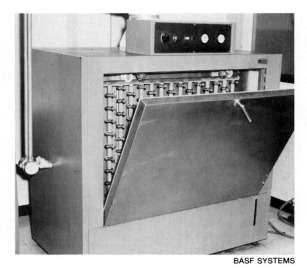

BASF SYSTEMS

Fig. 67-11. A washout machine containing many spray jets.

E.I. DU PONT DE NEMOURS

Fig. 67-12. Rigid flat photopolymer plates are used on cylinder letterpress machines.

solution of sodium hydroxide. This solution is made from 50 percent industrial grade caustic soda and water. The spray removes the parts of the plate that were not hardened by the ultraviolet light (Fig. 67-10). The washout machine has a large number of spray jets (Fig. 67-11). It goes through the complete processing cycle automatically.

Zinc original

Magnesium original

DYCRIL original

E.I. DU PONT DE NEMOURS

Fig. 67-13. Unretouched photomicrographs illustrate the high quality of photopolymer plates. Note the sharp edges, uniform shoulders, and the high relief of the image.

A processed plate is finished by trimming, beveling, or crimping the edges. This prepares it for use on the printing press.

USING THE PLATES

After plates are fully prepared, they can be attached to the printing press. Flat plates are attached to platen and cylinder presses (Fig. 67-12). Flexible and precurved plates are attached to rotary presses.

Photopolymer plates for letterpress use are better than metal ones (Fig. 67-13). Enlarged photographs show how the shoulders of the image areas are uniform. Also, the image surface is sharper, and transfers the ink more accurately.

UNIT 68 FLEXIBLE PHOTOPOLYMER RELIEF PLATES

Making flexible photopolymer relief plates is basically the same as making rigid photopolymer relief plates (see Unit 67). The differences depend on the company brand and the intended use of the plate. Each company that produces photopolymer relief plates gives specific instructions on how to make and use them.

FLEXIBLE LETTERPRESS PLATES

As the name implies, these plates are thin enough to attach easily to a press printing cylinder (Fig. 68-1). The photopolymer coating (emulsion) can be applied to several different support bases. These support materials include polyester film, aluminum, steel, and a special polymer composite material. The intended use determines which plate backing material to select.

The basic procedure used to make flexible photopolymer relief plates is shown in Figure 68-2. Processing these plates usually takes less than thirty minutes. Automated platemaking systems can turn out several plates an hour. Plates come in sizes to fit a variety of letterpress machines.

Once the plate is made, it can be mounted into the press. It is possible to attach plates to press cylinders of any size. Often presses have magnetic cylinders so that plates large and small can easily be positioned and held in place for printing (Fig. 68-3). For this system to work, the thin relief plates must have a conductive metal backing. It is possible for a 2-inch (5.08 cm) square plate to be held firmly in place during high-speed press runs. Magnetic cylinders save press makeready time and improve printing quality.

Flexible relief plates can also be attached to large printing belts (Fig. 68-4). Book-page-size plates are individually applied to the long flexible belt used on the *Cameron Book Production System.* This system is discussed in Section 10, Unit 82. A plate is made for each page of a book and applied to the long press belt with strong adhesive. The plates move through the press rapidly and transfer ink to the web of paper. Thousands of copies can be printed from these thin flexible letterpress plates.

E.I. DU PONT DE NEMOURS

Fig. 68-1. A steel-backed photopolymer wraparound plate being attached to a rotary letterpress.

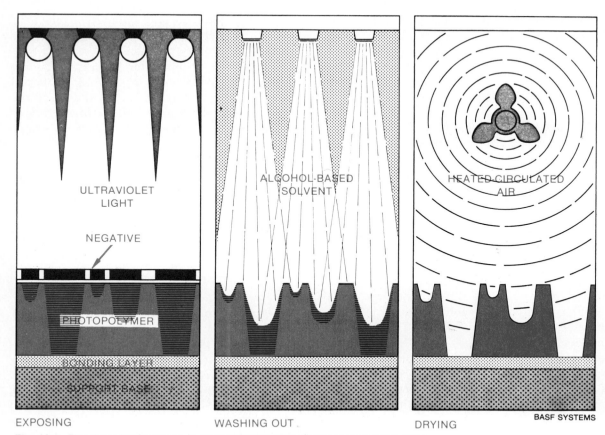

ULTRAVIOLET
LIGHT

NEGATIVE

PHOTOPOLYMER

BONDING LAYER

SUPPORT BASE

ALCOHOL-BASED
SOLVENT

HEATED CIRCULATED
AIR

EXPOSING   WASHING OUT   DRYING   BASF SYSTEMS

Fig. 68-2. The three basic stages in processing flexible photopolymer relief plates.

BUNTING MAGNETICS COMPANY

Fig. 68-3. A flexible photopolymer letterpress held in place with a magnetic printing cylinder on a small web press.

MIDLAND-ROSS CORPORATION

Fig. 68-4. A plate-mounting machine attachs flexible photopolymer relief plates to a special belt used on the *Cameron Book Production System.*

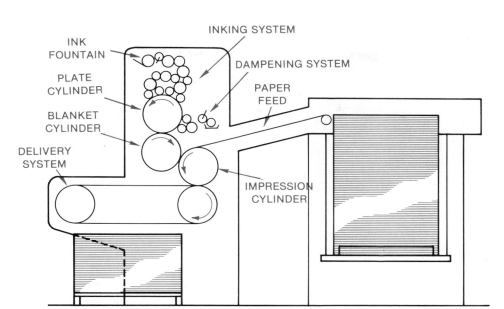

Fig. 68-5. A side view of a standard offset-lithography press.

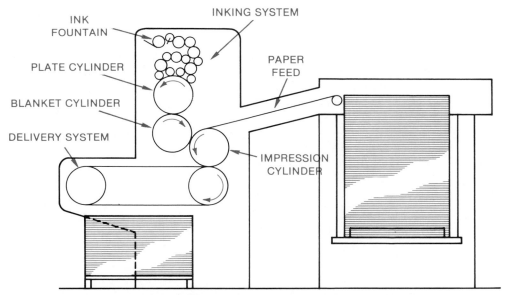

Fig. 68-6. A side view of a letterset press, a basic offset- lithography press without the dampening system.

LETTERSET PLATES

Letterset is a printing method that uses relief printing plates on an offset lithography printing press (see Section 13). Letterset does not need a dampening system as lithographic presses do. A standard lithographic press contains three main cylinders—plate, blanket, impression, a series of ink rollers, and a series of dampening rollers (Fig. 68-5). A letterset press contains the three cylinders and a series of ink rollers but does not have dampening rollers (Fig. 68-6).

Letterset plates have images in relief that transfer ink to the rubber blanket. Like a stan-

E.I. DU PONT DE NEMOURS

Fig. 68-7. Attaching a relief letterset plate to a specially designed offset press.

dard offset lithography press, the ink is then transferred to the paper. These plates usually have either polyester film or thin steel as the support for the photopolymer layer.

A letterset plate is attached to a press in the same way as a lithographic plate (Fig. 68-7). Using these special plates on an offset lithography press creates a process that technically should be called "offset letterpress." The plate cylinder of the lithographic press must be made smaller, or "undercut," to accept the thicker relief plate.

UNIT 69 STEREOTYPES AND ELECTROTYPES

Stereotypes and electrotypes are made by two different processes but both are used for the same purpose—to reproduce printed matter. Both plates are in the *duplicate* relief category because they must be made from original plates.

Stereotypes were made and used in the United States as early as 1813. The process itself dates back to Europe in the 1690s. The first electrotypes were made in 1840 to duplicate wood engravings. In the past, both of these plates played a major role in the graphic arts industry. Today, the graphic arts industry makes limited use of stereotypes and electrotypes, but it is still good to know the basic procedures for making them.

MAKING STEREOTYPES

The process of making a stereotype is basically simple (Fig. 69-1) but much research has perfected it. To make a stereotype, (1) type and

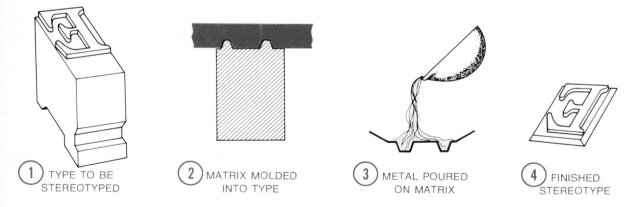

1. TYPE TO BE STEREOTYPED
2. MATRIX MOLDED INTO TYPE
3. METAL POURED ON MATRIX
4. FINISHED STEREOTYPE

Fig. 69-1. The basic stereotype process from the original image to the finished relief letterpress printing plate.

original image carriers are assembled, (2) a matrix or mold is formed, (3) the metal is poured on the matrix, and (4) a finished stereotype emerges.

The basic procedure

1. The type and original engravings are locked up, as outlined in Section 9. The engravings can be halftones or line illustrations. A good lockup must be obtained before proceeding to the next step.
2. A matrix of the type, halftones, and illustrations is then made (Fig. 69-2). The matrix material is made from wood pulp, rag fibers, and a filler, which is usually clay. This material is called matrix paper.
3. The moisture must be removed after the matrix or mat is made. If molten metal is poured against a wet matrix, the metal will form improperly. Special heating units are often used to dry the mats thoroughly.
4. The stereotype image carrier can now be cast. The mat is fastened to a flat or curved casting box and molten metal is poured against it. The metal, primarily lead, solidifies immediately. The casting can be removed from the casting box after pouring.
5. After casting, the flat and curved stereotype is cut to size using special saws.
6. The stereotype is planed to a predetermined thickness on a plate shaver. This is necessary to get exact type-high image carrier.
7. Excess metal is removed in the non-image areas with a router (Fig. 69-3). If this step is not completed, portions of the non-image areas may reproduce, causing poor reproductions.

After routing, the stereotype casting is ready for the press. Several curved castings are prepared for large rotary presses (Fig. 69-4).

MAKING ELECTROTYPES

Electrotype image carriers are metal reproductions of type, photographs, and illustrations. Electrotypes are made by depositing or plating

Fig. 69-2. A stereotype matrix or mat made by a heavy-duty roller. Mats are also made by direct pressure.

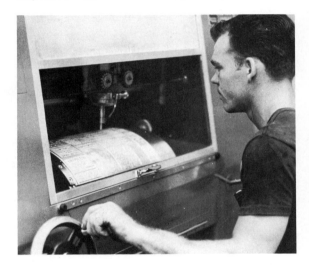

Fig. 69-3. A curved stereotype casting being routed on a completely enclosed unit.

Fig. 69-4. Prepared stereotype castings ready to be used on a high-speed rotary press.

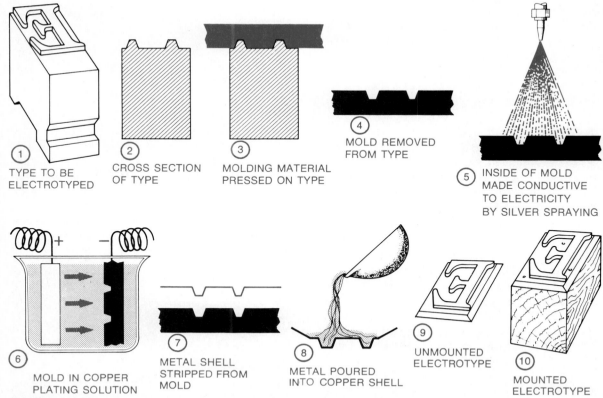

Fig. 69-5. The basic steps involved in producing an electrotype printing plate.

metal on a mold by the electrolysis or electro-chemical process.

The basic process for making an electrotype is illustrated in Figure 69-5. Graphic material to be electrotyped is molded in specially prepared material (steps 1 through 4). Silver or graphite is then applied to the mold to make it conduct electricity (step 5). The mold is hung in a tank of plating solution and the electrical connections are made.

Current is turned on and electrolysis takes place, forming multilayers of copper on the mold (step 6). The copper shell is stripped from the mold (step 7).

A metal supporting-material is applied to the back of the copper shell (step 8) and is shaved to proper thickness. The result is either an unmounted electrotype (step 9) or a mounted one (step 10).

UNIT 70 FLEXOGRAPHIC PRINTING PLATES

Flexographic printing is a relief method of printing. It had its beginnings in 1952. The word *flexography* was used to describe a printing method using flexible rubber printing plates on a rotary letterpress unit. Rapid drying, fluid inks are used.

Rubber plates are still used with flexographic printing, but in 1974 a photopolymer flexographic printing plate was introduced to the industry. Photopolymer is a very effective material for transferring fluid inks to various materials. A major advantage of photopolymer flexographic plates over rubber ones is that each plate is an original. Rubber flexographic plates, made by the traditional molding process, are considered duplicate plates and there is some loss in quality (Fig. 70-1). Quality printing can be obtained from both methods of flexographic platemaking. Products often printed with flexographic plates include paper bags, business forms, envelopes, food cartons, packaging materials made of transparent film, milk cartons, and many others (Fig. 70-2).

PHOTOPOLYMER FLEXOGRAPHIC PLATES

Photopolymer plates were created to overcome some problems with the traditional rubber

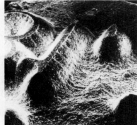

BASF SYSTEMS

Fig. 70-1. Enlargement of the image formation with (left) photopolymer and (right) molded rubber flexographic printing plates.

Fig. 70-2. Typical products printed with photopolymer flexographic printing plates.

plates. Photopolymer material was used because it could be made very sensitive to ultraviolet light. It could be bonded to a strong support material like polyester to make a stable but very lightweight and flexible plate.

A photopolymer flexographic plate is made of several layers (Fig. 70-3). The protective outer foils guard the relief and base layers against damage and soiling. The relief material layer is the light-sensitive photopolymer that will take the image. The stabilizing foil is often made of polyester and keeps the plate dimensionally stable. The backing material absorbs excess printing pressure and helps to prevent damage to the image areas.

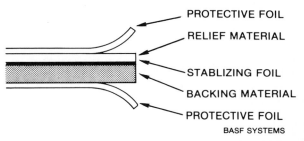

PROTECTIVE FOIL
RELIEF MATERIAL
STABLIZING FOIL
BACKING MATERIAL
PROTECTIVE FOIL

BASF SYSTEMS

Fig. 70-3. The several layers of a photopolymer flexographic plate.

Producing photopolymer flexographic plates

Processing steps for producing photopolymer flexographic plates vary, depending upon the manufacturer and type of plate, but six steps are typical (Fig. 70-4).

1. The back of the plate is exposed to ultraviolet light to harden the support material.
2. A film negative is placed over the light-sensitive photopolymer relief plate material. The negative can have either a line or halftone image, but it must have excellent density. Ultraviolet light is used in the exposure unit; it passes through the negative's transparent image areas and hardens the photopolymer.
3. The wash-out step is done to remove the unhardened (unexposed) polymer material. This leaves the hardened image areas in relief.
4. In the drying step, time and temperature are important. Plates not dried enough

1. PRE-EXPOSURE:

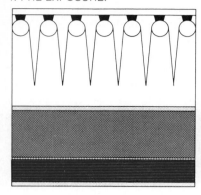

2. EXPOSURE:

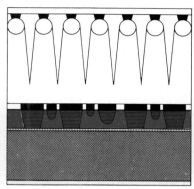

3. WASH-OUT:

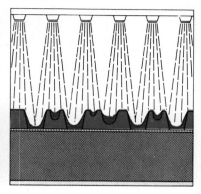

4. DRYING:

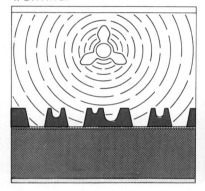

5. AFTERTREATMENT:

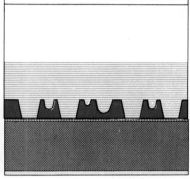

6. RE-EXPOSURE

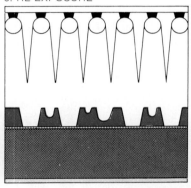

BASF SYSTEMS

Fig. 70-4. The six basic steps in the production of photopolymer flexographic printing plates.

may swell and become unlevel. Too much heat may cause plates to change dimensions.

5. To remove plate tackiness, the relief plate is immersed in a special solution.

6. An overall exposure of the plate to ultraviolet light is then made to harden all visible areas. This completes the curing of the plate and makes it ready for use.

RUBBER FLEXOGRAPHIC PLATES

Making rubber flexographic plates needs a mold, heat, and pressure to obtain a relief image. Rubber once was thought to be the best material to accept and transfer the special fluid printing inks to packaging containers and materials. As we have seen, photopolymers are now being used but rubber is still important in flexography.

Making a rubber flexographic plate is similar to making a rubber stamp (see Unit 71). The type form, including photoengravings, must be prepared and locked in a chase. A mold is made from a special material that gives a positive reading image that is sunken. The rubber layer is then placed over the mold and heat and pressure are applied. The rubber is pressed into the mold, giving a relief image. The rubber plates must then be mounted on material appropriate for the kind of press being used. A press with magnetic cylinders needs plates with a thin steel backing (Fig. 70-5). These plates will stay in their proper positions while being used to print at high speeds.

Rubber design rollers are used to print continuous images (Fig. 70-6). Typical products

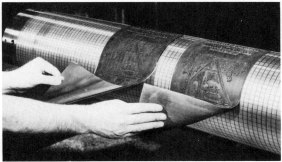

BUNTING MAGNETICS COMPANY

Fig. 70-5. Rubber printing plates with a thin steel support being positioned on a magnetic printing cylinder.

MOSSTYPE

Fig. 70-6. Rubber design rollers ready for printing continuous and non-continuous images on such products as wallpaper, gift wrap, and paper bags.

MOSSTYPE

Fig. 70-7. Fastening a rubber flexographic plate on a printing cylinder using an optical mounter and proofing machine.

printed in this way are wallpaper, wrapping paper, and paper bags. These rollers must be carefully made using highly specialized techniques (Fig. 70-7). These rubber plates are vulcanized to a special rubber base, which in turn is vulcanized to the press cylinder (roller). This procedure keeps the rubber plate in position during the high speed press runs.

LASER ENGRAVED FLEXOGRAPHIC CYLINDERS AND ROLLERS

Figures 70-8 and 70-9 show a laser engraving system. The artwork is mounted on a drum and scanned by a low-power laser. The resulting information is sent to a computer. The data stored in the computer is sent to the engraving unit so that the printing cylinder can be engraved in one continuous operation. In addition, the computer (Fig. 70-10) can be used to generate a pattern such as graph-paper lines. Direct image information can also be sent to the computer from electronic composition systems (see Unit 33). The controlling computer also allows an operator to prepare the next engraving job while a cylinder is being engraved.

The relief printing image is engraved by a high-power carbon dioxide laser, in rubber, ceramic, or another suitable substrate. This powerful laser can be controlled very precisely. Non-image material is selectively removed with great accuracy from the printing cylinder. Computer-controlled flexographic engraving equipment can be refined to the smallest detail. This enables high-quality flexographic printing cylinders to be made rapidly and accurately.

This system permits perfectly sized and positioned artwork to be engraved around the relief printing cylinder (Fig. 70-11). Step-and-repeat, or multiple images of the same artwork, can be easily created in flexographic printing plate cylinders.

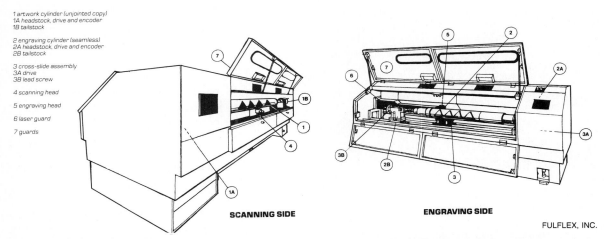

1 artwork cylinder (unjointed copy)
1A headstock, drive and encoder
1B tailstock

2 engraving cylinder (seamless)
2A headstock, drive and encoder
2B tailstock

3 cross-slide assembly
3A drive
3B lead screw

4 scanning head

5 engraving head

6 laser guard

7 guards

SCANNING SIDE

ENGRAVING SIDE

FULFLEX, INC.

Fig. 70-9. The major parts of laser scanning and engraving equipment used to prepare high quality flexographic printing rollers and cylinders.

ZED INSTRUMENTS AND FULFLEX INC.

Fig. 70-8. The major parts of laser scanning and engraving equipment used to prepare high quality flexographic printing rollers and cylinders.

COHERENT/LASER DIVISION

Fig. 70-11. An example of laser engraving. Note the exceptional quality and detail of the several different images.

ZED INSTRUMENTS AND FULFLEX INC.

Fig. 70-10. A computer is used to input data into the laser engraving system shown in figure 70-9.

UNIT 71 RUBBER STAMP MAKING

Making rubber stamps is very similar to making standard rubber flexographic plates for flexography presses. Rubber stamps are known to almost everyone because they are used in nearly every business establishment as well as in homes. They carry everyday messages like *Rush, Do Not Drop*, and *Special Handling*. The procedure for molding rubber stamps is outlined in this unit.

RUBBER STAMP PRESS

A rubber stamp press consists of two flat surfaces or platens parallel to each other, heating elements for each platen, and levers to force the two platens together (Fig. 71-1). Several companies manufacture small stamp presses. See the operator's manual for the specific procedure for operating each machine.

Press parts and uses

Top and bottom platens. These are the heated working surfaces that close when forming the matrix and the rubber stamp.

Platen levers. These two levers raise the bottom platen. The top platen is stationary.

Platen spacers. These tubular devices allow the two platens to be closed precisely the same amount each time.

Chase. This rectangular device is used to hold the type securely while the matrix is being made.

Compensating block. This is a thick rectangular metal block used in place of the type when the rubber stamp is being formed from the matrix.

Shim plates. These are used to protect the face of the platens. The plastic matrix material and gum rubber will stick to the platens if these are not used. Shim plates are also used to add thickness when necessary.

Preheat area. The compensating block, chase, and type are placed on this area for preheating before making the matrix and rubber stamp.

MOLDING RUBBER STAMPS

1. Compose the typeform. If available, use special heat-resistant type when making a rubber stamp. Because of the heat, standard foundry type may smash when the matrix is being made. Remember to proof the typeform.
2. Plug in the press. Heat until the platens reach approximately 300° F (149° C).
3. Lock up the typeform in the chase (Fig. 71-2). Use the procedure outlined in Unit 77. Be sure to place type-high bearers on each side of the line of type. There should be a minimum of one pica between the type

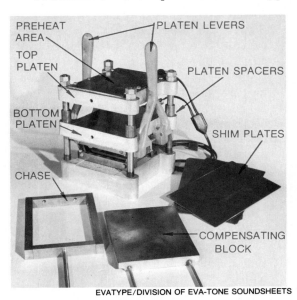

EVATYPE/DIVISION OF EVA-TONE SOUNDSHEETS

Fig. 71-1. A small rubber-stamp molding press.

and each bearer. The bearers prevent the typeform from being smashed while you are making the matrix.

4. Cut a piece of matrix board ¼-inch (6.35 mm) larger on all four sides of the typeform, including the bearers.

5. Place the chase and locked-up type form on the hot compensating block. It should rest on the preheat area of the press (Fig. 71-3) for at least 5 minutes.

6. Place the cut-to-size matrix board on the locked-up typeform. Note the correct side of the matrix board.

7. Place a shim plate on the matrix board.

8. Open the platen of the hot press and insert a shim plate on the bottom platen.

9. Place the chase, matrix board, and shim plate between the platens (Fig. 71-4). Check the edges of the shim plates. They should be clear of the corner posts so they will not be clamped between the platen spacers and the platens.

10. Let the typeform and matrix board heat for 2 minutes. Do not close the platens.

11. After the 2-minute period, close the platens until the top platen touches the shim plate. Let the press stay in this position for a few seconds.

12. Close the platens gently until they come in contact with the platen spacers (Fig. 71-5). Do not force the platen levers down. This could damage the type and result in a poor matrix. The press should stay in this position for ten minutes to let the matrix board cure completely.

13. Raise the platen levers after the 10-minute heating period.

14. Remove the entire contents from between the platens. Pry the finished matrix from the typeform with a screwdriver or similar instrument (Fig. 71-6). Be very careful not to damage the type or the newly formed matrix.

Vulcanizing the rubber die

1. Remove all shim plates from between the platens.

2. Heat the press and compensating block, if necessary.

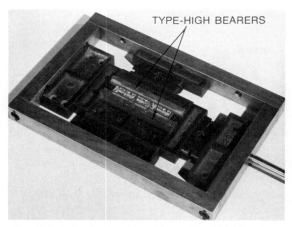

Fig. 71-2. A typeform properly locked in the rubber-stamp press chase (see Unit 77 for lockup procedure).

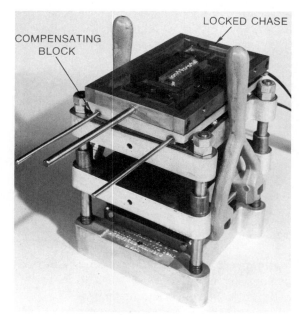

Fig. 71-3. Preheating the locked typeform.

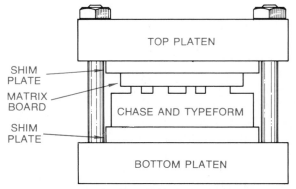

Fig. 71-4. Proper position for the matrix assembly.

Fig. 71-5. The platen in a closed position.

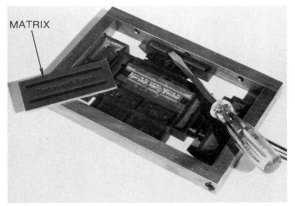

Fig. 71-6. The completed matrix removed from the typeform.

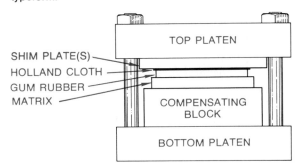

Fig. 71-7. The proper position for rubber vulcanizing assembly.

3. Cut a piece of gum rubber ¼-inch (6.35mm) larger than the type area in the matrix.
4. Remove the holland cloth from the gum rubber. Powder the newly exposed side liberally with release powder.
5. Place the gum rubber, powdered side down, on the matrix.
6. Place the matrix and gum rubber on the compensating block.

7. Place the holland cloth and a shim plate on top of the gum rubber. The holland cloth keeps the rubber from sticking to the shim plate.
8. Open the platens and insert the materials in the press (Fig. 71-7).
9. Close the platens until the top one touches the shim plate. Hold the press like this for a few seconds, then slowly close the platens completely. The rubber should vulcanize for 8 minutes.
10. Open the platens. Remove the contents by carefully pulling the rubber stamp die from the matrix (Fig. 71-8).
11. Let the rubber stamp die cool.

Mounting the die

1. Trim excess rubber as close as possible to the raised letters.
2. Select the proper width of cushion mounting block.
3. Cut a piece of mounting block the length of the rubber die.
4. Coat the cushion mounting block and the rubber die with rubber cement. Allow the rubber cement to dry on both surfaces.
5. Put the rubber die in the correct position on the cushion mounting. Press it firmly into place.
6. Test the rubber stamp (Fig. 71-9).

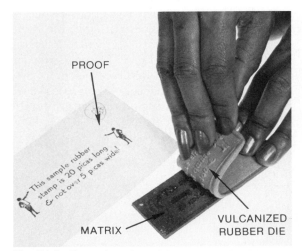

Fig. 71-8. Removing the rubber stamp die from the matrix.

7. Put an identification label in the window area of the mounting block.

MOLDING COMMERCIAL RUBBER-IMAGE CARRIERS

Large rubber image carriers used for standard letterpresses and flexography presses are made in the same way as rubber stamps. The main difference in the manufacture of large image carriers and rubber stamps is in the size of the equipment used. Hydraulic-operated molding presses with automated controls (Fig. 71-10) are used instead of the small molding presses used for rubber stamps. Control features on heavy-duty molding presses (Fig. 71-11) include microprocessor-based timers for preheat and cure periods. The heating platens can be either electrically

MOHAWK INDUSTRIES, INC.

Fig. 71-10. An automatic molding press.

Fig. 71-9. A completed rubber stamp and test print.

heated or drilled and channeled for use with steam or hot oil from external sources. The exact platen temperature is clearly displayed using light-emitting diode (LED) lights. Temperatures can be accurately controlled from very low heat up to 350°F. Automation through computerization gives operators precise control of every aspect of the process used to make rubber printing plates containing the full range of image detail.

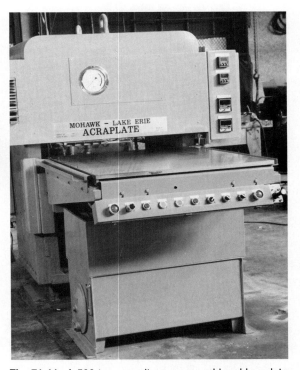

Fig. 71-11. A 500 ton capacity programmable rubber plate molding press.

UNIT 72 CREATING LINOLEUM BLOCKS

Wood blocks, wood cuts, and wood engravings have served as image carriers for many centuries. Before movable type was invented, entire pages of words were hand carved from wood to form the image carrier. Pictures or illustrations were also carved into this material to be reproduced. Even afer the invention of movable type, wood blocks were the only method that could be used to reproduce pictures.

The first peoples to experiment with block printing were the Chinese, Syrians, and Egyptians. They also attempted to use stone blocks. Actual block prints from as early as the eight and ninth centuries have been found in China and Japan. The earliest known wood blocks in Europe were used in approximately the fifteenth century.

Today, hand-cut block prints are seldom used in the commercial graphic arts because more sophisticated image carriers are available. These were discussed in previous units. Some hobbyists and craftsmen, however, prefer to cut their own blocks because of the economy and the personal pride of accomplishment.

Linoleum is the common material used today for block printing because it is easier to cut than wood. It is economical and has a smooth texture that gives excellent image transfer. For students of graphic arts, linoleum blocks provide an economical way to get an understanding of relief image transfer.

ILLUSTRATIONS FOR LINOLEUM BLOCK

Illustrations must be kept simple because linoleum blocks are cut by hand. Beginners should cut simple, basic designs, but with experience, more detail can be added to the block cut.

The positive design (Fig. 72-1) shows the illustration as a solid print or a silhouette. Little attempt is made to show detail.

The negative design shows a different illustration reversed from the positive (Fig. 72-2). The image area has been cut away. The background has been printed to form the outside edges of the illustration. The color of the image is the same as the paper color, but the background could be reproduced in any tint.

The *line-positive* design (Fig. 72-3) shows the illustration as lines only. Narrow border lines and detail lines have been left in relief; all the background has been removed. This type of illustration has a disadvantage—it may collapse under pressure during printing.

The *line-negative* design (Fig. 72-4) shows the illustration as narrow white or paper-color lines. Narrow portions of the linoleum have been removed so that they cannot print with this

Fig. 72-1. A positive design.

Fig. 72-2. A negative design.

Fig. 72-3. A line-positive design.

Fig. 72-4. A line-negative design.

Fig. 72-5. A linoleum block cut showing the four basic types of design.

type of design, there are no problems with breakage or collapse of lines.

Detail and emphasis can be added to the illustration if a combination of all four basic methods of design are used (Fig. 72-5). A well-cut linoleum block reproduction is sometimes hard to tell from one produced chemically or mechanically.

CUTTING

1. Select or develop an illustration.
2. Transfer the illustration to a plain sheet of white typing paper. Darken the area that will reproduce.
3. Reverse the illustration by placing the paper upside down on the light table. Trace the image. (The illustration must be reversed before it is transferred to the lino-leum block. Otherwise, the illustration will reproduce backward. This step could be omitted if the illustration were symmetrical.)
4. Transfer the illustration to the linoleum block. Place a sheet of carbon paper on the linoleum block. Place the reversed illustration on top of the carbon paper, then apply firm pressure on the pencil while tracing the illustration.
5. Place the linoleum block on a bench hook (Fig. 72-6) (1) to insure safety and (2) to provide firmness. Linoleum-block cutting tools are sharp and a slip of the hand could cause an injury. The bench hook also helps to hold the block while the image is being cut; it lets you keep your hands behind the sharp cutter tool. The block can be held firmly in place for more accurate cutting.
6. Select the smallest V-shaped cutter (called

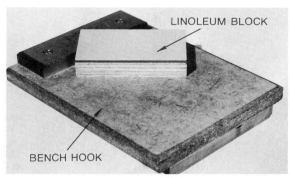

Fig. 72-6. A linoleum block properly positioned in a bench hook.

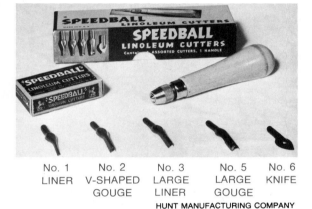

HUNT MANUFACTURING COMPANY

Fig. 72-7. A common set of linoleum-block cutting tools.

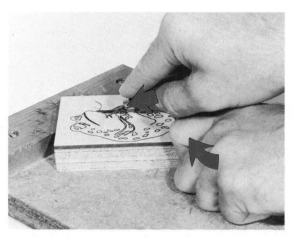

Fig. 72-8. Using a liner cutting tool to cut around the entire illustration.

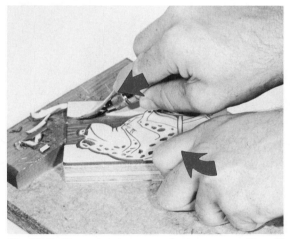

Fig. 72-9. Removing large non-image areas with a U-shaped gouge.

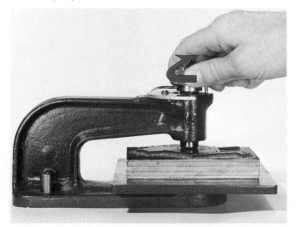

Fig. 72-10. Using a type-high gauge to determine block height. Just as for foundry type, it must be 0.918-inch high.

a liner) from a set of common cutting tools (Fig. 72-7).

7. Cut around the illustration (Fig. 72-8). Do not attempt to cut too deeply with the liner. The purpose of this first cut is to make a clean edge around the image area. NOTE: keep the hands behind the cutting tool.

8. Use a V-shaped gouge to cut the lines deeper. Do not cut on the image side of the narrow (liner) cut.

9. Remove all other non-image areas with the appropriate size U-shaped gouge (Fig. 72-9). The farther from the image it is, the deeper the cut must be. The nonimage areas may print if the cuts are not sufficiently deep.

10. Make the block type-high (0.918 inch) before it is proofed. Use a type-high gauge (Fig. 72-10) to determine accurately the proper backing needed. Use chip board and other papers of varying thicknesses to bring the block to the proper height.

11. Proof the linoleum block in a standard proofpress. Place the block in a galley, ink the image, and pull a proof just as if it were a standard typeform.

12. Make necessary corrections in the linoleum cut and reproof it. The linoleum block is now ready to be used on a platen or cylinder letterpress.

UNIT 73 LEARNING EXPERIENCES: LETTERPRESS IMAGE CARRIERS

KEY TERMS

Unit 64

First-generation plate
Image carrier
Laser engraving

Second-generation plate
Wraparound plate

Unit 66

Copper
Magnesium

Photoengraving
Zinc

Unit 67

Carbon dioxide conditioning
Heat sensitizing
Insoluble

Photopolymer
Photosensitizing
Sensitization
Ultraviolet

Unit 68

Flexible letterpress plate
Letterset

Offset-letterpress
Undercut (cylinder)

Unit 69

Casting box
Electrolysis
Electrochemical

Electrotype
Matrix
Stereotype

Unit 70

Flexographic plate
Flexography
Laser

Microprocessor
Vulcanized

Unit 71

Holland cloth
Matrix board

Mounting block
Rubber stamp

Unit 72

Wood block
Wood cut

Wood engraving

DISCUSSION TOPICS

1. Identify the several materials, metallic and non-metallic, that are used to produce letterpress image carriers.
2. According to research, when do most accidents occur in the school laboratory?
3. Why are printing presses equipped with magnetic cylinders?
4. How is the laser used in preparing flexographic printing rollers?
5. Why should a special heat-resistant type be used in the rubber stamp press?

ACTIVITIES

Units 64, 66–70

1. Obtain a sample of each kind of letterpress image carrier. These samples can be

obtained in local commercial graphic arts concerns if they are not available in your school graphic arts laboratory. Mount and build each image carrier to type-high. Proof each image carrier under the same proofing conditions. Using a magnifying glass, compare the results of each proof. Also carefully inspect the several image carriers and compare them with each other.

2. Visit several commercial graphic arts companies. Ask to see their production facilities for letterpress image carriers. Carefully observe the steps for producing each kind of first-generation and second-generation letterpress image carrier. Compare the methods used in each commercial concern and discuss them in class.

Unit 71

3. Prepare a rubber stamp. Compose the type, prepare the matrix, vulcanize the rubber, and mount the stamp. Carefully compare your stamp with a commercially made stamp. What qualities does a commercially made stamp have that yours does not, and vice versa?

Unit 72

4. Cut a linoleum block. Obtain or draw an illustration, transfer it to the linoleum, cut away the nonimage areas, make the block type-high, and proof the image. Carefully study the proof and make needed corrections until the linoleum block proof is a close reproduction of the original illustration. Retain the linoleum block until you have studied Section 10. You can then produce copies from the linoleum block.

Locking up a typeform in a skeleton chase on an imposing table.

LETTERPRESS IMPOSITION

INTRODUCTION TO LETTERPRESS LOCKUP AND IMPOSITION

Typeforms, or blocks of composed type, must be held tightly in metal frames so that they can be placed in a printing press. The frame that holds the type is called a *chase*. The procedure of putting typeforms in a chase and tightening them is called *lockup*. *Imposition* is placing the typeforms in relation to one another in the chase. This step makes sure that the printed pages will be in the proper order.

For many years lockup and imposition were done on a flat stone table, often one made from marble. Today the *imposing table* (still sometimes called an imposing stone) is made from steel. Lockup and imposition requires skillful and accurate work.

Several different kinds and sizes of typeforms can be printed on the same letterpress printing press. In one situation, only one typeform may need to be printed on a sheet of paper (Fig. 74-1). In another, two or more typeforms may have to be printed on the same sheet (Fig. 74-2).

Type is arranged in imposition so that it will print in the proper position on the printing

Fig. 74-2. Locking up several pages of type that will all be printed on a single sheet of paper.

Fig. 74-1. Locking up a single page for printing on the press.

Fig. 74-3. A page for a newspaper that has been locked up to make a stereotype mat.

CHALLENGE MACHINERY COMPANY

Fig. 74-4. A lockup to be used for making an electrotype plate.

press. The person doing the lockup and imposition must be familiar with the tools and procedures and with the operation of the printing press on which the type will be printed.

Typeforms also are locked up to make *stereotype* and *electrotype* plates (see Unit 69). These are made to duplicate original typeforms (Figs. 74-3 and 74-4). In this unit, we will discuss only methods of locking up type to be printed directly on a press. However, the procedures are basically the same as those used for locking up typeforms for making duplicate plates.

UNIT 75 TOOLS AND EQUIPMENT

Similar tools and equipment are used in most graphic arts companies for letterpress lockup and imposition. The tools should be kept in good working condition. The tools and equipment must also be organized for efficient use when making a lockup.

IMPOSING TABLE AND BASE

Modern *imposing tables* are metal surfaces on which the lockup process is done (Fig. 75-1). The top of the table has been machined to be as accurate as the bed of the press on which the type will be printed. The steel top has a rabbeted (recessed) edge on which the open side of a galley can rest while the typeform is moved from the table to a galley. The imposing table surface should periodically be lightly oiled to prevent rust.

Several styles of bases are used as supports for the imposing table. While the main purpose of the base is to establish a satisfactory working height, it is also used to store lockup equipment: chases, furniture, reglets, and galleys. Most bases also include a drawer and shelves to store quoins, quoin keys, type-wash containers, and planer blocks (Fig. 75-2). These terms are explained below.

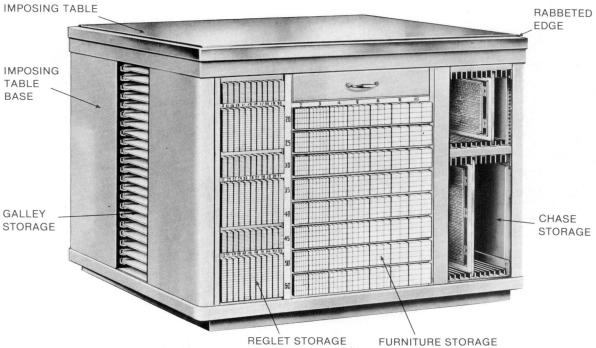

IMPOSING TABLE

IMPOSING TABLE BASE

GALLEY STORAGE

RABBETED EDGE

CHASE STORAGE

REGLET STORAGE   FURNITURE STORAGE

Fig. 75-1. An imposing table and the front side of a typical imposing-table base.

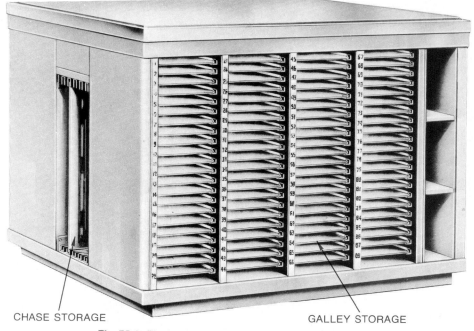

CHASE STORAGE

GALLEY STORAGE

Fig. 75-2. The back side of the base shown in Figure 75-1.

CHASES

A *chase* is a rectangular frame made from cast iron or steel. It is clamped into a platen press after type has been locked into it (Fig. 75-3).

Chases are sized to fit different presses. There are also several kinds of chases available for most presses. Figure 75-4 shows a *standard*

Fig. 75-3. Clamping a chase with a lockup into a small platen press.

Fig. 75-4. A standard chase for a platen press. Not all chases have handles at the top.

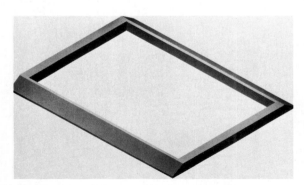

Fig. 75-5. A skeleton chase for a platen press.

chase for a platen press. It is used for most lock-ups. The standard chase often has handles at the top for easier handling. The *skeleton chase* in Figure 75-5 is the same size outside as the standard one but is larger inside. It is useful for locking up large amounts of type. The spider chase in Figure 75-6 is a special kind used to lockup small typeforms.

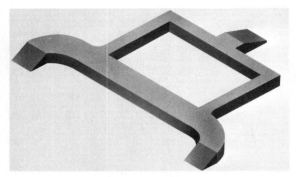

Fig. 75-6. A spider chase for a platen press.

The bottom (back) of the chase must be flat. If it gets warped, locking up and printing with the typeform will be very difficult.

FURNITURE AND REGLETS

Wood and metal blocks, called *furniture*, are used to fill the space between the typeform and the inside edge of the chase. Figure 75-7 shows an example of a lockup in which light-weight metal furniture is used to fill the space between the typeform and the chase.

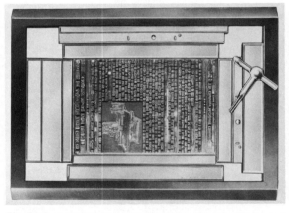

Fig. 75-7. A locked up typeform using metal furniture and high-speed quoins.

Several sizes of wood and metal furniture are available (Fig. 75-8 and 75-9). Furniture is stored in racks, according to standard pica lengths and widths (Figs. 75-1 and 75-10). These standard widths are 2, 3, 4, 5, 6, 8, and 10 picas. Standard lengths of furniture are 10, 15, 20, 25, 30, 35, 40, 45, 50, and 60 picas. Furniture can also be ordered in longer lengths when needed.

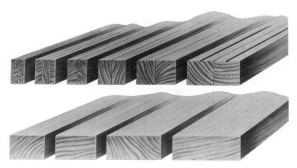

Fig. 75-8. End view of wood furniture and reglets.

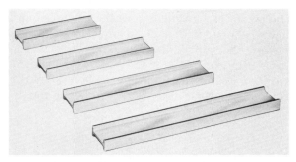

Fig. 75-9. Lightweight metal furniture.

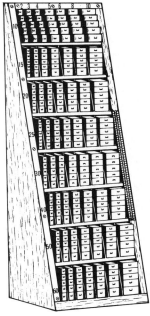

Fig. 75-10. A furniture rack used to store and organize wood furniture. Similar racks are used for metal furniture.

The length of the furniture is stamped on one end of each piece.

Reglets are thin pieces of wood furniture. They are stored in racks similar to those used for regular furniture (Fig. 75-10). Reglets are 6 and 12 points thick and vary in length in single-pica units from 10 to 60. They are often used as line spacing as well as for lockup.

QUOINS AND QUOIN KEYS

Quoins (pronounced *coins*) are metal devices that expand to tighten the furniture against the typeform and the chase. Wedge-shaped quoins (Fig. 75-11) and cam-type quoins (Fig. 75-12)

Fig. 75-11. A common wedge quoin.

Fig. 75-12. Cam quoins and a quoin key.

are used primarily for small typeforms. High-speed quoins, shown in Figure 75-13, are made in several sizes. They are extremely useful in locking up large forms and when a typeform must be placed very accurately so that it prints in a specific location on the paper (called printing in *register*).

The scale located on top of the high-speed quoin (Fig. 75-13) permits the person using it to tighten the quoin to a specific tension. When the quoin must be loosened for corrections, it

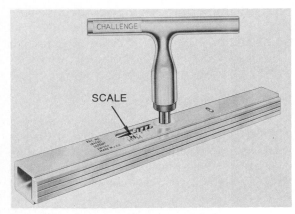

Fig. 75-13. High-speed quoin and key.

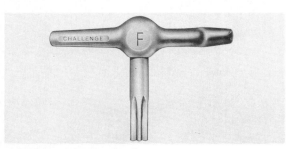

Fig. 75-14. A quoin key.

can be retightened so that the typeform is in exactly the same original position.

Quoin keys are tools used to tighten (expand) or loosen quoins. Each kind of quoin has a specific key (Fig. 75-14).

PLANER BLOCK

The *planer block* is a solid block of hard wood with one flat surface (Fig. 75-15). After the typeform has been locked up, the flat surface of the planer block is placed on the typeform and lightly tapped with a quoin key or mallet. This pushes the type characters and slugs in the typeform down. This makes the feet touch the steel surface of the imposing table so that the typeforms are perfectly level across the top.

Fig. 75-15. A planer block.

UNIT 76 KINDS OF LOCKUPS

Nearly all typeforms, regardless of size or shape, are locked up by one of two lockup methods: the *chaser* method or the *furniture-within-furniture* method. The only difference between the two is in where the first four pieces of furniture are placed around the typeform.

CHASER METHOD

A common method of locking up a typeform is the chaser method. This is better for typeforms whose measurements are not in standard pica lengths of furniture.

1. To begin the chaser method of locking up, measure the typeform to find its dimensions in picas. Figure 76-1 shows a typeform of 23 by 27 picas.

2. Select four pieces of furniture. Two should be longer than the ends (top and bottom) of the typeform; two should be slightly longer than the sides.

3. Place the furniture around the typeform. One end of each piece should be placed next to the corner of the typeform. The opposite end should extend past the other end of the typeform (Fig. 76-2). When all of the furniture is around the typeform, the edge of one piece should overlap the end of the next. The pieces of furniture appear to be chasing each other around the typeform (Fig. 76-2).

Fig. 76-1. Measure a typeform to find the proper length furniture for the chaser method of lockup.

Fig. 76-3. Measuring a typeform for the furniture-within-furniture lockup method.

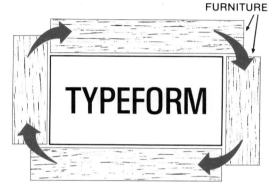

Fig. 76-2. The placement of the first four pieces of furniture around the typeform using the chaser method.

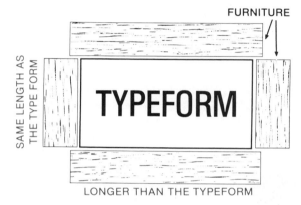

Fig. 76-4. The first four pieces in place for the furniture-within-furniture lockup method.

FURNITURE-WITHIN-FURNITURE METHOD

The furniture-within-furniture method is used with typeforms that have been composed to lengths that match standard pica lengths of furniture (10, 15, 20, etc.). Some printers prefer this method because of its stability. However, it cannot be used in as many situations as the chaser method.

1. To begin the furniture-within-furniture method of locking up, measure the typeform. The length of the ends of the typeform must equal standard pica length furniture before this method can be used. The dimensions of the typeform in Figure 76-3 are 24 by 30 picas.
2. Select four pieces of furniture. Two should be equal to the length of the ends of the typeform. The other two should be slightly longer than the sides.
3. Put the funiture around the typeform. The first two pieces should be placed at the ends so that the corners of the furniture are next to the corners of the typeform. The other

two are placed next to the sides of the form so they overlap the ends of the furniture at the ends of the typeform, as shown in Figure 76-4.

PLANING THE LOCKED-UP TYPEFORM

A locked-up typeform should always be made smooth and even across the top before printing. This procedure is called *planing*. The purpose of planing is to push down the type characters so that all the faces are at the same level (in the same plane). Typeforms that have not been planed, or have been improperly planed, could cause press makeready problems or damaged type.

To plane the locked-up typeform, place it in a flat position on the imposing table. Then adjust the quoins until the furniture is snug against the type. Be sure that the quoins are not too tight or too loose. Place the planer block on the top of the typeform and tap the planer lightly with a quoin key or mallet. Move the planer over the typeform to be sure that all type characters have been covered. Be careful, because type can be damaged if the planer is hit too hard or if it is not absolutely flat on the typeform. Tighten the quoins after the typeform has been planed.

After the typeform has been locked up, store it for later printing or place it directly in the press for immediate printing. Take special care when handling the lock-up. Type can be damaged quite easily, and any sudden jolt could pi (scramble) it.

UNIT 77 LOCKUP PROCEDURE

Every typeform uses almost the same lockup procedure. The only difference is where the first four pieces of furniture are placed around the typeform, as discussed in Unit 76. Before starting to make the lockup, all lines in the typeform must be justified. That is, they must be the same length. The typeform should be tied securely with a string to hold its parts together when it is moved to the imposing table.

LOCKUP

1. Clean the steel surface of the imposing table. Even a small bit of dirt under any type character can cause *embossing* (a raised type character). Dirt also causes excessive wear on the type character or slug.

2. Move the typeform from the galley to the imposing table (Fig. 77-1). Handle it very carefully, using both hands, so that you do not pi the typeform.

3. Place the appropriate chase over the typeform (Fig. 77-2). One of the long edges should be nearest you. The long edge of the chase that is farthest from you should be the *top* of the chase.

4. Position the typeform. If the head (top) is to be printed parallel to the short edge of the sheet of paper, place it to your *left* (Fig. 77-3). If the head is to be printed parallel to the long edge of the sheet, place it *nearest* you (Fig. 77-4).

5. Position the typeform in approximately the center of the chase. A smaller form can be positioned a little nearer the top of the

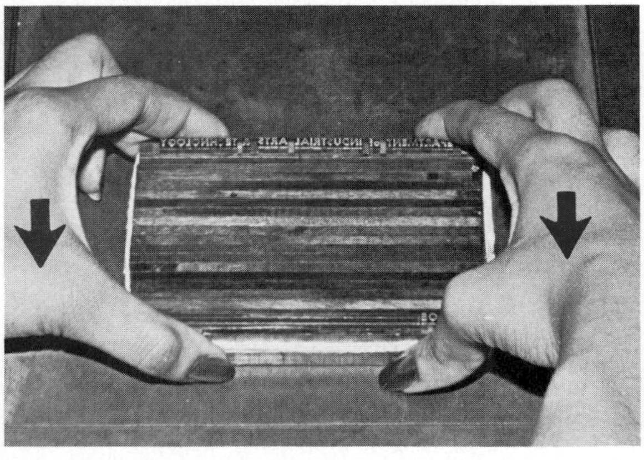

Fig. 77-1. Moving the typeform from the galley to the imposing stone.

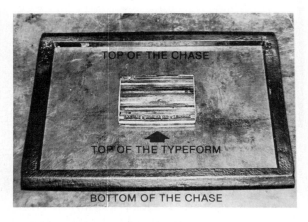

TOP OF THE CHASE

TOP OF THE TYPEFORM

BOTTOM OF THE CHASE

Fig. 77-2. A chase placed around the typeform.

Fig. 77-3. If the typeform is to be printed parallel to the short edge of the paper, the top of the form should be to your left.

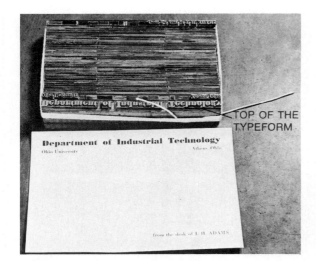

Fig. 77-4. If the typeform is to be printed parallel to the long edge of a sheet of paper, the top of the typeform should be nearest you.

chase to make feeding the press easier. When a typeform is to be printed at one end or on a corner of a piece of paper, position it

so the paper will be in the center of the platen of the press.

6. Decide what kind of lockup is right for the typeform. The size of the typeform shown in Figure 77-2 is 22 picas by 33 picas. Because it does not match the standard furniture sizes, the chaser method should be used (see Unit 76).

7. Select the first four pieces of furniture (see Unit 76).

8. Place the first four pieces of furniture around the typeform (Fig. 77-5). (Again, see Unit 76 for specific procedures.)

9. Place furniture in the space between the bottom of the chase, the left of the chase, and the typeform (Fig. 77-6). Notice that the length of the furniture becomes longer when nearer the edge of the chase. This makes the lockup more stable.

10. Place reglets next to the furniture between the type, the right edge of the chase, and the top edge (Fig. 77-7).

Fig. 77-5. Placement of the first four pieces or furniture for the furniture-within-furniture method of lockup.

Fig. 77-6. Furniture fills the space between the typeform, the bottom of the chase, and the left of the chase.

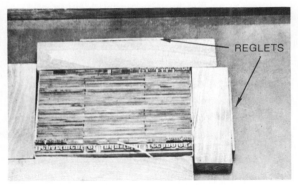

Fig. 77-7. Reglets placed between the furniture.

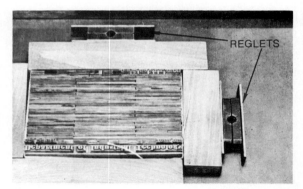

Fig. 77-9. Reglets in proper position between the quoins and the chase.

Fig. 77-8. Quoins are located at the top and right of the chase.

Fig. 77-10. Removing string from around the typeform.

11. Place quoins next to the reglets (Fig. 77-8). The size of the typeform will determine how many quoins should be used. NOTE: Quoins should always be placed at the top and right of the chase. This permits the press operator to keep the type *in register*. If the lockup has to be loosened for corrections, the typeform will remain the same distance from the bottom and left of the chase. This is very important when type must be located accurately on the paper.

12. Place reglets next to the quoins (Fig. 77-9). Reglets prevent quoins from damaging the regular furniture.

13. Carefully remove the string from around the typeform (Fig. 77-10).

14. Fill the remaining space at the top and right of the chase with furniture (Fig. 77-11).

15. Use the quoin key to tighten the quoins until they are snug but not tight.

16. Carefully lay a planer block on the typeform and tap it gently with a mallet or quoin key.

Fig. 77-11. Furniture that is properly placed around the typeform.

Fig. 77-12. Tightening the quoins.

17. Tighten the quoins (Fig. 77-12). Do this in stages. Tighten one quoin a little, then the next one a little. Continue to do this until all are tight. Take care not to tighten them too much. Too much pressure could break the chase.

Checking the lockup for loose lines

After type has been locked up it should be checked for loose lines. If any lines or pieces of type are loose, they could fall out when the locked-up form is lifted. If the type is loose, type could also be pulled out by the ink on the press when the typeform is being printed. This must be avoided.

To check for loose type, place a quoin key under one corner of the chase (Fig. 77-13). This lifts the chase off the imposing table. While the corner of the chase is off the imposing table, tap all areas of the typeform with your finger (Fig. 77-14). After tapping the lines, remove the

quoin key from under the chase. When the typeform is flat on the imposing table loosen the quoins. Correct any loose type in the typeform while it is in a flat position. Snug the quoins and give the typeform a final planing (Fig. 77-15). Tighten the quoins and check once again for lift.

Once this last step has been completed, the locked typeform is ready for the press. As we have stressed, care must be taken when placing the chase in the press to prevent damage to the type.

Fig. 77-14. Testing a lockup for loose lines.

Fig. 77-13. A locked up typeform resting on a quoin key before testing for loose lines.

Fig. 77-15. Planing a typeform.

UNIT 78 MULTIPLE-PAGE LOCKUP AND IMPOSITION

Often, several typeforms are placed in the same chase. The entire contents of the chase are printed on a single sheet of paper and the page is then cut into several smaller sheets. This procedure uses less press time to print an item and makes the finishing operations more efficient.

The procedure for locking up more than one typeform in the same chase is similar to that for locking up a single typeform. The typeforms are arranged next to each other so that they will print in the proper position.

Locking up several forms is easiest if the typeforms are arranged in a rectangle (Fig. 78-1). The rectangle can be treated as a single typeform as you complete the lockup.

The size of the press on which the printing will be done must be considered. The sheet size of the press must be large enough to hold all of the typeforms with ample margins between them.

DUPLICATE FORMS

When large quantities of items, such as letterheads and office forms, are printed, it is some-times more economical to print several identical items on a large sheet of paper. The sheet is cut to the correct size after the ink is dry. This procedure reduces the number of sheets to be fed through the press by the number of duplicate forms that are locked up. For example, if only one typeform were used for 30,000 copies, 30,000 sheets would have to be fed through the press. If six duplicate forms are locked up in a single chase, only 5,000 sheets have to be fed through. This is called printing *six-up*. If only four typeforms are used, it is called printing *four-up*.

Instead of actually composing several forms of type, duplicate plates are often used to reduce the typesetting time. In other situations, several typeforms are used. The cost of extra type or plate preparation must be considered before using this method. The procedure is not worthwhile if the extra cost is more than the savings from reduced press time.

Figure 78-2 shows a combination of duplicate plates being locked up. In this case, two plates of four different items are locked up together and printed at the same time. For this procedure to be economical, all items must be printed

Fig. 78-1. Four typeforms locked into one chase.

FOUR TYPEFORMS ARRANGED TO FORM A RECTANGLE

Fig. 78-2. Duplicate plates being locked up.

on the same kind of paper, have about the same number of copies to be printed with the same ink color, and be about the same size and shape.

IMPOSITION OF SIGNATURES

Items such as books, booklets, magazines, pamphlets, and programs are printed with several different pages on both sides of a single sheet of paper (Fig. 78-3). The printed sheets are then folded so that the pages are in the right order (Fig. 78-4). This printed sheet is called a *signature*. A signature has 4, 8, 16, or 32 pages.

Fig. 78-3. A printed signature.

Fig. 78-4. A folded signature.

The *saddle*, or center, of the signature is the side that will be stitched or stapled to hold it together after trimming (Fig. 78-5). The *head* is the top edge of the pages. There is usually a fold at the head; when folded, it is called the *closed head*. The *closed edge* and *open edge* of a signature form the right edge of the finished book or booklet. The closed edge is so named because there is a fold on that edge. On smaller signatures, there is no closed edge, and it is called only an edge.

Folio is the name given to the number of the page. The folio on the front page of a signature

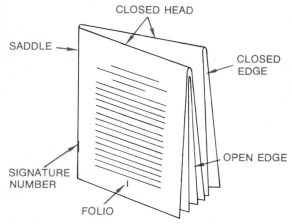

Fig. 78-5. Parts of a folded signature.

is the smallest number in the signature. When all signatures are bound together, the head and edges are trimmed so that the pages are separated and can be turned. The bottom is also trimmed to make it even and clean looking.

Imposition refers to the placement of the typeforms so that the pages will be in the right order after the sheet is printed and folded. A complete *page layout* is made before arranging

the typeforms. The page layout is a sheet of paper on which fold lines, page numbers, and page heads (tops) have been accurately placed (Fig. 78-6). The page layout determines the *imposition table layout*, which is a plan for placing the pages of type on the imposition table accurately. Notice that the imposition layout in Figure 78-7 is the exact reverse of the page layout.

Imposition considerations

Space between typeforms must be set accurately. You must allow for *margins, trimming*, and *creep* (Fig. 78-8). Margins are the spaces between the printed pages and the edges of the folded sheet. Trimming allows for some paper to be removed from the three outside edges after the signature is folded. Creep occurs when the signature is folded and the inside pages extend past the outside ones (Fig. 78-8). When the signature is trimmed, the inside pages will be slightly narrower than the outside ones. Also, the inside margin (next to the center) of the

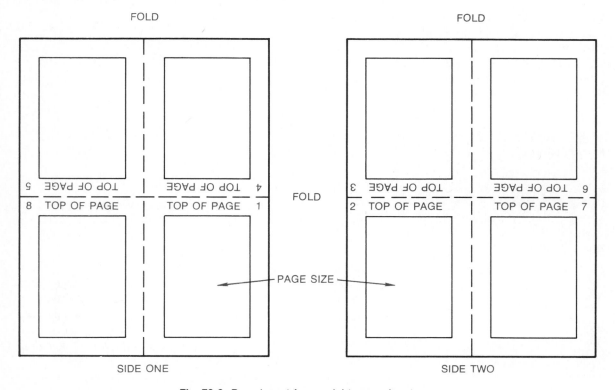

Fig. 78-6. Page layout for an eight-page signature.

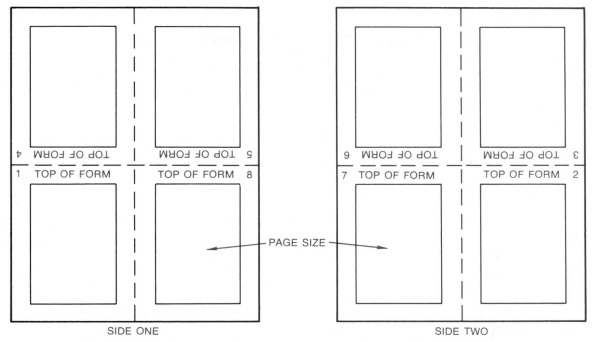

Fig. 78-7. Imposition layout for an eight-page signature. It is the opposite of a page layout.

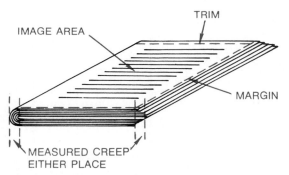

Fig. 78-8. Creep, trim, and margin.

inside pages will not line up with the inside margins of the outside pages. Creep is important only when the signature has several pages.

Signature imposition is critical to printing a quality product. Before it is done, the following questions should be answered:

1. What is the exact size of the image area of the largest page included in the signature? (Image area means the outside dimension of the typeform.)
2. What is the exact size of the margins for all four sides of the page?
3. How much will be trimmed from the three outside edges?

4. How much space should be allowed for creep? (This needs to be considered only for signatures of more than sixteen pages.)
5. What is the sheet-size capacity of the press on which the signature is to be printed? This determines the number of pages printed on a signature.

The precise sheet size can be calculated when the above questions are answered. It is necessary to know the sheet size to make accurate page and imposition table layouts. In Figure 78-7, the fold lines and image size of the pages have been identified. The head and page numbers have been clearly marked.

Determining page sequence

The *folding schedule* is determined before the actual page layout can be made. It refers to the location, sequence, and direction of each fold. Begin with the first page; number each one on both sides. This information is easily transferred to the imposition table layout. Remember that the imposition table layout is an *exact opposite* of the page layout.

Sheetwise method

Two impositions are required to print a signature by the *sheetwise* method. Figure 78-6 shows a page layout for this method, sometimes called *work-and-back* method. Half of the pages are locked into a chase and printed on one side of the sheet. When the ink is sufficiently dry, the remaining half is printed on the opposite side of the sheet.

Work-and-turn or work-and-tumble methods

Two other methods are used to print signatures. They are called *work-and-turn* and *work-and-tumble* impositions. These are used when there is a small number of pages in the signature, or when the pages are small enough to be locked into one chase. In both cases, all of the pages of the signature are printed on both sides of the sheet. The sheets are later cut in half. They are folded after the cutting operation. The sheet size must be *twice* the size of the finished signature sheet size.

In the work-and-turn method, the typeforms are located so the sheets are printed on one side of the sheets. The sheets are then turned over and printed on the second side. Sheets for the work-and-turn method are turned so the *lead edge* remains the same. The lead edge is the edge that is fed into the press first (Fig. 78-9). A page layout for a four-page work-and-turn signature is shown in Figure 78-10. The stone layout of a four-page imposition is given in Figure 78-11.

The work-and-tumble method is similar to the work-and-turn method. After the sheets are printed, they are turned so the opposite edge will feed into the press (Fig. 78-12). Because the lead edge is changed, this is not an effective method to use when close register is needed.

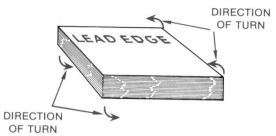

Fig. 78-9. Direction for turning a stack of sheets for a work-and-turn job.

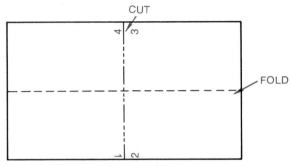

Fig. 78-10. Page layout of a four-page signature—work and turn.

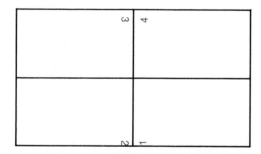

Fig. 78-11. Imposition layout of a four-page signature—work and turn.

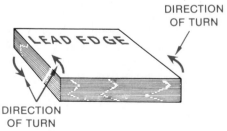

Fig. 78-12. Direction of turn for a stack of sheets for a work-and-tumble job.

UNIT 79 LEARNING EXPERIENCES: LETTERPRESS IMPOSITION

KEY TERMS

Unit 74

Chase	Imposition
Imposing table	Lockup

Unit 75

Furniture	Quoins
Planer block	Reglets
Quoin key	

Unit 78

Closed edge	Saddle
Creep	Sheetwise
Folio	Work-and-back
Head	Work-and-tumble
Lead edge	Work-and-turn
Open edge	

DISCUSSION TOPICS

1. Why is it important to know the size of the typeform before making a chaser lockup?
2. Why must care be taken when planing a letterpress typeform?
3. Why is it important that all lines of a typeform be exactly the same length?
4. What is meant by *imposition of signatures*?
5. What is the major advantage of using work-and-turn and work-and-tumble methods of imposition?

ACTIVITIES

Units 76 and 77

1. Take three sheets of sketching paper or grid paper, 8½ by 11 inches (21.5 by 28 cm). Make the following sketches and submit them to your instructor for evaluation. Take some time and perform this task as accurately as possible. Be sure to label each sketch.
   a. Placement of the first four pieces of furniture for a *furniture-within-furniture* lockup.
   b. Placement of the first four pieces of furniture for a *chaser* lockup.
   c. A complete lockup—either style, including the chase, furniture, typeform, reglets, and quoins. Identify which style you selected to sketch.

Unit 77

2. Obtain a photoengraving or wood block of standard pica length and width (25 by 40 picas). Lockup either one using both lockup methods. Have your practice lockup checked by your instructor.
3. Visit a local newspaper or printing plant. Watch the person who locks up typeforms. Ask about procedures, shortcuts, and problems that are encountered. Ask about what things a person has to know to do the job of lockup and imposition. Prepare a detailed report on your visit.

Unit 78

4. Get four or eight photoengravings, stereotypes, or electrotypes that have been mounted type-high. Make proofs and give each a page number. Lock them up as a sheetwise imposition; as a work-and-turn imposition; and as a work-and-tumble imposition. Linoleum blocks with numbers cut on them can be used if the suggested ones are not available.
5. Look at an old textbook and examine the back. Notice that it was assembled by placing signatures together. Count the number of pages in one of the signatures to determine the number of pages in the signature. Estimate the size of the original sheet of paper on which the signature was printed.

Preparing an automatic platen press for operation.

Transfer of an image by letterpress is accomplished from a relief surface, as we explained in Unit 5. There are three different letterpress press designs: (1) platen, (2) cylinder, and (3) rotary.

The letterpress printing process is used heavily by the specialty printers. Printing from a raised image surface works well for items like envelopes, imprinted company names and addresses on the covers of booklets, and pressure sensitive labels (Fig. 80-1). Many other products are printed from relief images, although a recent government report states that less than 25 percent of all printing is being done by the letterpress printing method.

automatically (Fig. 80-4). The size of a platen press is measured by the inside dimensions of the chase. Hand-operated platen presses generally have a maximum chase size of 6½ by 10 inches (16.5 by 25.4 cm). Power-operated platen presses commonly come in three sizes: 8 by 10, 10 by 15, and 12 by 18 inches (20.3 by 25.4 cm, 25.4 by 38.1 cm, and 30.5 by 45.7 cm). The top speed of an automatic platen press is about 5,000 IPH (impressions per hour).

CYLINDER PRESS

The cylinder-press operating principle is shown in Figure 80-5. The image is transferred to the

BRANDTJEN & KLUGE

Fig. 80-1. A multi-unit pressure sensitive label press that can print, die cut, and foil stamp.

PLATEN PRESS

The *platen press* operating principle is illustrated in Figure 80-2. The *impression* (image transfer) is made at one time as the entire typeform is pressed against the paper.

Platen presses can be hand-operated (Fig. 80-3), power-operated with hand feed, or fed

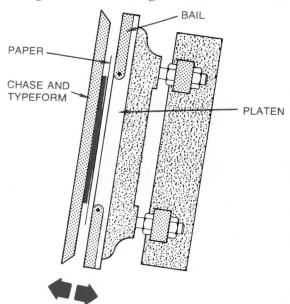

Fig. 80-2. The operating principle of the platen letterpress.

CHANDLER AND PRICE COMPANY

Fig. 80-3. A hand-operated platen press.

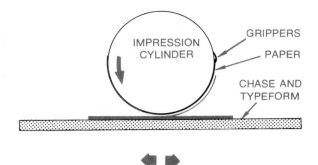

Fig. 80-5. The operating principle of the cylinder letter-press.

cylinder presses are the horizontal (Fig. 80-6) and the vertical (see Unit 86).

ROTARY PRESS

The operating principle of the rotary press is shown in Figure 80-7. Rotary presses can be sheet-fed or web-fed (by a continuous roll of paper). With many, two-image carriers can be attached to one image-carrier cylinder so that one revolution of the cylinder produces two complete impressions.

Large newspaper and magazine presses are designed for multiple pages, color, and high speed (Fig. 80-8). Magazine and most high speed

paper as the flat typeform moves against the impression cylinder. Only a small part of the sheet receives the image at one time.

Modern cylinder presses are designed for automatic feed and delivery of paper. The size of the press is measured by the maximum sheet size that can be run through it. Usual sheet sizes range from 15 by 23 to 31 by 44 inches (38.1 by 58.4 cm to 78.74 by 111.76 cm). Press speeds go to a maximum of 5,000 iph. Two basic designs of

Fig. 80-4. An automatic platen printing press which can be used for numbering, perforating, scoring, die-cutting, embossing, and hot-foil stamping, in addition to high quality printing.

OMNITRADE INDUSTRIAL CO. LTD.

Fig. 80-6. A standard horizontal cylinder letterpress that will print an 18 by 23-inch (45.7 by 58.4 cm) sheet.

HEIDELBERG USA

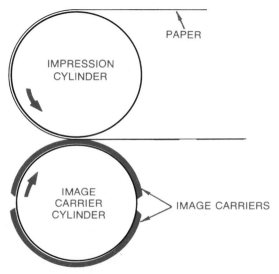

Fig. 80-7. The operating principle of the rotary letterpress.

presses must use a heating unit to dry the ink when printing on glossy paper. Both types of presses are equipped with folding units that cut and fold the web of paper to the finished size. The cylinders of a typical newspaper press turn at 35,000 revolutions per hour.

EARLY PRESSES

Gutenberg had to develop a press to print from his movable-metal type. He built his press roughly like a wine press. It applied the pressure that transferred the ink from the type to the paper.

For many years, improvements in press design were few and eighteenth-century printers were still using the same basic press as

Fig. 80-8. A web multiple-printing newspaper letterpress.

THE GOSS COMPANY

Fig. 80-9. A typical eighteenth century pressroom.

DIDEROT'S ENCYCLOPEDIA/COLONIAL WILLIAMSBURG

Gutenberg's. A typical pressroom of an eighteenth century printer is shown in Figure 80-9. Note that the presses were made of wood. Bracing them to the roof helped make them secure.

Two people were needed to operate these presses, and production was only a few hundred sheets per day. Two experienced press operators could print an average of 200 sheets per hour.

Robert H. Davis writes about the importance of the printing press in the following verse:

I AM THE PRINTING PRESS

I am the printing press born of mother earth. My heart is of steel, my limbs are of iron, and my fingers are of brass.

I sing the songs of the world, the oratorios of history, the symphonies of all time. I am the voice of today, the herald of tomorrow. I weave into the warp of the past the woof of the future. I tell the stories of peace and war alike. I make the human heart beat with passion or tenderness. I stir the pulse of nations, and make brave men do braver deeds, and soldiers die.

I inspire the midnight toiler, weary at his loom, to lift his head again and gaze with fearlessness into the vast beyond, seeking the consolation of a hope eternal.

When I speak, a myriad people listen to my voice. The Saxon, the Latin, the Celt, the Hun, the Slav, the Hindu, all comprehend me. I am the tireless clarion of the news.

I cry your joys and sorrows every hour. I fill the dullard's mind with thoughts uplifting. I am light, knowledge, power. I epitomize the conquests of mind over matter. I am the record of all things mankind has achieved.

My offspring comes to you in the candle's glow, amid the dim lamps of poverty, the splendor of riches; at sunrise, at high noon, and in the waning evening. I am the laughter and tears of the world, and I shall never die until all things return to the immutable dust.

I am the printing press.

UNIT 81 FLEXOGRAPHIC PRINTING

In flexography, the image transfer is made from a relief surface similar to a letterpress. By definition, flexographic printing is a method of rotary letterpress printing. Instead of rigid plates of metal or synthetic material, flexible rubber or synthetic plates are used. Also, fast-drying solvent-based fluid inks are used instead of the paste-type inks used for regular letterpress.

TYPICAL PRODUCTS

The primary growth of flexography has been in the packaging industry. Materials such as paper bags, polyethylene films, foils, gift wraps, and pressure sensitive tapes used to package manufactured goods are nearly all printed by the flexography process. The process is also being used in printing books, business forms, folding boxes, and specialty items such as shower curtains and drinking straws.

Color process printing is routinely done by flexography on flexible packaging materials. It is possible also to print halftones that have been made with 120, 133, and 150 line screens. Corrugated containers can be conveniently printed by flexography (Fig. 81-1).

IMAGE CARRIERS AND INK

Image carriers for flexographic reproduction are made of either rubber or synthetic materials. After the rubber is cured by heat and pressure, it is shaved to the right thickness. Etching methods are used to make the synthetic flexible plates. The completed image carrier is then fastened to the press cylinder by adhesives or mechanical anchors for printing. The process of producing relief, flexography image carriers is discussed in Unit 70.

Ink is very important to this process. Flexography is used to print packaging materials for

APEX MACHINE COMPANY

Fig. 81-1. A flexographic printing system that prints one or both sides of corrugated shipping containers.

food products, and the food and drug laws are very strict about anything that comes into contact with food. Flexographic ink is thin and dries quickly. Much research has gone to develop ink with opacity, heat resistance, gloss, alkali and acid resistance, and permanency. Seventy-five percent of the flexographic inks in use are water based and so they need no solvents. This helps meet the antipollution regulations established by the government.

IMAGE TRANSFER DEVICES

Standard flexographic presses are of the rotary type and are designed to print in one or more colors. They range in size from 6 to 60 inches (15.2 to 152.4 cm) wide but they can be specially built to take a wider web. Unprinted rolls (webs) of paper stock are threaded into the press, printed, force dried, and rewound into rolls.

Press speeds are measured in feet per minute. Common speeds range from 200 to 1000 FPM. Several variables determine press speeds—type of equipment, type of work, quality of work, kind of inks used, and kind of materials being printed.

Most flexographic presses fall into one of three major groups of press design. The original press construction, similar to rotary letterpress, is called the stack-type (Fig. 81-2). One to six color printing stations are available in this press design. A schematic of the four-color stack-type press in Figure 81-2 is shown in Figure 81-3.

Each of the printing stations has three basic parts—inking unit, image carrier (plate) cylinder, and impression cylinder (Fig. 81-4). In the inking section, a fountain roller carries the fluid ink to a transfer roller. Here the ink is metered accurately and carried by the transfer roller to the image carrier mounted on the plate cylinder. The surface of the transfer roller, often called the form roller, is either rubber, chrome-plated smooth steel, or chrome-plated engraved steel.

The second kind, the single-impression cylinder flexography press has an enlarged and centrally-located impression cylinder that serves all image transfer units. Assured fixation of the web is the most appealing advantage of this press over the stacked design. This type of press (Fig. 81-5) is similar to the stack type except for the printing unit. The large impression cylinder (Fig. 81-6) must be machined accurately to within .003 inch (.076 mm) to provide the printing surface needed for quality results.

The water-cooled cylinder is equipped with a temperature control system to keep a constant drum temperature. This prevents changes in the cylinder size that could affect printing quality and color register. Drying units, web tension

WINDMOELLER & HOELSCHER CORPORATION

Fig. 81-2. A four-color stack-type flexography press.

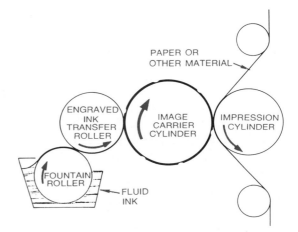

Fig. 81-4. A single-color image transfer unit of a stack-type flexography press.

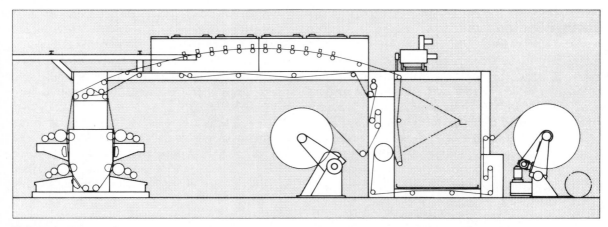

Fig. 81-3. A schematic drawing of the four-color stack-type flexographic press shown in Figure 81-2.

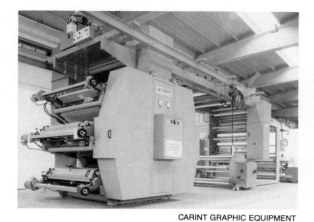

CARINT GRAPHIC EQUIPMENT

Fig. 81-5. A six-color, central impression cylinder flexographic press that can print speeds up to 1,000 feet a minute.

CARINT GRAPHIC EQUIPMENT

Fig. 81-6. A direct view of the large cylinder of the flexographic press shown in Figure 81-5.

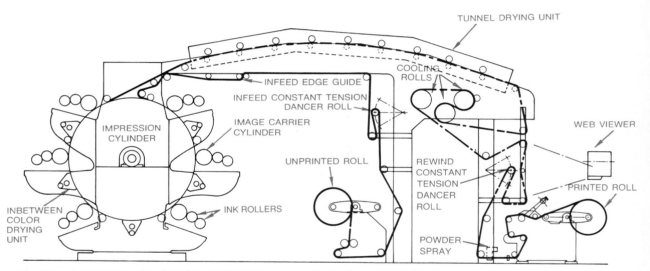

Fig. 81-7. A schematic of a six-color, central impression cylinder flexography press.

control, unwinding, and rewinding systems are part of flexographic presses (Fig. 81-7).

The third type of flexographic press is the inline press design (Fig. 81-8). This press design permits almost unlimited printing image repeats and better between-color drying as well. Flexographic presses that print labels often use the inline design because it is easy to change printing rollers (Fig. 81-9).

HISTORICAL HIGHLIGHTS

The first flexographic press was probably built in 1890 in England. The process came to the United States in the middle 1920s. Flexography was originally known as analine printing because analine dyes dissolved in alcohol were used as inks. In recent years, dramatic improvements have made this method of reproducing images one of the most important in the graphic arts industry.

ADVANTAGES OF FLEXOGRAPHY

The Flexographic Technical Association lists several advantages of this method of printing.

1. *Press makeready.* Since plate cylinders can be removed from the press, separate off-

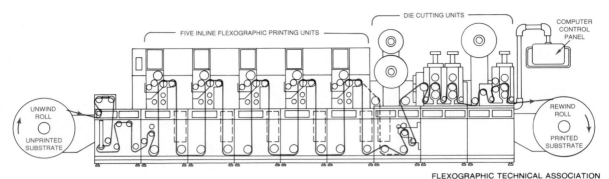

FLEXOGRAPHIC TECHNICAL ASSOCIATION

Fig. 81-8. A schematic of an inline design of a flexographic press.

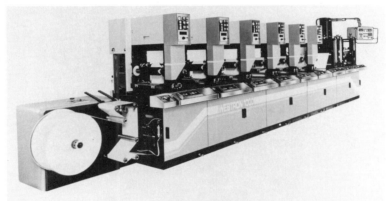

WEBTRON CORPORATION

Fig. 81-9. The inline press design is commonly used for flexographic label presses. These presses often have a die-cutting station where the label shapes are cut from the pressure-sensitive material.

press mounting and proofing operations are possible. Thus multi-color plates can be set-up in register in advance of a production run without affecting the operation of the press.

2. *Copy changes.* By using pre-makeready cylinders or plates, copy changes can be made during a run. Using vacant color stations, color changes can be made with only a slight increase in amount of time required for the total run.

3. *Plate life.* Properly made flexible printing plates last a long time. Long uninterrupted runs give millions of impressions without much loss of plate quality.

4. *Printing speeds.* Flexography can be very economical, with as many as six colors being printed at one time at speeds up to 2,000 FPM.

5. *Continuous printing.* A plate roller of any circumference can print a continuous pattern on stock which can then be cut to a specified length or width.

6. *Printed roll stock can be supplied.* With the development of high-speed wrapping and packaging machinery, printed roll stock—in some cases with flexographically applied heat-seal coatings—has become an important product.

7. *Fast-drying inks.* Quick-drying inks let the operator check the results right after printing. This continuous high-speed flexible process also lets the printing operation be tied in with other operations such as die cutting, coating, bagmaking, waxing, or sheeting for economy of production.

8. *Applicaton of tints or coatings.* Continuous or spot applications of tints and functional coatings, such as varnishes and heat-sealing materials, can be readily printed on flexographic presses. With proper equipment, such coatings can be applied on either or both sides of a web in a continuous operation.

UNIT 82 BOOK PRODUCTION SYSTEM

Complete books can be printed rapidly from start to finish with the *Cameron Book Production System.* This patented system goes from an unprinted roll of paper to manufactured books with only a single setup. Part of the system is shown in Figure 82-1.

The Cameron Book Production System is a web-processing machine that prints and automatically collates books at web speeds of up to 1,000 feet a minute. At this speed, a $4^3/8$ by 6 inch (11.11 by 15.24 cm) book of 160 pages can be produced at the rate of 200 a minute; a 640-page book of the same dimensions can be produced at 50 a minute. Paper of up to 38 inches (96.5 cm) wide is fed to the system from rolls of up to 50 inches (127 cm) diameter. The printing method is similar to rotary letterpress, but the plates are mounted on two continuous belt conveyors, one for each printing unit.

THE FLEXIBLE IMAGE CARRIER

The heart of Cameron Book Production System is the printing belt (Fig. 82-2). The printing

SOMERSET TECHNOLOGIES, INC.

Fig. 82-2. The printing belt of the Cameron Book Production System uses flexible, relief photopolymer plates.

plates for each book page are made of flexible photopolymer (see Units 67 and 70). The individual page plates are attached to a flexible belt that has excellent tensil strength. These plates must be carefully and accurately attached to the belt. A special mounting machine is used to align each page plate and apply the correct amount of pressure (Fig. 82-3). The adhesive that fastens the plates to the belt is strong and flexible because it must hold during high-speed printing.

A special proofing machine is used to proof the printing belt (Fig. 82-4). Correct page order,

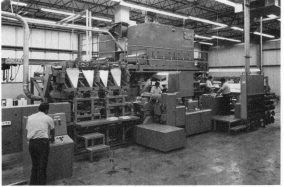

SOMERSET TECHNOLOGIES, INC.

Fig. 82-1. A partial view of the Cameron Book Production System showing the several working locations for the press operators.

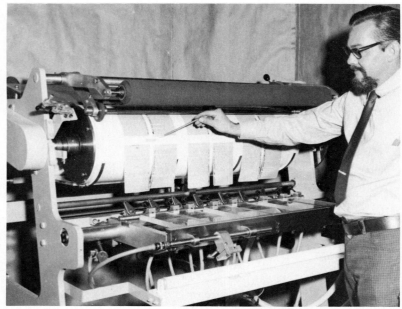

Fig. 82-3. A special plate-mounting machine is used to position and fasten the individual plates to the printing belt.

Fig. 82-4. The proofing machine is used to check printing page order, margins, and straightness of each page.

margins, and straightness of each page plate can be checked through proofing. Because spelling and content on each page are proofed before the individual plates are made, these items are not considered at this proofing stage. After proofing, the printing belt is ready to be installed on the printing portion of the book production system.

THE PRINTING CYCLE

The web of paper is pulled through two identical printing units so that both sides of the paper are printed. The schematic drawing shows the several parts of the total book production system (Fig. 82-5). Study this illustration closely to see how the web of paper travels through the entire system. Notice that there are two printing belts, one for each side of the paper.

The first printing belt prints all the pages that will appear on one side of the paper web. The ink is dried quickly as the web passes through a heated forced-air dryer. After this, two special turning bars turn the web over and the paper web passes through the second printing unit. Here the second side is printed with back-to-back register so the pages align accurately. Registration is achieved with automatic edge guides located in strategic places.

Printing quality is accurately controlled by micrometer settings that adjust the printing impression. Ink is distributed to the relief images of the plates with several precision-ground ink rollers. This system is best with type-set material, but line illustrations and coarse-screen halftones can also be used in the books produced on this total system (Fig. 82-6).

The length of the printing belts depend on

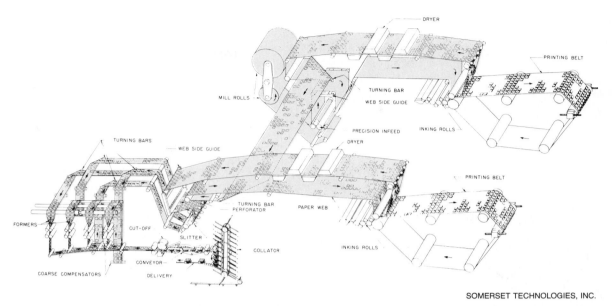

SOMERSET TECHNOLOGIES, INC.

Fig. 82-5. A general arrangement schematic of the patented Cameron Book Production System.

SOMERSET TECHNOLOGIES, INC.

Fig. 82-6. The printing results from the flexible printing belt.

SOMERSET TECHNOLOGIES, INC.

Fig. 82-7. The perforating (near top) and slitting (near bottom) section, of the Cameron Book Production System. This book production job requires slitting three ribbons of a two-page width and one ribbon of a single-page width.

the number of pages in the book being printed. Belts can be as short as 60 inches (152.4 cm) and as long as 378 inches (960.1 cm). Even greater lengths are possible. The printing belts, with plates still mounted in place, can be washed, rolled up, and stored. They are ready at any time for inexpensive short- or long-run reprinting. Any needed changes can be easily stripped in before starting a new run.

FINISHING AND BINDING

After leaving the second press unit, the printed web is pulled through the first bindery operation—perforating and slitting. Perforating cuts the paper in dashes so it will easily tear or fold.

Slitting is the operation that cuts the paper with a sharp roller (Fig. 82-7). Here the printed web is slit into 2, 3 or 4 ribbons. Each ribbon may be the width of two book pages. Just before slitting, the web is perforated along the centerline of each ribbon for subsequent folding. If one ribbon is single-page width, it will not be perforated. The perforation (or folding line) always follows the long grain of the paper (the direction of the web). The fold of each ribbon will be in the direction of the grain. This gives a flatter book than cross-grain folding.

MIDLAND-ROSS CORPORATION

Fig. 82-8. The forming and folding section of the Cameron Book Production System, where the cut ribbons are made into signatures of several pages.

Either sixteen-page signatures or single sheets, can be produced on this system, so there is no need to allow for margins when laying-up multipage signatures. Side-register controls correct the tracking position of the web both before printing and again before perforating and slitting to give uniform side and center margins on each page of the finished books.

After perforating and slitting, the ribbons of printing paper are pulled through former-folders (Fig. 82-8). Turning bars, ahead of the folders, change the direction of the slit ribbons 90 degrees. The system offers maximum flexibility in planning page widths and se-

quence of signatures. Course compensators adjust for differences in travel distance between one slit ribbon and another as they negotiate the 90-degree turn to restore the proper signature alignments.

The ribbons are then pulled down individually through folder rolls. The folded ribbons travel one above the other toward the rotary cut-off. The ribbons of printed, slit, and folded paper—stacked in signature alignment—are pulled through the rotary cut-off. Individual signatures are cut to the proper page depths. Each cut produces a packet of 4 to 32 pages, depending upon the overall setup for the run.

The individual packets are conveyed to a vertical collator, where they are stacked in page sequence (Fig. 82-9). Each compartment in the collator is timed to collect one complete book. The collator can be adjusted to accept various book thicknesses up to 2 inches (5 cm) compressed. Jogging discs square the books as they are lowered to an automatic outfeed delivery belt.

Automated perfect binding equipment (Unit 156) glues covers and trims the collated signatures to produce a completed book.

SOMERSET TECHNOLOGIES, INC.

Fig. 82-9. The page/signature packets are conveyed to the vertical collator where they are stacked in page sequence to make up complete books.

UNIT 83 SAFETY WITH LETTERPRESS PRESSES

Here is a checklist of precautions for safe operation of platen and cylinder presses.

Permission. Ask your instructor for permission before operating the platen or cylinder press.

Clothing. Wear tight-fitting clothing. Loose-fitting clothing can be dangerous. Remove ties and roll up or button long sleeves.

Jewelry. Remove wrist watches, bracelets, and rings. They can catch on the press and pull you into moving parts.

Hands and fingers. Be careful where you put your hands when a press is running. They could easily get caught in moving parts.

Adjustments. Make adjustments only when a press is stopped.

Guards. All safety guards should be in place and fastened securely before the press power is turned on. All belts, chains, gears, and shafts should be adequately covered.

Instruction manual. Read the instruction manual carefully before using the presses. Each manufacturer designs these machines differently; the operating controls and adjustments may be located in different positions from those shown on the presses in Units 84 through 87.

Press speed. Operate the hand-fed platen press at a slow speed until you develop the right rhythm for smooth feeding and delivery of sheets. The cylinder press should also be operated slowly until you gain adequate skill to operate safely.

One operator. Only one person should operate a platen or cylinder press at a time. These machines are one-operator machines and are very dangerous when two or more persons try to run the controls.

Stopping the press. Turn the power off and stop the press before leaving it.

Stance. Place your feet firmly when operating presses.

Clean floors. Keep the floor free of waste paper and oil. You could easily slip. Do not leave tools on the floor or on the press after making adjustments or repairs. Put them back where they belong.

Lubricating a press. Stop the press before oiling or greasing it.

Safety switch. Use the safety switch or device properly for each press. Power presses all should have electrical safety switches. Some also have mechanical devices that, when activated, will not allow the power to be turned on.

Carrying a locked chase. Carry the locked chase to the press with care, as a dropped one could hurt your foot. Keep your back straight when removing a locked chase from the storage rack or press.

Feeding the press. Feed and remove sheets of paper from the hand-fed press carefully but deliberately. Learn and remember the safe working areas of a press when hand feeding. Never try to pick up a printed sheet that has been dropped into a moving press.

Makeready knife. Always know where you have put your makeready knife. Use it with care when completing the makeready operation on the platen or cylinder press.

Ink solvents. Store the ink solvent in a safety can and use a solvent that is not flammable or has a low flash point. Do not strike matches near the solvent. Do not use carbon tetrachloride.

Air circulation. There should always be adequate air circulation to carry away solvent fumes that could cause headaches and drowsiness.

UNIT 84 PLATEN PRESS PREPARATION

You must prepare the platen press properly (Fig. 84-1). If you are careful with pre-printing details, you will have trouble-free operation and do a good job. The platen press is a very safe machine to use—when operated correctly. Safe operation is your responsibility. Be sure you observe all safety precautions.

Learn the names of the press parts and know what each does. Then thoroughly study the preparation and operation procedures before using the platen press.

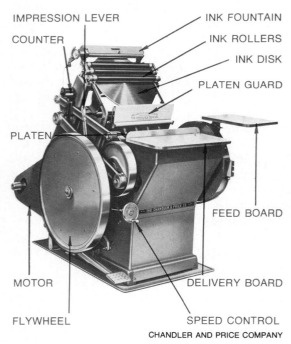

Fig. 84-1. A 10 by 15-inch (25.4 by 38.1 cm) hand-fed platen press.

PARTS AND USES

Platen. The smooth metal casting that provides the impression surface.

Ink fountain. The ink reserve that automatically puts ink on the ink rollers.

Ink disk. The ink rollers get ink from the disk on each turn of the press.

Platen safety guard. A safety device that keeps hands from between the platen and the typeform.

Feed board. Sheets to be printed are placed on the feed board.

Delivery board. After sheets have been printed, they are placed on the delivery board.

Impression lever. This lever controls whether an image is transferred. Pulling it backward permits impression. Pushing it forward keeps the typeform from striking the paper.

Counter. This device records the number of sheets printed.

PRESS PREPARATION

1. Move the grippers to the outer edge of the platen (Fig. 84-2).

Fig. 84-2. Moving the grippers to the outer edge of the platen.

2. Tighten the gripper nuts. This keeps them from sliding between the typeform and platen while the press is being prepared.
3. Dress the platen (Fig. 84-3). Use the following dressing materials in the order listed:

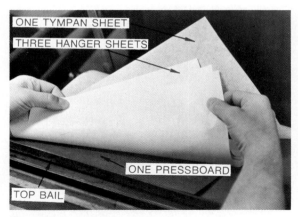

Fig. 84-3. Dressing the platen.

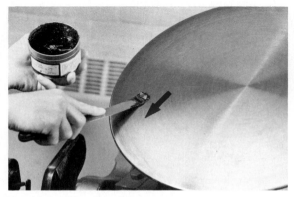

Fig. 84-4. Inking the platen press.

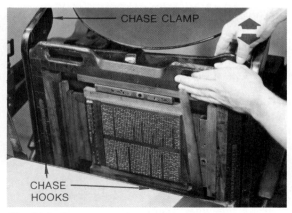

Fig. 84-5. Placing a locked chase in the press.

Fig. 84-6. An impression pulled on the tympan.

a. one tympan sheet of 0.006-inch (.152 mm) oiled manila paper
b. three hanger sheets, each of 0.003-inch (.076 mm) coated paper
c. one pressboard of 0.020-inch (.51 mm) smooth-finished hardboard.

The total thickness of these three materials is 0.035-inch (.89 mm). The tympan and hanger sheets are clamped under the bottom and top bails. Do not place the pressboard under the bails.

4. Ink the press (Fig. 84-4). Do not use the ink fountain for short runs; only place a small amount of ink on the ink disk. The amount of ink will vary, depending on the press and typeform sizes. About a thimbleful would be a good beginning. Additional ink can easily be added if needed.

5. Turn on the power. Allow the press to run until the ink is distributed.

6. Turn off the press.

7. Wipe the bottom of the typeform to remove any dirt. Then place the chase and typeform in the press (Fig. 84-5).

8. Set the bottom of the chase against the two chase hooks; secure the top with a chase clamp. The quoins should be positioned to the top and right sides of the press.

9. Pull an impression on the tympan (Fig. 84-6). Roll the press over by hand to print on the tympan. It is not necessary to obtain a high-quality print, but all parts of the typeform should be visible on the tympan.

10. Determine the paper position on the tympan.

a. To center the image on the paper measure the image length and width. Then subtract the image size from the paper size and divide the marginal area equally on all four sides (Fig. 84-7).

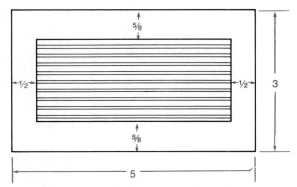

Fig. 84-7. An image centered on a sheet of paper.

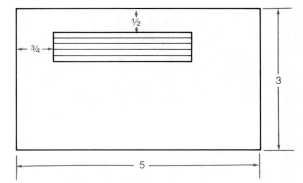

Fig. 84-8. Predetermined top and left margins.

b. A pre-determined margin can be selected for any of the four sides (Fig. 84-8).

c. After determining margins, mark guidelines on the tympan for the side and top edges of the paper (Fig. 84-9).

11. Secure the gauge pins to the tympan. Gauge pins are devices that hold the paper in place on the platen while the sheet is being printed.

a. Two gauge pins are positioned at the top edge of the paper, about ⅙ the width of the paper from the ends (Fig. 84-10).

b. One gauge pin is positioned at the left edge of the paper, about ½ the height of the paper from the top edge (Fig. 84-10).

c. Insert the center prong under the tympan ⅛-inch (3.17 mm) outside the guideline.

d. Extend the prong under the tympan ½-inch (1.27 cm) and force it back through the surface.

e. Continue sliding the gauge pin until the guide edge is in line with the guideline (Fig. 84-11). Do not let the prong extend through the hanger sheets.

12. Check gauge pins and gauge-pin tongues to see that they clear the typeform. If they do not, the type will be damaged.

13. Wipe the inked image from the tympan. Use a clean cloth slightly dampened with ink solvent.

14. To pull a trial impression (Fig. 84-12):

a. place a sheet of paper against the gauge pins

b. pull the impression lever

c. roll the press over by hand.

15. Measure the position of the image. If it is not correct, slide the gauge pins until the

Fig. 84-9. Guidelines drawn on the tympan for the top and side edges of the paper.

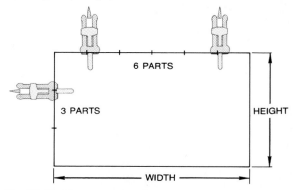

Fig. 84-10. The proper position of the gauge pins.

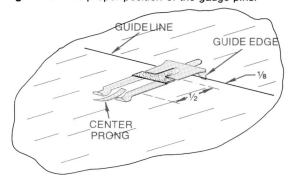

Fig. 84-11. A properly installed gauge pin.

Fig. 84-12. Pulling the trial impression.

Fig. 84-13. The gripper positioned over the margin of the printed sheet.

position is correct. After getting the proper printing position, lightly tap the top of the gauge pins to secure them in the tympan sheet.

16. If necessary, move grippers into position over the margin of the sheet (Fig. 84-13). Be sure that they clear the typeform and gauge pins.

17. Proceed with the makeready in an orderly manner.

UNIT 85 PLATEN PRESS OPERATION

An important process called makeready must be completed after the preliminary steps of press preparation have been done. In *makeready*, the press is adjusted so that all parts of the typeform make an equal impression as it prints on a sheet of paper. Proper makeready will result in perfect image transfer.

To operate a hand-fed platen press, you need hand and eye coordination that comes only with practice. Follow the steps given below to operate and complete a printed job safely.

PRESS MAKEREADY

1. Adjust the press for the proper printing position on the paper. Before doing this, inspect the type, "cuts," plates to see if they are type high, ".918."

2. Check for punch-through (excessive type pressure) to the back of the sheet. Lay a printed sheet upside down on a smooth, hard surface. Feel the back of the paper for raised areas caused by the typeform pressing too hard against the paper. If *punch* is detected, remove a hanger sheet and repeat inspection. If there is excessive punch, the height of the platen may need to be adjusted.

3. Find any image areas that are printing too lightly.

4. Circle the letters or areas on a printed sheet that need better impression (Fig. 85-1).

5. Place makeready paste inside the circled areas. Use the paste sparingly.

6. Lay a sheet of tissue paper over a circled area. Cut the tissue with a makeready knife to conform with the lines (Fig. 85-2). Be careful to cut only through the tissue.

7. Place the pasted-up sheet (now called a makeready sheet) in the press against the gauge pins.

8. Cut 2 caret marks (inverted V) through the makeready sheet and tympan (Fig. 85-3). The position of the marks should be directly across from the two gauge pins

Fig. 85-1. Finding and circling image areas that are printing too lightly.

Fig. 85-2. Adding tissue to the image areas that are printing too lightly.

Fig. 85-3. Cutting caret marks.

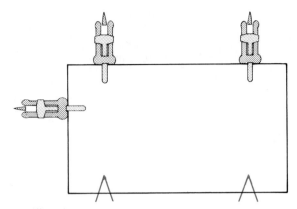

Fig. 85-4. The correct position of caret marks.

(Fig. 85-4). The caret marks are used to align the makeready sheet under the tympan.

9. Remove the makeready sheet.
10. Raise the top bail only; fold back the tympan.
11. Paste the makeready sheet on the top hanger sheet (Fig. 85-5) by lining up the caret marks in the makeready sheet with those that were cut in the hanger sheet. Use paste sparingly.
12. Remove a hanger sheet to compensate for the extra thickness of the makeready sheet.
13. Remove the pressboard from the bottom of the platen dressing. Place it between the tympan and top hanger sheet. This smooths the different thicknesses of the makeready sheet.
14. Lower the tympan sheet and reclamp the platen dressing under the top bail.
15. Take a trial impression.

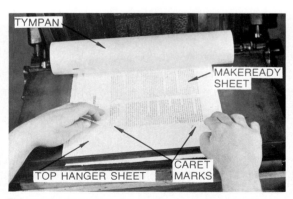

Fig. 85-5. Attaching the makeready sheet to the top hanger sheet.

16. Inspect the image. If more impression is still required, add tissue to the needed areas on the makeready sheet. Repeat this step until you are getting perfect impressions.

PRESS OPERATION

1. Re-study the safety guidelines in Unit 83.
2. Clear away all materials from the feed and delivery boards.
3. Place a pile of paper stock on the feed board.
4. Set the counter, turn on the power, and run the press at a slow speed.
5. With your right hand, place a sheet against the gauge pins when the platen is open (Fig. 85-6). Position the sheet against the bottom two pins. Slide the sheet over to the side pin.
6. Pull the impression lever back with your left hand.
7. Also, remove the printed sheet with your left hand.
8. Feed another sheet with your right hand (Fig. 85-7). These two operations must be completed during the few seconds that the platen is open.
9. Push the impression lever forward if the sheet is not being properly fed to the gauge pins.
10. On the next revolution of the press, straighten the sheet, pull the impression lever, and begin feeding and delivering the sheets again.

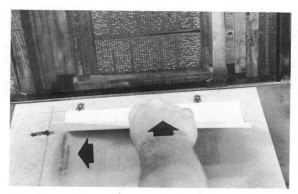

Fig. 85-6. Placing a sheet against the gauge pins.

Fig. 85-7. Feeding the hand-fed platen press.

11. Finish printing the correct number of copies.
12. Clean the press as outlined in Unit 87.

UNIT 86 CYLINDER PRESS OPERATION

The automatic cylinder press prints from flat typeforms. The type is either (1) in the form of hot composition or foundry type or (2) in the form of original or duplicate letterpress image carriers. It may also be a combination of the two.

In this printing procedure the press is inked, the paper is loaded on the feed table, and the locked chase is placed in the press. Suction delivers one sheet at a time to the impression cylinder grippers and guides. The sheet travels around the cylinder between the typeform and the cylinder to receive the impression or image. It is then taken from the cylinder grippers by the delivery grippers and deposited onto a delivery table. This is repeated as many times as there are sheets to be printed.

The cylinder press must be prepared properly (Fig. 86-1). Pay careful attention to preprinting details for trouble-free operation and a job well done.

PARTS AND USES

Typeform and chase bed. Here the locked typeform is placed in the vertically designed cylinder press.

Feeder unit. This unit automatically feeds single sheets of paper to the grippers on the impression cylinder.

Impression cylinder. This is a cylinder with grippers that presses the paper against the typeform for the image transfer.

Ink rollers. The several ink rollers deliver ink to the type after each impression.

Ink fountain. The ink reserve automatically refills the ink rollers.

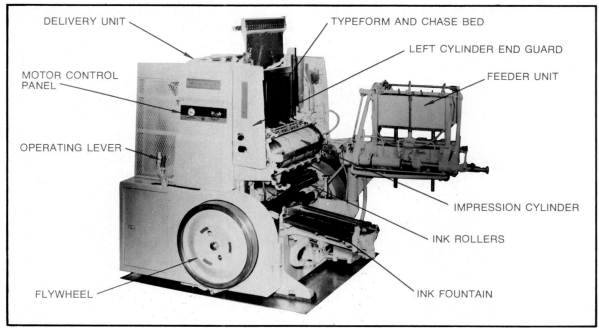

DELIVERY UNIT

TYPEFORM AND CHASE BED

LEFT CYLINDER END GUARD

MOTOR CONTROL PANEL

FEEDER UNIT

OPERATING LEVER

IMPRESSION CYLINDER

INK ROLLERS

FLYWHEEL

INK FOUNTAIN

THE MIEHLE COMPANY

Fig. 86-1. A cylinder letterpress machine.

Operating lever. This lever controls the starting and stopping of the press. It also acts as a brake.

Motor control panel. This panel contains the motor start-stop switches and the oil pressure gauge.

Left cylinder end guard. This guard encloses the left end of the cylinder. It protets the operator as the cylinder moves up and down. It also keeps the electric power switch from being turned on when the cylinder is open for making adjustments. The entire purpose of the guard is SAFETY.

Delivery unit. In this unit the sheets are delivered and jogged or straightened after receiving the image.

CYLINDER PRESS PREPARATION

1. Lubricate the press. Many printing presses have an automatic lubrication system. This should be checked to see that it is operating correctly.
2. Install the ink rollers. Follow the roller schedule given in the manufacturer's press manual.
3. Turn the flywheel by hand and roll the press through one entire cycle to see whether the ink rollers have been installed correctly. Repeat this step each time an adjustment or an addition is made on the press.
4. Put ink into the fountain (Fig. 86-2). The amount of ink needed depends upon the job to be printed. Do not overfill the fountain because ink dries rapidly in air, and too much will be wasted.

5. Close and adjust the ink fountain.
6. Ink the rollers. This is simply called *inking the press.* The press must be turned on for this step. When finished, turn the press power off.
7. Place the chase and locked typeform in the press. Position the chase in the press and secure it firmly with the chase clamp (Fig. 86-3).

Fig. 86-3. Securing a locked chase in a cylinder press.

8. Attach the feeding, or transfer, table with the impression cylinder up. Then rotate the press by hand until the impression cylinder is in the down position.
9. Set the side register guide so the image will be printed in the correct position (Fig. 86-4).

Fig. 86-2. Putting ink into the fountain.

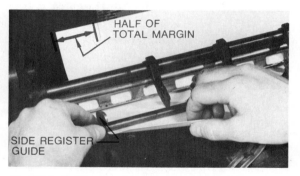

Fig. 86-4. Setting the side paper register guide.

10. Prepare the feeder. Swing the feeder from open position, lock it in operating position, and make any needed adjustments.

11. Load a supply of paper stock in the feeder and raise it to within one-half inch of the top of the front pile guides (Fig. 86-5).

12. Adjust the feeder air suction and the blow nozzles so the top few sheets of the pile are *floating on air*. This allows the air suction shoes to pick up one sheet at a time.

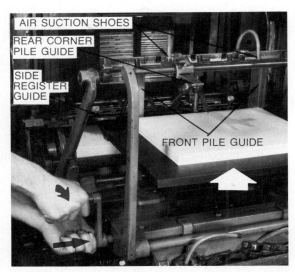

Fig. 86-5. Raising the feeder pile table to the proper feeding level.

13. Feed one sheet through and then stop the press just before the sheet is released by the delivery grippers. Adjust the delivery side and rear joggers to accept the sheet (Fig. 86-6).

MAKEREADY FOR A SPECIFIC FORM

1. Print a few sheets and obtain the proper printing position on the paper.

2. Check for punch-through to the back of the sheets. Lay a printed sheet upside down on a smooth, hard surface. Feel the back of the paper for raised areas caused by the paper pressing too hard against the typeform. If punch is detected, remove one or more hanger sheets from the impression cylinder packing.

Fig. 86-6. Adjusting the delivery joggers to accept the sheet.

3. Start the press and print one sheet, but stop the press just short of the delivery grippers. Check to see that contact is not made.

4. Turn the press power off and engage the safety.

5. Cut 2 caret (line-up) marks through the printed sheet, through the tympan, and into the top hanger sheet (Fig. 86-7). Figure 86-7 shows a special tool being used, but a standard makeready knife can also be used.

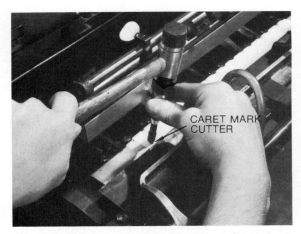

Fig. 86-7. Cutting caret marks through a printed sheet, through the tympan, and into the top hanger sheet.

6. Remove the sheet from the press and inspect it. Add tissue paper to the light areas, just as you did with the platen press makeready sheet (see Unit 85).

7. Glue the makeready sheet to the top hanger sheet according to the caret marks (Fig. 86-8). Remove a hanger sheet to compensate for the added thickness of the makeready sheet.

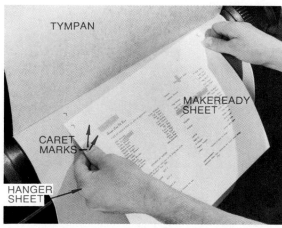

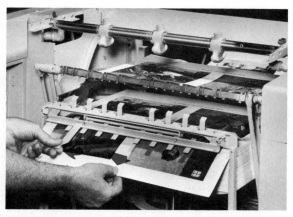

Fig. 86-8. Attaching the makeready sheet to a cylinder hanger sheet.

8. Print about 12 copies. Stop the press and examine the printed sheets. If better impression is needed, add tissue to the needed areas on the makeready sheet that is already attached to the impression cylinder packing.

CYLINDER PRESS OPERATION

1. Clear away all tools and materials used to set up the press.

Fig. 86-9. Removing a sheet from the delivery to check the printing quality.

2. Re-check all adjustments to make sure that the press will operate properly.
3. Set the automatic counter.
4. Begin to print the needed number of copies.
5. Check to see that the sheets are being printed properly during the press run (Fig. 86-9).
6. Regulate the ink fountain to get an even balance of ink across the printed sheet.
7. After printing the needed number of copies, stop the press and remove all printed and unprinted sheets.
8. Wash the press according to the procedure outlined in Unit 87.

UNIT 87 PLATEN AND CYLINDER PRESS CLEANUP

Cleaning a platen or cylinder letterpress is an easy but very important part of press operation. All ink must be removed from the ink rollers and press supply areas, such as the ink fountain, ink plate, and ink disk. This must be done after the press has been used because the ink dries and damages the ink rollers.

PLATEN PRESS CLEANUP

1. Have the power turned off and be sure that the safety switch is engaged.
2. Remove the chase from the press and place it on the imposing table.
3. Wash the typeform. Do this carefully so the typeform is not damaged.
4. Get two cloths, one clean and another somewhat used. Also get a can of solvent.
5. Pour solvent on the used cloth and wipe the ink disk and rollers. The press will need to be turned by hand so that the rollers will be positioned as shown in Figure 87-1.
6. Pour solvent on the clean cloth. Again wipe the ink disk and rollers. No ink should remain on the press rollers or ink disk. NOTE: Do not pour solvent on the disk itself. If you do, it will run down the front of the press and make a mess.
7. Put all materials that were used in the printing and cleanup operation back where they belong.
8. Unlock the chase and replace all items.

CYLINDER PRESS CLEANUP

1. Remove the chase from the press and place it on the imposing table.
2. Wash the typeform. Do this carefully so the typeform is not damaged.

Fig. 87-1. Washing the ink disk and rollers of a platen press.

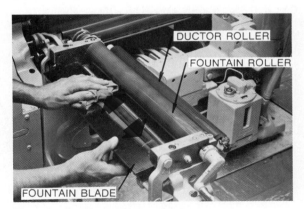

Fig. 87-2. Cleaning the ink fountain.

3. Slowly run the press until the impression cylinder is positioned to expose all ink rollers and the ink plate.
4. Turn off the power, set the brake, and engage the safety.
5. Remove the excess ink from the ink fountain with an ink knife and put the ink back in the original can.
6. Clean the ink fountain blade, the fountain rollers, and the ductor roller (Fig. 87-2).

Fig. 87-3. Washing a composition ink roller that has been removed from the press.

Fig. 87-4. Washing the ink plate of a cylinder press.

Wipe the fountain clean with a cloth and solvent.

7. Remove each composition ink roller and wash it thoroughly (Fig. 87-3).
8. Place the clean rollers in a special roller rack to keep them from getting flat on one side.
9. Wash each steel ink roller that is permanently mounted in the press.

10. Wipe the ink plate free of ink (Fig. 87-4). Ink allowed to dry on the plate will cause inking problems the next time the press is used.
11. Wipe down the press, using a cloth dampened with solvent. This removes ink and oil build-up. The press is now ready for the next job.
12. Unlock the chase and replace all items.

UNIT 88 LEARNING EXPERIENCES: LETTERPRESS IMAGE TRANSFER

KEY TERMS

Unit 80
Cylinder press
Impression
Platen press
Rotary press

Unit 81
Analine printing
Central impression flexographic press
Inline flexographic press
Flexography
Stack flexographic press

Unit 82
Paper ribbon
Perforating
Printing belt
Registration
Slitting

Unit 84
Counter
Delivery board
Feed board
Gauge pins
Ink fountain
Ink disk

Impression lever
Platen
Platen dressing
Platen safety guard
Tympan

Unit 85

Caret marks
Makeready   Makeready sheet

Unit 86

Floating on air   Left cylinder end
Grippers   guard
Joggers   Punch-through
Impression cylinder   Side register guide

DISCUSSION TOPICS

1. How are the sizes of the presses generally measured?
2. How is flexography different from the standard method of letterpress image transfer?
3. What is different about the image carrier in the Cameron Book Production System?
4. When should press adjustments be made?
5. Why is it important to clean the platen and cylinder presses soon after use?

ACTIVITIES

Unit 80

1. Research the history of each of the press designs and prepare a short paper on each design. Arrange an exhibit in one of your school display cabinets.

Unit 81

2. Obtain or prepare a flexographic image carrier. Fasten the image carrier to a metal can small enough to allow the image carrier nearly to encircle the can. Ink the image carrier with the hand brayer and transfer the image by rolling the cylinder (can) over a sheet of paper. If possible, attempt to prepare a working model of a flexographic press.

Unit 82

3. Obtain two or three books printed with a Cameron Book Production System. Inspect the books closely then explain to the class how it is possible to know the books were printed on this system. Determine if possible the number of Cameron Book Production System installations in the United States. Mark these locations on a map. Use this information to create a display board or fill a display case.

Units 84 and 85

4. Plan a job to be printed on a platen press. Compose and lock up the form correctly. Obtain or cut the paper that you will need for your job. Suggested jobs are name cards, book marks, stationery, and address cards. Print the needed number of items with the platen press. Set up, operate, and clean the press properly.

Unit 86

5. Plan a job to be printed on a cylinder press. Compose and lock up the form correctly. Obtain or cut the paper that you will need for your job. Suggested jobs are stationery, pamphlets, handbills, business forms, and newspapers.

Unit 87

6. Lubricate a platen or a cylinder press or both. Obtain the press operator's manual and study the procedures for lubricating that particular press. Be sure to locate the several points that need to be lubricated with oil or grease. Using a cloth dampened with ink solvent, wipe the entire press free from ink, oil, and dirt accumulation.

The printed page can live forever.

This is a spread from the Gutenberg bible, the world's first book printed from movable type.

The Gutenberg bible came off the press in 1455. Some 47 copies are still in existence today.

A message in print is not like a message in time.

A message in time will last for 10, 20, 30 or 60 seconds. Like a stroke of lightning, a message in time lives gloriously for a moment and then dies.

A message in print can die just as fast. On the other hand, a message in print can be read for 10 minutes, can be taken to the store a week later or perhaps saved for several lifetimes like this bible.

If you have something important to say, your message will last longer if you put it in print.

Your message in print will live as long as it is relevant to the needs and interests of your marketplace.

Your message in print can live forever.

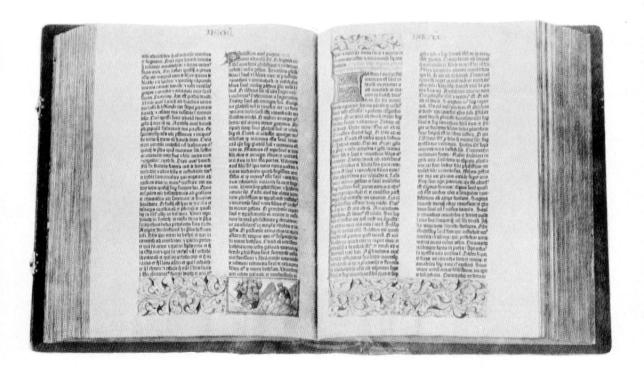

A stripper examines a halftone positive on a light table. He will prepare the positive for making a lithographic image carrier.

11 LITHOGRAPHIC IMPOSITION

89 INTRODUCTION TO LITHOGRAPHIC IMPOSITION

Lithographic imposition is commonly called *stripping*. The person who does the stripping is called the *stripper*. Another name often used is *litho artist*. The stripper's job is to make flats. *Flats* are used to make plates. Plates are used on offset lithography printing presses to make printed copies.

THE LITHOGRAPHIC FLAT

The flat is made of negatives or positives attached to a *masking sheet*. The masking sheet is usually yellow or orange paper, sometimes called *goldenrod*. This sheet keeps unwanted light from reaching the light-sensitive surface when the plate is exposed. After one or more negatives are attached to the masking sheet, the area covering the image areas is removed. This lets light pass through only the image areas of the negative.

The flat is then placed over a plate with a light-sensitive surface. A bright light source is used to expose the light-sensitive plate (Fig. 89-1). This operation is usually done with a special platemaking machine that puts the flat and plate in tight contact (Fig. 89-2). The light used to expose the plate is inside the cabinet of the platemaking machine.

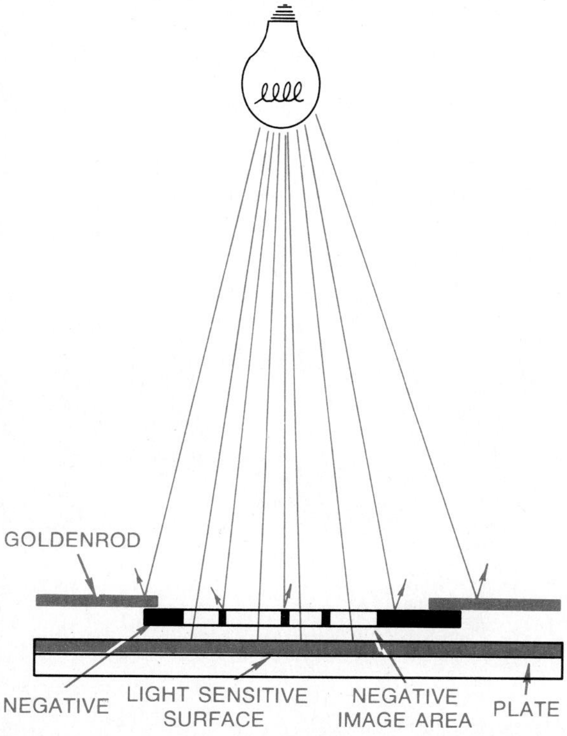

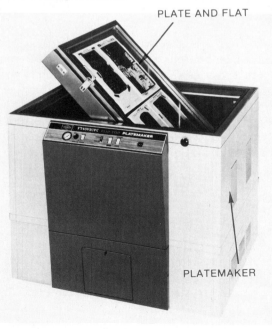

NUARC COMPANY

GOLDENROD

NEGATIVE   LIGHT SENSITIVE   NEGATIVE   PLATE
SURFACE   IMAGE AREA

Fig. 89-1. Flat and plate position when exposing a negative.

PLATE AND FLAT

PLATEMAKER

Fig. 89-2. A plate exposure unit with the flat and plate in position.

The flat is the negative master for making plates. Any number of plates can be made from one flat. Most graphic arts companies store and file flats so they can be used again. If the plate is damaged or wears out, a new one can easily be made from the flat. The new plate will be exactly like the old one and can be made in a few minutes.

WORK OF THE STRIPPER

The stripper has several tasks that must be done very accurately. The masking sheet must be prepared so that it matches the original artwork for the job. Negatives must be attached in the correct position on the masking sheet. The stripper must cut windows in the masking sheet to expose the image areas of the negative.

Unwanted areas of the negative must be covered with opaque material. Also, the stripper makes proofs to check whether the flats have been properly prepared.

The stripper must work carefully and be very precise. Problems in the printing process are often caused by poor stripping. Expensive adjustments on the printing press or bindery equipment may have to be made if flats are not properly prepared. Some printing jobs are ruined by errors made during stripping.

The stripper's jobs range from simple ones like accurately placing one negative on a masking sheet. More complicated jobs include making flats when several negatives must be placed on one masking sheet. The work becomes even more complicated when flats must be prepared for multiple color printing. Here, flats must be made so that when the plates are made and printed, the colors will line up precisely.

UNIT 90 TOOLS AND MATERIALS FOR STRIPPING

An offset lithography stripper requires several pieces of equipment and materials different from those used elsewhere in a graphics arts plant. The stripper must know each item very well to use it efficiently. Most strippers organize their equipment and materials so they can find them easily when needed. Equipment must also be kept clean and in good working order.

LIGHT TABLE

The stripper spends most of the time working at a light table (Fig. 90-1). The table has a solid frame, a frosted glass top, and lights below the glass top. Light below the glass helps the stripper see through film negatives and masking sheets. The edges of the light table should be straight and square so that a T-square and triangle can be used for accurate work.

When extremely precise work must be done, a line-up table is used. The line-up table is similar to the light table but has micrometer gauges for making exact measurements. Figure 90-2 shows a line-up table on which a flat has been made.

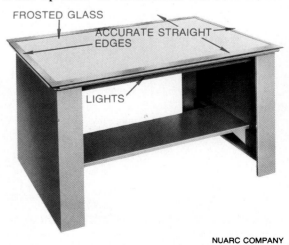

FROSTED GLASS

ACCURATE STRAIGHT EDGES

LIGHTS

NUARC COMPANY

Fig. 90-1. A light table.

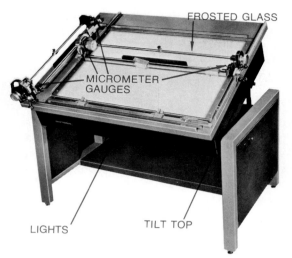

CRAFTSMAN TABLE COMPANY

Fig. 90-2. A line-up table.

T-SQUARE AND TRIANGLES

A T-square and triangles are needed to make layouts on masking sheets. They are also used to help align negatives and cut negatives and masking paper. The most popular ones are made of stainless steel, because they give an accurate guide when you cut along the edges with a knife. Stainless steel tools are not as easily damaged as plastic or aluminum ones. Figure 90-3 shows a T-square, two triangles, and a standard bevel rule, all made of stainless steel.

REGISTER PUNCH AND REGISTER PINS

Masking sheets and plates are often punched with a register punch (Fig. 90-4). The precision

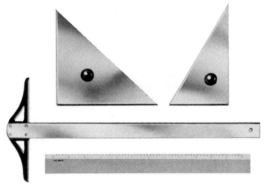

Fig. 90-3. Stainless steel T-square and triangles along with a beveled rule.

holes let the flats and plates be placed over register pins (Fig. 90-5). This lets the stripper locate the flat accurately on the plate. It is also used when preparing multi-color or complementary flats.

PROOF PRINTER

The stripper will need to have an exposure unit in order to make proofs. Many times the stripper will be able to use a platemaking machine to expose proofs. The exposure unit should be big enough to hold the largest flat that will be made in the plant.

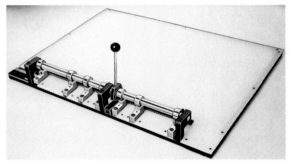

CHESLEY F. CARLSON COMPANY

Fig. 90-4. A pin register punch.

CHESLEY F. CARLSON COMPANY

Fig. 90-5. Register pin for pin registration.

RULES

Rules are used to make measurements on the masking sheets and negatives. Stainless steel rules are often preferred, but other kinds will work well, too. In addition to making measurements, rules are sometimes used as straight edges. A thin rule, or one with a beveled edge, is best because it is easier to use accurately.

MAGNIFYING GLASS

Magnifying glasses are used to examine negatives during stripping. Magnification helps you find small defects in the negatives and positives. Magnifying glasses are available in several styles (Fig. 90-6). They also come in styles that will magnify the image 6 to 10 times.

OTHER SMALL TOOLS

There are many other small tools that help the stripper in making flats. The tools discussed below are the common ones.

Knives. Knives are used by the stripper to cut negatives and masking materials. Knives should be kept very sharp. Strippers often like knives with blades that can be replaced, because less time is needed to replace a blade than to sharpen a dull one. Single-edge razor blades are sometimes used as substitute knives but they are not very safe.

Scissors. Scissors are used to trim negatives and positives. The cutting edes should be very sharp to make clean cuts.

Brushes. Artist brushes are used to opaque (block-out) pin holes in negatives. Several sizes of brushes, from very fine to medium, should be

Fig. 90-6. A swing-base magnifier is used to find defects in negatives.

available to the stripper. They should always be kept clean and in good condition.

MATERIALS

Many different materials are used or consumed during the stripping operation. An ample supply of these materials should be kept on hand. They should be stored so that they are easy to get and easy to keep in good condition.

Masking sheets. This material is used as a support for negatives when making flats. Masking sheets are yellow or orange. The color is important because it keeps ultraviolet light, which could expose the plate, from reaching the plate.

Masking sheets are translucent. This lets the stripper see through the masking sheet when it is on a light table.

Masking sheets are made from either paper or plastic. Paper is used for general work when only one flat must be made. Plastic is used when extreme accuracy is needed. Paper expands and contracts (gets larger or smaller) when the temperature and humidity change. Plastic masking sheets do not change size with changes in temperature or humidity. Plastic masking sheets are more expensive than paper masking sheets, but they are worth the cost if accuracy is needed.

Masking sheets come in several sizes. A masking sheet must match the plate size to be used on the printing press. Masking sheets larger than the plate are often used.

Some masking sheets are available with printed guidelines that make it easy to align the negatives (Fig. 90-7). Masking sheets for larger presses do not usually have pre-printed guidelines, so the stripper must draw the needed guidelines to align the negatives.

Opaque solutions. Opaque (say *o-pake*) is a water-soluble material available in cake, paste, or liquid form. Pinholes and other unwanted clear areas on negatives are blocked out with opaque. The opaque is usually thinned with water to make a creamy solution that is applied to the negative with a brush or pen. Opaque comes in black and red. Many strippers prefer the red opaque because it contrasts with the black negative, making it easier to see.

Fig. 90-7. A typical masking sheet for masking flats.

Fig. 90-8. Felt tip opaquing pens.

Special felt tip opaquing pens are convenient to use, but the tips dry quickly unless they are kept covered. Both large and small sizes are available (Fig. 90-8).

Tape. Both lithographer's tape and common clear pressure-sensitive tape are used during stripping. Clear tape is used to hold the negative to the masking sheet. Lithographer's tape is red or brown and is used to cover unwanted images on the negative. Like masking material, it keeps light from reaching the plate. Tape should be kept in dispensers ready for use near the light table.

UNIT 91 PREPARATION AND LAYOUT FOR STRIPPING

All stripping for offset lithography begins with planning and layout of the flat. Other preparatory work must also be done. Most errors in stripping are caused by incomplete or poor layout planning. The location of the negatives on the masking sheet determines their exact location on the printing plate.

PREPARING FOR STRIPPING

The stripper should first examine the negatives to be attached to the masking sheet. When possible, the negatives should be compared with the copy used to make the negatives. Inspection can sometimes be done without a magnifier, but often, when working with fine line work or halftones, magnification is helpful.

Specifications, including the original layout, should be carefully checked by the stripper. Before the layout can be made, you must know the sheet size, the location of the images on the press sheet, and the margins. You need to know if the printed sheets will be trimmed, folded, stitched, padded, or have other operations done after the printing is done. In most cases, the artist who prepares the copy should put registration marks on the copy to help the stripper. These marks are most helpful when the negatives are being positioned on the masking sheet. Stripping is very difficult without registration marks. If these marks do not appear on the negatives, the stripper will need to supply them.

LAYING OUT THE MASKING SHEET

Layout is done on masking sheets. Both pre-printed and plain (unlined) masking sheets can be used to make flats. Pre-printed masking sheets are often used with small presses and duplicators. Even though pre-printed masking sheets already have some lines printed on them, you may need to add some essential guidelines.

Figure 91-1 shows a drawing of the several lines that should be placed on a masking sheet. When there may be question about what a mark on the masking sheet means, the stripper should write out the meaning on the masking sheet.

Locating the leading edge. The stripper must place the negative on a masking sheet so that it will print in the correct position on the final printed sheet. To do this, you find the edge of the masking sheet that corresponds to the *lead edge* of the sheet to be printed. The lead edge is the side of the press sheet that feeds into the press first. One way to identify the lead edge on the masking sheet is to cut a triangle-shaped mark at the lead edge. This is shown as the *center mark* in Figure 91-1.

The lead edge of the press sheet is held in the printing press by grippers. The lead edge of the press sheet should be located at the top edge of the gripper margin (Fig. 91-2). The space between the masking sheet lead edge and gripper margin is called the *plate bend area* (Fig. 91-1). The size of the plate bend area is different for each printing press. You should learn the size of the plate bend for all presses in the graphic arts laboratory. The location of the lead edge is shown on most pre-printed masking sheets. These special masking sheets are designed for specific kinds and sizes of offset lithography presses and duplicators.

It is very important that the plate bend area of the press sheet be the same for each job on a press. This will save large amounts of time as the press operator will not have to make so many press adjustments.

Identifying the gripper margins. A stripper must know the size of the gripper margin for each press in the laboratory or plant. This is the distance between the lead edge of the press sheet and the position where the first part of the image can be printed. This portion of the printed sheet is held by the press grippers, which are the parts of the press that carry the sheet through the press. Figure 91-3 shows the gripper margins on a pre-printed masking sheet. The space is usually ¼- to ⅜-inch (6.35 to 9.5 mm). *No image will print within the gripper margin area.* You must draw the lower line of the gripper margin on masking sheets that are

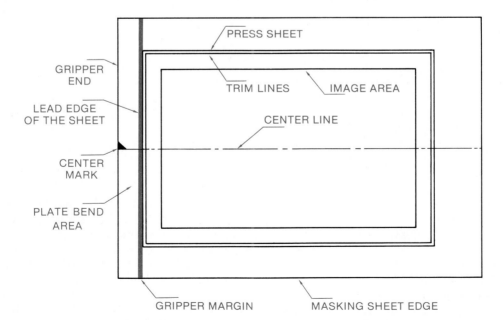

Fig. 91-1. The kinds of marks placed on a masking sheet layout.

LEAD EDGE

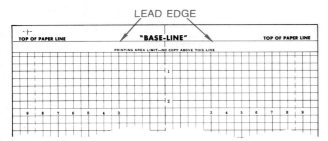

Fig. 91-2. Part of the masking sheet that corresponds to the lead edge of a printed page.

GRIPPER MARGIN

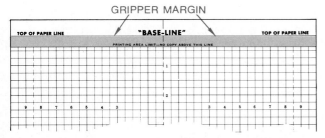

Fig. 91-3. The gripper margin is the space between the lead edge of the printed page and the place where the image will print.

BEST 8½ x 11 PAGE MARGIN

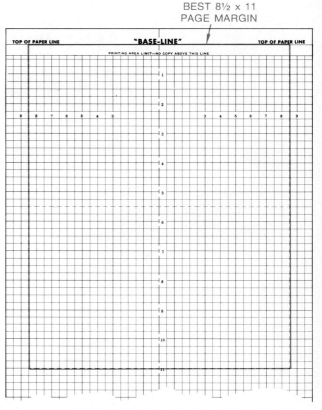

Fig. 91-4. Many masking sheets for duplicators have the best location for the sheet of paper marked by dotted lines.

not pre-printed. This is done by measuring the gripper margin distance from the lead edge line.

Locating the center line. Most jobs are positioned by the center line on a masking sheet (Fig. 91-1). As the term implies, the center line is the exact center of the masking sheet. Center lines are marked on pre-printed masking sheets, but must be drawn on other masking sheets. The center line of the press sheet should, in most cases, be located on the center line of the masking sheet. This procedure will help the press operator set up the job and will save valuable press time.

Determining the press sheet lines. The press sheet guidelines should be exactly the same size as the sheet of paper that will be printed on the press. Notice that the lead edge of the sheet is placed at the top edge of the gripper margin. In Figure 91-4 the sheet is located so that half of the press sheet is on both sides of the center line. The press sheet guidelines should be drawn on both preprinted and plain masking sheets.

Placing trim lines on the masking sheet. It is sometimes helpful to draw *trim lines* on the masking sheet. Trim lines show the size of the sheet after it has been printed and trimmed

(Fig. 91-1). The trim lines are the lines that should be used to locate the image area.

LOCATING IMAGES ON THE MASKING SHEET

The layout procedures described above are very important and need to be done accurately before attaching negatives to the masking sheet. Equally important is laying out for the placement of the images to be printed. This is done by drawing guidelines within the press sheet area. It can be done several different ways. One common method is to draw a guideline for placing the top line on the negative. When more than one negative is to be placed on a flat, a guideline should be drawn for each negative (Fig. 91-5).

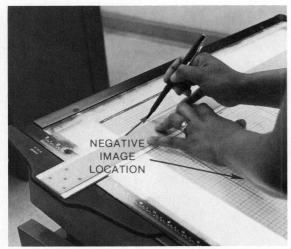

Fig. 91-5. Marking the image location within the page margins.

LOCATING SEVERAL PAGES ON A FLAT

Often you will need to print several pages on the same press sheet. The procedure is much the same as for locating a single page on the press sheet. The major difference is that the stripper must draw additional lines to show the position of the pages within the press sheet margins. Figure 91-6 shows a flat layout for one side of an eight-page booklet. In this case four pages will be printed on the reverse side of the booklet.

When both sides of the booklet are printed, it must be folded and trimmed.

In Figure 91-6 the same kind of guidelines have been drawn as for a single page on the masking sheet. Additional lines have been drawn so the stripper can properly locate the images on each page. The additional lines needed for a multi-page layout are fold lines and trim lines. In the layout the centerline identifies one fold line. This procedure should be used with both preprinted and plain masking sheets. When the flat is actually prepared, marks are made on the flat so that the marks will print in the trim areas. They guide the press operator and the people who will do the binding. These can be scribed (scratched) into the emulsion of the film attached to the masking sheet. Sometimes the trim lines and fold marks are made by making thin cuts in the masking sheet. The best way is to place them on the original paste-up.

PROCEDURE FOR FLAT LAYOUT

The stripper should follow the procedures below when preparing a masking sheet. Some strippers bypass these procedures to save time, but time will actually be lost if the flat is inaccurately prepared.

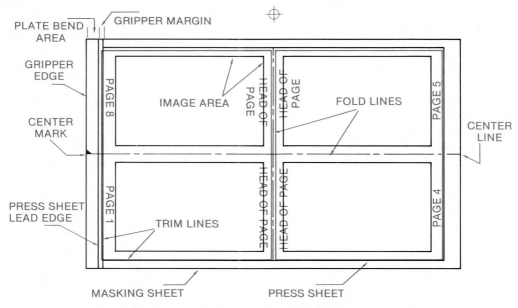

Fig. 91-6. A flat layout for one side of an eight-page booklet.

1. Look over the comprehensive layout and negatives for the job. These should give all of the information you need to complete the flat. If you have questions about how the job should be printed, ask the customer.
2. Fasten the masking sheet to the light table with masking tape. Be sure it is square to the left and bottom edges. Remember to use a T-square.
3. Find the gripper edge of the masking sheet and make the center mark.
4. Draw the center line of the masking sheet. This should be done with a ball-point or felt-tip pen. Use a thin, dark line.
5. Mark the plate bend area needed for the press that the job will be printed on.
6. Draw a line to identify the gripper margin. This space will be somewhat different for each printing press. *The gripper margin is very important because no image will print in this area.*

7. Draw the press sheet size on the masking sheet. This is the same size as the sheet of paper that will be printed on the press. Notice in Figure 91-2 that the lead edge of the sheet should be placed at the top line of the gripper margin.
8. Place the trim lines on the masking sheet when necessary.
9. Draw the fold lines on jobs that will be folded.
10. Draw lines to show the area where the image will be located on each page to be printed on the press sheet.
11. Draw lines to show the exact location of each image (negative) to be attached to the masking sheet.
12. When preparing a flat to print multiple pages on a press sheet, the top of each page should be given. This is sometimes called the *head of the page.*

UNIT 92 ATTACHING NEGATIVES TO THE MASKING SHEET

The stripper's job is to position the negative in the location where the image will print on the press sheet. You should start with the masking sheet layout. Making a good masking sheet layout will reduce the problems of attaching negatives to the masking sheet. Once the image positions are determined, negatives can be attached to the masking sheet with tape.

Two basic techniques are commonly used to prepare flats. One is done with the emulsion side of the negatives down and the other is done with the emulsion side of the negatives up. Both efficiency and accuracy must be considered when deciding which technique to use. The first concern should be accuracy, but it is also important to do the work as quickly as possible. You should use the technique that does accurate work in the least amount of time.

The stripper needs to have all of the necessary tools nearby for attaching the negatives

(Unit 9). Knives should be sharp. All tools and working surfaces should be clean.

ATTACHING NEGATIVES—EMULSION SIDE DOWN METHOD

To use this method, the negatives are placed under the masking sheet with the emulsion side of the film against the glass of the light table. The negatives are in the right-reading position (Fig. 92-1). The top surface of the masking sheet faces up.

This technique is simple to use and is most useful when working with smaller masking sheets. In most cases, flats can be made quickly and accurately in this way. Here is the procedure for attaching negatives with the emulsion side down:

1. Tape the masking sheet to the surface of

the light table. The top surface of the masking sheet should be face up. Often the masking sheet will already be attached to the light table, because the stripper usually attaches the negatives immediately after making the masking sheet layout. Place the tape only at the gripper edge of the masking sheet. Be sure to align the masking sheet with a T-square (Fig. 92-2).

2. Carefully draw guidelines to locate the images for the negatives on the masking sheet. This is sometimes done as part of the masking sheet layout. The images must be in the proper location and parallel or square to the press sheet. Note that some images may be placed at an angle to the press sheet edge (Fig. 92-3). Note also that the guidelines must provide for both horizontal and vertical placement of the image.

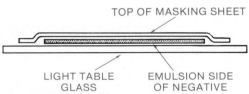

Fig. 92-1. A negative and masking sheet position for making a flat with the emulsion side down.

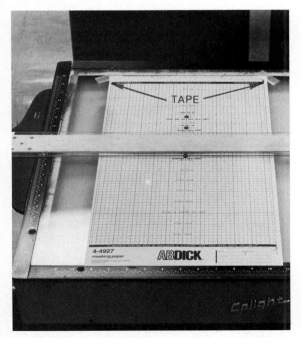

Fig. 92-2. Masking sheet placed in position on light table.

3. Place the negative under the masking sheet with the emulsion side against the light table glass. You should be able to read the image on the negative.

4. Move the negative until the image aligns with the guidelines drawn in step 2 above (Fig. 92-4). You will be able to see the image by the light of the light table.

5. Cut small football-shaped openings in the masking sheet near the edges of the negatives. Hold the negative in place by applying pressure to the masking sheet over the negative. Be careful to cut only through the masking sheet (Fig. 92-5). You may need several football-shaped openings to hold large negatives in place.

6. Place lithographer's tape over these openings and press the tape firmly into place (Fig. 92-6). This will temporarily attach the negative to the masking sheet.

7. Check the image in the negative with a T-square and triangle to be sure it is square on the masking sheet.

8. Remove the tape from the gripper edge of the masking sheet and turn the flat over. Place tape at the corners of the negative (Fig. 92-7). Clear tape can be used. When the negative is large, you may need to place small pieces of tape along the edges of the negative to hold it securely in place.

ATTACHING NEGATIVES—EMULSION SIDE UP METHOD

This method is done by first placing the masking sheet on the light table. The top surface of the masking sheet is placed against the glass of the light table. The negatives are placed on the masking sheet with the emulsion side up (Fig. 92-8).

The emulsion-up method of attaching negatives is often used with large masking sheets. In most cases, this method gives greater accuracy than does the emulsion-down method. One disadvantage of emulsion-up is that the negatives cover the guide lines on the masking sheet. Because of this, guidelines need to be scribed on the negative to align it with the guidelines on the masking sheet.

Fig. 92-3. Stripper marking guidelines on the masking sheet.

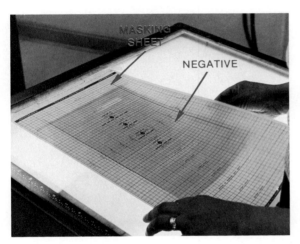

Fig. 92-4. Negative images aligned with masking sheet guidelines.

Fig. 92-5. Stripper cutting windows to tape negative temporarily in place.

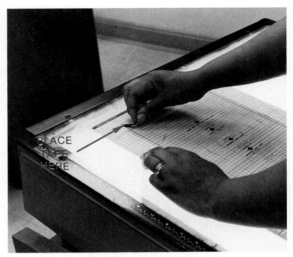

Fig. 92-6. Stripper placing tape over windows.

Fig. 92-7. Stripper taping negative to the back of the masking sheet.

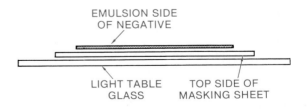

Fig. 92-8. Negative and masking sheet position for making a flat with emulsion side up.

Here is the procedure for attaching negatives with the emulsion side up:

1. Tape the masking sheet to the surface of the light table. The top surface of the masking sheet should be against the glass of the light table. The masking sheet must be squarely positioned and checked with a T-square. Tape the masking sheet at the gripper edge (Fig. 92-9).

2. Draw guidelines for positioning the negative. These lines should be extended beyond where the edge of the negative will be located (Fig. 92-10). Both horizontal and vertical guidelines should be drawn.

3. Guidelines (registration marks) should be scribed (scratched) in the emulsion side of the negative. This is done in the open area next to the image area. Both horizontal and vertical guidelines should be scribed (Fig. 92-11). Another method is to have registration marks on the paste-up. When the negative is made, these marks will be on it.

4. Line up the registration marks of the negative with the guidelines on the masking sheet (Fig. 92-12). The negative may need to be trimmed to aid in aligning the negative with the masking sheet.

5. While holding the negative in position, place clear tape over the corners of the negative. On large negatives, small pieces of tape can be placed along the edges.

Many times you will need to attach several negatives to a single masking sheet. This is done by repeating the procedure described above. Be careful that the negatives do not overlap (Fig. 92-13). Overlapped negatives may cause a bad plate exposure. Trim negatives to keep them from overlapping.

OPENING THE IMAGE AREA

The combination of negatives and the masking sheet is called a flat. However it cannot yet be used to make a plate because no light can go through the image area of the negatives. The image areas are still covered by the masking sheet (Fig. 92-14). The masking sheet covering

Fig. 92-10. Guideline for image placement for emulsion side up flat.

Fig. 92-11. Stripper scribing lines on the emulsion side of a negative.

Fig. 92-9. Masking sheet in position on the light table for emulsion side up flat.

Fig. 92-12. Aligning negative with masking sheet for negative side up flat.

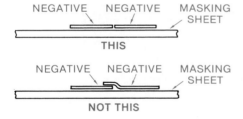

Fig. 92-13. Negatives should butt. They should not overlap.

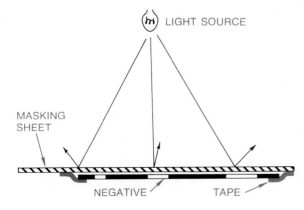

Fig. 92-14. The masking sheet keeps light from passing through the masked areas of the negative.

the image areas must be removed by carefully cutting through the masking sheet with a sharp knife.

Cuts should be made so that the masking sheet will be about ³/₈-inch (9.5 mm) from the edge of the image area (Fig. 92-15). The minimum image-to-cut distance should be ¹/₈-inch (3.2 mm). When there are large spaces between images on a negative, openings should be cut around each image instead of the whole masking sheet.

OPAQUING NEGATIVES

Negatives often have unwanted clear areas in them. The most common are called *pinholes*. These are tiny holes in the negatives caused by dirt on the paste-up or poor negative processing. If the pinholes are not covered, they will show up on the printing plate and be printed on the press sheet. You must cover *all* pinholes. This process is called *opaquing* or *spotting*.

Opaquing can be done on the negative either before it is attached to the masking sheet or after the flat has been opened. Because many pinholes may be covered by the masking sheet, it is best to opaque negatives after the flat has been made.

Opaque solution is placed on the base (right reading) side of the film. It can be applied with a brush or with a felt-tip pen (Fig. 92-16). Fingerprints should be cleaned from the surface of the negatives, because skin oils will keep the opaque from sticking to the negative. The opaque solution must be completely dry before the flat is used to make a plate. When opaquing, carefully cover the negative image areas. If opaque does get on the image areas, it should be removed with a damp tissue.

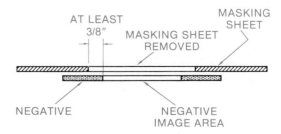

Fig. 92-15. Cut away the masking sheet at least ³/₈-inch from the image area.

Sometimes large areas of a negative need to be blocked out or opaqued. Lithographer's tape may be used to cover these areas. This is done by taping the right-reading negative or flat to the light table with the base side up. You then cover the entire area with lithographer's tape. The strips should slightly overlap. Then cut away the tape with a very sharp knife to expose areas to be printed.

OPAQUING

Fig. 92-16. Stripper opaquing a negative on the right-reading (base) side.

UNIT 93   COMBINING NEGATIVES AND PROOFING

Halftone negatives often must be attached to negatives of line copy. Halftone negatives must be made separately from the line negatives. For many printed jobs, halftone and line negatives must be combined to complete the job as ordered by the customer. There are also times when corrections are made in only a small part of a larger negative. The smaller negative is then stripped in register with the large negative to avoid having to make the entire negative again.

Combining halftone negatives with line negatives can be done before or after attaching them to the masking sheet. If the halftone is attached after the line negative is attached to the masking sheet, you must be very careful. It is quite easy to move the line negative on the flat.

There are two main ways to combine halftone and line negatives. The most effective way is to place the halftone negative behind a clear window in the line negative. A halftone negative can also be combined with the line negative by cutting a window (hole) in the line negative. The halftone negative to be combined with the line negative is cut to the same size as the window and is taped in place.

COMBINING NEGATIVES USING CLEAR WINDOWS

Black (or red) rectangular shapes should be placed on the paste-up where halftones will go. This will form clear areas in the line negative. This will save much stripping time and reduce the cost of printing the job. Here is the procedure for combining a halftone negative with a line negative, using a window:

1. Examine the line negative and the paste-up. The continuous-tone copy (photographs) that comes with the paste-up should also be examined. The artist should have given information about how the photographs should be cropped (which parts will be printed).
2. Compare the halftone negative to the window in the line negative. The window

should be large enough for all parts of the halftone to be printed.

3. Cut the halftone negative so that it will fit within the window area. The halftone is usually cut so that it is about ⅛- to ¼-inch (3.2 to 6.35 mm) larger than the window. Be careful not to let any of the halftone overlap into image areas on the line negative.

4. Turn the line negative upside down on the light table—that is, emulsion side up.

5. The halftone negative should be placed over the window in the line negative. The emulsion side of the halftone negative should also face up.

6. While holding the halftone in place, carefully tape it to the line negative. This should be done with clear tape. The tape should not extend into the image areas of the line negative (Fig. 93-1).

7. Turn the combined negatives over to right-reading position and check to be sure that the halftone is in the correct position.

The halftone negatives should always be placed on the emulsion side of the line negative. The image on the plate will be defective if the halftone negative is placed on top of the line negative.

CUTTING WINDOWS FOR HALFTONES

When a line negative does not have clear windows, the stripper must cut them. The stripper must also cut the halftone negative to fit inside the line negative window. This procedure, given below, is much more difficult than the clear window procedure.

1. Examine the line negative, paste-up and the original photograph for the job. Determine exactly where the halftone should appear in the line negative. Often the line negative

will already be attached to the masking sheet.

2. Cut the halftone to a size slightly larger than the final printed size. About ⅛- to ¼-inch (3.2 to 6.35 mm) should be left on all four sides for tape to hold the negative in place.

3. Turn the flat upside down. The emulsion side of the line negative should face up.

4. Mark the location on the line negative where the halftone will be placed. This can be marked by scribing the emulsion of the line negative. The window should be the same size as the halftone negative. A T-square should be used to help scribe the window area (Fig. 93-2).

5. Turn the flat over so the line negative is right-reading.

6. Carefully cut out the window with a very sharp knife (Fig. 93-3). It is best to cut the line negative from the base side (right-reading) because the emulsion side can be easily scratched.

7. After the window is cut, the halftone negative should be placed into the window area. Be sure the emulsion side faces in the same direction as the line negative.

8. With the halftone negative in place, put lithographer's tape over the lines where the negatives butt together (Fig. 93-4).

9. Trim the tape to the exact size for the illustration with a sharp knife.

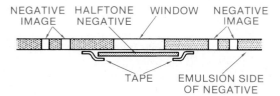

NEGATIVE IMAGE   HALFTONE NEGATIVE   WINDOW   NEGATIVE IMAGE

TAPE   EMULSION SIDE OF NEGATIVE

Fig. 93-1. Halftone negative taped behind a line negative.

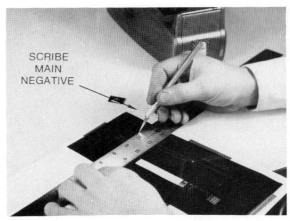

SCRIBE MAIN NEGATIVE

Fig. 93-2. Scribe the emulsion of the negative to locate the illustration on the main negative.

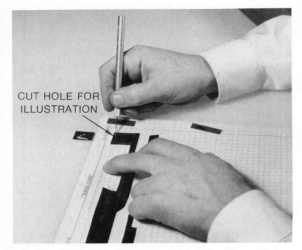

Fig. 93-3. Cut the main negative where it was scribed.

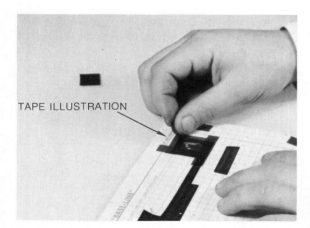

Fig. 93-4. Place the illustration in the hole and tape it to the main negative.

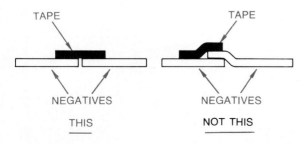

Fig. 93-5. Negatives should butt against each other, not overlap.

The two negatives should not overlap. They should butt against each other (Fig. 93-5). It is better to have a little space between the negatives than to have them overlap. The tape should always be placed on the base (right-reading) side of the film.

PROOFING

Proofs are often made of flats to find problems and errors. This should be done after the flat is complete and before the offset lithography plate is made. The proof is used in the printing plant to check for errors, and most customers will want to see proofs before the job is printed. Several printing plants even require customers to approve proofs before the jobs are printed. The customer can often find errors missed by the printer.

Several kinds of materials are available for making proofs. Some are developed in special solutions, others are developed in ammonia, and some need only to be exposed. Proofs are not meant to be permanent. They are needed only for short periods of time. In Figure 93-6 the stripper is exposing some proof paper.

Fig. 93-6. Stripper exposing a proof of a flat.

UNIT 94 STRIPPING FOR MULTIPLE EXPOSURES

It is often necessary to make more than one flat to effectively prepare the plates required to print a job. This will require special attention by the stripper because extreme accuracy is required to keep the flats in *register*. Flats are in register when all of the images are precisely lined up with each other. This unit will deal with some situations in which multiple flats are needed.

REGISTRATION METHODS

Strippers use different methods to register (align) the flats. Some jobs require more critical alignment than others. Regardless of how critical the registration, the stripper must have a frame of reference to register one flat with other flats. The same frame of reference should be used to align flats with plates.

Registration can be done using several methods. For jobs where critical alignment is not necessary, the edges of the masking sheet can be used. While this is not nearly as accurate as other methods, it is sometimes faster and requires less equipment.

Register Punch. It is recommended that strippers use a *register punch* and *register pins* to align flats. The same punch is often used to punch the plates so they too can be accurately aligned with flats.

The register punch (Fig. 90-4) cuts holes in the masking sheets and plates, all of which must be punched on the same edge, frequently the lead edge, of the masking sheet (See Fig. 91-1). For greatest precision, the punched holes should be the same distance from an adjacent edge of the flat. When this is done, all flats and plates will be in proper alignment (Fig. 94-1).

Some printing presses are built so plates can be precisely attached to the printing cylinders. This helps maintain accurate register throughout the printing process. Figure 94-2 shows a flat that has been punched for register pins. In Figure 94-3, a plate has been punched to match the register holes in the flat in Figure 94-2. The plate also has *plate position indents* on the edge to position the plate on the press cylinder. The plate position control indents are used to locate each plate in the same place on the cylinder (Fig. 94-4).

COMPLEMENTARY FLATS

Sometimes it is necessary to make multiple flats to expose one plate properly. For example, when line copy, such as a caption, must be placed near a halftone, *complementary flats* must be used. Complementary flats are also used when one image is printed over another

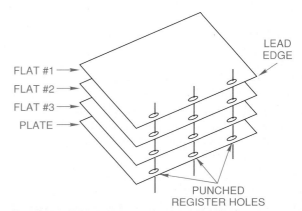

Fig. 94-1. Flats and plates are punched so they can be accurately registered.

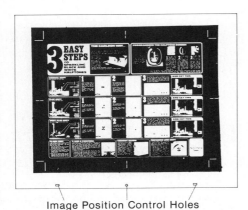

Image Position Control Holes

CHELSEY F. CARLSON COMPANY

Fig. 94-2. Flat punched with holes for register pins.

CHESLEY F. CARLSON COMPANY

Fig. 94-4. Press operator locating plate position indent in place on a press.

Plate Position Control Indents

CHELSEY F. CARLSON COMPANY

Fig. 94-3. Plate punched with holes for register pins.

image, such as when line copy is printed on top of a tint. In Figure 94-5, first the tint was exposed on the plate using one flat. Another flat that contained the type matter and border was then exposed on the same plate. Because both flats had been punched for register pins, the images were in register.

Any number of flats can be used to expose one plate, as long as the images are in the proper locations and register pins are used. Normally one flat is used as a *master flat*. All of the markings are made on the master flat. The other flats are registered to the master flat so that all images will be in position.

STEP-AND-REPEAT

Some printed jobs are done with the same image repeated several times on the same sheet of paper. After the job is printed, it is cut into the individual items. This saves considerable press time. Jobs like labels, decals, and business cards are done with this method.

Step-and-repeat can be done by making several duplicate negatives and placing each in the correct location on the masking sheet. However, this could require considerable stripping time if there are several images to be placed on the same flat.

More frequently, step-and-repeat is done by placing one negative on the flat. The flat is then exposed the correct number of times on the plate. Each time an exposure is made, the flat is moved horizontally or vertically to a new position on the plate. The space where previous exposures have been made is covered with masking paper to protect it from the platemaker light. If this is done by hand, care must be taken to be sure the images are accurately located on the plate.

Equipment such as that shown in Figure 94-6 is used to do extremely precise step-and-repeat work. This equipment is computer controlled and is necessary when doing step-and-repeat work with multicolor images. The head on the table moves horizontally and vertically to accurately locate the images.

PRINT OVER A TINT

Fig. 94-5. A print that needed two negatives to make the plate.

MASKING METHOD

Some simple multicolor jobs can be done by making one master flat and *masking* flats for each color. This method is appropriate when no images overlap other images or print on top of other images. The master flat is used to make two or more plates. The masking flats are used to block out images except those to be printed on a particular plate. Below is the procedure for the masking method:

1. Obtain a masking sheet and punch it for register pins. This will be the master flat.

2. Place register pins in the holes and line the masking sheet up with a T-square on the light table. Tape the register pins to the light table when the masking sheet is lined up.
3. Place all negatives, regardless of color, in the proper location on the master flat. Cut windows in the master flat for all images.
4. Punch a second masking sheet exactly like the master masking sheet. This will be used to mask (block out) all images except those to be printed in one color. Cut windows in this masking sheet for all images to be printed in that particular color.
5. Obtain another masking sheet for each additional color to be printed and repeat Step 4.
6. Punch a plate with holes exactly like the ones in the flats. Place pins through the holes.
7. Place the master flat over the plate so the register holes on the flat line up with those on the plate.
8. Place the first masking flat over the master flat and expose the plate.
9. Remove the plate and develop it.
10. Repeat Steps 6, 7, and 8 for each masking flat.

COLOR STRIPPING

Most color stripping requires that at least one flat be prepared for each color to be printed. If yellow, cyan, magenta, and black are to be printed, there will be at least four flats—one for each color.

In many ways, stripping for color reproduction is similar to that done for preparing complementary flats. For example, Figure 94-7 was printed with the same flats as the image in Figure 94-5. The only difference was that a plate was made to print the tint in a color and another plate was made to print the type in black.

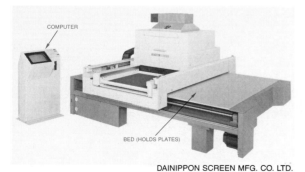

COMPUTER

BED (HOLDS PLATES)

DAINIPPON SCREEN MFG. CO. LTD.

Fig. 94-6. A step-and-repeat machine.

Register is particularly important when preparing process-color flats. Most negatives will have register marks that will assist the stripper in locating negatives. However, the stripper also must be sure the images line up, regardless of the register marks.

Usually one color is used as the master to prepare the first flat. This is frequently the cyan printer (negative or positive). All other flats are aligned with the master. Care must be taken to look straight down on the negatives or positives when aligning them with the master. It is easy to misalign the images when sighting is done at an angle.

Masks with windows are sometimes used so halftones will have accurate borders. These can be prepared by using masking film. In some plants the masks are prepared with special equipment. The equipment shown in Figure 94-8 is computer controlled. Information is placed into the computer by a digital tablet. The digital tablet locates the position and sizes of the windows very accurately. The plotter then cuts masking film or draws the windows. This is a much more accurate method than preparing them by hand.

As with complementary flats, it is sometimes necessary to make more than one flat for each color to be printed. This is done for the same reasons that complementary flats are made for single-color printing. The stripper must concentrate on what he or she is doing to be sure the flats are prepared properly.

PRINT OVER A TINT

Fig. 94-7. The same negatives used in Figure 94-5 will also print two colors.

It may be useful for the stripper to make notes on the flats to explain their purpose.

PROOFING

It is wise to prepare proofs of flats to be sure that all images have been properly located. Sometimes printers do not make proofs because it takes more time. However, it is much easier to find errors from a proof than to try to find them on a flat.

Many printers require that customers approve proofs before plates are made and the job is printed. Also, some customers want to see proofs before the job is printed to be sure the job has been done to their specifications. There are several different kinds of proofing materials for both single-color and multicolor proofs.

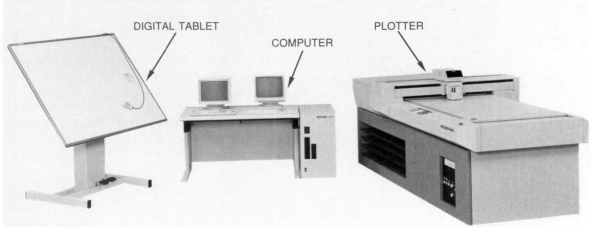

DIGITAL TABLET COMPUTER PLOTTER

DAINIPPON SCREEN MFG. CO. LTD.

Fig. 94-8. Digital plotting equipment used to prepare masks for color stripping.

UNIT 95 LEARNING EXPERIENCES: LITHOGRAPHIC IMPOSITION

KEY TERMS

Unit 89

Goldenrod
Masking sheet

Stripper
Stripping

Unit 90

Light table
Line-up table
Opaque

Register pin
Register punch

Unit 91

Center mark
Fold lines
Gripper edge

Gripper margin
Lead edge
Plate bend
Trim lines

Unit 92

Opaquing

Spotting

Unit 93

Proofing

Unit 94

Complementary flats
Masking
Step and repeat

Register
Register marks

DISCUSSION TOPICS

1. How is the flat used in the lithographic printing process?
2. Why is it important for the stripper to mark the gripper margin on a masking sheet?
3. Why are line and halftone negatives combined on a single flat?
4. Why should register marks be used on paste-ups, flats, and printing plates?
5. Why are register punches valuable for both single color and multiple color printing?

ACTIVITIES

Unit 91

1. Obtain a masking sheet and mark it to show the center mark, plate bend area, lead edge, gripper margin, center line, and press sheet for an 8 1/2-by-11-inch (21.5 by 28 cm) sheet of paper.
2. Layout a masking sheet for a four-page signature.

Unit 92

3. Secure a negative to a masking sheet using the emulsion-side-down technique.
4. Secure a negative to a masking sheet using the emulsion-side-up technique.

Unit 93

5. Prepare a single flat for a one-color job that contains one line negative and two halftone negatives. Attach one halftone using the clear window technique and attach the other halftone by cutting out the window. Proof the flat and inspect your results.

Unit 94

6. Prepare a single flat that will be used to expose offset lithography plates for a two-color job. Prepare the two masking sheets that will serve as color masks. Be sure to punch register the three masking sheets. Make a proof for each color. Compare these proofs with the original rough or comprehensive layout to determine their accuracy.

Preparing a plate to be used to print a student newspaper.

12 LITHOGRAPHIC IMAGE CARRIERS

UNIT 96 INTRODUCTION TO LITHOGRAPHIC IMAGE CARRIERS

A plate (image carrier) is used in the offset lithographic process to produce printed products. A plate can be made from paper, plastic, or metal. The material must be thin and strong enough to be wrapped around the plate cylinder of an offset lithography press (Fig. 96-1).

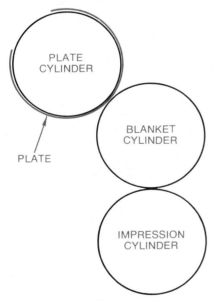

Fig. 96-1. The plate is wrapped around the cylinder.

The surface of a plate has *image* areas and *non-image* areas. The plate image areas repel water (fountain solution) and the non-image areas accept water. When ink is applied to the plate surface, ink will stick to image areas and will be repelled in the non-image areas. The ink from the image areas is transferred to the blanket from the plate. Ink is then transferred to the paper as it passes between the impression and blanket cylinders.

There are several methods used to make plates for offset lithography printing. It is important to select the best method and the best kind of plate to get the desired quality. The *platemaker* is the person who traditionally has made plates from flats. In recent years, however, several methods have been developed that do not require flats.

Quality printing plates are important when printed material is produced by the offset lithography method. Printing press operators can produce quality printed products only with printing plates that are made right. If poorly-made plates are sent to the press operator, production schedules will be delayed and materials wasted. The result is less profit made from the job.

Manufacturers of platemaking materials and equipment are developing new methods of producing quality plates. The manufacturers are also concerned with efficiency and economy in making plates. Commercial printers should be aware of the many kinds of plates now available.

UNIT 97 KINDS OF PLATES

Plates are usually grouped in two ways—as surface plates and as deep-etch plates. Surface plates are made by placing the images on the surface of the base material (Fig. 97-1). Deep-etch plates are made with images slightly below the surface of the base material (Fig. 97-2).

SURFACE PLATES

There are two kinds of surfaces on plates—smooth and grained. As the name suggests, *smooth surface plates* have a very flat, smooth surface, which is treated so that water adheres to it. Some printers believe that smooth surface plates produce greater detail than grained plates.

Grained surface plates have a rough surface. The rough surface helps hold the emulsion (photosensitive material) on the metal plate. It also helps balance the ink and water. Grain is applied to plates by mechanical or chemical methods.

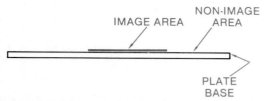

Fig. 97-1. Images are placed on the surface of lithographic surface plates.

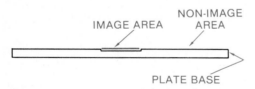

Fig. 97-2. Images on deep-etch plates are slightly below the surface of the base.

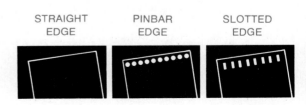

A. B. DICK COMPANY

Fig. 97-3. Lithographic plates are made with different kinds of ends.

Plates are made in many sizes to fit specific presses. Plates are also prepared with different kinds of edges. Most common are straight-edge, pinbar-edge, and slotted-edge plates (Fig. 97-3). The straight-edge plates are clamped into the plate cylinder of a press. Pinbar and slotted-edge plates are used on litho duplicators that have special plate-holding devices.

Surface plates are the most commonly used plates. Many kinds of surface plates are used to produce high-quality printing. They are more economical to use than deep-etch plates. While they do not last as long as deep-etch plates, many of the newer surface plates can be used to produce thousands of copies before they wear out.

Laser-imaged plates. The image to be printed is applied directly to the printing plate surface with a laser imagesetter (Fig. 97-4). This technology eliminates the need to print the image on phototypesetting paper, to make film negatives, to strip flats, and then to process a litho printing plate. The laser image-setter used to make this type of litho plate is described in Section 4. Direct laser-imaged plates are automatically processed after being exposed in the imagesetter. They can print from 25,000 to 50,000 high-quality impressions, and their cost is reasonable. There are considerable savings in time, material, and labor.

Pre-sensitized plates. Pre-sensitized plates have two main layers—a base and a light-sensitive coating (emulsion). Bases are made of paper, plastic or metal. Aluminum is the most common metal base.

Different kinds of photosensitive emulsions are placed on pre-sensitized plates. The most common kind of emulsion is called *diazo*. The areas exposed to light become insoluble (will not dissolve) in water. When lacquer is applied to the surface, it sticks to the image areas.

Pre-sensitized plates are either additive or subtractive. With the *additive* plate, the exposed image area is made visible by adding a lacquer-based coating. With *subtractive* plates, the emulsion coating (lacquer) is placed on the plate when it is manufactured and the non-image area is removed when the plate is processed. These are commonly used plates because of their low cost, ease of preparation, and excellent printing quality.

Electrostatic plates. These plates have a smooth water-receptive surface that is conductive. This conductive surface is given an electrical charge. When light strikes the plate surface, the electrical charge is released from the plate. The plate is passed through a material, called *toner,* which is attracted to the charged image area on the plate. The toner is heated to fuse it to the plate. The fused toner is ink receptive, and so the ink sticks to the image areas when printed. Plates are made on special machines similar to office electrostatic copiers. Electrostatic plates are used when a limited number of copies are needed and quality is less important.

Diffusion-transfer plates. The diffusion-transfer process can be used without a flat to make a plate. The copy is photographed directly from the paste-up to the negative paper. The exposed negative paper and a plate are developed in a processor. After the negative and the plate material are separated, the image is visible on the printing plate.

Photo-direct plates. Photo-direct plates are made with special equipment. A camera unit is used to expose a plate, much as a negative would be exposed. However, the image to be printed is placed directly on the plate without making a negative. Most equipment is de-

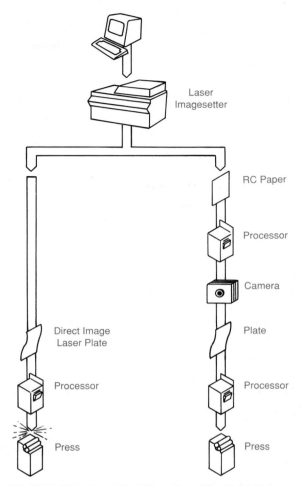

Fig. 97-4. Preparing a direct-image laser litho plate eliminates several steps involved in making conventional litho printing plates.

signed to cut plates to the correct length and then automatically process them. These plates are usually used on litho duplicators for short-run jobs.

Direct-image plates. The image to be printed is applied to the surface of the plate. Direct-image plates are made from paper or plastic, and have smooth water-receptive surfaces. They are usually used on lithographic duplicators, or when less than a hundred copies are needed. Images are placed on the plate with anything that will give an ink-receptive image, commonly typewriters, pencils, ballpoint pens, and crayons (grease pencil).

Direct-image plates usually have nonprinting guidelines printed on the plate to aid in drawing on the plate.

DEEP-ETCH PLATES

Deep-etch plates are used when a great many copies must be printed. Some kinds of deep-etch plates can be used to print over a million copies. There are many kinds of deep-etch plates and several different methods are used to make them. Deep-etch plates are expensive and are used for special long-run jobs. Because of the improved quality of pre-sensitized plates, deep-etch plates are not so popular as they once were.

UNIT 98 EXPOSING PRE-SENSITIZED PLATES

Flats are placed over plates to cover the entire surface. The masking sheet for the flat should be slightly larger than the plate so the edges are completely covered. When the flat and plate are in tight contact, light is passed through the image areas to expose the plate. The flat—which includes the masking sheet and the negative—holds back all light except in the image areas. After the plate is exposed and processed, it is ready for use on the printing press.

EQUIPMENT FOR EXPOSING PRE-SENSITIZED PLATES

Pre-sensitized plates are exposed in machines called *platemakers* (Fig. 98-1). Sometimes this piece of equipment is called a *plate exposure unit*. A platemaker has two important parts— the vacuum frame and exposing light. The *vacuum frame* holds the plate and flat in tight contact. The exposing light produces a very bright light to expose the plate.

The exposure unit in Figure 98-1 has the exposure light in the cabinet. The vacuum frame is hinged so it can be rotated. The plate and flat are placed in the vacuum frame when it is in the

NUARC COMPANY

Fig. 98-1. A typical lithographic exposing unit.

up position. When the plate and flat are in place, the vacuum frame is turned upside down so the plate and flat face the light. This kind of platemaking unit helps protect the operator's eyes. Some plate exposure units have an open vacuum frame (Fig. 98-2) with a movable exposing light (Fig. 98-3).

Fig. 98-2. Vacuum frame on a plate exposing unit.

NUARC COMPANY

Fig. 98-3. Open vacuum frame and movable exposing light.

Vacuum frame. An efficient way to hold the plate and flat in tight contact is with the vacuum frame. A vacuum frame consists of a rubber blanket, a glass cover, and a vacuum pump. The plate is placed in the frame and the flat is put over it. When the plate and flat are in position, the glass frame is closed (Fig. 98-4). The vacuum pump is turned on and the blanket compresses the plate and flat against the glass to produce tight contact (Fig. 98-5).

Light source. The ideal light source for exposing pre-sensitized plates is a point-source light (Fig. 98-6). This means that light comes from a single point rather than from

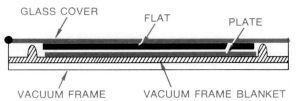

Fig. 98-4. A cross section of a vacuum frame, no vacuum applied.

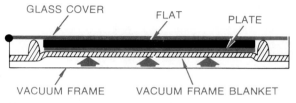

Fig. 98-5. A vacuum frame with vacuum applied.

many points. The point-source light must produce a bright ultraviolet light. Mercury vapor and metal halide are lights commonly used to expose plates.

The exposure unit in Figure 98-7 has a light source above the vacuum frame. A curtain is pulled around the unit when the exposure is made. Metal halide lights (Fig. 98-8) give large amounts of light.

Safety tip. The ultraviolet light used to expose plates is very bright and can damage eyes. Never look directly at the light in a plate exposure unit.

DETERMINING PLATE EXPOSURE

Pre-sensitized plates are exposed with bright ultraviolet light. Like film, plates can be underexposed or overexposed. Underexposure causes plates to have a short press life. *Short press life* means the image will wear off the plates much faster than normal. Overexposure may cause the image to spread, especially with halftones. The light may undercut (shine beneath) the small dots in the shadow area and fill in the image completely.

A *plate sensitivity guide* is used to determine the proper exposure time. The sensitivity guide, sometimes called a gray scale, is a piece of film that has several different densities of gray, ranging from clear to black. Each density is given a specific number called a *step* (Fig. 98-9).

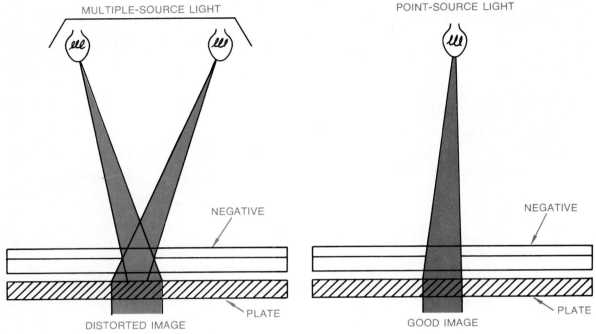

MULTIPLE-SOURCE LIGHT

POINT-SOURCE LIGHT

NEGATIVE

PLATE

DISTORTED IMAGE

NEGATIVE

PLATE

GOOD IMAGE

Fig. 98-6. The effects of multiple-source and point- source lights.

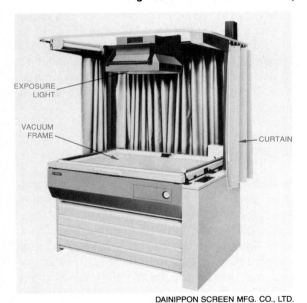

EXPOSURE LIGHT

VACUUM FRAME

CURTAIN

DAINIPPON SCREEN MFG. CO., LTD.

Fig. 98-7. The curtain is pulled around the exposure unit while the exposure is made.

NUARC COMPANY

Fig. 98-8. Metal halide lights.

The sensitivity guide is attached to the flat in the plate bend area as though it were a negative. The flat is then exposed. When the plate is processed, the sensitivity guide is treated exactly like all other images on the plate, except that it should be thoroughly rubbed over the gray area. If the plate has been exposed long enough, step 6 will remain on the plate (Fig. 98-10). Step 6 should be as dark and sharp as the step 1. If step 6 rubs off or becomes ragged, the plate was not exposed long enough and a longer plate exposure time should be used. If the sensitivity guide steps 7, 8, and 9 remain on the plate, the exposure was too long and the exposure time should be shortened.

Fig. 98-9. A platemaker's sensitivity guide (gray scale).

Fig. 98-10. A platemaker's gray scale developed on a plate.

The sensitivity guide need not be used with every plate. Once the correct exposure time is found, it will not change rapidly. However, a regular schedule should be established to check the accuracy of the exposure time.

PLATE EXPOSURE PROCEDURE

The following procedure is a guide to exposing most offset lithography plates. In exposing plates, you should be familiar with the exposure specifications for the specific kind of plate being used. You must also know thoroughly how to use the equipment.

Cleanliness of the glass frame is very important. Both sides of the glass should be checked each time a plate is made and cleaned if necessary. Even tiny pieces of dirt can block light from passing through an image on the flat. This will cause a broken image on the plate. Before you expose the plate, the flat should be examined to be sure it is clean, the opaque dry, and all images clear. Also, be sure that the plate is clean. Use the following procedure to expose a plate:

1. Check the flat, plate, and platemaker for cleanliness.
2. Load the plate and the flat into the plate exposure unit. Place the light-sensitive side of the plate toward the glass of the vacuum frame. Position the flat over the plate so that the image on the negative is readable. Align the plate accurately with the flat, using register pins. Close the glass frame when the plate and flat are aligned.
3. Turn on the vacuum pump. Pressure from the rubber blanket should make firm contact between the plate and flat up against the glass. Be sure the plate and flat remain aligned.
4. Move the vacuum frame into position so that the light will expose the plate.
5. Set the timer for the correct exposure time. *Remember this should be checked on a regular basis with a plate sensitivity guide.*
6. Turn on the light source. Expose the plate for the proper amount of time.
7. Turn the frame so the glass cover is up when the exposure is done.
8. Turn off the vacuum pump.
9. Remove the plate and flat from the vacuum frame.
10. Close the frame and cover the glass, or turn it over, to keep the glass clean.
11. If a two-sided plate is being used, both sides should be exposed before processing either side.
12. Process the exposed plate to make the image visible. See Unit 99.

Plates are sensitive to bright room light, so it is best to handle the plate in yellow light. If yellow light is not available, the normal white light brightness should be reduced. Heat and humidity also affect plates. Unexposed plates should be stored in a cool, dry place.

UNIT 99 PROCESSING PRE-SENSITIZED PLATES

After exposure, pre-sensitized plates must be processed before they can be used on the printing press. Processing is often called *rubbing-up* a plate. The purposes of processing are to remove the unexposed light-sensitive coating from the plate and to preserve the plate. The non-image areas of the plate will oxidize if not covered with protective gum.

There are two kinds of pre-sensitized plates—*additive plates* and *subtractive plates*. Images are placed on additive plates by placing a lacquer-type solution on the plate. Subtractive plates have a colored image material on the plate before it is exposed. This material is removed from the nonprinting areas during processing.

PROCESSING EQUIPMENT

Plates should be processed on a clean, flat surface. Special plate processing tables are very helpful. A plate developing sink with a water supply is excellent for plate processing (Fig. 99-1). A plate finishing table with a heater for drying plates rapidly is useful (Fig. 99-2). Clamps are used to hold the plate in place.

PROCESSING ADDITIVE PRE-SENSITIZED PLATES

Additive plates need to have a lacquer-type material applied to the plate for the image to be seen. Many different companies manufacture additive plates. Follow the instructions of the manufacturer. The following is a typical procedure for processing an additive pre-sensitized plate.

1. Collect all materials needed to process the plate (Fig. 99-3). They should be organized close to the work area.

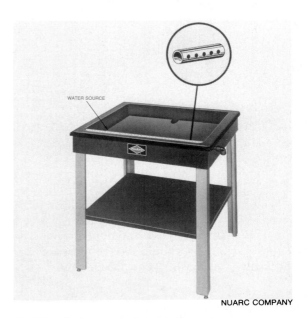

NUARC COMPANY

Fig. 99-1. A plate processing sink. The water source makes it convenient to spray water on the plate after it is processed.

NUARC COMPANY

Fig. 99-2. A lithographic plate-finishing table.

3M COMPANY

Fig. 99-3. Materials used to process presensitized additive plates.

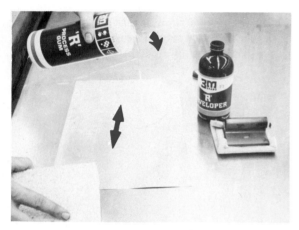

3M COMPANY

Fig. 99-4. Applying the desensitizing process gum solution which will remove the unused light-sensitive coating from the non-image areas.

2. Place the plate in the plate developing sink or on the processing table. The exposed surface should be face up.

3. Pour some *desensitizer* solution onto the plate. This solution is called process gum by some companies. The purpose of the solution is to remove the unexposed diazo material from the plate.

4. Wipe the entire plate with a sponge (Fig. 99-4). The plate should be thoroughly covered and wiped with the process gum. It is better to wipe a little too much than not enough. When this step is complete, the plate is light safe.

5. Pour developer on the plate. Only a small amount (a spot a little larger than a half-dollar) is needed for most plates. It should be poured on a non-image area of the plate. This liquid has a color like

red or blue. It is called lacquer by some companies. The main purpose of the lacquer developer is to make the image area visible. The developer also adds to the life of the plate so that long press runs are possible.

6. Use a sponge to rub the developer over the entire plate in a circular motion until a uniform medium color is obtained (Fig. 99-5). *Be sure to rub the plate bend areas to check the plate sensitivity guide.* It should show a solid step 6 that is as dark and sharp as step 1.

7. Wash the plate with water. You may need to rub the plate lightly with the developer sponge to remove the excess developer.

8. Drain the excess water from the plate by lifting it by one corner and letting the water run off into the sink.

9. Lay the plate on some dry newspapers on a nearby counter or table.

10. Pour a small amount of process gum on the dry plate (Fig. 99-6). The process gum is placed on the plate to keep the non-image areas from oxidizing. Any non-image area that oxidizes will pick up ink on the press just like the image areas.

11. Using a special litho wipe pad, polish the plate until it is dry. Use heated or unheated air to dry the plate more rapidly.

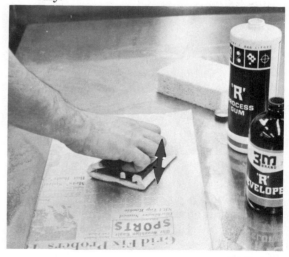

3M COMPANY

Fig. 99-5. Developing the plate.

Fig. 99-6. Applying process gum after developing the plate.

Fig. 99-7. Pour developer on the pad or sponge and plate.

12. Hang the processed plate in a dry, dirt-free area until it is ready to be printed.

Steps 9 through 11 can be omitted if the plate is to be used immediately on the press. The plate can also be used without doing steps 5 and 6, but it is difficult to see the images on

the plate. When two-sided plates are used, both sides should be wiped with desensitizer before applying the developer.

PROCESSING SUBTRACTIVE PRE-SENSITIZED PLATES

Subtractive pre-sensitized plates are somewhat different than additive plates. The emulsion (light-sensitive coating), including the colored lacquer, is placed on the plate when it is made. Processing is done to remove the unexposed light-sensitive diazo emulsion from the plate. This will leave the non-image areas clear. While the plates are quite different, the rubbing up procedure is similar:

Fig. 99-8. Develop the plate.

1. Be sure all materials are ready to be used.
2. Pour developer on the pad or sponge and the plate (Fig. 99-7).
3. Develop the plate. The pad should be moved in a circular motion. Firm pressure should be applied (Fig. 99-8).
4. The colored (usually red) non-image areas will be removed from the plate. The image areas will remain on the plate.
5. The plate should be cleaned. This can be done with a squeegee or a throw-away de-

NATIONAL MACHINE COMPANY

Fig. 99-9. An automatic lithographic plate processor. Machines of this type are frequently used in graphic arts plants where platemaking consistency and timesaving are very important.

veloping pad and water.

6. Lift the plate and let the water run off.
7. Gum the plate. Use the same procedure as with the additive plate.

Some subtractive plates are processed by dipping the plates in a developing solution after the plates have been exposed. The non-image areas will be removed by the developer. The plate is then washed and gummed.

AUTOMATIC PROCESSING

In plants where large numbers of plates are made, an automatic processor is often used (Fig. 99-9). The processor does all of the procedures needed to prepare the plate for use on the press.

100 PREPARING DIFFUSION-TRANSFER, DIRECT IMAGE, AND ONE-STEP PHOTOGRAPHIC PLATES

UNIT

Many different kinds of plates can be used in offset lithography printing. Several plates were described in Unit 97. Most of them were designed for use with litho duplicators or presses. The three kinds of plates presented in this unit can be made without using a flat. These plates are used most often when speed and cost are more important than quality.

DIFFUSION-TRANSFER PLATES

Plates are made directly from the paste-up using a process camera and a diffusion-transfer plate processor (Fig. 100-1). Instead of film, a piece of negative paper is placed in the camera. The exposed negative paper is placed in contact with the plate material and run through the plate processor, where the negative paper and plate material go through an activator solution. The plate material and exposed negative paper must stay in contact after being taken out of the processor for thirty seconds to one minute. The plate material and

EASTMAN KODAK COMPANY

Fig. 100-1. A typical diffusion-transfer processor that can be used when making paper prints, film positives, and litho plates.

negative paper are then separated. The paper or metal plate is then coated with special fixer before being used on the press.

Several companies manufacture diffusion-transfer materials and equipment. These companies may use different terms and have differ-

KODAK PMT METAL LITHO PLATES

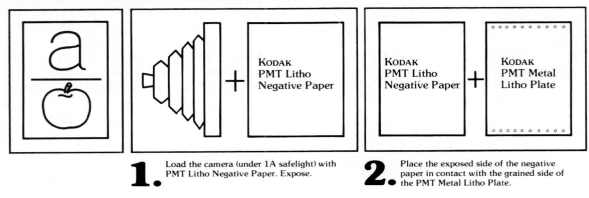

1. Load the camera (under 1A safelight) with PMT Litho Negative Paper. Expose.

2. Place the exposed side of the negative paper in contact with the grained side of the PMT Metal Litho Plate.

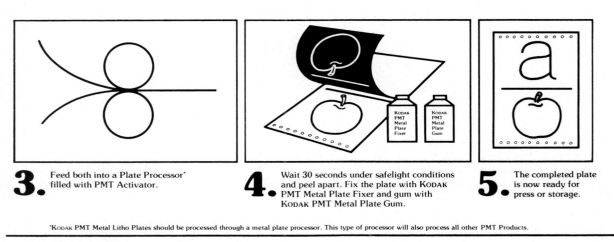

3. Feed both into a Plate Processor* filled with PMT Activator.

4. Wait 30 seconds under safelight conditions and peel apart. Fix the plate with KODAK PMT Metal Plate Fixer and gum with KODAK PMT Metal Plate Gum.

5. The completed plate is now ready for press or storage.

*KODAK PMT Metal Litho Plates should be processed through a metal plate processor. This type of processor will also process all other PMT Products.

EASTMAN KODAK

Fig. 100-2. Steps used to make a diffusion-transfer metal plate using the Kodak PMT process.

ent procedures for making diffusion-transfer plates. Figure 100-2 shows the steps used to make Kodak PMT (diffusion-transfer) metal plates. The steps for making paper and metal diffusion transfer plates are very similar.

DIRECT-IMAGE PLATES

The image to be printed is applied directly to the surface of the plate. Direct-image plates have a smooth, water-receptive surface. The image is placed on the surface with anything (grease) that will make an ink-receptive image. Direct-image plates are made from paper and plastic and are most often used on duplicators. Only a limited number of copies can be printed from direct-image plates. They are useful in situations where photomechanical equipment is not available.

Typing on direct-image plates

Typewriters are used to put images on direct-image plates (Fig. 100-3). Both cloth ribbons and one-time carbon ribbons can be used on the plates. One-time carbon ribbons give a much sharper image. Also, electric typewriters give better results than manual typewriters.

Typing on a direct-image plate is nearly as easy as typing on paper. The same procedures are used. The typewriter keys should be very clean. When typing, you must take special care in handling plates and making erasures. Fingerprints are greasy and will print if not completely cleaned from the plate. Some typists even wear white gloves when handling direct-image plates. Even pressure should be used on the typewriter. Too much pressure can create hollow spots on the plate image surface (Fig. 100-4). The low-pressure setting on an electric typewriter gives good impressions on the plate.

DIRECT IMAGE PLATE

Fig. 100-3. A direct-image plate used in a typewriter.

THIS TOUCH IS TOO HEAVY.

THIS TOUCH IS CORRECT.

Fig. 100-4. Correct typing pressure is needed to get a good image on a direct-image plate.

Drawing on direct-image plates

Drawing is done on direct-image plates with special pencils and pens that make a greasy image on the plate. (When making drawings, do not handle the plate more than necessary.)

Both freehand and mechanical drawings can be made. Guidelines are first placed on the plate with a non-reproducing pencil. The marks made with the non-reproducing pencil will be removed when the plate is printed. Special ball-point pens, reproducing pencils, and crayons can be used to draw on plates.

PHOTO-DIRECT LITHOGRAPHIC PLATES

Photo-direct plates are unique. Images to be printed are photographically placed directly on the plate material. This is done without the use of negatives or flats.

Equipment for photo-direct plates looks similar to process cameras used to make negatives (Fig. 100-5). However, there are some differences. The camera has a lens and a prism that places a readable image on the plate (Fig. 100-6). Also, most equipment includes a section where the plates are processed after they have been exposed (Fig. 100-7). Plates ready for printing are delivered from the equipment in a short time.

Photo-direct plates are used when speed of reproduction is important. Line copy is most frequently used when making photo-direct plates. However, prescreened halftones can be included as part of the copy to be photographed.

Photo-direct plates usually have a polyester base with a lithographic surface (accepts water). A photographic emulsion, which is a receptor (accepts ink), is on the surface. The photographic emulsion is removed from the plate—except from the image areas—when it is processed. Plate material comes in rolls that fit into the machine. The width of the plate material is the same as plate widths for litho duplicators and presses. The plate is cut to the proper length for the particular litho-duplicator/press during processing.

Photo-direct plates are commonly used on litho duplicators but they are also used on litho presses. Up to 10,000 copies can be obtained from these plates. Several companies make photo-direct platemaking equipment and materials. To obtain quality litho plates, care must be taken to follow the manufacturer's instructions.

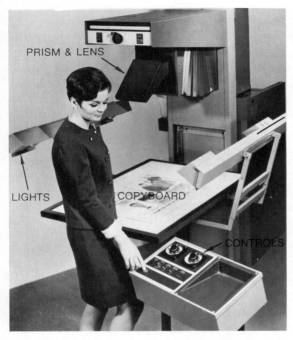

Fig. 100-5. An operator preparing to make a photo-direct litho plate using a camera-processor system.

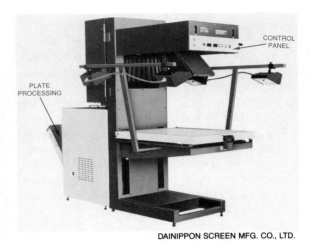

Fig. 100-7. A computer-controlled photo-direct platemaking system that is used to make quality litho plates.

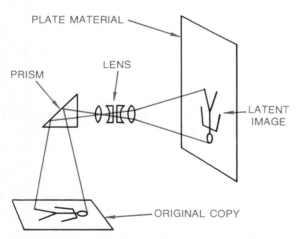

Fig. 100-6. A schematic illustration of the exposure system of the photo-direct platemaking equipment shown in Figure 100-5.

UNIT 101 CORRECTING, PRESERVING, AND STORING PRE-SENSITIZED PLATES

Pre-sensitized plates are sensitive to oxidation and scratches and must be handled with care to give satisfactory results when used on the press. But problems occur even when the most careful precautions are taken to protect the plates. The following procedures are like those suggested by plate manufacturers for correcting, preserving, and storing pre-sensitized plates.

MAKING CORRECTIONS

Plates are made to reproduce exactly what is on the negative of the flat. Once the plate is made, it is hard and at times impossible to make any changes. It is much easier and less costly to prevent errors than to correct them. However, two kinds of corrections can be made on the pre-sensitized plate. You can make deletions and some additions.

Deletions. Deletions are the removal of unwanted areas from the plate. Small areas, such as spots from pinholes on the negative, can be removed by rubbing lightly with a clean, soft rubber eraser that has been moistened with water or fountain solution. This is often done after the plate has been attached to the press. Be very careful not to damage or scratch the plate with the eraser.

Large areas are removed with a special *deletion fluid* provided by the manufacturer of the plate. It must be applied when the plate is dry by using a clean cotton swab or pad. After the image has been removed from the plate, the deletion fluid is flushed away with water.

Additions. It is often possible to repair broken lines, damaged letters, or holes in solid areas of a plate. Broken lines are repaired and minor additions are made by scratching the surface with a sharp needle held at a slight angle. The plate should be dry for this repair.

Holes in solid areas are repaired with *plate tusche* (a form of greasy lithographic ink) available from the plate manufacturer. The tusche is applied while the plate is dry but before it is gummed (preserved). It is rubbed on the area with a cotton swab for about 30 seconds. Neutralize the tusche with water and dry the plate immediately. Rub ink into the dry area where the tusche was applied; then gum the plate.

Correcting is not as satisfactory as producing a correct plate in the first place, and the procedures for correcting should be used only when it is not practical to make a new plate.

PRESERVING PLATES

Plates are preserved to prevent oxidation and minor abrasions and scratches. Most plates are

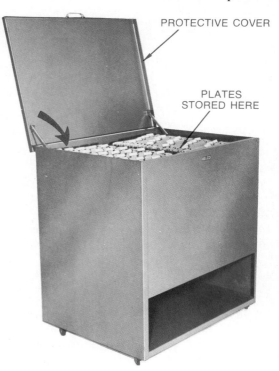

PROTECTIVE COVER

PLATES STORED HERE

FOSTER MANUFACTURING COMPANY

Fig. 101-1. A plate storage cabinet.

preserved before and after they are printed. Plates are kept after printing when it is likely that they will be used again. A protective coating of gum arabic is applied to the surface. You should follow the manufacturer's instructions because some plates need a special solution.

The same procedure outlined in Unit 99 for gumming the plate is usually suitable for preserving it. It is important to prevent air bubbles by polishing the gum dry. If the air bubbles break, oxidation will occur in that spot. The result is a plate that will print little specks. Before the plate is printed, the gum is removed with water or fountain solution.

STORING PLATES

Plates are sometimes made several days before they are printed. They can be damaged during this time unless special care is taken with them. A damaged plate delays production and increases the cost of the job.

It is always best to *hang* plates rather than stack them on top of one another. If they must be stacked, put protective paper between them. Take care that both sides are completely dry. Moisture attacks the protective gum coating and causes oxidation. Large envelopes should be used to store plates. This helps protect them from scratching and makes handling them easier.

Portable storage cabinets are useful in organizing and storing plates (Fig. 101-1). This type of cabinet can be rolled to the area where it is needed. It should be kept in an area of the plant away from moisture and excessive heat.

UNIT 102 LEARNING EXPERIENCES: LITHOGRAPHIC IMAGE CARRIERS

KEY WORDS

Unit 96

Platemaker

Unit 97

Additive plate
Deep-etch plate
Diazo
Diffusion-transfer
  plate
Direct-image plate

Electrostatic plate
Grained plate
Pre-sensitized plate
Subtractive plate
Surface plate

Unit 98

Gray scale
Mercury vapor light
Metal halide light
Plate sensitivity
  guide

Point source light
Pulsed-xenon light
Vacuum frame

Unit 99

Lacquer

Rubbing-in

Unit 101

Deletion fluid
Gum arabic

Tusche

DISCUSSION TOPICS

1. Describe *image* and *non-image* areas on a lithographic plate.

2. Describe the difference between surface plates and deep-etch lithographic plates.

3. Describe the difference between *additive* and *subtractive* pre-sensitized plates.

4. How is a plate sensitivity guide used in making a plate?

5. Describe the procedures for making diffusion-transfer plates.

ACTIVITIES

Units 98 and 99

1. Get a masking sheet and a plate sensitivity guide. Cut several windows in the masking sheet. Make them the same size as the sensitivity guide. Tape the sensitivity guide into one of the windows. Place the flat, with the sensitivity guide, over a plate in the exposure unit and cover up the additional windows. Make an exposure of slightly less time than that presently being used in the laboratory. After the exposure, remove the sensitivity guide and place it in another window. Cover the window from the first exposure and make an exposure of the sensitivity guide, using a little more time. Continue this procedure until all of the windows have been used. Process the plate to determine the best exposure time as recommended by the manufacturer.

Unit 100

2. Secure a direct-image plate and examine the markings on the plate. List the purpose of each of the markings.

3. Using several different tools, try to produce images on the direct image plate. Examples of tools:
   a. Non-reproducing pencil
   b. Reproducing pencil
   c. Regular graphite pencil
   d. Regular ball-point pen
   e. Ball-point pen made for drawing on direct-image plates
   f. Grease pencil (crayon)
   g. Typewriter with a regular ribbon
   h. Typewriter with a reproducing ribbon
   i. Typewriter with a one-time carbon ribbon

   In addition to using different tools to produce images on the direct image plate, apply various pressures when making the images.

4. Print the plate from Item 2 and examine the printed sheets to determine the best methods for preparing a direct-image plate.

5. Visit a printing plant that has equipment for making one-step photographic plates. Ask the operator to explain the process of making a one-step photographic plate. Prepare a detailed report on your visit and interviews.

**Attaching a lithographic plate to
the cylinder of a newspaper press.**
DOW JONES & COMPANY, INC.

13 LITHOGRAPHIC IMAGE TRANSFER

103 INTRODUCTION TO OFFSET LITHOGRAPHY PRESSWORK

The lithographic principle of image transfer is that grease and water do not readily mix. This principle allows an image to be transferred from one smooth surface to another smooth surface (Fig. 5-2). Large and small offset lithography presses are designed on this principle.

OFFSET LITHOGRAPHY DUPLICATOR AND PRESS SYSTEMS

Offset lithography presses (large or small, sheet- or web-fed, single- or multiple-color) contain five major systems (Fig. 103-1). These systems are: (1) feeding, (2) cylinders, (3) dampening, (4) inking, and (5) delivery. As an operator, you must understand each system thoroughly. Different brands and models of presses have their

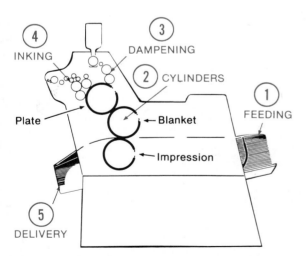

Fig. 103-1. The five systems of an offset lithography duplicator or press.

controls in various locations, but if you understand each of the systems, you can find the controls and make adjustments needed.

Feeding system. The feeding system includes the area of the press from the pile of single sheets or the roll of paper through the line-up mechanism, and into the blanket and impression cylinders. This system must be adjusted to feed and line up one sheet of paper at a time.

Cylinder system. The cylinder system contains the plate, blanket, and impression cylinders. The plate cylinder holds the thin lithographic plate, which when inked, transfers the image to the blanket (offsetting); the blanket in turn transfers the image to the paper. The impression cylinder holds the paper in contact with the blanket.

Dampening system. The dampening system, sometimes called the water system, contains a supply fountain and a few rollers that transfer a thin coating of ink-repellent solution to the plate as it revolves around the plate cylinder. The solution is basically water, but it contains some special additives to repel ink. With the development and use of the dry lithographic duplicator plate, this system can be eliminated from duplicators and presses. Such a plate has a special dry surface that transfers an inked image without the need of a water solution.

Inking system. As it revolves around the plate cylinder, the inking system, containing several rollers, carries and distributes a supply of ink to the image of the plate. Several ink rollers are needed to carry the proper supply of

319

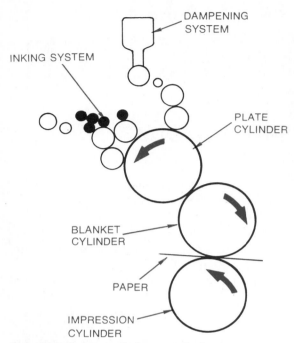

Fig. 103-2. A three-cylinder press design.

SOLNA CORPORATION

Fig. 103-3. An offset lithography press that incorporates the three-cylinder design.

ink to cover the image fully during each revolution of the press.

Delivery system. After being printed, the sheets must be delivered from the cylinders to a collection area. This system can hold several hundred printed sheets.

Three-cylinder press design

The *three-cylinder* press design (Fig. 103-2) has plate, blanket, and impression cylinders. A thin metal, plastic, or paper plate is fastened to the plate cylinder with specially designed clamps. As the cylinder revolves the plate receives a thin coating of water in the non-image areas and a coating of ink within the image area. The plate rolls against the blanket cylinder and the image is offset onto the blanket. As the blanket and the impression cylinders roll together with paper between them, the image is offset from the blanket onto the paper. Most offset lithography presses, large and small, use the three-cylinder press design (Fig. 103-3).

Two-cylinder press design

The *two-cylinder* press design (Fig. 103-4) has an oversized upper cylinder that includes the

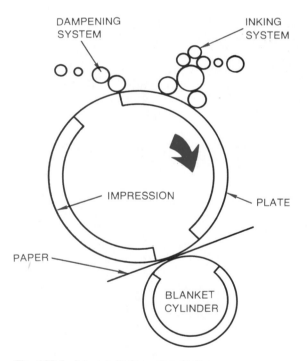

Fig. 103-4. A two-cylinder press design.

plate and the impression segment. The lower, smaller cylinder contains the blanket.

When no paper is traveling between the upper and the blanket cylinders, the plate is *offsetting* the image onto the blanket. When the plate area of the upper cylinder completes half a revolution, a sheet of paper begins to pass

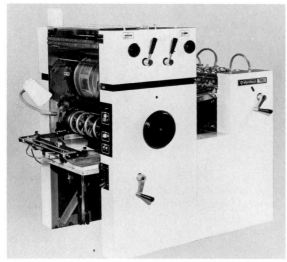

ATF-DAVIDSON COMPANY

Fig. 103-5. An offset lithography duplicator-press that incorporates the two-cylinder design.

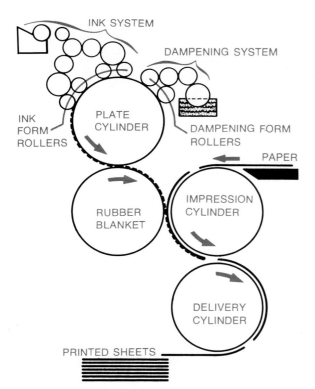

Fig. 103-6. The ink, dampening, and cylinder systems typical of a heavy-duty offset lithography press.

through the two cylinders. The impression segment of the cylinder forces the paper against the blanket cylinder, causing the image to offset

to the paper. During this time the plate is again receiving a new supply of water and ink, ready to complete another printing cycle. The offset-lithography press in Figure 103-5 uses the two-cylinder press design. These presses are commonly used for office and in-plant reproduction.

Heavy-duty press design

This press design uses plate, blanket, impression, and delivery cylinders (Fig. 103-6). The delivery cylinder, added to the typical three-cylinder press design, aids in precision delivery of the printed sheet. It is used on nearly all commercial heavy-duty offset lithography presses (Fig. 103-7). Another addition to this press design is the two dampening form rollers that

SOLNA CORPORATION

Fig. 103-7. A two-color, heavy-duty offset lithography press incorporating the press schematic in Figure 103-6.

roll against the plate, insuring proper application of the dampening solution. There are also four ink-form rollers for thorough application of ink to the image area of the plate.

OFFSET LITHOGRAPHY AND LETTERSET PRESS DESIGN

The offset lithography and letterset press design has features of both offset lithography and letterpress in a single unit. A schematic (Fig. 103-8) shows how these two principles of image transfer are used. The normal three cylin-

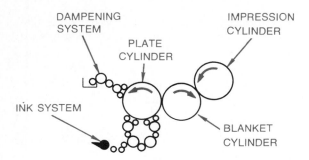

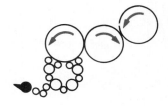

Fig. 103-8. Schematics of an offset lithography and letterset press. Left schematic: dampening system in place, making an offset lithography press. Right schematic: dampening system removed, making a letterset press.

ders (plate, blanket, and impression) are used with this press design.

When the press is used for offset lithography, the dampening and ink systems are in place (left schematic, Fig. 103-8). When used as an offset letterpress (letterset) press, the water-dampening system is removed (right schematic, Fig. 103-8). Shadow-relief image carriers are attached to the plate cylinder, which receives ink only on the raised image areas. As the cylinder revolves, the ink is transferred (offset) to the blanket cylinder. It, in turn, offsets the image onto the paper as it passes between the impression and blanket cylinders. This offset adaptation is used in several commercial presses (Fig. 103-9).

HEIDELBERG USA

Fig. 103-9. An offset lithography and letterset press incorporating the press schematics in Figure 103-8.

UNIT

104 OFFSET LITHOGRAPHY DUPLICATORS AND PRESSES

Offset lithography machines are designated as either *duplicators* or *presses*. A duplicator is not generally designed for high-quality reproduction. The adjustment and controls in the various systems are not as precise as those of a large, heavy-duty commercial press. There are not so many ink rollers, limiting the image area of the plate that can receive the proper amount of ink. There is also a limited set of dampening rollers.

Offset lithography machines that are considered to be presses are precision equipment. A press contains all the controls needed to turn out high-quality printed products.

Several manufacturers make offset lithography duplicators and presses. Each manufacturer has many models and sizes. The different sizes and designs allow the person buying duplicators and presses to choose from a variety of models. Some presses are designed for general uses; others are made specifically for certain kinds of printed products.

OFFICE DUPLICATORS

Offset lithography duplicators are designed for simple but fast operation. Persons with little instruction can use small table-top models (Fig. 104-1). Large offset lithography duplicators, such as those designed to handle 14- by 20-inch (35.5 by 50.8 cm) sheets (Fig. 104-2), can print large and small sheets. These duplicators take more skill to operate than the table-top models, but a person can learn this skill in a short time.

ROTAPRINT COMPANY

Fig. 104-3. The first offset lithography duplicator in the world. It was introduced in 1927.

A.B. DICK

Fig. 104-1. A tabletop offset lithography duplicator.

The first small offset lithography duplicator was introduced to the industry in 1927 (Fig. 104-3). Since then, thousands of these small image-transfer machines have been manufactured and put into use throughout the world.

Lithographic duplicators are designed with

PLANETA NORTH AMERICA INC.

Fig. 104-2. A 19 X 26–inch offset lithography press.

AM MULTIGRAPHICS/DIVISION OF AM INTERNATIONAL

Fig. 104-4. A high-speed offset lithography duplicator used in commercial printing plants and in in-plant printing/duplicating centers.

many special features (Fig. 104-4). The single-level control lets the operator dampen the plate, ink the plate, engage the impression between the plate and blanket cylinders, and begin feeding the paper. This saves a lot of time and effort. Some machines have *computer control* systems that allow the operator to select the number of sheets to be printed. The machine turns off when this number is reached. Also available is a *chain delivery,* which carries duplicated sheets from the cylinder to a stacking area. This avoids jam-ups, which are common to an ejection-type delivery.

FORM AND JOB DUPLICATORS

Several makes and models of offset lithography duplicators and presses are made to meet the needs of the business world. *Web-fed* multiple-unit duplicators (Fig. 104-5) print several colors

DIDDE GRAPHIC SYSTEMS CORPORATION

Fig. 104-5. A multiple-unit web press designed for specialty work.

ROCKWELL INTERNATIONAL/GRAPHIC SYSTEMS DIVISION

Fig. 104-6. A six-color sheet-fed commercial offset lithography press.

on one or both sides of the sheet. These presses can perforate, punch, trim, number, and insert carbon paper during one pass. They are limited in the width of paper they can take, but they have a very high printing speed.

COMMERCIAL PRESSES

Presses used to produce high-quality single- and multiple-color printed materials are precision-built equipment. They are used to print products ranging from advertising brochures to magazines, books, and newspapers. They can be either sheet fed (Fig. 104-6) or web fed (Fig. 104-7). They are also designed as single-, two-, four-, five-, and six-color presses.

Large-publication web-fed presses have a *printing unit*, a *drying section*, and a *folding unit.* The web of paper enters the machine and is printed with four colors. The web is dried as it passes through the drying oven and is then folded into signatures that make up a book or magazine. The press design shown in Figure

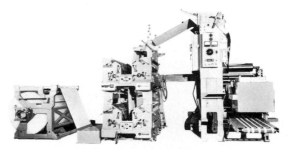

ROCKWELL INTERNATIONAL/GRAPHIC SYSTEMS DIVISION

Fig. 104-7. A web-fed lithographic press that can print book signatures, two colors per side, up to 25,000 folded 16-page signatures per hour.

MOTTER PRINTING PRESS COMPANY

Fig. 104-8. A four-color, web-fed, signature-offset-lithography press.

104-8 produces high-quality printing at speeds of 1,500 feet a minute.

High-speed, multi-unit lithographic presses are so complex that they need a central control station. These stations contain electronically controlled buttons and dials for every adjustable feature of the machines. Control stations let companies obtain high production hour-after-hour.

LITHOGRAPHIC PROOF PRESSES

Offset lithography proof presses simulate the production press sequence of dampening, inking, and printing (Fig. 104-9). The image carrier is attached to the proof press and the dampened rollers are rolled over the carrier to put water on the non-image areas. The ink rollers then are rolled over the image carrier to ink the image areas. The rubber blanket cylinder immediately follows the ink rollers. It picks up the ink from the image carrier and deposits it on the paper in the next revolution. After the proof is taken, the operator inspects it and decides whether the image carrier needs to be corrected.

A rotary four-color offset lithography proof press is shown in Figure 104-10. It simulates actual production press sequence and operating conditions. Each of the four image carriers has the image area for one of the four colors (yellow, magenta, cyan, and black) used in four-color reproductions. If corrections are needed, they can be made before the image carriers are placed on a high-speed production press.

BOBST GROUP, INC.

Fig. 104-9. A four-color offset sheet press

BOBST GROUP, INC.

Fig. 104-10. A four-color web proof press.

UNIT 105 SAFETY WITH THE OFFSET LITHOGRAPHY DUPLICATOR/PRESS

You must be careful in order to operate the off-set lithography press or duplicator. The following basic safety rules will help you get good printing results and use this precision equipment properly.

Permission. Ask permission before beginning work with the offset lithography press.

Clothing and jewelry. Wear suitable clothing and remove jewelry. Loose clothing, long hair, or bulky jewelry may get caught in the press.

Safety guards. Power equipment should have the proper safety guards placed over moving parts. Check the press to see that all guards are in place before using it.

Air circulation. Make sure there is enough air circulation. If necessary, start exhaust fans or open windows or doors before working on the press. Ink solvent fumes must be removed from the press area.

Electrical connections. Be sure that all electrical connections on the press are in good condition and that the press is properly grounded. Arrange the cords so that no one will trip and fall.

Good housekeeping. Keep the laboratory neat, clean, and orderly. Never let waste materials collect around the press working area. A messy work area invites accidents or fires.

Materials storage. Store containers of water-fountain solution, ink cans or tubes, and ink solvents on shelves within easy reach.

Illumination. Good lighting is needed for safety. Turn on all overhead and press lights while operating the machines.

Noise. Too much noise is a distraction and is unsafe. Keep talking and laughter to a minimum.

Fire. Keep fire extinguishers charged and located in conspicuous places in the laboratory. Handle all flammable materials with care.

Ink and solvent-soaked rags. Place all such rags in a metal safety-can with a tight metal lid. Spontaneous combustion is always a threat.

Hands and fingers. Be careful where you place your hands when a press is running. They can easily get caught in moving parts.

Adjustments. Do not make any adjustments while a press is running.

Instruction manual. Read the instruction manual carefully before you use any offset-lithography duplicator or press. Each manufacturer designs presses differently; the operating controls and adjustments may not be in the same place as those shown in Units 106 through 108 and Unit 111.

Press speed. Operate the offset-lithography press at a slow speed until you are skillful enough to increase the speed safely.

One operator. Only one person at a time should operate the offset-lithography press. Small presses are one-operator machines and it is dangerous for two or more persons to attempt to operate the controls.

Stopping the press. Turn off the power and stop the press before leaving it. A press running without an operator nearby is dangerous to other persons working in the area.

Lubricating the press. Do not oil or grease the press parts while the press is running. Use the oil can or grease gun on any piece of machinery only while it is stopped.

UNIT 106 THE OFFSET LITHOGRAPHY DUPLICATOR/PRESS

All brands and models of lithography presses have control levers, wheels, and knobs. It is important to know the function of these devices before you can operate a press efficiently. The procedures for operating the feeding, cylinder, dampening, inking, and delivery systems for the press/duplicator are given in Units 107, 108, 109, and 111.

A schematic drawing of a basic litho duplicator/press is shown in Figure 106-1. This illustration is helpful in understanding how paper is fed through the machine and how ink and dampening solution are transferred to the plate for printing.

FEEDING SYSTEM

These controls are shown in Figure 106-2. The following letters refer to the controls shown in Figure 106-2.

G. Register Board. The register board receives sheets as they are fed from the pile and transports them to a jogger, which positions them for good register just before they enter the duplicating head.

H. Automatic Paper Feeder. The automatic paper feeder stores a paper pile (stack of sheets) and maintains the pile at a constant height (set by the operator) as sheets are fed into the duplicator.

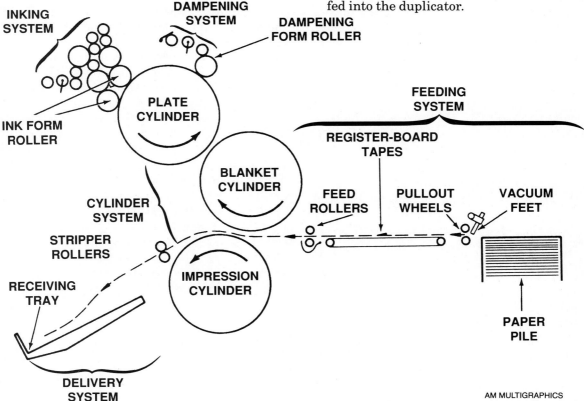

AM MULTIGRAPHICS

Fig. 106-1. The feeding system, cylinder system, and dampening system controls for a lithography duplicator/press.

J. *Paper-Guide Release Lever.* Used to lock the hinged paper guide assembly up (to load paper) and unlock the assembly so that it can be swung to the down position.

K. *Elevator Crank-Release Lever.* Used to lock and unlock elevator crank (item M below). Crank only lowers when lever is turned toward the paper pile.

L. *Vertical Side Guide Locking Lever.* Used to lock the vertical side guides once in place. Raise lever to unlock side guides. The side guides can then be positioned. Lower the lever to lock the side guides.

M. *Elevator Crank.* Used to raise or lower elevator to convenient height for loading paper. Turning the crank clockwise raises elevator. Turning the crank counterclockwise lowers elevator.

N. *Vacuum and Blower Controls.* The vacuum control allows adjustment of vacuum applied to suction feet for pickup of paper sheets from the top of the pile. The blower control regulates an airstream that separates the topmost sheet of paper in the pile.

R. *Pump Motor On/Off Switch.* Used to control operation for the pump that creates vacuum for the suction feet and pressure for the blower tubes.

CYLINDER SYSTEM

The letters refer to the controls shown in Figure 106-2.

E. *Single-Lever Control.* Four-position lever used to select the different phases of the duplication cycle: off, moist, master ink, and print.

F. *Handwheel.* Allows manual rotation of rollers and cylinders for easy cleanup and certain other procedures.

O. *Operating-Speed Indicator.* Shows speed at which duplicator has been set to operate in thousands of cylinder revolutions per hour.

P. *Speed-Control Knob.* Used to adjust duplicator operating speed in the range of 5,000 to 10,000 cylinder revolutions per hour.

T. *Machine Start/Stop.* Dual pushbuttons that control machine action: green to start and red to stop.

DAMPENING SYSTEM

The two major controls are shown in Figure 106-2. Other controls are actually present on the duplicator/press, but are difficult to show in this illustration. Typically, there is a ratchet system to regulate the amount of dampening solution added per press revolution. Also, there is often a lockout device so no dampening solution will be added to the system while the duplicator/press is being operated. The letters refer to the controls shown in Figure 106-2.

C. *Moisture-Fountain-Roller Knob.* Allows manipulation of moisture fountain roller for initial moistening procedure and cleanup procedure.

D. *Moisture-Form-Roller Knob.* Used to lock the moisture form roller in or out of contact with the master cylinder.

INKING SYSTEM

These controls are shown in Figure 106-2. Like the dampening system, other controls are present in inking systems of most duplicators/presses. A ratchet system to regulate the amount of ink applied to the ink rollers on each duplicator/press revolution is always available. Also, some devices known as ink fountain "keys," or adjusting screws, are built into the ink fountain. These adjusting screws permit specific area regulation of the amount of ink that will be added to the rollers. The letters refer to the two major controls shown in Figure 106-2.

A. *Ink-Fountain-Roller Crank.* Used to turn the ink fountain roller manually for the purpose of making a faster initial transfer of ink when preparing for operation.

B. *Ink-Form-Roller Knobs.* Used to lock the ink form rollers either in or out of contact with the master cylinder.

DELIVERY SYSTEM

The paper receiver tray is shown in Figure 106-2. With a simple "catch" tray, there are two sets of "stripper" rollers that help remove the printed sheets from the impression cylinder. These rollers also help guide the printed sheets into the receiving tray. The position of the stripper rollers can be seen in Figure 106-1. Chain delivery systems are attached to some small duplicators/presses. These units are very helpful in removing the printed sheets from the cylinder system. They are de-

signed to place the individual sheets of paper into a well-organized pile. This makes it easy to control and handle the printed sheets. The letter S refers to the receiving tray shown in the figure.

S. Copy Receiver. The copy receiver can be either a receiving tray (standard equipment) or a chain delivery (optional accessory).

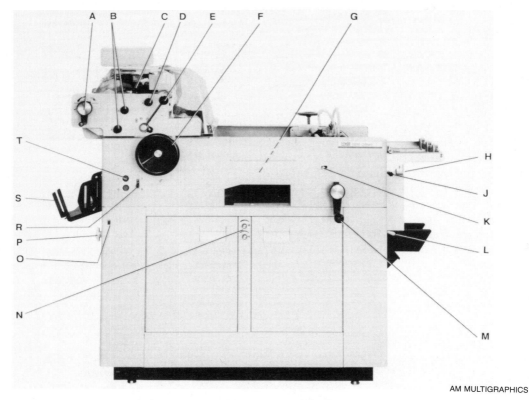

AM MULTIGRAPHICS

Fig. 106-2. The delivery system and ink system controls for a lithography duplicator/press.

UNIT 107 PREPARING THE OFFSET LITHOGRAPHY DUPLICATOR/PRESS

Several pre-operating preparations must be done before printing can begin. The four press systems that need attention are the (1) feeding, (2) delivery, (3) inking, and (4) dampening.

FEEDING SYSTEM PROCEDURE

1. Lower the paper platform by turning the elevator crank counterclockwise. Move the release lever toward the paper pile.
2. Set the inside of the left paper stack corner guide on the scale marking for the size sheet to be run (Fig. 107-1).
3. Lay a sheet of the proper size paper stock in position; set the right-hand paper stack corner guide so that it will be about ¹⁄₁₆-inch (1.6 mm) away from the edge of the paper.

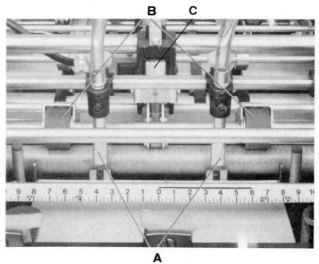

AM MULTIGRAPHICS

Fig. 107-2. Parts of the in-feed portion of the total feeding system: A, suction feet; B, feed rollers; and C, double sheet detector.

Fig. 107-1. Loading paper on the feeding platform. Parts of the feed end of the duplicator/press: A, release lever for front corner guides; B, front corner guides; C, positioning bar; D, paper pile platform board; and E, paper pile support.

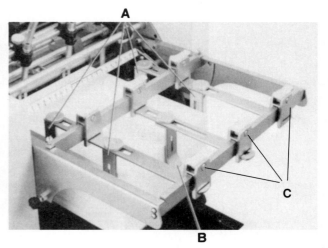

AM MULTIGRAPHICS

Fig. 107-3. Parts of the paper pile area of the feeding system: A, side guides; B, end guide; and C, guide clamps.

4. Set the sheet separator plates to a line representing ¼ the width of the front edge of the paper (Fig. 107-4).

5. Center the two suction feet directly above the thin metal sheet separators (Fig. 107-2).

6. Position the front air-blower in the center of the paper lead edge if one is available.

7. Load the paper platform and raise the paper stack to within ⅛-inch (3.2 mm) of the sheet separators.

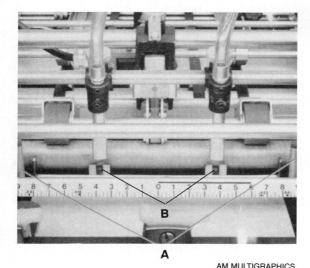

Fig. 107-4. Correct positions of the side air blow and the thin metal sheet separators: A, side air blow; and B, sheet separators.

8. Set the side guides to lightly contact the paper. They should be about 2 inches (5.08 cm) from the back of the paper pile, or at their extreme when running larger-size stock (Fig. 107-3).

9. Center the paper pile end guide to lightly contact the paper pile (Fig. 107-3).

10. Set the side air blow paper separators to blow into the top of the paper pile (Fig. 107-4).

11. Lower the paper platform to one inch (2.54 cm). Turn on the drive motor switch. Let the paper platform raise automatically. Adjust the elevator control knob (Fig. 107-2) so that the paper pile stops about ⅛-inch (3.2 mm) below the metal sheet separators. (Turning the knob clockwise lowers; turning it counterclock-

Fig. 107-5. Jogger micrometer adjustment controls; A, locking lever; B, micrometer adjustment wheel; and C, rotation direction arrows.

wise raises the height of the pile of paper.)

12. Set the double sheet eliminator. Follow the procedure as listed in Unit 109.

13. Set the feedboard jogger (Figs. 107-5 and 107-6). The paper is picked up from the paper pile, moved to the paper pull-out roll by the suction feet, and then delivered to the paper feedboard. It travels down the feedboard by way of the con-

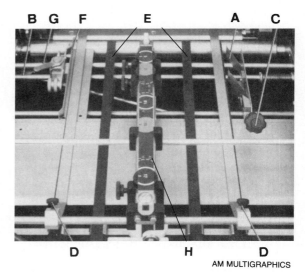

Fig. 107-6. Parts of the paper feed and register board: A, register springs; B, jogger shaft; C, set-screw knob for register spring assembly; D, set-screws for paper retainers; E, conveyor tapes; F, jogger; G, jogger locking lever; and H, skid roller assembly.

veyor tapes to the paper stop bar and jogger. It is then jogged (moved) into correct feeding position.

On some litho duplicator/presses, paper may be jogged from either the operator's side or the non-operator's side. The latter is used most often when running copy on *both sides* of the paper, in which case, for good printing, use the operator's side jogger the first time through and the non-operator's side for the second time through for the backup. This uses the same paper edge for jogging during each printing cycle. For work printed on *one side only,* the operator's side jogger is most often used.

14. Set the register springs (Fig. 107-6). These should be set so they are depressed no more than 1/16-inch (1.6 mm) when the jogger moves a sheet for lineup.

15. Adjust the skid rollers assembly and the metal paper retainers (metal strips) over the conveyor tapes. It is best to equally space the conveyor tapes over the paper width area. The skid roller should help move each sheet to the paper stops before jogging begins, but keep turning at the trailing edge of the sheet.

16. Adjust the impression between the blanket and impression cylinders for the paper being printed. The procedure is presented in Unit 109.

17. Raise the delivery platform to the uppermost position by turning the delivery pile hand-crank (Fig. 107-7).

18. Feed a sheet of paper through the machine letting it drop into normal delivery position on the delivery board. The two side guides and one end guide should be at the maximum sheet size positions when this step is done.

19. Loosen the delivery side guide clamp knobs. Bring the stationary side guide against the sheet of paper. Tighten the clamp knob. Turn the press handwheel until the automatic side-jogging guide is in the extreme inward position. Slide it over to lightly touch the paper when the paper is against the stationary guide (Fig. 107-7). Tighten the clamp knob.

20. With the paper against the front guide, turn the handwheel until the back jog-

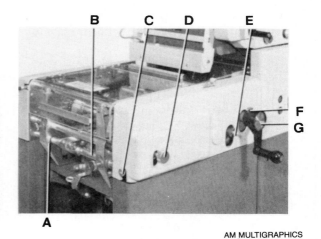

Fig. 107-7. The chain delivery system controls: A, side jogger; B, printed paper platform; C, paper platform descent adjustment; D, jogger fine adjustment; E, low-speed raise/lower shaft; F, crank release lever; and G, high-speed raise/lower shaft and crank.

ging guide is in the extreme inward position. Loosen the guide setscrew, slide the guide to lightly touch the paper, and retighten the set-screw.

21. Run several sheets through the duplicator/press to check all adjustments. Turn on the drive motor switch; slow the press to slowest speed; turn on the air-vacuum pump switch; and engage the paper feed control lever. Carefully inspect the sheets as they pass through the machine and make necessary adjustments. The paper

INK ROLLERS   DAMPENING ROLLERS

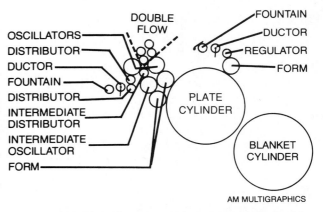

Fig. 107-8. The roller names and arrangements for the ink and dampening systems of a litho duplicator/press.

must feed through the machine efficiently and smoothly to give maximum reproduction quality.

22. Install the inking system rollers (Fig. 107-8). Make sure all rollers are perfectly clean. Follow the procedure as outlined in the duplicator/press manual.

23. Fill the ink fountain at least half full with a suitable ink for the image content and the kind of paper being used (Fig. 107-9).

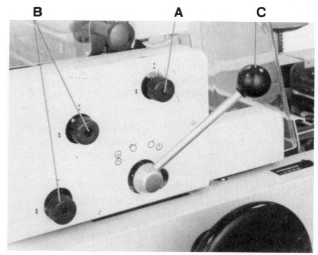

AM MULTIGRAPHICS

Fig. 107-11. Locations of important ink and dampening controls; A, water form roller knob; B, ink form roller knobs; and C, single-lever control.

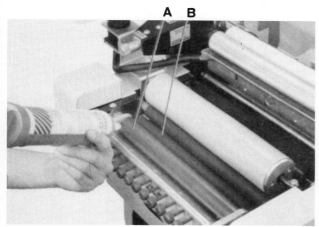

AM MULTIGRAPHICS

Fig. 107-9. Using an ink gun to deposit an even bead of ink along the entire ink fountain. Identified parts are: A, ink fountain roller and B, ink ductor roller.

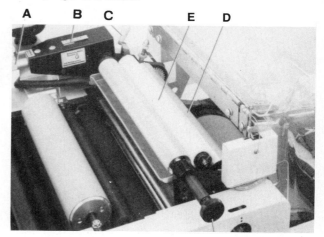

AM MULTIGRAPHICS

Fig. 107-12. Important dampening system parts: A, feed rate control knob; B, feed rate gauge; C, ductor lever; D, ductor roller; E, fountain roller; and F, fountain roller knob.

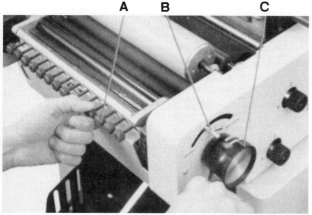

AM MULTIGRAPHICS

Fig. 107-10. Adjusting the ink flow to the rollers with the ink fountain adjusting screws. Identified parts are: A, ink fountain screws; B, ink feed rate control; and C, ink fountain roller crank.

24. With the ductor roller against the fountain roller turn the ink-fountain roller control knob counterclockwise; turn the ink-fountain adjusting screws in or out until a thin film of ink is spread evenly over the fountain roller (Fig. 107-10).

25. Place the ink-feed rate control (Fig.107-10) on the third notch. Turn the two ink form roller knobs to the ink position (Fig 107-11). Also, turn the "night-latch" ink

form roller lever so all ink rollers are in contact with one another.

26. Turn on the press power switch. Run the machine until all ink rollers are covered with a thin film of ink.

27. Return the rate control lever to the neutral position. Turn the duplicator/press off. The inking system is now ready to transfer ink to the plate image.

28. Install the dampening system rollers (Fig. 107-8). Make sure all rollers and covers are clean. Follow the procedure as outlined in the duplicator/press manual.

29. Fill the dampener fountain bottle with the proper mixture of fountain solution and water for the plate that will be printed. The pH (potential of Hydrogen) value of dampening fountain solutions should be between 4.0 and 5.6 on the pH scale. Manual and electronic testing devices are available to check pH values.

30. Turn the bottle upside down with the spout down over a sink or wastebasket. Be sure the float valve does not leak. Bring the bottle over the side of the machine, being careful not to spill any solution on the ink rollers, and insert it in its holder (Fig. 107-12).

31. Dampen the fabric coverings on the ductor and form rollers (Fig. 107-8). Adjust the dampener volume control to the 4th or 5th setting and turn on the duplicator/press power. Run the duplicator/press until the fabric coverings feel slightly damp to the touch. Safety Note: Only touch the rollers when the machine is stopped and the safety switch is on.

32. Re-set the volume control to the 1 or 2 positions. The duplicator/press is now ready for operation.

UNIT

108 OPERATING THE OFFSET LITHOGRAPHY DUPLICATOR/PRESS

PRINTING COPIES

1. Check all systems of the duplicator/press using the information given in Unit 107.

2. Get the prepared plate (image carrier) and inspect it for flaws.

3. Inspect and clean the plate cylinder. It must be clean before the plate is attached.

4. Turn the duplicator/press with the handwheel until the plate cylinder lead plate clamp is in proper position (Fig. 108-1).

5. Attach the lead edge of the plate to the lead plate cylinder clamp (Fig. 108-1). Start at the far side or right side of the plate and place each clamp hook in a plate hole.

6. Hold the trailing edge of the plate with the right hand and turn the press clockwise with the handwheel until the trailing plate clamp is in view (Fig. 108-2).

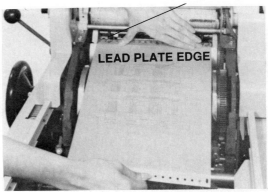

LEAD PLATE CLAMP

LEAD PLATE EDGE

AM MULTIGRAPHICS

Fig. 108-1. Attaching the lead plate edge to the lead clamp of the plate cylinder.

7. Bring the trailing plate clamp up with spring tension and attach the trailing edge of the plate to the clamp (Fig. 108-2).

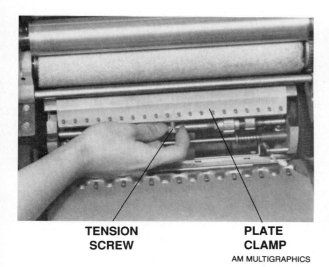

**TENSION
SCREW**

**PLATE
CLAMP**

AM MULTIGRAPHICS

Fig. 108-2. Tightening the plate around the cylinder with the tension screw.

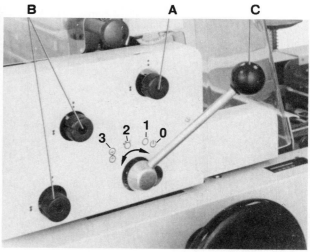

AM MULTIGRAPHICS

Fig. 108-3. Positions of the single-lever control (C): O = neutral position; 1 = dampening position; 2 = inking position; and 3 = impression position (between plate and blanket). A = moisture-form-roller knob; B = ink form-roller knobs.

8. Tighten the plate clamp by turning the tension screw clockwise (Fig. 108-2). Secure the lock nut.
9. If a metal plate is used, moisten it with cotton that has been dipped into the dampening fountain solution to remove the gum protective coating. If using a plate made of paper, pre-etch it with the recommended plate brand solution before putting it on the plate cylinder.
10. Turn on the duplicator/press.
11. Move the form roller control lever to the number one (1) position (Fig. 108-3). This places the dampening form roller against the plate. Let the duplicator/press make 8 to 10 revolutions.
12. Move the form roller control lever to the number two (2) position (Fig. 108-3). This places the ink form rollers and dampening form roller against the plate. Let the rollers make several revolutions.
13. Move the control lever to number three (3). This moves the plate and blanket cylinders into contact to transfer (offset) the ink from plate to blanket.
14. Turn on the air-vacuum pump switch.
15. Return the control lever to the neutral (0) position and turn off the duplicator/press.
16. Inspect the printed sheets to be sure that the image is in the correct position. Make any needed adjustments in this order: (1)

angular positioning, (2) vertical positioning, and (3) horizontal positioning.
(1) Angular Positioning.
   a. Check a printed test sheet with a T-square or by folding the sheet and comparing the registration marks to the original copy (paste-up).
   b. If the image is not square on the printed sheet, either the plate or the paper must be twisted.
   c. Loosen the trailing plate edge tension screw, but do not remove the plate from the clamp (Fig. 108-4).
   d. Turn the adjusting knob, left or right, on the angular adjustment bar to move the trailing edge of the plate.
   e. Re-tighten the plate tension screw.
   f. Print more test copies and check for squareness.
   g. Continue making the angular adjustments until the printed image and registration marks are straight on the sheet of paper.
(2) Vertical Positioning.
   a. Turn the duplicator/press with the handwheel until the gear clamp wrench knob is aligned with the gear clamp bolt head located at the end of the plate cylinder (Fig. 108-5).

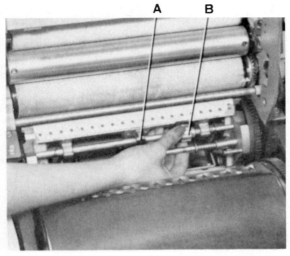

Fig. 108-4. Moving the trailing plate edge either left or right will square the image on the printed sheet. Important components are: A, trailing plate edge tension screw and B, adjusting knob on the angular adjustment bar.

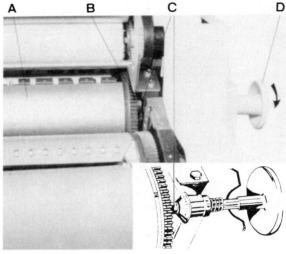

Fig. 108-5. The vertical image adjustment mechanism. The important components are: A, plate cylinder; B, plate cylinder gear; C, gear clamp bolt head; and D, gear clamp wrench knob.

    b. Engage or mesh both by pushing and holding in the gear clamp wrench knob.

    c. Turn the gear clamp wrench knob to the left to unlock the cylinder.

    d. Turn the gear clamp wrench knob to the right to relock the plate cylinder safety. NOTE: Never try a vertical adjustment while the press is running.

    e. Print 3 or 4 more copies, inspect, and adjust again if needed.

    f. Repeat steps a through e until the image is correctly positioned vertically.

(3) Horizontal Positioning.

    a. Move the paper stock either left or right to position the image correctly.

    b. Adjust the jogger and register springs toward the operator to move the paper to the left or away to move the paper to the right (Fig. 107–6).

    c. Print 3 or 4 more copies, inspect, and adjust again if needed.

    d. Repeat steps b through d until the image is correctly positioned horizontally.

17. Check for adequate ink coverage.

18. Set the copy counter to 00000 and print the correct number of copies.

UNIT 109 LITHOGRAPHY DUPLICATOR/ PRESS ADJUSTMENTS

FEEDING SYSTEM

Double sheet eliminator. This unit should be positioned in the center of the paper (Fig. 109-1) whenever possible.

1. To move the unit, loosen the assembly thumb screw and slide the unit to the correct position.

2. Get a strip of paper about 2 inches (5.08 cm) wide of the kind that will be used for

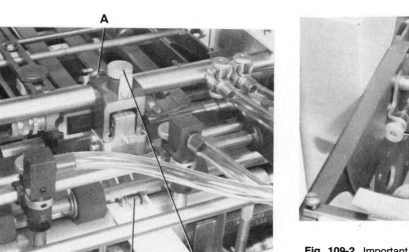

AM MULTIGRAPHICS

Fig. 109-1. The double sheet eliminator unit. Important parts are: A, assembly thumbscrew; B, adjustment knob; and C, detector roller.

AM MULTIGRAPHICS

Fig. 109-2. Important controls for establishing the correct paper pile height: A, adjusting screws on the paper height control bar; and B, paper pile height adjusting screw.

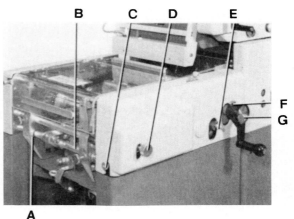

AM MULTIGRAPHICS

Fig. 109-3. Controls for the delivery system of the litho duplicator/press: A, jogger guide; B, paper receiver platform or table; C, descent adjustment knob; D, jogger micrometer adjustment; E, lowspeed raise/lower shaft; F, crank release lever; and G, high-speed raise/lower shaft.

printing. Fold it end-to-end but do not match the edges closer than 1 inch.

3. Turn on the power and the vacuum.
4. Place the single and then the double areas of the paper strip under the thickness control.
5. Turn the double-sheet eliminator adjustment knob, left or right, until the ejection mechanism does not engage with a single thickness but will take hold with the double sheet.

Paper pile height. The adjusting screw (Fig. 109-2) is used to regulate the maximum height to which the top of the paper pile will be elevated automatically. Turn the adjusting screw clockwise to lower the pile; counterclockwise to raise it.

Printing speed. The duplicator/press speed can be either increased or decreased by a speed-control knob (see Fig. 106-2). The knob is turned left to increase the speed and right to decrease it.

DELIVERY SYSTEM

Delivery rate descent control. This control (Fig. 109-3) sets the rate of descent of the delivery paper platform. A general rule of thumb for correct adjustment of this control is that if the top of the paper stack remains at a point about halfway up on the side and jogger guides, the control is correctly adjusted.

If the top of the paper stack climbs higher than halfway up, turn the control clockwise to increase the rate of descent. If the top sinks below this halfway point, turn the control counterclockwise to decrease the rate of descent.

INKING SYSTEM

Form rollers position test.
1. Attach a clean, dry plate to the plate cylinder.
2. Turn the handwheel until the plate clamps face the feeder.
3. Drop the ink form rollers momentarily by placing the control lever in the ink (2) positon (Fig. 108-3).
4. Lift the ink form rollers.
5. Revolve the plate cylinder until the 2 strips of ink are in view (Fig. 109-4).
6. Both strips should be nearly the same and about 3/16-inch (4.76 mm) wide.

DAMPENING SYSTEM

Form roller position test.
1. Attach a plate to the plate cylinder.
2. Cut 2 strips of 16-pound paper to 1-inch (2.54 cm) widths or obtain pre-made plastic test strips.
3. Insert one strip on the right side. Insert the other on the left between the plate and dampener form roller (Fig. 109-5).
4. Drop the form roller onto the plate by placing the form roller control lever in the dampening (1) position (Fig. 108-3).
5. Pull on the test strips. Each should have a slight but equal amount of resistance.

A   A

AM MULTIGRAPHICS

Fig. 109-5. Testing dampener form roller pressure against the plate using strips of 16-pound bond paper (A).

Oscillator roller position test.
1. Place the 2 test strips between the oscillator roller and the form roller.
2. Make the same check for resistance as with the form roller and plate.
3. Carefully install or remove this metal roller so the form and ductor roller coverings are not damaged (Fig. 109-6).

Ductor roller position test.
1. Turn the handwheel until the ductor roller contacts the oscillator roller.

B

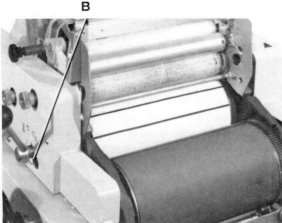

AM MULTIGRAPHICS

Fig. 109-4. Identical ink strips 3/16 inch (4.76 mm) wide on the plate indicate properly adjusted ink form rollers: B, locking bolt.

AM MULTIGRAPHICS

Fig. 109-6. The oscillator roller must be installed carefully so the coverings on the dampener ductor and form rollers are not damaged.

2. Place 2 test strips between these 2 rollers.
3. Make the same resistance check and adjust if necessary.

CYLINDER SYSTEM

Plate-to-blanket impression.
1. Attach a used plate to the plate cylinder.
2. Start the duplicator/press.
3. With the auxiliary dampener form roller control in the *off* position, drop the form rollers until the plate is solidly inked.
4. Stop the duplicator/press.
5. Turn the handwheel until the plate is in position to contact the blanket about halfway around.
6. Place the impression between the plate and blanket cylinder to *on* and release the impression immediately.
7. Revolve the blanket cylinder until the ink strip is visible. It should be even and about 3/16-inch wide (Fig. 109-7).

Blanket-to-paper impression.
1. Release the pressure between the blanket and impression cylinders using the adjusting mechanism shown in figure 109-8.
   a. Loosen the clamp screw with the t-wrench.
   b. Turn the pressure adjusting screw to release the pressure.

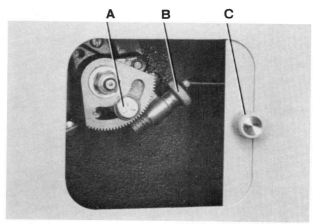

AM MULTIGRAPHICS

Fig. 109-8. The blanket-to-impression cylinder adjusting mechanism on the litho duplicator/press: A, clamp screw; B, pressure adjusting screw; and C, protective cover knob.

   c. Tighten the clamp screw.
   d. Close the protective cover.
2. Feed one piece of paper which will be used for the printed job. Stop the duplicator/press when the sheet is halfway between the blanket and impression cylinders. The impression mechanism is automatically activated when the sheet strikes a sensitive control lever.
3. Set the pressure between the blanket and impression cylinders.
   a. Open the protective cover exposing the adjusting system.
   b. Loosen the clamp screw with the t-wrench (Fig. 109-8).
   c. Turn the pressure adjusting screw to increase the pressure. This should be turned "finger" tight.
   d. Tighten the clamp screw.
   e. Close the protective cover.
4. Print a few sheets, inspect for quality, and re-adjust if needed.

BLANKET INSTALLATION

Although the blanket is made of high-quality material, it must be replaced from time to time because chemicals and ink soak into the surface and make the blanket brittle.
1. Turn the handwheel until the lead blanket clamp is in position (Fig. 109-9).

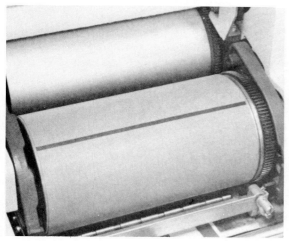

AM MULTIGRAPHICS

Fig. 109-7. The ink strip should be about 3/16 inch (4.76 mm) wide on the blanket for the correct plate-to-blanket pressure.

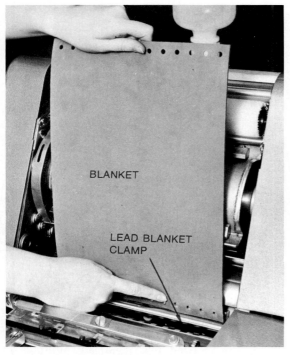

Fig. 109-9. Hooking the blanket to the lead blanket clamp.

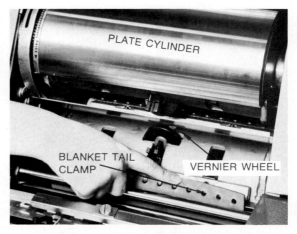

Fig. 109-10. Hooking the tail end of the blanket to the blanket tail clamp. The vernier wheel (more frequently called tension set-screw) is then used to tighten the blanket.

2. Hook the blanket onto the lead blanket clamp (Fig. 109-9). Be sure that all hooks are securely fastened into the holes of the blanket.
3. Hold the blanket tight, using your right hand. Turn the handwheel with your left hand until the blanket tail clamp comes into view.
4. Hook the tail end of the blanket onto the blanket tail clamp (Fig. 109-10).
5. Turn the tension set screw clockwise until tight.
6. Check to see that all hooks are correctly in place in the holes punched into the blanket.
7. Run about 15 sheets of paper through the duplicator/press. Stop and retighten the tension set screw. Secure it with the locknut.

BLANKET CONSTRUCTION AND PRESERVATION

A lithographic blanket has two, three, or four plies of cotton fabric laminated with thin layers of rubber. This laminated structure is covered with about a 0.020-inch (.51 mm) thick top layer of rubber compound.

The most important part of blanket maintenance is *wash-up*. Never let ink dry on it. As a general guide, the blanket should be washed at the following times:
1. Before being used for the first time.
2. After every 3,000 to 4,000 impressions, or when the printing quality deteriorates.
3. During a paper load change.
4. When the press is stopped for any length of time.

Soak a good lint-free rag with blanket solvent. Wipe the entire surface of the blanket evenly with the rag. Wipe it again until it is dry, using a completely dry rag.

A blanket should rest. After being used for a period of time, remove it from the duplicator/press cylinder. Clean it thoroughly and hang it up to dry and rest for several days. During this period the blanket will be restored as swelled edges or smashes disappear. Two blankets should be used alternately on duplicator/press runs.

UNIT 110 LITHOGRAPHIC PRINTING PROBLEMS

Many times the quality of reproduction needs to be made better while the job is being printed. The duplicator/press operator must then decide what is wrong and solve the problem as well as possible. The following problems and remedies may help you.

PRINTED SHEET PROBLEMS AND CAUSES

Good copy has images with crisp, dark lines and solids; a clean background; clear halftones, screens, and reverses; good registration; and completely dry sheets (Fig. 110-1).

Background dirty, scumming (Fig. 110-2). Dirty copy may be caused by too much ink, not enough moisture, dirty dampener-roll covers, or dampener covers tied too tightly on ends.

Gray, washed out image, dirty background (Fig. 110-3). This problem may be caused by glazed ink rollers, glazed blanket, too much

3M COMPANY

Fig. 110-2. The background is dirty.

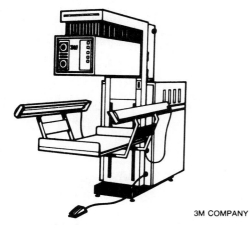

3M COMPANY

Fig. 110-1. A good image.

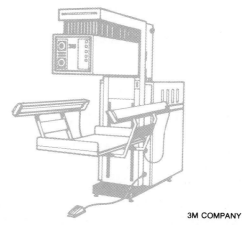

3M COMPANY

Fig. 110-3. A gray washed-out image, plus a dirty area (unwanted ink) in the non-image area.

ink form roller pressure, or too much damp-ener form roller pressure.

Too dark (Fig. 110-4). Too much darkness, when halftones and fine reverses fill in or sheet dries slowly, may be caused by too much ink, too much impression-to-blanket pressure, or not enough plate-to-blanket pressure.

Weak spots (Fig. 110-5). Weak spots may be caused by incorrect plate-to-blanket pressure, incorrect impression-to-blanket pressure, low spots in the blanket, blind image on plate caused by dried gum or overly strong fountain solution, or a glazed blanket.

Non-image area filling (Fig. 110-6). This may be caused by a poor or old plate, a plate fogged from room light, or poor plate processing.

Image breaks down while plate is running (Fig. 110-7). Image breakdown may result from too much dampener form roller pressure against the plate, too much ink form roller pressure against the plate, too much plate-to-blanket pressure, overly strong fountain solution, or end play in form rollers.

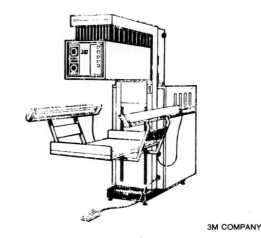

3M COMPANY

Fig. 110-5. Weak spots throughout.

3M COMPANY

Fig. 110-6. Non-image area filling.

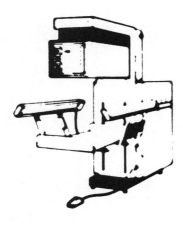

3M COMPANY

Fig. 110-4. The print is too dark.

3M COMPANY

Fig. 110-7. The image breaks down.

UNIT 111 CLEANING THE OFFSET LITHOGRAPHY DUPLICATOR/PRESS

The litho duplicator/press must be cleaned thoroughly after each day of use. The three systems that need attention are the (1) inking; (2) dampening, and (3) cylinder systems.

CLEANING THE DAMPENING SYSTEM

1. Remove the fountain supply bottle. Discard the remaining dampening solution. Rinse the bottle with plain water. A new solution should be made when the duplicator/press is used again.
2. Remove the water from the dampening system trough by soaking it out with cotton pads.
3. Remove the three dampening system rollers ductor, oscillator, and form—and clean them if necessary. Ink can be removed from molleton-covered (cotton fabric) rollers by using a soft bristle brush and a mild soap. Special machines are used to clean large press dampening rollers (Fig. 111-1). It is very important to keep the dampening fountain rollers clean.
4. Put these rollers in a rack so no pressure is against the soft roller surfaces. A flat spot can be a severe problem the next time the rollers are used.
5. Inspect the dampener fountain roller. If any ink has collected on the roller, remove it with a cloth and a soft bristle brush soaked in ink solvent. There are special cleaners that remove ink easily.

CLEANING THE INKING SYSTEM

1. Remove the ink from the fountain with an ink knife. Save unused ink, if possible.
2. Remove the ink fountain; lay it on a newspaper-covered table and clean it thoroughly. The fountain is removed by

JOMAC INCORPORATED

Fig. 111-1. A roller cleaning machine used to clean the ink from dampening system rollers.

AM MULTIGRAPHICS

Fig. 111-2. Removing the ink fountain from the litho duplicator/press.

tilting it up toward the ink rollers, and then lifting it upward (Fig. 111-2).
3. Clean the ink fountain roller with a solvent-soaked cloth.
4. Attach a cleanup sheet (made of blotter stock) to the plate cylinder. The cleanup sheet is attached just like a plate. NOTE: After the printed copies are completed,

the plate should be removed from the press and properly cared for.

5. Turn on the duplicator/press.
6. Put an amount of solvent across the large ink roller (Fig. 111-3). Use an oil can or plastic squeeze-bottle. Allow the duplicator/press to run for several turns.
7. Drop the ink rollers on the cleanup sheet by moving the form roller control lever to the third position (see Fig. 108-3). Be sure that the dampening system rollers have been removed.
8. Add a little more solvent to the large ink roller as the cleanup sheet absorbs the ink and solvent from the rollers.
9. Stop the duplicator/press. Replace the cleanup sheet with a new one. Repeat steps 6 through 8. Do this until the ink rollers are completely clean.
10. Remove the cleanup sheet. Save the sheets until the next duplicator/press cleanup and use the other sides.
11. Hand wipe each of the ink rollers with a soft cloth containing a small amount of solvent. Ink often accumulates on the ends of the rollers, thus wipe them clean too.
12. Place the removable ink rollers on a roller rack where they will not press against themselves or a hard shelf. The soft rollers can easily develop flat spots from prolonged pressure in one spot. This will cause severe printing problems in the future.

   NOTE: Ink roller cleaning devices, sometimes called wash-up trays, are available for most lithography duplicator/presses. A unit of this type is convenient to use and assists in removing ink from the rollers quickly. A rubber or fiber blade presses against one of the hard ink rollers and scraps the ink and solvent into the tray. Solvent is added to the ink rollers in the same manner as when clean-up sheets are used. After use, the wash-up tray should be thoroughly cleaned.

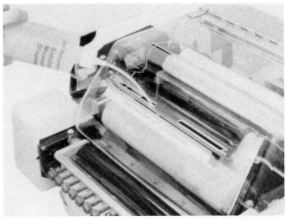

AM MULTIGRAPHICS

Fig. 111-3. Placing solvent on the large ink distributor roller during the cleaning operation.

CLEANING THE CYLINDER SYSTEM

1. Using a wiping cloth dampened with ink solvent, wipe the three cylinders (plate, blanket, and impression) free of ink. Dry the cylinders with a dry wiping cloth.
2. Remove glaze from the blanket with a special glaze remover.
3. Inspect the impression cylinder for hardened ink buildup and remove it with ink solvent or a special cylinder cleaner.

SECURING THE TOTAL DUPLICATOR/PRESS

1. Wipe down the entire machine.
2. Lubricate needed parts in preparation for the next printing job.
3. Turn off all electrical power to the duplicator/press.
4. Cover the duplicator/press with a dust-protector.

UNIT 112 LEARNING EXPERIENCES: LITHOGRAPHIC IMAGE TRANSFER

KEY TERMS

Unit 103

Cylinder system
Dampening system
Delivery system
Feeding system
Inking system

Letterset
Offset
Three cylinder design
Two cylinder design

Unit 104

Duplicator
Forms duplicator

Press

Unit 106

Dampener
Jogger

Vacuum

Unit 108

Lead plate edge
Single lever control
Vernier wheel

Tension screw
Trailing plate edge

Unit 109

Blanket
Ductor roller

Form roller
Oscillator

Unit 110

Image breakdown

Scumming

Unit 111

Cleanup sheet
Cylinder cleaner

Molleton

DISCUSSION TOPICS

1. Compare the offset lithography duplicator and the offset lithography press.
2. What are the advantages in using a central control station on a large offset lithography press?
3. What should be done to the inking system of the press before placing ink in the fountain?
4. How can the surface and body of the lithographic blanket be preserved?
5. When the non-image area of the lithographic plate accepts ink during a press run what are the possible causes?

ACTIVITIES

Unit 107

1. Get 100 sheets each of three different sizes of 20-pound bond paper. These sheets should vary in width as well as length. Make the necessary adjustments on the feeder and delivery systems on the offset lithography duplicator/press for each of the three paper sizes. Make the adjustments accurately enough so that all 100 sheets of each size go flawlessly through the press.

Units 107 and 109

2. Prepare the dampening and inking systems of the duplicator/press. Make the necessary checks of the dampening system rollers, the inking system rollers, and the cylinder system pressure. If any of these checks show a need for adjustments, get proper supervision and make the adjustments. Use the operators manual provided by the company.

Unit 108

3. Get or prepare a lithographic plate. Also get 300 to 400 scrap sheets of paper cut to a size suitable for the image on the plate as well as for the duplicator/press. Set the machine up and practice running the duplicator/press by printing the scrap sheets. Make all necessary adjustments and reproduce the job to the best of your ability.

4. Start from the beginning and print a job by using the offset lithography duplicator/press. Plan, typeset, complete the photography work, prepare the photo-sensitive image carrier, and print the job. Suggested jobs are personal stationery, business forms, pamphlets, and small newspapers. Use ink other than black if you wish. Remember to clean the duplicator/press thoroughly when you have finished printing the job.

Units 109 and 110

5. Visit a commercial printing plant that has offset lithography presses. Ask to watch these presses in action. Carefully watch the skilled operators as they prepare, operate, and clean the presses. Take special note of the operator's skill and knowledge in making the adjustments needed for a quality printed job. Interview an operator about the needed job skills and training. Prepare a detailed written report.

The Story of My Life in the Printing Industry

By DR. BENJAMIN FRANKLIN

Philadelphia—I was born in Boston, New England, on January 17, 1706. My father had seven children by his first wife and by a second wife ten more. I was the youngest son and the youngest child.

My elder brothers were all put apprentices to different trades. I was put to the grammar-school at eight years of age, my father intending to devote me, as the tithe of his sons, to the service of the Church. My early readiness in learning to read and the opinion of all his friends, that I should certainly make a good scholar, encouraged him in this purpose of his.

I continued at the grammar-school not quite one year until my father, from a view of the expense, took me from the grammar-school and sent me to a school for writing and arithmetic. I acquired fair writing pretty soon, but I failed in the arithmetic and at ten years old I was taken home to assist my father in his business of a tallow-chandler and sope-boiler. I disliked the trade.

My bookish inclination, at length, determined my father to make me a printer, though he had already one son (James) of that profession. In 1717 James returned from England with a press and letters to set up his business in Boston. I signed the indentures when I was yet but twelve years old, to serve as an apprentice till I was twenty-one.

In 1720 or 1721, James begun to print a newspaper, the New England Courant, the second that appeared in America. I remember his being disuaded by some friends from the undertaking, as not likely to succeed, one newspaper being, in their judgment, enough for America. Not long later, some problems at the printinghouse and action by the Assembly came to the return of my old indenture to me, and when a difference arose between my brother and me, I took upon me to assert my freedom, presuming that he would not venture to produce new indentures.

When he found I would leave him, he took care to prevent me getting employment in any other printingh-ouse of the town by going round and speaking to every master. By selling some of my books for passage I went to New York on a sloop. I was then a boy of but 17.

I could find no employment in New York, but was sent on by a gentleman to one Keimer's printinghouse in Philadelphia. Keimer asked me a few questions, put a composing stick in my hand to see how I worked and then said he would employ me.

The printers at Philadelphia were wretched ones, and I, appearing a young man of promising parts, was asked by the governor to have my own business he would set up. I would first go to London to improve myself so that on my return to America I could set up to greater advantage.

In England, I immediately got into work at Palmer's, then in a famous printing-house in Bartholomew Close, and here I continu'd near a year, before I went to work at Watt's, an even greater printing-house, near Lincoln's Inn Fields, where I continued all the rest of my stay in London. At my first admission into Watt's, I took to working on a press, later going to the composing-room. We sail'd from Gravesend on the 23rd of July, 1726, and landed in Philadelphia on the 11th of October. I was then only 20 years old.

In my own Philadelphia printing-house in 1726, my partner was Hugh Meredith, 30 years of age, who had worked at press with Keimer. From the Quakers we procured the printing of forty sheets of their history, the rest being to be done by Keimer. It was a folio, pro patria size, in pica, with long primer notes. I composed of it a sheet a day, and Meridith worked it off at press.

It was often eleven at night, and sometimes later, before I had finished my distribution for the next day's work, for the little jobbs sent in by our other friends now and then put us back. But so determined I was to continue doing a sheet a day of the folio, that one night, when, having imposed my forms, I thought my day's work over, one of them by accident was broken, and two pages reduced to pi. I immediately distributed and compos'd it over again before I went to bed; and this industry, visible to our neighbors, began to give us character and credit.

Our partnership was dissolved about 1729, and soon after I obtained through a friend, the printing of the Newcastle paper money, another profitable jobb as I then thought it. He procured for me, also, the printing of the laws and votes of that government, which continued in my hands as long as I followed the business. In 1729, I purchased the Pennsylvania Gazette from Keimer.

In 1737, I was offered and accepted the commission of deputy at Philadelphia to the postmaster-general. I found it of great advantage, for it facilitated the correspondence that improved my newspaper, increased the number demanded, as well as the advertisements to be inserted, so that it came to afford me a considerable income.

My partnership with printers at Carolina having succeeded, I was encouraged to engage in others, and to promote several of my workmen, by establishing them with printing-houses in different colonies. Most of them did well, being enabled at the end of our term, six years, to purchase the types of me and go on working for themselves. I had, on the whole, abundant reason to be satisfied with my being established in Pennsylvania.

The rest of my story and my services to my country the reader already knows.

(Courtesy of *Printing Impressions*)

Modern printing presses are capable of the most complex jobs.
GRAVURE ASSOCIATION OF AMERICA

14 GRAVURE PRINTING PROCESS

UNIT 113 INTRODUCTION TO THE GRAVURE PRINTING PROCESS

The *gravure printing process* is one of the major graphic reproduction methods. It is also known as the rotogravure process. It differs from the other graphic reproduction methods in several important ways. But like other processes, the gravure process is used to reproduce images for the purpose of visual communication. It has advantages and disadvantages. People who need printed materials should understand its limitations.

In the gravure process, the image areas of the image carriers are sunk below the non-image surface (Unit 5). *Intaglio* is another method that reproduces images from a sunken surface, but intaglio uses lines produced either by hand or mechanical means. Gravure uses tiny, shallow ink wells to make dots of ink on the paper.

Gravure, with its repetitive ink cell pattern, is an adaptation of the original intaglio process. The image material has a screen-like pattern that produces dots in the gravure process. Gravure images can include photographs, artist's renderings, illustrations, and type matter. The dots are so small that they are hard to see without a magnifying glass.

PRODUCTS PRODUCED BY GRAVURE

The gravure process is used for products such as newspaper supplements, packaging, wrappers, advertising brochures, trading stamps, and magazines (Fig. 113-1). Other items include mail order catalogs, gift wrappings, food-package labels, floor covering, automobile upholstery material, handbags, table and counter top high-

pressure laminate, and wood-grain coverings for furniture (Fig. 113-2). The applications seem unlimited.

About 56 percent of gravure printing is used for publication work, 27 percent for packaging, and 17 percent for specialty items. From 12 to 15 percent of all commercial and publication printing is done by gravure. According to industry surveys, numbers of products printed by gravure are increasing at a steady rate.

One gravure technique lets rolls of completely seamless material be printed with absolute uniformity of design. This makes possible authen-

Fig. 113-1. Some of the products printed by the gravure process.

Fig. 113-2. Specialty products printed with the gravure process.

tic reproduction of unbroken wood and leather grains, marble patterns, linen weaves, and similar effects.

The United States Bureau of Engraving and Printing uses the intaglio process to produce paper currency and postage stamps. A specially designed press produces postage stamps at a speed of 1,700,000 an hour.

PRODUCTION STEPS

Gravure production follows the normal pattern of all graphic reproduction processes (Unit 3). Because the design and layout, type composition, and photoconversion phases are similar to those in other processes, we will not discuss them again in this section.

There are, however, notable differences of treatment in the photoconversion phase. Instead of the halftone film negatives used in letterpress and lithography reproduction processes, continuous-tone photographs and film positives are used. The production of gravure image carriers (Unit 114) and the image transfer presses (Unit 115) are significantly different and are treated in detail in the following units.

ADVANTAGES AND DISADVANTAGES OF GRAVURE

There are several advantages and disadvantages in gravure reproduction. You should consider them when planning products to be printed by gravure.

Advantages

1. The color looks almost like continuous-tone printing. It is similar to color photographic prints.
2. The image carriers have a long image life.
3. Gravure can produce images on a great variety of materials with high quality and visual impact.
4. High quality reproduction is possible on inexpensive printing substrates such as newsprint paper. The color impact is usually better than with the other printing methods—letterpress, lithography, and screen.
5. The ink is fast-drying.
6. Press speed is exceptionally high—up to 2,500 feet a minute.
7. Wide presses give good flexibility and more pages per publication.

Disadvantages

1. The initial cost of producing image carriers like wrap-around plates and cylinders is high.
2. Type size and styles are limited. Type smaller than 8 point should not be used unless absolutely necessary, and the typeface cannot have hairline strokes. The type should be medium-to-bold style without fine detail.
3. If one part of the whole image area needs to be changed, the entire cylinder may need to be remade. This takes time and is expensive.
4. More precision and time are needed to get quality results than with the other printing processes.

HISTORICAL HIGHLIGHTS

No one knows exactly how gravure began. The process seems to have started in Italy as a way of engraving gold and silver plates. As the art of intaglio engraving by hand developed, techniques were discovered that have continued through the centuries. Today intaglio is still considered a valuable art. Etching and dry point are much used fine art methods today (Unit 117).

The need to reproduce the newly invented photographs pushed development of the gravure method. During the 1880s and 1890s Karl Kleitsch (pronounced Klik) of Vienna, Austria, successfully used photographic methods to produce a gravure image carrier and a press having cylinders (rotogravure). He used a carbon-tissue process invented in 1864 by Joseph Swan, an Englishman.

The first large-scale commercial use of gravure took place in 1914 when the *New York Times* newspaper built its own rotogravure facility. The process was somewhat slow to advance because some details of how to make the image-carrier cylinders and the actual printing presses were kept as trade secrets. However, in recent years, great progress has been made in perfecting this image-transfer method.

Some products have long been printed by the gravure process (Fig. 113-3). The quality of the

printing and the possibility of long press runs were recognized quickly by both the graphic arts industry and buyers of printing. Currently, there are over 400 commercial and publication printers in the United States using the gravure process. It is used throughout the world and its future is limited only by the creative minds of the technicians and artists.

R.R. DONNELLEY AND SONS

Fig. 113-3. Many catalogs have been printed and continue to be printed by the gravure process.

114 GRAVURE IMAGE CARRIERS

The three main types of gravure image carriers are the flat plate, wrap-around plate, and cylinder. All three carriers reproduce images from recessed image areas (see Unit 5).

Flat plates are used on special sheet-fed presses that produce stock certificates and other high-grade limited-copy materials.

Wrap-around plates are used to print art reproductions, books, mail order booklets, calendars, and packaging materials. The wrap-around plate is thin and flexible. It attaches to cylinders similar to those on lithography presses. Wrap-around plates can be used economically only on short runs (30,000 copies or less). They cannot be used to produce a contin-

ROTO CYLINDERS

Fig. 114-1. An engraved gravure cylinder being inspected for accuracy before being placed in the printing press.

uous design or pattern because of the area needed to clamp the plate to the cylinder.

Cylinder image carriers are the most commonly used carriers in the industry. Preparation of a gravure cylinder is a very critical process. Each step in its production must be done with exacting care in order to get quality results (Fig. 114-1). Many "wood grain" products, some packaging designs, floor and wall coverings, textiles, and some newspaper printing jobs have continuous patterns. To print these continuous patterns, the never-ending-cylinder type of production is used.

PREPARING THE COPY

Preparation in gravure printing, as in all printing methods, is very important. The final printed results can be no better than the prepared copy. Words, sentences, and paragraphs of type are composed using the traditional methods, as presented in Section 4. Photographic and electronic generated typesetting methods are most often used because of their crisp reproduction.

Reflection copy, such as a regular paste-up, can provide copy information to the cylinder engraving machine. Transparency copy similar to a 35 mm color slide (except for size) is often used for input copy. When color separations are needed, a color separation electronic scanner is used (Fig. 114-2). This machine is used to separate the four standard colors of yellow, magenta, cyan, and black accurately. Copy can be converted to digital bits of infor-

CROSFIELD ELECTRONICS, INC.

Fig. 114-2. Preparing an electronic color scanner used to prepare four-color separations for engraving gravure cylinders.

mation and stored in computer memory. From there, it can be transmitted to an electronic engraving machine.

READYING THE CYLINDER

While the type matter, photographs, and color separations are being created, the surface of the gravure cylinder is being prepared to accept the image. It is very important to prepare the cylinder carefully before engraving the image on it.

Cylinders are made of high-quality steel. They are balanced so they don't vibrate when they are turning at high speeds on the gravure press. The steel outer surface of the cylinder must be perfectly round, smooth, and clean. The cylinder is then copper plated through the standard electroplating process briefly explained in Unit 69. Once plated with copper, the surface must be finished to an exact size. This is done with a high precision, metal-cutting machine (Fig. 114-3). The cylinder is sized and super-finished to the exact specified diameter and smoothness.

MAX DAETWYLER CORPORATION

Fig. 114-3. A computer-controlled, high-precision machining and finishing center for gravure cylinders.

PREPARING THE CYLINDER

The properly surfaced cylinder must be moved into the engraving and etching equipment with utmost care. An overhead crane is often used to move the cylinders because they are too heavy and cumbersome for engraving personnel to handle without help.

Electromechanical engraving.

The engraving machine has two synchronized rotating cylinders (Fig. 114-4). One is the copy cylinder; the other is the actual cylinder that will be put on the gravure press. The original copy to be reproduced is attached to the copy cylinder.

As the copy cylinder rotates, the image is scanned by a light beam and a photo-optical system. The reflected light is converted into electrical impulses that act as control signals for each diamond-cutting stylus.

The engraving stylus cuts cells that are shaped like inverted pyramids into the gra-

HELL GRAPHIC SYSTEMS, INC.

Fig. 114-4. An electronic gravure cylinder engraving machine, which scans the copy on the image cylinder (left) and electronically transfers the information to the cutting head to be engraved on the printing cylinder (right).

vure printing cylinder. The up-and-down movement of the stylus controls the depth of each cell, and this affects the amount of ink the cell can hold. This in turn controls the tonal values. A viewing system composed of a microscope and a high-resolution monitor are used to measure the pyramid-shaped cells (Fig. 114-5).

Chemical etching.

A film called *rotofilm* is exposed with a process camera, and then processed like the film used in the lithography printing method. Rotofilm consists of several layers, including an emulsion-resist layer. The film-positive image

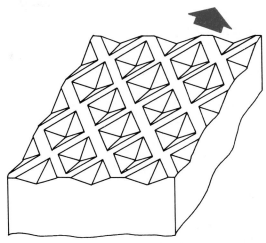

DIRECTION OF ENGRAVING

STORK INTER-AMERICAN CORPORATION

Fig. 114-5. An example of electronically engraved cells.

is tightly secured to the copper-surfaced gravure cylinder using pressure and a thin layer of water. Hot water is used to remove the soft emulsion-resist where it was not hardened by light during exposure. This leaves the screened image on the cylinder.

The cylinder is revolved in an etching bath of concentrated iron chloride (Fig. 114-6). This solution erodes the copper, biting through the film emulsion-resist. Water is then used to rinse the cylinder.

Electronic engraving.

Electronic engraving is often referred to as "filmless engraving" because no photographic film is needed (Fig. 114-7). Pasteups are read by scanning heads. The information is directly converted to electronic signals, which operate the engraving heads that cut the image cells into the copper cylinder. This procedure greatly reduces cylinder preparation time, but it is not a perfect process.

PROOFING AND CORRECTING

After close inspection, the cylinder is proofed on a special gravure proofing press (Fig. 114-8). The proof results are compared with the original copy. If flaws are found in the cylinder, a

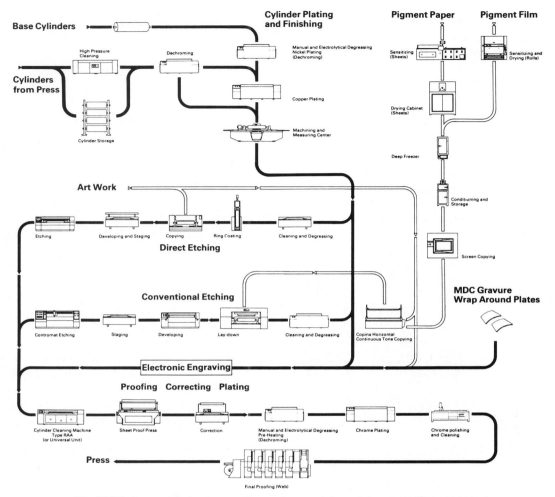

Fig. 114-6. A complete laser engraving system contains a color separation scanner, a page make-up unit, input devices, magnetic memory, and the printing cylinder engraving machine.

Fig. 114-7. The engraving head of the laser engraving machine shown in Figure 114-6.

Fig. 114-8. Proofing the cylinder on a gravure proof press.

skilled finisher will hand-correct them. When electromechanical and filmless engraving methods are used, hand corrections are not often needed. If major problems are found, it actually takes less time and materials to re-engrave the entire cylinder.

FINISHING THE CYLINDER

Once the cylinder is engraved, proofed, and corrected, it can be placed in a gravure press and used. In almost all instances, the cylinder is chrome plated. (Fig. 114-9). Chrome is much harder than copper, it wears better, and it gives many more copies. Also, it produces less friction and allows the doctor blade to wipe excess ink off the surface with little wear to the image carrier.

Fig. 114-9. A chromium-plating machine used to coat the engraved gravure cylinder for very long printing runs.

MAX DAETWYLER CORPORATION

UNIT 115 GRAVURE PRINTING PRESSES

Gravure presses and equipment were first manufactured and used in England late in the nineteenth century. In 1924 the *New York World* newspaper printed the first four-color newspaper gravure supplement. The press was German in design and was equipped with a folder, a flat sheet delivery, and a reel that accepted a web of paper. Shortly after that, several other four-color gravure presses began operation in both the United States and in Canada.

BASIC OPERATING PRINCIPLES

The basic operating principle of a gravure press, whether sheet fed or web fed, is the same (Fig. 115-1). The image-carrier cylinder, or flat plate, must be covered with a thin, liquid ink. The ink is removed by the doctor blade from non-image areas, and the plate or cylinder is pressed against the receptor (usually paper) to transfer the image.

While all gravure presses use this basic reproduction principle, many presses also use a system called *electrostatic assist* (explained below). Sometimes the term *retrogravure,* first used in 1912, is used instead of gravure printing. *Roto* simply refers to the web on the roll-fed presses. Today most gravure printing is done on roll-fed presses.

The early gravure presses ran 8,000 to 10,000 impressions per hour (IPH), but pro-

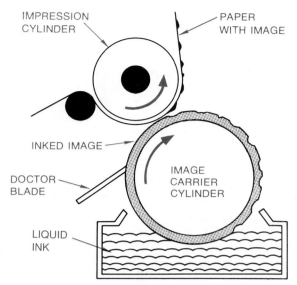

Fig. 115-1. The operating principle of a gravure printing press.

R.R. DONNELLEY AND SONS

Fig. 115-3. Millions of full-color catalogs can be produced on multistory gravure printing presses in a short time.

duction quickly increased to 12,000 to 15,000 IPH. The maximum web width was 60 to 66 inches (152 to 168 cm). Today, presses can print webs up to 120 inches (3m) wide at speeds of 3,300 feet per minute (fpm) (Fig. 115-2).

THE GRAVURE PRESS

The gravure process is used to reproduce fine color printing. Multi-unit presses are therefore

REGAR WORLD CORPORATION

Fig. 115-2. A six-station rotogravure press in operation. It handles a web 43 ½ inches wide (1105 mm).

common (Fig. 115-3). The paper web is fed from rolls that are sometimes below the first floor, coming up through the floor to enter the press. A five-unit color press prints on one side of the paper (unit A), then turns the paper over and prints four colors on the second side (units B, C, D, and E) (Fig. 115-4). With one pass through the press, both sides of a sheet are printed and four-color reproductions appear on one of the sides.

The usual gravure presses print webs from about 20 to 50 inches (51.8 to 127 cm) wide. These presses can have from one to eight color units placed in a line. As the width of the web increases, the construction of the press becomes more massive. A close-up view of a heavy-duty rotogravure press shows castings and bearings (Fig. 115-5). A rotogravure press is a precision machine that weighs many tons. As a precision machine, it must be properly maintained (Fig. 115-6). Gravure printers schedule regular equipment cleaning and repair. It is good business to keep equipment in top working condition.

Electrostatic assist is an important development in the gravure image transfer process. An electronic charge is created between the printing and impression cylinders, which causes ink containing metalized particles to transfer to the receptor (surface being printed) much more efficiently. This has improved gravure printing quality.

Computers have been integrated into the press control systems to make possible many

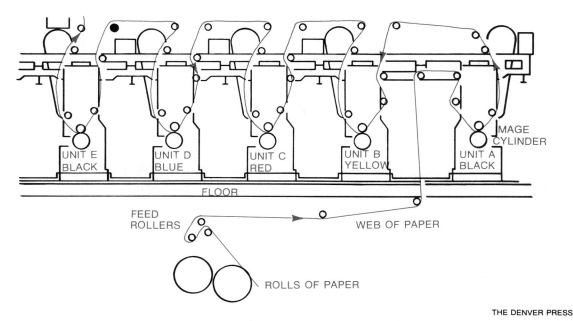

UNIT E
BLACK

UNIT D
BLUE

UNIT C
RED

UNIT B
YELLOW

UNIT A
BLACK

IMAGE
CYLINDER

FLOOR

FEED
ROLLERS

WEB OF PAPER

ROLLS OF PAPER

THE DENVER PRESS

Fig. 115-4. Schematic of a rotogravure press indicating color units and paper feed.

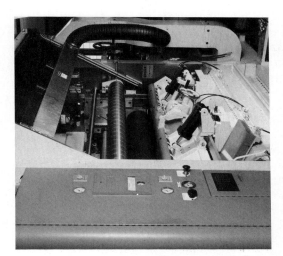

MOTTER PRINTING PRESS COMPANY

Fig. 115-5. A close-up view of a heavy-duty rotogravure press printing station.

prepress run adjustments and settings (Fig. 115-7). With the computer it is possible to pre-register and keep in register the multi-color images.

As press speeds have increased, precision operation and management of the total system have also increased. Printed, often finished, products are delivered from gravure presses at very high rates. Die cutting, creasing, and other

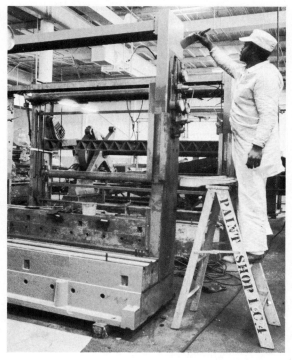

R.R. DONNELLEY AND SONS

Fig. 115-6. Good maintenance of printing presses and other equipment is necessary for efficient operation of a graphic arts production plant.

Fig. 115-7. This multiple unit gravure press control panel lets press operators control most functions important to quality printing. Computers are important parts of this and other press controls.

Fig. 115-8. Gravure press tenders removing die-cut cartons from a high production printing and finishing system.

finishing equipment (see Section 18) can be attached in-line to the gravure press. When this is done, people must work hard to remove finished products as fast as they come off press (Fig. 115-8). Proper handling of the products at this point is essential for profitable operations.

THE DOCTOR BLADE

The *doctor blade* is made of fine steel, 0.006-inch (.15mm) thick; it wipes ink from the non-image area of the cylinder (Fig.115-9). It has one edge that is carefully honed to a tapered shape, much like a large razor blade. This blade is the key to quality reproduction. If it fails to remove ink from unwanted areas, they will be printed, and the quality of the reproduction will be reduced. The blade is held in firm contact with the cylinder, and oscillates (moves) back and forth to keep grooves from forming in either it or the cylinder. Nearly all doctor blades are purchased "pre-honed" from suppliers who specialize in this product and service (Fig. 115-9). When a doctor blade becomes worn and does not properly remove the ink from the cylinder, it is discarded and replaced with a new blade.

GRAVURE PROOF PRESSES

Gravure proof presses are designed to check the image that has been engraved into the surface of the image carrier. Most reproduc-

Fig. 115-9 A doctor blade being reground on a precision grinder.

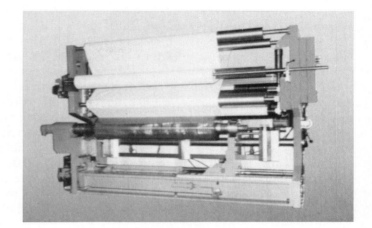

Fig. 115-10. A gravure-cylinder proof press.

MOTTER PRINTING PRESS COMPANY

tions made by the gravure reproduction process are printed from cylinders. Before a cylinder is put on a high-speed production press, a proof is taken to check the correctness and quality of the gravure cylinder. A proof press for a gravure cylinder must work like an actual production press (Fig. 115-10).

The cylinder receives a small quantity of ink and the doctor blade removes the ink from the non-image area. As the paper travels between the impression cylinder and the gravure image carrier cylinder, the ink is transferred from the tiny cells of the cylinder to the paper. As in letterpress and lithographic processes, the proofs are inspected. If corrections are needed, they can be made before the cylinder is placed on a high-speed press.

UNIT 116 SAFETY WHEN ETCHING AND ENGRAVING

Etching and engraving entail the use of sharp tools and toxic solutions. Follow the cautions listed in this unit to do quality work safely.

Permission. Get permission from someone in charge before beginning either etching or engraving.

Clothing and jewelry. Secure loose clothing and remove jewelry and wrist watches. Loose clothing and long hair can get caught in moving equipment.

Safety guards. Have the safety guards installed over moving parts of both the plate-whirler and the thermography machine. Hand-operated machines such as the etching and engraving press must also have the proper safety guards over moving parts.

Air vents. Start exhaust fans before working with chemicals, acids, or solvents. Check to see that the exhaust system is working properly. If there is no power exhaust system, open windows or doors or both.

Eye and face protection. Wear safety glasses or a face shield when working with etching solutions and when making a hand engraving.

Body protection. Wear rubber gloves and an apron when using etching solutions. Gloves should come up to the elbows, and the apron should be large enough to cover the entire front of the body.

Good housekeeping. Keep the laboratory orderly. Never let waste materials collect on the floor because of the danger of fire. Accidents are more likely to happen in a messy setting.

Floor drain. There should be floor drains near sinks and containers holding liquid etching solutions. For safety purposes, most chemicals should not enter the sanitary drain system.

Illumination. Have good lighting. Not being able to see clearly to work can be dangerous.

Materials storage. Store containers of etching solutions and ink solvents near the floor. Put boxes, tools, and other items on storage shelves so that you can reach them easily and they will not be shaken off the shelf.

Noise. Too much noise is unsafe. Talk and laughter should be kept to a minimum.

Fire. Fire extinguishers *must* always be kept charged and located in conspicuous places in the laboratory. Be careful when using the hotplate or thermography machine. Do not leave these units unattended when they are turned on. These two units can start fires.

Sharp objects. Handle and use sharp tools with care. Engraving tools must be used with great caution. Do not carry them in your pocket unless protective caps are in place.

Ink- and solvent-soaked rags. Put rags containing ink or solvents in a metal safety can that has a tight metal lid. Spontaneous combustion could occur if these rags are not placed in this kind of container.

Burns. Electrical burns are painful. Be careful when using the hotplate and when operating the thermography machine.

Safety shower. Whenever chemicals are used in any laboratory, a safety shower must be near. Persons who spill caustic chemicals or solutions on their bodies or in their eyes should immediately flush the affected areas with large volumes of cool water.

UNIT 117 FLAT-PLATE GRAVURE ETCHING

Flat-plate gravure etching can be done in most small laboratories. The method described here is not foolproof but it will help you to understand the procedures and problems of making gravure cylinders.

We suggest that you use aluminum because it is easy to get and easy to etch. The main problem is that it is very soft. This is most noticeable during the proofing operations.

MAKING THE PLATE

1. Get a piece of aluminum. A size of 4 by 5 inches (10.16 by 12.7 cm) is big enough.
2. Clean one side very thoroughly with water and pumice. Use a soft cotton pad to scrub the metal with the pumice. Use plenty of water because it is very important that the metal is clean. Keep fingerprints from the metal surface.
3. Dry the metal with forced air from an air hose, or use the heat of two 250-watt infrared heat bulbs.
4. Apply a photoresist solution formulated for aluminum. Pour the liquid resist on the plate; distribute it by tilting the plate from side to side. NOTE: Room illumination must be *low* when working with photoresist.
5. Place the plate in a whirler (Fig. 117-1). Allow it to whirl for 5 minutes *without* heat. The turning action distributes the photoresist solution evenly over the plate.

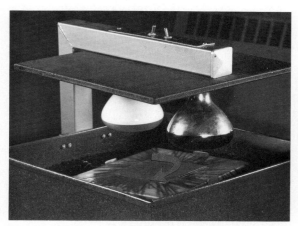

Fig. 117-1. Whirling a plate to distribute the photoresist.

Fig. 117-2. Etching an aluminum gravure flat-plate.

6. Dry the photoresist while in the whirler. Allow the whirler to continue turning, and turn on the heating element. Two 250-watt infrared heat bulbs will work well. Ten minutes are generally enough for drying.

7. Expose the plate. Position a halftone film positive emulsion-side up, on the plate. Any good exposure unit can be used and the length of exposure depends upon the light source and the speed of the photoresist. You will have to conduct exposure tests with available equipment.

8. Develop the exposed plate in the appropriate developer that is compatible with the aluminum photoresist. The developer softens the image area of the plate that was not struck by the light.

9. Wash away the softened photoresist with a bath of warm water.

10. Etch the plate in the appropriate aluminum etch (Fig. 117-2). Let the etch bite into the plate approximately 0.002 to 0.003 inch (.05 to .076 mm). NOTE: The halftone film positive contains various dot sizes and when the plate is etched the wells will all be the same depth. This is unlike conventional gravure cylinder methods (Unit 114).

11. Flush the plate with cold water to remove the etching bath.

12. Immerse the plate into the developer again. This softens the remaining photoresist. Flush with water.

13. Dry the plate with compressed air. Inspect the final etching with a magnifying glass.

PROOFING THE PLATE

Proofing the plate is like printing a dry-point engraving (Unit 118). It is possible, however, to remove the ink from the non-image area with either a hard rubber squeegee or plastic straightedge. This will simulate the gravure press doctor blade action.

UNIT 118 HAND ENGRAVING AND PRINTING

The terms *hand engraving* and *etching* are often used interchangeably but actually should not be. To *engrave* is to cut an object with a tool and to *etch* is to remove by chemical-acid means.

Both engravings and etchings are true intaglio methods of reproducing images. Lines are cut or etched below the non-image surface of the image carrier. The image carrier, made of copper, steel, or plastic, is then inked over the entire surface. The ink is wiped from the non-image high portion, leaving the lines filled with ink. The image carrier is then pressed against a paper receptor to transfer the image.

COPPER AND STEEL HAND ENGRAVINGS

Copper and steel image carriers are used in making commercial hand engravings. Both types are made in the same basic way. Copper, a relatively soft metal, can be engraved more easily than steel, but it will make fewer impressions. Steel can produce almost unlimited impressions if it is hard chromed after engraving.

An engraver must be able to engrave the image in the copper or steel in reverse (Fig. 118-1). Engravers use several tools, called gravers, that have different cutting edges to produce many different widths and shapes of lines. A magnifying glass can be used while making small images with the gravers.

The engraved plate, or die, is mounted in a die stamping press and engraved copies are produced (Fig. 118-2). The press automatically inks the plate and presses it to the paper with great pressure. The counter, a fiberboard material, is cut by hand to force the paper into the die or plate. The pressure causes the ink to transfer, and also causes a raised image on the paper. This gives the final product a distinctive look.

Up to 200 copies can be reproduced from copper engravings, 250,000 from steel ones. With hard chrome plating, it is possible to make up to 1,000 impressions from copper engravings and unlimited impressions from steel engravings. Automatic feed die stamping presses (Fig. 118-3) die stamp and emboss at speeds of over 6,000 IPH.

Stationery, business cards, announcements, and invitations are examples of hand engraving and embossing. United States paper currency is reproduced from steel engravings, as are negoti-

JOSTEN'S SCHOLASTIC DIVISION

Fig. 118-1. An engraver cuts the image into a copper plate.

JOSTEN'S SCHOLASTIC DIVISION

Fig. 118-2. Carefully hand feeding a die-stamping press.

Fig. 118-3. An operator tends a high-speed automatic-feed die-stamping press.

Fig. 118-4. A reproduction of a dry-point engraving.

able stock and bond certificates. In blind embossing, an image is produced in relief without ink.

DRY-POINT ENGRAVING AND PRINTING

Dry-point engravings are produced by scratching lines in a piece of plastic, inking the plate, and pressing paper against it to make the print. Dry-point engravings are composed entirely of lines and can be very intricate (Fig. 118-4). With practice, high-quality prints can be made at an economical price. Greeting cards, bookplates, bookmarks, artwork, and many other items are possible with this intaglio process.

Selecting the copy

It is important to select an illustration that can be drawn with lines only. Landscapes, people, and animals are excellent illustration subjects. Many more topics can be reproduced. Areas of solid color cannot be reproduced, but near-solid ones are possible with the use of crosshatching or lines drawn close together.

Preparing the plate

1. Prepare the copy of the illustration on white bond paper. It must be made the same size as the desired final print. Use black ink when preparing the copy illustration.
2. Tape the copy upside down on the glass of a light table. The plate must be prepared in reverse if the final prints are to be right-reading.
3. Place a transparent plastic sheet 0.15 to 0.040-inch (3.81 to 1.02 mm) thick over the copy. Tape it securely in place. The light from the light table makes the image visible through the paper and plastic.
4. Take a dry-point engraving tool and scratch the lines of the copy (Fig. 118-5). The sharp-pointed tool can be a sheet metal scriber, a sharpened nail imbedded in the end of a 3/8-inch (9.5 mm) dowel, a large sewing needle, or the metal point of a bow compass.

Fig. 118-5. Using a sharp-pointed engraving tool to make a dry-point engraving.

5. Scratch or engrave the entire illustration on the plastic plate. Dark and heavy lines must be engraved more deeply than thin, light ones. A burr must develop on each line to make a good reproduction.

Reproducing the prints

1. Prepare the paper. Select a soft-surfaced paper such as uncoated book paper or mimeograph stock. Special etching paper can be bought. Dampen the paper slightly. Stack it and allow it to stand under a weight for 24 hours.
2. Mix the ink. Use the special etching ink or letterpress or lithography all-purpose ink. Mix a drop of reducing varnish with a thimbleful amount of ink. Use a glass ink plate and ink knife to prepare it.
3. Using a cloth dauber, work the ink into the engraved lines on the plate. It is better to get too much ink on the plate than not enough.
4. Remove the ink from the non-reproducing area of the plate by wiping it with a cotton cloth or paper towel (Fig. 118-6). You may also use the heel of your hand to polish the non-reproducing surface completely clean.
5. Place the inked plate on the bed of the engraving and etching press (Fig. 118-7), engraved side up.
6. Lay a pre-dampened sheet of paper stock over the plate. Also put two felt blankets over the paper and plate.

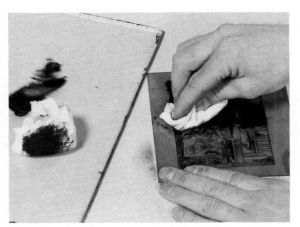

Fig. 118-6. Removing ink from a dry-point engraving with a cotton cloth.

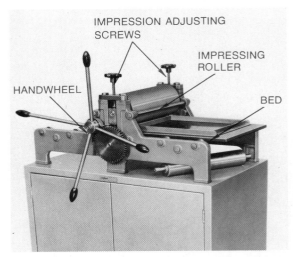

THE CRAFTOOL COMPANY

Fig. 118-7. A hand-operated engraving and etching press.

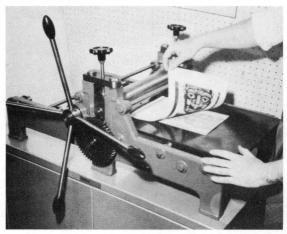

THE CRAFTOOL COMPANY

Fig. 118-8. Removing the sheet from the engraving after it has been printed.

7. Adjust the press impression roller with the adjusting screws so that a high amount of pressure in pounds per square inch will be exerted on the paper and plate as they pass between the roller and the bed.
8. Turn the wheel of the press to move the bed under the impression roller. This causes the ink to transfer from the engraved lines of the plate to the paper.
9. Remove the felt blankets and the printed sheet carefully (Fig. 118-8). Inspect the sheet for flaws and decide what caused

imaging or inking problems. More lines can be added and existing ones made deeper.

10. Make corrections or alterations if necessary.
11. Make additional prints. Repeat steps 3 through 9.
12. Multi-color prints can be made by inking different portions of the illustration with different colors of ink. Remove the ink and print the plate in the usual manner.
13. Clean the plate. Remove all ink from the engraved lines with ink solvent. The plate can be stored and used again.

UNIT 119 THERMOGRAPHY

Thermography is a process that produces raised printing. The word *thermography* is a combination of the words *thermo* meaning heat, and *graphy* to write, and it means, literally, *heat writing*. It has been used for years to add an attractive quality to different printed materials.

The raised printing results from sprinkling special rosin powder over a freshly printed sheet. Excess powder is removed from the non-inked areas and the powder that sticks to the wet ink is heated. The heat melts the powder, and, after cooling, a raised effect results.

There are several models of commercial thermographic equipment. A hand-fed model is shown in Figure 119-1. Figure 119-2 shows a model placed in-line with a printing press. With hand-fed models, the operator must powder the sheet before placing it in the machine. Automatic in-line machines, which accept freshly printed sheets from nearly any kind of a press, powder the sheet, remove excess powder, heat the sheet and powder, and cool the sheet to complete the process. A commercial plant installation is shown in Figure 119-3.

Thermography products include greeting cards, stationery, business cards, and formal announcements. Thermography also enhances package design, ceiling tile, hardboard panels, wall coverings, metal containers, children's furniture and accessories, and home appliances.

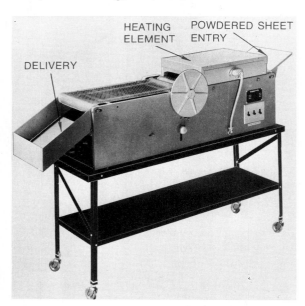

VIRKOTYPE CORPORATION

Fig. 119-1. A hand-fed thermography machine with a heating element and wire belt.

PRODUCTION PROCEDURE

1. Complete the design and layout, type composition, photography, plates, and printing steps. Letterpress, offset lithography, or screen printing image transfer methods can be used to produce printed sheets. It is important to do a good job of printing the image on the receptor sheet.
2. Apply the special thermography powder to the sheets while the ink is still wet. Immerse the entire image area of the sheet in the pan of powder (Fig. 119-4).

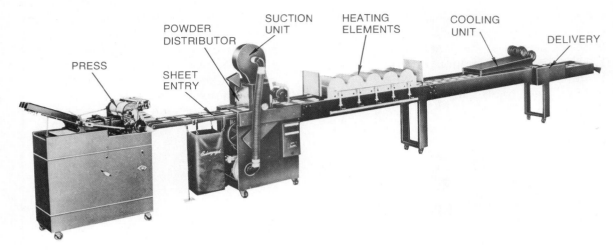

VIRKOTYPE CORPORATION

Fig. 119-2. An automatic thermography machine placed in-line with a printing press.

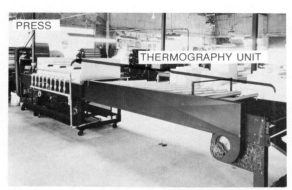

VIRKOTYPE CORPORATION

Fig. 119-3. A commercial installation of a thermography unit in-line with a press.

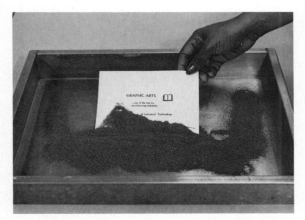

Fig. 119-4. Immersing freshly printed sheets in the thermography powder.

3. Remove the excess powder by tapping the sheets sharply over the pan containing the powder.
4. Heat the sheet to melt the powder and fuse it with ink by:
   a. Putting the sheets through a hand-fed thermography machine (Fig. 119-5), or

Fig. 119-5. Placing freshly printed sheets through a hand-fed thermography machine.

   b. Holding the sheets over the heat of a standard hot plate (Fig. 119-6) until the powder melts and fuses to the ink.
5. Allow the sheets to cool before stacking and packaging.

Fig. 119-6. Holding the freshly powdered sheet over a hot-plate to melt the thermography powder.

DESIGN LIMITATIONS

Type, halftone reproductions, and pen-and-ink illustrations are suitable for thermography. Getting very fine detail is difficult, but with care and the use of correct ink and powder, finely detailed illustrations are possible.

Mostly, type less than 6 point in size should not be used. However, 5 point can be used satisfactorily, if it is open face and in the sans-serif family. Letters with delicate serifs, particularly in small sizes, should be avoided as they tend to fill in with powder after heating.

POWDERS AND INKS

Neutral powders permit the color of the base ink to show through. Opaque colors have complete hiding power. Opaque colors are available in white, orange, red, yellow, pink, and green. Metallic and fluorescent colors are also available.

The ranges of the granulation powders are from coarse to very fine. The choice depends upon the image. If the image has fine lines, use a fine powder. A coarse powder will cause fine lines to fill in and lose their individual detail.

Almost all inks can be used in the thermography process, because ink serves only as an adhesive for the powder. For high-quality work, use special inks having little or no dryer in them.

UNIT 120 LEARNING EXPERIENCES: GRAVURE PRINTING PROCESS

KEY TERMS

Unit 113

Halftone gravure   Ink cell

Unit 114

Copy cylinder   Filmless engraving
Chrome plating   Gravure cylinder
Electromechanical   Laser engraving
Engraving

Unit 115

Doctor blade   FPM
Electrostatic assist   Rotogravure

Unit 117

Etching   Whirler
Photoresist

Unit 118

Blind embossing   Embossing
Dry pont engraving

Unit 119

Thermography

DISCUSSION TOPICS

1. How does the image-transfer principle of gravure differ from the principles of letterpress, lithography, and screen printing?
2. How does the electromechanical engraving machine form ink cells in the copper surface of the gravure cylinder?
3. What have electrostatic assist and computers done for the gravure method of image transfer?
4. Why should there always be a safety shower in an area where caustic chemicals or solutions are used?
5. Compare *engraving* and *etching*.

ACTIVITIES

Units 113–115

1. Visit a gravure printing plant. Carefully observe the methods used to prepare the gravure cylinders. Carefully watch the gravure printing press. Are these presses sheet-fed or web-fed? How fast can they produce printed products? Get example products that the company produces, especially gravure products. Look at these products carefully with a magnifying glass and see their quality. Analyze your observations.

Unit 117

2. Prepare a flat-plate gravure etching. Get the materials you need, prepare the film positive, and make the etching. Proof the finished plate and compare the proof with the original copy used to prepare the film positive. Carefully inspect the plate with a magnifying glass to see the depth of the ink wells.

Unit 118

3. Prepare a dry-point engraving and reproduce several copies from it. Use different engraving tools to discover which tool does the best job and is easiest to use. During the printing operation, try reproducing prints on dry paper as well as on dampened paper. Also experiment with different kinds, consistencies, and colors of ink.

Unit 119

4. Plan, compose, and print items such as personal stationery, announcements, or invitations suitable for thermography. Follow the procedures that are needed to produce raised printing (thermography). If possible, experiment by using different kinds and sizes of type, by using different kinds and colors of ink, and by using different colors and grades of thermography powder. Compare the results of each of these several experiments.

The printed page can live forever.

> **M**EN WANTED for Hazardous Journey. Small wages, bitter cold, long months of complete darkness, constant danger, safe return doubtful. Honor and recognition in case of success — Ernest Shackleton.

This advertisement, written by Ernest Shackleton, the famed polar explorer, appeared in London newspapers in 1900. In speaking of it later, he said: "It seemed as though all the men in Great Britain were determined to accompany me, the response was so overwhelming."

Seventy years later, people still refer to the "hazardous journey" ad when they talk about the power of print.

If you have something important to say, your message will last longer if you put it in print.

Your message in print can last forever.

**Cleaning a printing unit on
a web screen printing press.**
THE ADVANCE GROUP

15 SCREEN PRINTING

121 INTRODUCTION TO SCREEN PRINTING

Screen printing, also called silk screen printing, stencil printing, mitography, or screen process printing, differs from other methods of reproduction. Where letterpress, lithography, and gravure printing transfer ink *from* an image carrier, the screen printing method prints *through* an image carrier. Heavy-bodied inks are forced through a fine-mesh screen to be directly printed on any type of product, whether flat or three-dimensional.

Among the parts needed for screen printing are the (1) screen fabric, (2) frame to hold the screen fabric, (3) stencil, (4) squeegee, and (5) ink (Fig. 121-1). A sheet is positioned on the printing base, the screen frame is lowered, the squeegee is pulled to force ink through the mesh to make the print, the frame is raised, and the stock is removed. On some presses, the screen stays still and the squeegee moves to make the print. On others the squeegee is fixed and the screen frame and bed underneath both move.

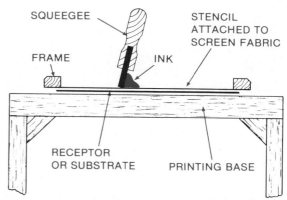

Fig. 121-1. The basic components of a screen-printing unit.

Fig. 121-2. Screen printing as done by the ancient Japanese.

HISTORICAL HIGHLIGHTS

The stencil principle used in screen printing has been traced back to ancient times. The Egyptians, Chinese, and Japanese pounded colored pigments through stencils reinforced with human hair onto a variety of objects, including pottery, fabrics, and decorative screens (Fig. 121-2).

During the Middle Ages the stencil method spread throughout Europe for making such diverse items as religious images and playing cards. In the seventeenth century, stencils were used in England to make wallpaper decorations. Early American colonists stenciled designs directly on walls, furniture, and textiles.

Although commercial screen printing plants were set up early in the twentieth century (there was one in California in 1906), the process was largely a hand craft until the Second World War. No one individual or invention caused the rapid rise of screen printing, which began in 1940. It resulted from a combination of many improvements in presses, drying equipment, screen materials, and inks.

The Second World War created a demand for permanent identification of huge quantities of

Fig. 121-3. A few products printed by the screen-printing method.

Fig. 121-4. Additional products printed by the screen-printing method.

military equipment and supplies. A wide range of materials and shapes, from small ampules (medicine vials) to tanks, were successfully marked by screen printing. Wartime requirements for fluorescent and phosphorescent coating and markings were best satisfied by screen printing. This led to the post-war boom in the display industry.

As late as 1953, screen printing was described as the least industrialized of all graphic arts. Today it is a mechanized industry, having moved from a low output hand operation to a process having considerable mechanization. In the United States, for example, the Census Bureau reports that screen printing is one of the fastest growing segments of the graphic arts industry.

PRODUCTS

Screen printing has many uses. Figure 121-3 shows a few examples of printing on flat, curved, cylinderical, and other shapes. The materials include paper, wood, metal, glass, cloth, rigid and nonrigid plastics, rubber, and fiberglass. Figure 121-4 shows other products—advertising displays, designs on dishes and decorative china, decals of any type, reflective decorations, bolt fabrics, wallpaper, and packages of every kind and surface.

Other products include braille dots on thin paper for lightweight books for the blind, and electrical circuits for portable radios, televi-

sion, hearing aids, and other small electronic equipment. Color dots on the inside of color television picture tubes, and capacitors for micro-miniature circuitry are also made with the help of screen printing. The majority of the circuits in missiles and spacecraft are screen printed.

An important feature of screen printing is its use of a wide range of printing inks. The present inks include solvent-based, water-based, plastisol, and ultraviolet inks. Solvent and water-based inks are commonly used to print on paper, plastics, metals, wood, glass, and textiles. They can either be air dried through evaporation or heat dried.

Plastisol inks are used primarily for textile printing and are cured by subjecting them to heat. Plastisol inks do not air dry, but cure or fuse to create a solid ink film.

Ultraviolet (UV) screen inks let the ink cure instantly, after printing. The ink does not dry in the screen, but, once printed, is cured by a special UV drying system. The ink actually does not "dry"—that is why the process is called "curing." On being exposed to UV energy, the ink molecules are cross-linked. This has greatly increased the production speeds of commercial screen printing.

Water-based, plastisol, and UV screen inks are solventless. This has simplified the screen-printing process. It has also made screen printing safer and more environmentally sound.

PREPARING IMAGE CARRIERS

There are three basic kinds of screen printing image carriers: (1) knife-cut film (2) photographic, and (3) washout (tusche). Knife-cut paper is also used, but more by individuals than industries.

Knife-cut films. A greatly used technique is the knife-cut method (Units 127 and 128). A coating of transparent colored film is bonded to a piece of transparent plastic or backing paper. Image areas are only cut through the top layer of the film and removed. Solvent is used to fasten the stripped film to the bottom of the screen. After drying, the backing paper is removed and the screen is printed.

Photographic methods. Photographic methods use the same principles as do other photomechanical processes. Light-sensitive emulsions harden when exposed to intense light.

Emulsions may be applied directly to the printing screen or coated on a semi-permanent carrying support such as paper or transparent plastic, usually polyester.

Film positives are made from original copy and placed in a vacuum frame in contact with either the sensitized emulsion-coated screen in the direct process or with the photographic film. They are then exposed to light. After exposure, soft or unexposed areas are developed and washed away. The non-printing hardened areas stay to form a stencil.

Washout (tusche) method. This method is primarily an art technique in which the desired image is first outlined on the screen. The image area is then coated with tusche block-out material. Liquid glue is applied to both the non-image and image areas of the screen. The tusched image areas are then washed away with a solvent, leaving a clear-screen image area.

UNIT 122 INDUSTRIAL EQUIPMENT AND PRODUCTION METHODS

In recent years, many ways have been found to mechanize screen printing. Experimental work goes on, and no single press has become standard. The various screen press principles are listed below.

Rotary screen. In machines of this type, the printing screen is attached to a cylinder or drum with a stationary squeegee and ink in the center. As the drum rotates, cloth or paper is fed onto a cylinder and brought into contact with the drum at the point where the squeegee is located. The rotary screen cylinder press makes web printing possible in the screen process.

Rocker-type machines. The *Selectasine* machine is an example of the oldest type of screen press. An oscillating curved platen carries the stock to a stationary squeegee. The ink is forced through the screen, which is attached to a reciprocating frame sliding back and forth under the squeegee.

Bottle-printing machines. In these the squeegee is stationary; a flat screen makes a reciprocating movement; and the stock is fed to a rotating drum.

Flatbed-type machines. These look like the setup used in hand-letterpress printing. The flatbed, however, is a much larger, motor-driven operation.

COMMERCIAL HAND-OPERATED PRESSES

Automatic screen printing presses print on a variety of products, but they may never completely replace hand-screen printing. There are many variations in hand-screen printing equipment and techniques.

The typical commercial screen printing unit has gained some simple improvements that increase quality and speed. Vacuum table units

Fig. 122-1. A hand-operated screen-printing unit containing a vacuum table.

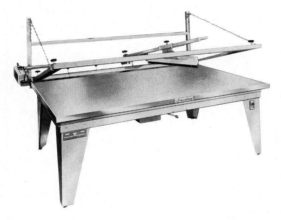

THE ADVANCE GROUP

Fig. 122-2. A one-armed hand-operated screen-printing unit with a vacuum table.

THE ADVANCE GROUP

Fig. 122-3. A semi-automatic hand-fed screen-printing press.

(Fig. 122-1) improve register and printing quality. Adding bars and handles to the squeegee (Fig. 122-2) increases the printing speed. Other adaptations are available from commercial sources. Many plants have designed their own equipment.

Flatbed screen printing presses

The *flatbed* screen press was developed in the 1930s. This simple clam-shell press can screen print posters, cardboard displays, metal signs, and decals. In it, the hand action of the squeegee and the raising and lowering the screen are mechanized. Feed and delivery operations are still done by hand (Fig. 122-3).

The flatbed press now includes many refinements, such as automatic feed and delivery, vacuum stock holding beds, micrometer adjustments, and automatic timers. Speed has gone from a few hundred impressions an hour to as many as 2,000. Size has increased from small 12-by 18-inch (30.5 by 45.7 cm) presses to popular 52 by 60 inch (132 by 152.4 cm) ones; special large ones of 66 by 144 inches (168 by 366 cm) are also available.

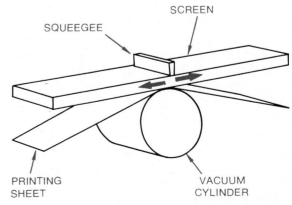

Fig. 122-4. The principle of a cylinder screen-printing press.

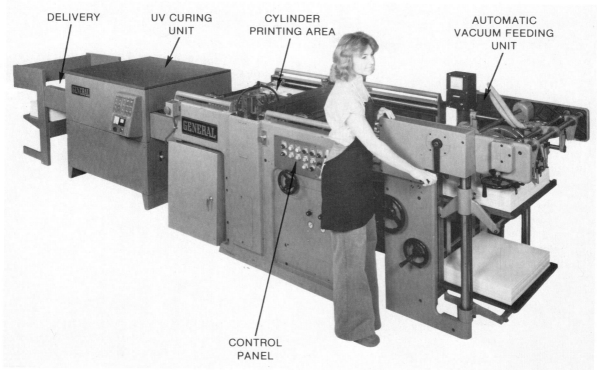

DELIVERY   UV CURING   CYLINDER   AUTOMATIC
             UNIT   PRINTING AREA   VACUUM FEEDING
                                       UNIT

CONTROL
PANEL

GENERAL RESEARCH

Fig. 122-5. A cylinder-type screen-printing press.

Cylinder screen printing presses

Major progress in the design of screen printing presses was made in 1949 when a press was perfected using the cylindrical platen principle (Fig. 122-4). Because the flat screen travels on top of the cylinder, the cylinder-screen frame arrangement looks like a letterpress flatbed cylinder press turned upside down. The revolving vacuum cylinder is perforated so that suction can keep the sheet from moving.

The squeegee is stationary during the printing cycle. The chase and cylinder are reciprocal in action—the stock is moved forward at the same speed as the screen frame. Sheets are fed automatically, printed, and delivered flat. The squeegee lifts and the cylinder and screen frame move back to starting positon after each impression.

Cylinder press operation includes high-speed press refinements used in letterpress and lithography. With the development of this press it was possible for the first time to feed, print, and deliver automatically (Fig. 122-5). Web-fed cylinder presses make up to 6,000 IPH, and sizes go as high as 52 by 76 inches (132 by 193 cm) (Fig. 122-6).

GENERAL RESEARCH

Fig. 122-6. A cylinder, web-fed screen-printing press with five color printing units, each equipped with a drying system.

Rotary screen printing presses

Rotary screen printing presses permit high speed printing. In this press design, the squeegee and ink are located inside a cylinder. The image stencil is fastened to the outside of the cylinder face. When the web of paper or cloth passes between the stencil cylinder and impression cylinder, the squeegee forces the ink through the open image areas, causing the print to be made.

Specialty screen printing presses

Screen printing is a versatile method of reproducing graphic images. To print on many different shapes and kinds of objects, special presses have been built. Many round, cylindrical, and flat objects are printed. Several press designs have been adapted to handle these situations. Some are hand operated with special object holders (Fig. 122-7). A cylindrical press is very different from a flatbed one: the squeegee is sta-

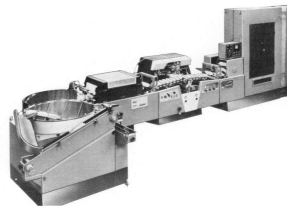

AMERICAN EQUIPMENT/DIVISION OF ADVANCED PROCESS SUPPLY

Fig. 122-8. A completely automatic printing line for one-color screen printing of plastic containers.

ATLAS SCREEN PRINTING SUPPLIES, INC.

Fig. 122-7. A hand-operated screen-printing press designed for cylindrical objects.

HOPKINS INTERNATIONAL

Fig. 122-9. A multi-color textile-garment screen printing unit. It can print up to six colors in perfect register.

TURCO MANUFACTURING COMPANY

Fig. 122-10. A screen-printing unit for printing multi-color spiral patterns around a long cylindrical object.

CINCINNATI PRINTING AND DRYING SYSTEMS

Fig. 122-11. A multi-shelf wooden drying rack.

Drying equipment

Freshly printed sheets direct from the screen-printing press cannot be laid on top of one another like the ones from letterpress and lithography presses. The ink deposit is too heavy to set and dry immediately, although the improved inks now dry more quickly. UV-cured inks, however, let many screen-printed products be handled almost immediately.

Wood or metal drying racks (Fig. 122-11) are commonly used in smaller commercial screen printing plants.

Wicket dryers are used to increase space production. They contain an endless belt of lightweight metal racks that hold the printed sheet as it travels over the drying distance (Fig. 122-12). Circulating air dries the sheets. Wicket dryers may have forced-air heating units to shorten the drying time.

Drying ovens hold portable drying racks (Fig. 122-13). The freshly printed sheets are placed on the racks and completely dried in a short time.

Fig. 122-12. A screen-printing wicket dryer with an enclosed heating unit.

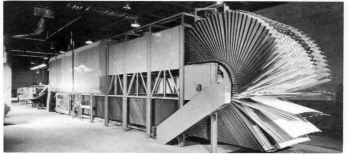

GENERAL RESEARCH

tionary except for up-and-down movement, and the frame moves back and forth as the object revolves during the printing.

Figure 122-8 shows a large commercial packaging plant with a completely automatic screen printing line. It includes a product unscrambler unit, a flame treater, a cleaning and destaticizing unit, a screen printer, and a heat-drying unit. Production speeds of 3,600 IPH are possible.

Manufacturers of products that need printed images often have screen printing facilities within their plant. Textile-garment (Fig. 122-9) and playground equipment (Fig. 122-10) manufacturers are typical examples.

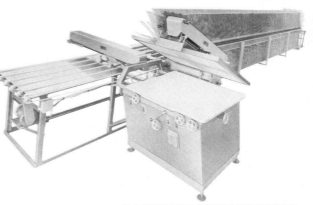

M & M RESEARCH ENGINEERING COMPANY

Fig. 122-13. A semi-automatic screen-printing press with an attached wicket dryer.

CINCINNATI PRINTING AND DRYING SYSTEMS

Fig. 122-14. A screen-printing drying oven.

AMERICAN EQUIPMENT/DIVISION OF ADVANCE PROCESS SUPPLY

Fig. 122-15. A forced-air, high-speed drying screen printing unit.

Continuous conveyor-belt dryers (Fig. 122-14) are placed in line with a high-speed screen press. Heated air constantly circulates around the printed product and dries or cures it very rapidly. These drying units also remove ink fumes and cool the sheets after they dry. There are also ovens or kilns for firing ceramic screen-printed products.

Ultraviolet (UV) curing units look much like the heated belt dryers used for rapid curing of plastisol and drying of water-based and solvent-based inks (Fig. 122-15). The major difference is that an UV bulb, which emits UV light waves, is housed in the hooded unit instead of the standard heating elements.

UNIT 123 SCREEN PRINTING EQUIPMENT FOR HAND PRODUCTION

Screen printing equipment for hand production includes a frame, some screen fabric, a squeegee, film cutting tools, and drying equipment. You will also need supplies such as film and chemicals for the image carriers, ink, solvent, and plenty of wiping cloths. The cost is small compared with cost for the letterpress and lithography printing methods. Some of the equipment can easily be made in the home or school laboratory.

SCREEN PRINTING FRAMES

Screen frames suitable for hand production can be built as shown in Unit 125, or bought from commercial supply houses (Fig. 123-1). The frame can be of a size useful for general work, it can be designed for specific jobs. A screen printing unit has a frame stretched with fabric, a baseboard, hinges, and the hinge lock.

SCREEN FABRIC

Many kinds of materials are used as *screen fabric*. The Silk fabric was probably first used as a screen to hold the image carrier in the United States. Samuel Simon, of Manchester, England, obtained the first patent relating to using silk for screen printing in 1907. Other materials used besides natural silk include nylon, polyester, stainless steel mesh, and metalized polyester.

DICK BLICK

Fig. 123-1. A typical hand screen-printing frame and base.

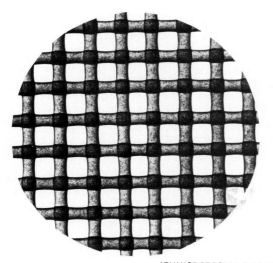

ADVANCE PROCESS SUPPLY

Fig. 123-2. A highly magnified view of a monofilament (single strand) of synthetic screen fabric.

When looking at screen fabrics made of nylon and polyester with a magnifying glass, you can see that they are finely woven meshes with openings that allow liquid ink to pass through (Fig. 123-2). Screen fabric is graded by the number of threads it has per linear inch. Mesh count is identified by number; the larger the number, the finer the screen fabric, because the threads are much closer together. Here are some typical mesh counts:

Number	Mesh Count
6xx	74
8xx	86
10xx	109
12xx	125
14xx	139
16xx	157
18xx	166
20xx	173
25xx	200

Numbers 6xx and 8xx are considered *coarse;* 12xx and 14xx are *medium* and should be used for most work. Numbers 18xx and 25xx are *fine* and mesh counts higher than 200 are considered *very fine*. Fabric is now being made with 508 threads per linear inch (200 cm) for extremely detailed images.

Most fabric is available in either *monofilament* or *multifilament*. Monofilament fabric contains one strand of fabric or material in each thread. Multifilament is made from several strands twisted together to form each thread. Monofilament fabric is made only from polyester and stainless steel. Multifilament is used for most screen-printed products. It provides good adhesion and good ink coverage. Polyester fabric is excellent for form-color process printing and textile products.

SQUEEGEE

The squeegee (Fig. 123-3) is used to press the ink across the screen, causing it to go through the openings of the image carrier at the point of contact. This penetration produces the print. Squeegees for hand use are a smooth strip of wood with a hard rubber or synthetic blade fastened to it. The blades are usually 3/16 to 1/2 inch (4.8 to 12.7 mm) thick, and project from the wooden handle 3/4 to 1 3/4 inches (19 to 31.75 mm). The blades must be kept clean and free of nicks. Quality printing on different materials calls for specially shaped blade edges (Fig. 123-4):

A. *Square-edged—for flat objects and all general use.*

Fig. 123-3. A squeegee used for hand screen-printing.

Fig. 123-4. Squeegee blade angles, each designed for a specific purpose.

Fig. 123-5. A fixed-blade film knife.

Fig. 123-6. A swivel-blade film knife.

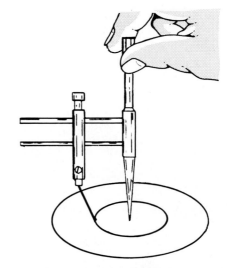

Fig. 123-7. An adjustable circle cutter that can make circle diameters of from $^1/_{16}$ to $3^7/_8$ inches (0.16 to 9.8 cm).

Fig. 123-8. A beam circle cutter to make diameters of from $^7/_8$ to $26^1/_8$ inches (2.2 to 67.3 cm).

Fig. 123-9. A loop-knife film-line cutter.

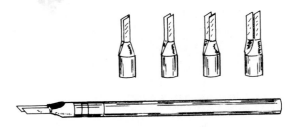

Fig. 123-10. Dual-knife parallel-line cutters.

B. *Square-edged with rounded corners*—for extra-heavy ink deposits, for printing light colors on dark backgrounds, and for printing with fluorescent inks.

C. *Rounded edge*—for textile printing with heavy ink deposits.

D. *Single-sided bevel edge*—for glass and nameplates.

E. *Double-sided bevel edge, flat point*—for ceramic printing.

F. *Double-sided bevel edge*—for direct printing on uneven surfaces such as bottles and containers; also for delicate textile designs.

Besides different blade shapes, squeegees come in different hardness values—hard,

Fig. 123-11. An adjustable dual-knife parallel-line cutter.

medium, or soft. For general printing, use a squeegee with a medium hardness grade and square edges.

FILM-CUTTING TOOLS

A sharp cutting tool is needed to prepare hand-cut lacquer and water-soluble films (Units 127 and 128). A single-edged razor blade will do, but a standard *film knife* (Fig. 123-5) has a fixed blade with an aluminum handle and is ideal. The blade can be replaced when it becomes dull. *Swivel-blade knives* (Fig. 123-6) are used when the illustration has a great many curves or irregular lines. The blade turns freely within the handle to let you cut irregular lines without twisting the handle. Small *circle cutters* (Fig. 123-7) and large *beam cutters* (Fig. 123-8) are available. A drafting *bow compass* can be adapted to cut circles in film by placing a razor-sharp blade in the pencil-lead holder.

There are cutting knives for cutting various widths of lines. A *loop-knife film-line cutter* (Fig. 123-9) has the cutting edge in a circle. When this knife is drawn along the film, it removes a specific width of the lacquer or water-soluble film. It comes in three sizes. *Dual-knife parallel-line cutters* produce several widths of lines. A *fixed-width parallel-line cutter* (Fig. 123-10) contains four cutters. *Adjustable dual-knife parallel-line cutters* (Fig. 123-11) are handy tools, also. The same amount of pressure must be placed on each blade while cutting.

Other high-precision cutting tools are available for quality work. For the professional, complete sets that contain several different cutting tools are available.

DRYING EQUIPMENT

Screen printing must have some kind of drying arrangement because the solvent- and water-based inks do not dry fast enough to allow stacking of the freshly printed sheets. A rack arrangement for flat objects is shown in Figure 123-12. These individual racks can be stacked very easily and let the air circulate freely among the printed sheets. Commercial drying racks that have individual racks hinged to a framework are also available.

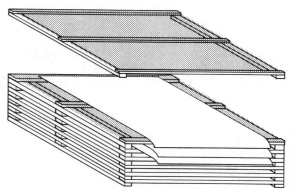

Fig. 123-12. Easy-to-build drying frames.

Fig. 123-13. A hanger-clothesline method of drying garments.

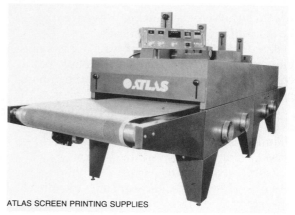

ATLAS SCREEN PRINTING SUPPLIES

Fig. 123-14. A typical small, electric, infrared conveyor dryer that is used to cure plastisol inks printed on textile garments.

Garments such as T-shirts and sweatshirts can be dried after printing by placing them on a clothes hanger and hanging them on a line. (Fig. 123-13.) Heated air or infrared dryers must be used to cure plastisol inks (Fig. 123-14). These types of dryers can also be used to assist in drying solvent- and water-based inks.

UNIT 124 SAFETY WITH SCREEN PRINTING EQUIPMENT AND MATERIALS

Screen printing is a very safe division of graphic arts. You should, however, always be safety conscious when working and experimenting with screen-printing equipment and materials.

Permission. Get permission from someone in charge before beginning work in the screen-printing area.

Clothing and jewelry. Secure loose clothing and remove jewelry before working in the screen-printing area.

Safety guards. Work carefully when building a screen-printing press. Use safety guards as needed.

Air vents. Start exhaust fans before working with chemicals or solvents. If there is no power-exhaust system, open the windows or doors or both.

Electrical connections. Be sure that all electrical connections on power equipment used for the screen-printing press are in good repair and are properly grounded.

Eye and face protection. Wear safety glasses and face shields when using power equipment and when mixing the photographic chemicals.

Floor drains. There should be floor drains near sinks and tanks where photographic chemical solutions are used. There should be a safety shower with a drain nearby.

Body protection. Wear a rubber apron when working with photographic chemicals, adherents, and ink solvents.

Good housekeeping. Never let waste materials collect on the floor or shelves.

Materials storage. Store containers of photographic chemical solutions, lacquer thinner, and ink solvents near the floor. Place boxes, tools, and other items carefully on storage shelves.

Illumination. Have good lighting. Being able to see well can let you avoid dangerous situations.

Fire. Fire extinguishers must always be kept charged and handy nearby. Be extremely careful when handling flammable materials such as lacquer, adhering liquid, lacquer thinner, and ink solvents.

Sharp objects. Handle and use sharp objects carefully. Knives used to prepare hand-cut films are very sharp.

Hand-skin protection. Lacquer-adhering liquid and lacquer thinner may irritate your skin. Wear protective gloves and aprons as needed.

Hot water. Do not irritate your skin with the hot water used to remove photographic film from the screen fabric.

Ink and solvent-soaked rags. Put all rags containing ink or solvents in a metal safety can with a tight metal lid.

Solvents. Do not pour screen-printing solvents down the sanitary drain. Place them in a special noncorrosive container for later disposal according to the safety guidelines established by federal, state, and local authorities. The screen-printing method of graphic reproduction is very versatile (Unit 121). The design and layout artist has a great deal of freedom in preparing the artwork. The type of artwork depends much on the method used to prepare the screen image carrier or the printing stencil.

UNIT 125 BUILDING A SCREEN PRINTING PRESS

Building screen printing press units is not hard. With some basic woodworking skills and power equipment, building the units takes only a short time. Wood for the frame is usually white pine or poplar. White pine, fir plywood, or masonite can be used for the base.

FRAME CONSTRUCTION

The frames can be any size, but the screen usually has a two-by-three proportion. The inside dimensions of the frame should be at least 5 inches (12.7 cm) longer and wider than the material to be printed. To keep the edges of the squeegee from distorting the printed image, the total fabric area should at least be double the image area.

The dimensions (width and thickness) of the wood for the frame must be larger as the overall frame size increases, because strength is important. If the frame is weak or poorly built, the printing results will be poor. Take the following steps in building the press units.

1. Select the screen size from the table. It gives the inside frame dimensions according to the largest image area to be printed.

SCREEN AND IMAGE SIZE RATIO
(inches)

Suggested Largest Image Size	Inside Screen Dimensions	Frame Wood Dimensions
3 by 6	9 by 12	1 by 1½
6 by 9	12 by 18	1¼ by 1½
9 by 15	15 by 23	1¼ by 1¾
12 by 20	18 by 27	1¼ by 2
15 by 24	22 by 30	1¼ by 2¼

2. Select and cut the framing stock to the right length. Use one of three corner joints: miter, end-lap, or miter-spline as shown in Figure 125-1.
3. Cut the groove for the cord in the bottom side of the framing stock (Fig. 125-2). The cord tightens and holds the screen fabric over the frame.
4. Assemble the frame, using glue, nails, or corrugated fasteners. The frame must be very firm.

BASE CONSTRUCTION

The screen base is a hinging support for the frame. Plywood or masonite ¼ to ¾-inch (6.35

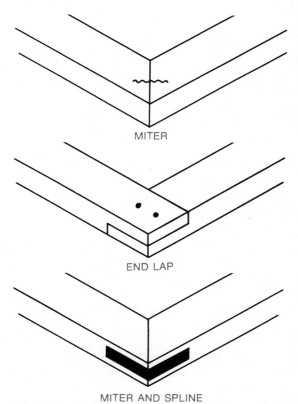

MITER

END LAP

MITER AND SPLINE

Fig. 125-1. The three common screen-frame corner joints.

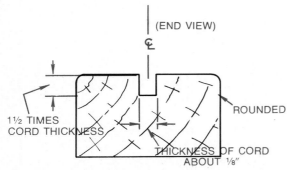

(END VIEW)

1½ TIMES
CORD THICKNESS

ROUNDED

THICKNESS OF CORD
ABOUT ⅛"

Fig. 125-2. The size, depth, and position of the groove for the cord in the framing stock. Note the rounded edges on the groove side of the stock.

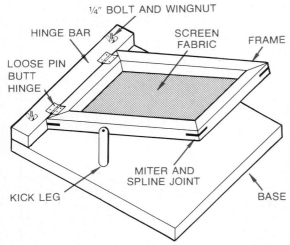

¼" BOLT AND WINGNUT

HINGE BAR

SCREEN
FABRIC

FRAME

LOOSE PIN
BUTT
HINGE

MITER AND
SPLINE JOINT

KICK LEG

BASE

Fig. 125-3. A typical home/school screen-printing unit.

to 19 mm) thick works well. The larger the screen frame, the thicker the plywood or masonite should be. The base is also used as a surface to locate and hold the paper or other material to be printed.

5. Cut the base. It should be about 2 inches (5.08 cm) larger on each side than the outside dimensions of the frame.
6. Cut a piece of stock the same as that used for the frame (Fig. 125-3). This will be the hinge bar.
7. Fasten the hinge bar flush, or even, with the end of the base board (Fig. 125-3). Use ¼-inch (6.35 mm) carriage bolts and wing nuts.
8. Center the screen frame from side-to-side on the base board and place it in contact with the hinge bar.

9. Fasten the frame to the hinge bar with loose pin-butt hinges (Fig. 125-3).
10. Fasten a kick-leg to the side of the frame. This keeps the screen up while a printed sheet is being removed and a new one inserted.
11. Apply two coats of sealer to the frame and base. The sealer makes it easier to remove the ink from the frame and base after completing the printing operation.

Commercial hinges can be used instead of a hinge bar (Fig. 125-4). Commercial hinges are used when several screen changes are needed throughout a work period. The hinges attach directly to the base, and the screen frame is held in place by turning down the clamp bolt or wing nut.

ATTACHING THE SCREEN FABRIC

12. Cut a piece of screen fabric (either organdy, silk, nylon, or polyester) 2 inches (5.08 cm) larger on each side than the groove in the frame.
13. Cut 4 pieces of cord to fit the grooves in the frame. They should be slightly shorter than the actual groove lengths to eliminate overlap at the corners when the screen is attached.
14. Lay the frame, groove side up, on a table or workbench and center the screen fabric over the frame.

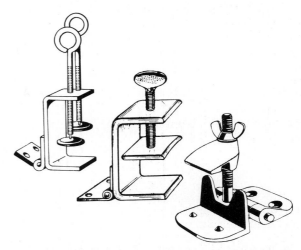

Fig. 125-4. Three types of commercial hinges to hinge the screen frame to the base.

15. Fasten the fabric by pressing the cord and fabric into the grooves (Fig. 125-5). Use a bookbinder's folding bone or some other narrow, rounded object, or a specially designed commercial tool. Stretch the screen fabric so that it is tight and even. A good method is to start by fastening the center of each of the four sides. Then work to the corners in an equal manner. A loose screen will give poor reproduction. Commercial screen stretching units help to get an evenly stretched screen (Fig. 125-6). For quality printing and high production, a commercial fabric stretching unit is essential.

16. Using a sharp art knife, cut and remove excess fabric from beyond the grooves. Leave about a $\frac{1}{4}$ inch (6.35 mm) of the fabric extending beyond the grooves.

17. Apply a coat of finish sealer around the groove side of the frame and let it dry thoroughly. This sticks the fabric to the frame and helps to hold the screen taut.

TAPING THE FRAME

18. Apply masking tape to the bottom grooved side of the frame. The tape should cover the entire bottom and extend onto the screen approximately $\frac{1}{2}$ inch (12.7 mm).

19. Apply masking tape to the top side of the frame. Position it even with the bottom tape on the screen and extend it up the inside walls of the frame. This keeps the ink

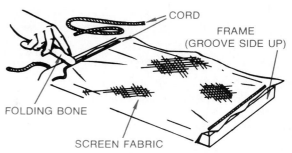

Fig. 125-5. Attaching the screen fabric to the screen frame by the cord and groove method.

THE ADVANCE GROUP

Fig. 125-6. An air-bar fabric-stretching system stretches fabric uniformly over a wooden or metal frame. A special liquid adhesive is then used to bond the fabric to the frame.

from the corners and grooves and helps in cleanup.

20. Apply a coat of sealer to the tape to make cleanup easier. The screen printing unit is now ready for use.

UNIT 126 ARTWORK FOR SCREEN PRINTING

The screen printing method of graphic reproduction is very versatile (Unit 121). The design and layout artist has a great deal of freedom in preparing the artwork. The type of artwork depends much on the method used to prepare the screen image carrier or the printing stencil.

ARTWORK FOR HAND-CUT FILMS

Hand-cut films are used to produce large lettering for posters and basic illustrations that do not have a great amount of detail. Finished art-work will help the person cutting the screen-printing film to produce quality work. It is hard, for example, to cut perfect letters from sketchy artwork.

ARTWORK FOR DIRECT PHOTOSENSITIVE SCREENS

Artwork for direct *photosensitive screens* can be prepared by several methods (Unit 129). A common method is to prepare a film positive either by the orthochromatic film method (Unit 58) or the diffusion transfer method (Unit 59).

If *type* is to be used, several compositon methods can be used: (1) dry transfer, Unit 31; and (2) hand mechanical, Unit 31; (3) photographic, Unit 32; (4) electronic, Unit 33; and (5) desktop, Units 182, 183, 184, and 185.

The *silhouette method* is another way to prepare artwork for direct photosensitive screens (Fig. 126-1). The image, an actual object or one cut from black paper or red stripping film, is laid on the photosensitive screen and the light exposure is made. The image must be very dense. Light must not pass through the image while the photographic exposure is being made.

ARTWORK FOR INDIRECT PHOTOGRAPHIC SCREEN FILM

Whether hand-drawn illustrations or mechanically composed type, artwork for the *indirect photographic screen film* should be prepared carefully (Unit 130). Because this type of reproduction can give high-quality results, the artwork should be very well done.

All methods of type composition can be used.

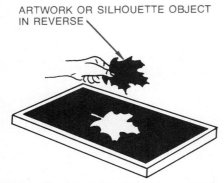

ARTWORK OR SILHOUETTE OBJECT IN REVERSE

Fig. 126-1. Silhouette artwork can be used to prepare direct photosensitive screens.

After the type and illustrations are prepared by an artist, a paste-up is made and a film positive is made. The film positive is used to expose the photographic screen film.

Five different kinds of positives can be used to expose light-sensitive indirect film or direct photosensitive screens. Each of these should be as high in quality as possible. They are:

1. A right-reading photographic film positive. This is one with the film emulsion up when the image is right-reading. When making a film positive from a negative for screen printing, be sure to expose the negative to the positive film, emulsion-to-emulsion.
2. Diffusion transfer film positives. See Unit 59.
3. Dry transfer lettering and images attached to a transparent piece of acetate. See Unit 31.
4. Black ink drawings on transparent acetate. Be sure to use special ink made for acetate so that the image areas will be dense. See Unit 31.
5. Stripping film, sometimes called masking film, in either deep red or orange. Positives are cut directly from this film and can be used many times to expose indirect photo-screen film. See Unit 42.

NOTE: A process camera is needed with the photographic film positive and the diffusion transfer positive. The three kinds of positives made without a process camera are very effective and are used throughout the screen printing industry.

ARTWORK FOR PAPER STENCIL AND WASHOUT SCREENS

These two screen-preparation methods do not require highly finished artwork (Unit 134). Rough sketches are good enough because much of the lettering and illustrations can be done during the screen image-carrier preparation.

DIVIDING FOR COLOR

With all graphic reproduction methods, you must do a separate piece of artwork for each area of the illustration or full page that is to be reproduced in a different color. Three methods can be used for the screen-process reproduction method.

Artwork with an overlay sheet. This method is the simplest and can be used with hand-cut films, paper stencil, and washout screens. The artwork is prepared either by hand or mechanical means on one sheet, in black and white.

A tissue overlay sheet similar to a comprehensive overlay sheet is placed over the artwork (Unit 24). The colors and other information are marked on this sheet. During the preparation of the image carriers, careful attention must be given to the sheet for proper preparation of an image carrier for *each* color.

Artwork with full color. When two or more colors are to be used on a screen printing reproduction, it is often a good idea to prepare the artwork in full color, just as it will appear when finished. This way, you do not have to guess what the result will look like. It also gives practice in selecting and handling several colors on one reproduction.

A set of colored pencils or felt-tip markers can provide the necessary colors, although these colors do not really match screen printing ink colors. Artwork with full color can be used for hand-cut films, paper stencil, and washout screens.

Artwork with overlays. This method is the most exacting and time consuming. The basic color or key area of the copy is prepared on a base paper or plastic sheet. The other colors are each placed on separate overlay sheets (Fig. 126-2) of translucent paper, plastic or transparent plastic. The content for each color is also placed on the overlay sheet. The overlay sheets are securely fastened together. Note the register marks (Fig. 126-2). These must be included on each overlay, including the base sheet. Also, mark each overlay with the proper color. This artwork method is used when preparing multiple-color work for direct photosensitive screens and indirect photographic screen film. Commercial stripping film can be used in preparing each overlay.

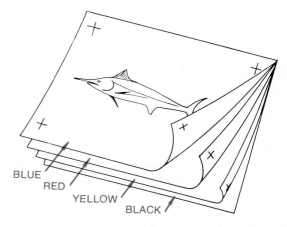

Fig. 126-2. The overlay method used for color division.

UNIT 127 LACQUER-SOLUBLE HAND-PREPARED FILM

UNIT 127 LACQUER-SOLUBLE HAND-PREPARED FILM

Hand-cut films with a lacquer base revolutionized the screen printing industry around 1930. Until that time, crude methods of preparing the screen stencil or printing screen were used. The film made possible more detailed and higher-quality screen reproduction.

Lacquer film has three layers (Fig. 127-1). The *film* and the *backing* are held together with a special *cement* that releases when the backing

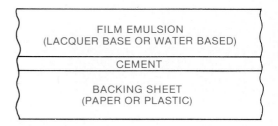

Fig. 127-1. The three layers of hand-cut film.

must be removed before printing. The backing sheet makes the film stable and holds film elements in place until it is attached to the screen.

CUTTING THE FILM

1. Prepare the artwork, including illustrations and words.
2. Fasten the artwork securely to a hard, flat surface by using small pieces of masking tape. Use a drawing board, table top, or piece of glass.
3. Get a piece of lacquer film; fasten it down over the artwork. The film should be at least one inch (2.54 cm) larger on each side than the image area of the artwork.
4. Begin cutting the film (Fig. 127-2). Cut the curved areas freehand or use the necessary special tools. Be sure to use a sharp knife and cut *only* the lacquer film. For best results, keep the knife blade perpendicular (vertical) to the film during cutting. Use a metal T-square and triangle to help guide the knife on straight cuts. NOTE: The backing sheet should not be cut.
5. Lift the lacquer film from the image areas by using a special stripping blade and a finger, as shown in Figure 127-3. A stripping blade is stronger than a knife blade and lifts the film more easily because it does not tend to cut it.
6. Remove all loose pieces of film from the lacquer film image carrier. A piece of masking tape wrapped around a finger, adhesive side out, will help you pick up small pieces.

Fig. 127-2. When hand cutting lacquer film, cut the film layer and not the backing sheet.

NOTE: If pieces of film from the non-image areas are accidentally removed during cutting, they can be reattached to the backing sheet with thinned rubber cement. With polyester-backed films, the film emulsion can be re-attached without using thinned rubber cement.

7. Carefully remove the film (now an image carrier) and illustration from the board or glass after cutting. Preserve the cut film until it is to be attached to the screen.

FABRIC PREPARATION

All screen fabric, new or used, must be properly prepared so the film stencil (image carrier) will stick tightly. Fabric preparation includes a *mechanical treatment* for synthetic material and a *degreasing* for all fabric. Silk does not need the mechanical treatment because the threads are naturally rough and have enough surface area for films to adhere to.

MECHANICAL TREATMENT

1. Get some powdered cleanser specially prepared for use on screen fabric. This must be a very fine grit powder so it does not clog the screen fabric. *Do not* use household scouring powders. They may damage the fabric. They also have particles that will clog the fabric and will not wash out.
2. Put the stretched frame in the sink and dampen the fabric with a warm water spray.
3. Sprinkle the fine-powdered cleanser on the printing side (bottom) of the screen fabric (Fig. 127-4). Apply a liberal amount of the cleanser.

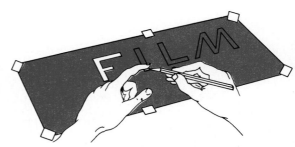

Fig. 127-3. Removing the lacquer film from the image areas after it has been cut.

Fig. 127-4. Sprinkling a fine-powdered cleanser on the printing side of the screen fabric.

4. Scrub the fabric, using a cotton cloth. Continue scrubbing until the cotton cloth fibers begin to fray. Be careful to not push on the stretched fabric hard enough to damage the fabric mesh.
5. Rinse the fabric from both sides with a soft warm water spray. Be sure to remove cleanser from the frame and all corner areas where the fabric and frame join.

DEGREASING

6. With the screen fabric still wet, apply the commercially prepared degreasing liquid to both sides of the fabric. Be sure to do this in a sink.

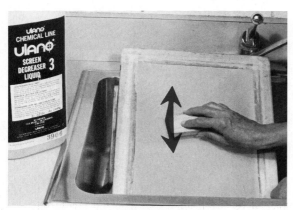

Fig. 127-5. Degreasing the screen fabric by scrubbing it with a medium-stiff hand brush and liquid degreasing solution.

7. Scrub both sides of the screen with a medium-stiff brush (Fig. 127-5). A good-quality hand-scrub brush will work. Continue to scrub until a foam develops on both sides of the screen.
8. Stop scrubbing and let the screen stand until the degreasing liquid quits foaming. While there is foam, the degreasing liquid is actively dissolving any oily substance on the screen fabric.
9. Rinse the screen thoroughly with a soft warm water spray. Spray both sides of the fabric, as well as the frame and all corner areas. All degreasing solution must be removed from the fabric so the film image carrier will adhere properly.
10. The screen fabric is now ready to receive the screen printing image carrier.

ADHERING THE FILM

1. Check the screen. Be sure the screen material is perfectly clean and dry. Also be sure the screen is stretched tightly over the frame.
2. Lay the cut film (emulsion side up) on a *build-up*. A good build-up is a piece of thick—¼-inch (6.35 mm) or more—frosted glass that is slightly smaller than the inside dimensions of the frame.
3. Place the clean screen (fabric side down) over the film. Position the screen and film so that the material to be printed can fit under the frame without touching the hinges.
4. Get a 4- to 5-inch (10.16 to 12.7 cm) square piece of cotton cloth and fold it into a pad about 2 inches (5.08 cm) square. It will be used to apply the film-adhering liquid.
5. Fold a cotton cloth about 12 to 16 inches (30.5 to 40.6 cm) square into a loose pad to fit the hand.
6. Saturate the small, neatly folded pad with the proper adhering liquid for the film being used. Wipe over a small 4 to 6 inch (10.16 to 15.2 cm) square area of the film.
7. Wipe this area immediately, using the larger dry cloth. Continue this action until the entire cut film is adhered (Fig. 127-6). The adhering liquid softens or dissolves the film slightly to stick it to the screen. If the

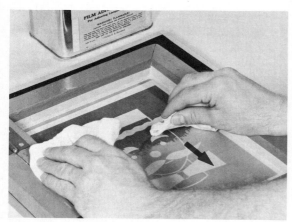

Fig. 127-6. Adhering the cut lacquer-based film to the screen.

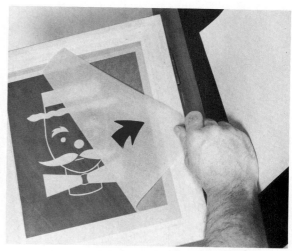

Fig. 127-7. Removing the backing sheet from the cut film.

adhering liquid is allowed to stand on the film it will dissolve it too much and make ragged edges along the image. CAUTION: Begin adhering *one* side of the film and continue across until all is adhered. This will help avoid most wrinkles and air bubbles.

8. Revolve the drying cloth constantly so that the film is always wiped with a dry surface. Keep the adhering pad well saturated with adhering liquid.

9. Look over the entire surface of the cut film. Properly adhered areas will turn darker when the adhering liquid is applied. If light spots remain, touch them up carefully by wiping with the adhering pad; then wipe immediately with the drying cloth.

10. Let the adhered film dry for about 5 to 10 minutes. Stand the frame up so that air can reach both sides.

11. Remove the backing sheet (Fig. 127-7). Grasp a corner and pull as parallel as possible to the screen. Be careful to avoid excessive stretching of the screen.

12. If an area of the film pulls away from the screen, *stop.* Let the backing sheet go back to its original position, and lay the frame

back down on the build-up. Adhere the area again, allow it to dry, then continue removing the backing sheet.

13. The film is now properly adhered. Continue the screen printing procedure given in Unit 131.

REMOVING FILM FROM THE SCREEN

1. Remove all ink with the proper solvent, as outlined in Unit 133.

2. Place several newspapers under the screen and pour lacquer thinner over the lacquer film. Thoroughly saturate it and allow it to soak for 2 or 3 minutes.

3. Lift the screen, leaving the dissolved lacquer film on the newsprint.

4. If any lacquer film remains in the screen, repeat steps 2 and 3.

5. To remove remaining small areas of the lacquer-based film, put solvent on 2 clean wiping cloths. Wipe both sides of the fabric at the same time. (See Fig. 133-2). The screen fabric should be left perfectly free of the lacquer-based film.

128 WATER-SOLUBLE HAND-PREPARED FILM

UNIT

The two main classes of knife-cut stencil-forming materials are (1) a thin film of *lacquer-type material* supported by a plastic or paper backing sheet, and (2) a *water-type film* material supported by translucent plastic. Both are prepared in the same way—the material to print is removed from the film. When cut, they are adhered to the stretched fabric to form the printing screen.

Flammable adhering liquid is not needed with water-soluble, hand-cut films. Water is far less expensive than the adherents and thinners used for adhering and cleaning, and the final printing quality of water-soluble film compares favorably with that of lacquer-type film. Also, water soluble film is compatible with nearly all inks except, of course, those with a water base.

CUTTING THE FILM

Water-soluble film is cut the same way as lacquer-soluble film. Use a sharp knife for the best results. During the cutting, if the film is accidentally lifted off in a non-image area, it can be re-adhered without special adhesives.

This type of film picks up moisture and gets softer when the humidity is high. Keep the film in the original container in an air-conditioned room. While you cut, put a piece of sheet plastic under your hands. This helps keep perspiration and skin oils off the film.

FABRIC PREPARATION

The importance of preparing the fabric before adhering the film cannot be over-emphasized. A water-based film will not adhere as tightly as it should to a poorly prepared fabric. Care taken at this important stage will save time and trouble later on.

See the fabric preparation guide in Unit 127. The technique and the materials listed there are the same for all stencil preparation methods.

ADHERING THE FILM

1. Check the fabric to be sure it is clean and ready to accept the water-based film.
2. Wet the stretched screen material thoroughly with a soft water spray. Wipe the excess water from the frame but leave the screen fabric damp.
3. Put the cut film on a hard-surfaced build-up, with the film side up (right reading) as shown in Figure 128-1. A surface of frosted glass slightly smaller than the inside of the screen frame makes a good build up.
4. Place the stretched screen over the cut film.
5. Position the frame, making sure there is perfect contact between the screen and film (Fig. 128-2).
6. Place 2 or 3 layers (sheets) of newsprint (unprinted newspaper stock) on top (squeegee side) of the fabric. Pre-cut the newsprint so that the sheets will fit inside the frame.
7. Gently wipe over the newsprint with a soft, clean cloth. Not much pressure is needed to blot and absorb the excess moisture.

Fig. 128-1. The hand-cut water-soluble film is properly positioned on the glass build-up.

Fig. 128-2. The screen positioned over the film.

8. Change the newsprint several times and repeat wiping over the screen area with the cloth. Some small amount of film emulsion may transfer to the newsprint during the blotting. This shows that the film emulsion is being drawn up into the screen mesh.

9. Leave the screen on the build-up for 4 to 6 minutes. After this period of time, the screen can be carefully lifted.

10. Gently wipe the excess moisture from the bottom (printing) side of the screen and film.

11. Stand the screen in a safe place, where it will not be damaged. Let it dry for at least

one hour. A longer drying time is better. The drying process can be speeded by a small fan blowing cool air over the screen.

12. If liquid masking blockout is to be used, apply it now. See Unit 131 for details. For paper blockout, proceed to the next step.

13. Peel the backing from the film. Carefully lift one corner and pull as parallel to the screen as possible (see Fig. 127-7).

14. Check the film for tears and pin holes. If necessary, apply a screen filler with a small artist brush.

15. The stencil is now ready for printing. If the non-printing areas have not been masked, proceed to Unit 131 for details.

REMOVING FILM FROM THE SCREEN

1. Remove all ink with the proper solvent, as outlined in Unit 133.

2. Spray both sides of the screen with cold water. Use a stiff-bristled brush to be sure the film is thoroughly wetted.

3. Let the wet screen film soak for 4 to 10 minutes.

4. Put the screen in a sink and flush away the film with hot water (See Fig. 130-4).

UNIT 129 DIRECT PHOTOGRAPHIC SCREENS

Photographic screens are prepared by (1) the direct photosensitive screen method, as explained in this unit, (2) the indirect, photographic screen method (see Unit 130) and (3) the direct/indirect photographic method (see Unit 130). To use these methods, you must know basic photographic principles and have a few pieces of special equipment. More detail in the copy is possible with photographic screen methods than with hand-prepared ones. Photographic-prepared screens, therefore, can be used for a wider variety of projects.

Direct photographic screens have a light-sensitive liquid emulsion coated directly into the screen fabric. After the emulsion is exposed to light through some specially prepared artwork and developed with water, the screen becomes the screen printing image carrier. This durable printing screen produces thousands of impressions without wearing out.

The *direct method* of making printing screens is widely used in textile, electronic, ceramic, and chemical industries. It is also popular for making point-of-purchase displays, decals, and pressure-sensitive labels. One screen can easily stand up to printing runs of over 100,000 impressions.

SENSITIZING THE SCREEN

When sensitizing the screen, you do not need to work in total darkness, but too much light will ruin the screen. Use just enough *indirect* light to see and work comfortably. Yellow fluorescent tubes or yellow bug lights give good light for seeing and are *safe* for the light sensitive liquid emulsion. Yellow light will not expose the material because photostencil materials are sensitive in the upper ultraviolet and visible blue part of the spectrum.

It is also important to work in a dust free location. For best results, use a room or area where the environment can be completely controlled—lighting, temperature, and cleanliness.

MATERIALS NEEDED

To print with a direct photographic screen, you will need the following things:

1. A screen printing frame stretched with fabric of good quality and average mesh.
2. An emulsion coating blade made of non-oxidizing metal with rounded edges. It should be slightly shorter than the inside narrow dimension of the frame.
3. Two small electric fans or a controlled heat drying cabinet.
4. Light-sensitive, diazo-based screen emulsion material.

PREPARING THE LIGHT-SENSITIVE EMULSION

Two basic parts make up the light-sensitive emulsion material—the sensitizer and the emulsion. When bought, they are packaged separately and the user must mix them together properly. Once mixed, the emulsion is light and temperature sensitive.

Mix the light sensitive emulsion, following the directions supplied by the manufacturer. Basically, the sensitizer is poured into the emulsion and mixed thoroughly. If the sensitizer comes as a liquid, it can be poured directly into the emulsion. If the sensitizer is in crystal form, water must be mixed with the crystals to form the liquid sensitizer. After mixing, allow the light-sensitive emulsion to stand in a closed container for one to two hours until all air bubbles have disappeared.

Any emulsion not used immediately should be stored carefully. Unsensitized emulsion should be kept at 50 to 68° F (10 to 20° C). The emulsion can be frozen during storage but for use it should be thawed slowly at room temperature. Do not store unsensitized emulsion for more than nine months.

Sensitized emulsion should be stored in a cool dark location, but the storage time is limited. At room temperature of 73° F (23° C) it will keep as long as six weeks, but stored in the refrigerator, it may keep for four months.

COATING THE SCREEN

1. Clean and thoroughly prepare the screen. See Unit 127 and follow the directions for Fabric Preparation closely. Let the screen fabric dry completely.
2. Work on a counter that has a convenient height. Cover the counter with newspapers for easy clean-up after the coating is done.
3. Set up a subdued work light or yellow safelight.
4. Hold the screen at a nearly vertical position. Somewhere between 60 and 90 degrees is best.
5. Pour some liquid light-sensitive emulsion into the metal scoop of the coating blade.
6. Coat and dry the screen. Select and use one of the following three methods.

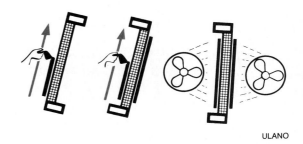

ULANO

Fig. 129-1 The basic method of coating a direct photosensitive screen.

The basic method (Fig.129-1).

   a. Apply a coat to the printing side. Begin at the bottom, put medium pressure on the screen with the coating blade. Tilt the blade up so the liquid solution runs against the screen. Pull the blade up and across the fabric in one smooth movement. It is important always to hold the screen frame at the same angle, to use the same pressure of the coating blade against the screen fabric, and to pull the coating blade across the screen fabric at the same speed.

   b. Turn the screen 180°.

   c. Apply a coat of emulsion to the squeegee side.

   d. Dry the screen at room temperature in a horizontal position with the printing side down. Keep this area as dust free as possible. Put a fan about 4 feet (1.2 m) away to blow on the screen.

   e. Once dry, the light-sensitive screen can be stored for future use or be immediately exposed through a film positive.

An improved method (Fig. 129-2). Read and follow all suggestions presented in "The basic method."

   a. Apply a coat to the printing side.

   b. Turn the screen 180°.

   c. While the first coat is still wet apply a second coat to the printing side.

   d. Turn the screen 180°.

   e. Apply from 2 to 5 coats to the squeegee side. This is done wet-on-wet. Remember to turn the screen 180° after each coating.

   f. Dry the coated screen in a horizontal position with the printing side down.

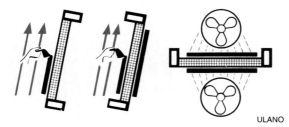

Fig. 129-2. An improved method of coating a direct photosensitive screen means placing two coats of emulsion on each side.

Use circulating air at 86° to 104° F (30° to 40° C). The screen should not be dried in a vertical position.

   g. Expose or store the light-sensitive screen.

The industrial method for high quality (Fig. 129-3). Read and follow all suggestions presented in "The basic method."

   a. Apply a coat to the printing side.

   b. Turn the screen 180°.

   c. While the first coat is still wet, apply a second coat to the printing side.

   d. Turn the screen 180°.

   e. Apply from 2 to 5 coats to the squeegee side. This is done wet-on-wet. Remember to turn the screen 180° after each coating.

   f. Dry the coated screen in a horizontal position with the printing side down. Use circulating air at 86° to 104° F (30° to 40° C). The screen can also be dried in a vertical position if necessary.

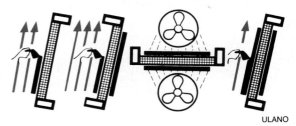

Fig. 129-3. The industrial method of coating a direct photosensitive screen.

   g. Apply one more coat to the printing side.

   h. Dry the screen as in step *f*.

   i. Repeat steps *g* and *h* if you need a thicker emulsion.

   j. Expose or store the light sensitive screen.

STORING SENSITIZED DRY SCREENS

Sensitized screens usually should be exposed within twenty-four hours of being coated. However, sensitized screens can be stored for several days or even up to two weeks, depending upon the recommendation of the manufacturer. Thus several screens may be sensitized at the same time, stored, and used as needed. But the storage place must be completely light-safe. Screens can be stored in an envelope or a cabinet.

ing direct photo-sensitive screens. These units have an exposure vacuum frame with clear glass on one side and a flexible rubber blanket on the other (Fig. 129-4). With the frame closed and

AMERICAN EQUIPMENT/DIVISION OF ADVANCED PROCESS SUPPLY

Fig. 129-4. A vacuum frame for direct photosensitive screens. It can expose several screens at once.

the vacuum on, the rubber blanket fits tightly to the screen and frame, holding the positive in close contact with the emulsion-coated screen. Use a separate light source to make the best exposures. Light sources include carbon arc, metal halogen lamps, mercury vapour, quartz iodide, and pulsed xenon.

A convenient exposure unit is shown in Figure 129-5. It can be used to expose thin photographic materials, such as lithographic plates and indirect screen photo-sensitive film, in the standard vacuum frame. The deep-well vacuum frame has the flexible rubber blanket for the direct photo-sensitive screen. The light source and all controls are located in this unit.

Materials needed

A basic method of making exposures calls for the following materials:

1. A light exposure source such as a number 2 photo-flood or a 200-watt frosted light bulb with a reflector.
2. One piece of clean window glass as large as the screen or the positive copy.

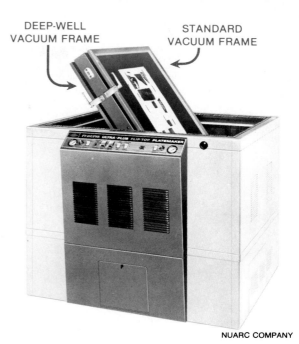

DEEP-WELL VACUUM FRAME   STANDARD VACUUM FRAME

NUARC COMPANY

Fig. 129-5. A self-contained exposure unit.

3. The positive copy. (See Unit 126 for a description of the five common kinds of positives that can be used to expose photographic screens.)
4. A wood block, or thick book covered with black felt, about the same size as the screen but thicker than the screen frame.
5. The coated screen.

Exposing the coated screen

1. Place the felt-covered block or book directly under the light source. The light should be 24 to 36 inches (60 to 91 cm) away from the screen. Be sure the light rays flood the entire exposure area (screen frame) evenly.
2. Put the screen, printing side up, in position over the block or book. The block or book must be thicker than the frame to put the needed pressure on the screen.
3. Place the prepared positive transparency (copy) over the screen. The right-reading side must be in contact with the printing side of the coated screen.
4. Put the piece of clear glass over the positive transparency, pressing it into perfect contact with the sensitive screen. Bar-shaped

weights can be added to the ends of the glass to help hold the positive and screen in perfect contact. This arrangement of materials are now ready for exposure (Fig. 129-6).

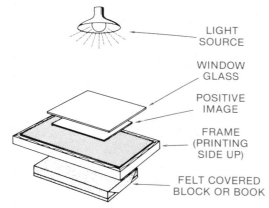

Fig. 129-6. The correct arrangement before making the exposure on a direct photosensitive screen.

5. Expose the sensitive screen to light. The exposure time depends on the light source, distance of the light from the screen, and the size of the screen. It also depends on the coating technique used and the color of the screen fabric. Make a series of trial exposures to find the correct time of each exposure for each condition. This is called a *step-wedge* or *test strip* and the procedure is described in Unit 142. An exposure of 5 minutes is a good one to start with. If the positive transparency (copy) has been prepared properly, there is less chance that you will overexpose it. Underexposure causes poor adhesion of the emulsion, tacky emulsion, and ragged image edges. The light-sensitive emulsion is hardened when struck by light. That is why you need positive copy on a transparent or translucent sheet.

6. After the exposure, remove all materials from the screen. Keep the exposed screen in a safelight area until after the image area is washed out. The image area is still sensitive to light because it was protected by the positive transparency during the exposure.

Washing out the image

To wash out the screen areas where the image will be, you will need the following materials:

1. A deep sink with a temperature-controlled water spray unit.
2. A device to hold the screen at an angle of about 60° against the inside of the sink.
3. Several sheets of unprinted newsprint as large as the screen frame.
4. An electric fan or drying cabinet.

To proceed with the washout, follow the instructions below:

1. Put the exposed screen, squeegee side out, in the sink at about a 60° angle. Be sure the sink is in a safe light area.

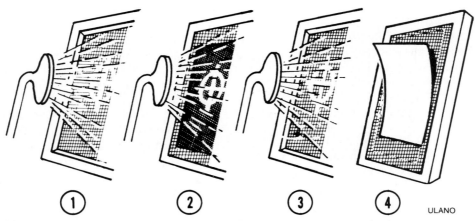

Fig. 129-7. Washing out and blotting the stencil on a direct phootsensitive screen: 1. Gentle spray from the squeegee side; 2. Intense spray from the printing side; 3. Gentle rinse spray from the squeegee side; and 4. Blotting the stencil from the printing side.

2. Wet both sides of the screen with water whose temperature is between 59° and 104° F (15° and 40° C).

3. Using a gentle spray, wash the squeegee side until the image opens up (Fig. 129-7). Do this as quickly as possible.

4. Turn the screen around and use an intensive spray against the printing side. Hold the spray about 12 inches (30.5 cm) away from the screen. Move the spray around the entire image area until all visible image area has been removed.

5. Turn the screen back around and rinse the photo stencil from the squeegee side with a gentle spray. NOTE: At this point the regular room lights may be turned on. If you find that some non-image area of the light-sensitive emulsion has washed away, make another screen, increasing the exposure time.

6. Take the screen out of the sink. Let the excess water run off the screen.

7. Lay the screen on a counter or table, printing side up, and blot the screen and stencil with unprinted newsprint. Do not push too hard on the unsupported screen fabric.

8. Dry the stencil and the entire screen with an electric fan or place it in a drying cabinet. It is best to use room-temperature air for drying. Heated air can shrink the image, causing register problems, especially in multi-color work.

ULANO

Fig. 129-8. Applying degreasing solution to the screen. Apply solution liberally to both sides and scrub with a medium stiff brush until a foam develops.

9. Check the screen carefully for pinholes in the emulsion. Hold it up to a light or place it over a light table to see if there are any pinholes.

10. Use some liquid screen filler, thinned with water, and put it on the pinholes with an artist brush. For best printing results, put the touch-up filler on the printing side of the stencil. Be very careful to not add thickness to the emulsion, because an uneven surface will cause printing problems.

11. After the screen filler is dry, you can start the printing procedure, as outlined in Units 131, 132, and 133.

RECLAIMING THE SCREEN

When you have finished printing, you should clean the screen for further use. You will need the following materials:

1. Photodirect stencil remover, liquid or paste.
2. Degreasing solution.
3. A round, medium-stiff, nylon bristle brush.
4. A deep sink with intense water spray unit.

Follow the steps given below to complete the screen cleaning.

1. Put the screen in the sink.
2. Be sure all ink is removed from the screen and frame, as shown in Unit 133. Remove ink residue with the proper solvent.
3. Thoroughly wet the screen and stencil from both sides with water.
4. Apply a degreasing solution liberally to both sides of the screen. Use a medium-stiff brush and scrub the screen-stencil until a foam develops (Fig. 129-8).
5. Let the screen stand until the foam is almost gone.
6. Rinse the screen and frame with a high-pressure water (hot or cold) spray.
7. Apply stencil remover (liquid or paste) to the wet screen. Brush quite a lot of remover on the screen from both sides. Let the screen stand 5 minutes to let the stencil remover soften the stencil emulsion.
8. Spray the screen with a strong-pressure water spray from one side and then from the other.
9. Repeat Steps 7 and 8 if there is still some emulsion in the screen fabric.
10. Let the screen dry. It can now be used for another screen printing stencil.

UNIT 130 INDIRECT AND DIRECT/INDIRECT PHOTOGRAPHIC SCREENS

Photography plays an important role in screen printing. In fact, most stencils have been made photographically since the mid-1950s. The image detail and overall quality possible with photographic screen stencils have made screen printing very competitive with other printing methods.

There are three methods of preparing photographic screens (stencils): *direct emulsion,* presented in Unit 129, in which light-sensitive emulsion is placed directly in the screen; *indirect film,* in which special light-sensitive film is prepared separately and attached to the screen fabric; and *direct film,* which is presensitized sheet film that is attached to the screen fabric and then exposed in the usual manner with a film positive.

PREPARING THE COPY

The *copy,* a positive transparency, can be prepared either by hand or by photographic methods outlined in Unit 126. Review the following mechanical-photographic methods in order to prepare high-quality photographic film transparencies.

1. Complete the design and layout work and compose the type by one of the several methods presented in Section 4.
2. Get or make the illustrations and photographs, and prepare the paste-up (see Unit 46; also review Section 6).
3. Make a film positive, using thin-base film (Unit 58). Use a right-reading positive when exposing indirect photographic screen film.

HANDLING AND STORAGE OF INDIRECT FILM

Indirect films do not need a darkroom for handling, but they should be protected from sunlight and bright fluorescent lighting. The best type of lighting is yellow. Indirect photographic screen films can be used under yellow fluorescent tubes and yellow incandescent bug lamps without having exposure problems.

Proper storage of indirect photographic screen film is important. This film must contain a proper moisture balance to work effectively. The best relative humidity level is 50 percent, although quality can be maintained if the relative humidity drops to 40 percent or slightly less. Relative humidity higher than 50 percent can cause the film emulsion to become tacky. Boxed indirect photographic screen film should never be stored near heat or in direct sunlight.

EXPOSING THE FILM

Materials needed:
1. Copy (positive transparency) of high quality.
2. Indirect photographic screen film.
3. Exposure unit with a vacuum frame and controlled bright light source.
4. One piece of red or black plastic about 1 or 2 mm thick. A good material is the kind used in thermoplastic forming machines.

Procedure:
1. Open the vacuum frame of the exposure unit and clean the glass thoroughly on both sides. A dirty glass may keep light from striking the photographic film, causing parts of the emulsion not to harden.
2. Place the piece of red or black plastic in the center of the vacuum frame blanket. Be sure it is larger than both the indirect photoscreen film and the positive transparent copy. This sheet provides a smooth surface for the film and positive copy.

3. Position the indirect photographic screen film in the center of the plastic sheet. The emulsion side must be down and the base (vinyl or polyester) side must be up.
4. Place the positive copy, emulsion down, over the photoscreen film (Fig. 130-1).
5. Close the frame and turn on the vacuum pump. For proper positive and film contact, 25 psi should register on the vacuum dial. Let the vacuum pump run another 30 seconds to be sure all air has been removed from the frame.
6. Make the exposure. The length of exposure will vary depending on the light source and the distance of the film from the light. A 3000-watt metal halide lamp placed 40 inches (100 cm) from the film should give the proper exposure in about 50 seconds. The longer the exposure, the thicker the film; the shorter the exposure, the thinner the film. To find the best exposure, make a set of test strips ranging from short to long exposure times.
7. Carefully remove the materials after the exposure. Put the positive copy in a file folder or envelope where it will not get damaged. It may be needed again for another exposure.

DEVELOPING AND WASHING OUT THE FILM

Materials needed:
1. Packaged A and B developing powders.
2. Photographic tray big enough to hold the photoscreen film.
3. Graduate, 16-ounce or larger.
4. Thermometer.
5. Plastic stirring rod.
6. Sink with a water temperature control and a soft spray or aerator nozzle.
7. Thick piece of glass with smooth edges or a clean stretched screen to use for washout.
8. Sheet of clean white paper.

Procedure.
1. Mix the pre-weighed A and B powders with water to make up the developer and pour it into a photographic tray big enough to hold the photoscreen film. The A and B powders often come in packages

that make 16-ounces of liquid developing solution. The temperature of the developer should be between 64° and 75° F (18° and 24° C). The developing tray should contain developer at least 1/2-inch deep (12.5 mm).
2. Immerse the exposed photoscreen film in the developer with the emulsion side up. Develop the film for 90 seconds. Slowly agitate the developer solution during the entire developing time. The developer hardens the parts of the gelatin-based emulsion that were struck by the light during exposure.
3. Wash out the image area right after the 90-second development. Put the film, emulsion side up, in a sink on a sloping but flat surface. A piece of glass or a stretched screen works very well.
4. Set the water temperature between 97° and 104° F (36° and 40° C) to wash out the image area of the film.
5. Using a soft spray or an aerator nozzle, cover the entire emulsion surface of the film (Fig. 130-2). The water will wash away the image areas of the film. Also, the light hardened exposed non-image areas will lose over half their thickness during washout. The washout process will take 3 to 5 minutes to remove soft emulsion from the film completely.

ADHERING THE FILM

Materials needed.
1. A properly prepared screen.
2. A *build-up*—a piece of solid material at least 1/2-inch (12.5 mm) thick and slightly smaller than the inside of the screen frame.

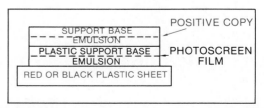

Fig. 130-1. The order and position of the materials when exposing a piece of indirect photoscreen film.

3. Several sheets of unprinted newsprint, also slightly smaller than the inside of the screen frame.
4. The washed-out indirect photostencil.
5. A clean wiping cloth.

Procedure.

1. Be sure the screen fabric is clean and properly prepared. See Unit 127 for the fabric preparation procedure and follow it closely. The screen fabric should be fully prepared before the film is exposed.
2. Place a build-up on a table top or counter near the washout sink. Cover the build-up with a piece of unprinted newsprint the same size.
3. Put the washed-out, chilled film stencil, emulsion up, in the middle of the build-up.
4. Gently lower the slightly damp screen, printing side down, onto the film stencil (Fig. 130-3). Do not apply pressure, because the weight of the screen frame is enough to make complete contact.
5. Lay 2 or 3 sheets of unprinted newsprint on the squeegee side of the screen. Gently wipe over the newsprint with a clean wiping cloth (Fig. 130-4). The newsprint will soak up the excess water from the film and the screen. Change the newsprint sheets 4 to 5 times. A roller can be used to

Fig. 130-2. Using a gentle water spray at between 95° to 100°F [35 to 38°C] to wash out the image areas of the photoscreen film.

apply light pressure across the screen. Some film emulsion color will show on the newsprint of the first few blottings.

DRYING AND PEELING THE STENCIL

Materials needed.

1. A clean, dry wiping cloth.
2. A small electric fan.

Procedure.

1. Let the screen stay on the build-up for at least 5 minutes. Do not move it. Then carefully and slowly lift it off and remove the newsprint. Wipe the excess moisture from the polyester or vinyl support. Do this carefully.
2. Stand the screen vertically and let it dry in a dust-free place. A small electric fan can be used to speed drying, but the photoscreen should dry for at least one hour. Longer is better. *Do not* use heat to dry the stencil!
3. When the photoscreen stencil is dry, peel off the support material. Begin at a corner and pull back the support at 180°, parallel to the fabric. If there is any resistance, let the stencil dry longer.
4. Go on to the masking and printing operations.

RECLAIMING THE SCREEN

Materials needed.

1. Powdered enzyme for indirect photoscreens.
2. Degreasing solution.
3. White vinegar or 5% acetic acid.
4. A round, medium-stiff, nylon bristle brush.
5. A deep sink with hot water hose or spray unit.

Procedure: An indirect photoscreen is reclaimed as is a direct photoscreen (see Unit 129), except the indirect photostencil is removed with a powdered enzyme instead of the liquid or paste stencil remover used to remove the direct emulsion.

1. After degreasing, sprinkle the powdered enzyme liberally on both sides of the screen.

2. While wearing thin rubber gloves, scrub the screen, both sides, for 1 to 2 minutes.
3. Let the screen stand for a few minutes, then hose it off with hot water.
4. Wipe the screen with white vinegar or 5% acetic solution to deactivate the enzyme.
5. Finish by rinsing the screen thoroughly with cold water.

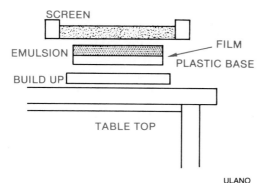

Fig. 130-3. The order of the materials used when adhering the indirect photostencil to the printing side of the screen.

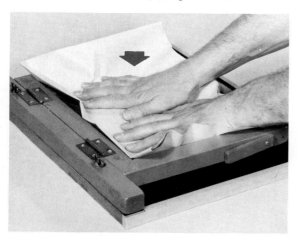

Fig. 130-4. Gently wiping over the unprinted newsprint to blot the excess moisture from the photostencil and screen fabric.

DIRECT FILM STENCILS

The direct-film stencil is the most recent advance in screen-printing stencil-making. The direct-film stencil method consists of a factory presensitized emulsion coating over a plastic (polyester) support base. The film layers are much like those of indirect presensitized stencil film (see Fig. 130-1). This film is often referred to as "capillary" film.

Using Direct (Capillary) Stencil Film

The first step is to attach a sheet of the presensitized film to the screen fabric. The fabric must be clean, degreased, and mechanically treated in the usual manner. Next, a sheet of film should be placed on a flat surface, emulsion side up. The screen frame is placed over the film and the fabric is wetted with a spray bottle of water (Fig. 130-5).

A regular printing squeegee is pulled across the screen (Fig. 130-6). This should be done in the same manner as when printing with ink (Fig. 130-7). The excess water must then be wiped with a soft cloth from all areas of the fabric and frame.

Fig. 130-5. Wetting the prepared fabric after it has been placed over the sheet of direct stencil film.

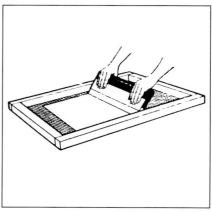

Fig. 130-6. Squeegeeing the direct stencil film to assist its bonding with the fabric mesh.

ANN GARVIN

Fig. 130-7. Pulling a squeegee across the screen.

The emulsion is dried by using a fan or drying cabinet. The backing sheet (film base) is now carefully removed. The remaining procedures of exposing, image washout, and stencil drying are done in much the same manner as with direct emulsion stencils presented in Unit 129.

UNIT 131 MASKING THE NON-PRINTING AREAS

For quality printing, you must carefully mask or block out the non-printing areas around the edges of the screen after the film (stencil) has been attached to it. There are several kinds of masking material. Choose the right one for your job.

PAPER MASKING

Paper masking can be used when no more than 100 copies will be printed. The ink used in the printing operation will eventually go through the masking paper and spots will leak onto the finished prints. Bond paper, 16 or 20 pound, is suitable. The masking paper can be applied to either the top or bottom sides of the screen.

Top-paper masking
1. Lay the screen frame on a flat surface, squeegee side up.
2. Use 4 sheets of paper; 2 sheets for the width of the inside of the frame and 2 for

the length. All 4 sheets should be wide enough to cover the unused screen and the frame on each side.

3. Tape the 4 sheets in place around the image (Fig. 131-1). Leave a minimum of a 1/4-inch (6.35 mm) space between the image and the tape. For best results, use 3/4-inch (19 mm) masking tape.

4. Tape the sheets at the corners and any other places where ink may leak through to the material being printed.

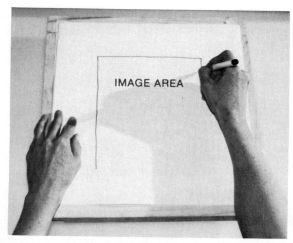

Fig. 131-2. Marking the paper masking where the opening is to be made for the image.

Fig. 131-1. A screen masked with paper from the squeegee side of the frame.

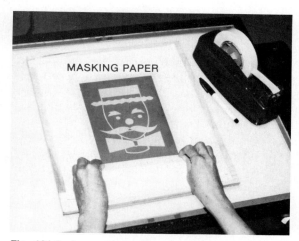

Fig. 131-3. A properly positioned and fastened masking sheet on the printing side of the screen.

4. Remove the sheet and cut it to the outside dimensions. Also cut the opening for the image. An art knife works well.

5. Attach the masking sheet to the underside of the screen by taping all inside and outside edges with masking tape (Fig. 131-3). During printing, the ink will hold the masking sheet very securely to the screen fabric.

Bottom-paper masking

1. Lay the screen frame on a light table, printing side up.

2. Use a sheet of paper as large as or larger than the outside dimensions of the screen frame.

3. Lay the sheet over the screen. Use a *pencil* to mark the opening needed for the image (Fig. 131-2). The opening should be at least one inch (25.4 mm) *larger* than the image area. Also mark the maximum sheet size one inch (25.4 mm) *smaller* than the frame on all four sides.

LIQUID MASKING

Two main types of liquid masking materials are lacquer-base and water-base. Both are applied to the screen in the same way. The ink to be

Fig. 131-4. Using a chipboard squeegee to apply liquid masking to non-printing areas of the screen.

1. Lean the screen, back or bottom side up, against a support.
2. Take a piece of paperboard about 2 by 4 inches (5.08 by 10.16 cm). A piece of chipboard similar to the back of a writing tablet works well.
3. Place this paperboard squeegee against the screen near the bottom and pour a small amount of block-out on the screen (Fig. 131-4).
4. Draw the squeegee upward, distributing the block-out throughout the non-printing areas of the screen. Continue until the screen has been covered and allow the block-out to dry.
5. Apply a second coat to cover any areas not filled during the first application.
6. Check the screen for pinholes and put on more liquid mask or opaque if necessary.

used determines which masking liquid to use. If you will use water-base ink, you will need a lacquer block-out.

Transparent and opaque masking liquids are available in both water- and lacquer-base materials. Transparent block-out lets you see what is to be printed. Liquid block-out can be used to patch open areas or pinholes in the screen film (image carrier).

TAPE MASKING

If small areas of open screen remain between the film and the frame, masking tape may be used to block out the ink. Apply the tape to the underside of the screen and overlap enough to be sure that the ink will not get through and spoil the material being printed.

UNIT 132 THE SCREEN PRINTING OPERATION

After you have prepared the image carrier and masked the non-printing areas, it is time to print. The basic operation is not difficult and you can get excellent results with just a little practice.

SCREEN PRINTING INK

It is important to select the proper ink for the material to be printed. For screen printing work, many types of inks are used because of the extremely wide variety of surfaces on which printing is done.

There are many qualities to select from in choosing an ink. The most important characteristics are color and gloss. Other things to consider are ease of printing, air drying time, forced heat drying time, weather resistance, durability, thickness after printing, and penetration into the material. The thickness of the ink deposit depends mostly on the fabric. Coarse fabric such as 6xx and 8xx (less than 100 mesh count) will let more ink pass through the image area. Textile products are best printed using a coarse fabric screen because a heavy deposit of ink is needed to give an opaque image.

There are five main classes of screen printing inks. One special group makes six. Each class has its own characteristics, purposes, handling methods, and solvents.

Water-base inks. These inks are subdivided into two main classes: those for indoor work on paper and those for printing on textiles. The inks for paper mix readily with water, are easily printed, dry quickly after printing, and are easily cleaned from the screen. The textile inks are chemically very complex, and they can be used on cotton, silk, linen, and other cloth.

Oil-based inks. These are often called poster inks. They are scuff-and-wear resistant and come in a very wide range of colors. They dry somewhat slowly, but usually can be force-dried in a very few minutes or even seconds. The average air-drying time is 30 minutes.

Synthetic enamel inks. When dry, this type of ink looks like glossy enamel. The vehicle, or base, is made of synthetic varnishes and resins. Synthetic enamel inks are used to print decals and outdoor signs. They can be printed on sheet metal, plastics, wood, glass, and previously painted surfaces.

Lacquer-base inks. Lacquer-base inks are slightly more volatile than are the three classes just presented. When printed they are quite flexible, and tend not to crack or break. These inks are very fast drying, which makes them useful in printing packaging containers on a production line.

Plastisol inks. Convenience of use is the primary advantage of plastisol inks. These inks will not air dry. Thus they can be left on the screen stencil for long periods of time. These inks are cured through the use of infrared heating elements and high-intensity, heated-air dryers. Most textile products are printed with plastisol inks.

Ultraviolet (UV) inks. These inks do not dry by air or heat. After printing, UV inks cure, not dry, by means of a high-output UV-light source. Pulse xenon lamps are often used on conveyor-belt curing units. These inks are used for printing on most surfaces—paper, metal, glass, plastics, and other synthetic materials.

Special formulations. Several special inks and materials are used in screen printing. Among them are flock adhesive, printed circuit formulations, cloth decorating mediums, heat transfer ink, and materials in the ceramic family.

PRINTING PROCEDURE

1. Attach the prepared screen frame to the base unit, using one of the methods presented in Unit 125.
2. Raise the hinge bar of the screen printing unit so the stencil will be about 1/16 inch (1.6 mm) above the substrate (paper or other material) being printed. A spacer should be placed between the hinge bar and the base (see Fig. 125-3). Spacers of the same thickness should be placed under the two front corners of the frame. These can be held in place with masking tape. During printing, the only point of contact between the stencil and the substrate is where the leading edge of the squeegee presses down. Off-contact printing keeps the movement of the squeegee from smearing the wet ink that makes the image.
3. Place a sheet of paper or other material to be printed under the screen. Position it according to the image in the screen.
4. Carefully raise the screen, leaving the paper in the correct location on the baseboard.
5. Find or cut three chipboard guides about 3/4 by 1 inch (1.9 to 2.54 cm).
6. Fasten the guides to the baseboard with masking tape. Place two guides on the long side of the sheet and one on the short side (Fig. 132-1). Lower the screen and get a squeegee slightly longer than the image width.
7. Spread newspapers on the table under and around the screen printing unit. The newspapers speed up cleanup. Prepare the ink, and following the manufacturer's directions carefully to obtain good results.
8. Place a sheet to be printed against the guides.
9. Pour a bead of ink the width of the image on the hinge side of the screen (Fig. 132-2).

Fig. 132-1. Guides properly positioned and fastened to the screen-printing baseboard.

Fig. 132-2. Pouring a bead of ink on the hinge side of the screen before printing.

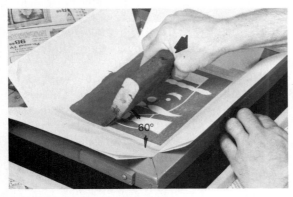

Fig. 132-3. Making a printed copy.

10. Grip the squeegee firmly and pull the ink across the image to be printed (Fig. 132-3). Firm pressure on the squeegee removes excess ink from the top of the screen. Hold the squeegee at about a 60° forward angle and make only one pull per print.

11. Lift the screen and make a *flood stroke* with the squeegee. In a flood stroke, ink is drawn back over the screen leaving a deposit of ink in the image areas of the stencil. This action does two things: it keeps the image area from drying and plugging between printings and it keeps a ready supply of ink in the image area for the next print.

12. Put the squeegee against the hinge side of the frame so it doesn't fall over and get covered with ink.

13. Remove the printed product and check it closely for flaws and needed corrections. Fill pinholes by brushing on liquid screen filler from the printing side. Masking tape can also be used to cover pinholes. Be sure to keep the tape at least a ½-inch (12.7 mm) from any image area, because the tape thickness will keep the stencil from making good contact with the substrate.

14. Repeat steps 8 through 13 for additional printed copies. Add ink when necessary.

15. Place the freshly printed products on drying racks until they are completely dry.

16. Clean the screen printing unit using the steps given in Unit 133.

PRINTING ON SPECIAL MATERIALS

Screen printing can be used to print on many different kinds and shapes of materials. To print on thick or round objects, the printing units must be adapted. In some cases, units must be specially designed to accept the product to be printed.

Thick, flat objects. The screen and baseboard can be easily separated for thick objects (Fig. 132-4). It is also possible to print on boxes and other three-dimensional products by building up the screen to accept them.

Cylindrical objects. Bottles, cans, and other cylindrical objects can be printed on specially designed screen presses. Commercial cylindrical screen printers are available, but

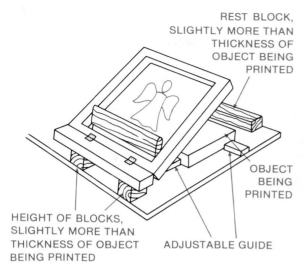

Fig. 132-4. A method for preparing the screen-printing unit when printing thick objects.

REST BLOCK, SLIGHTLY MORE THAN THICKNESS OF OBJECT BEING PRINTED

OBJECT BEING PRINTED

HEIGHT OF BLOCKS, SLIGHTLY MORE THAN THICKNESS OF OBJECT BEING PRINTED

ADJUSTABLE GUIDE

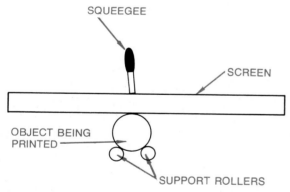

Fig. 132-5. The principle of a cylindrical screen-printing unit.

SQUEEGEE

SCREEN

OBJECT BEING PRINTED

SUPPORT ROLLERS

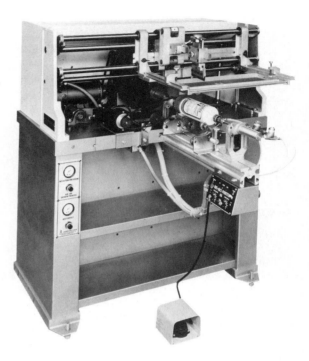

Fig. 132-6. A screen-printing press used to print on three-dimensional products of many different shapes.

units can also be made in the school laboratory (Fig. 132-5). When printing on cylindrical objects, the screen moves horizontally, the squeegee remains stationary (permanent), and the object being printed revolves under the screen. Some commercial screen printing presses can be used to print three-dimensional objects of nearly any shape—flats, rounds, ovals, conicals, spheres, and special shapes (Fig. 132-6).

UNIT 133 SCREEN CLEANUP PROCEDURES

The screen printing unit must be cleaned immediately after the printing operation. If the ink is not removed soon after printing, it will dry and cake in the fabric, and the screen will have to be thrown away. Cleaning up takes less time and money than preparing a frame with a new piece of screen fabric and stencil.

All screens are cleaned in the same basic way, even though different image carriers and inks are involved. You must use the correct solvent for each kind of material to be removed. Check the manufacturer's recommendations for suggested solvents for different image carriers and inks.

The cleanup operation can be messy, but you, the screen, and the working area can be neat and tidy in the end. Have plenty of newspapers available and wrap all ink-soaked materials except rags in clean newspaper before putting them in the wastebasket. Place soiled solvent-soaked rags in a metal safety can.

REMOVING THE INK

1. Place several sheets of newspapers under the screen as soon as the printing operation is completed.
2. Remove excess ink from the screen and squeegee, using a piece of chipboard of about 3 by 4 inches (7.6 by 10.16 cm) as a spatula (Fig. 133-1).

Fig. 133-1. Using a chipboard spatula to remove excess ink from the screen during the clean-up operation.

3. Put the ink back into the original can if no drier or other material was added to it for the printing operation.
4. Throw away the chipboard spatula by wrapping it in newspaper.
5. If a top or bottom paper mask was used, remove it now. Carefully remove the tape, holding the paper so you do not put much stress on the screen fabric.
6. Pour some ink solvent on the screen. Be sure to use the correct solvent for the type of ink. Use water for water-base ink, mineral spirits for oil-base ink, and lacquer thinner for lacquer-base ink. Let the solvent soak briefly.

7. Wipe the inked area of the screen with a medium-size cloth about 12 inches (30 cm) square. The cloth absorbs much of the ink; the newspaper sheets under the screen absorb the rest.
8. Remove 1 or 2 of the top saturated sheets of newspaper from under the screen to renew the absorbent surface.
9. Repeat the cleaning process until all the ink has been removed from the screen.
10. Saturate two clean cloths about 12 inches (30.5 cm) square with the ink solvent.
11. Wipe both sides of the screen at the same time (Fig. 133-2).
12. Store the screen after all traces of ink have been removed. It can be used for future copies, or the emulsion or coating making up the image carrier can be removed to free the screen for another job.

Fig. 133-2. Wiping both sides of the screen to remove ink and foreign material.

REMOVING THE IMAGE CARRIER

The image carrier, which may be screen printing film or coating, can be taken off after all ink has been removed. Removing it from the screen destroys it, however, so save it on the screen if you will need to print from it again.

Follow the proper procedure for removing image carriers of each kind. If a liquid mask was used to block out the non-printing areas of the screen, it must also be removed. Use the correct solvent and repeat Steps 6 through 11 under "Removing the ink."

STORING THE SCREEN

Screens must be stored properly to preserve them. Stacking several frames on top of one another on a bench is likely to damage the screens. Frames should be placed vertically in a rack to protect the screen fabric (Fig. 133-3).

The storage rack should be built with all sides enclosed except the front. This helps keep heavy deposits of dust and other foreign material from gathering on the screens. It also keeps them from being punctured and ruined for future use.

Screens handled with care will give long service. One screen can accept several image carriers and be used in printing several thousand impressions.

Fig. 133-3. A screen storage rack that holds thirty frames.

UNIT 134 PAPER STENCIL AND WASHOUT SCREENS

The paper stencil and the washout (tusche and glue) are two of the earliest and cheapest methods of preparing screen printing image carriers. *Tusche* is a substance like lithographic ink in crayon form that is used as a resist in screen work. These two screen preparation mediums will give good results, although they are not widely used commercially.

PAPER STENCIL IMAGE CARRIERS

One of the simplest ways to prepare a screen is to make a *paper stencil* image carrier. A paper mask or stencil is adhered to the screen fabric with the ink used to print the copies. The image is cut out of the paper with a sharp knife (an art knife works well). Copies are printed in the usual way. The paper stencil method can be used for work involving simple illustrations or large lettering. It is possible to print up to 200 copies with this method.

Preparing the stencil

1. Select the copy; remember to keep it simple.
2. Take a piece of white bond paper (20 pound is best). It should be slightly smaller than the outside dimensions of the frame.
3. Place the copy on a light table. Tape it down and then tape the white bond sheet over the copy (Fig. 134-1).
4. Cut out the image, using an art knife (Fig. 134-1). If letters or parts of the illustration contain centers, you must leave connecting links. Avoid these if you can.
5. Get a clean screen printing frame and base. Place a sheet of clear newsprint paper on the base and place the cut stencil sheet on the newsprint paper. Lower the screen and position it if necessary.
6. Complete the printing operation as outlined in Unit 132. The ink will hold the paper stencil sheet on the screen fabric.
7. Remove the paper after printing and clean the screen as outlined in Unit 133.

THE WASHOUT SCREEN

The *washout method* is sometimes called the tusche and glue method because originally glue was used as the masking or block-out material. Commercial water and lacquer base block-out materials are now available.

This method of preparing the screen image carrier uses a liquid or crayon tusche material. The image areas of the screen are filled with the tusche material and a liquid is used to fill the remaining areas of the screen. The tusche is then removed to form the image carrier.

The washout screen method is often used for fine-art compositions, which generally are produced in limited editions. These compositions can be reproduced to look much like the original. Cost of this method is less than that of most graphic reproduction methods.

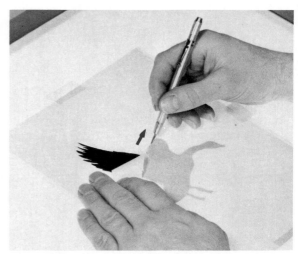

Fig. 134-1. Preparing a paper stencil by cutting out the image to be printed.

Preparing the washout screen

1. Select the copy. Landscapes and artist's renditions are best for this method.
2. Thoroughly clean the screen fabric with cleanser and water.
3. Tape the copy to a flat table top and lay the screen over the copy.
4. Trace the image onto the screen, using a soft pencil. Accuracy is important.
5. Lift the screen and prop it against a support at a slight angle.
6. Apply liquid tusche to the image area of the screen, using a lettering or art brush (Fig. 134-2). Let the tusche dry thoroughly.
7. If a crayon tusche stick is used, lay the screen on a flat, hard surface when applying the tusche. You can get interesting texture patterns by laying heavily grained wood or other porous material under the screen and rubbing over the screen with the tusche stick. The tusche will stick to the screen only in the high areas of the underlying material.
8. After the tusche is completely dry, apply the masking or block-out. Use water or lacquer base liquid block-out, depending upon the ink to be used.
9. Apply the liquid block-out with a brush or a chipboard squeegee, as outlined in Unit 131. Apply the block-out to the squeegee side of the screen.

10. After the liquid block-out is dry, remove the tusche. To do this, saturate two cloths with solvent. Work from both sides of the screen and wash out the tusche (see Fig. 133-2). Use the correct solvent (usually turpentine, benzene, or naphtha) to dissolve the tusche.

11. Mask out the screen around the edges of the frame with paper or tape (see Unit 131).

12. Print the copies as outlined in Unit 132. Several hundred copies can be reproduced before the block-out material begins to break down.

13. Clean the screen according to the instructions in Unit 133. Remove the block-out with water or lacquer thinner.

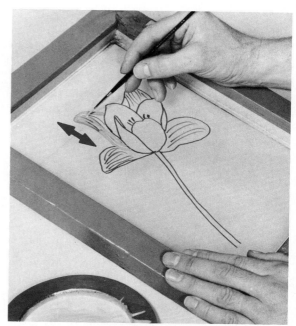

Fig. 134-2. Applying liquid tusche to the image area of the screen.

UNIT 135 MULTI-COLOR SCREEN PRODUCTION

One advantage of screen printing is the ease with which colors can be used. There are several mechanical ways to register (position) colors and print them in combinations. Only one method will be discussed in this unit. With ingenuity and planning, however, other register and printing methods can be developed. Register marks should be used in all multi-color screen production.

COPY PREPARATION

Precise preparation of copy for multi-color work is essential for quality reproduction. The number of colors to be printed is not important. The reproduction of two colors uses the same basic steps as the reproduction of three or more.

The following procedure should be followed for hand-cut (lacquer or water-base) films:

1. Obtain multiple-color copy that is appropriate for hand cutting.

2. Divide the color. Each color area should be shaded with a corresponding colored pencil or should be marked to indicate the proper colors (Fig. 135-1). Use colored pencils or felt-tip markers.

3. Place center register marks on the copy. They should be placed on each side a minimum of 1 inch (2.54 cm) from the nearest copy. Use an ink ruling pen and make the lines 1/8 to 1/4 inch (3.175 to 6.35 mm) long. Preprinted register marks that have an adhesive backing can also be used.

4. Cut one piece of film for each color. If colors are next to each other, take extreme care in cutting the film. Carefully cut the register marks in each piece of film.

5. Adhere the film to the screen. It is more convenient to have one screen for each color, although this is not necessary. If only one screen printing unit is available, print the first color, clean up the screen, adhere the film, and then print the second color.

6. Mask the screen or screens as outlined in Unit 131. If multiple pages are being printed, check the imposition carefully.

7. Print the first color. Normally, the lightest color is printed first, although this is not necessary. Print about 6 copies with the register marks, then cover the marks from the underside with masking tape. Also print approximately 10 percent more copies per color than the number of final copies needed. These extra prints are necessary to allow for normal spoilage during printing.

8. After the first color has dried, the second color can be printed. Prepare the screen in the usual manner. To register the second color, place one of the first prints containing the register marks under the screen. Move it around until the printed register marks of the first color and the register marks cut into the film of the second color align. Raise the screen carefully and position the guides.

9. Make one or two trial prints of the second color which has the register marks. Inspect for the correct position and make guide adjustments if necessary. Cover the register marks and complete the second color printing.

10. Complete additional colors.

11. Clean the screens thoroughly.

Fig. 135-1. Multicolor copy for screen printing hand-cut film. Note the center register marks on each of the four sides.

136

KEY TERMS

Unit 121

Mitography
Screen process
    printing

Silk screen printing
Stencil
Stencil printing

Unit 122

Cylinder screen press
Drying oven
Flatbed screen press

Rotary screen press
Wicket dryer

Unit 123

Beam cutter
Circle cutter
Dual knife
Film knife
Loop knife
Mesh count

Monofilament fabric
Multifilament fabric
Screen fabric
Squeegee
Swivel-blade knife

Unit 125

Kick-leg
Screen base

Screen frame

Unit 126

"Right-reading" film
    positive

Silhouette method

Unit 127

Build-up
Degreasing fabric
Hand-cut film
Lacquer soluble film

Mechanical fabric
    treatment
Stripping blade

Unit 128

Blotting

Water soluble film

Unit 129

Direct emulsion
Direct photoscreen
Emulsion
Emulsion coating blade
Light-safe
(Light-proof)
Light sensitive emulsion

Sensitizer
Step-wedge (Test-strip)

Unit 130

Capillary film
Enzyme
Indirect photoscreen
Presensitized direct film
Presensitized indirect film

Printing side
Positive transparency
Squeegee side
Washing out

Unit 131

Block out

Masking

Unit 132

Fabric mesh
Flood stroke
Hinge bar
Lacquer-base inks
Off-contact

Oil-base inks
Plastisol inks
Synthetic enamel inks
UV inks
Water-base inks

Unit 134

Paper stencil
Tusche

Washout screen

DISCUSSION TOPICS

1. How does *screen printing* differ from letter-press, lithography, and gravure image-transfer methods?
2. Name and briefly describe the principle press designs in common use today.
3. Why is it important to prepare artwork in full color for screen printing?
4. Why should screen fabric, new or used, always be *degreased* before attaching a screen stencil?
5. Why is it important to select the correct screen printing ink for the material being printed?

ACTIVITIES

Units 121–122

1. Collect as many products as possible that have been printed by the screen printing method. Carefully examine the quality of the images. What improvements could have been made to obtain a higher-quality product? If possible, determine the kind or class of ink used on each printed example.

Units 123–125

2. Build a screen printing unit. Prepare a unit for flat materials or for cylindrical objects or for both. Carefully design the unit for high-quality printing and maximum efficiency.

Units 124–135

3. Plan, prepare, and print a product suitable for screen printing. Select the best image carrier for the particular job. Remember to use the correct ink.

Units 127–130 and 134

4. Compare the several methods of preparing the screen printing image carriers. Select an illustration for a particular product and try to prepare an image carrier by each of the several methods. Print and critically analyze the results from each of these image carriers. Repeat this experiment with a different type of illustration for another product.

Units 126–135

5. Produce a four-color poster advertising an event in your school. Use a different method of preparing the image carrier for each color. Remember to choose the appropriate image carrier for each color element. Have friends or fellow students critique the poster.

16 PHOTOGRAPHY

137 INTRODUCTION TO PHOTOGRAPHY

For thousands of years people have tried to make pictures of what they have seen with their eyes. Cave dwellers drew pictures on the walls of caves to show the animals they hunted. Later artists tried to show buildings, people, or scenes by making very detailed marks. Until recently, such drawing was the only way to keep visual records.

In the mid-1800s, the first process for making permanent photographic images was invented by a French painter named Daguerre. Photography was made available to many people in the late 1800s when an American named George

Eastman first made roll film to fit standard camera sizes. Many changes in photographic materials, equipment, and processes have taken place since Eastman's first film and cameras.

Fig. 137-3. A negative is made from the film that is exposed in the camera.

Fig. 137-1. Some photographers like to make their own prints to get special effects.

Fig. 137-2. Film is exposed in the camera.

Fig. 137-4. A photographic print is made from a negative.

Photography has become an important part of our daily lives. Photographs in books, newspapers, and other printed matter help people better understand the printed word. In some cases, photographs alone tell a story. Photographs in catalogs and advertisements show people what they are buying. Scientists explore the unknown by using photography. Photographs help physicians cure patients. Engineers use photography to design better roads, bridges, buildings, and automobiles. Police use photography in investigating crimes and accidents. Almost everyone uses photography to record their experiences.

Nearly anyone can own a camera and take pictures. Even low-priced cameras take very good photographs when used correctly. Automatic photographic processing equipment has made possible low-cost black-and-white or color photographs. The same automatic equipment has also made it possible to get the photographs in a short time. Many people make pictures as a hobby. They experiment to get special effects. Figure 137-1 shows a scene photographed at night. The photographer wanted to get the special effects of the lights.

In this section, we will discuss black-and-white photography, but much of what is learned can also be used to make color photographs. There are three steps in making a black-and-white photograph. The first step is to expose film in a camera (Fig. 137-2). The second step is to make negatives from the exposed film (Fig. 137-3). The third step is to make a positive print, or photograph, from the negative (Fig. 137-4).

UNIT 138 THE CAMERA

A camera is used to expose film. The exposed film is processed in chemicals to make negatives. Some cameras are so simple that almost anyone can make exposures with them. Others are more difficult to use and need to be used by persons who understand the camera parts.

The major purpose of a camera is to hold film so that light will not reach the film until the pictures are taken. Most cameras have four main parts. The first part is a light-tight box called the *body* of the camera. The second part is the *lens*, which makes the image clear and sharp on the film. The third part is the *aperture*, which controls the amount of light that enters the camera. The fourth part is the *shutter*, which determines the length of time that light will enter the camera.

SIMPLE CAMERAS

The *box* camera is the simplest kind of camera. Nearly all box cameras have only one shutter speed and a lens with the focus fixed in one position. Box cameras usually use roll film and are mostly used for making snapshots.

The *cartridge* type camera is the most widely used simple camera. Film for it is packed in hard plastic cartridges. The two sizes are 126 and 110. The 126 size film is larger than 110 size.

110 CAMERA AND FILM

126 CAMERA AND FILM

Fig. 138-1. 110- and 126-size cameras with film cartridges.

The cartridge is very simple to load in the camera. Most cartridge cameras, like box cameras, have a fixed focus, shutter speed, and aperture. However, some companies make very complicated cameras that use 110-size cartridges. The size of the 110 cartridge makes it possible to make a small camera. Figure 138-1 shows 110 and 120 cartridge cameras with their film cartridges.

TWIN-LENS REFLEX CAMERAS

A *twin-lens reflex* camera has two lenses (Fig. 138-2). The two lenses are usually similar. One lens is placed above the other lens. The photographer views the subject and focuses through the top lens. The lower lens is used to expose the film.

Twin-lens reflex cameras are often used by professional photographers. The camera body is small, but the 120-size roll film gives a negative 2 1/4 inches (57.15 mm) square. This is much larger than 35 mm size film. Very good lenses are often found on twin-lens reflex cameras. In recent years, however, single-lens reflex cameras (discussed later) have reduced the use of twin-lens reflex cameras.

One problem with the twin-lens reflex camera is with what is called the *parallax*. The scene is framed through the top lens but the picture is exposed through the bottom lens—so the photographer does not see exactly the same picture that is taken. The problem is greatest with close-up exposures and lessens as the photographer moves away from the subject. Parallax will be discussed in detail later in this unit.

RANGEFINDER CAMERAS

The most common kind of rangefinder camera is a 35 mm camera. The rangefinder (focusing mechanism) is located above and usually to the side of the camera lens (Fig. 138-3). The focusing ring is connected with the rangefinder. The photographer turns the focusing ring until the camera is in focus. There are two common kinds of rangefinders on cameras. The first is a *double-image* rangefinder. The second kind is the *split image* rangefinder.

Most rangefinder cameras are focused with a double-image rangefinder, which shows two images of the subject when the camera is not in focus. One image is a sharply defined image of the subject. The other is a filtered (dim) image of the subject, usually a pale color like yellow. The camera is in focus when both images are exactly on top of each other.

Many rangefinder cameras have automatic controls. These include automatic focus and

VIEWING AND FOCUSING LENS EXPOSURE LENS ELECTRONIC FLASH

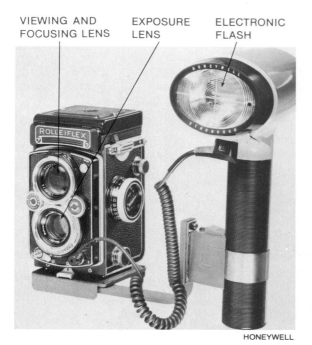

HONEYWELL

Fig. 138-2. A twin-lens reflex camera with an electronic flash attached.

RANGEFINDER

YASHICA

Fig. 138-3. A typical rangefinder camera.

automatic exposure controls. Photographs are easily made with these cameras.

The rangefinder camera is a very good camera for making medium-range photographs. Its fixed focal-length lens is not very good for making close-up or long range photographs. Parallax is a problem with the rangefinder camera when making close-up photographs. Expensive attachments are needed to make telephoto photographs.

SINGLE-LENS REFLEX CAMERAS

The most common kind of 35 mm camera in use today is the single-lens reflex camera (Fig. 138-4). Photographers see the subject, focus the camera, and make the exposure through the same lens. The camera shows exactly what will be on the film before the picture is taken.

The image is viewed through the lens by being reflected by a series of mirrors in a prism (Fig. 138-5). When the shutter release is pressed, the mirror behind the lens lifts out of the way to let the film be exposed.

Another advantage of single-lens reflex cameras is that many lenses can be used on the camera. Wide angle and telephoto lenses can be fitted on, as well as other special purpose lenses.

SHUTTER RELEASE ⟶

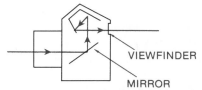

VIEWFINDER

MIRROR

Fig. 138-5. The image is reflected with mirrors to the viewfinder.

MINOLTA CORPORATION

Fig. 138-6. A 35 mm single-lens reflex camera with a flash attachment.

YASHICA

Fig. 138-4. A typical 35 mm single-lens reflex camera.

NIKON

Fig. 138-7. Modern 35 mm cameras use electronic controls.

Nearly all single-lens reflex cameras have an exposure meter behind the lens of the camera. This lets the camera measure the light that actually enters the camera lens for very accurate light readings.

Other attachments are available for many single-lens reflex cameras. One popular attachment is the *auto-winder*. After an exposure is made, the auto-winder automatically advances the film for the next exposure. Electronic flashes are also available for most single-lens reflex cameras. Electronic flash attachments give very good light without the bother of flash bulbs. The camera in Figure 138-6 has an auto-winder and an electronic flash.

Electronics have made single-lens reflex cameras very complicated in recent years. Figure 138-7 shows the inside of a modern camera. Electronics in cameras permit greater flexibility and accuracy in making exposures. The use of electronics has also made cameras smaller and lighter.

VIEW CAMERAS

Ground glass on the back of a view camera lets the photographer see the subject. This type of camera is used for portrait photography because it takes 4 by 5 inch (10.2 by 12.7 cm) or larger sheet film (Fig. 138-8).

View cameras have bellows between the camera lens and body, which lets the photographer adjust for distortion in the subject being photographed.

Because of the large camera size and the view-focus mechanism with its ground glass and bellows, the view camera is most often used for still subjects. Also, the sheet film must be loaded in film holders in a darkroom. The film holders are placed in the camera as needed.

PRESS CAMERA

Press cameras like the ones in Figure 138-9 were once used by all newspaper photographers. They were bulky and heavy but could take rough treatment. Most press cameras used 4-by-5-inch (10.2 by 12.7 cm) sheet film. The film was loaded into film holders, which were placed in the back of the camera. In recent years, newspaper photographers have changed to twin-lens reflex cameras and single-lens reflex cameras, because they are easier to handle.

Several other cameras are available for special purposes. *Subminiature* cameras use film as small as 9 mm wide. *Aerial* cameras are used to photograph large land areas. *Underwater* cameras take pictures in water. You can find a camera for nearly any purpose.

VIEWING
GROUND GLASS   BELLOWS   LENS

CALUMET MANUFACTURING COMPANY

Fig. 138-8. A view camera.

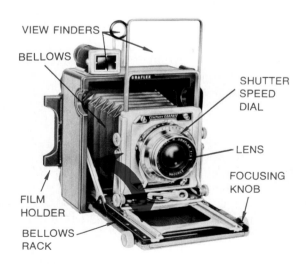

VIEW FINDERS

BELLOWS

SHUTTER
SPEED
DIAL

LENS

FOCUSING
KNOB

FILM
HOLDER

BELLOWS
RACK

Fig. 138-9. A typical press camera.

PARALLAX

Parallax happens when the lens that the photographer looks through is not the same as the one the picture is taken through (Fig. 138-10).

Most parallax problems take place during close-up exposures. The photographer must adjust the camera angle to avoid having the subject in the wrong place on the negative. If the photographer does not allow for the differences in the viewing angles of the lenses, part of the image may be missed. Parallax is usually not a problem when exposures are made more than 10 feet from the subject.

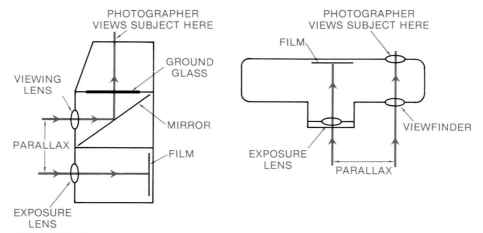

Fig. 138-10. The photographer must adjust for parallax in aiming the camera.

UNIT 139 PHOTOGRAPHIC FILMS

Photographic films are exposed in cameras and processed in chemicals to produce negatives. There are several kinds of photographic films. You should know the important characteristics of each film so that you can select the right one for different purposes.

KINDS OF FILM

Films used for general photography produce continuous-tone negatives. Prints made from continuous-tone negatives should have a full range of gray tones from black to white.

The film most used in black-and-white photography is *panchromatic* film. Panchromatic film is sensitive to all colors. It must be handled in total darkness until it is fully processed.

Orthochromatic film and *infrared* films are sometimes used for special effects. Orthochromatic film is sensitive to all colors except red. Infrared film is sensitive to invisible heat rays, which are just beyond the red end of the spectrum we can see. Infrared pictures look like ones taken on panchromatic film, but green plants look white. Infrared photographs can be made in total darkness.

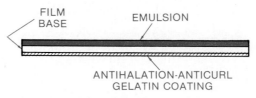

Fig. 139-1. Cross section of a piece of film.

STRUCTURE OF FILM

Most films are made by coating both sides of a thin, flexible, transparent material called the *base*. The base usually is made of a plastic material, but some films are made on glass. Films are made with extremely high quality materials and workmanship so that each kind of film will give the same results time after time.

An *emulsion* is coated on top of the film base. The emulsion is light-sensitive silver halide particles suspended in a gelatin material. The gelatin absorbs water and is transparent (Fig. 139-1). The image for the photographic negative is formed on the emulsion side of the film.

Another layer of gelatin is coated on the other side of the base. This coating reduces curling of the film and includes an *antihalation* dye. The antihalation dye absorbs light that passes through the emulsion so that reflections do not result in unwanted exposures.

When the film is exposed to light through the lens, a *latent image* is formed on the emulsion. When the film is developed, the bright parts of the latent image turn to black metallic silver. This produces a reverse of the original image (subject). Areas of the subject that were white will be black on the negative. Areas that were dark on the subject will be clear (or light gray) on the negative. Other colors will appear as different shades of gray on the negative.

FILM SPEED

Film speed refers to sensitivity to light. Film that is very sensitive (requires little light to cause a latent image) is called *fast* film. Film that is not very sensitive to light is considered *slow* or *medium* speed film. Fast film is used when there is not much available light. When there is a lot of light, you may select a much slower film.

The speed of a film is given in an ISO/ASA number. Fast films have ISO/ASA numbers above 200. Some ultra-fast films have ISO/ASA numbers above 6400. Medium speed films have ISO/ASA numbers between 64 and 200. Slow films have ISO/ASA numbers below 50. The ISO/ASA number is marked on the film package (Fig. 139-2). You must know the ISO/ASA number to determine the proper exposure.

GRAIN

The emulsion of film is made up of millions of tiny silver halide particles called *grains*. When the film is processed, the grains become visible. In photographic prints, the greater the enlargement, the more the grain can be seen.

Grain is related to film speed. Faster films have larger grains than slower films. Because of this, enlargements made from fast film negatives will usually show more grain than enlargements made from negatives made with slower films. In most cases you should try to avoid noticeable grain. Sharp detail is lost with grain; heavy grain looks like snow on television.

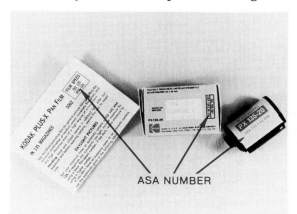

Fig. 139-2. The ISO/ASA number is given on the film package, cartridge, or data sheet.

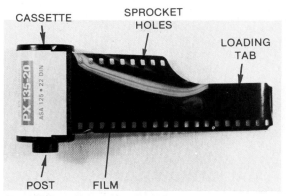

Fig. 139-3. A 35 mm film cassette.

Grain can also become more visible because of improper exposure and film processing. Grain size can be controlled by good exposure and developing techniques.

Grain in a photographic print is always the result of grain in the negative. Some ways to reduce grain are:

1. Use the slowest film possible.
2. Expose the film accurately.
3. Develop the film correctly.
4. Use a camera that produces the largest possible negative.
5. Crop the subject in the camera viewfinder as close as possible.
6. Keep enlargement size to a minimum.

FILM SIZES

Camera manufacturers make their cameras so that a certain size film will fit the camera. Film is packaged in four ways: cartridges, cassettes, rolls, and sheets.

The 110 and 126 size film are packaged in cartridges (Fig. 139-1). Cartridges are easily loaded into the camera. The cartridge is destroyed when the film is removed for processing.

Cassettes are used to package 35 mm film. To save money, you can buy 35 mm film in bulk packages with re-usable cassettes. Bulk film is usually purchased in 25-, 50-, or 100-foot (7.6, 15, or 3 m) rolls. A bulk film loader is used to load the cassettes. A 35 mm cassette will have a strip of film extending from the opening of the cassette (Fig. 139-3).

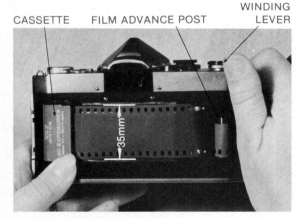

Fig. 139-4. Loading 35 mm film.

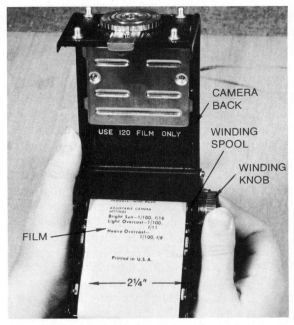

Fig. 139-5. Loading a roll of 120 film into a camera.

The most common roll film is the 120 size. The film is protected on a spool by colored paper. The spool and paper are thrown away when the film is processed.

Sheet film is loaded into film holders that are placed in the back of a view camera or press camera. Film holders must be loaded and unloaded in a darkroom. Sheet films for film holders can be obtained in sizes ranging from 2¼ by 3¼ inches (5.7 by 8.3 cm) to larger than 8 by 10 inches (20.3 by 25.4 cm) and larger.

LOADING FILM

Film must always be properly loaded in the camera in a place where there is only low light. Many good photographs have been spoiled because film was exposed to light (fogged) while being loaded into the camera.

The 35 mm camera is probably the most difficult camera to load. You should be sure that the film tab is wrapped completely around the film advance post (Fig. 139-4). Also, the sprocket holes on the film must line up with the sprockets in the camera.

When cameras are loaded with 120 roll film, the marks on the protective paper should line up with marks on the camera (Fig. 139-5). The paper is placed in the slot in the winding spool and the winding knob is turned until the marks

line up. After the camera back is closed, the winding knob is turned until the film is in place for the first exposure.

UNIT 140 MAKING THE EXPOSURE

Film is exposed when light strikes it. The correct amount of light entering the camera and striking the film causes the negative to have the most detail in all areas. Possibly the most important part of black-and-white photography is making a good exposure. Good exposure and proper processing make a good negative, and a good negative is necessary to make a good print.

The lightest areas of a photograph are called *highlight* areas (Fig. 140-1) and the darkest areas of a photograph are called *shadow* areas. The gray, or in between, areas are called *middle tones*. On the negative these areas will be just the opposite. The highlights will be the darkest part of the negative and the shadows will be the lightest part of the negative. Good photographs will have detail in all areas of the picture.

When too much light enters the camera, the highlight areas of the negative will be too dark. There will be no detail in the lightest areas of the final print. This is called an *overexposure*.

If too little light enters the camera, the shadow areas will be too light. They will be nearly clear and the print (positive) will have no detail in the shadow areas. This is called *underexposure*.

Film speed and the *amount of light* determines the exposure. You must adjust the camera properly for both the film speed and amount of light.

AMOUNT OF LIGHT

The amount of light let into the camera for an exposure is very important. Light can come from natural (the sun) or from artificial sources.

Fig. 140-1. Photographs have highlight, middle tone, and shadow areas.

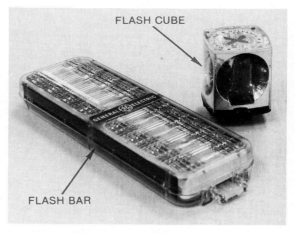

Fig. 140-2. A flash bar and flash cube.

There are two kinds of artificial light—continuous, as in flood lights, and flash lighting.

There are two kinds of flash systems—*electronic flashes* and *flash bulbs*. The electronic

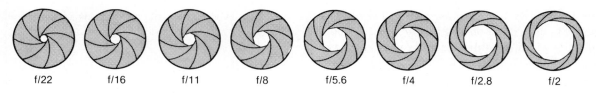

APERTURE SIZES

Fig. 140-3. Metal leaves mesh together to form different size apertures.

flash has a lamp and a reflector (see Fig. 138-4). The lamp of the electronic flash can be used several thousand times. The flash bulb is placed in a reflector socket and can be used only once. *Flash cubes* and *flash bars* have been developed in recent years (Fig. 140-2). A flash cube has four bulbs and reflectors built into the unit. The unit automatically turns a quarter-turn each time an exposure is made. The flash bar has eight or ten flash bulbs with built-in reflectors. Each time a picture is taken, the camera uses a different bulb. The flash cube and flash bar are thrown away after use. A camera must be built to use flash cubes or flash bars.

The amount of natural or constant artificial light is measured by a light meter. Many cameras have a light meter built into the camera case. Flash attachments have a scale or table on the back of the flash unit to indicate correct exposures. The steps in deciding proper exposures will be explained later in this unit.

Film exposure depends both on the amount of light entering the camera and the length of time that light is admitted into the camera. The amount of light is controlled by the lens aperture and the time by the shutter. For good results, you should know how to adjust both the aperture and shutter speed.

Lens aperture

The *lens aperture* is the size of the lens opening. The aperture is formed by a device called the iris. The iris is formed by several metal leaves that work together. When the aperture ring on the camera lens is turned, the opening in the center of the leaves gets bigger or smaller (Fig. 140-3). Simple cameras do not have irises but only one or two fixed openings. More complex cameras have a range of aperture adjustments.

Apertures are measured in *f-numbers* or *f-stops*. Common f-stops on a lens are f/1.2, f/1.4, f/1.7, f/2, f/4, f/5.6, f/8, f/11, f/16, f/22. *Each f-stop lets in half as much or twice as much light as the f-stop next to it.* For example, f/5.6 lets twice as much light into the camera as f/8 but f/11 lets only half as much light into the camera as f/8.

The smaller the f-number, the larger the aperture opening. This can be seen in Figure 140-3. The opening next to f/2 is larger than the opening next to f/16. The smallest f-number (largest opening) indicates the *speed of the lens.* The lens speed measures the largest amount of light a lens will let pass. If the smallest f-number on a camera is f/2, the speed of the lens is f/2.

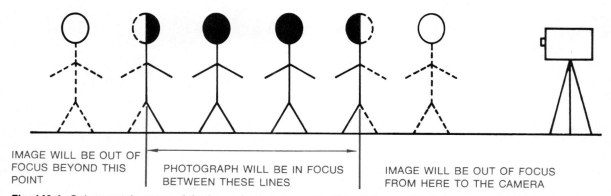

IMAGE WILL BE OUT OF FOCUS BEYOND THIS POINT

PHOTOGRAPH WILL BE IN FOCUS BETWEEN THESE LINES

IMAGE WILL BE OUT OF FOCUS FROM HERE TO THE CAMERA

Fig. 140-4. Only a certain range of the image in a photograph will be in focus. This is known as the depth of field.

The size of the aperture also determines *depth of field,* or *depth of focus.* Depth of field is the range of distance in a photograph that will be in focus (sharp image). The distance from the closest image that is in focus to the farthest image that is in focus is the depth of field (Fig. 140-4).

The smaller the aperture opening (larger number) the longer the depth of field. An aperture setting of f/16 will have more of the photograph in focus than will an aperture setting of f/2.8. The photograph in Figure 140-5 shows a photograph taken with an aperture of f/2.8. The same subject in Figure 140-6 was photographed at f/11. Notice how much more of the subject is in focus in Figure 140-6 than in Figure 140-5.

Shutter speeds commonly found on cameras range from 1 second to 1/2000 of a second. A common series of shutter speeds are 1 second, 1/2 second, 1/4 second, 1/8 second, 1/15 second, 1/30 second, 1/60 second, 1/125 second, 1/250 second, 1/500 second, and 1/1000 second. *Each shutter speed is either half as fast or twice as fast as the shutter speed next to it.* For example, 1/250 second is half as fast as 1/500 second and 1/1000 second is twice as fast as 1/500 second.

Fig. 140-6. The depth of field is much greater with an aperture of f/11.

Fig. 140-5. The depth of field is not great with an aperture of f/2.8.

Shutter speeds

A camera *shutter* lets light into the camera for a certain amount of time. The shutter release is pressed to open the shutter and make an exposure. Simple cameras have only one or two shutter speeds. More complicated cameras adjust for many shutter speeds.

Shutter speeds are very important when making an exposure of a moving subject. If the subject moves while the shutter is open, the photograph may be blurred unless a fast shutter speed is used. The best shutter speed to make an exposure of a swimmer, for example, may be 1/250 second, but 1/60 second may be best to photograph a building. Moving subjects generally should be photographed at shutter speeds of 1/250 second or more.

DETERMINING EXPOSURES WITH A LIGHT METER

Most adjustable cameras have a light meter built into the camera body. The camera shown in Figure 138-3 has a light meter just above the camera lens. Most single-lens reflex cameras have a light meter that measures the light that passes through the lens.

To give useful readings, the light meter must be adjusted to the speed of the film being used in the camera. Different cameras and light meters are adjusted in different places. The camera or light meter should be adjusted until the correct ISO/ASA number is in place. On the light meter in Figure 140-7, the ISO/ASA speed is set at 100 in the ISO/ASA window. Once the meter (or camera) has been adjusted for the film speed, the photographer is ready to find the correct exposure setting for the selected picture.

Using in-camera light meters

When the light meter is built into the camera, the meter reading can be seen in the viewfinder. Since camera makes and models are different, it is hard to show what you will see in a viewfinder. Manufacturer's instruction books will be your best source of information.

Most cameras are either *shutter priority* or *aperture priority*. On shutter priority cameras, the photographer hand sets the shutter speed for the exposure. The meter will then show what f-stop should be used for the selected shutter speed. On an aperture priority camera, the photographer will hand select the f-stop and the meter will show the best shutter speed to use.

In other type cameras with meters, a needle pointer in the viewfinder shows the correct setting. On these cameras, either the aperture or shutter can be adjusted until the needle points to the correct spot on the scale.

Using a hand-held light meter

Finding correct aperture and shutter settings for an exposure is somewhat different when using a hand-held meter (Fig. 140-7). A hand-held meter is used when the camera has no meter or when a photographer wants a more accurate reading.

To get a reading with a hand-held light meter, point the light-gathering cell toward the subject. Point the meter slightly down, to avoid

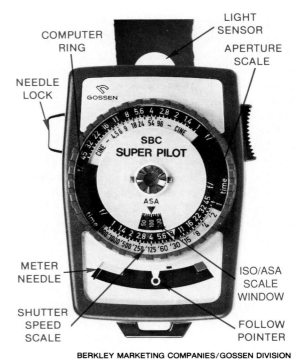

BERKLEY MARKETING COMPANIES/GOSSEN DIVISION

Fig. 140-7. The front side of a hand-held light meter.

the glare of sky or overhead lights. When the meter switch is turned on, a needle will move to a point in the window. Turn the computer ring until the follow pointer lines up with the meter needle. This automatically lines up the combinations of aperture numbers and shutter speeds that will give a correct exposure. In Figure 140-7, you would get accurate exposures if the camera were set at f/2 for 1/500 second, at f/2.8 for 1/250 second, f/4 for 1/125 second, f/5.6 for 1/60 second, f/8 for 1/30 second, f/11 for 1/15 second, or f/16 for 1/8 second.

RECIPROCITY

Different exposure conditions will need different shutter speeds and aperture settings. For example, say that a good exposure would be made at f/11 for 1/60 second. But if you want to make an exposure of a runner, the picture would be blurred at 1/60 second. An exposure with a shutter speed of 1/500 second would reduce the chance of a blur, but, with a f/11 lens opening, light would enter the camera for too short a time. You must change the aperture along with the shutter speed. In this example you would need to change the shutter speed four places—from $1/60$ to $1/125$ to $1/250$, to $1/500$. The aperture would also be moved four f-stops—from f/11, to f/8, to f/5.6, to f/4. In other words, if the exposure meter showed that a good exposure would result from f/11 for $1/60$ second, any of the camera settings in Figure 140-8 would also give a good exposure.

A knowledge of reciprocity is useful not only when you want to stop action but also when you are concerned with depth of field. When you want to have a great deal of the subject in focus from near to far, a large aperture number (small aperture opening) should be selected. Choose f-stops of f/11, f/16, or f/22.

f/22	-	1/15 sec.
f/16	-	1/30 sec.
f/11	-	1/60 sec.
f/8	-	1/125 sec.
f/5.6	-	1/250 sec.
f/4	-	1/500 sec.
f/2.8	-	1/1000 sec.

Fig. 140-8. The same amount of light will enter the camera with any of these aperture/shutter speed combinations.

SPECIAL EXPOSURE SETTINGS

We have been discussing camera settings for making normal exposures. To work under special conditions or to get unusual effects, check the manufacturer's directions that came with your camera or light meter.

Sometimes, you may not have a meter handy. Good exposures can also be made by using the guidelines on the instructions found in the film package. The guidelines suggest aperture settings and shutter speeds for different lighting conditions. NOTE: when it is very important to get one good exposure, you can use the *bracket* exposure technique. That is, you guess at the best exposure setting and make an exposure. Then, for insurance, you make two more exposures, for one f-stop larger and one f-stop smaller. By doing this, you will probably get at least one good exposure.

HOLDING THE CAMERA

Images on the photograph can be blurred if the camera is not held still. For sharp detail in the negative, it is important to have little or no camera movement when an exposure is made. Cameras can be hand held when exposures are made with shutter speeds of $1/60$ second or faster. When the shutter speed is slower than $1/60$ second, you should use a tripod or other device. Even the slightest movement of the camera while the camera shutter is open will cause the subject to be blurred on the negative.

When making an exposure, you should take a comfortable position. Keep your elbows close to your body and squeeze the shutter release rather than push on it. On windy days or when using slow shutter speeds, lean against something like a door frame or a tree to help reduce movement.

A tripod should be used when you are concerned about camera movement. A cable release is very useful with a tripod. When using a cable release, you do not have to touch the camera to take the picture. A self-timer on the camera can be used in place of a cable release, if one is available.

UNIT 141 FILM PROCESSING

A good print is made from a good negative. Correct film exposure is the first step toward a good negative. The next step is to process the film correctly. In this unit, we present the background and procedure for successful continuous-tone film processing.

As we discussed in Unit 139, when film is exposed, a *latent* image is produced on the film. *Latent* means that the image cannot be seen until the film is processed. When a roll of exposed film is processed, it becomes a series of *negatives*. Negatives are the opposite of the original subject. Where the subject was bright, that part of the negative will be dark. Where the subject was dark, the negative will be light. Areas that were somewhere between the lightest and darkest will be gray on the negative. The negative will have a series of continuous tones from light to dark.

LOADING FILM

Panchromatic film (the type used most for continuous-tone photography) must be handled and processed in total darkness. Even the smallest amount of any kind of light beyond the camera exposure will overexpose the film. Film can be processed in either of two ways—in a tank or in

a tray. Both sheet and roll film are usually processed in a tank. Tray processing is sometimes used to develop sheet film.

Several pieces of equipment are needed to process film. In addition to the needed chemicals, you should have the right size of developing tank, thermometer, graduate, funnel, timer, and scissors. When working with 35 mm film, a bottle opener is also useful.

Developing tanks

There are several kinds of tanks for developing both roll and sheet film. Tanks are sometimes called daylight developing tanks. The film is loaded into the tanks in total darkness. After the tank is loaded, it can be used in daylight.

Tanks are made from plastic, stainless steel, or hard rubber. Some tanks can be adjusted to fit several sizes of film (Fig. 141-1). The reel squeezes together to fit different film sizes. Other tanks are made to fit only one film size (Fig. 141-2).

Developing tanks simplify film processing. Without them, the film would have to be handled in trays in the darkroom. Using a tank, the film is loaded on the reel and placed in the tank. With the lid on, the tank can be used in room light. Chemicals are poured in and out of the tank to process the film.

Loading roll film

There are two general kinds of developing tank reels. On one reel, the film is loaded from the center (Fig. 141-3). On the other reel, the film is started from the outside (Fig. 141-4). In loading the reel, the film must be separated by the grooves so that processing chemicals can freely circulate on both sides of the film.

Fig. 141-1. The parts of an adjustable daylight developing tank.

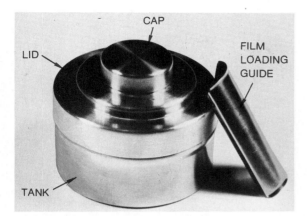

Fig. 141-2. The parts of a stainless steel developing tank.

The photographer should prepare the darkroom before loading the film into the developing tank. The items needed to load the tank should be set out in order of use. This will avoid hunting for the equipment in total darkness.

Continuous tone film is packaged in rolls (120 size) and cassettes (35 mm size). The 120 size is packed with a protective paper over the film. This paper must be removed as the film is loaded into the tank. The film for a 35 mm roll is inside a metal cassette (see Fig. 139-3). The leader on 35 mm film is rolled completely into the cassette when rewinding film in a 35 mm camera. The film is removed from the cassette by prying the cap off the cassette with a bottle opener (Fig. 141-5). The narrow leader on 35 mm film must be cut off with scissors before the film is loaded (Fig. 141-6).

With a stainless steel reel, the end of the film is placed in a clip in the center of the reel (Fig. 141-3). You must slightly cup (bend) the film to make it fit into the spaces in the reel. This is sometimes done with a film loading guide. You must handle the film only by the edges because fingerprints will leave skin oil on the film, damaging the image.

Film is loaded from the outside edge of several brands of reel. The film is started by feeding the film into two slots on the outer edge of the reel (Fig. 141-4). Once the film is started, you hold it in place with your thumb (Fig. 141-7). The sides of the reel work like a ratchet (Fig. 141-8). You feed film into the slots in the reel by turning one side of the reel while holding the film against the other side of the reel. When the side of the reel stops, you hold the film against the reel and turn the other end backwards. This ratcheting movement will feed the film into the reel.

Film is taped to the spool on 35 mm rolls and this end should be cut off. Ratcheting is continued until the film is advanced completely into the reel. Film is sometimes easier to feed onto a ratchet-type reel if the corners of the end of the film are trimmed. Also, be sure the reel is completely dry before starting to load film. If the reel is wet, the film will stick in the slots and will not feed properly.

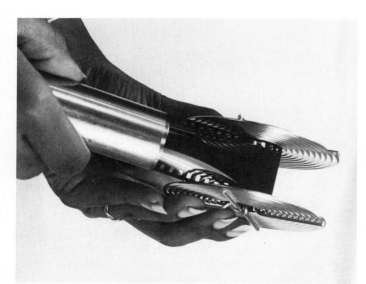

Fig. 141-3. The film is loaded from the center toward the outside of the reel.

Fig. 141-4. The film is loaded from the outside on some reels.

Fig. 141-5. Pry off the cap to remove the film from a 35 mm cassette.

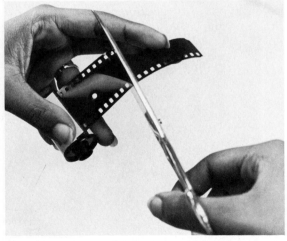

Fig. 141-6. A photographer must cut the tab off a roll of 35 mm film before loading the film.

You should practice loading film onto a reel with a dummy roll until you can do it with your eyes shut. Remember—the film must be loaded on the reel and put in the tank in total darkness. Attach and secure the top of the tank before turning on the room lights. Loading film into a

HOLD FILM WITH THUMB

Fig. 141-7. When loading film from the outer edge of the reel, hold film with thumbs.

Fig. 141-8. The ends of the reel turn like a ratchet.

developing tank is an important step toward successful film processing.

PROCESSING CHEMISTRY

Continuous-tone film is processed in five basic solutions: developer, stop bath, fixer, water, and wetting agent. It is a good idea to decide on a specific kind or brand of chemicals and use them for all of your work. By always using the same chemistry, you know exactly what to expect each time. The best way to begin processing film is to follow the instructions that are found in the film package.

Developer. The developer changes the exposed silver halide crystals (latent image) to black metallic silver. Developers also are known as *reducers*. Several developers are available, each designed for a specific purpose. Some produce extremely fine grain negatives. Others help with contrast. The beginning photographer should use a developer recommended by the film manufacturer.

Stop bath. Stop bath is used to stop the action of the developer. It also washes most of the developer from the film. If too much developer gets into the fixer, the fixer will be ruined. A mild *acetic acid* solution or clear water can be used for stop bath. But the best thing to use is prepared stop bath concentrate.

Fixer. The fixer removes unexposed and undeveloped silver halide crystals. Fixer also contains a hardener to firm up the emulsion of the film. This helps prevent scratches on the negative. After film has been in the fixer for the correct amount of time, the negatives are safe in white room light.

Water. When processing film, you should have plenty of clean water available. Chemicals used to process the film must be washed from the film with running water.

Wetting agent. Film is placed in a wetting agent solution after it has been washed. This last step in processing reduces the number of water spots on the film.

PROCESSING THE FILM

When you process film, you should pour the right solutions into the developing tank in the right order and in the right way. Much of the negatives' quality depends on how well the film is processed. The most important factors in film development are *development time, temperature of the developing solution*, and *agitation of the film during development*. The beginner should follow the film manufacturer's recommendations in each case.

Temperature of processing solutions

The temperature of the chemical solutions is a major concern in film processing. *All solutions used to process a roll of film should be the same temperature.*

The best temperature is 68° F (20° C) because most continuous-tone film chemistry has been

made to work at that temperature. If any of the solutions is at a different temperature, excessive grain may show in the negatives. One way to be sure all chemicals are the same temperature is to put the containers in running water of the desired temperature for 10 to 15 minutes.

Processing procedure

Film can be processed in slightly different ways, but the general procedure is the same. The following steps will give good negatives.

1. *Pre-wash the film.* After the film has been loaded in the tank, pour clean water into the tank. The temperature of the water should be the same as the temperature of the other chemicals to be used to process the film. Rap the tank on a table or hard surface to remove air bubbles from the film. The purpose of this step is to wet the film. After about 15 to 20 seconds, pour the water out of the tank.
2. *Prepare the developer.* Put the correct amount of developer into a graduate. Some developers are used full strength. Others are mixed with water.
3. *Find the temperature of the developer.* Use a thermometer to find the temperature of the developer. This temperature determines how long the developer should stay in the tank. A chart on the information sheet that comes with the film will give development time for a specific temperature. The developer should be the same temperature as the pre-wash water.
4. *Set the timer.* Set a timer for the correct amount of developing time.
5. *Pour the developer into the tank.* The developer should be poured into the tank as quickly as possible. As the developer solution is poured, the timer should be started. The developer should stay in the tank for the length of time on the timer.
6. *Agitate the film during development.* Agitating the film brings new developer into contact with the film. Agitate the film for 5 seconds every 30 seconds. Too much agitation will cause the film to develop too quickly. Not enough agitation will cause

ARKAY CORPORATION

Fig. 141-9. A film drying cabinet.

Fig. 141-10. Preserve negatives by putting them in protective containers.

streaks to form on the film. When the time is gone on the timer, pour the developer out of the tank.

7. *Pour the stop bath into the tank.* The stop bath should be poured into the tank as quickly as possible after the developer has been poured out. Developing action will continue until the stop bath is poured into the tank. Shake the tank rapidly with the stop bath. Pour the stop bath out of the tank after about 15 to 30 seconds.

8. *Pour the fixer into the tank.* You can use rapid-working fixer or regular fixer. The rapid fixer fixes the film faster than regular fixer. Fixing time can vary between 5 and 10 minutes. Follow the directions of the film manufacturer. Since the fixer solution can be reused, be sure to return the fixer to the used container after the film has been fixed.

9. *Wash the film.* After the fixer has been poured from the tank, the film should be thoroughly washed. When possible, the film should be washed in running water

at the same temperature as the other developing solutions. Check the manufacturer's recommendations for the correct amount of washing time. Many beginners try to cut this step short. Don't. Hypo (fixer) clearing agent can be used to reduce washing time.

10. *Place the film in the wetting solution.* Water spots can be avoided by placing the film in a *wetting agent* immediately after washing the film. The wetting agent may form bubbles on the film, but the bubbles will disappear as the film dries. Squeegee the excess water and wetting agent from the film.

11. *Dry the film.* The film should be hung in a dust-free place to dry. Clips should be placed at the top and bottom of the film. Because film can be easily damaged while it is wet, it should not be used until it is completely dry. The drying cabinet in Figure 141-9 helps to keep film free of dust and dirt.

12. *Cut the film into strips, and place the strips in negative envelopes.* When the film is dry, it should be cut into strips of several exposures. The strips should be put into negative envelopes like those shown in Figure 141-10. These protect the negatives from dust, dirt, fingerprints, and scratches.

Be sure to clean the developing tank thoroughly after each use. It should be washed in running water to get rid of all chemicals. Be sure to dry all parts of the tank and store it in a dust-free place.

UNIT 142 PHOTOGRAPHIC PAPERS

The final step in photography is to make a print on light sensitive paper. There are many kinds of photographic paper. You must select the right kind of paper for the results you want.

PHOTOGRAPHIC PAPER CHARACTERISTICS

Photographic paper works much like photographic film. It has a light-sensitive emulsion coated on a paper base. The emulsion is a gelatin with silver halide crystals suspended in the gelatin. When light hits the emulsion of the paper, it forms a latent image. When the paper is developed, the latent image becomes visible.

Bases

Photographic paper bases must be high quality, white, and free of impurities. The paper must be strong enough to withstand processing in chemicals and drying with heat. It must also remain in good condition for many years.

Two kinds of bases are used for photographic paper: *fiber bases* and *resin-coated bases*. Fiber-base papers are made as single weight (SW) and double weight (DW) (Fig. 142-1). Resin-coated papers most often are made in medium weight (MW) (Fig. 142-2). Single-weight papers are light and cost less than either double-weight or medium-weight paper.

The emulsion on each kind of paper is essentially the same. The biggest difference between fiber-base and resin-coated paper is that resin-coated paper can be processed faster and easier than fiber-base paper. Fiber-based paper must be washed for long periods of time in order to remove the chemicals. Resin-coated papers have a thin coating of resin (plastic) on the paper base that keeps chemicals from being absorbed into the base. This means that less

time is needed for fixing, washing, and drying prints. Resin-coated papers will dry in the air without curling.

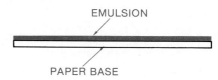

Fig. 142-1. Fiber base photographic paper is coated with an emulsion.

Fig. 142-2. Cross section of resin-coated (RC) paper.

Emulsions

The emulsion on photographic paper is made of silver chloride, silver bromide, or a combination of both. The combination of silver chloride and silver bromide is called silver chlorobromide. More light is needed to expose silver chloride paper than silver bromide or silver chlorobromide paper. Chloride paper is mostly used to make contact prints. This is because, in making contact prints, the light is usually closer to the paper.

Most enlarging paper is made with silver chlorobromide emulsions. This kind of emulsion needs much less time to make exposures. Silver bromide paper is very fast and requires the least amount of time to make an exposure. Some enlarging papers are called *rapid* paper. These are used when large numbers of prints must be made or when very large prints are made.

Nearly all black-and-white photographic papers are not sensitive to some colors of light—most often, red or yellow light. Because of this, most papers can be used in a darkroom with safelights. The manufacturer gives the recommended safelight for each photographic paper.

Emulsion contrasts

Two kinds of photographic papers are made with two kinds of contrast emulsions: *graded contrast papers* and *variable contrast*. Graded papers come in grades or contrasts ranging from 0 to 5. Numbers 0 and 1 are the softest (least contrast) and numbers 3, 4, and 5 are the hardest (most contrast). Most photographs are printed on a medium contrast paper that gives good whites and blacks with several gray tones. There is only one kind of variable contrast paper and different color filters in the enlarger are used to give different amounts of contrast. Variable contrast paper is popular because it is much more convenient to use than graded paper. The cost per sheet is generally higher, but the time saved is worth the extra cost.

Sizes

Papers are packaged in sizes ranging from $3\frac{1}{2}$ by 5 inches (8.9 by 12.7 cm) to 20 by 24 inches (50.8 by 61 cm). Some papers even come in rolls for very large prints. The most popular sheet sizes are 4 by 5 (10.2 by 12.7 cm); 5 by 7 (12.7 by 17.8 cm); 8 by 10 (20.3 by 25.4 cm); and 11 by 14 inches (27.9 by 35.6 cm).

Papers come with different numbers of sheets in a package. Some larger sizes come in packages of as few as 10 sheets. Others can be bought in packages of up to 500 sheets. Paper costs less per sheet when bought in large quantities.

Finishes and tones

Photographic printing papers are made in several finishes. The most common has a very shiny surface and is called *glossy*. Other finishes include semi-matte, matte, silk, pearl, and linen. Finishes are shown on the package by letters. For example the letter *F* is used for paper with a glossy surface.

Papers are also made with different degrees of whiteness, often referred to as *tone*. Some of the tones include cream white, white, snow white, and old ivory. Some seem warm and others cold. They add an emotional effect to a print. Dealers usually have paper samples from which you can select the finish and tone for the results that you want.

HANDLING AND STORING PAPER

Photographic paper needs to be handled and stored properly in order to give the same results time after time. Many different things can damage paper.

Temperature and humidity. It is best to store paper in cool places. Paper can be stored at room temperature (68° F to 72° F—20 to 22° C). However, if paper is to be stored for long, it should be kept at lower temperatures.

Humidity (moisture in the air) and dryness can also cause problems. Too much humidity can cause fungus to grow on the emulsion. Too much dryness may cause the emulsion to become brittle and crack. It is best to store

Fig. 142-3. Photographic paper should be held by the edges.

paper where the humidity will be about 40 percent.

Paper packages. Paper is packaged in envelopes or boxes. Inside, the photograhic paper will be in a black envelope or wrapped in black paper. The black wrapping protects the paper from light and humidity. Do not remove the photographic paper from the wrapper until it is ready to be used.

Handling sheets of paper. Paper should always be handled by the edges (Fig. 142-3). Paper can be scratched very easily if handled carelessly. Moisture and oil from fingerprints can also damage the paper. Keep your fingers dry and free of chemicals when you handle paper.

UNIT 143 PHOTOGRAPHIC PRINTING

Photographic prints are made by passing light through a negative onto photographic paper. This printing technique makes a picture exactly like the original subject that was photographed with the camera. The two ways to make photographic prints are by *contact* and *projection*. Projection printing is often called *enlarging*.

With processing, photographic emulsions turn dark where they were exposed to light. This means, as we have seen, that a negative is dark, or opaque, where the subject was bright. It is clear where the subject was dark. When this negative is used to make a photographic print, the light passes through the clear places to turn the emulsion on the paper dark. The dark places on the negative block the light so that the paper in those areas will stay white. The gray places on the negative let through a little light and turn the paper a little dark—or a shade of gray. Thus the light shining through the negative recreates the lights and darks of the original subject on the photographic paper.

CONTACT PRINTING

Contact printing produces a photograph the same size as the image on the negative. Some well-known photographers prefer to make contact prints because they give better detail and lack grain. However, large negatives must be used. Contact printing is not often done with small negatives.

Contact printing is the simplest method of making photographic prints. The negative is placed in contact with the photographic paper, with the emulsion side of the negative next to the emulsion side of the paper (Fig. 143-1). Light is passed through the negative to strike the paper. The paper is then processed in developer, stop bath, fixer, and water.

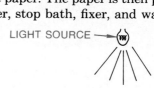

LIGHT SOURCE

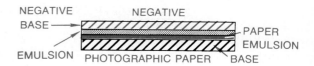

NEGATIVE
BASE ———→ NEGATIVE
PAPER
EMULSION
EMULSION PHOTOGRAPHIC PAPER BASE

Fig. 143-1. Contact prints are made with the negative emulsion pressed tightly against the photographic paper emulsion.

Several devices can be used in making contact prints. Figure 143-2 shows a hand-made contact printing frame. The printing frame shown in Figure 143-3 was used several years ago when large negatives were common. Contact printer units use pressure to hold the negative and photographic paper together. With 35 mm size film, most contact printing is done to make proof sheets.

Fig. 143-2. A hand-made contact printing frame.

BASE WITH
LIGHT INSIDE   TIMER

ARKAY CORPORATION

Fig. 143-3. A contact printer.

Proof sheets

Proof sheets are made so that the photographer can see what is on each negative frame. They are mostly used with 35 mm negatives. Unless a proof is made, it is hard to see how a negative will look because the images are small and in reverse of the original subject.

Proof sheets are usually made with several negative strips on the same sheet of paper (Fig. 143-5). The proof sheet was exposed in a

vacuum frame like the one shown in Figure 143-4. To make the proof sheet, 35 mm negative strips are placed on a piece of photographic paper. The glass cover is closed over the negatives and paper. The vacuum pump is turned on to force the rubber blanket against the glass and put the negatives in tight contact with the paper.

A similar result can be obtained by using a negative file sheet. The negatives are placed in the file sheet with the emulsion side of all of the negatives facing the back of the sheet (Fig. 143-6). To make the proof sheet, the file sheet is placed on top of the photographic paper. The vacuum frame brings the paper and

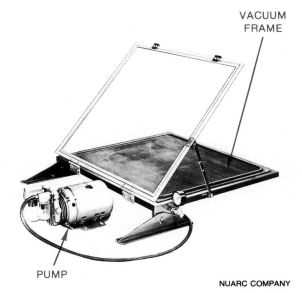

VACUUM
FRAME

PUMP

NUARC COMPANY

Fig. 143-4. Vacuum printing frame with pump.

Fig. 143-5. A proofsheet made in a vacuum frame.

the file sheet into tight contact. The negatives are better protected by this technique. They are also easier to find.

If a vacuum frame is not available, the file sheet can be used with a piece of glass or clear plastic and a piece of foam rubber. Place a piece of photographic paper on the foam rubber, emulsion up. Put the file sheet, with negatives, on the photographic paper. Put a piece of glass or clear plastic on top of the file sheet. Put light weights on both ends of the glass (Fig. 143-7). The light from an enlarger can be used to expose the proof sheet.

Different methods can be used to expose contact prints and proof sheets (Fig. 143-8). Some contact printers have a built-in light. In other cases, room light or light from an enlarger is used. The photographer will quickly learn how much time is needed to get a good proof sheet.

PROJECTION PRINTING

Projection printing is used to make prints that are larger than the negatives. An *enlarger* is the device used to make projection prints (Fig. 143-9).

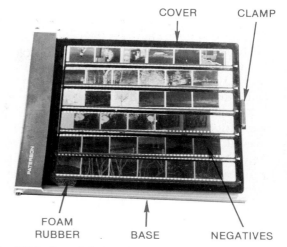
Fig. 143-8. A proof sheet maker.

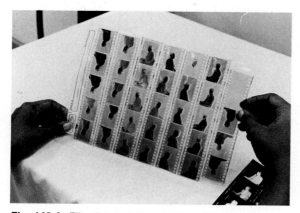
Fig. 143-6. File sheets with negatives, like this one, can be used to make proofsheets.

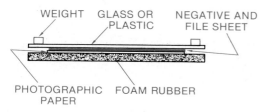
Fig. 143-7. Cross section of a proof sheet maker.

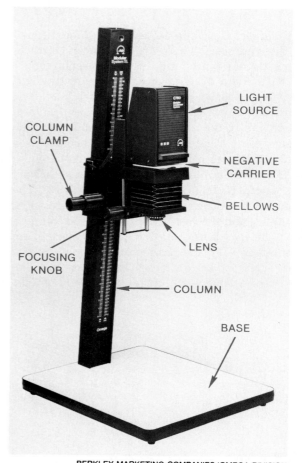
BERKLEY MARKETING COMPANIES/OMEGA DIVISION
Fig. 143-9. Parts of an enlarger.

Projection printing has several advantages over contact printing. The main advantage is the larger prints. Also, parts of a negative can be chosen to make a print. In addition, contrast can be controlled and corrections made in the image.

The greatest disadvantage of projection printing is that prints often have much more visible grain structure. The popular 35 mm cameras make negatives that must be enlarged for the prints to be useful. The larger the print, however, the greater the chance of noticeable grain. With a small enlargement, very little grain can be seen (Fig. 143-10). When a small part of the photograph in Figure 143-10 is greatly enlarged, the grain structure is much more visible (Fig. 143-11).

Enlargers

Enlargers are available in several different qualities and sizes. There are also several attachments that can be used with most enlargers.

The main parts of an enlarger are the light source, negative carrier, filter holder, base, lens, focusing knob, and bellows (Fig. 143-9). Enlargers can have different light sources. The enlarger in Figure 143-12 has a light source used to make color prints.

The negative carrier is a frame used to hold the negative in a flat position (Fig. 143-13). The negative is placed between the two plates (Fig. 143-14) and the carrier is placed in the enlarger.

The lens is the most important part of an enlarger. The lens can cost as much as the enlarger. Enlarging lenses have apertures like lenses on cameras to control the amount of light that reaches the paper.

The base supports the column of the enlarger. The easel is placed on the base and holds the photographic paper in place.

The negative carrier fits between the enlarger light source and the lens. As the head of the enlarger is moved up the column, the image on the base gets larger (Fig. 143-15). The image is focused by turning the focusing knob. This causes the bellows to move up and down, varying the distance between the lens and the negative.

Fig. 143-11. When a print is enlarged, the negative grain can be seen.

Fig. 143-10. Very little grain shows in a small print.

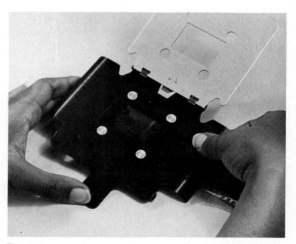

Fig. 143-14. A negative being placed in a negative carrier.

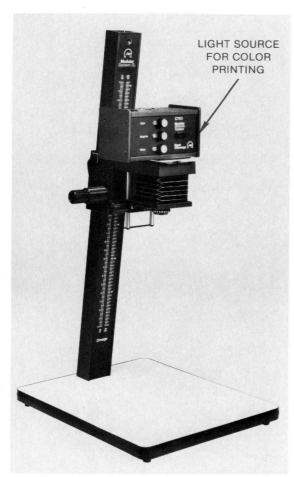

LIGHT SOURCE FOR COLOR PRINTING

BERKLEY MARKETING COMPANIES/OMEGA DIVISION

Fig. 143-12. An enlarger to do color printing.

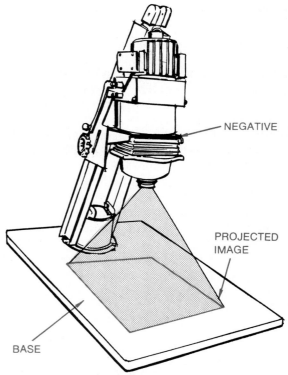

NEGATIVE

PROJECTED IMAGE

BASE

Fig. 143-15. The projected image spreads out as the negative moves away from the base of the enlarger.

Fig. 143-13. A negative carrier.

Other enlarging equipment

There are several items of equipment that can be used to make enlargements. Some items are necessary and others are just handy.

Easels hold the photographic paper in position and keep it flat. The easel in Figure 143-16 is adjustable and creates borders on the print.

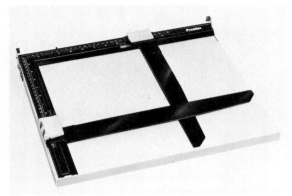

PHOTO MATERIALS COMPANY

Fig. 143-16. An adjustable enlarging easel.

The paper is placed on the base and the border guides are adjusted to the right print size. An adjustable easel holds the paper so that no borders will appear on the print (Fig. 143-17). Speed easels are made for specific sizes of paper and automatically put borders on the print (Fig. 143-18).

Timers are needed to time the length of exposure for an enlargement (Figs. 143-19, 143-20, and 143-21). Enlargers can be plugged into the timer so that when the switch is turned on, the timer will automatically start the enlarger. The timer in Figure 143-19 automatically resets itself. The timer in Figure 143-22 is more accurate and can be programmed to time several operations including exposure time and developing time. A simple timer will work well for most situations.

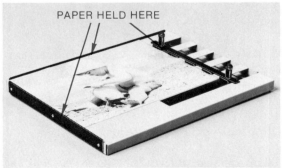

PAPER HELD HERE

PHOTO MATERIALS COMPANY

Fig. 143-17. Adjustable borderless easel.

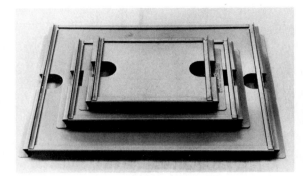

Fig. 143-18. Speed easels.

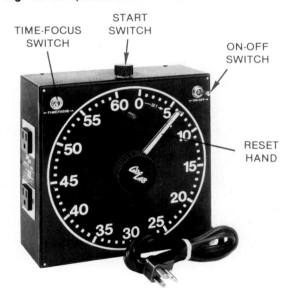

START
SWITCH

TIME-FOCUS
SWITCH

ON-OFF
SWITCH

RESET
HAND

DIMCO-GRAY COMPANY

Fig. 143-19. Enlarging timer with reset controls.

A *focusing magnifier* can be used to help make sharp exposures. The magnifier is placed on the easel in any part of the image area. The magnifier increases the image size so that you can sharply focus the enlarger.

Making the exposure for an enlargement

Enlarging paper must be exposed for the correct length of time to make a good print. But differences in negative densities and differences in enlargement sizes make it hard to determine the right exposure times. In most cases, it is best to make a test exposure for each negative and each enlargement size. The test exposure will let you

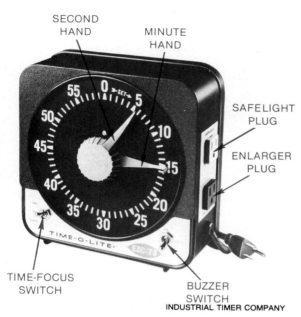

Fig. 143-20. Enlarging timer.

DIMCO-GRAY COMPANY

Fig. 143-21. Enlarging timer for timing from 1 second to 59 minutes 59 seconds.

PHOTO MATERIALS COMPANY

Fig. 143-22. A timer that can be programmed for different darkroom operations.

FALCON SAFETY PRODUCTS

Fig. 143-23. Compressed air for cleaning negatives and photographic equipment.

know how long to expose the enlargement.

Place the negative in the negative carrier so the emulsion side of the negative is toward the enlarger base. The negative should be cleaned to remove any lint or dirt. This can be done by blowing on the negative with compressed air (Fig. 143-23) or by brushing it with a special static-free brush.

A *test exposure* is a series of short exposures on a small piece of enlarging paper. The test strip of enlarging paper should be the same kind that will be used to make the enlargement (Fig. 143-24). The test strip is processed by the same procedure used to make the final enlargement. The exposures for the test strip in Figure 143-24 were 2 seconds apart. The developed test strip is inspected to find the area that gives the best density. In this case, the 8-second exposure was the best one. The other exposures were too light or too dark. The resulting print is shown in Figure 143-25.

Once the best time is found from the test

OVEREXPOSURE | CORRECT EXPOSURE | UNDEREXPOSURE

12 SEC   10 SEC   8 SEC   6 SEC   4 SEC   2 SEC

Fig. 143-24. A test strip made to find the proper exposure time.

Fig. 143-25. A print made by using the test exposure time from Figure 143-24.

exposure, making the print is simple. Set the timer for the best exposure time found from the test strip. Check to see that the easel is in the correct position. The image should be located within the borders of the easel. Also check to see that the negative is in proper focus. Put a piece of photographic paper in the easel with the emulsion side toward the lens. Make an exposure for the same time as the best test exposure and process the exposed paper.

Processing photographic paper

Exposed paper must be accurately processed. To do this, use exactly the same procedure for all photographic prints, including test exposures. That helps find the source of problems if they occur and to tell what changes to make if different results are wanted.

The steps in processing photographic paper are similar to processing film. The paper goes through four solutions—developer, stop bath, fixer, and water wash. The manufacturer gives recommendations for processing on the data sheet included in the photographic paper package.

Before developing paper, prepare the solutions in three trays—the developer, stop bath, and fixer. (To wash prints, you can also use a tray or you can use a sink with running water.) Trays should be placed so the paper is processed from left to right. Use the manufacturer's recommendations to mix the solutions.

Place the paper in the developer so that the entire surface is covered as quickly as possible. The time that the print is in the developer can vary from 1 to 2 minutes. A common development time is 90 seconds. Be sure to use the same developing time for all prints.

Developer wears out after several prints have been made. It may need to be replaced if you are processing a large number of prints in a given period of time.

Developer solutions are usually stored in colored bottles to keep light from getting to

FALCON SAFETY PRODUCTS

Fig. 143-26. Bottles used to store paper developing chemicals.

them (Fig. 143-26). Light, high temperature, and air will all cause developer to spoil. Some specially designed bottles collapse to get rid of excess air as the chemicals are used (Fig. 143-26).

After the paper has been in the developer for the correct amount of time, put it in the stop bath. This stops the developing action and helps to wash the developer from the paper. The stop bath can be clear water or weak acetic acid solution, but it is best to use commercially prepared chemistry. The paper should stay in the stop bath for 5 to 10 seconds.

After the stop bath, put the paper in the fixer for 2 to 10 minutes. The time that the print will stay in the fixer depends on the kind of paper being used. Fiber-base paper can stay in the fixer much longer than resin-coated paper. In fact resin-coated paper can be damaged if it stays in the fixer for too long.

Prints should be washed in running water to remove all chemicals from the paper. Fiber-base papers should be washed 15 to 30 minutes, which is much longer than resin-coated paper because they absorb more chemicals. Resin-coated paper should not be washed for more than 3 or 4 minutes.

When the photographs have been processed, they are dried or otherwise finished or mounted. These procedures will be discussed in Unit 144.

UNIT 144 FINISHING AND MOUNTING PRINTS

Finishing operations usually consist of drying and mounting the photographs. Surface finishes are usually put on papers during the drying operation. The finishing techniques are determined by the kind of paper used and what the photographer or customer wants.

Photographs that are to be made into halftones should be finished with a glossy surface. The type of finish increases the quality of the black areas and gives the print more tonal range.

When photographs are to be displayed, it is often best to select a paper with a non-gloss surface. For example, portraits are often printed on matte surface papers to give a softer effect. Billfold-size prints are sometimes printed on a linen-surface paper. This is a semi-gloss surface that does not soil as easily as matte surface paper.

DRYING RESIN-COATED PAPERS

Resin-coated papers have surface water on them after washing because the coating does not absorb moisture. The surface water should be removed so the paper can air dry. The water can be blotted with paper or a squeegee can be pulled across the surface of the paper (Fig. 144-1). Excess water can also be removed from the paper surface with a chamois.

Resin-coated paper can dry flat or standing on edge. Figure 144-2 shows a roller for removing surface water and a rack for holding the prints while they dry. A dryer that blows warm

Fig. 144-1. Squeegee used to remove excess water from photographic paper.

air over the prints helps to dry them more quickly (Fig. 144-3).

DRYING FIBER BASE PAPERS

Fiber-base papers soak up a lot of water during processing and it must be removed before the print can be used. Air drying fiber-base paper will make it curl and wrinkle. The moisture must be removed while the paper is held flat. In many cases heat is used.

The simplest way to dry fiber-base paper is with a ferrotype plate—a metal plate with a shiny chrome surface. The paper is placed on the plate and the water is removed with a squeegee. To get a glossy surface print, the surface of the paper is placed against the shiny

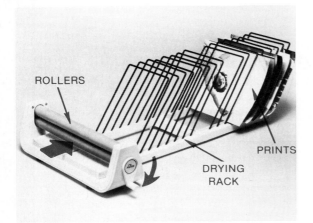

Fig. 144-2. Drying equipment for RC paper.

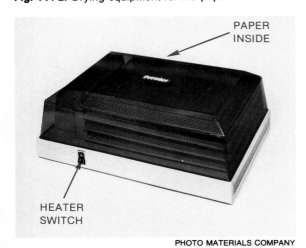

Fig. 144-3. Dryer for drying RC paper with heat and air.

surface. For a flat or matte surface, the base is placed against the plate. As the print dries, it will pop off the plate.

Heated roll-type dryers are widely used (Fig. 144-4). Be sure, however, that the dryers are not too hot. Excess heat can damage the prints. It is also important that the prints are totally washed. Prints will discolor if not clean and completely free of processing chemicals.

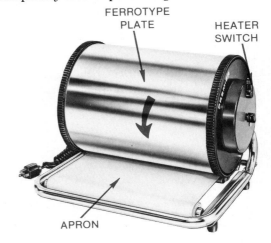

Fig. 144-4. Roll-type heated print dryer.

MOUNTING PHOTOGRAPHS

Photographs should be mounted on heavy paper board material when they will be handled or displayed. A good mounting makes the photograph look better by focusing attention on it.

Photographs are fastened to a heavy material called *mounting board*. Several colors and surfaces can be purchased at art and photographic supply stores. White, black, and gray are used most often with black and white photographs. Colored mounting board also can be used.

The best way to mount prints is to use dry mounting tissue and a mounting press. *Mounting tissue* has an adhesive coating on both sides and looks like wax paper. It is placed between the photograph and the mounting board. When heated, the mounting tissue sticks to the back of the photograph and the front of the mounting board (Fig. 144-5).

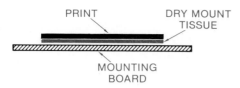

Fig. 144-5. Cross section of print mounting.

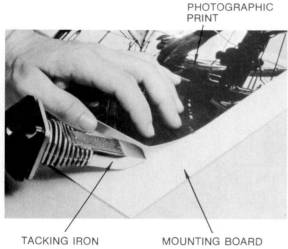

Fig. 144-6. Dry mounting tissue is attached to the print and mounting board with a tacking iron.

Fig. 144-7. Print trimmer.

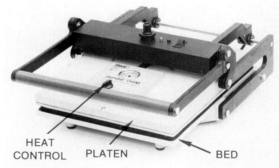

SEAL, INCORPORATED

Fig. 144-8. Dry mounting press.

To mount a photograph, attach a piece of dry mount tissue to the back of the photograph. The tissue should be the same size or a little larger than the photograph. A tacking iron or household iron is used to attach the dry mount tissue (Fig. 144-6). The dry mount tissue then should be trimmed to the exact size of the photograph with a hand shears or bar cutter. No tissue should be seen around the edges of the photograph.

Some photographs may need trimming to remove the borders or to change the size of the print (Fig. 144-7). It is important that the prints are trimmed to a perfect rectangle.

Mounting board should be cut so that it will have proper margins at the edges of the print. The margins at the top and sides are usually equal and the bottom margin is slightly larger. This will make the print look centered.

When mounting, mark the board where the photograph's edges will be located. This can be done with three very light pencil marks at the bottom and one side of the board.

Position the print so it is square with the board. Lift the corners of the print while holding the print in place and spot attach the print to the board with the tacking iron. This will keep the print from moving out of place.

The entire unit—of the print, mounting tissue, and mounting board—is then put into a mounting press (Fig. 144-8). You can put a piece of plain white paper over the print to protect the photographic surface. The best temperature for mounting a print will vary with the kind of paper, the thickness of the mounting board, and the kind of mounting tissue. You may need to make several tests before you find the correct combination of time and temperature.

UNIT 145 LEARNING EXPERIENCES: PHOTOGRAPHY

KEY TERMS

Unit 138

Aperture
Camera body
Camera lens
Parallax
Rangefinder

Shutter
Single lens reflex
   camera
Twin-lens reflex
   camera

Unit 139

Antihalation dye
ASA/ISO number
Emulsion
Grain

Latent image
Orthochromatic film
Panchromatic film

Unit 140

Aperture priority
   camera
Bracket exposure
f-stop
Highlights
Light meter
Middle tones

Reciprocity
Shadows
Shutter priority
   camera

Unit 141

Acetic acid
Daylight developing
   tank
Developer

Fixer
Negative
Stop bath
Wetting agent

Unit 142

Fiber-base paper
Resin-coated paper
Safelight

Unit 143

Contact print
Easel
Enlarger
Photograph

Projection print
Proof sheet
Timer

Unit 144

Ferrotype plate
Print dryer

DISCUSSION TOPICS

1. What are three advantages of a single-lens reflex camera?
2. How are film speed and grain found in negatives related?
3. How do the aperture numbers relate to the size of the aperture?
4. What are the purposes of each of the solutions used in processing film?
5. How should you determine the correct exposure for an enlargement?

ACTIVITIES

Unit 138

1. Obtain and examine several different kinds of cameras. Compare them by identifying the differences in essential parts.

Unit 140

2. Compare the light meters on five kinds of adjustable cameras. Are there differences? If so, why?

Units 139–142

3. Expose a roll of film using the following procedure. The procedure is designed for roll film with twelve exposures, but it can be done with larger or smaller rolls.
   a. Expose the first frame 3 f-stops greater than a normal exposure.
   b. Expose the second frame 2 f-stops greater than a normal exposure.
   c. Expose the third frame 1 f-stop greater than a normal exposure.
   d. Make a normal exposure on the fourth frame.
   e. Expose the fifth frame 1 f-stop smaller than a normal exposure.
   f. Expose the sixth frame 2 f-stops smaller than a normal exposure.
   g. Expose the seventh frame 3 f-stops smaller.
   h. Record the settings and expose the next five frames, varying the f-stop and shutter speed to obtain a normal exposure.

Process the film to obtain normal negatives. Look at the negatives and note the differences among them. Make good projection prints from the negatives, using normal contrast paper, and process the prints.

Units 137–144

4. Visit a photographic retail store and see the kinds of equipment available. Learn the cost of the equipment and supplies.
5. Visit a local professional photographer and ask about some of the techniques used to make photographs. What kinds of equipment does the photographer use? Prepare a detailed report on your visit.

Color reproduction can be made easily by using electrostatic copiers.
XEROX CORPORATION

17 DUPLICATING AND SPECIAL PRINTING PROCESSES

146 INTRODUCTION TO DUPLICATING AND SPECIAL PRINTING PROCESSES

Often information must be reproduced faster and cheaper than is possible when using the methods previously discussed in this book. The quality of the print is sometimes not as important as the time needed to pass on the information. Many industries need daily inventory records, production schedules, and production reports distributed to a limited number of persons. A real estate broker may need copies of official documents. School officials need daily records of students to distribute to teachers.

Limited-copy duplication is so important to

Fig. 146-1. A typical office offset lithography duplicator.

business and industry that extensive research has gone into developing new processes and machines. There are so many different kinds of processes and machines on the market that we cannot discuss them all in this section. In fact, many office copying methods and machines do not stay on the market long. Regular changes in technology have improved the quality and speed of reproduction processes. Many types of machines are now available. Improvements are making them even more versatile and efficient.

There are two kinds of fast, informal graphic reproduction. In this section, we will call them *duplicating* and *copying*. Which one to use depends on how rapidly the information must be distributed, what kind of equipment is available, which method is most economical (including labor), how many copies must be made, and how closely the original must be reproduced.

Inkjet printing and *heat transfer* will also be presented in this section. They do not fit well into other units of the book and they are important to know about.

DUPLICATING

There are several duplicating processes. In each, copies are made from an image carrier. An example is offset lithography duplication.

A direct image master, or other kind of master (plate) is prepared. It is placed on the printing press (duplicator) and copies are produced. The copies look exactly like the image on the master or plate. Figure 146-1 shows a small offset lithography duplicator. Offset lithography printing procedures are discussed in Sections 11–13 of this book and will not be included in this section. Two traditional graphic reproduction methods are *spirit* and *mimeograph duplication*. These are discussed in Unit 147.

COPYING

Copying is different from duplicating, because in copying, exact prints are made directly from an original. No additional image carrier is needed. Copying can be done much more quickly than most duplicating processes. Because of this, copying is more widely used than duplicating processes to make limited copies.

Nearly every business office has at least one copying machine. Some offices have several different machines with one or more special features. Each has advantages and disadvantages. These are discussed in Unit 148.

UNIT 147 SPIRIT AND MIMEOGRAPH DUPLICATION

Two methods of making limited numbers of copies are *spirit duplication* and *mimeograph duplication*. These methods have been popular because they make copies cheaply and easily. In both, little equipment is needed to prepare the masters for making copies. Electrostatic office copiers have reduced the use of these two methods. Nevertheless, the spirit and mimeograph duplicating processes are still useful for some purposes.

SPIRIT DUPLICATION

Spirit duplicating uses a special fluid (alcohol) to dissolve the aniline dye on the master (image carrier). The dissolved dye, usually purple, is what is seen on the duplicated sheet. Because the image on the master is eventually used up, the spirit duplicating process can produce only about 100 to 300 good copies from one master.

The duplicator consists of a master cylinder, an impression cylinder, a fluid container, and a fluid applicator (Fig. 147-1). The sheets are fed into the duplicator and pass against the appli-

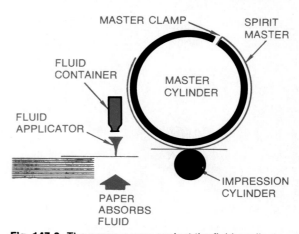

Fig. 147-1. Fundamental parts of a typical office spirit duplicator.

Fig. 147-2. The paper moves against the fluid applicator.

cator (Fig. 147-2). The paper absorbs a small amount of the duplicating fluid from the applicator. The paper then passes between the master and the impression cylinders (Fig. 147-3). The sheet of paper, still damp from the fluid, is pressed by the impression cylinder against the master on the master cylinder. The damp sheet dissolves a very small amount of the aniline dye from the master each time an image is duplicated. When the dye is gone, the master is discarded.

Spirit duplication master unit

The two main parts of a spirit duplication *master* are a piece of specially prepared paper called the master sheet and the analine dye sheet. (The aniline dye sheet is sometimes called the carbon sheet because it looks somewhat like a sheet of carbon paper.)

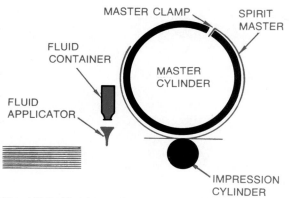

Fig. 147-3. The image is created because of pressure between the master cylinder and the impression cylinder.

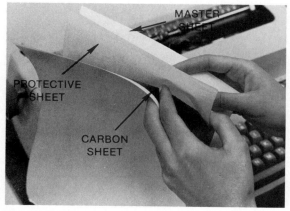

Fig. 147-4. The master unit.

The two parts of the master are often attached to each other, with a plain protective sheet of paper between them. This keeps the dye from transferring to the master sheet until desired (Fig. 147-4). When the master is prepared, the dye sheet is detached and the master sheet, on which the image has been deposited, is placed on the duplicator.

Master sheets and dye sheets can be bought separately. Masters come in several colors, such as red, green, black, blue, and purple. Purple is the color most often used because the dye can produce many more copies than the other colors.

Preparing the master

Spirit duplicator masters are prepared by putting pressure on the front side of the master sheet while the dye is on the back side. The dye image on the back side of the master sheet is in reverse. It must be in reverse because the image on the master sheet is again reversed when it is duplicated.

Spirit masters are usually prepared either by *typing* or *drawing* on them. Whatever method is used, the work is done on the front side of the master sheet.

Before typing on the spirit master, you should thoroughly clean the typewriter keys so they will make a clean, sharp image on the master. Do not forget to remove the protective sheets between the sheets of the master unit before inserting it into the typewriter. The

Fig. 147-5. Insert the master sheet with the open part up.

master unit should be placed in the typewriter so that the front part of the master sheet faces the typist. It is easier to make corrections on the master sheet if the open end of the master unit is put in the typewriter first (Fig. 147-5). Once the master unit has been rolled into place, type on it as you would on a regular sheet of paper. Keystrokes must be crisp so that the type strikes the master firmly and evenly but does not cut through it.

The spirit duplicating process can easily duplicate drawings. Drawing should be done with the master on a hard surface to get clean, sharp lines. Leave the protective sheet between the master unit and dye sheet while you sketch guidelines. When the guidelines are complete, remove the protective sheet and draw over the lines with a ball-point pen (Fig. 147-6). Replace the protective sheet until you are ready to print so unwanted marks or scratches will not be made on the master.

Multiple colors are easy with spirit duplicating. When making a master, just use a different color dye sheet for each color you want. All colors are duplicated at the same time on the spirit duplicating machine.

Making corrections

Corrections are made on spirit masters by scraping the dye off carefully with a sharp knife or razor blade. A small piece of new dye sheet paper should be placed where the error was removed and a new image placed on the master sheet.

This is done by rolling the master up in the cylinder until the error can be seen. Pull the master sheet back toward you and scrape off the

Fig. 147-6. Drawing lines on the master sheet.

Fig. 147-7. Scrape carbon off the back of the master sheet.

Fig. 147-8. A spirit duplicator with a spirit master attached to the master cylinder.

A.B. DICK COMPANY

dye where the error was located (Fig. 147-7). Then place a small unused dye piece behind the area with the dye surface toward the master. The master unit is rolled back into place in the typewriter and the correction made by striking the correct typewriter key. Then remove the small dye piece and continue to prepare the master.

Duplicating with the spirit master

Spirit masters are reproduced on duplicators similar to the hand-operated one shown in Figure 147-8. The master is attached to the master cylinder and the sheets are fed into the duplicator. When the desired number of copies are made, the master sheet is removed and discarded, or placed in a folder for future use.

MIMEOGRAPH DUPLICATING

The mimeograph duplicating process, sometimes called *stencil duplicating*, is an inexpensive and efficient printing method. More copies can be run from a mimeograph stencil or image carrier than from a spirit master. For mimeograph duplicating four things are needed—the stencil, ink, paper, and a mimeograph duplicator.

Mimeograph stencil

The *stencil* is a key part of the mimeograph process. A stencil is made from a fibrous, porous tissue that ink will pass through. The fibrous tissue is coated on both sides with a wax material that does not let ink pass through. The coating is made so that nearly any pressure applied to the surface will push the coating to the side, exposing the fibrous material (Fig. 147-10). Ink may then be squeezed through the stencil onto the paper below the stencil (Fig. 147-9).

A basic stencil has a stencil sheet, a typing cushion, and a backing sheet. Stencils also come with a plastic typing film over them. Typing film gives a broader image with heavier letters. It also reduces the chance of the typewriter cutting out areas of certain letters in the stencil, such as an *o*.

Most mimeograph stencils have several guide markings. These help the person preparing the stencil to know the best place to put the image and to see the duplicating area limit or boundaries. The holes at the top of the stencil hold it on the mimeograph duplicator.

A useful method of preparing mimeograph stencils is with an *electronic stencil maker* (Fig. 147-11). The instrument makes a stencil that looks exactly like the original copy. A paste-up copy is prepared as if for offset lithography printing. The paste-up is placed on one cylinder

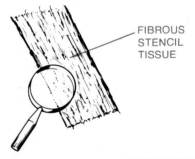

FIBROUS STENCIL TISSUE

A.B. DICK COMPANY

Fig. 147-10. The core of a stencil is made from a fibrous material.

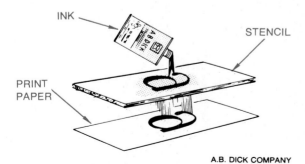

INK

STENCIL

PRINT PAPER

A.B. DICK COMPANY

Fig. 147-9. Ink passes through spots on a stencil to produce an image on paper.

GESTETNER CORPORATION

Fig. 147-11. An electronic stencil maker that can make color separations.

of the stencil maker and a special mimeograph stencil is put on the other. The stencil maker electronically scans the image on the original and reproduces the copy on the stencil. Some stencil makers can be used to make color separations. A mimeograph stencil maker is an excellent example of the large electronic scanners used in making four-color process separations and gravure printing cylinders.

Mimeograph inks and papers

Mimeograph inks are more fluid than most printing inks. Several inks are available for

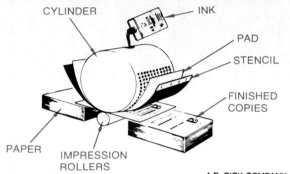

A.B. DICK COMPANY

Fig. 147-12. The paper is pressed against the stencil by pressure from the stencil cylinder and impression rollers.

mimeograph duplication—quick drying, paste, emulsion, and oil-base inks. Most kinds of inks come in black and in colors. Your duplicator dealer can help you choose the right one for your situation.

One of the single most important factors in successful mimeograph duplication is using the right paper. The paper should be absorbent or the ink will smear or set-off. Bond paper and card stocks for mimeograph duplication are available in several colors.

Operating the mimeograph duplicator

The essential parts of the mimeograph duplicator are the cylinder, impression roll, and ink pad. Duplicators also have mechanisms to feed the paper between the cylinder and the impression roll. Ink is put inside the cylinder and the stencil is attached to the ink pad. When pressure is created between the cylinder and the impression roll, the ink passes through the open parts of the stencil and creates the image on the paper (Fig. 147-12).

Hand and power mimeograph duplicators are equally efficient if operated correctly. The fol-

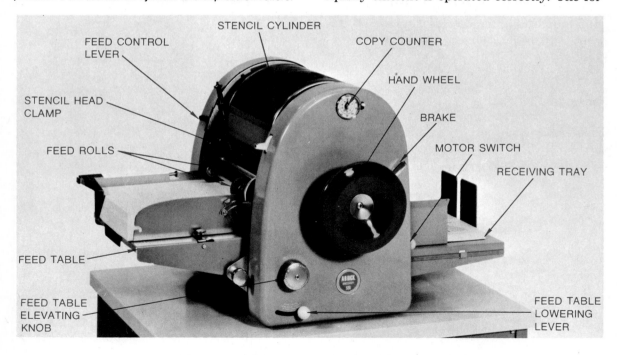

Fig. 147-13. An electrically operated mimeograph duplicator.

lowing procedure is used to produce copies with a power-operated duplicator (Fig. 147-13).

1. Clamp the stencil to the cylinder, using the head clamp. The stencil is placed on the cylinder so that the image is upside down.
2. Load the paper in the feed table.
3. Lower the feed rolls to touch the paper.
4. Turn on the duplicator. The sheets are fed through the machine between the cylinder and the impression rolls and into the receiving tray.
5. When the desired number of copies has been duplicated, stop the duplicator.
6. Remove the stencil and place it in an absorbent storage folder for future use.
7. Cover the cylinder with the protective cover sheet. The cover sheet keeps ink from drying on the pad. It is also wise to keep the entire duplicator covered to protect it from dust and dirt.

UNIT 148 OFFICE COPYING METHODS

In recent years, office copying methods have caused many changes in both large and small businesses. Copying equipment saves time and money for business operations large and small. Most offices have at least one copier and many have several.

Copiers are most often used when few copies are needed of several originals. They are also used when there is not time to have copies printed or duplicated by other methods. Sometimes copier quality is not as good as with some duplicating methods, but in general the quality of today's copiers is excellent.

Many different companies make copiers. Some companies have added features like automatic feeding of originals and sorting of copies. Office copiers even make copies in colors. Some copiers make copies from information from computers.

In this unit, we will discuss the most commonly used copiers. The most popular type of copier uses the electrostatic process. In a few situations, *thermographic* (heat) copiers are used.

ELECTROSTATIC COPIERS

Electrostatic copiers are the most widely used copiers. The quality of electrostatic copiers has improved and in some models is extremely good. Some copiers can make more than 100 copies per minute. Copiers are also made that reproduce images on both sides of the sheet.

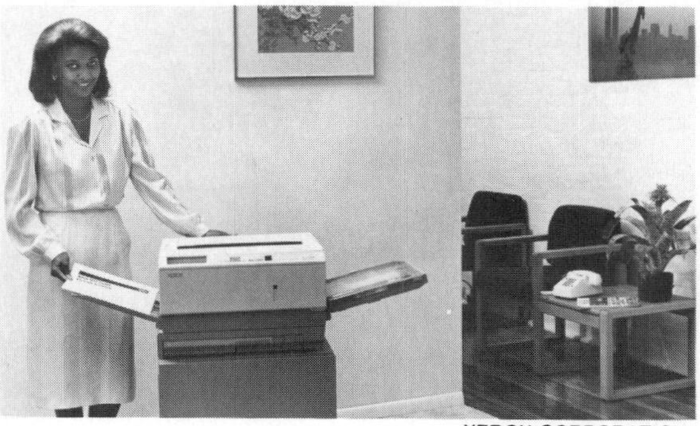

XEROX CORPORATION

Fig. 148-1. A small electrostatic copier.

XEROX CORPORATION

Fig. 148-2. A large copier with a variety of special features.

There are two types of electrostatic copiers. The first is the *transfer-electrostatic copier*. It is the most popular because it makes copies on regular bond paper. It is sometimes called the *plain-paper copier*. The second kind of electrostatic copier is the *direct-electrostatic copier*. It needs a special paper with a coated surface.

Transfer-electrostatic process

Several different models of direct-electrostatic copiers are made. Smaller copiers, like the one in Figure 148-1, are commonly used in offices where only a few copies are needed. Other copiers are much larger and can make over 100 copies a minute (Fig. 148-2). Originals are fed into the machine automatically and images from different originals are placed on both sides of a sheet of paper. Also, the copies can be sorted into the same order as the original manuscript.

The transfer-electrostatic process uses a selenium plate or drum. Selenium is a material that, when combined with metal, has an electrical conductivity that varies with the intensity of illumination or light.

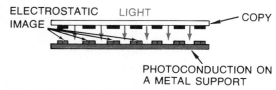

Fig. 148-3. Light reflected from the non-image areas of the copy causes the electrostatic charges to leave the drum in those areas.

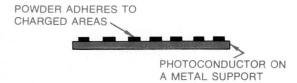

Fig. 148-4. Toner adheres to the electrostatic charge on the drum.

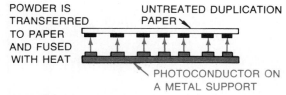

Fig. 148-5. Toner is transferred to the paper to form the final print.

When making a copy by this process, the selenium drum first is coated with a uniform positive electrostatic charge. This is done inside the machine in total darkness. As long as the selenium drum remains in darkness the electrostatic charges will remain on it.

After the drum is charged, it is exposed to the original copy through a lens system much like that in a process camera. Where light is reflected from the non-image areas on the copy and hits the drum, the electrostatic charge leaves the drum. But dark areas of the copy reflect little or no light and so the areas on the selenium drum that correspond to the dark areas of the copy will keep the positive electrostatic charge. No image can be seen on the drum at this time, but it has an *electrostatic image*. (NOTE: To show the electrostatic principle more clearly, Figure 148-3 uses a flat surface instead of the usual curved drum.)

When the electrostatic image has been placed on the drum, *toner* is distributed over the drum. Toner contains a pigment (color) and is negatively charged. The toner is attracted to the positively charged selenium drum and forms a visible powder image in reverse on the drum (Fig. 148-4).

A sheet of regular, untreated bond paper is placed over the powder image on the drum. The paper is given a positive electrostatic charge. The toner transfers from the drum to the paper

XEROX CORPORATION

Fig. 148-6. A color electrostatic copier.

(Fig. 148-5). The toner is only lightly attracted to the sheet of paper and can be removed easily by brushing the image. To make the image permanent, the toner is fused by heating the paper. The toner powder melts and bonds to the paper. Last, the machine cleans the drum to make it ready for the next copy.

Most electrostatic copiers make only black and white copies. Some copiers can make full color copies from color originals (Fig. 148-6). Copies can be made from color photographs, color prints, drawings, or transparencies. The machine will copy on plain paper, mylar (plastic) sheets, adhesive-backed paper, card stock, and cover materials. The quality does not yet match that of printing processes. But electrostatic imaging has many uses and shows much promise for the future.

Direct-electrostatic process

The direct-electrostatic copying process is similar to the transfer process. The primary difference is that the electrostatic image is produced directly on the print paper and is not transferred to the paper from a drum. Paper treated with zinc-oxide is used. The coating makes the paper heavier than the regular sheets used with the transfer-electrostatic process.

The special paper is first given a negative electrostatic charge inside the copier in total darkness. It is then exposed to the original copy with a lens system similar to the one in a process camera. Light from the non-image areas of the copy neutralizes the negative charges on the treated paper. The areas on the special paper

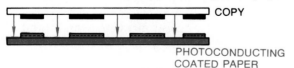

COPY

PHOTOCONDUCTING COATED PAPER

Fig. 148-7. Direct electrostatic process.

PHOTOCONDUCTING COATED PAPER

Fig. 148-8. Powder adheres to the electrostatic charges that remain on the paper.

that correspond to the image areas of the original copy keep the electrostatic pattern to form an electrostatic image that is a duplicate of the original copy (Fig. 148-7).

The image is made visible by the positively charged toner powder that adheres to the paper when it is applied (Fig. 148-8). As in the transfer-electrostatic process, the paper is heated to fuse the toner to the paper. If the copier is working right, the copies will be exact duplicates of the original.

THERMOGRAPHIC PROCESS

The thermographic process was once popular as an office copying method. However, since the advancements of electrostatic copying, it is used much less. The major use of thermographic copying today is to make transparencies for overhead projectors.

The thermographic process produces an image by a heat reaction. The image of the original copy must contain carbon black or a metallic compound in order to produce an image on the print paper. A specially treated paper is used that is coated with compounds that form a colored substance when heated.

The treated sheet of paper is placed over the original copy, with the treated side up. Infrared radiation passes through it and strikes the original. The infrared radiation that strikes the image of the copy below is absorbed and becomes heated (if the image is carbon black or metallic). The heat that comes from the image areas of the original copy is transmitted to the heat-sensitive paper. This causes the compound to form a colored image that corresponds to the image areas of the original copy (Fig. 148-9).

INFARED RADIATION

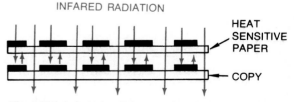

HEAT SENSITIVE PAPER

COPY

Fig. 148-9. Infrared radiation produces an image on heat-sensitive paper.

UNIT 149 INKJET PRINTING AND HEAT TRANSFER

This unit describes two graphic arts technologies that are different from those included in other units: inkjet printing and heat transfer. Both have special applications. They are limited in their use when compared with other major printing methods—letterpress, lithography, gravure, and screen printing. These technologies facilitate printing on certain products on which it would otherwise not be possible to print.

INKJET PRINTING

All of the printing methods discussed in this book make images by pressing ink against another material. In contrast, inkjet printing is done by spraying tiny drops of ink on material. The only thing that touches the material being printed is the ink.

Inkjet printing is one of the dot matrix technologies. In these techniques, images are formed by dots that overlap each other. Each dot is formed by a drop of ink that comes from a *drop generator*. Ink is forced through a tiny

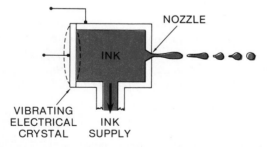

Fig. 149-1. A drawing of a drop generator for an inkjet printer. The crystal forces ink drops out of the very tiny nozzle.

nozzle by a vibrating electrical crystal. This creates drops that have the same size, speed, and spacing (Fig. 149-1).

Each drop passes through a *charge electrode* that gives different electrical charges to the

drops. The amount of electrical charge given to the drops of ink is determined by an electrical control unit (Fig. 149-2).

The drops then pass through *deflection plates* that have a constant high voltage. The amount of charge on the drops will cause them to deflect in different directions. Drops that are not used to form the image are caught by a *gutter*. The ink that is caught in the gutter is returned to the system to be reused.

Inkjet printers are controlled by computers. The computers (input device) form images (words, illustrations, etc.) by defining their digital matrix. A control unit, called a *character generator,* transforms the input information into electrical charges, which then form the drops of ink. The drops are given precise electrical charges so they will deflect and form images on the material being printed (Fig. 149-3).

Images formed by inkjet printing have slightly uneven edges (Fig. 149-4). Notice that the normal size print looks like ordinary typewriter type. However, the enlarged type shows the individual dots. The more drops in an image, the better the appearance. Larger characters need more drops.

There are many applications of inkjet printing in the printing industries and in other areas of manufacturing. Because it is controlled by a computer, inkjet printing can rapidly

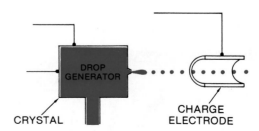

Fig. 149-2. Ink drops get an electrical charge from a charge electrode.

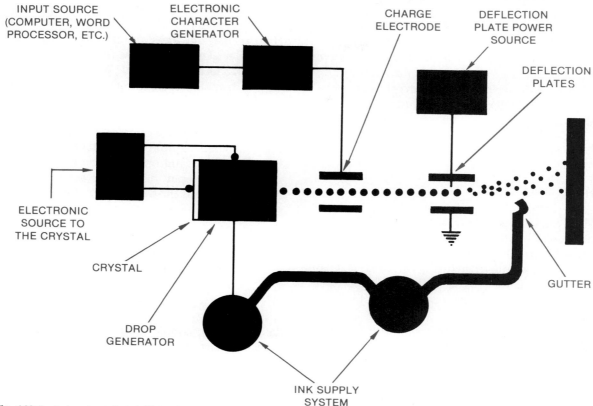

INPUT SOURCE
(COMPUTER, WORD
PROCESSOR, ETC.)

ELECTRONIC
CHARACTER
GENERATOR

CHARGE
ELECTRODE

DEFLECTION
PLATE POWER
SOURCE

DEFLECTION
PLATES

ELECTRONIC
SOURCE TO
THE CRYSTAL

CRYSTAL

DROP
GENERATOR

INK SUPPLY
SYSTEM

GUTTER

Fig. 149-3. A drawing of an inkjet printing system.

change the images being printed from one item to another. A major application of inkjet printing is to place mailing addresses on magazines and other printed material. Inkjet printing is also widely used to customize printed material by adding different messages to the material.

Another advantage of inkjet printing is that image size and shape image can be formed. The main limitation is the amount of information in the computer. Inkjet printers, in many cases, now do work automatically that was previously done on typewriters. They work much faster and are much quieter than typewriters.

Because the inkjet printer does not touch the surface of the material, it can print on uneven surfaces. It is used to print dates on the surface of eggs and codes on the surface of electrical wire. Inkjet printing can also be done on material that must be kept sterile during its production and packaging.

Fig. 149-5. A color graphics printer used to produce copies from a computer in full color.

ABCDEFGHIJKLMNOPQRSTUVWXYZ
abcdefghijklmnopqrstuvwxyz
±@#$%¢&*()_+°":?.,1234567890

LMNOP

Fig. 149-4. When letters from an inkjet system are enlarged, the shape of the dots can be seen.

A major application of inkjet printing is to place code numbers and dates on food packages. For example, most soft drink cans have numbers printed on the bottom with inkjet to identify when and where the drink was made. Figure 149-5 shows an inkjet printer used to produce color prints from a computer.

HEAT TRANSFER

Heat transfer is not considered a new printing process. The regular printing processes are used to produce the heat transfer patterns. The most common printing method is gravure, but screen, offset lithography, letterpress, and flexography are all used to print heat transfer patterns.

In the heat transfer process, patterns or designs are printed on paper with special ink. The ink (sometimes called dye) is transferred to another material by heat and pressure. Heat transfer designs are usually transferred to textiles. The designs are printed in reverse (wrong-reading) on the paper. When the design is transferred to the polyester fabric, it will be right-reading.

Inks used for heat transfer are called *heat sublimation inks* or dyes. They look like regular ink when printed on the transfer paper, but when heat and pressure are applied, the ink turns to vapor. The vapor goes into the material to form the design (Fig. 149-6).

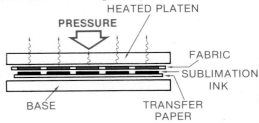

Fig. 149-6. Fabric and heat transfer paper are placed under heat and pressure. The ink turns to vapor and transfers to the fabric.

UNIT 150 LEARNING EXPERIENCES: DUPLICATING AND SPECIAL PRINTING PROCESSES

KEY WORDS

Unit 146
Copying   Duplicating

Unit 147
Mimeograph duplication
Spirit duplication

Unit 148
Direct-electrostatic   Thermographic copier
Electrostatic copier   Transfer-electrostatic

Unit 149
Heat sublimation ink
Heat transfer
Inkjet printing

DISCUSSION TOPICS

1. What is the difference between *duplicating* and *copying*?
2. In addition to its primary purpose of making mimeograph stencils what value is there in using an electronic stencil maker?
3. Explain the difference between *transfer electrostatic* and *direct electrostatic* copiers?
4. What is inkjet printing?
5. What are some ways to print heat transfer patterns on the transfer paper?

ACTIVITIES

Unit 147

1. Take a spirit duplication master and identify the parts of the master. With the protective sheet in place, sketch a drawing on the master sheet. Remove the protective sheet and complete the drawing on the master by using several different writing instruments, such as wide, medium, and fine pencils and ball-point pens.
2. Prepare a mimeograph stencil by using an electronic stencil maker. You will need to make a high quality paste-up first. Plan to use body type, display type, and an illustration in your copy. After you have made the stencil, duplicate 100 copies on a mimeograph duplicator.

Unit 148

3. Make copies on two or more different office copiers. Use a prepared paste-up or create one that contains different kinds of copy—line illustration, halftone positive print, body type, and display type. Locate a transfer-electrostatic copier, a direct-electrostatic copier, and, if possible, a thermographic copier. Make 10 copies on each machine using the same paste-up. Most copiers have light-to-dark copy adjustments; make your copies at different settings. Keep accurate records on each copy—the process, kind of machine, and light-dark setting. When finished, compare your results and share your findings with your instructor and fellow class members.

Unit 149

4. If your instructor can arrange it, take a field trip to a company that has an inkjet printing system. Observe the operation of this system very closely. If possible, have the operator show how the system works. Find out why the company chose to use inkjet printing over other available imaging methods.
5. Produce two or three heat transfer prints on T-shirts or sweat shirts. Use either screen printing or offset lithography to print the single or multiple-color image on the transfer paper. You will need to prepare high quality artwork if you want heat transfer prints. Use the heat transfer press with care, because it becomes very hot when the images are transferred to the textile product. Compare your results with a commercial heat transfer print.

Cutting thumb indexes in the body of a dictionary.

SMYTH MANUFACTURING COMPANY

18 FINISHING AND BINDING

SECTION

151 INTRODUCTION TO FINISHING AND BINDING

UNIT

Finishing and binding make the products of design and layout personnel, typesetters, camera operators, platemakers, and press operators ready for use by the public.

Books have played an important part in the development of the civilized world. The oldest books were baked clay tablets used in Asia Minor about 5,500 years ago. Another early form of books was the scroll, a roll of animal skins or crude paper used by the Egyptians, Chinese, Greeks, and Romans.

The art of hand bookbinding developed rapidly after the invention of movable metal type by Johann Gutenberg in 1450. When machines could print hundreds and thousands of sheets an hour, binding methods had to keep pace. The book form used today was developed and has proved its value.

Early bookbinders did everything by hand. Most of the equipment and hand tools were made by the bookbinder. Using them took long hours of hard work.

Figure 151-1 shows a typical eighteenth-century bookbindery. Note that all operations

CHALLENGE MACHINERY COMPANY

Fig. 151-2. A complete binding system gathers the pages, binds them with wire stitches, trims them to size, and prepares them for use.

Fig. 151-1. A typical eighteenth-century bookbindery. Several important binding operations can be seen. Left, A. Beating folded screens of a book so that they will lie flat; B. Stitching folded sections to the heavy cords that hold the book together; C. Trimming the edges of a freshly sewn book on a ploughing press; and D. Pressing freshly bound books in a large standing press. Right, 1-3. The blocks and hammer used by the binder;

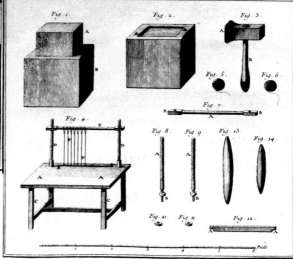

DIDEROT'S ENCYCLOPEDIA/COLONIAL WILLIAMSBURG

4. The sewing frame, 5-6; Twine; 7-12, Parts of the sewing frame; and 13-14. Wood or bond folders.

were done by hand. Modern binding methods and equipmnent have improved book construction quality beyond the dreams of the early bookbinders. Thousands of high-quality books are produced in a single day by automated equipment (Fig. 151-2).

Not all printed sheets are bound into books. Some have only to be cut to size, folded, or perforated to be useful. These several operations are commonly called *finishing the sheets*. Several things can be done to a printed sheet of paper to make it more useful without binding it into a book. These specific items and many others are discussed in detail in Unit 153, "Finishing Methods."

UNIT **152** SAFETY IN FINISHING AND BINDING

Finishing and binding tools and equipment must be used carefully. Read and follow these safety suggestions very closely to protect yourself and fellow students.

Permission. Always get permission from someone in charge before using the paper cutter, hot stamp press, wire stitcher, and other power equipment.

Jewelry. Remove rings, bracelets, and wrist watches before operating machines with moving parts such as those just mentioned.

Paper cutter knife. Keep your fingers away from the razor-sharp cutter-knife edge. Always keep the clamp below the knife.

Hands. Keep both hands on the lever or control buttons when cutting. Be careful when using the hot stamp machine not to burn your hands. Keep hands and fingers out from under the head of the wire stitcher.

Hand shears. Use hand shears with care. Never point them at fellow classmates or workers. Eyes can easily be injured when hand shears are used carelessly.

Electrical wire. Keep electrical wire from touching the heated part of the hot stamp machine. If the insulated covering of the wire shows wear, repair or replace it.

Wire stitcher head. Be sure not to have anything under the stitching head when you turn the power on. Sometimes the trip pedal has been pushed accidentally while the machine was turned off. Check this. Don't be surprised.

Safety glasses. Wear safety glasses when operating the wire stitcher.

Removing staples. Use a special puller and not your fingernails to remove staples. Staple ends are sharp.

Binder's knife. Handle the binder's knife carefully. Keep it sharp for easier use.

Hot glue pot. Keep the glue pot clean. Put it where it will not be knocked over or touched accidentally.

Sewing needle. Always know where the sewing needle is. Use it with care and protect your fingers while sewing.

Backing press. The clamping pressure of the backing press is tremendous. Keep fingers and hands from between its jaws.

Back or dovetail saw. Handle the saw carefully when cutting the sewing opening in the binding edge of the signatures. Keep it sharp.

Machine operation. Only one person at a time should operate a machine. It is not safe for two or more persons to try to use the same machine at the same time.

UNIT 153 FINISHING METHODS

There are several finishing operations that can make printed sheets of paper more useful. It is not always necessary to bind two-dimensional graphic materials into a book. Study the following operations to understand the various finishing methods.

CUTTING

Several different types of machines may be used to cut and trim sheets of paper. They vary from the office-style bar cutter in Figure 153-1 and the single-knife hydraulic cutter in Figure 153-2 to the fully automatic hydraulic three-knife book trimmer shown in Figure 153-3.

Each of these machines is designed to do *cutting* and *trimming* with accuracy and speed. The operation of a hydraulic paper cutter is described in Unit 154. Cutting is probably the most common finishing operation, regardless of the binding used.

FOLDING

Folding is the act of doubling over a sheet of paper to make creases or folds. Paper can be doubled over several times to form several pages. Many attractive folders and brochures can be made by creatively folding paper. Figure 153-4 illustrates some common paper folds.

Sizes and designs of paper-folding machines vary from light-duty office types (Fig. 153-5) to heavy-duty types (Fig. 153-6). Large complex folding machines that cut and fold the printed web of paper into book or magazine signatures can also be attached directly to roll-fed presses.

CHALLENGE MACHINERY COMPANY

Fig. 153-2. A single-knife hydraulic paper cutter.

Fig. 153-3. A fully automatic three-knife book trimmer.

MICHAEL BUSINESS MACHINES

Fig. 153-1. A table-top bar paper cutter.

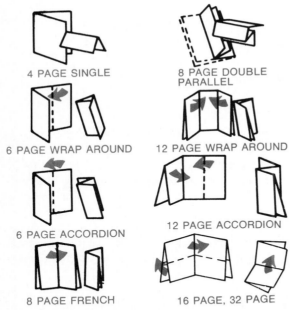

Fig. 153-4. Several common ways of folding paper.

BAUMFOLDER CORPORATION

Fig. 153-6. This industrial folder can fold a 32-page signature.

CHALLENGE MACHINERY COMPANY

Fig. 153-5. A typical office letter-folding machine.

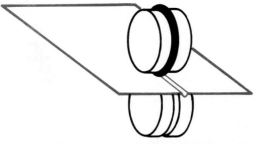

Fig. 153-7. A tongue-and-groove set of scoring rollers.

SCORING

Scoring puts a crease in a sheet of paper to help it fold properly. Creasing or scoring the paper in a narrow line weakens paper fibers and makes the sheet fold easily.

Two methods are commonly used to score.

The oldest uses a type-high, round-face scoring rule. A straight piece of rule is locked in a chase and placed in a platen press or in a special scoring machine. The paper is creased when the rule strikes it.

The second method of scoring is done by the rotary principle. A special set of tongue-and-groove rollers (Fig. 153-7) can be attached to many presses and folding machines. Special perforating machines also score by this principle (Fig. 153-10).

Most heavy or thick papers must be scored before folding. This is done on the paper folder during the folding operation. It is good practice to score the sheet as shown in Figure 153-8. Scoring a sheet on the wrong side can make a poor fold.

PERFORATING

Perforating means cutting a series of slits or punching a series of holes in a sheet of paper to make it easy to tear. There are three common methods of perforating (Fig. 153-9):

1. The perforating rule, used on a platen or cylinder press.
2. The pin bar, used on a special machine which punches holes in a sheet.
3. A perforating wheel, attached to the ejector section of a press or to the delivery end of a paper folder.

Specially designed equipment can score and perforate at a high rate of speed (Fig. 153-10). This machine uses the scoring and perforating wheel arrangement. Commercial graphic arts plants that have a large volume of perforating and scoring use machines of this type. The small community printer, however, uses the platen press, pin-bar punch perforator, or folding machine.

GATHERING AND COLLATING

Gathering is the assembling of signatures (large sheets folded to form pages) in the correct order before binding. It is done by either hand or machine. Most people have collected several sheets of paper and then stapled them to form a booklet at one time or another. On a larger scale, this is an important phase in the completing of a published work.

Collating is often confused with gathering. To *collate* means to gather single sheets of paper in proper order. A booklet of several pages can be made by stapling these pages. Office personnel

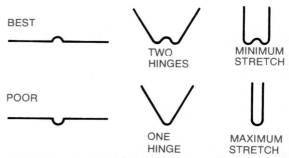

Fig. 153-8. The proper and improper way to fold a sheet of paper after scoring.

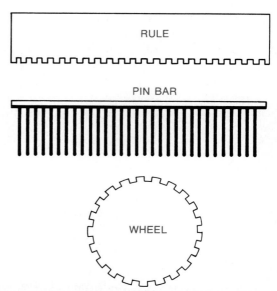

Fig. 153-9. Three common ways to perforate sheets of paper.

F. P. ROSBACK COMPANY

Fig. 153-10. A high-speed scoring and perforating machine.

do a lot of collating, putting together business reports, market predictions, and other duplicated items.

Page-gathering equipment ranges from the desk-top, semi-hand-operated type in Figure 153-11 to the programmed automatic sorter shown in Figure 153-12.

The latter is placed at the delivery end of a duplicator or offset lithography press. It delivers the sheets to individual bins. After the several pages of a booklet have been reproduced, the gathered ones are bound and the job is complete.

Large binderies use equipment that can gather single sheets or folded signatures. A multi-station, side-gathering machine is shown in Figure 153-13. Machines like this gather, straighten, and deliver signatures to the binding unit. Usually these machines also stitch the pages or signatures together and often trim all three sides in one operation.

PUNCHING AND DRILLING

Punching and drilling are necessary when pages need holes for inserting in ring binders. The hand paper-punch or the three-hole notebook punch are used in offices. Heavy-duty *punching* equipment is used by graphic arts binderies to produce holes in large-volume work. Specially shaped holes can be punched in a sheet of paper (Fig. 153-14) with the same equipment used to punch standard round holes.

PITNEY-BOWES

Fig. 153-12. An automatic sorting machine used with a duplicator to gather sheets.

MCCAIN MANUFACTURING CORPORATION

Fig. 153-13. This multi-station gathering machine opens signatures and positions them for wire stitching and trimming.

PAPER EDGE

Fig. 153-14. Specially shaped holes can be punched in sheets of paper.

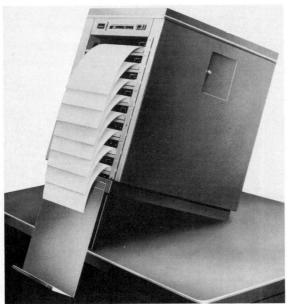

PITNEY-BOWES

Fig. 153-11. A desk-top semi-automated gathering machine.

Drilling machines are used primarily for round holes, but special attachments can make some different shapes. Also cornering of sheets can be done. With drilling, several hundred sheets can be drilled at one time, where only a few sheets can be punched at one time. Drilling machines vary from the single-head bench model in Figure 153-15 to the multiple-head floor model shown in Figure 153-16.

DIE CUTTING

Die cutting is the process of cutting paper or other sheet materials into special shapes. The cutting die is prepared by sawing the shape that is to be die cut into a piece of ¾-inch plywood. The cutting rule is then inserted into the space made by the saw blade. Cork or rubber squares are fastened to the wood near the die. They force the stock from the die after an impression is made. Laser cutting equipment is now being used to prepare die cutting boards.

Standard platen and cylinder letterpresses can be used for die-cutting if rollers are removed, but special heavy-duty machines are needed for high-volume work (Fig. 153-17). Almost any shape can be die cut.

HOT STAMPING

Hot stamping is used to put type or illustrations on covers of casebound books. Basically, hot stamping is an image-transfer process. It is commonly thought of, however, as a finishing pro-

CHALLENGE MACHINERY COMPANY

Fig. 153-16. A multiple-head floor-model paper drill.

BRANDTJEN & KLUGE

Fig. 153-17. A heavy-duty, automatic die-cutting and embossing press.

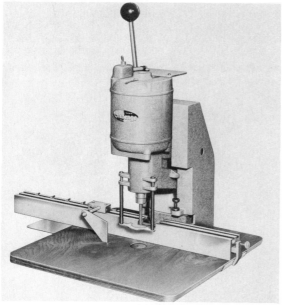

CHALLENGE MACHINERY COMPANY

Fig. 153-15. A single-head bench-model paper drill.

cess because it is part of the completion of bound books. Gold, silver, or colored foil is placed between the type and the book cloth, and, through heat and pressure, a permanent image is formed. Machines for this process vary from small hand-operated ones (Fig. 153-18) to heavy-duty hydraulic operated types (Fig. 153-19).

LAMINATING

In the graphic arts, *laminating* is the process of placing a thin layer of transparent film, polyester or polyethylene, on both sides of a printed sheet. This protects the printed materials from rough use, water, oil, and chemical materials (Fig. 153-20). Laminating also brings out the full brilliance of materials printed in color.

Methods of applying the transparent film range from hand-operated devices to completely automatic laminators (Fig. 153-21). All methods of transparent-film lamination work by heat and pressure.

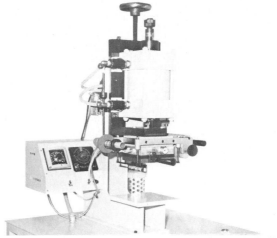

APEX MACHINE COMPANY

Fig. 153-19. A heavy-duty, hydraulic hot-stamping machine with a maximum stamping area of 4¼ by 6 inches (107.9 by 152.4 mm).

GENERAL BINDING CORPORATION

Fig. 153-20. This special unit laminates documents between sheets of tough plastic film.

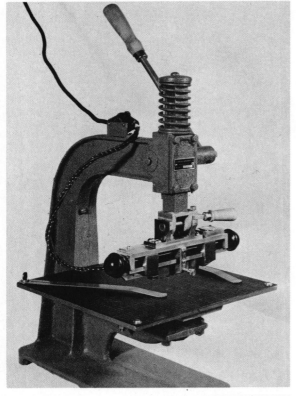

HALVORFOLD-KWIKPRINT COMPANY

Fig. 153-18. A table-model hot-stamping machine.

GENERAL BINDING CORPORATION

Fig. 153-21. A table-model laminating machine. It holds two rolls of polyester film and can laminate products continuously.

UNIT 154 PAPER-CUTTING PROCEDURES

Throughout the process of preparing and completing printed materials, paper must be cut. Paper often must be cut to size before it can be printed. Paper coming off a press generally needs to be cut or trimmed. Paper cutters are important machines in the graphic arts industry.

Hand- and power-operated paper cutters work in much the same way. The primary rule with all paper cutters is *Think and Practice Safety*. A machine containing a razor-sharp knife is not a toy.

When cutting paper to size, planning the best cut is important. Many hundreds of dollars can be wasted quickly by thoughtless cuts. An operator of a paper cutter should prepare a cutting chart before making the first cut. The operator must figure how many smaller press sheets can be cut from one large stock sheet, the number of stock sheets needed, the amount of waste that can be expected, and the best order for making cuts.

PLANNING FOR CUTTING

1. Determine the sheet size for printing. This is called a *press sheet*.
2. Select the kind of paper to be used.
3. Measure the large stock sheet size.
4. Calculate the number of press sheets that can be obtained from the stock sheet. Figures 154-1 and 154-2 illustrate methods of finding this information. Study the illustrations closely to understand each method.
5. Figure the number of stock sheets needed. After you know how many press sheets you can get from a stock sheet, use simple division to find how many stock sheets you will need. A 10 percent press spoilage is commonly figured for average press runs of a few hundred to a few thousand copies.

How to figure the number of stock sheets needed.

Number of copies wanted	= 750
10% press spoilage	= 75
Total press sheets needed	= 825

17 press sheets can be cut from each stock sheet.

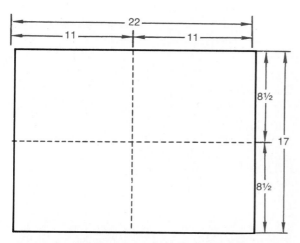

Fig. 154-1. A drawing method of calculating the number of press sheets obtainable from one stock sheet; stock sheet 17 by 22 inches (431.8 by 558.8 mm); press sheet 8½ by 11 inches (215.9 by 279.4 mm); four press sheets obtained.

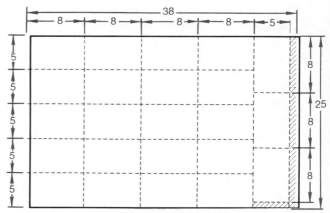

Fig. 154-2. A second drawing method of calculating the number of press sheets obtainable from one stock sheet; stock sheet 25 by 28 inches (63.5 by 71.1 cm); press sheet 5 by 8 inches (12.7 by 20.3 cm); 23 press sheets obtained.

$825 \div 17 = 48^9/_{18} = 49$ stock sheets needed to get 825 press sheets.

NOTE: Always round up.

6. Make a cutting chart like the one in Figure 154-3 to plan the paper cutting operation. The order of cuts is important. Referring to Figure 154-2 will help you to make the right cuts. Prepare your cutting chart so that you make the least possible number of paper cutter settings.

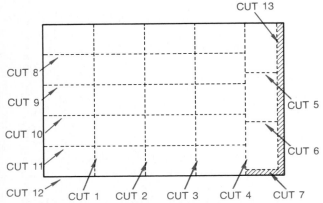

Fig. 154-3. Cutting chart to determine the order of cuts.

PAPER CUTTER PARTS

Learn the parts of the paper cutter and their purposes (Fig. 154-4). This will help you become a careful, safe, and efficient operator.

Backgage. An adjustable part against which paper is placed for cutting to the desired size.

Backgage handwheel. The wheel that adjusts the depth of the backgage from the cutting knife. Turning the wheel clockwise moves the backgage back to leave the sheet larger. Turning it counterclockwise makes the sheet smaller.

Backgage indicator. A lighted dial indicator with a magnified image so the backgage can be positioned accurately in inch or millimeter measurements.

Clamp. A pressure bar that lowers onto the paper to keep it from moving while being cut.

Clamp control. This hydraulic control raises and lowers the clamp.

Cutting stick. A strip of wood or special synthetic material that the knife strikes after cut-

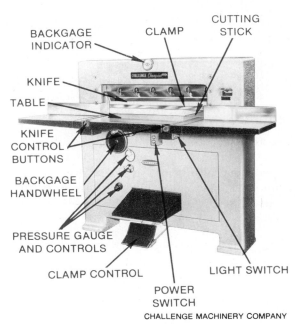

CHALLENGE MACHINERY COMPANY

Fig. 154-4. A hydraulic paper cutter that can cut paper up to $30^1/_2$ inches (77.5 cm) wide.

ting through the paper. If the sharp steel knife pressed against the steel table, it would rapidly dull.

Knife. The knife should always be razor-sharp. It is the heart of a paper cutter.

Knife control buttons. Both of these control buttons must be pushed at the same time to make the knife cycle down and back up. The two control buttons are safety devices. Because both hands are needed, they cannot be placed under the knife during the cutting cycle.

Light switch. This switch controls the light located in the framework above the center-front table.

Fig. 154-5. Turning the backgage handwheel to position the backgage before inserting the paper.

Power switch. This is an electrical off-on switch used to start the hydraulic system that operates the clamp and knife.

Pressure gauge and controls. The gauge is used to determine clamp pressure, measured in PSI (pounds per square inch). The controls make necessary pressure adjustments.

Table. The flat, smooth horizontal surface on which the paper rests while being cut.

PAPER CUTTER OPERATION

1. Move the backgage to the proper cutting size by turning the backgage hand wheel (Fig. 154-5). Read the backgage position indicator, which shows the depth of cut to be made in either inch or metric measure (Fig. 154-6).

Fig. 154-6. The backgage can be positioned very accurately with the magnified image in the backgage indicator.

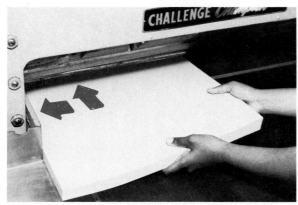

Fig. 154-7. Placing the paper against the backgage and left side of the paper cutter.

2. Tighten the locking screw for the backgage wheel when the backgage is where you want it.

3. Jog the paper.
4. Position the paper on the table against the backgage and the left side of the paper cutter (Fig. 154-7).
5. Lower the clamp by pushing against the top part of the clamp control with your foot (Fig. 154-8).

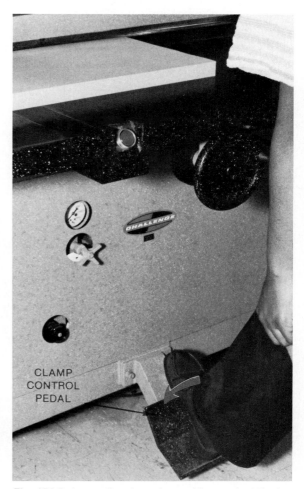

Fig. 154-8. Lower the clamp by pushing against the top portion of the clamp control pedal.

6. Push the knife control buttons to activate the knife (Fig. 154-9). When the knife reaches the cutting stick, release the buttons and the knife will return to the upward position. The hydraulic clamp will also return to the raised position.
7. Remove the cut paper from the front table. Place it on a nearby table or counter in a neat stack. Turn each lift of paper (the

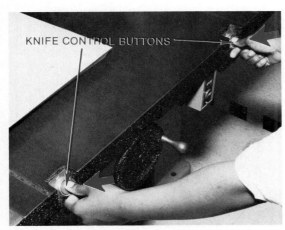

Fig. 154-9. Push the two knife control buttons to cut. When the knife reaches the cutting stick, release the control buttons to return the knife and clamp to their raised positions.

Fig. 154-10. Turning each lift of paper after cutting helps the operator pick up the paper for successive cuts.

amount of paper convenient to handle) slightly so each lift will be easy to pick up for successive cuts (Fig. 154-10).

8. Remove the paper that is against the backgage. It is perfectly safe to put your hands under the knife when removing this lift of paper—*if* the cutter hydraulic system is in proper working condition and *if* you are the

only operator of the cutter. Remember: the paper cutter is to be operated by *one* person at a time.

9. Make additional cuts as needed. Handle the paper carefully and follow your cutting chart for accurate cutting. If press sheets are cut to even slightly different sizes, they will be difficult to run through a duplicator/press.

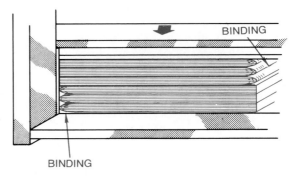

Fig. 154-11. Trimming saddle-stitched books. Note the slicing action of the knife.

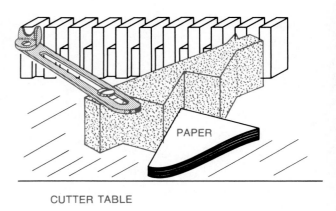

Fig. 154-12. Paper stock guide for cutting paper at any angle.

SPECIAL CUTS

In addition to plain and printed flat paper, booklets also are trimmed and cut with paper cutters. Figure 154-11 shows saddle stitched booklets properly positioned in the paper cutter. Note that half of the books should be turned with the bound edge to the left side, and half to the right. This helps to level the books and to equalize the pressure so the clamp will hold all sheets securely.

Angle cuts can be made by using a jig that attaches to the backgage (Fig. 154-12). This device can be adjusted to any angle. The paper to be cut is placed against it before the clamp is lowered. You then follow normal cutting/trimming procedure in making the special cuts.

UNIT 155 BASIC BINDING METHODS

Sheets of paper, folded or unfolded, can be bound together in several different ways. Notice the great variety of bindings—sizes and styles—in books you see around you every day (Fig. 155-1).

Methods of binding, or holding, the sheets of paper together are important to the use of the book. Some binding methods are meant for low cost and short life, others for a long life and hard use. Most people who use a book don't think about the binding method that holds the sheets together. They think only of the graphic information contained on the sheets.

BINDING METHODS

There are five basic kinds of bindings used to fasten booklets, magazines, and books: mechanical, loose-leaf, wire staple, perfect, and sewn. There is a sixth kind, called welding, but it has limited use and is unlike the other categories.

Mechanical. Mechanical bindings are not highly permanent, but they withstand some rough use. The sheets do not need to be uniform in size and the bound book lies flat when opened. The two common mechanical bindings are *spiral wire* and *plastic cylinder*. Spiral wire

Fig. 155-1. Books of various sizes and thicknesses bound by common binding methods.

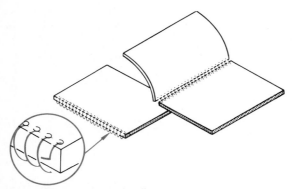

Fig. 155-2. Spiral-wire binding.

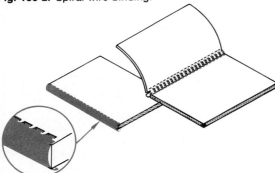

Fig. 155-3. Plastic-cylinder binding.

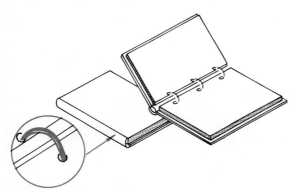

Fig. 155-4. A ring binder.

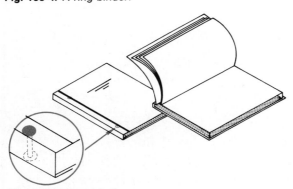

Fig. 155-5. Post binding.

Fig. 155-6. Base-and-prong binding.

Fig. 155-7. Friction binding.

Fig. 155-8. Saddle-wire binding.

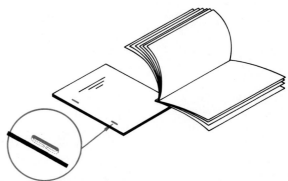

Fig. 155-9. Side-wire binding.

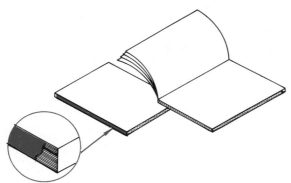

Fig. 155-10. Perfect binding.

Fig. 155-12. Sewn hard-cover or case-bound binding.

Fig. 155-11. Sewn soft-cover binding.

Fig. 155-13. Ultrasonic (welding) binding.

binding (Fig. 155-2) is often used for school notebooks. Plastic-cylinder binding (Fig. 155-3) is used for business reports and books such as monographs.

Loose-leaf. This style of binding lets sheets be added or removed easily. The *ring binder*, usually three-ring, (Fig. 155-4) is the most popular. The *post-binding* method (Fig. 155-5) is used for photograph albums and catalogs.

The *base-and-prong* method (Fig. 155-6) is similar to post binding. Both methods can be used to bind single sheets of uneven size into thicknesses of up to three or four inches. *Friction binding* (Fig. 155-7) uses a plastic U-shaped strip that is slid on the binding edge, clamping the paper edges. This method is used in the temporary binding of business and educational reports. Booklets of a few pages can be bound in this way.

Wire staple. Two common binding methods use wire staples. The *saddle-wire* method (Fig. 155-8) is used to bind magazines and small booklets. The *side-wire* type (Fig. 155-9) is used for binding thicker magazines and books. In saddle-wire binding, staples are placed through the fold. In side-wire binding, the staples hold

sheets together on the left margin. Both methods are economical and printed materials can be rapidly bound by hand or with automatic equipment.

Perfect. Perfect binding (Fig. 155-10) was developed to fill a need for a binding method that did not require sewing and hard covers. Perfect binding holds sheets of paper together by a flexible adhesive. Pocket-size books are almost exclusively bound in this manner and with automated equipment. It is fast, economical, and gives an attractive product. Hard- and soft-cover books can be bound by the perfect binding method.

Sewn. Sewn bindings are the most permanent way to hold sheets of paper together. Strong thread is placed through the binding edge of each sheet and securely holds all sheets in place between the covers of a book.

Sewn binding with soft covers (Fig. 155-11) will take hard use for a limited time. Technical information is often bound in this manner because the book will pass through many hands during its brief but valuable life. Technical material would be useless if individual sheets or signatures were to fall out.

Sewn bindings with hard covers (Fig. 155-12) are used when hard use and long wear are expected. *Case bound*, and *case binding* are other names given to this common bookbinding method. Most library books and school textbooks, like this one, are bound with hard covers or cases. This is the most expensive bookbinding method but it is also the most durable.

Welding. Binding by welding is a recent development in fastening a book together (Fig. 155-13). The binding edge of the book is treated with ultrasonic radio waves that fuse the sheets with heat and friction. The sheets may then be bound with either a soft or hard cover. This has proved to be a very effective binding.

UNIT 156 SOFT-COVER BINDING

Soft-cover binding is a popular and practical method of holding sheets of paper together. Economy, binding speed, and versatility are among the advantages of this type of binding. Several soft-cover binding methods are presented in this unit.

PLASTIC-CYLINDER BINDING

Materials.
Printed sheets
2 Covers
1 Plastic cylinder
Tools and equipment.
Paper cutter
Special multiple-hole punch
Plastic-cylinder binding machine (Fig. 156-1)
Hand shears

1. Gather the sheets and the covers in correct order, either by hand or by machine.
2. Trim the gathered sheets to the right size. Paper measuring 8½ by 11 inches (21.5 by 28 cm) is not usually trimmed because it is a common booklet size.
3. Punch holes in the binding edge with the special multiple-hole punch (Fig. 156-2). Adjust the punch accurately. Plastic cylinders are available in several diameters that need different punching positions. Punching specifications are listed on the machine. Note that the holes are rectangular.

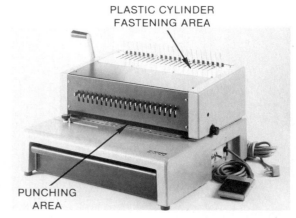

Fig. 156-1. A plastic-binding machine with a combination electric punch and hand-operated plastic cylinder fastening system.

4. Attach the plastic cylinder to the punched sheets. A special machine opens and holds open the several tongues on the cylinder while the sheets are positioned (Fig. 156-3). The diameter of the cylinder should be slightly larger than the thickness of the booklet.
5. With a pair of shears, trim the plastic cylinder to the height of the booklet. Plastic cylinders are usually 11 inches (28 cm) long to conform to the standard 8½ by 11-inch (21.5 by 28 cm) sheet of paper.

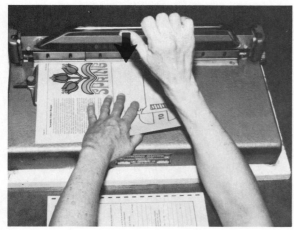

Fig. 156-2. Punching holes in the binding edge of a book-let with a multiple-hole punch.

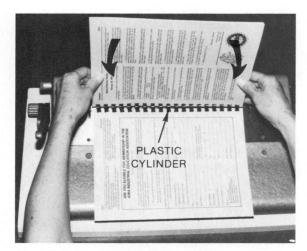

Fig. 156-3. Attaching the plastic cylinder to the punched sheets.

POST BINDING (LOOSE-LEAF)

Materials.

Printed sheets
2 Binder's board covers
2 Binder's board strips
2 Binding cloth coverpieces
2 Binding cloth end sheet pieces
Glue
Hot stamping foil
2 Binding posts

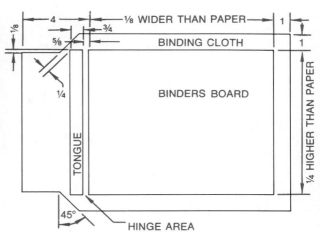

Fig. 156-4. Post tongue and cover construction.

Tools and equipment.

Board shears
Rule
Glue brush
Folding bone
Hand shears
Paper cutter
Hot-stamp press
Type
Paper punch

1. Gather the sheets of paper and trim them to the specified size. NOTE: The following information is given for the front cover only. All steps also should be followed for the back cover, omitting Step 16.
2. Cut the heavy binder's board material used for the stiff cover. Use heavy-duty board shears (Fig. 153-1). This piece should be ⅛-inch (3.175 mm) wider and ¼-inch (6.35 mm) higher than the sheets of paper.
3. Cut a binder's board strip ¾-inch (1.9 cm) wide and the same length as the height of the binder's board cover. This piece will be used for the tongue.
4. Cut the binding cloth that will cover the binder's board. It should be 5 inches (12.7 cm) larger than the cover width and 2 inches (5.08 cm) larger than cover height.
5. Apply glue to the binder's board cover. Use hot or cold bookbinder's glue.
6. Place the cover, glued side down, on the binding cloth. Position this piece 1 inch (2.54 cm) from each of three sides of the binding cloth (Fig. 156-4). Rub the glued

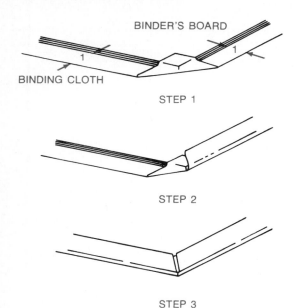

Fig. 156-5. Steps in making the library corner.

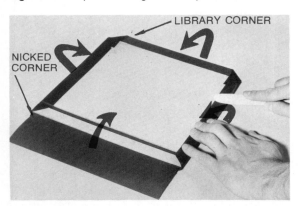

Fig. 156-6. Gluing the binding cloth over the edges of the binder's board.

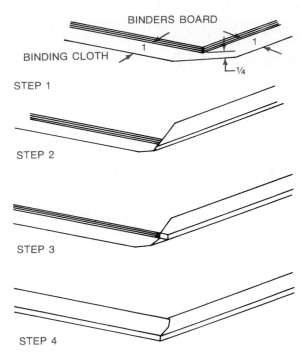

Fig. 156-7. Steps in making the nicked corner.

area with a folding bone to remove wrinkles and air pockets.

7. Apply glue to the binder's board strip. Position it $^2/_{16}$ inch (7.94 mm) from the cover board (Fig. 156-4). This strip forms the tongue of the book cover.

8. Trim the corners of the binding cloth to the left of the tongue (Fig. 156-4).

9. Glue and fold over the binding cloth on the front corners (opposite the tongue side) at a 45° angle (Fig. 156-5). This begins a library corner.

10. Glue and fold the top and bottom pieces of binding cloth over the binder's board (Fig. 156-6).

11. Glue and fold the binding cloth at the 2 remaining corners over the tongue to form nicked corners (Fig. 156-7).

12. Glue and fold the remaining binding cloth over the binder's board cover and tongue (Fig. 156-6). Firmly rub the area between the tongue and binder's board with a folding bone. This area is the hinge.

13. Cut a piece of binding cloth or end sheet $^1/_4$-inch (6.35 mm) smaller than the width and $^1/_4$-inch (6.35 mm) smaller than the height of the binder's board cover.

14. Apply glue. Position the piece on the inside of the cover. Allow a $^1/_8$-inch (3.2 mm) margin on all 4 sides. This hides the binding cloth edges and makes an attractive cover both inside and out.

15. Press the cover in a bookpress or under heavy weights for 24 hours.

16. Hot stamp the book title and any other information on the front cover (Fig. 156-8).

17. Punch holes in the sheets and the cover tongues.

18. Assemble the book with binding posts. These are bolt-like devices available in $^1/_2$-inch (1.27 cm) to several-inch lengths.

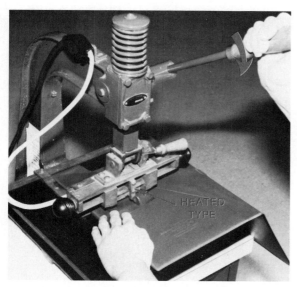

Fig. 156-8. Hot stamping the loose-leaf cover with gold leaf foil.

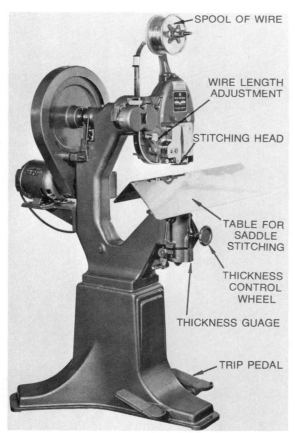

SPOOL OF WIRE

WIRE LENGTH
ADJUSTMENT

STITCHING HEAD

TABLE FOR
SADDLE
STITCHING

THICKNESS
CONTROL
WHEEL

THICKNESS GUAGE

TRIP PEDAL

INTERLAKE STEEL CORPORATION

Fig. 156-9. A wire-stitching machine ready for saddle stitching.

SADDLE-WIRE STITCHING

Materials.
Pamphlet content (printed pages)
1 cover

Tools and Equipment.
Wire stitcher
Paper cutter

1. Fold the printed sheets into signatures. This can be done either by hand or by a folding machine (Fig. 153-5).
2. Gather the signatures and the cover. Be sure all pages are in correct order. Gathering is done either by hand or by a mechanical gathering device (Fig. 153-13).
3. Prepare the stitcher for saddle stitching (Fig. 156-9). Stitchers are used to make wire-staple bindings—saddle-wire and side-wire.
   a. Place the saddle-stitching table on the stitching machine.
   b. Adjust the thickness control by placing the pamphlet (the signatures and cover) in the thickness gauge. Remember to open the pamphlet before inserting it into the gauge.
   c. Adjust the wire for length. The number on the wire-length adjustment lever should correspond to the number on the thickness gauge.
   d. Check to see that the wire on the machine is the right one for the pamphlet thickness being stitched.
   e. Check the maintenance manual for other necessary adjustments.
4. On a practice pamphlet, make several staples to see that all machine settings are correct. Step on the trip pedal and release it immediately to obtain one staple. (If the trip pedal is held down, the stitcher will continue to operate.) Make the necessary adjustments.
5. Place staples evenly (2 or 3, depending on pamphlet height) in the fold of the pamphlets. See Figure 155-8 for the specific locations.
6. Trim the 3 unbound edges to give the pamphlet a neat appearance. Follow the cutting procedure outlined in Unit 154.

The machine in Figure 156-10 can gather, stitch and trim several thousand pamphlets an hour. Such machines are essential for high-speed quality production.

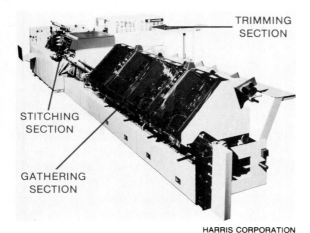

HARRIS CORPORATION

Fig. 156-10. This machine system gathers, stitches, and trims saddle-stitched pamphlets, magazines, and books.

SIDE-WIRE STITCHING

Materials.
Book or pamphlet content
2 Book covers
1 Binding tape
Tools and Equipment.
Wire stitcher
Folding bone
Paper cutter

1. Fold the printed sheets into signatures.
2. Gather the signatures or the single sheets. Side-wire binding permits the use of single sheets.
3. Prepare the stitcher for side-wire stitching (Fig. 156-11).
   a. Place the flat table on the stitching machine.
   b. Attach the back and side guides to the table. Adjust the guides to the approximate stitching positions.
   c. Finish preparing the stitcher according to Steps 3a, b, c, d, and e under "Saddle-Wire Stitching."
4. Use a practice pamphlet or book. Make several stitches to see that all machine settings are correct. If not, make the needed adjustments.

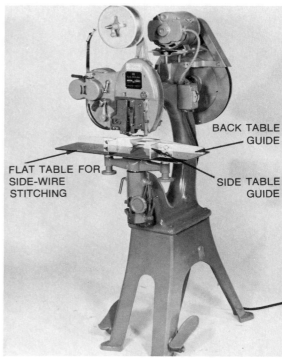

INTERLAKE STEEL CORPORATION

Fig. 156-11. A wire-stitching machine ready for side-wire stitching.

5. Place 2 or 3 staples evenly along the binding edge of the booklet (Fig. 155-9). Make final adjustments of the back and side guides at this time.
6. Place binding tape, a colorful paper or cloth with an adhesive backing, around the binding edge (Fig. 156-12). This covers the staples and binding edge to improve the appearance of the book. Smooth this tape with a folding bone.
7. Trim the 3 unbound edges. Follow the cutting procedure outlined in Unit 154.

A bookstitcher or side-wire stitcher used in industry is shown in Figure 156-13. It has 6 stitching heads.

PADDING

Materials.
Sheets of paper, printed or unprinted, to be bound into scratch pads or forms.
Chipboard, same size as the sheets of paper.
Padding adhesive

Fig. 156-12. Placing binding tape around the binding edge of a side-stitched book.

Tools and Equipment.

Glue brush
Rule
Heavy flat weight or a padding press
Binder's knife
Paper cutter

1. Gather the paper into piles of 25 to 50 sheets each.
2. Place a piece of chipbord between each pile of paper. Be sure there is a piece of chipboard on top and bottom of the pile.
3. Jog the sheets and position the entire pile on the edge of a table or counter. Place the heavy weight on top (a builder's brick works fine). The sheets may be placed in a padding press, which has a clamping device to hold the sheets together.
4. Apply the padding adhesive with the brush (Fig. 156-14). Two thin coats work best, with about 15 minutes drying time between coats.
5. After the adhesive is thoroughly dry, use the binders knife to separate the pads. Carefully draw the knife between a chipboard and top sheet of each pad, including the top pad and piece of chipboard.
6. It is well to trim a small amount from the 3 unbound edges to make these pad edges even and clean. Trim the pads to the correct size with a hydraulic paper cutter.

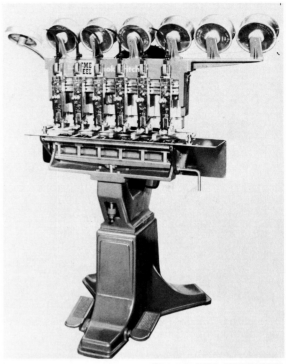

Fig. 156-13. A bookstitcher or side-wire stitcher with six stitching heads.

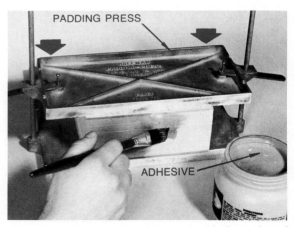

Fig. 156-14. Applying adhesive to the binding edge of several book piles being perfect-bound.

There are padding presses of many designs for use with this important binding method. One such machine is shown in Figure 156-15. On it, one operator can produce 1,400 single paper pads per hour. When more than one pad image is printed per sheet, production can be much higher.

Fig. 156-15. A multi-unit power padding press that can produce 1,400 single paper pads per hour.

STANDARD DUPLICATING MACHINES

Fig. 156-16. A small perfect binding machine is useful for business and in-plant printing operations.

MULLER MARTINI CORPORATION

Fig. 156-17. This high-speed perfect binding machine can produce 12,000 books per hour.

Perfect binding is like padding in that adhesive is the primary binding material. Heat, pressure, and some gauze-like material called *crash* are used to get quality binding by this popular method. A small office-size perfect binding unit can be used to bind a limited number of books (Fig. 156-16). These units have an adhesive application roller, a heating system, and a clamping mechanism. Such small units are useful to a company business office or an inplant printing operation.

Commercial binderies and publishers use large automated perfect binding equipment (Fig. 156-17). This equipment can produce thousands of high-quality perfect bound books day after day. Figure 156-18 shows the several stages in binding fully covered, perfect bound books.

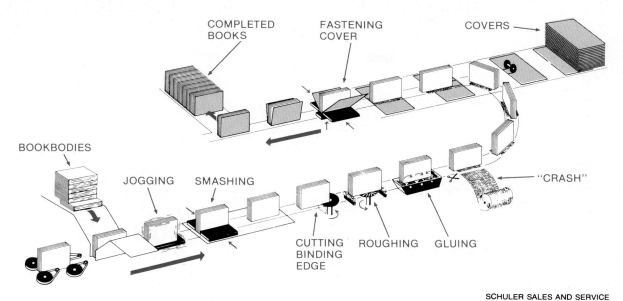

Fig. 156-18. A schematic of a perfect binding machine similar to the one in Fig. 156-17.

UNIT 157 CASE BINDING

Case binding is the most durable method of binding. A *case* (a hard cover) is wrapped around the book to protect the pages from damage. Several materials are combined to form a case-bound book (Fig. 157-1).

PARTS OF A BOOK

Body. The block of pages or signatures to be bound.

Case. The covers of a hardbound book.

End sheets. The blank sheets of paper placed at the front and back of a book. They help hold the body in the case and protect the first and last printed pages.

Backbone. The back, or binding, edge of any bound book. Also called *spine*.

Super. This is the gauze-like fabric glued to the backbone and case. This material is often called *crash*. It makes a permanent link between them.

Binder's board. A thick gray rigid paper board used to make the case.

Book cloth. A fabric made either from synthetic or natural materials. It covers the two pieces of binder's board that form the case.

Backing paper. A stiff but flexible paper strip placed between the two binder's boards. It holds the book cloth in place around the backbone.

Lining. A heavy kraft paper glued to the backbone to give a smooth, even surface.

Headbands. Colorful beads of thread placed for decoration at the top and bottom of the backbone.

Gummed tape. Strong reinforcement tape glued to the edges of the end sheets.

Thread. The thread, usually linen, that sews the book signatures together.

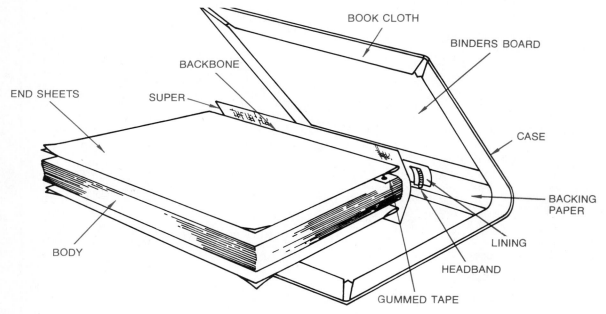

Fig. 157-1. Parts of a case-bound book.

Fig. 157-2. A saddle-sewn book.

CASE BINDING

There are several separate steps in case binding a book. By studying these, you can understand the basic manufacturing procedures.

1. Large printed sheets of paper (the pages for the book) are folded into signatures by special paper-folding machines (Fig. 153-6).
2. End sheets are cut to size, taped, folded, and glued to the first and last signatures of the book. Usually an end sheet is placed on the front and at the back of the book.

3. The several signatures that make up one book are then gathered in their proper order by machines designed for this job (Fig. 153-13).
4. The signatures are then sewed together. One of four methods is used, depending upon the style, intended use, and thickness of the book.
   a. *Saddle sewn.* Signatures are sewn through the fold (Fig. 157-2) with a heavy-duty sewing machine. This method is used for notebooks, stamp collection books, and account books.
   b. *Flat sewn.* Two to several signatures or single sheets up to 1 inch (2.54 cm) in thickness are sewn through the side of the sheets (Fig. 157-3). Side-sewing machines can sew more than 1,000 books an hour (Fig. 157-4). This method is used for school textbooks and other books to be given hard use.
   c. *Signature-to-signature sewn.* Two to any number signatures can be sewn together. The thickness of the book is limited only by the problem of handling the bound edition. In this method of sewing, the books have an individual hinge at each signature because the signatures are sewed one to another (Fig.

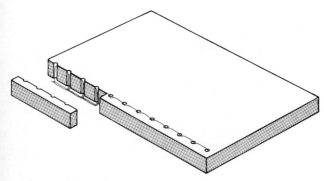

Fig. 157-3. A side-sewn book.

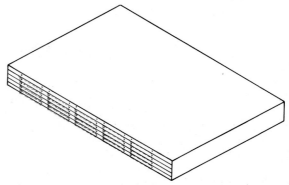

Fig. 157-5. A signature-to-signature or "Smyth sewn" book.

MCCAIN MANUFACTURING CORPORATION

Fig. 157-4. A high-speed side-sewing machine.

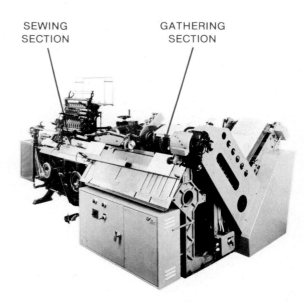

SEWING SECTION   GATHERING SECTION

SCHULER SALES AND SERVICE

Fig. 157-6. An automatic signature-to-signature book-sewing machine.

157-5). In the industry this method is known as *Smyth Sewn*. Sewing machines used for this method are either hand-fed or completely automatic (Fig. 157-6). An automatic machine sews up to 85 signatures a minute.

Signature-to-signature sewing is the most expensive binding method. It gives a strong book that opens and stays open easily. Unlike the side sewn methods, only a small binding margin is needed.

d. *Cleat sewn.* Loose pages or narrow tight signatures are notched and a single needle tightly laces a figure eight through the pages and around the notches. A coating of adhesive is then applied, which holds the thread and fills the cleats (Fig. 157-7).

5. After the body has been sewn together, it must be prepared to receive the hard cover. Several operations make it ready for the cover. All of these together are called *forwarding.*

a. *Nipping and smashing.* During the sewing operation, the binding edge of the book body has got thicker because of the thread. To make the finished book more attractive and easier to handle, the binding edge and the total book body are pressed under great pressure. This makes it the same thickness throughout.

The *nipping* operation places heat and pressure only on the sewing or binding edge of the body. Metal bars under hydraulic pressure are forced against each side of the book to press the sewn edges firmly (Fig. 157-8).

Right after the book has been nipped, the body moves to the next station in the machine and the entire unit is smashed. Metal plates are forced against both sides of the book body under pressure. This *smashing* makes the body the same thickness. During nipping and smashing, glue is applied mechanically to the binding edge of the book body. The glue dries rapidly and helps to hold the book body in its compressed state.

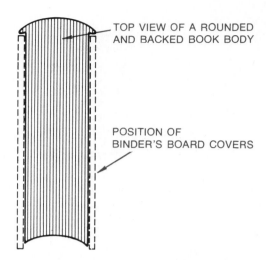

Fig. 157-9. The shape of a book body after it has been rounded and backed.

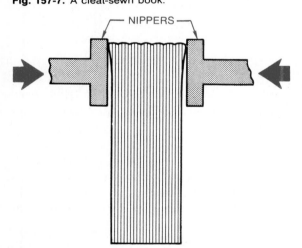

SMYTH MANUFACTURING

Fig. 157-7. A cleat-sewn book.

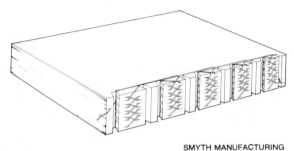

Fig. 157-8. Nipping a sewn book body. Heat and pressure form the binding edge together.

b. *Trimming.* Once the book has been nipped and smashed, it gets its final trimming. In most large book binderies, an automatic 3-knife book trimmer is used (Fig. 153-3).

SCHULER SALES AND SERVICE

Fig. 157-10. A rounding and backing machine.

c. *Rounding and backing.* The final bound book is rounded and backed to make it more attractive and usable. The backbone will be given a convex shape; the front edge a concave shape (Fig. 157-9).

After the book is rounded, it is *backed.* This is the process of flaring the binding edge (Fig. 157-9). The binding edge, or backbone, is flared or backed to a thickness of the binder's board used to make the cover.

Both operations are done not only to improve appearance but also to help the reader to open, keep open, and close the book. An automatic machine that rounds and backs a book body is shown in Figure 157-10.

Fig. 157-11. An automatic lining and headbanding machine.

d. *Attaching super, headbands, and lining.* A lining and headbanding machine (Fig. 157-11) attaches the 3 backbone materials. A coating of glue is applied to the backbone. The next operation attaches the super or gauze-like material. Another coating of glue is then applied and the headbands and lining are attached. The super is the bridge between the book body and the book case. Headbands are only decorative. The lining of heavy kraft paper gives the backbone a smoother surface.

Book bodies travel from the rounding and backing machine directly to the lining and headbanding machine. When ejected they are completely forwarded and ready to receive the hard book covers.

6. While the book bodies are being prepared, the covers are also constructed and stamped. It is very important that the cover fit the book body. Elements such as book

cloth, binder's board, and backing strip must be cut and handled accurately. A case-making machine (Fig. 157-12) combines these three cover materials by gluing, positioning, pressing, and folding them into a usable book case.

After being completed, each case is stamped with the book title, author, publisher, and any additional information. Standard automatic printing presses are specially equipped to accept the thick covers and to use heat and foil to put images on them. The platen press produces the image just as does the hot-stamping machine (Fig. 153-19).

7. The book bodies and book cases are now ready to be united. This is called *casing in.* Glue is applied to the front and back end sheets of the body; the case is properly positioned on the body. These operations are done at the same time on a casing-in machine (Fig. 157-13). It is very important that the body be properly positioned in the case.

8. The cased-in books travel to a book forming and pressing machine (Fig. 157-14). There,

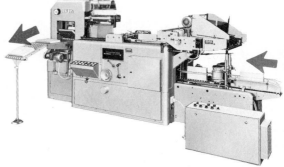

Fig. 157-13. The casing-in machine join the body and cover to form a complete book.

Fig. 157-12. An automatic casemaker for hard-cover construction.

Fig. 157-14. A book-forming and pressing machine.

heat and pressure adhere the end sheets to the cover and form the hinges in the front and back.

9. The books are now complete and can be used. Publishers often put a book jacket around the book to protect the cover and to give space for promotional information.

These jackets are put on by hand or by a special book-jacketing machine.

10. The books are ready for distribution. Corrugated cardboard cartons are made in specific sizes to accept certain sizes of books. The books are carefully packed and shipped for distribution.

UNIT 158 HAND CASE BINDING

Hand case binding can be done in the school laboratory with a few pieces of equipment. The same procedure is carried out in hand case binding as in commercial case binding. After you complete a hand case binding job, you should understand basic industrial book-binding procedures.

For experience, you will bind a year's volume of professional journals or any magazine using the signature-to-signature sewing method. You can, however, saddle sew a single issue of a journal, or several could even be flat sewn. All other basic hand case binding operations would be carried out without change.

Materials.
Issues of journals
Transparent mending tape
2 Binder's boards
1 Piece binding cloth
4 End sheets
2 Pieces lining paper
2 Headbands
3 Sewing tapes
1 Piece super
Sewing thread
Hot stamping foil
Binding glue (hot or cold)
Tools and Equipment.
Board shears
Paper cutter
Hand shears
Folding bone
Pressing boards
Book clamp

Sewing frame
Backing press
Backing hammer
Back saw
Hot-stamping machine
Glue brush
Glue pot
Rule
Sewing needles

BINDING

1. Arrange the journals in chronological order. Place the December index issue in the back. NOTE: For this binding procedure, the term *signature* will be used instead of *journal*.

2. Remove the staples from each signature. Be careful not to tear the pages.

3. Repair torn pages with transparent mending tape. Each signature may need tape over the staple holes on the inside of the center. Remove advertising inserts. They date rapidly.

4. Prepare the 4 end sheets:
   a. Using heavy-weight book paper, cut 2 end sheets $3/4$-inch (1.9 mm) wider than the signatures, but the same height. Fold the extra $3/4$-inch (1.9 mm) over and lay these two sheets aside.
   b. Cut 2 end sheets the same size as the signatures.
   c. Cut 2 binding cloth strips $2^1/2$ inches (6.35 cm) wide and the same height as the signatures.

d. Glue each of these 2 end sheets to the binding cloth strips with a ½-inch (1.27 cm) overlap.

e. Fold a ¾-inch (1.9 mm) strip of binding cloth over, good side up. Study Figure 158-1.

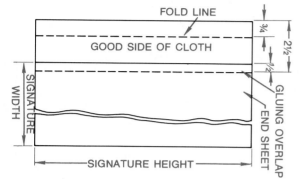

Fig. 158-1. The dimensions for preparing end sheets.

5. Attach the end sheets to the first (top) and last (bottom) signatures:

a. Apply glue inside the ¾-inch (1.9 mm) folded flaps, using the all-paper end sheets.

b. Place one of the end sheets on the front of the first signature, with the ¾-inch (1.9 mm) flap folded around the back of the signature.

c. Place the second all-paper end sheet on the back of the last signature, with the flap around the front of the signature (Fig. 158-2).

d. Apply glue to the ¾-inch (1.9 mm) folded flaps of the other paper-and-cloth end sheets.

Fig. 158-2. Placing an end sheet on the last or bottom signature.

e. Attach them directly over the all-paper ones in the same way.

f. Place the 2 signatures in a book press.

g. Let the glue dry thoroughly. Place waxed paper above, between, and below the signatures to keep them from sticking together.

h. Replace the signatures in their correct chronological order when they are dry.

Sewing signatures together

6. Jog the signatures and place saw-guide boards on each side. Put the assembly in a clamp: you can use 2 1-by-4s with two bolts, 2 wood handscrew clamps, or a standard backing press.

7. Mark lines for the saw cuts on the binding edge of the signatures (Fig. 158-3). The lines must be square across the binding edge of the signatures. They must also conform to the width of the sewing tape that is used.

8. Cut into the saw-guide boards and the binding edge with a backing or dovetail saw

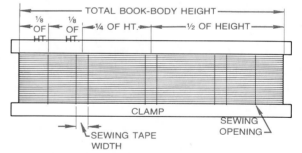

Fig. 158-3. Suggested position for the sewing tapes and end sewing openings. All eight lines represent saw cuts and sewing openings in the signatures.

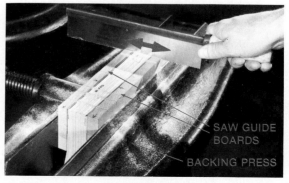

Fig. 158-4. Sawing the binding edge of the signatures to make openings for sewing.

according to the lines marked. See Figures 158-3 and 158-4. Saw about ¼-inch (6.35 mm) deep to pierce the inside center pages of the signatures. The saw cuts make openings for the sewing operation. The saw-board guides can be used many times, saving the time needed to measure and mark the binding edge each time a new group of same-size signatures is bound.

9. Unclamp the signatures and position them on a sewing frame.
10. Fasten the sewing tape to the front edge of the sewing frame according to the saw cuts (Fig. 158-5).

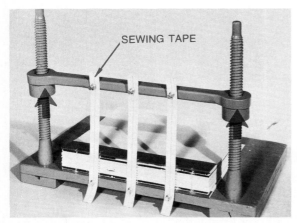

Fig. 158-5. The signatures and sewing tape properly positioned on the sewing frame.

11. Prepare the needle and thread. Estimate the length of thread needed by multiplying the signature height by the number of signatures. Begin the sewing operation with the last signature:
    a. Open the signature to the center. From the outside, insert the needle through the sewing opening on the right side.
    b. Bring the needle back out at the first opening or saw cut to the left.
    c. Go around the sewing tape, back into the signature, out, around the tape. Continue until the left sewing opening is reached.
12. Lay the next signature in position.
    a. Begin sewing from left to right. After reaching the first tape (left one), loop the thread of the first signature. Continue sewing (Fig. 158-6).

b. Tie the two signatures together when the right end of the second is reached.
    c. Continue with the remaining signatures. The sewing technique at the end-sewing openings is shown in Figure 158-6. When the last signature has been sewn, take several of these end stitches to hold it firmly. This sewing technique gives a tightly sewn one-unit book body.
13. Release the sewing tapes from the sewing frame. Cut them so they extend 1 inch (2.54 cm) on each side of the book body.

Forwarding the book body

14. Nip and smash the book body (see step 5, Unit 157). Use the backing press for nipping and the book press for smashing.
15. Apply a coating of glue to the backbone and allow it to dry thoroughly while under pressure.

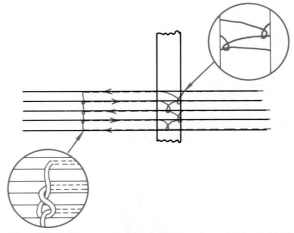

Fig. 158-6. The sewing techniques around the sewing tapes and at the end openings.

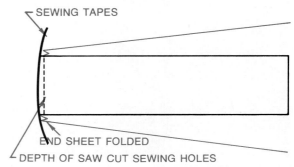

SEWING TAPES

END SHEET FOLDED

DEPTH OF SAW CUT SEWING HOLES

Fig. 158-7. Binding cloth of top and bottom end sheets folded to cover saw cuts or sewing holes.

16. Fold the binding cloth on the top and bottom end sheets to cover saw cuts (Fig. 158-7).

17. Trim the 3 unbound sides with a standard paper cutter (Unit 154). Trim the front first, the bottom second, and the top last.

18. Round the back of the book body (see Fig. 157-9):

   a. To round by hand, hold the front edge with one hand and hit the binding edge with a bookbinder's hammer (Fig. 158-8). Push on the center pages and pull on the front and back pages while hitting the binding edge.

   b. To back the book body, place it in a backing press with the binding edge extending ⅛-inch (3.175 mm) above the

jaws. Use a bookbinder's hammer to hit the backbone with light, glancing blows (Fig. 158-9). Strike the backbone from the center toward the edges.

19. Attach the super, headbands, and lining:

   a. Cut a piece of super ½-inch (1.27 cm) less than the body height and 3 inches (7.62 cm) more than the body thickness.

   b. Apply glue to the book backbone.

   c. Attach and center the super.

   d. Cut 2 headbands ½-inch (1.27 cm) longer than the body thickness.

   e. Apply glue to the ends of the backbone.

   f. Position the headbands with the bead edge toward the body.

   g. Trim them to exact body thickness with hand shears.

   h. Cut a piece of heavy kraft paper the same size as the backbone and glue it to

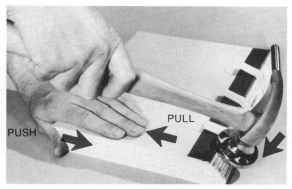

Fig. 158-8. Rounding a book body by the hand method. Note the position of the thumb and fingers on the book body.

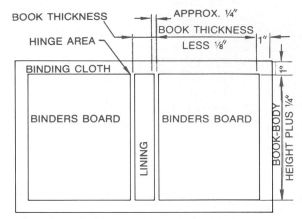

Fig. 158-10. Parts, sizes, and positions of a book case.

Fig. 158-9. Backing a book body by the hand method. The backbone should extend ⅛ inch above the backing press jaws.

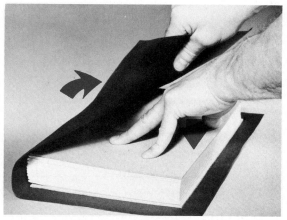

Fig. 158-11. Pulling the binding cloth over the second (or top) binder's board.

the backbone. This strip (called lining) helps smooth the backbone.

Preparing the case

20. Cut binder's boards and binding cloth (Fig. 158-10):
    a. Cut 2 binder's boards (Fig. 156-3). Determine the size by adding ¼-inch (6.35 mm) to the body height and subtracting ⅛-inch (3.175 mm) from the body width.
    b. Cut a piece of binding cloth 2 inches (5.08 cm) larger than the binding board height and 3 inches (7.62 cm) larger than the 2 combined board widths plus the body thickness.
    c. Apply glue to one binder's board.
    d. Press it to the reverse (inside) of the binding cloth. Let the binding cloth extend 1 inch (2.54 cm) beyond the board on 3 sides.
    e. Position the book body on the glued binder's board. Let the board extend ⅛-inch (3.175 mm) beyond the top, front, and bottom.
    f. Spread glue on the second binder's board.
    g. Place it on the book body with the glued side up. It must be in perfect alignment with the bottom binder's board.
    h. Pull the binding cloth over the second binder's board (Fig. 158-11) and smooth down. Make sure the boards do not move.

    i. Remove the book body and thoroughly press the binding cloth to the boards, using a folding bone. NOTE: Be sure that the two binder's boards are parallel.
21. Cut and attach the cover lining strip (Fig. 158-10):
    a. Cut a piece of heavy kraft paper the same size as the backbone.
    b. Glue the lining strip midway between the binder's boards. Be sure it is parallel to the top and bottom of the boards (Fig. 158-10).
22. Fold the binding cloth over the binder's boards.
    a. Make nicked or library corners (see Figs. 156-5 and 156-7).
    b. Glue and fold the binding cloth over the 4 edges.
    c. Place the case in a book press for several hours. Be sure 2 pressing boards are in place with flanges to form the book hinges.
    d. Let the case dry thoroughly.
23. Hot stamp the desired lettering on the case:
    a. Compose the type with special hot stamp type.
    b. Heat the stamping unit.
    c. Place the type in the pallet.
    d. Align the case, clamp, and stamp (see Fig. 156-8).
24. Hang the volume into the case (this is called *casing-in*):
    a. Place the book body into the case in the correct position.

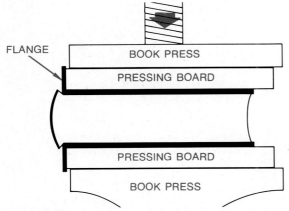

Fig. 158-12. The order and arrangement of the book and pressing boards in the book press.

Fig. 158-13. A bound volume between two pressing plates in a book press.

b. Open the top cover. Place a sheet of scrap paper between the sewing tapes and the end sheet.

c. Apply glue to the super and tapes.

d. Remove the scrap paper; replace it with a sheet of waxed paper.

e. Close the top cover. Turn the volume over.

f. Repeat Steps b, c, d, and e for the back cover.

g. Place the book between 2 pressing boards.

h. Clamp in a book press for 8 hours. The pressing boards, along with pressure, help form the cover hinge (Fig. 158-12).

Note the flange on the pressing board and how it forms the hinge.

25. Complete casing-in the book:

a. Open the top cover and place a sheet of scrap paper between the 2 end sheets.

b. Apply glue to the outside end sheet.

c. Replace the scrap paper with a sheet of waxed paper.

d. Close the cover and turn the book over.

e. Repeat Steps a, b, c, and d for the back cover.

f. Place the volume between 2 pressing boards (also called pressing plates). Clamp in a book press for another 8 hours (Fig. 158-13). Book completed.

UNIT 159 MICROSTORAGE AND RETRIEVAL SYSTEMS

Microstorage and retrieval systems use materials commonly called *microform*, a general term for all very small (micro) images. Most of the forms use photographic film in rolls, strips, or small pieces (Fig. 159-1). All methods of microform follow six basic steps (Fig. 159-2): (1) the original document is exposed and coded, (2) the film is processed, (3) the film is duplicated, (4) the film is stored, (5) the film is retrieved,

and (6) images are displayed on a screen and paper copies produced.

Microform systems are becoming more and more important in business and industry. Microform systems are used to keep records and to save space in their storage. Many papers turn yellow and crumble with age, but film keeps its original condition for many years.

Saving space is probably the chief advantage of microform. The entire Bible can be put on one microfilm card less than two inches square. If books were published in micro-image form, an encyclopedia could be carried in a pocket; a book could be mailed in a small envelope for the price of first-class postage. The several million volumes in the Library of Congress could be filed in fewer than ten small cabinets. The astronauts take thousands of pages of reference material on their missions—all contained in very small units of microform.

Microform is used mostly for reference and for getting graphic information from one place to another. Libraries relay information by copying their original document of a microform. Keeping documents available and protected is

EASTMAN KODAK

Fig. 159-1. Examples of the several microforms.

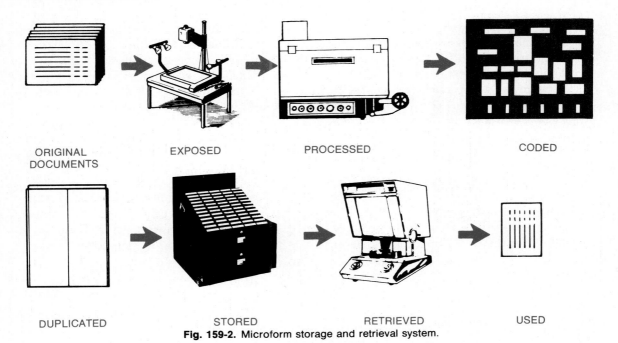

Fig. 159-2. Microform storage and retrieval system.

one of the most important benefits of using microform.

MICROFORM STORAGE

Four common microform storage methods are in use (Fig. 159-3): (1) the *roll film,* usually 35 mm; (2) the *film magazine* or cartridge, usually 16 mm; (3) the *aperture card* (Fig. 159-4), which holds a small clip of film attached to a data processing card; and (4) the *microfiche* (Fig. 159-5), a sheet of film containing several hundred pages of the original document. Usually 35 mm film is used to record material that is not often needed.

The magazine cartridge is used to record company documents and customer records. The aperture card is used to record the micro-images of large engineering drawings. The microfiche system is used to record company documents and entire books, magazines, and even libraries. Most daily newspapers use micro-imaging to store their daily newspaper on film in file cabinets instead of keeping stacks of original newspapers.

With all microform storage systems, special equipment is needed to (1) reduce the original document to micro-image form, (2) process the microfilm, (3) duplicate the micro-images, and (4) retrieve the information. The micro-imaging process begins with a camera. Several styles are available and most reduce the original document by sixteen to twenty times

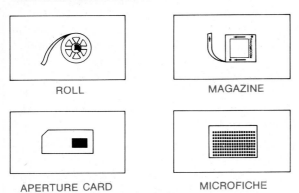

Fig. 159-3. The several microform storage methods.

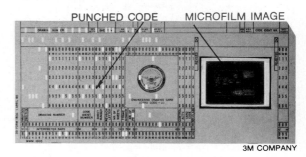

Fig. 159-4. A coded aperture card.

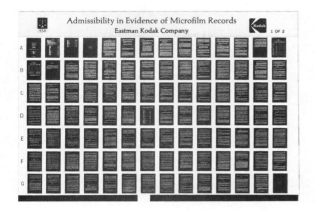

EASTMAN KODAK

Fig. 159-5. A microfiche that records 98 pages.

or more. Some cameras only expose the film; others photograph the image and process the film.

MICROFORM RETRIEVAL

Each of the four microform storage methods needs a retrieval system. Most machines accept only one kind of microform, but some can accept more than one. The reel film can be viewed by using a machine that enlarges the micro-image to the original size and projects

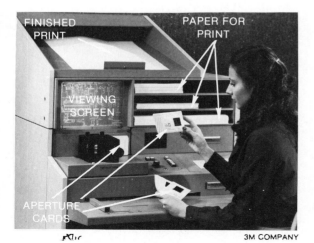

3M COMPANY

Fig. 159-6. An enlarger-printer that makes standard-size prints from aperture cards on plain paper, on vellum, and on lithographic printing plates.

it on a screen or reading area. It can also produce hard-copy paper prints.

The magazine micro-image system, as has been noted, is used to store company records. It uses a sophisticated retrieval system that can locate information in seconds.

Aperture cards, because of their punched coding system, can also be located quickly. Put into a reader-printer, the information is enlarged to a size that is very readable. If a print is needed, a turn of the dial produces a hard copy in seconds at small cost. If many prints are needed, offset lithography printing plates can be made (Fig. 159-6). These plates can be used on most lithographic duplicators to produce low-cost printed copies.

A BRIEF HISTORY

Microfilm began in the late nineteenth century. An enterprising Frenchman, Rene-Prudent Dragon, photographed 1,000 telegrams on a film strip two inches wide. He attached the film to the leg of a pigeon to send on a communications mission. In the Second World War, the military made great use of microform images. Following that war, a few forward-looking business people developed and promoted uses for this system. In recent years the potential of microform systems has been realized. Use of microform storage and retrieval systems will be expanded greatly in business, industry, government, publishing, and education.

VIDEODISK STORAGE AND RETRIEVAL

Videodisks are available in several sizes. They can be used for storing great amounts of information. These disks are sometimes called optical disks. Lasers are used to file and retrieve information on the videodisks. Sophisticated equipment makes it convenient to input information on disks. This equipment can then be used to locate, view, and make hard copies (paper copies) of the stored data (Fig. 159-7). The contents of six four-drawer file cabinets, or 50,000 documents, can be stored on one 12-inch optical disk.

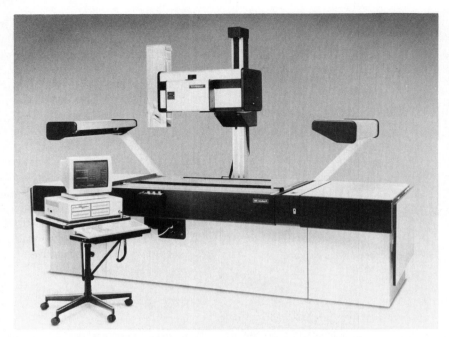

Fig. 159-7. A complete laser-optical disk system for storing, filing, and retrieving information. It also contains a laser printer for making paper print copies of filed data.

UNIT 160 LEARNING EXPERIENCES: FINISHING AND BINDING

KEY TERMS

Die cutting   Perforating
Gathering   Scoring

Unit 151

Binding   Scroll
Finishing

Unit 154

Cutting stick   Press sheet
Backgage   Stock sheet

Unit 155

Unit 153

Creasing   Hot stamping
Collating   Laminating

Case binding   Sewn binding
Loose-leaf binding   Welding binding
Mechanical binding   Wire staple binding
Perfect binding

Unit 156

Folding bone   Plastic cylinder
Library corner   Post binding
Nicked corner   Saddle-wire stitching
Padding   Side-wire stitching

Unit 157

Backbone   Nipping
Backing   Rounding
Binders board   Smashing
Casing-in   Super
Headbands

Unit 158

Book press   Pressing boards
Forwarding   Sewing frame
Lining   Sewing tape

Unit 159

Microfiche   Microstorage
Microform   Optical disk
                        Video disk

DISCUSSION TOPICS

1. Why have binding improvements followed developments in book production?
2. Why should a planning sheet be made before cutting a large amount of paper?
3. In producing saddle-wire and side-wire bound books, what is the main advantage of a wire stitching machine over a stapling machine?
4. What would happen if a book body did not receive either of the two operations called *nipping* and *smashing*?
5. How is information located that has been stored by one of the microform methods?

ACTIVITIES

Units 151–159

1. Visit a commercial bookbinding plant. If possible, also visit a large graphic arts printing plant that has a bindery department. Notice the methods of binding and the procedures by which each commercial plant operates its bindery. Prepare a detailed report on your visit.

Units 153–156

2. As a class project, plan and produce from 50 to 100 copies of a booklet. Complete the necessary paper cutting, trimming, folding, scoring, and binding operations. Use either the side-wire or saddle-wire method of binding.

Unit 156

3. Bind five books by each of the methods described in Unit 156.

The largest fine paper mill in the world located in Ashdown, Arkansas.
NEKOOSA PAPERS, INC.

PULP AND PAPER MANUFACTURING

INTRODUCTION TO PULP AND PAPER MANUFACTURING

Paper manufacturing is a basic industry that began about 2,000 years ago. Today it is increasingly an industry of technological change and dynamic growth. In the United States alone, there are over 5,000 manufacturing plants for pulp, paper, and paper products with nearly a million employees. Paper is a major industry in Canada and many other countries as well (Fig. 161-1).

Paper has many forms other than sheets to be written or printed on. Some of these are paper bags, packaging, gun cartridges, diapers, drinking cups, filters of all kinds, and polishing cloths. Other forms include roofing materials, soda straws, towels, wallpaper, sandpaper, building paper, and wrappers. There are even paper clothing and paper tents.

HISTORICAL HIGHLIGHTS

Thousands of years ago people expressed themselves by etching pictures and symbols on

stones, walls of caves, and bones. Later they used other surfaces such as beeswaxed boards, palm leaves, bronze, silk, and clay tablets. The ancient Greeks used a parchment made from animal skins. Four thousand years ago the Egyptians discovered how to make a writing surface of the papyrus plant. They formed a cross-woven mat of reeds and pounded it into a hard, thin sheet. The word *papyrus* is the source of our word *paper*.

Paper as we know it today was invented in A.D. 105 by Ts'ai Lun, a Chinese court official. He mixed mulberry bark, hemp, and rags with

R. R. DONNELLEY AND SONS

Fig. 161-1. A large publishing and printing company uses tons of paper in rolls and sheets every day.

NEKOOSA PAPERS

Fig. 161-2. A tall stand of tree-farm timber to be used in making paper.

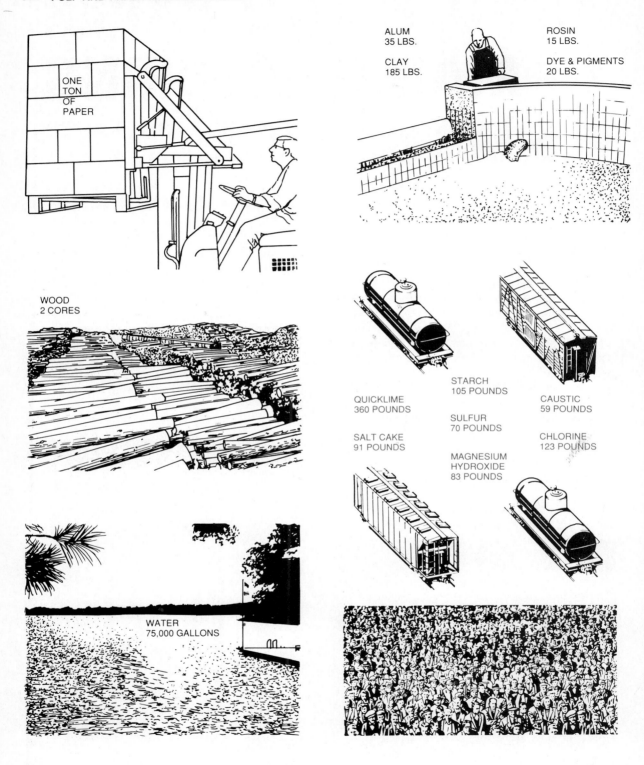

Fig. 161-3. Many elements make up a ton of paper.

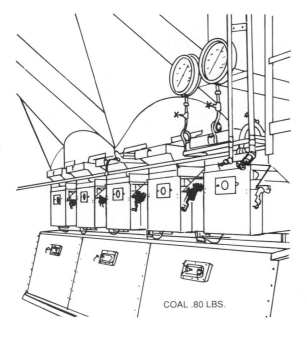

COAL .80 LBS.

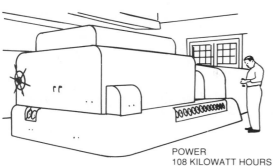

POWER
108 KILOWATT HOURS

CAPITAL INVESTMENT
PLANTS AND EQUIPMENT

NEKOOSA PAPERS

water, mashed them into a pulp, pressed out the liquid, and hung the thin mat to dry in the sun. This basic wood mixture set off mankind's greatest revolution in communications. In China, one emperor had a library of 50,000 books at a time when most of the great leaders of Europe could not even write their names.

After nearly a thousand years, the Chinese technique of papermaking was brought into Europe by the Moors of North Africa. But somehow the method of making paper from wood was lost. Until the early 1800s, the Western world made paper from rags and cloth. Each sheet was individually turned out by dipping a screen into a vat of water-suspended fibers and then draining the water away from them. A skilled worker could produce about 750 sheets of paper a day. It was an expensive, tedious process that did not answer the urgent demand for paper.

During the Revolutionary War, the colonists were very short of paper. Soldiers tore up old books to make wadding for their guns. Washington's generals sent him messages on mere scraps of paper. John Adams, in a letter to his wife, wrote, "I send you now and then a few sheets of paper; this article is as scarce here as with you." In desperation, Washington ordered some paper makers discharged from military service and sent back to the mills.

In 1798 Nicholas-Louis Robert, a clerk at a papermaking mill in Essenay, France, devised a machine that replaced hand dipping and produced paper in a continuous roll. It was a large, endless wire screen turned by hand to filter the pulp.

Robert could not get financial backing for his idea in France, so he sold the patent to the Fourdrinier Brothers in England. They built a practical machine but still could not meet the need for cheap and plentiful paper. The industry was held back by a lack of raw materials; rags were expensive and hard to get.

In 1850, Friedrich Gottlob Keller of Germany read a book by Rene de Reaumur, a French scientist who lived a hundred years earlier. Reaumur noted that wasps used wood fiber to make paper-like nests. He wrote, "The wasp invites us to try to make fine and good paper from the use of certain woods." Keller developed a machine for grinding wood into fibers. A few years later Hugh Burgess, an Englishman, advanced mechanized papermaking another step by inventing a chemical pulping process.

In 1865, C. B. Tilghman, an American scientist, solved a major chemical problem when he invented the sulphite process for dissolving unwanted resins in wood. The age of economical mass production of paper was beginning.

Newspapers increased; more and cheaper magazines were published. The small slates used by students gave way to notebooks and lined paper. Between 1889 and 1900 in the United States, the production of paper doubled to about 2½ million tons a year.

TREES, THE RAW MATERIAL

The tree farm system was started in 1941 near Montesano, Washington, U.S.A. Seedlings were planted and fire control begun in a 120,000-acre area.

Trees are the basic raw material for paper (Fig. 161-2). A Douglas fir must be between thirty and forty years old before it can be used for pulp. Careful, long-range management of this important raw material is essential for economic growth.

WHAT GOES INTO A TON OF PAPER

Many other ingredients besides wood are needed to produce a ton of paper. A supply of fresh water is essential. Other elements and power sources needed are shown in Figure 161-3.

⊃$_Z$162 PULP MANUFACTURING

Wood fiber was first used to make paper in 1844 and now makes up 95 percent of all the papermaking fiber in the world. Wood fibers have short-length fibers that come from deciduous, or hardwood, trees whose leaves fall each year. Fibers that are long, thick, and strong, come from coniferous or cone-bearing, softwood trees.

WOOD SOURCES

Even though millions of acres of forests over the world supply wood for papermaking, constant replanting is necessary (Fig. 162-1). Paper companies are buying more and more timberland, but most mills are supplied by small woodlot farmers.

In the past, most logs moved by rail or water, but better transportation and highways increased the number of logs moved by truck (Fig. 162-2). After the wood is weighed and purchased, it is placed in storage piles (Fig. 162-3).

S.D. WARREN COMPANY

Fig. 162-1. Seedlings are planted to renew pulp and timber lands.

DEBARKING

From the piles, stacks, or lagoons, the logs are placed either on a conveyor or in a flume (a flowing trough of water) to go to the debarkers. There are both mechanical and hydraulic types of debarkers. The *mechanical debarker* shown in Figure 162-4 is the oldest and most widely used. A drum with vertical slotted plates rubs the logs clean and, if they are not completely debarked on the first pass, they are sent through the drum a second time (Fig. 162-5). Tons of logs can be debarked in less than thirty minutes.

Hydraulic debarkers strip the bark from the log by means of water jets. The log is placed in a revolving stand and jets of water peel the bark from it with 1500–2000 psi of pressure.

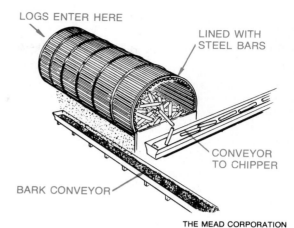

THE MEAD CORPORATION

Fig. 162-4. A debarking drum can be operated either dry or submerged in water.

NEKOOSA PAPERS

Fig. 162-5. Pulp logs are sorted after leaving the debarker. Logs not fully debarked are returned to the machine.

S.D. WARREN COMPANY

Fig. 162-2. Loading pulpwood onto a truck with a forklift.

U.S. FOREST SERVICE

Fig. 162-3. Pulpwood is stacked in piles or dropped to form stacks.

CHIPPING

After debarking, the logs travel to a *chipper*, which is a disk fitted with knives that radiate from the hub to the edge. The log drops into this spinning disk at about a 45° angle and in seconds a five-foot log is reduced to a jumble of chips.

The chips go over a series of screens. Over-sized ones are sorted out and sent to a rechipper. The sawdust and undersized chips are used for fuel or other profitable purpose. The chips that measure about one-inch (2.54 cm) go to a storage area.

PULPING

Pulping methods can be grouped in three broad classes: (1) chemical, (2) mechanical (groundwood), and (3) a combination of chemical and mechanical. The purpose of all pulping processes is to release the fibers from the log. In the chemical process, the non-cellulose material that holds the fibers together is removed chemically. The mechanical process rips the fibers from the log by friction. The chemical-mechanical method uses chemical action to loosen the fibers and mechanical action to tear them apart.

Chemical pulping

A slab, chip, log, or any wood substance is made of fibers held together by a glue-like material called *lignin*. Chemical pulping dissolves the lignin binding agent, freeing the fibers. The main chemical pulping processes use soda, sulfate, and sulfite in the cooking liquors. The chips are conveyed from a storage area to the digesters (Fig. 162-6) where they are cooked in these chemicals.

The mixture is heated in one of two ways (Fig. 162-7). In direct heating, live steam is added directly to the digester. In the alternate method, the liquor is pumped through a heat exchanger which is heated.

When the cooking is done, the pressure is released and the chips (almost in pulp form) are sent into a blow tank. They next go to a washer that removes as much as possible of the cooking chemicals and the dissolved non-cellulose. The pulp, now called *brown stock*, is ready for the next operation. In the case of printing paper, the next step is *bleaching*.

In recent years there has been a great deal of interest in a continuous digester, which has a steady in-flow of chips and a constant output of pulp (Fig. 162-8). This equipment is easy to automate, cheaper to install and operate.

Mechanical pulping

In the mechanical pulping process, the logs are taken from the debarker to a grinder that tears

Fig. 162-6. Chips are moved from the storage bins to the giant digesters by covered conveyor.

NEKOOSA PAPERS

Fig. 162-7. The lid of a digester is closed before cooking the chips.

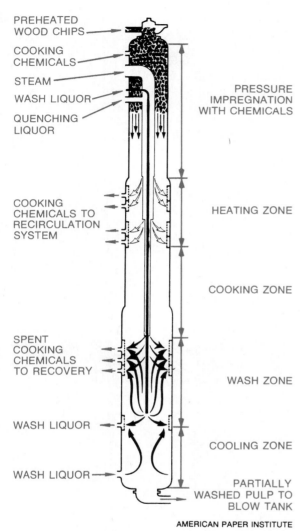

PREHEATED WOOD CHIPS

COOKING CHEMICALS

STEAM

WASH LIQUOR

QUENCHING LIQUOR

PRESSURE IMPREGNATION WITH CHEMICALS

COOKING CHEMICALS TO RECIRCULATION SYSTEM

HEATING ZONE

COOKING ZONE

SPENT COOKING CHEMICALS TO RECOVERY

WASH ZONE

WASH LIQUOR

COOLING ZONE

WASH LIQUOR

PARTIALLY WASHED PULP TO BLOW TANK

AMERICAN PAPER INSTITUTE

Fig. 162-8. A continuous digester over 200 feet tall can produce 700 tons of pulp a day.

the fibers from the logs (Fig. 162-9). Logs are held against the grindstone by hydraulic pressure. The ground-off fibers mix with the cooling water spray on the stone to form a slurry of pulp. The slurry passes over a series of screens where the good pulp, called *accepts*, is removed and sent to a cleaning unit.

Groundwood pulp has both good and bad qualities. It is very efficient because from 90 to 95 percent of the wood is turned into fiber. But grinding the wood takes a lot of power and, unless hydro-electric power is available, the cost is high.

Chemical-mechanical pulping

In the combination process, the wood substance is reduced partially by chemicals and then completely separated mechanically. In the chemical stage the chips are lightly cooked to dissolve the binding material partially. The half-cooked chips are next sent to mechanical grinders where the separation is completed. This process produces an intermediate pulp with both a relatively high strength and a high yield.

BLEACHING

Bleaching removes stains and produces a bright white pulp. It is an extension of the pulping process (Fig. 162-10). Main bleaching agents are chlorine gas, calcium hyprochlorite, hydrogen peroxide, and chlorine dioxide. These chemicals

A—THREE POCKET GRINDER   B—MAGAZINE GRINDER   C—CHAIN GRINDER   D—RING GRINDER

Fig. 162-9. The four types of mechanical pulpers.

hold the color-bearing materials in solution or release oxygen that destroys them.

Groundwood is bleached by peroxide under controlled conditions. After bleaching has taken place, the bleaching agent is neutralized and the pulp is ready for use without washing.

BEATING AND REFINING

In the sequence of operations called stock preparation, beating and refining are important steps. The pulp is carried from the pulping and bleaching operations to beaters and refiners.

Beating. A modern beater (Fig. 162-11) does two things: (1) it completely separates fibers so they will not form *shives*, or lumps, when formed into a sheet, and (2) it changes the individual fibers so that the papermaker can *felt*

them into a smooth, even sheet that will handle, look, and wear well.

Refining. The refiner (Fig. 162-12) has a bar-studded rotating element which fits closely together. The water-suspended pulp is pumped through the refiner continuously. The fibers are cut and shortened to produce a more uniform pulp.

Pulping. Pulping—or more accurately, repulping—resuspends dried pulp or paper in water. No attempt is made to change the fibers' fiber properties. The purpose is to break the pulp or paper down to individual fibers before further processing. There are many types of pulpers, all of which are either *batch* or *continuous* (Fig. 162-13).

NEKOOSA PAPERS

Fig. 162-10. The pulp is bleached to remove lignin stains and produce a bright white material.

THE MEAD CORPORATION

Fig. 162-12. A battery of disc refiners.

Fig. 162-11. Side view of a typical beater.

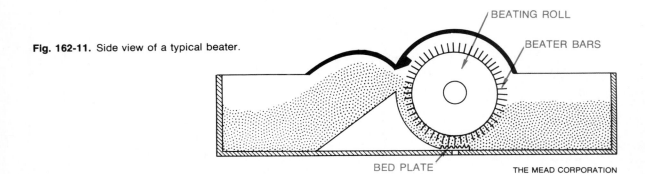

BEATING ROLL

BEATER BARS

BED PLATE

THE MEAD CORPORATION

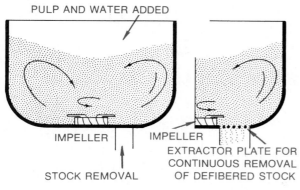

THE MEAD CORPORATION

Fig. 162-13. A batch hydrapulper is shown on the left. The continuous hydrapulper (detail on the right) uses a screened outlet so that defibered pulp can be continuously withdrawn.

ADDITIVES

Many non-cellulose items are added to the *fiber furnish* before it is carried to the paper machine. They can be added at almost any point in the stock-flow system, but most are added at the beaters because that is the least expensive and most convenient place, and no special equipment is needed. At this point the additives are absorbed uniformly into the fibers before they bond.

Additives are used to improve the pulp before it goes to the paper machine. The four common additives are: (1) material to change inter-fiber bonding, (2) materials to improve looks and handling properties, (3) internal sizing to improve water resistance of the paper, and (4) dye-stuffs and pigments to give color to the paper.

CLEANING

The final step in preparing the pulp before it reaches the paper machine is cleaning. The two chief methods of cleaning stock are by screening and by pressure drop cleaners.

Screening. The stock must be screened for uniform fiber dispersion until it is free of fiber

clumps and dirt and other foreign matter. Stock clumps are formed from undercooked wood chips, wastepaper, slime growth, and similar hard-to-break-up materials.

Centricleaner. The pressure drop, or cyclone-type cleaner (Fig. 162-14) works because dirt, fiber bundles, uncooked pulp, and other unwanted materials are heavier than acceptable fiber. When the pulp is spiraled at high velocity, the heavier foreign matter moves to the outside of the spiraling flow.

The cyclone cleaner has a tapering tube into which the stock comes in at the side and near the top. The spiraling pulp moves down toward the small end of the shaft. At the same time an inner spiraling column, or vortex, moves up to the top of the shaft where the acceptable stock is removed. The dirt, fiber bundles, and other materials are heavier and cannot make the up-turn and are rejected at the bottom of the shaft.

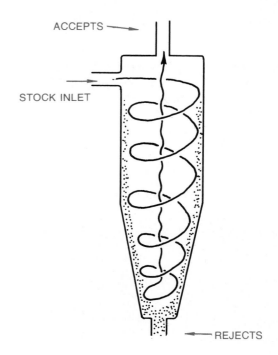

THE MEAD CORPORATION

Fig. 162-14. A centricleaner used to clean pulp.

UNIT 163 PAPER MANUFACTURING

Papermaking machines are monsters of modern mechanization. Some of the larger ones are as long as two football or soccer fields and are among the largest machines in industry (Fig. 163-1). They can produce paper over 380 inches wide at more than 4,000 feet per minute. Today, many processes controlled by computers, but operator skill is one of the best controls for paper quality. (Fig. 163-2).

FORMING PAPER

Paper pulp is delivered to the continuously moving *Fourdrinier* wire through the head box. The mixture can be as much as 99 percent water at the wet end. As the pulp travels the length of the wire, water is removed by gravity and vacuum, and the remaining solids form a mat of paper. At the end the pulp passes through a first set of press rolls. It continues through the drying, sizing, and finishing stages of the Fourdrinier paper machine.

WATERMARKS

Watermarks are designs that are placed into the paper without using ink. A watermark is often

considered to be a sign of high quality. Good grades of bond paper are used for letterheads, envelopes, and other business materials. A watermark often advertises the company that produced the paper or the business concern that uses it.

Two means of producing watermarks are (1) the dandy roll method (Fig. 163-3) and (2) the rubber stamp roll method (Fig. 163-4). The *dandy roll* produces the true watermark. A cylinderical frame, wrapped with wire cloth, rides on top of the Fourdrinier wire near the end where the pulp leaves the screen and enters the first press drying section. The dandy roll may have either a recessed design or raised letters. As the wire watermark form touches the still-fluid paper, it displaces some of the fibers to produce a specific pattern.

The *rubber stamp roll* is generally used on lower-cost papers which are produced at higher speeds. It is located in the wet press section of the paper machine. Rubber stamp watermarking produces a sheet that is slightly embossed because of the raised images upon the rubber.

WATER REMOVAL AND DRYING

The jet press section of the paper machine is

NEKOOSA PAPERS

Fig. 163-1. The wet end of a giant papermaking machine. It features a combination of Fourdrinier and twin-wire (a Fourdrinier wire on both the bottom and top of the paper).

S. D. WARREN COMPANY

Fig. 163-2. A control room where the pulp is watched while it is prepared and delivered to the papermaking machine.

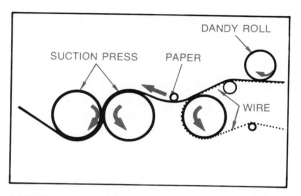

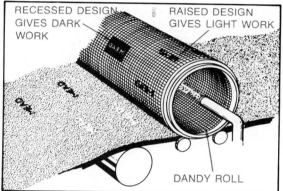

Fig. 163-3. A watermark produced by the dandy-roll method.

just behind the Fourdrinier wire. The wet sheet, still over 80 percent water, passes between rolls covered with wool and other rollers made of granite, brass, or hard rubber. The thickness (or caliber) of the sheet is partially controlled at the wet press section. Constant adjustment and control are necessary (Fig. 163-5).

The paper sheet leaves the wet press section with about 60 percent moisture and enters the drying section. It passes over steam-heated drying rolls about four to five feet in diameter (Fig. 163-6). The paper is heated on one side and then the other as it passes from roll to roll.

Drying is expensive because of the large cost of installing and maintaining the many steam-heated rollers. The cost is a large part of the cost of the finished paper.

In most drying sections, there is a sizing press to improve the surface quality of the paper. The web of paper, now about 5 to 10 percent moisture, enters the sizing press, which has two large rollers and a vat of sizing liquid. It runs through

the sizing liquid and then between two rollers that squeeze out excess sizing solution. Sizing the paper hardens its surface to resist penetration of ink, lets it resist the effect of handling, and fastens the loose surface fibers to the base sheet. The paper leaves the sizing press containing about 25 percent water.

The paper goes to another drying section similar to the previous one. It then leaves and enters a calendar stack (Fig. 163-7), which has eight or nine highly polished steel rolls 16 to 24 inches (40.6 by 61 cm) in diameter. The paper passes over and around each roll, being smoothed and getting a more uniform thickness. The felt and wire marks that were in the paper from the Fourdrinier wire and the drying cylinders are smoothed.

The paper leaves the calendar section and is taken up on a reel at the dry end of the papermaking machine (Fig. 163-8). On the larger machines paper is wound in rolls with diameters up to 88 inches (223.5 cm).

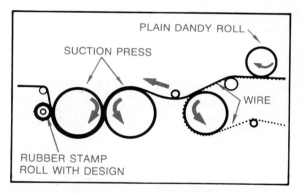

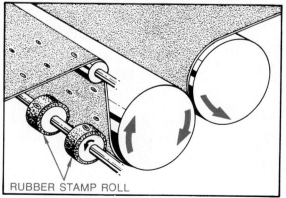

Fig. 163-4. A watermark produced by the rubber stamp roll method.

Fig. 163-5. Two operators, the machine tender and the back tender, make adjustments in the wet-press section of a paper-making machine.

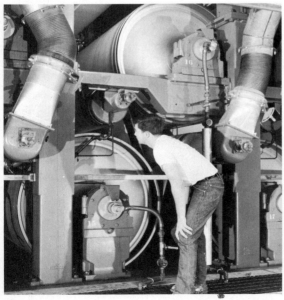

Fig. 163-6. An operator checks the adjustments of a pocket ventilating roll in the drying section of the paper-making machine.

METHODS OF MANUFACTURING PAPER AND PAPERBOARD

The three principle methods of manufacturing paper and paperboard—(1) the Fourdrinier, (2) the cylinder, and (3) the inverform—are illustrated in Figure 163-9. Each method is used to produce certain types of paper products.

Fourdrinier. Much of the paper made for printing and writing purposes is manufactured on this type of machine. The pulp mixture, forced from the head box (Fig. 163-9), travels about 30 feet along an endless wire. The pulp then mats semi-dry as the water drops away. The matted fibers are thrown off the wire and proceed through press rolls and a set of dryers. If the paper is to get a slick, shiny surface, it is coated before the drying process. If it is to have a smooth, hard surface, the paper goes through a calender stack before being wound onto a core or reel.

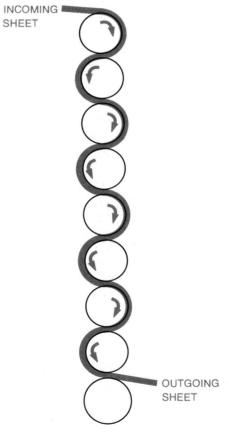

INCOMING SHEET

OUTGOING SHEET

Fig. 163-7. A calender stack of nine polished steel rolls.

Cylinder. The cylinder method is used to manufacture paperboard and building paper. In this process, successive layers of fibers and other stock preparations can be formed to produce packaging materials. A series of vats contain the various mixtures that are fed into the top liner, filler, and back liner (Fig. 163-9). For example, a board can have a good printed surface, a filler of inexpensive pulp, and another protective surface. The machine is also used to manufacture tissue and other absorbent papers.

Inverform. The inverform is a relatively new machine (Fig. 163-9) used to produce several types of board. It uses an endless wire similar to the Fourdrinier's but mounted over its top are a number of head boxes and forming-wire units, each for a different type of stock. It offers high-operating speeds and lower cost manufacture of some special boards.

FINISHING PAPER

After it comes off the papermaking machine, the paper must go through several finishing steps: inspecting, sheeting, special finishing, and packaging. After these steps, the paper is ready to be shipped to the customer.

When the large roll of paper is taken off the machine, it must be re-wound. During this process the edges of the paper roll are trimmed and it can be cut into desirable widths.

Some papers are run through a set of calender steel rolls again and are *super-calendered*. This places special finishes on the paper to fit it for specific uses.

The art of raising or depressing areas of a paper surface by applying pressure in a repeating pattern is called *embossing*. It is usually done by passing a web of paper through a pair of engraved rolls that press the pattern into the sheet (Fig. 163-10). There are a number of methods, which can give one- or two-sided embossed patterns.

Rolls of paper to be cut into sheets can come directly from the rewinder or from any of the other finishing processes. The rolls are placed on reel stands, which hold one to a dozen rolls. From the reel the paper passes through *slitters* (Fig. 163-11), which cut the paper into the correct width. The paper then goes through a *cutter* where a knife revolves on a cylinder. Each time the cylinder revolves, the knife cuts the sheet to a specified length.

After being cut, the sheets are taken on moving belts to machines called *layboys* which jog the sheets into uniform piles. Most modern layboys have counters that automatically insert a marker at the required number of sheets.

Workers inspect, count, and wrap the sheets into packages of the right amount (Fig. 163-12). High grade paper is usually hand sorted or inspected but machines have been developed that will do all of the necessary operations from cutting through wrapping without human help.

Fig. 163-8. The dry end of a paper-making machine.

NEKOOSA PAPERS

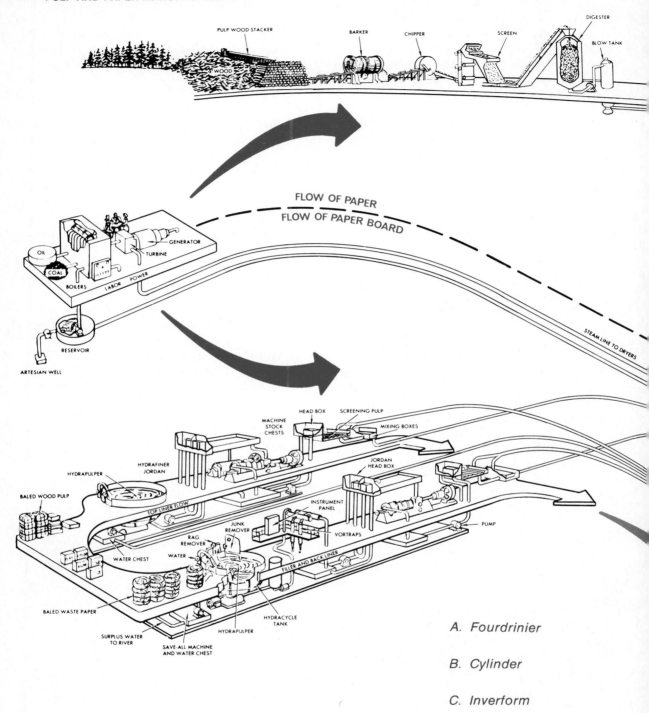

Fig. 163-9. The three principle methods of manufacturing paper and paperboard.

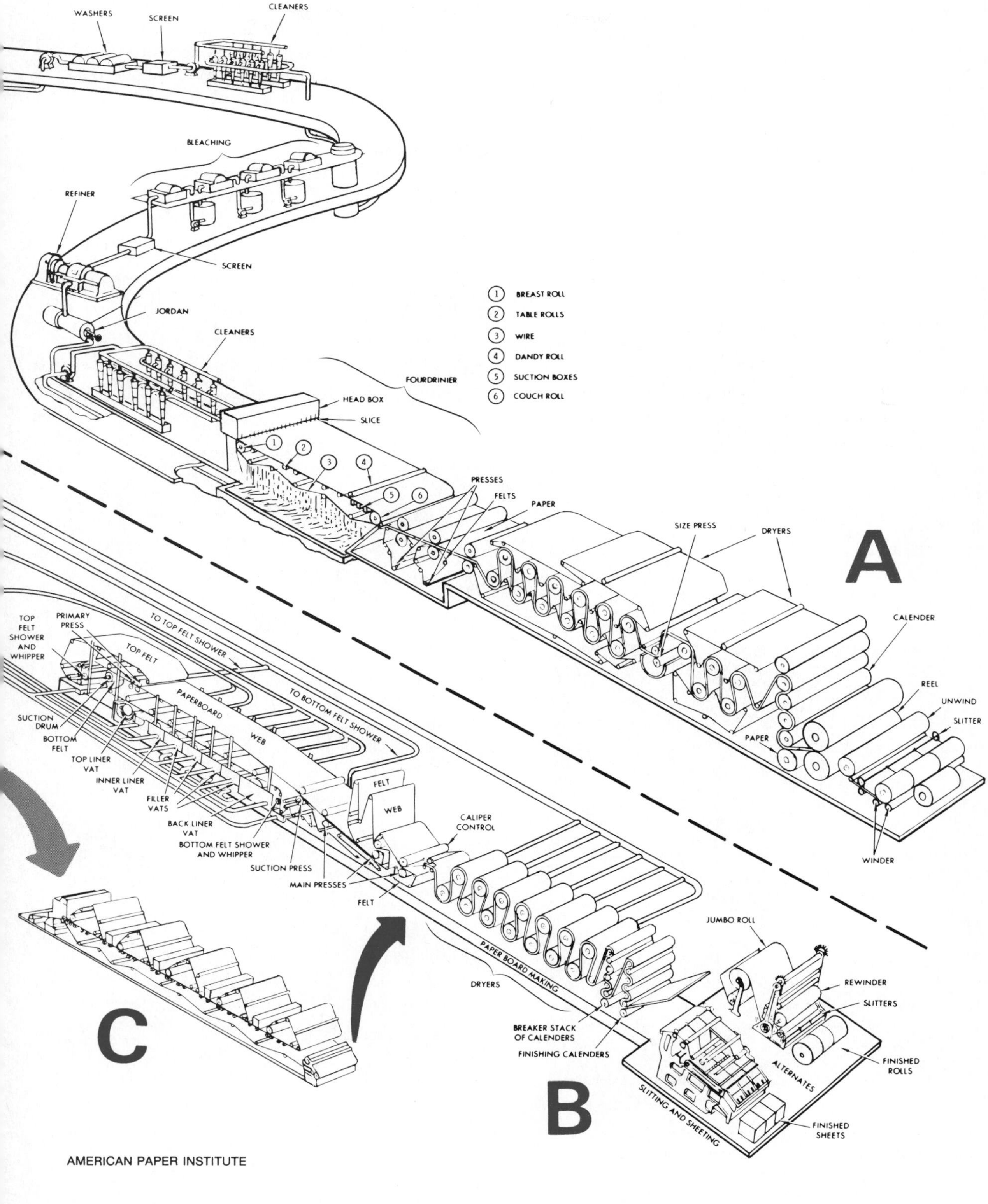

WASHERS
SCREEN
CLEANERS
BLEACHING
REFINER
SCREEN
JORDAN
CLEANERS

1 BREAST ROLL
2 TABLE ROLLS
3 WIRE
4 DANDY ROLL
5 SUCTION BOXES
6 COUCH ROLL

FOURDRINIER
HEAD BOX
SLICE

PRESSES
FELTS
PAPER
SIZE PRESS
DRYERS

A

CALENDER
REEL
UNWIND
SLITTER
PAPER
WINDER

TOP FELT SHOWER AND WHIPPER
PRIMARY PRESS
TO TOP FELT SHOWER
TOP FELT
SUCTION DRUM
BOTTOM FELT
TOP LINER VAT
INNER LINER VAT
FILLER VATS
BACK LINER VAT
BOTTOM FELT SHOWER AND WHIPPER
SUCTION PRESS
MAIN PRESSES
FELT
PAPERBOARD WEB
TO BOTTOM FELT SHOWER
FELT
WEB
CALIPER CONTROL

C

PAPER BOARD MAKING
DRYERS
BREAKER STACK OF CALENDERS
FINISHING CALENDERS

JUMBO ROLL
REWINDER
SLITTERS
ALTERNATES
FINISHED ROLLS
SLITTING AND SHEETING
FINISHED SHEETS

B

AMERICAN PAPER INSTITUTE

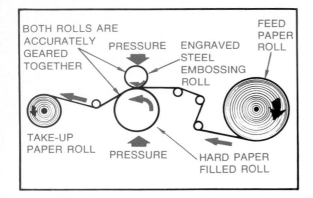

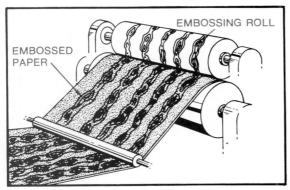

THE MEAD CORPORATION

Fig. 163-10. Embossing paper.

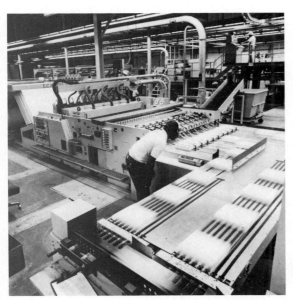

NEKOOSA PAPERS

Fig. 163-11. High-speed, cut-size sheeters are used in the finishing operations of many paper companies.

Large rolls of paper, to be used on large presses designed for a continuous web of paper, are handled with great care while being wrapped (Fig. 163-13). If the rolls are mishandled, hundreds of dollars worth of fine paper can easily be ruined. The boxed and wrapped paper is shipped to customers by truck, railroad, airplane, and ship.

Paper Research

The paper industry stresses research in many areas. Research specialists work in laboratories, prelogging and tree-thinning procedures, tree farming, and soil conservation.

NEKOOSA PAPERS

Fig. 163-12. The inspecting, counting, and wrapping room of a paper mill.

THE MEAD CORPORATION

Fig. 163-13. A paper roll conveying system and packing operation in a paper mill.

Many firms in the pulp and paper industry have research laboratories that employ chemists, chemical engineers, physicists, biologists, and foresters. They investigate improved processes and products, more scientific uses of wood and other raw materials, and development of by-products from waste materials. The paper industry has established the Institute of Paper Science and Technology to deal with broad research problems. It is located on the campus of the Georgia Institute of Technology in Atlanta, Georgia.

Research is done not only to improve paper products, but to develop better equipment and methods of using energy for specific operations when making paper (Fig. 163-14). Millions of dollars are spent annually by the paper industry to continue its successful research program.

S. D. WARREN COMPANY

Fig. 163-14. A research specialist tests paper for opacity. Paper samples are also laboratory-tested for fold, tear, gloss, strength, and thickness.

UNIT 164 KINDS, WEIGHTS, AND SIZES OF PAPER

There are too many kinds, weights, and sizes of paper to discuss in this unit. A list of all the available varieties would be impossible to remember.

Basic papers used by the commercial printer are bond, book, bristol, cover, ledger offset, text, newsprint, duplicator, and mimeograph. Each is discussed briefly in this unit. Other kinds of paper available are onionskin, tracing vellum, kraft wrapping, and paperboard. Special papers for specific uses have been and will continue to be developed.

WEIGHTS AND SIZES

Papers are said to have a *specific weight* and a *basic size*. Weight usually refers to thickness, but not always. In figuring weight, one constant is the quantity, which is always one ream of 500 sheets.

When a paper is said to be 24-pound bond, it means that 500, 17- by 22-inch (43 by 56 cm) sheets of that paper weigh 24 pounds (10.9 kg). This is called the *basis weight*. Even if this same paper were available in 34- by 44-inch (86.4 by 111.8 cm) sheets (four times the size) it would still be a 24-pound bond, although 500 sheets would weigh 96 pounds (43.6 kg) or four times as much.

Bookpaper weights are figured differently. Many books and papers, but by no means all, are printed from 25- by 38-inch (63.5 by 96.5 cm) sheets, and so the paper mills have settled on this as the basic size for computing weights of book papers.

You might expect a 24-pound bond paper and a 24-pound book paper to be the same weight and thickness, but the book sheet is over twice as large as the bond sheet. That means it is somewhat less than half as thick. A 60-pound (27.2 kg) book paper would be the same as a 24-pound bond paper.

Throughout this book, we have given the metric equivalents when mentioning weights and sizes. In discussing paper sizes in the following pages, however, we will not give metric measurements. Papers in metric countries follow a different system. A conventional piece of typing paper, for instance, is 210 by 297 mm—8¼ by 11⅝ inches. Giving the metric translation of the U.S. standard size of typing paper—8½ by 11 inches—would be meaningless since that size of paper is not used in metric-measure countries.

BASIC PAPERS

Bond

The many bond papers come in as many different varieties as there are uses for them.

Common uses: Stationery, letterhead, business forms, direct-mail advertising, announcements, price lists, office systems, invoices, and so on.

Requirements: Strength, permanence, good appearance and a crisp "snap," ink-receptive surface, good erasing qualities, freedom from fuzz.

Characteristics: Bond papers are manufactured from rag fiber, cotton fiber, or chemical wood pulps in a wide range of qualities. Rag content bonds may be 25, 50, 75, or 100 percent rag. The non-rag material in the first three grades consists of bleached chemical wood pulp made from various combinations of bleached sulfite, sulfate, soda, and semi-chemical wood fibers. Bond papers have a hard, even finish on both sides of the sheet and are sized so that they do not absorb writing or printing ink into the body of the paper. Size may be added in three different ways: (1) engine, or beater, sizing in which sizing is added while the paper is in the beater, (2) tub sizing, in which paper is dipped or immersed in the sizing solution, and (3) surface sizing, in which size is sprayed on both sides of the paper as it comes off the papermaking machine and before final drying. Rag bonds are usually watermarked and, like chemical wood bonds, have either a laid or wove formation and are produced in a variety of finishes.

Weights: Basis 17 by 22/500: 9, 13, 16, 20, 24 pounds.

Sheet sizes: 17 by 22, 17 by 28, 19 by 24, 22 by 34, 24 by 38, 28 by 34, 34 by 44 inches.

Cut sizes: 8½ by 11, 8½ by 13, 8½ by 14 inches.

Book

Book papers may be coated or uncoated and are adaptable to any printing process.

Common uses: Books, pamphlets, folders, brochures, catalogs, direct-mail advertising.

Requirements: The requirements are variable, depending on use of the printed product. Appearance, strength, opacity, permanency, and with coated papers, good bond between paper and coating are considerations.

Characteristics: Book papers are made from raw materials such as mechanical and chemical wood pulps, straw, and reclaimed wastepaper. Usually two or more of these are mixed to form the basic solution, then mineral filler, size, and dye are added. Book papers may or may not be surface sized. Five different finishes are standard for the uncoated variety: antique, eggshell, machine, English, and supercalendered. Antique offers the roughest surface, with eggshell close behind. Smoothest of the uncoated book papers is the supercalendered, which is rolled or ironed down under pressure to make a smooth printing surface. Base stock for coated book papers is the same as for uncoated, but it is faced with mineral pigments mixed with adhesives and sometimes also a wax or soap to enhance the finish, or feel. Coating may be either dull or glossy, on one or both sides of the paper.

Weights: Basis 25 by 38/500: Uncoated, 35, 40, 45, 50, 60, 70, 80, 100 pounds; Coated One Side, 50, 60, 70, 80 pounds; Coated Both Sides, 50, 60, 70, 80, 90, 100, 120 pounds.

Standard sizes: 20 by 26, 22½ by 35, 24 by 36, 25 by 38, 28 by 42, 28 by 44, 32 by 44, 35 by 45, 36 by 48, 38 by 50, 41 by 54 inches.

Bristol

Bristols are a group of stiff, heavy papers in thicknesses from 0.006 inch up to and including index and postcards. Two or more plies (layers) of the same kind of paper may be pasted together for greater durability.

Common uses: Records and filing, identification and time cards, business and commercial cards, self-mailers, programs, menus, announcements, file folders, booklet covers, and many more.

Requirements: Smooth, hard, uniform surface, free from lint, sturdy enough to take much handling.

Characteristics: A bristol is usually made from sulfite or sulfate pulp, or both, but may also include rag pulp. Index bristols are thoroughly sized to give them good writing and printing surfaces, and good wearing and recording qualities. They are primarily used for card files of all kinds. A variety known as printing bristol is somewhat stiffer and less durable under heavy use than index. Postcard bristols may be either uncoated or coated in dull or glossy finish on one or both sides. Both types are used for postal and return cards. Cast-coated postcard stock has the best printing quality and is used for picture postcards, menu covers, and others. There is also a class known as folding bristol, which has long, flexible fibers that let the paper be folded more easily.

Weights: Index (Basis 25½ by 30½/500, 90, 110, 140, 170, 220 pounds; Postcard (Basis 22½ by 28½/500), 94, 100, 105 pounds; Printing and Folding (Basis 23 by 35/500, 110, 125, 150, 175, 200, 250 pounds.

Standard sizes: Index, 20½ by 23¾, 22½ by 28½, 22½ by 35, 25½ by 30½, 25½ by 35½, 8½ by 11 (cut size); Postcard, 22 by 28, 22½ by 28½; Printing and Folding, 17 by 22½, 22½ by 28½, 22½ by 35, 23 by 29, 23 by 35, 35 by 46 inches.

Cover

Cover paper is a term applied to a great variety of papers used for the outside covers of catalogs and brochures.

Common uses: Booklet and manual covers, binders, programs, directories, self-mailers, broadsides, announcements.

Requirements: Resistance to handling and abrasion, good appearance, permanent color, ability to accept standard types of printing plus such others as screen printing and embossing, foldability, holding to binding glue.

Characteristics: Cover papers are usually made from rag pulp, chemical wood pulp, or a mixture of the two. They may also contain mechanical pulp. Cover papers may be uncoated or coated on one or both sides. Most have a wove formation; some have a laid finish and are watermarked or deckle-edged. Many of the uncoated papers are given a textured finish to imitate linen, leather, corduroy, and other specialties. Others are calendered to accept halftone printing, cloth lined (by a lamination process), or pasted back-to-back to provide a cover material with extra strength, or with a different color on each side. Coated papers may be cast coated for smoothness and gloss, metallic coated for special effect, surface sized for offset lithography printing, or plastic coated with a transparent film. There are also plain-coated covers with either dull or glossy finishes similar to coated book paper except that they are made in heavier weights.

Weights: Basis 20 by 26/500: Uncoated, 40, 50, 65, 80, 90, 100, 130 pounds; Plain Coated, 50, 60, 65, 80 pounds.

Standard sizes: 20 by 26, 23 by 29, 23 by 35, .26 by 40, 35 by 46 inches.

Text

Text papers were originally used in the manufacture of books and textbooks, but now they have much broader applications.

Common uses: Booklets, brochures, pamphlets, manuals, portfolios, menus, announcements, letterheads, self-mailers, annual reports, catalogs, surveys, promotional material.

Requirements: Appearance, opacity, strength, pick resistance, foldability.

Characteristics: Text papers come in many decorative colors and a variety of finishes, including antique, vellum, smooth, felt-marked, patterned and laid, and often have a deckle edge. Some are made from rag pulp, but most are made from chemical wood pulps or a combination of rag and wood pulps. Fillers are added for opacity.

Weights: Basis 25 by 38/500: 60, 70, 80 pounds.

Standard sizes: 23 by 29, 23 by 35, 25 by 38, 26 by 40, 35 by 45, 38 by 50 inches.

Newsprint

Newsprint is the lowest grade of paper used for quantity printing.

Common uses: Newspapers, handbills, telephone directories.

Requirements: Low permanence and strength, low light glare to reduce eye strain.

Characteristics: Grayish in color. Newsprint is produced by the ground-wood or mechanical method; the fibers are very short. Because of the short fibers, it will fold easily either direction. It will yellow and become brittle after a time. Very absorbent to ink so that little dryer needs to be used in the ink.

Weights: Sheet Basis 24 by 36/500: 34 pounds; Roll Basis 24 by 36/500; 32 pounds.

Standard sizes: Sheets: $8^{1}/_2$ by $15^{1}/_8$, 22 by 30, 22 by 32, 22 by 35, 24 by 35, 24 by 36, 26 by 40, 28 by 42, 30 by 44, 32 by 44, 35 by 44, 36 by 48 inches. Rolls: 35, $52^{1}/_2$, 70 inches.

Ledger

Ledger papers are similar to bonds but are somewhat smoother, harder, heavier.

Common uses: Primarily for bookkeeping and records, but also for statements, legal documents, and other forms.

Requirements: Strength, tear resistance, water and ink resistance, erasability, smooth, nonglare surface, adaptability to binding, resistance to splitting, flexibility.

Characteristics: Ledger papers are commonly made from rag pulp, bleached chemical wood pulp, or a mixture of the two. They are available in several grades. Because of their longer fibers they are stronger than equivalent weight bonds. Most are sized, calendered.

Weights: Basis 17 by 22/500: 24, 28, 32, 36 pounds.

Standard sizes: 17 by 22, 17 by 28, 19 by 24, 22 by 34, 24 by 38, 28 by 34, $22^{1}/_2$ by $22^{1}/_2$, $22^{1}/_2$ by $34^{1}/_2$, $24^{1}/_2$ by $24^{1}/_2$ inches.

Offset

Offset papers are essentially book papers, specially made to meet offset lithography needs.

Common uses: Reports, proposals, manuals, form letters, advertising and promotional material, forms and so on.

Requirements: Proper moisture content and *pH* value, freedom from lint and paper dust, good pick strength.

Characteristics: Some grades of offset paper are made from rag pulp and bleached chemical wood pulp; others from a combination of bleached chemical and mechanical pulps. All offset paper is engine sized and often tub sized as well. Papers may be uncoated or clay coated on one or both sides. All are processed to eliminate distortion.

Weights: Basis 25 by 38/500: 50, 60, 70, 80, 100, 120, 150 pounds.

Sheet sizes: 25 by 38, $22^{1}/_2$ by 35, 28 by 42, 28 by 44, 32 by 44, 35 by 45, 36 by 48, 38 by 50, 38 by 52, 41 by 54, 44 by 64 inches.

Cut sizes: $8^{1}/_2$ by 11, 10 by 14, 11 by 17 inches.

Duplicator

These papers are used as either masters or copies for the spirit duplicating processes.

Common uses: Office systems, form letters, notices, bulletins, announcements, manuals, menus, news and publicity releases, production schedules, and many other applications where inexpensive, limited volume duplication is required.

Requirements: Master papers: Freedom from lint, ability to accept dye image and release readily for duplication, imperviousness in spirit masters to solvent. Copy papers: Smooth surface, good strength, freedom from lint.

Characteristics: Coated and uncoated book papers are used for both masters and copies. Spirit master paper is specially coated or enameled to meet the needs of the process. Copy papers are coated and have smooth surfaces and good strength.

Weights: Basis 17 by 22/500: Master Papers, 24, 28 pounds; Copy Papers, 16, 20, 24 pounds.

Sheet sizes: 17 by 22, 17 by 28, 19 by 24, 22 by 34, 24 by 38, 28 by 34 inches.

Cut sizes: 8½ by 11, 8½ by 13, 8½ by 14 inches.

Mimeograph

Mimeograph paper is similar to bond but has a rougher finish.

Common uses: Reports, announcements, notices, manuals, form letters, schedules.

Requirements: Opacity, rapid ink absorption, strength, lint-free surface.

Characterisitics: Toothy surface minimizes the amount of ink received from the stencil and aids in setting ink.

Weights: Basis 17 by 22/500: 16, 20, 24 pounds.

Sheet sizes: Basis 17 by 22, 17 by 28, 19 by 24, 22 by 34, 24 by 38, 28 by 34 inches.

Cut sizes: 8 by 10½, 8½ by 11, 8½ by 13, 8½ by 14 inches.

RECYCLED PAPER

Recycling is an idea with new importance because of the increasing amount of solid waste generated by industry, business, and the general population. Recycling is simply the reuse of resources and materials of all kinds that have been worn out or thrown away in their original manufactured form. Recycling is reclaiming and reprocessing previously wasted used products and raw materials to make them into useful products again. Metals and glass and water are recycleable, for example. Even land can be recycled through reforestation.

Perhaps more than any other material, paper is recycleable. A principal source of waste paper for recycling is the waste of business, industry, and the general waste of America's cities. New York City alone produces thousands of tons of solid waste each hour, of which 40 to 60 percent is paper and paperboard. Recycled paper is defined by the federal government as follows:

The various paper stocks shall contain mini-

mum specified percentages, by weight, of fibers reclaimed from solid waste or waste collected as a result of a manufacturing process but shall not include those materials generated from and reused within a plant as part of the papermaking process.

There are forty-six grades of waste paper as defined by the Paper Stock Institute. In addition, there are several hundred specialty grades of waste paper that do not clearly fit into the forty-six grades. These are frequently called high grades and low grades. *High grades* is used in the trade for waste that can be recycled into fine printing papers. *Low grades* can be recycled into folding cartons, building board, and/or roofing materials. Furthermore, old newspapers can be recycled into new newsprint.

A large amount of paper waste is created in a commercial graphic arts plant. This includes trimmings from booklets, paper needed for machine set-up, and printing overruns. This waste paper is made into bales that can easily be shipped to a recycling papermaking facility and re-made into useable paper (Fig. 164-1).

CALIPERS AND WEIGHTS

Different kinds and weights of paper have different thicknesses. Although paper is graded

R. R. DONNELLEY AND SONS

Fig. 164-1. Paper trimmings from graphic arts plant operations are baled for shipping to a recycling papermaking facility.

according to pounds, press operators often need to know the thickness of paper being printed or bought. Tables have been prepared to save time (Fig. 164-2). Note the thickness similarities among the several papers and the differences in weight.

Weights of special sizes

The Constant Factor Schedule (Fig. 164-3) offers a quick way to find the 1,000-sheet weights of special-size sheets. First, find the number of square inches in the proposed size. Then, multiply the number of square inches by the constant factor. The answer is the 1,000-sheet weight of the special size.

Example: The proposed size is 46 by 58 inches. Substance weight is 80 pounds, 46 by 58 is 2,668 square inches.

Under the heading of book paper in Figure 164-3, locate 80 lbs. and the corresponding factor of 0.1684. Multiply 2,668 sq. in. by 0.1684, which equals 449.2912. This rounds out to 449 lbs. per 1,000 sheets in size 46 by 58 inches. The factors in Figure 164-3 represent the *weight of 1,000 sheets one inch square.*

The *MM* system of basis-weight determination refers to the weight of 1,000 sheets, size 25 by 40 inches. Therefore, the *MM Basis Weight* of any basis weight listed is found by moving the decimal point of the factor three places to the right.

Example: The MM Basis weight of 70-pound book paper is 147.4 pounds.

The MM basis weight of 140-pound Index Bristol is 360 pounds.

The calipers listed are approximate averages. Variations will be found from one mill run to another, either to the light or heavy side of the basis weight, within trade custom tolerances. One point equals 1/1000 of an inch.

BOND, MIMEO, DUPLICATOR

bs. 17 x 22	13#	16#	20#	24#
Sulphite Bond	.003	.0035	.004	.0045
Cotton Fiber Bond				
Cockle Finish	.003	.0035	.004	.0045
Smooth Finish	.0025	.003	.0035	.004
Mimeo		.004	.005	.0055
Duplicator		.0025	.003	.0035

LEDGER

bs. 17 x 22	24#	28#	32#	36#
Smooth Finish	.0045	.005	.0055	.006
Posting Finish	.005	.0055	.006	.0065

BOOK PAPERS

bs. 25 x 38	45#	50#	60#	70#
Offset				
Regular	.0035	.004	.0045	.005
Antique	.004	.0045	.005	.006
Bulking			.0055	.0066	.0077
English Finish	.0032	.0035	.004	.0045
Supercalendered	.0022	.0025	.003	.0035
Gloss Coated		.0025	.003	.0035
Dull Coated		.003	.0035	.004
Coated 1 Side			.0032	.0037

bs. 25 x 38	80#	100#	120#	150#
Offset				
Regular	.006	.0075	.009	.011
Antique	.007	.009	.011	.013
Bulking	.0088	.011	.0135	
Gloss Coated	.004	.0055		
Dull Coated	.0045	.006		
Coated 1 Side	.004			

COVER PAPERS

bs. 20 x 26	50#	60#	65#	80#	90#	100#	130#
Uncoated							
Smooth			.0065		.011		.013
Antique	.007		.010				.020
Coated	.005	.0055	.006	.008	.009	.010	

bs. 20 x 26	50#		65#	80#	94#	110#	
Lusterkote	.0055		.0065	.008	.010	.012	

INDEX BRISTOL

bs. 25½ x 30½	90#	110#	140#	170#
Smooth Finish	.007/.0075	.008/.009	.0105/.0115	.013/.014

Leslie Paper Company

Fig. 164-2. Table of calipers and weights.

BOOK PAPER		NEWSPRINT, TAG AND CRAFT		BRISTOL	
Basis wt. 25x38/500	1000 Sheet Factor	Basis wt. 25x36/500	1000 Sheet Factor	Basis wt. 22½ x28½/500	1000 Sheet Factor
25	.0526	32	.0741	67	.2090
30	.0632	34	.0787	80	.2489
35	.0737	35	.0810	82½	.2573
40	.0842	40	.0926	90	.2807
45	.0947	50	.1157	100	.3119
50	.1053	60	.1389	120	.3743
60	.1263	100	.2315	140	.4366
70	.1474	125	.2894	160	.4990
80	.1684	150	.3472	180	.5614
100	.2105	175	.4051	200	.6238
120	.2526	200	.4630		
140	.2947	250	.5787		
150	.3158				

BRISTOL		COVER PAPER		BONDS, WRITINGS AND LEDGER	
Basis wt. 23x35/500	1000 Sheet Factor	Basis wt. 20x26/500	1000 Sheet Factor	Basis wt. 17x22/500	1000 Sheet Factor
100	.2484	50	.1923	8	.0428
125	.3106	60	.2308	9	.0481
150	.3727	65	.2500	11	.0588
175	.4348	80	.3077	12	.0642
200	.4969	90	.3462	13	.0695
250	.6211	100	.3846	16	.0856
		130	.5000	20	.1070
				24	.1283
INDEX BRISTOL				28	.1497
Basis wt. 25½ x30½/500	1000 Sheet Factor			32	.1711
90	.2314			36	.1925
110	.2829				
140	.3600				
170	.4372				
220	.5657				

Leslie Paper Company

Fig. 164-3. Constant factor schedule.

UNIT 165 BUYING AND FINDING COST OF PAPER

Most paper is bought in either sheet form or roll form. In each of these two useful paper forms, several different amounts of stock are available from the paper supply company. Rolls of paper are packaged and sold by weight; sheets of paper are normally packaged and sold according to the number of sheets.

Individual sheets of paper are commonly sold by the package, carton, or bundle. The number of sheets in each of these three packaging media varies according to the kind of paper. For example, a package of bond paper normally contains one ream, or 500 sheets, where a package of index bristol paper normally contains only 100 sheets. The different amounts makes for handling convenience. Five hundred sheets of index bristol paper would be too heavy for one person to handle.

BUYING PAPER

Paper can be bought by the package, the carton or bundle, the four carton or four bundle, and the sixteen carton or sixteen bundle (Fig. 165-1). The same paper will have different prices depending on how it is packaged or the amount of paper that is bought at one time. The price difference of the varying amounts of paper depends mostly on the labor cost. It takes more time to handle and distribute one package of paper that contains from 100 to 500 sheets than to handle and ship sixteen cartons of paper that could contain 64,000 sheets. The labor charge per sheet is therefore much less when handling larger quantities of paper.

In most cases, paper supply houses will not require you to buy sixteen cartons of one specific weight and color to get the sixteen-carton price. They will let an assortment of full packages make up a complete carton.

Some materials are hard to classify as packages, cartons, or bundles; these items are called

---

Package Price applies only on orders for not less than an original package of one item.

Carton or Bundle Price applies only on orders for not less than an original carton or bundle of an item.

4 Carton or 4 Bundle Price applies only on orders for not less than 4 original cartons or bundles. May be assorted so long as each item assorted is an even carton or a multiple thereof.

16 Carton or 16 Bundle Price applies only on orders for not less than 16 original cartons or bundles. May be assorted so long as each item assorted is an even carton or a multiple thereof.

Carton Assortments - Full packages of sealed goods may be assorted for a carton multiple under 4 or 16 carton assortment privilege.

This assortment privilege applies only to printed papers listed from page 11 through page 122.

Wrapped Goods Equivalents:
$$500 \text{ lbs.} = 4 \text{ cartons}$$
$$2000 \text{ lbs.} = 16 \text{ cartons}$$

LESLIE PAPER COMPANY

Fig. 165-1. Packaging and pricing.

JET STREAM BOND — 0207
Economy Bond (Sulphite)
Unwatermarked
Trimmed Four Sides
500 Sheets to the Package

WHITE

				Pkg.	Ctn.	4 Ctn.	16 Ctn.	Bkn. Pkg.
						Price Per 100 Pounds		
Basis 17x22 — 16 lbs.				$31.50	$26.00	$22.70	$21.10	$59.00
Basis 17x22 — 20 lbs.				30.30	25.00	21.80	20.30	57.00

Size	Wt. Per M	Basis Wt. 17x22	Shts. to Ctn.	Pkg.	Ctn.	4 Ctn.	16 Ctn.	Bkn. Pkg.
					Price Per 1000 Sheets			
17½ x22½	34	16	4000	$10.71	$ 8.82	$ 7.71	$ 7.18	$19.82
17x28	41	16	3000	12.92	10.66	9.31	8.65	24.19
19x24	39	16	3000	12.29	10.14	8.85	8.23	23.01
22x34	64	16	2000	20.16	16.64	14.53	13.50	37.76
24x38	78	16	1500	24.57	20.28	17.71	16.46	46.02
28x34	82	16	1500	25.83	21.32	18.61	17.30	48.38
17x22	40	20	3000	12.12	10.00	8.72	8.12	22.80
17½ x22½	42	20	3000	12.73	10.50	9.16	8.53	23.55
17x28	51	20	3000	15.45	12.75	11.12	10.35	29.07
19x24	49	20	3000	14.85	12.25	10.68	9.95	27.93
22x34	80	20	1500	24.24	20.00	17.44	16.24	45.60
24x38	98	20	1500	29.69	24.50	21.36	19.89	55.86
28x34	102	20	1500	30.91	25.50	22.24	20.71	58.14

COLORS — Canary, Pink, Blue, Green

				Pkg.	Ctn.	4 Ctn.	16 Ctn.	Bkn. Pkg.
					Price Per 100 Pounds			
Basis 17x22 — 16 lbs.				$34.00	$28.05	$24.50	$22.80	$63.00
Basis 17x22 — 20 lbs.				32.80	27.05	23.60	21.95	61.00

Size	Wt. Per M	Basis Wt. 17x22	Shts. to Ctn.	Pkg.	Ctn.	4 Ctn.	16 Ctn.	Bkn. Pkg.
					Price Per 1000 Sheets			
17x22	32	16	4000	$10.88	$ 8.98	$ 7.84	$ 7.30	$20.16
17½ x22½	34	16	4000	11.56	9.54	8.32	7.75	21.39
17x22	40	20	3000	13.12	10.82	9.44	8.80	24.40
17½ x22½	42	20	3000	13.78	11.37	9.92	9.23	25.49
17x28	51	20	3000	16.73	13.80	12.04	11.19	31.11
28x34	102	20	1500	33.46	27.59	24.07	22.44	62.22

LESLIE PAPER COMPANY

Fig. 165-2. Paper breaking points.

wrapped goods and are sold according to poundage, which in turn is equal to so many cartons. For example, 500 pounds normally equals 4 cartons and 2,000 pounds equals 16 cartons.

Figure 165-2 indicates the number of sheets that can be bought in broken package quantity before the price equals the amount for a full package. If only 312 sheets of bond paper were needed to produce a specific commercial printing job, it would be unwise to buy that amount of paper from the paper supplier. It would be more economical to buy an entire package containing 500 sheets and get 188 sheets free. As you study the chart, you will see why the commercial printer should be well aware of the breaking point when buying paper.

FINDING THE COST OF PAPER

Upon selecting a specific kind, size, and weight of paper, it is easy to find the cost of the paper. Paper supply catalogs list several items for each kind of paper—the color, sizes, weight, packaging, and pricing information (Fig. 165-3). From this price schedule, note that a 17- by 22-inch sheet will weigh 40 pounds per thousand sheets. The basis weight is 20 pounds and is packaged 3,000 sheets per carton. The cost of the paper is figured by the thousand sheets and varies by how the paper is bought—for example, by the package quantities of carton, four carton, sixteen carton, or broken package. You can see that the cost per 1,000 sheets becomes less as the quantity of paper increases. Note that the broken package price is nearly twice as much as the full package price.

It is easy to find the cost per sheet. This is done by moving the decimal three places to the left. For example, if the package price for 1,000 sheets was $12.12, one sheet would cost $0.012, or slightly more than one cent.

Information about the price per 100 pounds of paper is also given in paper catalogs. Before paper was priced per 1,000 sheets, all paper stock was sold by the pound. This pricing system was cumbersome and confusing. In recent years the pricing system has been changed to the present one.

FLAMBEAU BOND
Flambeau Paper
Packaged: 500 Sheets
Grain: Second Dimension

		PRICES PER CWT		
	Package	1 Carton	4 Carton	16 Carton
WHITE 16LB	85.85	75.15	65.70	60.55
WHITE 20LB	79.80	69.85	61.05	56.25
COLORS 16LB	90.90	79.55	69.55	64.10
COLORS 20LB	84.85	74.25	64.90	59.80

Basis 17X22-500

Item Number	Basis	Size	Wt. M	Shts Ctn	Color	Package	1 Carton	4 Carton	16 Carton
						PRICES PER 1000 SHEETS			
WHITE									
109-018	16	17x22	32	4000		27.47	24.05	21.02	19.38
109-019	16	17.5x22.5	34	4000		29.19	25.55	22.34	20.59
109-020	16	19x24	39	3000		33.48	29.31	25.62	23.61
109-021	20	17x22	40	3000		31.92	27.94	24.42	22.50
109-022	20	17.5x22.5	42	3000		33.52	29.34	25.64	23.61
109-023	20	19x24	49	3000		39.10	34.23	29.91	27.56
COLORS									
109-024	16	17.5x22.5	34	4000	Canary	30.91	27.05	23.65	21.79
109-025	20	17x22	40	3000	Blue	33.94	29.70	25.96	23.92
109-026	20	17x22	40	3000	Buff	33.94	29.70	25.96	23.92
109-039	20	17x22	40	3000	Canary	33.94	29.70	25.96	23.92
109-040	20	17x22	40	3000	Cherry	33.94	29.70	25.96	23.92
109-041	20	17x22	40	3000	Goldenrod	33.94	29.70	25.96	23.92
109-042	20	17x22	40	3000	Green	33.94	29.70	25.96	23.92
113-440	20	17x22	40	3000	Grn Tint	33.94	29.70	25.96	23.92
109-048	20	17x22	40	3000	Gray	33.94	29.70	25.96	23.92
113-439	20	17x22	40	3000	Ivory	33.94	29.70	25.96	23.92
109-049	20	17x22	40	3000	Pink	33.94	29.70	25.96	23.92
109-050	20	17x22	40	3000	Salmon	33.94	29.70	25.96	23.92

Fig. 165-3. Typical price schedule.

UNIT 166 MAKING PAPER BY HAND

You can get a better understanding of papermaking by actually doing it yourself by hand. The American Paper Institute has provided the following easy-to-follow instructions.

EQUIPMENT

1. A fine-meshed wire screen.
2. A metal pan, such as an old biscuit pan, refrigerator tray, aluminum frozen food container, or some similar shape.
3. A forming rack or mold. This can be made from a second pan that will fit inside the first. Cut out the entire bottom, leaving only the sides.
4. A basin that will hold at least 10 quarts of water.
5. Thirty sheets of facial tissue, not the *wet strength* kind.
6. Two sheets of blotting paper, pan size.
7. Laundry starch. One tablespoon of instant starch to two cups of water provides what commercial papermakers call *size*.
8. An egg beater or blender and a rolling pin.
9. A household electric iron.

PROCEDURE

1. Tear sheets of tissue and place them in the basin.
2. Pour in the starch sizing and add water to make about 10 quarts of liquid.
3. Beat until thoroughly mixed (Fig. 166-1). This forms the pulp.
4. Prepare the paper machine, which is the combination of the pan, screen, and forming rack (Fig. 166-2). The pan and rack shown came from an old refrigerator tray.
5. Hold the forming rack firmly on the screen and dip it sideways into the pulp mixture (Fig. 166-3).
6. Clean the excess pulp from the outside of the forming rack.
7. Lift out the screen on which the pulp has formed (Fig. 166-4).
8. Dry the screen and wet sheet of pulp between two pieces of blotting paper (Fig. 166-5). The sheet will stick to the blotting paper.
9. Press out excess water with a rolling pin.
10. Iron dry (not too hot) the sheet, which is still between the blotters (Fig. 166-6).
11. Trim the edges with scissors. You now have a sheet of handmade paper.

AMERICAN PAPER INSTITUTE.

Fig. 166-1. Beating the tissue sizing mixture to make the pulp.

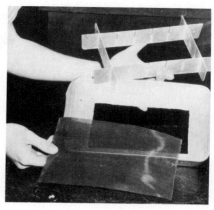

AMERICAN PAPER INSTITUTE.

Fig. 166-2. Preparing the paper machine.

AMERICAN PAPER INSTITUTE.

Fig. 166-3. Dipping out the pulp mixture.

AMERICAN PAPER INSTITUTE.

Fig. 166-4. Lifting out the screen with pulp deposited on it.

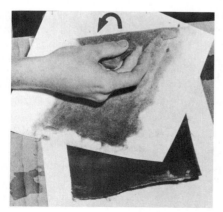

AMERICAN PAPER INSTITUTE

Fig. 166-5. Blotting the wet sheet of pulp between two pieces of blotting paper.

AMERICAN PAPER INSTITUTE.

Fig. 166-6. Drying the sheet of pulp between blotters.

UNIT 167 LEARNING EXPERIENCES: PULP AND PAPER MANUFACTURING

KEY TERMS

Unit 161

Papyrus

Unit 162

Additives	Debarking
Beating	Deciduous
Bleaching	Lignin
Centricleaner	Pulping
Chipping	Refining
Coniferous	

Unit 163

Dandy roll	Watermark
Fourdrinier	

Unit 164

Basis weight	Mimeograph paper
Bond paper	Newsprint paper
Book paper	Offset paper
Cover paper	Recycled paper
Duplicator paper	Text paper
Ledger paper	

DISCUSSION TOPICS

1. Why is fresh water essential in the production of paper?

2. Why is a combination of the two wood categories generally used in paper production?
3. Why must the paper pulp contain much water when it enters the papermaking machine?
4. What are the different ways of finishing paper after it has been delivered from the papermaking machines?
5. What is the advantage in purchasing large amounts of paper at one time?

ACTIVITIES

Units 161–166

1. Visit a paper manufacturing facility. Carefully observe the pulping and paper-forming stages in the paper manufacturing process. Also take special notice of the finishing and shipping departments. Prepare a detailed report of your visit.

Units 162–163

2. Get as many different kinds of paper products as you can. Look closely at the paper used in each product and think what special treatment the raw paper received to make it useful for each particular use. Which pulping process was used to prepare the basic paper for each product? Report in detail your investigations.

Unit 164

3. Get samples of each of the several basic papers that are used for producing printed products. Look closely at each sample. Compare the surface finish of each paper, the thickness, the opacity, the strength, and the general quality. Use instruments such as a magnifying glass, microscope, and densitometer.
4. Compare the printability of each of the several kinds of papers. Make the comparisons by using the letterpress, lithography, and screen-printing image-transfer methods.

Unit 165

5. Find the paper cost for one issue of your school newspaper or yearbook. Find the cost of the paper used in a midterm test for an entire class. Do these costs surprise you? Is paper cheap or expensive? Defend your answer.

Unit 166

6. Make a batch of paper using the information given in Unit 166. Make several sheets; after the sheets are fully dry, attempt to write with a pencil, ballpoint pen, and an ink pen. Also print on the sheets by using a platen press. Compare the writing and printing results on handmade paper with commercially made paper.

Lithographic ink being processed on a three roll mill.

20 PRINTING INK MANUFACTURING

168 INTRODUCTION TO PRINTING INKS

The printing process coats one material onto another. *Ink* is the most common coating material. *Receptors*, sometimes called *substrates*, are the materials on which the ink is coated or printed. The problem of coating would be simple if all receptors were the same. However, there are thousands of materials to be coated, including paper, glass, wood, metal, and plastic. New materials are always being developed. These often require special inks.

The different printing processes also complicate the situation. Each needs a special kind of ink developed just for that process. In addition, each printing process can use several kinds of ink. For example, water-base, oil-base, enamel, lacquer, textile, and epoxy inks are a few used in screen printing.

Inks are made to withstand the effects of heat, abrasion, acids, alkalines, and other chemicals. The ink manufacturers also face the challenge of making inks that will print at the high speeds now common in the graphic arts industry. It is estimated that nearly one million new ink formulas are developed each year.

Ink was manufactured and used by the Chinese during the third century B.C. to print with blocks. Figure 168-1 shows an early Chinese signature hand stamp. The manufacture of ink was well established in China several hundred years before Johann Gutenberg invented movable metal type in about 1450.

This section has been prepared in cooperation with the National Association of Printing Ink Manufacturers.

Ink manufacturing is a growing chemical industry. In the United States alone, 200 printing ink companies have sales of over 600 million dollars a year. The plants are located near the centers of the graphic arts industries.

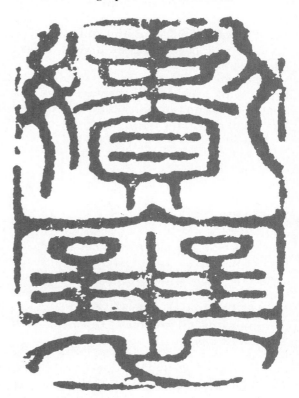

NATIONAL ASSOCIATION OF PRINTING INK MANUFACTURERS

Fig. 168-1. Early Chinese hand stamp.

UNIT 169 FORMULATION OF PRINTING INKS

The makeup of printing inks varies considerably, depending on the printing process, the substrate on which the printing will be done, and the system needed to dry the ink. Letterpress inks are very different from gravure inks because of the different requirements of these printing processes. The ingredients in two different inks for a single printing process may be different and have different drying requirements.

There are three groups of ingredients in printing ink: vehicles, pigments, and others, such as driers and waxes (Fig. 169-1). Vehicles are liquid; they carry the pigment and a binder to make the ink adhere to the receptor. Pigment is the ingredient that provides color.

VEHICLES

The vehicle is the ingredient that makes one kind of ink different from others. The *vehicle* carries the pigment and holds it. Vehicles from different inks may not be compatible. You should be careful when mixing inks.

Non-drying oil vehicles. These consist of penetrating oils that do not dry, such as petroleum oils and resins. The oils are often used in combination to get different printing qualities. This kind of vehicle is used to print on materials that absorb the ink, such as newsprint.

Drying-oil vehicles. Drying-oil vehicles dry by oxidation. They absorb oxygen, which causes the ink to harden or *set*. Most letterpress and lithographic inks have drying-oil vehicles. Linseed oil and litho varnish are most often used. Examples of others are Chinawood oil, castor oil, cottonseed oil, fish oil, and synthetic drying oils.

Linseed-oil varnishes distribute well on printing plate images, and they transfer and adhere well to the receptor. Litho varnishes are labeled by numbers. The numbers refer to the viscosity (thickness) of the varnish. Litho varnish numbered 00000 is very thin, 00 and #1 are medium, #5 and #6 are heavy, and #9 and #10 are very heavy (sometimes called body gum).

Solvent-resin vehicles. Resin-oil vehicles contain resin, oil, and a solvent. When ink is printed, the solvent is absorbed into the receptor almost immediately. Only a nearly dry coating of oil and resin remains on the surface, and this coating dries by oxidation. Some letterpress and lithographic inks are made with resin-oil vehicles that are called *quick-setting inks*.

Other vehicles. These include glycol, resin-wax, and water-soluble vehicles. Ink chemists

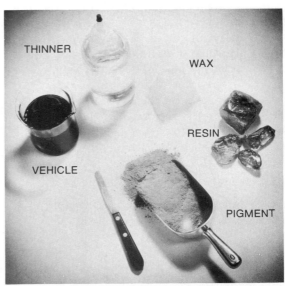

NATIONAL ASSOCIATION OF PRINTING INK MANUFACTURERS

Fig. 169-1. Ingredients of printing ink.

continue to develop printing ink vehicles that will support the needs of new pigments and printing substrates.

PIGMENTS

Pigments are what you see when the ink is printed. Pigments are thoroughly mixed with different vehicles for use with different printing processes.

Black pigments. These are primarily carbon, produced by burning gas or oil. Some common black pigments are channel black, furnace black, and lamp black. Some minerals are also used to produce black pigments for special printing purposes.

White pigments. There are two kinds of white pigments: opaque whites and transparent whites. Printed opaque whites cover the receptor like any other pigment. Materials used are titanium dioxide, zinc sulfide, and zinc oxides. Opaque whites can be divided into cover white and mixing whites. *Cover white* pigments can be used directly without support from other pigments. *Mixing white* pigment is used with other inks.

Transparent whites let light pass through the pigment so that the color below the ink can be seen. Some of the materials used to produce transparent white pigments are aluminum hydrate, magnesium carbonate, calcium carbonate, and clays.

OTHER INGREDIENTS

Special ink characteristics are gained by adding ingredients such as driers, waxes, lubricants, gums, starches, and wetting agents. These are added at different times during the manufacture of ink. When a special ingredient is added after manufacture, it must be mixed well with that particular type of ink.

Driers. Driers speed the oxidation and drying of the vehicle. Driers are sometimes added to ink by press operators. This must be done carefully. The drier must be the right kind for the particular ink. Too much drier may cause drying on the press, fill-in of halftones, and excessive sticking. As a general rule, one ounce of drier for each pound of ink will help the ink to dry in 4 to 8 hours.

Waxes. Waxes are used to combat setoff, which is the transfer of ink from a printed sheet to the back of the sheet above. They also improve abrasion resistance. Waxes are added either during the cooking of the varnish or after the ink is prepared. Paraffin wax, beeswax, and carnauba wax are kinds used frequently.

Greases and lubricants. Greases and lubricants are used to help lubricate ink, reduce stickiness, and increase setting and drying. Cup grease, wool grease, and petroleum jelly are some types of lubricants. Too much lubricant will cause ink to print poorly.

UNIT 170 MANUFACTURE OF PRINTING INKS

Printing inks are manufactured by mixing pigments and other compounds with a vehicle. Mixing solid ingredients like pigments and compounds in the vehicle is called *wetting down.* Most inks are made by the *batch* method. This means that one quantity is made, then everything is cleaned up. Only standardized inks, like news ink, are made by a continuous process.

Inks are ground after mixing. Grinding reduces the size of the solid particles and helps distribute the pigment and compounds into the vehicle. The three-roll mill (Fig. 170-1) works well, even though it is one of the old means of grinding inks. The three rollers of the mill are adjusted until there is only a small space between them. The center cylinder turns at a

Fig. 170-1. A three-roll mill.

NATIONAL ASSOCIATION OF PRINTING INK MANUFACTURERS

Fig. 170-2. A ball grinder.

NATIONAL ASSOCIATION OF PRINTING INK MANUFACTURERS

different speed than the other two. The combination of the very small clearance between the cylinders or rolls and different speeds grinds the ink to extreme fineness after several passes through the mill.

Other methods of grinding inks use ball mills, colloid mills, sand grinders, and turbine mixers. Figure 170-2 shows a ball grinder consisting of a rotating horizontal drum. The ingredients and steel balls are placed inside and as the grinder turns, the balls fall on the mixture with a grinding action. The longer the drum turns, the finer the ink will be.

The fineness of the ink is measured to see whether it has been ground enough for the quality desired. Tests are made often to check the fineness of the ink mixture (Fig. 170-3). It is vital that printing inks meet the high requirements demanded by quality work.

NATIONAL ASSOCIATION OF PRINTING INK MANUFACTURERS

Fig. 170-3. Testing the fineness of grind of an ink.

UNIT 171 KINDS OF PRINTING INKS

New kinds of printing inks are developed every year to meet the demands of the graphic arts industry. Some major considerations in the search for new inks are the requirements of printing processes, the speeds of printing presses, the uses of the printed items, and the kinds of receptors.

PRINTING PROCESSES

Inks are made to meet the requirements of each printing process. Often special printing inks are developed for use in producing a single printed product, such as a magazine.

Letterpress. Inks for letterpress printing must distribute well on raised surfaces like type, line plates, and halftone plates. Letterpress inks have moderate *tack* (stickiness) and flow. *Flow* is the characteristic that causes ink to level out

(Fig. 171-1).

Different printing presses need different qualities in the ink. Inks for platen presses are

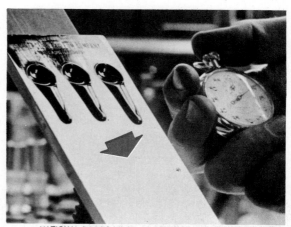

NATIONAL ASSOCIATION OF PRINTING INK MANUFACTURERS

Fig. 171-1. Testing the flow characteristics of ink.

rather *short* and tacky and lack good flow ability. Cylinder press inks must have less tack and more *length*—the ability to stretch out to a long fine thread without breaking. Inks for rotary presses must have even less tack and more length. They should be able to dry rapidly.

Lithography. Lithographic inks are made to cover a flat surface smoothly. These inks are longer and more *viscous*. They have more body than letterpress inks. Lithographic inks must be resistant to water and to the mild acids in the dampening systems of offset lithography presses.

Gravure. Gravure printing inks must have enough body to be pulled from the printing plate. Hand gravure printing requires a short ink; high speed presses require longer ones. Drying speed is not as important a consideration for hand gravure printing as for rotogravure. Inks for hand printing can dry by oxidation, but rotogravure ink must dry by absorption or evaporation.

Screen Printing. Probably more inks or paints are available for screen printing than for any other type. These inks must pass through small openings in the screen without clogging. They must not damage the stencil or dry in the screen while being printed. They should adhere to the material being printed on, and should dry rapidly. Check the manufacturer's specifications and recommendations before using a screen-printing ink. In general, screen-printing inks are thinner and more fluid than inks of the other printing processes.

USE OF PRINTED ITEMS

The use of the printed item should be considered when ink is chosen for a job. For example, packages used to hold foods must be printed with an odorless ink. Those used outdoors should use inks that are weather resistant. Books need ink that withstands aging. Bottles that will be handled and washed must be printed with inks that withstand abrasion.

RECEPTORS

Inks should fit the material, or receptor, as well as the printing process. Many problems are avoided when the correct ink for a specific kind of receptor is used.

Paper

Paper is the most common material used as a receptor. When you have inking problems with papers, consult the manufacturer of the specific product.

Newsprint. This is the least expensive paper, having coarse, open fibers. It contains little or no sizing and is absorbent. Inks commonly used for newsprint are very thin and dry by absorption. They contain little or no binder, leaving only pigment on the surface of the paper.

Uncoated papers. Bond, book, and vellum papers usually use inks that dry by oxidation. These inks should have medium viscosity.

Coated papers. These papers have surfaces that resist any ink penetration, so quick-setting inks are usually used. The inks are fluid and the pigments are extremely well dispersed because coated papers are used primarily for fine printing that calls for extreme detail. Heat-set inks that dry by evaporation are also used. Many other papers—cardboard, parchment, glassine, and kraft—require inks that meet the needs of both the material and the process used.

Non-paper

Non-paper materials include glass, fabrics, plastics, metals, woods, and ceramics. Because of their irregular surfaces and the nature of the substance being printed, many of these materials must be printed by either the screen printing or flexography methods.

Nearly all non-paper materials require rapid-drying inks. In some situations, instantaneous drying is necessary. It is best to have the ink manufacturer make special inks for these specific materials. For example, a manufacturer of screen printing inks will not recommend an ink for plastics until it is tested on the material.

TYPES OF INKS

Some common types of inks used in the graphic arts industry are listed below. Many more kinds of ink are available. The best detailed information on inks is provided by the manufacturers.

Heat-set inks. These are used on high-speed presses. The vehicle or bonding agent in heat-set inks must evaporate rapidly when heat is applied to the printed material while resins and the pigment stay on the surface of the paper. Presses using this type of ink must have a heating device and an exhaust system.

Quick-set oil inks. These inks have vehicles that are combinations of oil and resin. When the ink is printed, the oil penetrates the surface of the receptors and the film of resin and pigment dries by oxidation. They are used in both letterpress and offset lithography printing processes.

Gloss inks. High gloss is obtained in printing by using inks having a minimum penetration into the paper. Several paper characteristics, such as porosity, surface sizing, and coatings affect the gloss. The vehicle must be one that does not penetrate the paper rapidly.

News inks. News inks are made to dry by absorption. They are made of mineral oil and carbon black and are usually very thin and fluid. News inks are designed for presses that run at high speed.

Metallic inks. These are inks with metal powders suspended in a vehicle. Aluminum powders are used to simulate silver. Bronze powder makes the inks appear to be gold. The powders usually are added to the vehicle just before printing. The powders must be mixed thoroughly into the vehicle.

Magnetic inks. Magnetic inks have pigments that can be magnetized. They are used to print forms and checks so that characters can be read electronically. These inks must be precisely formulated. They are usually used in lithographic printing.

Sublimable inks. Sublimable inks are used in heat-transfer printing of textiles. The inks contain sublimable dye instead of pigments. Inks are printed on paper and transferred to the textile by applying heat and pressure. With the heat and pressure, the dye becomes a vapor that is absorbed by the textile product. Dyes from sublimable ink transfer well to synthetic cloth, but they do not work well with natural cloth like cotton.

Ultraviolet curing inks. In some situations ultra-violet radiation is used to cure special inks. These inks react to radiation causing the ink to adhere to the receptor. Unlike heat-set inks, these inks do not need high temperatures.

Most ink manufacturers provide samples of their inks on different kinds of paper or other materials. The printer can then find the kind and color of ink needed for a particular job.

UNIT 172 DIFFICULTIES WITH PRINTING INK

Poor ink quality is a common alibi in the graphic arts industry, but poor results can have many causes. Difficulties can be caused by inaccurate matching of receptor to ink, poor press conditions, or the use of the wrong additives. Changes in the conditions of the receptor often must be allowed for by changing the characteristics of the ink after consulting the recommendations of the manufacturer. Following are some of the common problems.

OFF COLOR

Color can vary for many reasons. Most often, the cause is dirtiness of the press. Also, the same ink (color) printed on two different materials will give different results. Further, the thinness or thickness of the layer of ink on the printed product will give a difference in color.

The person preparing the ink to be used on the press should have a sample of the color to be matched, a sample of the paper on which the ink will print, and as much other information as possible. When the ink is formulated, a *draw-down* is made. The draw-down is made on a pad on which both the sample and the formulated ink are deposited with a thin blade. Figure 172-1 shows a draw-down being made to check new ink against a standard one for color, strength, and tone.

SETOFF

Setoff occurs when wet ink from the printed sheet transfers to the back of a sheet placed on

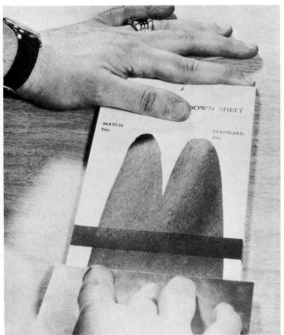

NATIONAL ASSOCIATION OF PRINTING INK MANUFACTURERS

Fig. 172-1. Draw down test.

top (Fig. 172-2). This usually happens in the delivery section of a printing press. Some common causes of setoff are static electricity, excessive heaviness of the ink film, slow penetration of ink into the paper, and improper handling of the printed material.

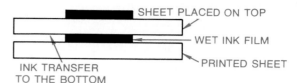

Fig. 172-2. Setoff occurs when one sheet is placed on top of another printed sheet.

Be alert to prevent setoff as soon as possible. Watch for setoff particularly when printing large areas like solids and halftones. You can reduce or avoid setoff by depositing only a minimum amount of ink on the receptor, by adding some static elimination device to the press, by using only the appropriate ink, by not pressing down on the top of freshly printed material, and by not letting the paper stack up too high.

IMPROPER DRYING

Sometimes ink does not harden or dry as rapidly as expected. If this happens, you may be using the wrong receptor for the ink. You may be using old ink that has lost its drier. If the ink is old, you may be able to solve the problem by adding a drier. But take care to use the right drier and to measure it carefully.

Poor drying can also mean that the paper or receptor has a high moisture content or is not porous. Low temperature and high humidity also cause drying problems. Temperature and humidity in the printing press area should be controlled when possible. Adding a drier to the ink may help solve temperature and humidity problems.

STICKING

Two pieces of printed paper may be stuck together by an ink film. The causes are often the same as for setoff and improper drying. Some remedies that reduce setoff and increase drying also eliminate sticking. For example, too much drier slows ink penetration into the paper. When ink lays on top of the receptor, it naturally sticks to the sheet above. It is best to print the thinnest possible ink film, which results in better drying and more rapid penetration.

CHALKING

In *chalking,* the ink film is dry and is easily removed from the receptor by abrasive action. Both chalking and inadequate drying can cause the ink to smear.

One way to solve a chalking problem is to add a varnish that does not easily penetrate the paper surface. Probably the best solution, however, is to select a more appropriate ink for the particular job. If chalking occurs on a completed job, you many need to print a clear protective coating over the ink.

SPECKING

Specking means that small dots appear between the dots on halftones or in the non-printed areas between line work. If this happens, the ink may be contaminated by dust, lint, setoff spray, and paper fibers. Other causes are heavy ink film, too much impression, and poor makeready. Ink that is not properly ground can also cause specking.

STRIKE-THROUGH

Strike-through is the problem of ink going through (penetrating) the sheet of paper to the reverse side. Either the ink dries too slowly or you have used too much non-drying oils. Strike-through often occurs on absorbent paper.

Strike-through is often confused with setoff, and show-through. *Show-through* happens when thin or not very opaque paper is printed, so that the image can be seen on the reverse side. The ink in this case has not penetrated the paper.

PLATE WEAR

Too much wear on printing plates can be caused by inks that are not properly ground. Other causes are inks that contain too much pigment and pigment that is too abrasive. Too much roller pressure or papers that contain abrasives may also cause wear.

UNIT 173 MIXING PRINTING INKS

The purpose of mixing printing ink is to get new or different colors or to adjust the characteristics of a certain ink. Mixing is done both in the printing plant and at the ink manufacturing plant. To get a color that you want, you may have to blend two or more different color inks that have the same characteristics. When you adjust inks to improve printing results, you use much the same procedure and tools as for color mixing.

Inks mixed at the manufacturing plant usually give better results than those mixed by the press operator. If inks are mixed by the printer, the mixture must be thoroughly prepared so it is uniform in blend and quality.

TOOLS FOR MIXING

To mix inks, you will need a slab, ink knife or spatula, and a set of scales. These tools must be clean and in good condition to mix ink properly.

The *slab* should be made of non-porous material. Porous ones hold ink from previous mixings and this old ink could ruin new mixtures. A piece of heavy plate glass about 12 by 18 inches (30.5 by 44.7 cm) with ground edges makes a good, safe slab. Badly scratched glass should not be used because ink will stay in the scratches and spoil new mixes.

An *ink knife* is used to blend the ingredients on the slab and to remove ink from containers.

Stiff, straight-edged knives, similar to putty knives, may be used to remove ink from containers. Use a long flexible knife with a rounded end to blend the ingredients. It also helps avoid scratching the slab. This type of knife is commonly called a *spatula*.

Scales are used to measure precise quantities of ingredients. Scales with a five-pound capacity are suitable for most jobs. Scales are most useful when the person who mixes the ink must make more than one batch of a particular kind or color.

When an ink is mixed only once, scales are not always needed. When ingredients are weighed, they are usually placed on materials such as plastic or other non-absorbent matter so that the scales can be kept clean and ready for other jobs. The plastic material must be weighed and this figure subtracted from the combined weight of the ingredients for an accurate weight.

INGREDIENTS

You should carefully select ingredients for mixing inks or making adjustments in ink characteristics according to the needs of the particular situation. When possible, you should use inks formulated by the ink manufacturer. Unfortunately, printing deadlines do not always allow time to ask for this service.

Mixing materials can be divided into two groups: (1) ingredients for adjusting characteristics of inks, and (2) inks for developing new colors. It is a good policy to order inks and additives, including driers and varnishes, that come from the same manufacturer and have the same characteristics.

The following is a minimum list of mixing and formulating ingredients for printing press operators who often use conventional oil ink for letterpress and lithographic printing:

1. Several grades of litho varnish: 00, 1, 4, and body gum.
2. Driers.
3. Waxes and compounds.
4. Two or more kinds of black ink.
5. Gray ink.
6. Transparent and mixing white inks.

7. Several strong colors, including blue, yellow, red, green, brown, and purple.

MIXING

Ink is mixed to match an existing color, to adjust its characteristics to meet a specific need, or to duplicate a previous formula. Ink is more often mixed to match a needed color or to adjust its characteristics than to duplicate a formula. To mix inks according to a formula, the formulator only has to measure accurate amounts of certain ingredients and then blend them (Fig. 173-1).

When mixing inks, hue, value, and chroma must be considered. *Hue* is the shade, or characteristic, of a color that makes it different from another one. *Value* is the lightness or darkness of a color. *Chroma* is the strength (brightness or purity) or grayness of a color.

It is helpful to refer to a color chart before starting to mix ink, because the chart shows how to get the colors you want. For example, the primary colors of yellow, red, and blue can be used to mix many tints and shades. If yellow is mixed with red, you get orange. You get greens from mixing blues and yellows. Red and blue make violet.

NATIONAL ASSOCIATION OF PRINTING INK MANUFACTURERS

Fig. 173-1. Mixing printing ink in a printing plant.

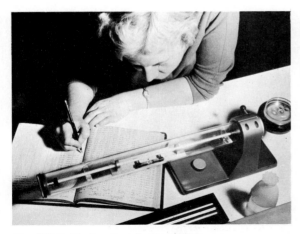

Fig. 173-2. Testing for ink penetration.

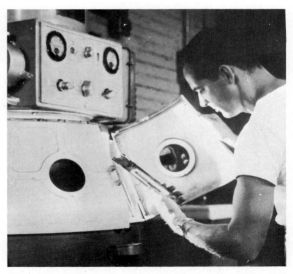

Fig. 173-3. Testing ink for fading and weathering under ultraviolet light.

Before mixing colors, all tools must be thoroughly cleaned to be sure that the mixture will not be contaminated. Use a color chart to select the proper hues for making the new ink color. Always place the lighter color ink on the slab first; then add the darker color to it. It is easier to make a light color dark than to make a dark color light. Add only a little of the dark color to the light color at a time. The colors should be blended until all streaks are gone. It is best to use a separate ink knife for each ink color and a different spatula for blending the inks. Be sure to mix enough ink to print the entire job, because it is very hard to duplicate a color.

Inks should be tested after mixing. Manufacturers make many tests for flow and fineness of grind, such as the test made to check ink penetration into the receptor (Fig. 173-2). Inks are also tested under ultraviolet light for fading and weathering tendencies (Fig. 173-3). A draw-down test is useful in judging color qualities.

Such tests are not usually made in a printing plant. A draw-down test is useful in judging color qualities. Many times the only real test possible in the plant is to print with the ink on the actual substrate. Penetration and drying qualities can only be tested by drying a print made on an appropriate receptor under normal conditions.

UNIT 174 LEARNING EXPERIENCES: PRINTING INK MANUFACTURING

KEY WORDS

Unit 168

Ink

Receptors
Substrate

Unit 169

Driers
Pigment
Vehicle

Varnish
Waxes

Unit 170

Ball mill
Batch method
Three-roll mill
Wetting down

Unit 171

Glassine
Gloss Ink
Heat-set Ink
Magnetic Ink
Metallic Ink

Quick-set Ink
Sublimable Ink
Ultraviolet Ink

Unit 172

Chalking
Chroma
Hue

Setoff
Specking
Strike-through
Value

Unit 173

Ink knife
Slab

Spatula

DISCUSSION TOPICS

1. What must printing ink withstand once it has been printed?
2. What is the difference between *opaque* and *transparent white* ink?
3. What is the purpose of grinding printing inks?
4. Describe two special requirements of gravure ink.
5. What is the best test for a printing ink?

ACTIVITIES

Units 168–171

1. List the kinds of inks in your school graphic arts laboratory. What printing processes would they be used with? What are some of the materials they could be printed on?
2. Collect several different printed items. Name the printing process used to print them. Try to decide what kind of ink was used to print them.

Unit 173

3. Mix some inks to get different colors. Keep a record of the amounts of ingredients. Try to match the ink with a second mix. Then try to match the ink a few days later.

Pressmen's Crossword Puzzle

By William C. Curr
New York, School of Printing

ACROSS:

1. Opposite side guide of near.
3. If feeder misses a sheet the press should ....
6. Gravure is known for its fine reproduction of ....
8. When on impression the cylinder must ride on the ....
10. Electric .... control.
11. Type of electric current.
12. Square of type body.
13. An excess of .... will cause setoff.
14. Printing Pressmen (abbr.).
15. Highest skilled craftsman in the graphic arts.
17. Will cause a slur.
19. A wheel containing a high and low spot.
21. Pressman's parent.
22. Requires careful setting to eliminate a wrinkle.
25. Solids should be .... type high.
26. 1,000,000 impressions.
28. Printing unit of measure (abbr.).
31. Newsprint is made from ....
33. Reducing varnish.
34. Right side of paper.
35. For folding against the grain it is sometimes necessary to .... a job.
36. Pressman's other parent.
38. A means of preventing setoff.
39. Result of over packing.
40. Strong brown paper.
41. Halftones are composed of various sized...............

DOWN:

1. Product of wood and rags for paper making.
2. Used to cut tissue.
3. To bundle.
4. Term used when coating pulls off a sheet.
5. Holds a sheet to packing.
6. When overprinting, second down ink must .... on the first down.
7. An ink .... before it dries.
9. Type measure.
11. Indefinite article.
13. Moving a press showly.
14. Jumbled type.
16. 500 sheets of a standard size.
18. A form that has not yet been printed.
20. What stereotypes are cast from.
23. Used to distribute ink.
24. Sized and super-calendered.
27. World's largest international printing trade union (abbr.).
29. Another name for a platen press.
30. An interlay is put between the plate and
31. Results of a bowed form.
32. Used for coating paper.
33. Reducing varnish.
34. Reward for spoiling job.
37. When it is doubtful it is advisable to

JUSTICE represents the administration of that which is just and also merited reward or punishment. (Shelburne, Vermont Museum)

21 LEGAL CONSIDERATIONS FOR THE PRINTER

175 LEGAL RESTRICTIONS OF PRINTED MATERIALS PRODUCTION

Printers and publishers of graphic materials must be on guard at all times to keep from getting in trouble with the law over counterfeiting, pornography, and violations of copyright. Graphic arts personnel have a responsibility to know the laws and ethical considerations involved in manufacturing printed products.

Copyright is the legal right of authors, artists, composers, to protect their writing, art, or music against unauthorized copying (Fig. 175-1). In the United States, the first federal copyright act took effect on May 31, 1790. The first document to be copyrighted was *The Philadelphia Spelling Book*. Since that time, millions of published works have received copyright protection.

Fig. 175-1. Books and magazines are usually copyrighted to protect the creative works and financial investments of authors and publishing companies.

In any country, the copyright office has three main purposes:

1. Register copyrights for those literary, artistic, and musical works that qualify.
2. Officially record and catalog all copyright registrations.
3. Examine legal claims to copyright in all classes of work that are eligible for protection.

The first complete revision of the United States copyright law since 1901, took effect on January 1, 1978. This revised law, "Public Law 94-553," is a result of more than twenty years of work by the copyright office, lawyers, and members of Congress. Under this law, the author, creator, or designer is given protection for life, and the protection can be renewed for an additional 50 years after death. The old law only gave a 28-year protection with the option of an additional 28-year renewal.

Copyrighting has two main purposes. First, it gives the creator or owner of a message or artistic creation the exclusive right of selling it or making money from it. Second, it gives the owner or creator of a message or artwork control over its publication. No one can print or use the material without the permission of the copyright owner. Since the owner must give permission, the owner can be sure that the material is quoted or reproduced accurately and is not used in any way that would be objectionable.

UNIT 176 HOW TO OBTAIN A COPYRIGHT

A *copyright* is a form of protection given by the law of a country or by international agreement. Owners of a copyright is granted, by law, certain exclusive rights of their work. In addition to the exclusive right to copy the work, the rights include: (1) the right to sell or distribute copies of the work, (2) the right to transform or revise the work, and (3) the right to perform and record the work.

WHAT CAN BE COPYRIGHTED

Copyright laws let any creative work designed to communicate thoughts and ideas to be registered by the copyright office. Works can be registered in five classifications: non-dramatic literary, performing arts, visual arts, sound recordings, and renewal registrations. This book you are now reading is classified as "non-dramatic literary."

There are seven categories or classifications of authorship: (1) literary works, (2) musical works, (3) dramatic works, (4) pantomime and choreographic works, (5) pictorial, graphic, and sculptural works, (6) motion pictures and audiovisual works, and (7) sound recordings. Again, this book is included in the category of literary works.

WHAT CANNOT BE COPYRIGHTED

There are several items that do not qualify for a copyright under United States law. Laws in other western countries are similar. These non-copyrightable items include the following:

1. Ideas, plans, methods, systems, or devices when they are not full descriptions or illustrations
2. Titles, names, short phrases, slogans
3. Common symbols and designs

4. Slight variations of typographic ornamentation, lettering or coloring
5. Listings of ingredients or contents
6. Time cards, account books, diaries, bank checks, score cards, address books, report forms
7. Calendars, measuring devices, sporting event schedules, tables of information taken from public sources.

However, original artwork used with some of the above items may be copyrighted. When the originator or the commercial printer is in doubt, the copyright office should be consulted. It is always better to take some time and effort to check copyright than to guess and be wrong.

COPYRIGHT CLAIMS

Only authors or those deriving their rights through them can rightfully claim copyright. Mere possession of a work does not give the possessor the right to use it. For instance, a letter belongs to the person to whom it was sent, but it cannot be printed without the permission of the person who wrote it.

STATUTORY COPYRIGHT FOR A PUBLISHED WORK

In the United States, three steps should be taken to secure and maintain statutory copyright in a published work: (1) produce copies with a copyright notice printed in them, (2) publish the work, and (3) register a claim in the U. S. Copyright Office. Under item one, you must first produce the work in copies by printing or other means of reproduction. All copies must have a copyright notice in the required form and position. Communications should be addressed to the Register of Copyrights,

Library of Congress, Washington, D.C. 20559.

Promptly after publication, the following material should be sent to the above address: (1) application form (this form may be requested from the Copyright Office), (2) two copies of the best edition of the work as published, and (3) the $10.00 registration fee for a published or unpublished work.

COPYRIGHT NOTICE

The copyright notice, as a general rule, should consist of one of the three forms shown in Figure 176-1. For a book or other publication printed in book form, the copyright notice should appear on the title page, or on the page immediately following. The page immediately

```
Copyright
John Doe
1900

Copr., John Doe, 1900

©John Doe, 1900
```

Fig. 176-1. The three forms of displaying the copyright notice.

following is normally the reverse side of the page bearing the title. Note the copyright in this book.

On periodicals, the copyright notices should appear either on the title page, the first page of text, or under the title of the periodical. Musical works should have the copyright notice on either the title page or the first page of music. For other types of materials qualified for copyright, consult the official publications available from the copyright office.

UNIT 177 COPYRIGHT INFRINGEMENT

When the United States was founded, people were so interested in protecting intellectual creations that the principle was written into the Constitution (Art. 1, Sec 8):

> The Congress shall have the power to promote the Progress of Science and the useful arts, by securing for limited times to authors and inventors the exclusive right to their respective writings and discoveries.

The concept of *writings* has been extended to include, "... original works of authorship fixed in any tangible medium of expression from which they can be perceived, reproduced, or communicated either directly or with the aid of a machine."

In early days the only means of reproducing writings was by the printing press. Infringement and unlawful printing were almost synonymous. Now reproduction of writings can include many different means including copying machines and electronic recording and transmission.

BREAKING THE LAW

What will you do when someone from another department or area comes to you for three copies of a page from a magazine? You usually go to the office copier in your room and run them off. You probably will never think that this is illegal. In many libraries, schools, and business establishments people are making copies of printed material every day, even though the work is copyrighted. Schools and libraries are among the most serious violators of this law and many have been taken to court because of it. Judgments against copyright violators are harsh.

Commercial printers must be very careful to not print a document that they know is protected by copyright. A printer must be careful to review each item brought by a customer for printing. Printing a copyrighted publication without knowing it can get a printer taken to court as an "infringer of the original copyright."

It is not always easy to say whether a reproduction is an infringement. The copyright owner may sue for damages and the court can award almost any amount of damage, but it is hard to catch the offender. The only solution at this time seems to be an honor system. Remember how many times you have seen the copyright law broken by other people.

COPYRIGHT GUIDELINES

Libraries and educational institutions are constantly concerned with people breaking the copyright law. Copyright is the only legal way to prove ownership of a published or unpublished document. Copyrighting a document should not mean that the author wants to limit use of the product, such as a piece of music or this textbook. It is meant to establish who is the legal owner, just as a deed shows ownership of a house and a title shows ownership of an automobile.

The large number of photocopying machines have made it easy for educators and library personnel to copy publications (Fig. 177-1). It is

Fig. 177-1. Educators and library personnel must be very careful to comply with legal guidelines when making photocopies of copyrighted publications.

important for people in these positions of responsibility to know what can and cannot be copied. The general public should also respect a copyrighted work and not take advantage of someone else's property unless they pay for using it. Many times an author or publisher can and will grant a request to make duplicate copies of a copyrighted work without payment. But the user must take the first step to get permission or face the possibility of being charged with infringement of copyright.

Educators may:

1. Make single copies of a chapter of a book; an article from a periodical; a short story, essay or poem; a chart, graph or diagram for research or class preparation.
2. Make multiple copies (one per pupil) if copying "meets the tests of brevity and spontaneity" and carries a notice of copyright.

Brevity is defined as a complete poem of less than 250 words; a complete article or essay of less than 2,500 words; an excerpt from any prose work of not more than 1,000 words or 10 percent of the work, whichever is less; one chart, diagram or other illustration per book or periodical; and 2 pages or 10 percent of short "special works."

Spontaneity means that the "inspiration of the individual teacher . . . and the decision to work" are so close to "the moment of its use for maximum teaching effectiveness" that there would not be enough time to write for permission.

Educators may not:

1. Copy to replace or create selected literary pieces or passages.
2. Photocopy consumable works such as workbooks and worksheets.
3. Copy publications as a substitute for buying books.
4. Charge students more than the actual cost of copying.

UNIT 178 PORNOGRAPHY

Pornography is material, such as books or photographs, that is intended to cause sexual excitement. Any discussion of freedom of the press or freedom of speech must include the First Amendment of the United States Constitution which prohibits Congress from abridging freedom of press or speech. Still, in a complex society, it would be naive to believe that anyone may write or say anything without restriction.

An effective law is one that is sound and enforceable. It must meet the test of constitutional acceptability. It should provide realistic penalties and should have the genuine support of the public.

The role of the printer in laws of obscenity is much clearer than that of the publisher. The printer is technically vulnerable at only two points: (1) in accepting the copy, and (2) on delivery of the completed product. When a printer gives legally pornographic copy to the typesetter and pressman, he or she has distributed obscene literature. The printer also distributes obscene literature when the finished product is delivered to the customer. Between these two activities the printer is doing nothing illegal since he or she only possesses the litera-

ture. In a few cases, printers have turned questionable material over to authorities, but not often. Printers should try to make objective judgments about what is or is not obscene. Their reputations are often at stake.

Publishers are more vulnerable to the laws of obscenity because they actually distribute the material directly for sale or supply a vendor with the material to sell. The laws are a bit clearer about the sale and distribution of pornography than they are about the printing of it.

The U. S. Supreme Court, by a decision in the 1960s, enabled pornography to run virtually uncontrolled for almost ten years. It said that to be obscene any printed matter must be totally without *social redeeming* value. Some printing firms openly printed hard-core pornography without fear of prosecution because practically anything can be shown to have *some* socially redeeming value. However, in 1973 the U.S. Supreme Court ruled that standards for obscene material could be set by local governments. This resulted in many local court actions in which publishers and distributors of hard-core pornography lost.

UNIT 179 COUNTERFEITING

Counterfeiting (imitating with intent to deceive) of money is one of the oldest crimes in history. In some periods it was considered to be treason and was punished by death. During the American Revolution, the British counterfeited American currency in such large amounts that the Continental currency became worthless.

During the Civil War, about one-third of the currency in circulation was counterfeit.

The late Robert H. Jackson, Associate Justice of the United States Supreme Court, described counterfeiting by saying, "Counterfeiting is an offense never committed by accident, nor by ignorance, nor in the heat of

Fig. 179-1. The procedure and result of counterfeiting.

passion, nor in extremity of poverty. It is a crime expertly designed by one who possesses technical skill, and lays out substantial sums for equipment." See Figure 179-1.

Modern photographic and printing equipment has lessened the amount of skill needed for counterfeiting. Counterfeiting is again on the rise because of the ease and speed with which large quantities of counterfeit currency can be produced and transported.

FACTS ABOUT UNITED STATES CURRENCY

1. Genuine currency is printed on special paper and manufactured under strict government control.
2. The paper contains many small red and blue fibers almost invisible to the naked eye.
3. Genuine notes are printed from engraved plates by master craftsmen who use the most sophisticated equipment.
4. There are eleven important identifying features of paper currency (Fig. 179-2).

Genuine paper money looks good because of the above-listed items. It is made by experts, made on costly machines and distinctive paper designed solely for that purpose, and printed from steel plates produced by expert engravers who produce clear lines (Fig. 179-3).

Counterfeit paper money looks bad because it is usually a product of inferior workmanship. It is usually made with equipment designed for other purposes; it is printed from a plate made by a photomechanical process, causing loss of detail (Fig. 179-4); and it is printed on paper which does not contain the distinctive red and blue threads.

WHAT IS PERMISSIBLE

The United States Secret Service is the federal enforcement agency charged with safeguarding

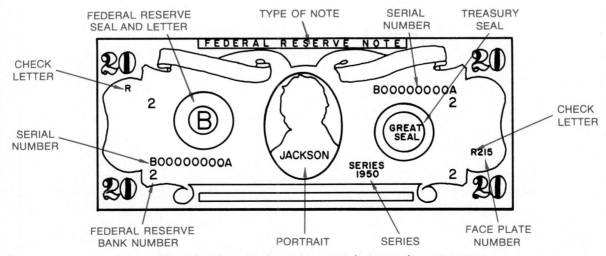

Fig. 179-2. Positions of eleven important features of paper currency.

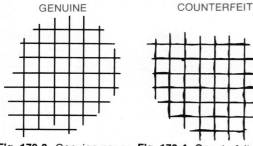

Fig. 179-3. Genuine paper currency has clear lines.

Fig. 179-4. Counterfeit paper currency has lines that are not sharp.

the nation's currency. The Department of the Treasury has sponsored legislation to clarify permissible use of illustrations of paper money, postage and revenue stamps, checks, bonds, and other currency of the United States and foreign governments.

Printed illustrations of paper money must be in black and white and must be less than ³/₄ or more than 1¹/₂ times the size of the original. Illustrations of paper money, checks, or bonds *must not* be printed in color. These illustrations must be for educational, historical, or newsworthy purposes. They cannot be used just for decoration or to get attention.

Printed illustrations of canceled and uncanceled United States postage stamps are permissable for articles, books, journals, newspapers, or albums. This is true for educational, historical, and newsworthy purposes. Black and white stamp illustrations may be any size. Colored illustrations of canceled United States postage stamps may be of any size. However, illustrations in color of uncanceled United States postage stamps must be less than three-fourths or more than one and one-half times the size of the genuine stamp.

PENALTIES

Counterfeiting and forgery are national offenses and carry heavy penalties. Making, possessing, or passing counterfeit bills can result in a $5,000 fine and up to fifteen years in prison.

UNIT 180 MORAL AND ETHICAL CONSIDERATIONS

Printers and publishers, no matter how large or small their establishments, must have a code of ethics that applies to what they print. Book, newspaper, and magazine publishers, and also the ordinary printing firm must be aware of the values of the materials they print. Some of the items have a great deal of merit; some have no significant value. Some should never be printed at all.

Many people think that anything printed must be true (Fig. 180-1). They are not entirely naive, because they know completely false statements cannot be printed without risking prosecution for libel or misrepresentation. Thus the very daring involved in printing a misrepresentation makes people believe it. The greater the exaggeration, the more believable it may become.

Especially when dealing with copyright, it is often difficult to prove that material has been stolen. Both the printer and owner of the copyright can find themselves in an embarrassing situation. Think about this case. A customer asks to have an advertising brochure printed. The printer starts from scratch, doing design and layout work, type composition, camera work, platemaking, and printing (Fig. 180-2). The next time the customer wants more of the same brochures printed, the job is taken to another printer. The second printer could do it much cheaper, because all the preliminary work has been done. Has anything illegal been done? No, but there certainly is a question of ethics, or fairness. A company, especially a small one, could be forced out of business by such irregular actions by its customers. Much more than just good quality finished products must be considered when any printing or publishing is done.

R. R. DONNELLEY AND SONS COMPANY

Fig. 180-1. Printed publications ready for shipment to customers.

Fig. 180-2. An artist puts much time and effort into developing printed products like advertising brochures.

UNIT 181 LEARNING EXPERIENCES: LEGAL CONSIDERATIONS FOR THE PRINTER

KEY TERMS

Unit 175

Copyright Public Law 94-553
Copyright office

Unit 176

Copyright notice

Unit 177

Copyright Infringer
  infringement

Unit 178

Obscenity Pornography

Unit 179

Counterfeiting

DISCUSSION TOPICS

1. How does the United States' Constitution protect authors and writers?
2. Why must a commercial printer be careful to not print a document protected by copyright?

3. Why is a publisher more vulnerable to the laws of obscenity than the printer?
4. Explain how counterfeiting can hurt the economy of a country.
5. What could happen to the printer who printed an untruth about an individual or a group?

ACTIVITIES

Unit 176

1. Search through several different kinds of published materials. Note the location of the copyright notice in each of the publications. Also note the styles or method of displaying the copyright notice. Which positions and methods of display are found most often?
2. Write to the Copyright Office for information and forms and report on your findings and information.

Unit 177

3. Discuss copyright violations with your parents, friends, teachers, and librarians. Get their opinions regarding copying activities and compare their attitudes and opinions.

Unit 178

4. Research and discuss recent court decisions on the publication of pornographic materials. Discuss your local standards on obscene materials.

Unit 179

5. Watch the local newspapers for accounts of counterfeiting offenses. Note the amounts of money involved and the penalties given to those persons caught. Talk with local law enforcement authorities to get more information about counterfeiting problems in your city or area of the country. How do counterfeiting problems in your geographical area compare to those of the whole nation? Prepare a detailed report on your visit.

Unit 180

6. Discuss the various moral and ethical problems of the printer and publisher.

Desktop composition has greatly improved the efficiency of many graphic arts operations.

22 DESKTOP COMPOSITION

182 WHAT IS DESKTOP COMPOSITION?

Desktop composition is an important part of the future of publishing and graphic arts. *Desktop composition* is the use of specialized computer software programs to create and integrate text and graphics in a page layout. Desktop composition also is called *electronic publishing* and *desktop publishing*. Briefly, computers using software programs designed for specific tasks allow the user to lay out pages of text and graphics on the screen. This is a new concept. Traditionally, computers used programs that were either text based or graphics based. With text-based programs, only one style of type could be viewed on the screen. With graphics-based programs, only graphics were shown. There was no high-resolution text.

Desktop composition is the marriage of text and graphics on the screen. It offers the flexibility of combining multiple typefaces and graphics on one page. It also allows many users to work together with their computers networked to share information and files quickly and easily.

In traditional publishing, each person involved in the project usually works alone at a specific task (Fig. 182-1). For example, the writers use typewriters or computers to input text. They then give their printed hard copy to the artist who will do the layout and design. The artist then sketches the layout. Type is specified. The copy is then sent for typesetting. The typesetter retypes the document, coding it for typesetting. To make the individual page paste-ups, the artwork is created and adhered to a board along with galleys of type from the typesetter. If the type

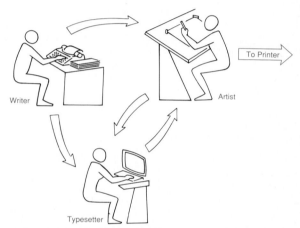

Fig. 182-1. In a traditional publishing environment there are constant revisions and editing changes to be made. The writer gives the copy to the artist, who works with the art director. The page is designed. The copy is then typeset and pasted to the layout. Each change in copy causes the cycle to begin again. This can be time consuming and costly.

does not fit the layout, the manuscript and type must be revised. This effort can be costly and time consuming.

In desktop composition, the writer works on a computer. The designer and artist also work on computers. Their information is passed from one to another electronically, with the designer controlling the layout and copyfitting. The designer can easily and quickly change type styles and sizes. Artwork can be resized to accommodate the copy. The completed document can then be printed on a laser printer or sent out for high-resolution

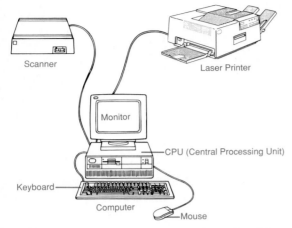

Fig. 182-2. The main components in an electronic publication system.

printing. Because the text and graphics are printed together, traditional cutting and pasting are eliminated. Color can be added by using the high-resolution typeset page as the paste-up and printing the product in the traditional manner. The computer permits considerable design innovation. The most difficult part of using computers for design is finalizing the design.

If computers are to be cost effective, the work done on them must be done by competent, skilled, and disciplined operators. These operators must be willing to reorganize their usual work patterns. They must learn new skills. Such adjustments are worthwhile. In most organizations, the cost savings and flexibility of electronic publishing make it a very attractive alternative to traditional methods of preparing imageset material.

HARDWARE AND SOFTWARE

To get started with electronic publishing, you must have the right hardware and software. *Hardware* is the computer itself, whereas *software* refers to the computer programs.

The required hardware includes a central processing unit (CPU), monitor, keyboard, mouse, scanner, and printer. Software pro-

grams include word processing, page makeup, graphics, and scanning programs.

The biggest decision will be the selection and purchase of the hardware. In desktop composition, the two major vendors of computers are IBM and Apple Computer. In the IBM desktop environment, there is also the option of buying IBM-compatible computers. These are usually fully compatible with IBM systems, and cost less. Apple Computer has not allowed its Macintosh operating system to be cloned, so its cost is usually higher.

Any type of document or graphic can be produced with either system. This was not the case, however, until the mid to late 1980s. Apple's Macintosh was the first computer to combine text and graphics, and output to the laser printers. Today IBM-compatible computers are gaining in popularity and becoming easier to use. They also have a graphic user interface similar to the one that made the Macintosh so popular. The choice of which system to buy should be based on budget, existing hardware considerations, and software preferences.

Hardware

An electronic publishing system usually consists of six major pieces of hardware: computer CPU, monitor, keyboard, mouse, scanner, and printer (Fig. 182-2).

Computer CPU. The speed at which a computer CPU (central processing unit) operates is of prime importance. A fast computer with a speedy hard disk is necessary in the production environment. A hard disk is necessary to store programs and files. Graphic and page makeup programs create large files, thus they need a lot of random access memory (RAM) in which to manipulate the files. Stored on a hard disk, such files can take up a large amount of space.

Monitor. Full color and monochrome (one-color) monitors, or screens, are available. Black-and-white monochrome large-screen monitors are easiest on the eyes for page makeup. Type on color monitors tends to be fuzzy because it takes red, green, and blue colors together in close register to create black. Color monitors are best used to create graphics.

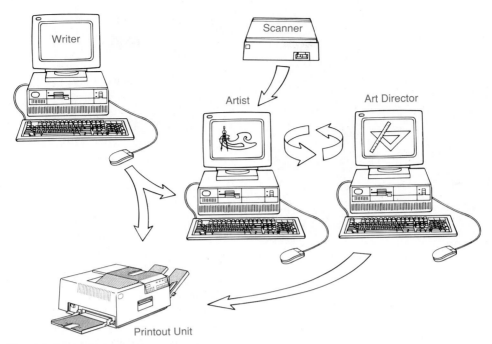

Fig. 182-3. The work flow in electronic composition.

Size is not as important for graphic applications because it is possible to zoom into work on the details of a drawing. For page makeup, it is important to see a full page to design a document. Some monitors are designed to show two full pages side by side.

Keyboard. The computer keyboard is a means of inputting information into the computer. It is much like the keyboard of a typewriter and serves as the primary input device for the computer.

Mouse. The mouse is an alternative device for inputting information into the computer. It has a rolling ball that sends X and Y coordinates to the monitor. It is attached to the computer by a wire. Digitizer pads and trackballs are also very popular. These operate on the same principle as the mouse.

Scanner. The scanner is another input device. A scanner is similar to a photocopy machine. However, the image is printed on the computer's monitor, instead of being printed on paper. Scanners can be used to import (transfer) images or text from hard copy (images on paper) to electronic signals as part of the computer software.

Printer. Almost any print-out device may be used with a computer, but laser printers are best for electronic publishing. Color printers may be used, but the colors usually do not match the screen colors on the monitor. Much progress has and will continue to be made in this area.

Software

Several software programs are essential in desktop composition. Computer software is available on diskettes. These diskettes, often called floppy disks, are available in 3.5 inch and 5.25 inch sizes (Fig. 182-4).

DOS (Disk Operating System). This software is the brain of the computer. It is designed to copy files, create directories, format disks, and keep track of where files are stored in the computer memory. The Apple Macintosh disk operating system has been easier to use than the IBM disk operating system because it is graphical, rather than text based.

Fig. 182-4. Computer diskettes.

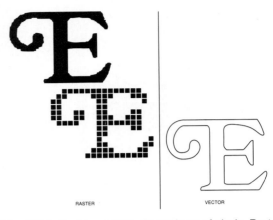

RASTER | VECTOR

Fig. 182-5. Raster graphics are made up of pixels. Raster images have a jagged stairstep look when enlarged. Vector graphics are outlines made from mathematical formulas. With vector images, the output device determines the quality of the final printed product. No quality is lost when enlarging vector images.

The text-based IBM disk operating system will soon be converted to a graphical user interface similar to the Macintosh's operating system. This will help make the IBM and IBM-compatible computers as easy to use as a Macintosh computer.

Word processing. Electronic publishing is the marriage of text and graphics. However, page-makeup software is really neither a word processor nor a graphics package. A good word processor allows the writer to use specialized features not normally found in page-makeup software. Word processing features include spell checking, find and replace, and grammar checking.

Optional scanning recognition (OCR). This software works with scanners to read typewritten text into a word processing format for text editing. Some OCR programs read copy set in different typefaces.

Image scanning software programs. These work with scanners to bring line art and photographs into the computer memory. Images are saved in a raster graphic format.

Page makeup. Page makeup software allows you to combine text and graphics on the same page. Text and basic graphics can be created and added in the desktop composition program. With these programs, it is possible to see different sizes and styles of type with pictures on the screen. Pictures can be stretched to size or distorted. Programs are available for both IBM and Macintosh. Some of the more popular, professional quality programs for IBM systems are PageMaker®, Ventura Publisher®, Interleaf®; for the Macintosh, PageMaker®, Quark Xpress®, Ready Set Go®.

Graphics. Graphic software programs fall into two distinct categories: raster graphics and vector graphics (Fig. 182-5).

Raster graphics are binary. They consist of picture elements, or pixels. Each *pixel* is a square that is either black or white. The image is created by "painting" these pixels in the graphics program. Raster graphics are usually of low-resolution and are created with software programs or scanners. They are distinctive by their stair-step edges. The resolution of this type of graphic is not improved by the resolution quality of the print-out device. The resolution remains at the level it was created. For example, an image scanned at 300 dots per inch (dpi) and printed on a 2540 dpi imagesetter still gives a resolution of 300 dpi.

Vector graphics are created by mathematical formulas. X and Y coordinates are defined to the computer, along with information on curved angles and line weights. Vector graphics are also called "draw" graphics. These graphics are device-dependent for their quality. Sending vector graphics to a high-resolution printer will result in graphics of the highest quality. For example, a graphic created on a 72 dpi screen with a vector drawing program printed on a 300 dpi laser printer gives a resolution of 300 dpi. The same image printed on a 2540 dpi imagesetter gives a resolution of 2540 dpi.

UNIT 183 INPUT IN DESKTOP COMPOSITION

PROGRAMS

Desktop composition programs are designed to transfer information from word processing programs into graphic programs. In some desktop composition programs, all text files are combined into one text file. Other page makeup programs save only the address of the text file. This allows the computer to operate faster. Having the address of the file, the desktop composition software retrieves the file at the time of printing. Because of this, it is important to include the original disk files when the final document is ready for copy creation on an imagesetter.

Although desktop composition programs are not full-featured word processing packages, copy can be directly entered into a document. Some programs even have word processing features such as find-and-replace and spell checking. Simple drawing features such as the capability to draw lines, circles, and squares are also included in desktop publishing programs. To create more complex images, though, a full-featured graphics program is required.

MENUS

Most software programs used to create documents and graphics use pull-down menus to select options. These menus appear across the top of the monitor's screen (Fig.183-1). Among other options, these pull-down menus make it possible to open an existing document, create a new document, and save a document. It is also possible to select type styles and sizes, drawing tools, and colors. All of the

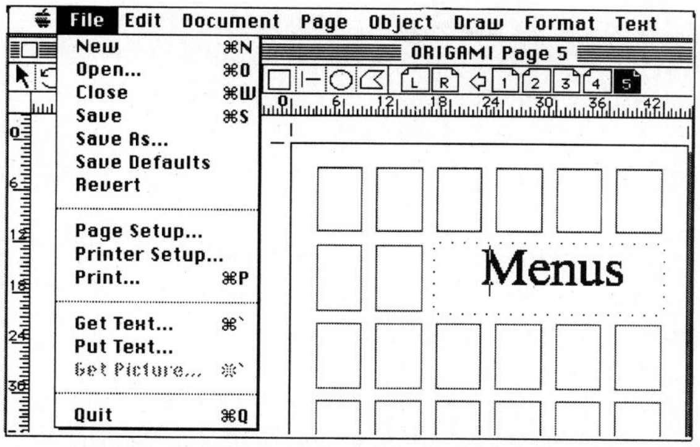

ELIZABETH WOOD, EGELAND WOOD & ZUBER, INC./ ELECTRONIC PUBLISHING & DESIGN CENTER

Fig. 183-1. All the popular desktop composition and graphics programs use a menu structure to access commands. Menu options are selected by pointing the mouse on the menu bar and activating the mouse button. Submenus appear and can be selected again with the mouse.

programs used in electronic composition have similar menus, regardless of the hardware used.

FORMATS

A *format* is the specific arrangement in which data is saved. A file format is like a language. Every software program saves the files it creates in its own format. Most software programs provide alternative formats in which to save a file. The key to using multiple software programs with different file formats is to find the format that is common to both programs, and that will allow the file to be transferred from one program to another. Most desktop composition software has been designed to input popular word processing and graphics file formats. Sometimes, though, it is necessary to use another software program as a translator.

Text Formats

Word processing software saves the file in its native format. Most word processing software has been designed to permit the saving of files in formats of other popular word processing packages too. It can also be saved in the most basic of formats—ASCII, which is a text-only format.

Graphic file formats

Graphic files are saved in their own formats. Text and graphic material cannot be saved in the same file because they use different formats. They can, however, be viewed together within standard desktop composition software.

GRAPHIC SOFTWARE

Graphic software programs contain features that allow free-hand drawing, painting, duplicating, rotating, stretching, and distorting of objects and type (Fig. 183-2). Vector drawing packages may be used to trace over

Fig. 183-2. Drawing packages and paint programs allow graphic artists to enhance already existing drawings.

scanned artwork to produce high-resolution drawings. The quality of vector graphics depends on the output device. Using raster paint programs, interesting fill patterns and quick sketches can be produced. In either program, sections of the image may be selected and manipulated to create special effects.

DOCUMENT CREATION

Document creation might begin with the copywriter using word processing software on a computer to create the text. The copywriter can enter coding into the word processing file to preformat the text. At the same time, but on another computer, the artist is creating artwork and scanning illustrations to be used in the document. The art director could also be laying out the document on another computer.

When the copy is ready, it is brought into the art director's computer. This is done either through a network or by transferring the word processing file to a floppy disk, which is then placed in the art director's computer.

The copy is then imported into the desktop composition software in which the art director created the layout. The text flows onto the page frame, where it is formatted in the typeface chosen by the art director.

Next, the illustrations and scanned images from the artist are imported, as the text was, from the artist's computer. The artwork is placed into the document. The text automatically reflows around the artwork. The artwork can be scaled or cropped to achieve the best positioning on the page. This is all done in the desktop composition program.

When the art director is satisfied with the design of the document, he or she prints the document on a laser printer. The document is then proofread. Final output can be from the laser printer or from a high-resolution imagesetter. The created pages of text and graphics are then duplicated by using an electrostatic copier or printed using the lithographic process.

UNIT **184** PAGE LAYOUT AND OUTPUT IN DESKTOP COMPOSITION

TRADITIONAL PAGE LAYOUT

It is important to follow good design and layout practices when preparing graphic content with computer software. The standard five design principles—page proportion, balance, contrast, unity, and rhythm—should be remembered and practiced when working at the keyboard of a computer (see Unit 20). The output from a desktop composition system will be only as good as the operator input.

Page layout on an electronic composition system is very much like traditional page layout. All the components of traditional design apply to electronic page makeup. Observe the following guidelines:

- Have an idea of how you want the page to look.
- Design your document with a purpose: to get the message to the reader.
- Keep the design simple.
- Avoid clutter.
- Use a minimum number of typefaces, dominant elements, and optical magnets.
- Unify the design with the graphics related to it.

ELECTRONIC PAGE LAYOUT

The first thing to do when designing a document using a page makeup program is to lay out the page. Choose the overall page size, margins, and the number of columns. These are determined by the type of document. However, basic design guidelines still apply.

The document consists of the base page. The *base page* is the page on which any repeating elements, such as logos or lines, are

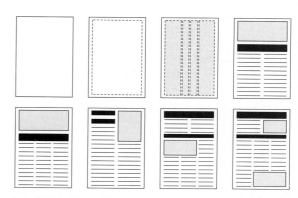

Fig. 184-1. The grid is the basis of all good page layout. This basic four-column grid allows for design flexibility within a document.

placed. The text and graphic files are placed into frames on top of this base page. A frame is like the paper that a galley of type is placed on. Frames can be sized and moved on the page just as in the traditional manner of sizing and moving them by cutting the galleys of type to create the layout of the page. With that in mind, a grid is created on the base page frame to help align the elements on the page (Fig. 184-1).

STYLE SHEETS AND TEMPLATES

In Ventura Publisher®, the predefined paragraph styles are called *tags*. With PageMaker®, Quark®, and Ready Set Go®, they are defined as *styles*. In IBM Interleaf Publisher®, they are called *components*. No matter how they are identified, each paragraph of text needs to be defined by typeface, alignment, spacing, and size. All of the styles or tags together make up the style sheet, or template.

These *style sheets,* or templates, as they are called in some programs, will become design standards for a consistent image across all documents. Because of their importance, they should be protected against change or accidental deletion. Style sheets or templates should be created for all the documents that a particular company will produce.

A style sheet created by a skilled designer can be easily used by someone with no design skills. All the nondesigner needs to do is to point at the paragraph of text and select the appropriate tag name, style sheet, or component name. The paragraph is quickly reformatted using the designer's chosen typeface, spacing, and alignment.

Documents can be created that will look professionally produced even if a designer is not on the staff. Many third-party vendors sell style sheets and templates for use with page makeup programs. Custom style sheets also can be created by design firms and advertising agencies.

TYPE AND TYPEFACES

With the wealth of typefaces now available to computer users, it is easy to be kidnapped into designing "ransom note documents." Ransom note documents are those documents in which the document's creator used every available typeface on the printer—all on one page! This, of course, should never be done.

In choosing typefaces, it is important to remember that less is actually more. A maximum of two basic typefaces should be chosen for each document. For example, a sans serif typeface such as *Helvetica* can be used for the headlines and a Roman typeface such as *Times* can be used for the body copy. Studies have shown that Roman typefaces are more easily read, especially when used as body text.

The typeface chosen should be consistent with the corporate image of the company for which the document is being produced. If the company is conservative, a flowery, decorative typeface should not be used. The typefaces chosen should reflect the capabilities of the company (Fig. 184-2).

After the appropriate typefaces have been

Fig. 184-2. The typeface chosen for a printed piece will depend partly on the image that is to be conveyed.

chosen, they must be placed on a page. Text is more easily read when line lengths are shorter than the full page width. If type extends all the way across the page, it is difficult for the eye to pick up the next line to continue reading. A two- or three-column layout should be used if the document is heavy on text. With the other extreme, narrow columns of text are very difficult to read. Line lengths from 15 to 25 picas are generally best for high readability of a printed document. Justified or ragged-right lines are commonly used in printed publications.

PAGE BALANCE

Good use of photos, text callouts, illustrations, and white space can offer graphic relief to the eye. The reader's eye will tend to be drawn to large or dark elements and away from small, light elements. A top, bottom, or side-heavy page is unbalanced and generally harder to read. It is also important to avoid extreme formal balance. Elements having equal weight, size, or shape should not be placed opposite each other. This will produce an artificial look. It is often better to strive for informal balance (see Unit 20).

STYLES

Desktop composition programs make it possible to electronically specify the type for each paragraph style that will appear in the document. Each style is given a name such as *headline, body text,* or *subhead* that will serve to describe it. After defining these styles through the use of pull-down menus, the paragraph copy can then be selected and tagged. This is done by "pointing and clicking" on the appropriate style name. The text then takes on the attributes of that style. These style names can also be entered with the text using the word processing software. Thus, the text can be brought into the desktop composition software preformatted.

The advantage of creating a document on the computer becomes obvious when it comes time to edit the document or create another document for the same company. Global style changes can be made quickly and consistently throughout the document by changing the style definition. All paragraphs with that style name will automatically assume the change made to the style definition. The computer software automatically changes the headline of the chosen typeface, size, and alignment. It also will place the correct amount of space between paragraphs.

Don't cut and paste by eye. The computer will do it for you automatically when you use style definitions. Similar documents for the same company can reuse the style sheet information and will require only modest changes. You will not need to create a new document each time. This is a more structured approach to document design. It also allows you to maintain a consistent image between documents.

This type of power made sophisticated desktop composition programs such as Ventura Publisher® and IBM Interleaf Publisher® seem difficult to use. One change in a style, tag, or component can alter the way the whole document looks. It is important to understand this and use it to your advantage. As users become more knowledgeable of page makeup programs, they will use the power of computers to eliminate the tedious, uninspiring job of positioning blocks of type on the page by hand methods.

OUTPUT PRINTERS

Once the document has been created, it is output (printed) to paper or film. Many options are available for creating this printed copy, which is referred to as *hard copy* (Fig. 184-3).

Dot matrix printers

The least expensive printer for printing a document is a dot matrix printer. This printer contains either nine or twenty-four pins in

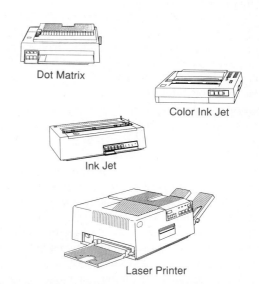

Fig. 184-3. Many types of printers can be used for electronic composition. Dot matrix has the lowest cost, and gives the lowest quality. Color is possible with dot matrix, inkjet, or PostScript® printers. PostScript® laser printers give the best quality, next to high-quality imagesetters.

the printing head. These impact through a typewriterlike ribbon to create the letter form on the paper. This type of printer is really not suited for producing quality copy. It is effective as a proofing printer. These units have serious limitations. The size of the letters they produce is not consistent with the size of letters on the high-resolution printers. This sometimes makes line lengths vary, causing type to break inconsistently between the proofing printer and the printer used for the final output.

Inkjet printers

Inkjet printers use a well of ink attached to the print head to spray ink onto the paper. Inkjet printers print in black or in colors. Type quality is better than that produced by dot matrix printers. However, the problem of inconsistent line lengths between proofing printer and final printer still exists.

Laser printers

Laser printers offer images of high quality. The technology of the laser printer is similar to that of the photocopier. The computer sends the description of the page to the memory of the laser printer. The laser translates the page into beams of light and they shine on a photosensitive drum. The part of the drum that has been exposed to light picks up toner. The drum then rolls over the paper and the toner is deposited on the paper. The paper is then heated to seal the toner to the paper. Laser printers offer resolutions of 300 to approximately 1000 dots per inch (dpi). This output is sometimes suitable for the final document when high quality is not required.

PostScript laser printers

For a laser printer to be compatible with high-end imagesetters, it must be able to interpret a page description language. One such language is called PostScript. It is currently the industry standard printer page-description language, and is used by both desktop laser printers and high-end imagesetters. Just as desktop composition software is designed to recognize the memory format of the text and

graphics, the printer needs to be able to understand the page description language, so the copy is interpreted correctly for printing.

The laser printer needs a raster image processor (RIP) to interpret the PostScript text file and rasterize it so that it can be imaged with the laser beam of light. To *rasterize* a file is to break the image down into a given number of dots per inch, which the printer then places on the paper with the laser light and toner. Because of the need for a RIP, PostScript laser printers are more expensive than non-PostScript laser printers.

Imagesetters

The current generation of imagesetting equipment also contains lasers to image the paper or film. Instead of placing dots of toner onto the page, imagesetters use laser beams of light to directly expose the light-sensitive paper or film. Because toner is not used, the resolution from typesetters is as high as 2540 dpi. The newest generation of imagesetters uses laser technology with or without a raster image processor (RIP). Because RIP technology is expensive, some imagesetting equipment does not contain this valuable feature.

TYPE FONTS

PostScript laser printers usually have up to thirty-five typestyles built into the memory of the printer. Additional type fonts are available through manufacturers who specialize in this area. These additional fonts are stored in the computer and transmitted to the printer when they are needed for a document. This process is called *downloading*.

Graphic files are usually large files. The laser printer or imagesetter must receive the description of the entire page before it can print a page. If the printer does not have enough memory to hold the complete description of a page, it will use the computer's memory. For this reason, it is recommended that the printer have at least 3 megabytes of memory. During the transfer of information from the computer to the printer, the computer is not available to receive input from the keyboard, mouse, or scanner.

SERVICE BUREAUS

Service bureaus are an extension of the traditional typesetting bureau. They have imagesetting equipment that is capable of reading electronically produced documents. Service bureaus may also have equipment to convert files from one format to another. Some service bureaus are set up to do scanning and slide making as well. It is important to check with the service bureau manager to make sure the selected typefaces are available. If not. other typefaces will need to be substituted.

UNIT 185 LEARNING EXPERIENCES: DESKTOP COMPOSITION

KEY TERMS

Unit 182
CPU (central processing unit)
Desktop composition
DOS (disk operating system)
Hardware
Monitor
Mouse
OCR (optical scanning recognition)
Scanner
Software

Unit 183
Format
Menu

Unit 184
Base page
Dot matrix printer
Downloading
Hard copy
Imagesetters
Inkjet printer
Laser printer
Service bureau
Style sheet

DISCUSSION TOPICS

1. What guidelines should be observed in designing a page?
2. What is the base page?
3. What is a style sheet?
4. What guidelines should be followed in choosing typefaces?

5. What is the least expensive printer for printing a document?
6. What is a service bureau?

ACTIVITIES

Unit 182
1. Obtain several different magazines. Examine the design of several pages in each of the magazines. In analyzing the pages, pay particular attention to the number of columns, the placement of photos and artwork, and the typeface. Do these help the reader gain information? Is the page layout attractive? Do you have any suggestions for improving the layout of the pages?

Unit 183
2. If you have available a word processing program with a spell checker, enter a sample document of 1,000 words. Practice using the spell checker to check the spelling on the document you have entered. Remember that the document you plan to import into a page layout program should be as complete as possible. Don't import into a page layout program a document that you have not spell checked.

Unit 184
3. If you have available a page layout program, use it to design a simple one-page, advertising flyer on an 8 1/2-by-11-inch sheet of paper. The flyer will be printed on one side. It will not be folded. Select a product. Then create your advertising

copy in a word processing program. Remember to cover the main points of the product. Emphasize the product's benefits, design, and price.

Select the margins and the number of columns. Then import your document from a word processing program. After importing the document, select typefaces for the various parts of the flyer. In selecting the typefaces, remember to follow the guidelines outlined in Unit 184.

The development of computer technology has resulted in a variety of new career opportunities in graphic arts.
JAMES L. SHAFFER

23 GRAPHIC ARTS CAREER OPPORTUNITIES

186 INTRODUCTION TO CAREERS IN GRAPHIC ARTS

The graphic arts industry constantly needs qualified people. Graphic arts offers many career opportunities, ranging from minimum-skill jobs to top management positions. People interested in working in this dynamic field must have high creative ability and craftsmanship.

The growth of the graphic arts industry has been caused by technological developments in such areas as computers, copy and duplicating devices, microimage, electronic transmission methods, and the constant development and refinement of present processes. People who choose this industry can know that they are making a contribution to society (Fig. 186-1).

Fig. 186-1. The graphic arts industry needs people with creative talents who can use computers and electronic imaging systems.

QUALIFICATIONS

Apprenticeship is a common way of entering the skilled areas of graphic arts. In some cases it is the only way that you may be trained to become a *journeyman* (skilled worker) in a unionized commercial plant. Formal apprenticeship is also required to become a journeyman in many large plants not covered by union contracts.

A registered apprentice is an employee who, under an expressed or implied agreement, is taught an occupation for a given period of time. This person must also be em-

ployed in an apprenticeship program that is registered with a state apprenticeship agency or with the U.S. Department of Labor, Bureau of Apprenticeship and Training.

Apprenticeship in the graphic arts usually lasts from four to six years, depending on the area of skill and the geographic location of the commercial plant. It covers all phases of the particular trade, and it usually includes classroom or correspondence study in related technical subjects in addition to training on the job. Applicants are usually between 18 and 35 years of age and must pass a physical examination.

You may also become qualified through formal education. Courses are available in technology education and vocational-industrial education. Post-high school opportunities include vocational-technical institutes, trade schools, and college-university programs. Several technological and managerial graphic arts programs are offered in many higher education institutions. These four-year programs, which lead to a bachelor's degree, qualify the graduate to enter the industry in supervision and management positions. Graduate programs that lead to the master's degree will qualify people for higher management positions.

EARNING AND WORKING CONDITIONS

Earnings of production workers in the graphic arts industry are among the highest in the manufacturing field. These include the unskilled, semi-skilled, and skilled workers. Recent statistics indicate that workers in all three categories are paid more per hour than other production workers. The wage varies from one classification in this occupation to another, and it is usually higher in cities than in smaller communities. It also varies with the type of commercial printing establishment.

The standard work week is between 35 and 40 hours, depending on the labor-management contract and also on the geographical location of the plant. Time-and-a-half is usually paid for overtime and for work on Sundays and holidays. In newspaper plants, however, the work week often includes Sunday; there is therefore no additional rate of pay. Night-shift workers generally receive pay above the standard day rate.

Annual earnings of skilled workers depend not only on the hourly rate of pay but also on how regularly they are employed. The graphic arts industry has fewer seasonal fluctuations than do many other industries. This is one of the reasons it offers steadier employment and higher average annual earnings.

Working conditions within the industry, in general, are quite good (Fig. 186-2). Many larger plants are air conditioned for quality control.

Fig. 186-2. A neat and well-organized working environment helps people who must provide management and operations services for a large graphic arts printing company.

Fig. 186-3. Preparing a printing press for operation.

EMPLOYMENT OUTLOOK

Opportunities in graphic arts range from the production and installation of equipment, to working with raw materials from production phases (Fig. 186-3) to service, sales, and management. These opportunities reflect the continued rise in the volume of printed materials. They are based on population growth, the increasingly high level of education, the expansion of industry, and the trend toward greater use of printed materials for information, packaging, advertising, and other industrial and commercial purposes.

A PERSONAL BUSINESS

Young people often wonder how they can start a business of their own (see Unit 193). Large amounts of capital are necessary to begin almost any private business. It is possible, however, to enter the graphic arts production industry without a great amount of money. Small business loans have helped many persons start their own shops.

Of the 50,000-some graphic arts production businesses in the United States, about one-third are one-person operations. This means that the concern is owned and operated by one person who may employ a few other workers.

UNIT 187 OPPORTUNITIES IN PRE-PRESS PREPARATION

Preparing material to be printed is an important part of the printing task. *Pre-press* involves design and layout, type composition, art and copy preparation, photography, and image carriers. Each of these specific areas is important to the completed product. A well-managed commercial plant gives careful attention to scheduling printing jobs through the production stages (Fig. 187-1). Finished products can be completed on time only when each production stage is completed on schedule.

DESIGN AND LAYOUT

The person involved in *design* and *layout* originates the graphic product. With the imaginative planning and development of the original ideas, the completed item results.

Design and layout people must have artistic talent. They should enjoy working at drawing tables (Fig. 187-2), handling computers, and arranging type and illustrations into

Fig. 187-1. A work schedule board helps control the production time of printing jobs.

usable form. Designers must have a good knowledge of color and how it affects people psychologically. The final result must have visual impact.

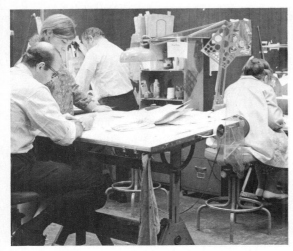

M. KORN PACKAGING

Fig. 187-2. Design and layout personnel get materials ready for publication.

Fig. 187-3. Persons who operate typesetting machines must understand the control functions of computer-based equipment.

TYPE COMPOSITION

A *compositor* is a person who puts together letters, words, sentences, and paragraphs in a form that can be duplicated many times. There are several methods of composition, as we have mentioned earlier. The person involved in composition must enjoy working with small materials and with delicate mechanical equipment.

In recent years, sophisticated procedures and equipment have entered the composition phase of the graphic arts industry. Computers and photographic techniques have made this work complicated. Persons working in composition must know how to operate the latest types of equipment (Fig. 187-3). They may have to attend an industrial or technical night school to obtain this knowledge.

PHOTOGRAPHY

Photography plays an important role in the graphic arts. Photographs are part of the copy to be printed. Photographic techniques are used in composition. Photographic film negatives and positives are involved in preparing image carriers.

People interested in photography have many outlets for their talents. They may work for a daily newspaper, for an advertising firm, or possibly even as a free-lance photographer. They not only take photographs but may also develop and print the final pictures.

Other technicians may use enlargers to prepare prints. They may operate special copying cameras (Fig. 187-4) to make prints of artists' renditions. Many persons may be involved with process cameras and normal darkroom activities, as discussed earlier in this text. People with a flair for photography have no problem obtaining work. In fact, the problem will be selecting the phase of graphic arts photography that they most prefer.

Fig. 187-4. A process camera operator should have a good understanding of optics and light-sensitive imaging.

IMAGE CARRIERS

The area of preparing image carriers is changing rapidly. New developments have forced many people to be retrained, and new persons with different backgrounds have been trained to do the work. A knowledge of chemistry is often useful.

The tools of the image carrier specialist are the many different kinds of plate making materials. These range from metal to plastic, rubber, and glass. Other new materials are being developed yearly. People in the image carriers area (Fig. 187-5) work amidst chemicals, sinks, and etching tanks. Other items of equipment are exposure units, etching machines, and light-sensitive emulsion applicating machines.

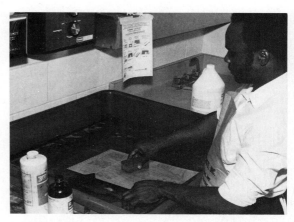

Fig. 187-5. Persons who make lithographic printing plates must have a basic understanding of chemistry.

UNIT 188 OPPORTUNITIES IN PRINTING AND FINISHING

The two main production phases are image transfer (press operations) and finishing and binding (putting materials into final usable form). The press operators and bindery employees work directly with the printed products that are eventually distributed to consumers.

IMAGE TRANSFER

The actual *image transfer* or printing operation, is performed on a press. Press operators are responsible for making certain that type, photographs, and illustrations are reproduced correctly. They must see that the right amount of ink is applied in all areas of each page. It is also their job to see that the total image is positioned properly on the page.

A press operator may work on large, web-fed presses (Fig. 188-1) or on large sheet-fed presses (Fig. 188-2) that require several people to operate. They may work on smaller machines needing two or three persons, or on a small machine where only one operator is needed. The techniques of operating several styles and brands of presses vary, but all work basically in much the same way.

FINISHING AND BINDING

Finishing operations include cutting, folding, punching holes, and several processes that make the printed materials usable. Special skills are needed to use several different finishing machines, such as the high-speed die cutter and creaser (Fig. 188-3).

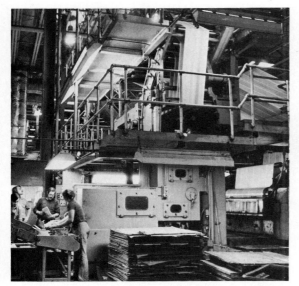

Fig. 188-1. Press operators inspect the printed signatures being produced on a high-speed web offset lithography press.

Fig. 188-2. Press operators keep constant watch on a four-color sheet-fed lithographic press.

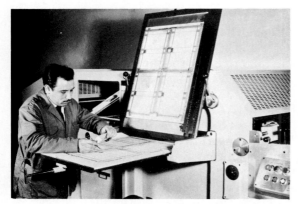

Fig. 188-3. A specialist gets a high-speed die cutter and creaser ready for operation.

Fig. 188-4. Four people are needed to keep an 18-pocket automatic gathering machine operating at top capacity.

Binding includes the several different methods of fastening sheets of paper together to make the final product. Books, magazines, pamphlets, business forms, and advertising literature all are bound together. Several different machines are used to complete the many phases of binding, and skilled operators are in demand to work them (Fig. 188-4). Binding machines and all graphic arts equipment also need constant servicing. Much of the maintenance work is done by hand.

Two types of binderies are *edition,* or case binding, and *pamphlet* or paperback binding. Edition binderies are plants that produce large numbers of hardbound books by mass production. Paperback binderies produce books, magazines, and pamphlets, often by methods similar to those used by edition binders. However, many paperbacks are printed, bound, and packaged in one continuous operation. Job binderies do binding on contract for printers, publishers, or other customers. They can be large commercial plants.

If you want to become a *journeyman binder* you probably will have to complete a four- to five-year apprenticeship program. As in other areas of graphic arts, you can shorten this period of time by taking graphic arts training in a high school or a technical and vocational school, or by doing other formal graphic arts work.

189 OPPORTUNITIES IN MANAGEMENT AND SALES

UNIT

Management and sales are necessary in all business enterprises, including the graphic arts industry. The managers of tomorrow must know the newer business tools, such as computers, operations, and research. Schools must turn out graduates who are specialists in change; people who can cope with the still-newer tools and machinery of tomorrow.

MANAGEMENT

A key responsibility of management is to motivate people. A manager must create an atmosphere that inspires people to produce their best work efficiently. This is more important than relationships with each individual. A manager should:

1. Know how to guide others.
2. Know where to look for experts who can strengthen weak areas.
3. Be creative and not be afraid to be different in actions and thought.
4. Be mature.
5. Have a good personality.
6. Be willing to look for help in understanding the personnel and their job responsibilities.
7. Develop the ability to find and act on facts rather than on opinions about certain business operations.
8. Be constantly concerned with self-motivation which, in turn, will motivate others.
9. Care about the successful operation of the company almost more than anyone else.

Management personnel must constantly be on the job (Fig. 189-1). They must want to devote more time to it than the average 8-to-5 shift. Special evening and weekend conferences and out-of-town trips are part of the job.

M. KORN PACKAGING

Fig. 189-1. Management personnel at work.

Young people interested in management must develop their potential. They are likely to find the positions they seek in this area. Management personnel is scarce and will become more so as business and the complexity of management increase.

SELLING

The sales phase of graphic arts is an exciting challenge. A sales representative must be dedicated to informing as many people as possible about the product. Graphic arts sales opportunities range from demonstrating and selling equipment to selling the printed product (Fig. 189-2).

Profit is the goal in almost all business efforts. A successful company makes a profit. One of the key persons who maintains the proper balance between sales and production is the sales representative. The more that is sold, the more the company can produce. In-

COVALENT SYSTEMS

Fig. 189-2. Most people in sales spend considerable time at computer keyboards updating and reviewing their customer accounts.

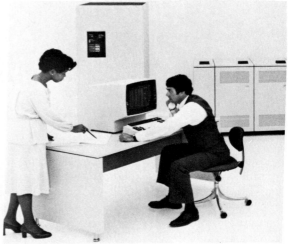

COVALENT SYSTEMS

Fig. 189-3. Sales personnel obtain extensive amounts of information from computer printouts, telephone, and fax machines.

creased production, in most cases, helps to increase the profit margin.

A sales representative in the graphic arts should have:

1. An interest in the industry.
2. A desire to learn as much about the industry as possible.
3. A desire to work closely with people.
4. Long hours to give to the work.
5. Good intelligence.
6. A desire to be constantly on the move.
7. Good grooming.
8. A sense of humor.
9. A good personality.

Computers are valuable to modern day sales personnel (Fig. 189-3). Access to information stored in computer memory can help the sales person meet customer demands. Qualified people backed up with quality equipment make business operations function effectively.

UNIT 190 OPPORTUNITIES IN TEACHING GRAPHIC ARTS

Teaching is a field with excellent career prospects. Teaching is one of the largest of all professions. Graphic arts presents many opportunities to persons who are interested in teaching and who especially like the graphic arts technical area. Over 4,000 schools in the United States offer courses and programs dealing with graphic arts. There are also great numbers of courses and seminars organized by industry.

GRAPHIC ARTS TEACHING OPPORTUNITIES

There are teaching positions at almost any level in which a prospective graphic arts teacher would be interested. Technology education/graphic arts curricula are offered in many secondary schools (grades 7–12) (Fig. 190-1). New programs requiring more qualified teachers are being offered each school year.

Many vocational high schools offer courses that deal directly with teaching the skills needed to work in commercial graphic arts plants. Students who complete these technical-vocational programs can begin work immediately after leaving school. Such career instruction requires teachers with knowledge and skills in many areas. For example, a teacher must be able to work with process cameras and darkroom film products.

Technical institutes and terminal technical programs in junior colleges provide further instruction in skills. Teachers for these types of programs must be highly knowledgeable in graphic arts production. Universities and colleges offering graphic arts management and technical curricula are in constant need of professors (Fig. 190-2). Industry needs people with special graphic arts skills who can teach employees the techniques needed to keep up with new techniques and machines. Because industry in our society changes constantly, necessary training often can only be given on-the-job in an industrial plant.

Teacher qualifications

No two teachers are alike, but those considering teaching as a career should have:

1. A personality acceptable to the people with whom they will work.
2. Above-average intelligence.
3. An interest in a specific subject.
4. An attitude that motivates and inspires students.

Fig. 190-2. A university professor discusses a technical graphic arts topic with some students.

5. Patience.
6. Ability to work long and hard with people until the educational objectives have been reached.
7. The ability to organize information.
8. The ability to demonstrate specific technical knowledge.

A bachelor's degree is the usual requirement for teaching in secondary schools, most technical-vocational high schools, and technical institute positions. However, in many

Fig. 190-1. A teacher shows young graphic arts students how to operate a lithography duplicator/press.

DOW JONES & COMPANY

Fig. 190-3. Formal education prepares people for highly technical positions in the graphic arts industry.

trade and vocational schools, skilled graphic arts personnel are providing very effective instruction based on their own job experience. To teach in colleges and universities, a master's degree is necessary. A doctor's degree is often necessary for teaching at the college/university level.

Industry does not always require formal education of instructors in their training programs, but people with formal education seem to have a better opportunity to fill these positions (Fig. 190-3). If you want a career in industrial training, you should gain as much technical and general knowledge about graphic arts as possible.

UNIT 191 PULP AND PAPER MANUFACTURING OPPORTUNITIES

There are many career possibilities in the pulp and paper manufacturing industry. Many kinds of talent are needed in the scientific, engineering, and liberal arts fields to fill a variety of technical, operating, and commercial positions.

Paper of all kinds is made or marketed all over the United States and in many other countries. The industry offers its employees an extremely wide choice of working locations and living environments.

ENGINEERING OPPORTUNITIES

Those persons with degrees in *industrial, civil,* or *mechanical* engineering have five possible areas of employment in the pulp and paper manufacturing industry:

1. Industrial engineers maintain and improve operating performance, reduce waste, prevent delays, reduce costs, and keep a high level of production efficiency.
2. Power plant engineers and their employees are concerned with design, supervision of construction, and operation of generating plants that furnish power.
3. Production, planning, and control employees help establish schedules that will make maximum use of available equipment, labor, tools, and capacity. They also coordinate production operations to meet delivery dates.
4. Mill or plant production needs quality control and production engineers, as well as employees with a bachelor of science degree in either chemistry, chemical, or industrial engineering and who have from three to five years work experience. Responsibilities include installing product-inspecting and testing procedures to establish quality standards. Promotions may lead to the office of quality control executive or manager.
5. Production time-and-motion employees maintain efficient plant operation for maximum production with minimum loss of effort by machine operators.

SCIENTIFIC OPPORTUNITIES

Persons having an advanced degree in *organic chemistry, physical chemistry* or *biochemistry* and experience in *paper engineering* perform the following basic chemical research:

1. They conduct independent investigations to develop new products or processes.
2. They contribute to solving technical problems.
3. They solve problems of high-output production and manufacturing.
4. They work to extend product usefulness.
5. They work closely with the chemist.

RESEARCH OPPORTUNITIES

Two other areas of basic research are carried on by mills dealing with products from their own forests: (1) basic research in timberland management, which deals with the acquisition, culture, harvesting, and continued use of forest stands and, (2) basic research in wood technology. Both require degrees from a college of forestry with additional education in botany, chemistry, geology, zoology, physics, environmental protection, and some general courses in economics and government.

Most papermaking companies maintain their own research facilities to improve existing products and develop new ones. Research personnel include engineers, chemists, physicists, and foresters. College graduates with degrees in forestry analysis can find a variety of positions in timber management, forestry and genetic research, and many other specialized fields.

MANAGEMENT, BUSINESS, AND LEGAL OPPORTUNITIES

Mill management and legal administration need:

1. Lawyers in corporate, patent, tax, and real estate law.
2. Specialists on exports.

3. Engineers skilled in the operation of the entire plant.
4. Experts on labor, industrial, community, and employee relations.
5. Administrative heads to manage large staffs of office workers.
6. Traffic consultants.
7. Purchasing agents for materials and equipment.
8. Public relations, advertising, sales, and sales-service staffs.

PLANT OCCUPATIONS

There are three groups of pulp and paper mill workers: (1) production workers who operate the various machines and equipment (Fig. 191-1), (2) maintenance workers who maintain, install, and repair physical equipment, and (3) workers such as material handlers and stock clerks. Additional staff people include checkers and sorters for quality control, laboratory chemists, and packing and shipping operators.

THE MEAD CORPORATION

Fig. 191-1. A paper machine operator feeds production information to a computer which controls most functions on the machine.

UNIT 192 BEING A SUCCESSFUL EMPLOYEE

Gaining employment in a graphic arts company may be the beginning of a long and successful career. Getting a job and keeping a job are important for those desiring stability in their lives. The receipt of a paycheck and the knowledge that one has done a good job provides great satisfaction.

GETTING A JOB

It is assumed that a person will have some preparation before looking for a job. This could mean that the person completed a program of graphic arts courses in high school, at a vocational/technical college, or at a university. Sometimes previous work experience alone will be enough to gain employment in a graphic arts printing company. This, however, is the exception rather than the norm. Usually, a combination of formal preparation and on-the-job experience gives an applicant the best job opportunities.

Where to look: Graphic arts employment opportunities are available in cities large and small, and in companies of every description. The previous units in this final section of the book contain much information about graphic arts companies and job opportunities.

Company personnel directors, plant managers, and business owners place job notices in the want ad sections of newspapers and magazines (Fig. 192-1). They may also post job announcements in the windows of their graphic arts businesses. They may contract with a job-service agency to locate prospective employees. High schools, colleges, and universities often have job placement and career centers. Company personnel directors frequently look for employees with educational

---

Employment Opportunity

Copy Preparation Supervisor

An energetic and knowledgeable person in graphic arts copy preparation is needed for the 2nd shift. The individual must have formal preparation in design and layout, typesetting and/or imagesetting, and desktop composition. Industry experience is a plus, but is not required for employment.

There are 35 employees in the 15 year old company. The company specializes in all areas of pre-press for lithography and screen printing. Wages and salaries are very competitive. A resume <u>must</u> be included with the letter of application.

Apply by letter to:

Mr. Joseph Z. Smith
Personnel Director
Graphic Arts Color, Inc.
1000 Graphic Communications Road
City, State, Zip

Fig. 192-1. An example of an announcement of a graphic arts employment opportunity that often appears in newspapers, industry journals, and company newsletters.

preparation in graphic arts. They send their needs for employees to academic job placement and career centers. Seeking employment advice from school counselors, graphic arts teachers, professors, and academic advisors can lead to job contacts (Fig. 192-2).

Making contact: Upon learning about a job, it is important to make contact as quickly as possible. There may be many people looking for employment. Job applicants are sometimes assigned a priority ranking based upon when they apply after a job has been announced or posted.

Fig. 192-2. Graphic arts students should seek employment opportunity advice from their academic advisor.

Job notices should always contain information about how to apply for the job. For example, the applicant may need to write a letter of application (Fig. 192-3). Application letters should specify why you want the job, your qualifications, and when you will be available for employment.

It is often beneficial to send a copy of your resumé along with your letter of application. A resumé should accent your strengths by presenting highlights of your background (Fig. 192-4). Most resumés contain personal information such as your name, birthdate, and birth place. They also include information about academic preparation, work experience, career goals, and hobbies.

Frequently, it will be necessary to complete a job application form. You may receive one in the mail as a result of sending an application letter. Possibly, the company personnel director will ask each applicant to come to the company location to complete a job application form. In either case, it is important to fill out the form neatly, accurately, and completely. This application form may be the one and only factor used to determine whether you are offered the job.

Interviewing for a job: Personnel directors frequently believe it is important to conduct a face-to-face interview. If so, this is your opportunity to put your best foot forward. Think about the interview and plan how you will conduct yourself. Write down those questions you would like answered. In this way, all important questions will be asked. It can be frustrating to forget to ask one or more questions that you would like answered. Also, think about questions that you should not immediately ask. Two such questions might be "How much money will I make?" and "When can I expect a promotion?" Be ready to ask questions. Be prepared also to answer questions. It is valuable to have some established goals and to be able to explain your experiences and accomplishments.

Personal grooming and health are important in the initial and follow-up interviews. In fact, they are often critical to getting, keeping, and being successful in a job. A suit and tie or a dress and nice shoes do wonders in improving how we feel about ourselves. Personal hygiene and health are critical to how people look at us. A bath, shower, clean fingernails, a bright skin complexion, and reserve energy contribute to a successful interview.

After the interview, make a sincere effort to express appreciation. Inform the personnel staff member that you appreciated the opportunity to interview for the available job. This should be done orally at the conclusion of the interview and in a written letter a few days later. A firm handshake and direct eye contact with the interviewer will add to your creditability.

KEEPING A JOB

Once a job has been secured, it is important to retain the job. There are many opportunities in the graphic arts industry. There usually is a shortage of qualified employees. However, company management should not and will not keep employees on the payroll who are not providing a positive benefit. Make every attempt to perform your responsibilities. Do the highest quality work you know how to perform. A person hired to operate a printing press or work in the copy preparation department of a graphic arts company has a major responsibility. That responsibility is to produce work that will contribute to the financial profit of the company.

April 1, 1999

Mr. Joseph Z. Smith
Personnel Director
Graphic Arts Color, Inc.
1000 Graphic Communications Road
City, State, Zip

Dear Mr. Smith:

The copy preparation supervisor position announcement which
appeared in the last evening's newspaper interests me very much.
I am planning to graduate with a Bachelor of Arts degree in
graphic communications from the University of Northern Iowa in
early May.

The program at the University of Northern Iowa is designed to
prepare people with a broad knowledge in graphic communications,
but I do believe that it will be possible for me to fulfill your
job expectations. I have an overall grade point average of 3.32
and an average of 3.56 in my major. During my cooperative
education experience, I worked in a copy preparation department
of a large graphic arts company.

Enclosed is a copy of my resume for your review. Letters of
reference or telephone numbers of the people who have agreed to
give me references will gladly be provided at your request. I
look forward to hearing from you with the hope that I will have
the opportunity to interview for the position.

Sincerely,

Mark Andrew Johnson
106 Star Street
City, State, Zip

Ph. (319) 010-2232

Enclosure

Fig. 192-3. An example of a letter of application for the job announcement shown in Figure 192-1.

MARK ANDREW JOHNSON

106 Star Street
City, State, Zip
Phone: (319) 010-2232

JOB OBJECTIVE

Obtain an entry level position in the graphic communications industry within the production management or customer service areas.

EDUCATION

8/1986—8/1990

Bachelor of Arts Degree   **August 1990**
University of Northern Iowa, Cedar Falls, IA
Major: Graphic Communications

Technical Courses: Communication Systems, Communications Technology, Power Technology, Computer Aided Drafting, Technical Illustration, Screen Printing Technology, Graphic Arts Technology, Lithographic Technology, Electronic Typesetting and Copy Preparation, Desktop Composition, Applied Photography, Principles of Chemistry, General Physics 1.

Business and Management: Principles of Marketing, Fundamentals of Management, Applied Industrial Supervision and Management, Graphic Arts Estimating and Management, Industrial Safety, and Report Writing.

EMPLOYMENT

1/1989—5/1990

Graphic Communications Laboratory Assistant: University of Northern Iowa
Department of Industrial Technology
Cedar Falls, IA 50614-0178

Supervise open lab, verify directions demonstrated by the professor, and help lab users as needed. The job provided practical experience in all of the major graphic communications areas. Have assisted in the printing of a pamphlet and promotional materials for the department.

Summers
1987—1988

Dishwasher / Kitchen Mainenance: Twin Lakes Bible Camp
RR. 1 Box 194
Manson, IA 50563

This employment provided opportunities to develop people skills. I also trained and supervised an employee.

ACTIVITIES AND INTERESTS

—Sports, Movies, Music
—Student Member of the Graphic Arts Technical Foundation.
—Joint Projects With Faculty
—Attended Graph Expo 1989
—Cooperative Education

REFERENCES & PORTFOLIO

Available upon request.

MARK A. JOHNSON

Fig. 192-4. An example of a resumé of a student who has studied graphic arts in school, but has had limited work experience.

Being a fully informed employee is valuable for the company, fellow employees, and yourself. Know your rights as a citizen and as an employee. All employees are entitled to a safe working environment, time for meals, and facilities for personal needs. If these and other appropriate services are not available, take time to find out why and how the problems can be remedied.

An important attribute of a successful employee is the ability to get along with fellow employees. This obviously includes your immediate supervisor and higher level management. Accepting criticism gracefully and using it to improve your future actions will increase your personal rate of success. Favorable behavior—both on and off the job—can lead to an enjoyable career.

Quality work performance is impressive and will be recognized. Although recognition may come slowly, it will come. It is better to improve steadily rather than unevenly. Another important attribute of a quality employee is *follow through*. Making certain that a job is finished on time will impress company management and the customer.

Maintaining a high level of competency is difficult with today's technology. While much can be learned on the job, this has its limitations. There is real value in pursuing continued education through college and university courses, and by attending workshops, seminars, and expositions sponsored by graphic arts associations and companies. New ideas and information will help maintain a level of excitement that contributes to keeping a job in the graphic arts industry.

CHANGING JOBS

There sometimes comes a need to make a change in employment. This can be a very positive experience, as it usually means a step up the ladder of success. There is, however, a right way and a wrong way to make a job change.

First, ask yourself why you believe a job change would have value. Possibly it means a promotion in job responsibilities, a higher wage or salary, greater long-range opportunities, or possibly the geographical location is more to your liking. Once this answer has been determined, resign your current job in a professional manner. Prepare a letter of resignation stating your intentions and reason for resigning. Include a statement of appreciation. Deliver the letter to your supervisor in person. Be sure to provide sufficient lead time of two to four weeks so your replacement can be found.

Making a job change is not always easy. However, it can help pave the way to a successful career in the graphic arts industry. Generally, job changes should be made infrequently, and made only when the benefits outweigh the negative factors.

DEVELOPING LEADERSHIP ABILITIES

Leadership is a key to having a successful graphic arts career. *Leadership* means to take the lead and get a job completed on time and at an acceptable quality level. It also means gaining the respect of co-workers, thus making it possible to lead and guide them in achieving common goals. For example, a plate-making department supervisor must possess leadership abilities in directing the activities associated with the several employees readying printing plates for pressroom use.

Student leadership: It is valuable to gain leadership skills while still in school. Such skills will serve as a foundation for leadership opportunities during full-time employment. Seek out, join, and become involved in student clubs such as the Graphic Arts Technical Society and the Technology Student Association (TSA). Volunteer to serve on organizational committees. If possible, run for elected office in the club. Part-time work at a local graphic arts company will also provide leadership experience.

Employee leadership: Graphic arts employment provides many leadership opportunities. Larger companies often have departments where supervisors are identified to organize and coordinate the specified responsibilities. Much can be learned about leadership by observing, listening, and participating in small group activities. Graphic arts organizations need people who are willing to become involved.

Leadership skills are closely associated with organizing and directing your personal life. Setting personal career goals is a critical leadership function. This takes planning, organization, and knowing oneself. Typical career goals involve identifying your work specialty, the type and size of company where you wish to be employed, the skill level or management level you wish to achieve, and the wage you need to earn.

Career goals cannot be achieved overnight. Small steps in a planned direction are important. For example, you might have the goal to achieve an advanced education degree while being employed part time or full time. To achieve this worthy goal, it is valuable to determine how many courses or academic credits must be completed each year to finally reach graduation day. Planning and following through with dedication will lead to career success.

Citizen leadership: There are many opportunities to become involved in community activities. This is true whether the community is a large city or a small town. Service clubs such as Rotary International, Lions, Kiwanis, and Sertoma are always looking for quality members. These groups call on their members for committees and leadership. Of course, the organization itself needs officers to establish policy and carry out the required and planned business.

People function best when there is structure. That is why national, state, and local governments exist. One way to experience and learn leadership is to participate in government. Cities and towns need citizen input. As a resident of a community, you might seek to be appointed or elected to positions of responsibility.

The local public and private school systems need direct input from citizens. Organized committees conduct research, secure citizen input, and prepare reports for the Board of Education and the school system administration.

IN REVIEW

Being successful in today's graphic arts job market requires appropriate preparation and follow through. It means that you must know how to get a job, keep a job, and change from one job to another. Success in one phase contributes to success in succeeding phases. Taking the initiative helps to insure career happiness.

Leadership is being able to accomplish something by yourself and with other people. The best way to gain leadership skills is to practice them through involvement in groups. Making the effort to search out opportunities that will provide positive influence will pay dividends in succeeding years.

UNIT 193 OWNING A GRAPHIC ARTS BUSINESS

The owner of a graphic arts company should have a clear idea of what is expected from the enterprise. Also, the owner must know the ways in which these expectations relate to the overall industry and ultimately to profits. Owners must have a knack for being competitive. Through a competitive approach, the owner-manager can use strategies for such important business fundamentals as establishing markets for the printed products and handling the finances for all aspects of the company.

To be successful, the owner of a graphic arts business must be motivated. This person must have a strong desire to get ahead. Working hard, working long hours, and being willing to accept responsibility are characteristic of company ownership. The willingness to take risks and be adventuresome are critical to the long-term success of a company owner.

Company owners are frequently identified as entrepreneurs. *Entrepreneurship* is the practice of being creative in the initiation of a business or product and having the knowledge and ability to be successful in the endeavor. Do you want to be an entrepreneur in the graphic arts business? If so, you will need educational preparation in graphic arts technology and management. You must be willing to seek help from wherever it can be found. You also must be willing to work very hard to achieve your established goals. Other characteristics of an entrepreneur are listed in Figure 193-1.

Entrepreneurship Self-Rating Scale

Needed Characteristics	Highly Needed	Minimum Needed	Seldom Needed	Not Needed
Attitude toward others	Positive; friendly interest in people	Pleasant, polite	Sometimes difficult to work with	Inclined to be quarrelsome or uncooperative
Leadership	Forceful, inspiring confidence and loyalty	Order giver	Driver	Weak
Responsibility	Responsibility sought and welcomed	Accepted without protest	Unwilling to assume without protest	Avoided whenever possible
Organizing Ability	Highly capable of perceiving and arranging fundamentals in logical order	Able organizer	Fairly capable of organizing	Poor organizer
Industry	Industrious; capable of working hard for long hours	Can work hard, but not for too long of period	Fairly industrious	Hard work avoided
Decision	Quick and accurate	Good and careful	Quick, but often unsound	Hesitant and fearful
Sincerity	Courageous, square-shooter	On the level	Fairly sincere	Inclined to lack sincerity
Perseverance	Highly steadfast in purpose; not discouraged by obstacles	Effort steadily maintained	Average determination and persistence	Little or no persistence
Physical energy	Highly energetic at all times	Energetic most of time	Fairly energetic	Below average

Fig. 193-1. A self-rating scale for determining needed entrepreneurship traits. Future entrepreneurs should be able to identify themselves with needs listed in columns 1 and 2.

WALDMAN GRAPHICS

GETTING STARTED

Getting started is sometimes the most difficult part of being an entrepreneur. Ideas and thoughts of beginning a business sometimes come easy. To put them into action is another story. People are often overheard saying that they should write a book, paint a picture, and start a business. It is the rare few who actually set their minds to the stated task and get the job accomplished.

What kind of business? The graphic arts industry is vast, as is shown throughout the units and sections of this book. Much more is taking place in the graphic arts industry than can ever be presented in a single publication. Thus research should be done to determine the best type of business for you to enter. For example, should you get involved in general commercial printing or in specialty product printing? What printing process should be used—letterpress, lithography, or screen? Would it be best to consider a specific line of printed products? If so, it will be necessary to research and select the best printing process to accomplish the task.

An entrepreneur, a person willing to step out and strive for success, should analyze his or her own abilities and interests before making the business decision. In graphic arts course work or work experiences, were you particularly capable or interested in a specific graphic arts area? If so, clearly identify this area and chart your course of action. Marketing opportunities or limitations will often dictate the type of business that is best. For example, if printed sweatshirts, T-shirts, and school athletic program clothing are purchased from outside the local area, there is probably room for a screen printer to establish a business. With good transportation and communication so readily available, it is possible to start a business that can serve regional and national markets, as well as the local market.

Financial considerations: How much money does it take to start a small graphic arts business? It depends on the kind of business and its intended scope. Much also depends on the national, regional, and local location. Some geographical locations are much higher priced than others, even within a few blocks in the same city.

Successful graphic arts businesses have been started with limited funds, but this can be risky. It is much more satisfactory to have adequate capital (funding). Adequate capital means more than just enough money to purchase equipment, furnishings, and supplies. It means having enough money in reserve to adequately operate the business before sales begin to be made. The reserve amount depends upon such expenses as salaries (including your own), building rent, utilities, and day-to-day unexpected expenses.

Estimating how much money will be needed is a difficult question to answer, even for financial planning experts. It is, however, possible to conduct some personal research using one or more standard financial planning forms (Fig. 193-2). Most planning experts for small businesses agree that there should be sufficient capital to operate a business for a minimum of six months without substantial income.

Having enough personal money (capital) to get started in a business is not often possible. It is important to have a large percentage of the total needed for initial capital expenditures and six months of operating expenses. There are ways and sources of funds that will provide money for these two major financial categories. Four sources of funding that can be beneficial to an entrepreneur are family and friends, banks, venture capital groups, and governmental agencies. It is often risky to borrow money from family and friends because strained relationships can develop over such things as the repayment schedule, amount of interest, and differing opinions on management strategies.

Better sources of funding are those that are "strictly business." Bank loan officers are generally interested in assisting entrepreneurs in their local communities. These people are often excellent sources of capital funding. Venture capital groups are made up of people who have extra money to invest in high-risk businesses. A venture capital group may be a

BUSINESS START-UP COSTS

Item	Estimate
Start-up investment	$ _____
Inventory	_____
Fixtures and equipment	_____
Installation of fixtures and equipment	_____
Remodeling and decorating	_____
Licenses and permits	_____
Professional (legal and accounting)	_____
Cash cushion	_____
Total start-up investment	$ _____

Operating expenses for 6 months

Salaries and wages	$ _____	Mo x 6	_____
Rent	_____	Mo x 6	_____
Telephone	_____	Mo x 6	_____
Utilities (light, heat)	_____	Mo x 6	_____
Office supplies	_____	Mo x 6	_____
Shop supplies	_____	Mo x 6	_____
Debt interest	_____	Mo x 6	_____
Advertising	_____	Mo x 6	_____
Maintenance	_____	Mo x 6	_____
Taxes	_____	Mo x 6	_____
Legal and accounting	_____	Mo x 6	_____
Insurance (fire, casualty, worker's compensation, disability, liability, etc.)	_____	Mo x 6	_____
Miscellaneous	_____	Mo x 6	_____

Total estimated costs for start-up and 6 month operation $ _____

Fig. 193-2. Entrepreneurs are people seriously interested in creating and pursuing a challenging career path.

good source of funds. It is important to remember, though, that the interest rate is usually high. This is because the people involved want to receive a good return on their investment because of the risk they are taking.

Governmental agencies have been created to help people get started in business. Obviously, it is in the best interest of a country, state, or city to have a new business be successful.

Many times the government agency's interest rate and repayment schedule are more generous than that of private groups and banks. Applicants for these loans must often meet special qualifications, such as being a military veteran.

Ownership options: When establishing a business, it is necessary to decide what type of business organization to have. There are four types to choose from. All are discussed below. The first two are most frequently selected by those starting a small graphic arts business.

1. *Sole Proprietorship.* This is a one-owner business. The major advantages are that all profits belong to the owner and business decisions can be made quickly. Sometimes there is difficulty with obtaining long-term financing. The lack of available capital for major purchases and operating expenses can be a serious disadvantage.

2. *Partnership.* This type of organization consists of two or more co-owners engaged in a business for profit. The motivation factor is involved when people work together, and can be a great advantage. Difficult times in the business can usually be worked out effectively when two or more minds work together on possible solutions. Disadvantages stem from possible incompatibility of the partners and the difficulties in disposing of partnership interests.

3. *Corporation.* This business organization is a legal entity, separate and distinct from the shareholders who own it. An elected board of directors are responsible for electing or appointing corporation officers who take charge of the day-to-day business operations. The ability of the corporation to draw on the expertise of more than one individual is a major advantage to a corporate structure. Securing capital in large amounts is another excellent benefit for corporations. Two of the several disadvantages to a corporate structure are that it is more expensive to organize and profits distributed to shareholders are taxed twice. First the corporation pays taxes on the profits. Then stockholders pay taxes on the dividends that are paid based upon the corporation profits.

4. *Sub-Chapter S Corporation.* The advantages of a partnership are combined with those of a corporation to form this business structure. The limitation of each stockholder's liability to a fixed maximum amount is a major advantage of this business arrangement. Another advantage is that there is no regular corporate tax. Disadvantages include a limitation of fifteen shareholders.

Getting into business: Basically, there are three ways of becoming involved in a business as an owner. These are: (1) starting a new business, (2) buying an existing business that is either well established or struggling to exist, and (3) investing in a franchise, such as a printing chain.

1. Starting a new business. Having a new idea for a graphic arts business will probably require the establishment of a new business. Advantages include being the first within a given geographical location. This makes it easier to capture and retain a customer base. There is also the challenge of succeeding where no one else has made the effort. Of course, this can also be a disadvantage in that it may be difficult to become established. Customers, of course, are people who may or may not desire products or related services. Just because a graphic arts business is located in a populated area does not mean that you will succeed. A thorough analysis of the geographical location is valuable—before deciding where to locate (Fig. 193-3).

2. Buying an existing business. This is sometimes the best way to become the owner of a business. Advantages include the possibility of buying the business at a bargain price, saving time and effort in equipping and stocking supplies, and continuing the customer base of the former owner. Paying too much for the business, living down the poor reputation of the former owner, or the physical location of the building might be disadvantages that must be closely studied before selecting this option.

3. Investing in a franchise. A franchised business is part of a chain of many individually-owned businesses. The business headquarters' management personnel provide considerable information to the franchise owner. The right to market a standard series of products and/or services that are well known is a strong advantage to owning a franchise business. Training and management assistance are also valuable assets. Disadvantages include loss of a certain amount of control in the business. Also a user fee or a share of the profits must be paid on a regular basis to the franchisor. This method of getting

into business should be thoroughly studied before signing the contract.

Regulations to consider: Business owners are required to know the federal, state, and local regulations that affect their business operation. There are many such regulations. A few of the most common are discussed here. A competent attorney should be consulted for legal assistance with the laws and regulations affecting your business.

1. *Licensing.* Most licenses require payments of fees and are usually issued on an annual basis.

2. *Protection of the environment.* Considerable attention continues to be given to decreasing air, water, and land pollution. Depending on the type of graphic arts business, there may be local, state, or federal laws affecting what you can or cannot do. For example, check out the ordinances regarding chemical disposal, the landfill requirements for paper trimmings, and the burning regulations.

3. *Fair labor standards.* If you have one or more employees, the Fair Labor Standards Act specifies the minimum wage that must be paid, the maximum hours that employees are allowed to work, and the working conditions required within the business establishment. All businesses are not subject to this and other fair labor laws. It is important to check with the local office of the Department of Labor.

4. *Safety.* Working in a safe environment should be the right of every citizen. Unfortunately, this is not always the situation. In 1970, the Occupational Safety and Health Act (OSHA) was enacted to require employers to provide places of employment free from recognized hazards for their employees. OSHA officials visit businesses unannounced to inspect the safety practices and conditions in a plant.

5. *Taxes.* Business owners must be prepared to pay federal, state, and local taxes. They must also withhold federal, state, and local

---

BUSINESS SITE SELECTION ANALYSIS

Factor	Score
1. Centrally located to reach my market	_____
2. Physical suitability of building	_____
3. Type and cost of lease	_____
4. Provision for future expansion	_____
5. Overall estimate of quality of site in 10 years	_____
6. Adequacy of utilities (sewer, water, power, gas)	_____
7. Parking facilities	_____
8. Transportation availability and rates	_____
9. Nearby competition situation	_____
10. Traffic flow	_____
11. Taxation burden	_____
12. Quality of police and fire protection	_____
13. Environmental factors (schools, cultural, community activities, enterprise of business people)	_____
14. Quantity of available employees	_____
15. Prevailing rates of employee pay	_____
16. Housing availability for employees	_____
17. Merchandise or raw materials readily available	_____

APPLIED GRAPHICS TECHNOLOGIES

Fig. 193-3. This score sheet can be used to help determine the quality of selected graphic arts business sites. Each factor should be graded: "A" for excellent, "B" for good, "C" for fair, and "D" for poor.

income taxes from employee paychecks. Also, there are property, sales, FICA, and unemployment compensation taxes. A competent tax accountant is usually a good investment for business owners.

6. *Insurance.* Insurance is essential for a graphic arts business owner. The major types of insurance to consider are fire, general liability, vehicle, and workmen's compensation insurance.

Consideration must also be given to obtaining insurance coverage for crime, business interruption, glass, group life, group health, and disability. It is always wise to consult with two or more insurance agents to discuss the type and amount of insurance that should be purchased (Fig. 193-4).

MANAGING A BUSINESS

The first important step in owning a business is to give some thought to managing it. A business is an ongoing activity. Once started, it must receive attention on a regular basis. Most of the time, this means daily attention. Managing includes setting goals, structuring the company, and working closely to obtain the desired financial structure. It also means being attentive to promotion and marketing, being competitive, and managing employees. It means practicing fiscal responsibility through personal and business record-keeping. Managing means to know the business from top to bottom, and from side to side. It also requires those skills needed to work well with people.

IMPORTANCE OF PLANNING

Planning means setting goals and establishing a timetable for completing those goals. It also means determining how to measure results so you know exactly how well you are doing. These goals should be written in measurable terms. For example, a measurable goal might be, "To buy a building large enough to house my graphic arts business within three years of opening the front door

---

Insurance Checklist

Inventory
Building
Office equipment
Show equipment
Vehicles
Records
Currency or security
Employee personal
  property

Floaters
Theft and burglary
Floods
Windstorm and hail
Explosion
Riots
Vandalism
Glass
Lightning
Business interruption

Vehicle accidents
Collision
Bodily injury
Towing
Theft
Property
Liability

Life and health losses
Worker's compensation
Disability
Key executive insurance
  (partner)
Hospitalization and
  medical care
Life insurance
Worker's compensation
  claims (if caused by
  improper repair or
  negligence by service
  technicians)

Liability claims
Product
On-premises accident
  employees
Non-employees

Fig. 193-4. This checklist can be helpful in determining the needed insurance coverage for a graphic arts business.

---

for business." If this is a realistic goal based upon your known and expected financial conditions, it can be easily measured. Either you will or will not own a building. The building will either be of adequate size or too small. If possible, all goals should be written in this manner.

Adequate planning helps control stress both in yourself and in your employees. Knowing what should happen helps decrease the worry of being a business owner. Most of the time, a company owner with "controlled" stress will serve as an example to his or her employees. Some stress is good because it can serve as motivation to reach business goals.

STRUCTURING THE COMPANY

Most small businesses have a simple structure because there is no need to have anything different. A complex business organization is necessary only when the number of employees plus the products and services grow beyond a manageable situation for the one or two top people in a company.

The organizational structure serves as the framework for operating a business. It reflects the work and skill relationships of the people involved in a business. As with any structure, there should be flexibility to allow for changes without upsetting the established operations and goals.

Organizational charts are not essential, but they do help illustrate how various departments or individuals should work together to reach company goals. Charts are visual aids that show lines of authority. The complexity of organizational charts varies, depending on the size of the company.

RECORD KEEPING

Good record keeping is crucial to success. Eighty percent of small businesses fail within the first five years. Often, the reason for such failure can be attributed to poor record keeping. An entrepreneur must be prepared to keep adequate records or pay someone to keep them.

Keeping up-to-date records helps the owner determine which way the business is going. Is money being made or lost? Were printing jobs greater in number last month than one year ago? Records serve as a business barometer. They can be read and analyzed to determine if the business is financially sound. An accountant can usually look at the records of a company and tell if the business is stable and solvent. This assumes that the records are accurate and up to date.

One form of record keeping is the use of checks to pay bills. Checks are pieces of paper that serve in the place of cash. They are prepared (written) based upon the amount of money in a bank checking account. Each time a check is cashed by the recipient, the cashed check is returned to the original bank. The amount of the check is then deducted from the company account. The canceled check, one that has been cashed and recorded, is then returned to the company. The check is properly filed and serves as a legal record of the financial transaction. Most federal and state tax laws require companies and individuals to keep records for five years.

Personal checks serve the same function as checks do for businesses. They permit the individual to carry less cash on his or her person and provide excellent financial records. Banks provide monthly statements of financial activity, listing all checks written on the account. Each time a check is presented as payment to a business or another person, the transaction must be recorded. This record provides the individual with information on how much money is still left in his or her checking account.

HIRING AND SUPERVISING EMPLOYEES

Careful choice of employees is essential to the successful operation of any business. Before each employee is hired, a *job description* should be written. This is a statement describing what a person must and should do to be successful in the company. With the job description, it will then be possible to interview and hire employees. The job description also provides the employee and the employer with a basis for the evaluation of work performance.

Training is an important part of having employees. Employees need to know how you expect them to perform. They also need to know how to use the latest in equipment and supplies. A training plan, including the distribution of information and actual classroom presentations, is valuable for insuring the success of your employees.

Good supervision of employees is essential. Employees need to know when they are doing well and not doing well on the job. If errors are corrected early, employees will get more satisfaction from their jobs and perform better.

REMAINING COMPETITIVE

To stay in business means to watch and respond to what is happening to other graphic arts businesses within your market area. A business owner must expect competition from other entrepreneurs. To stay competitive, it is essential to keep technically up-to-date and provide quality products and services for every customer.

SOURCES OF HELP

There are several sources of assistance for anyone interested in starting a business. These sources include government, private, state, and local development agencies; universities; and private individuals. Being resourceful in determining where help can be found is the first major step in operating a successful business.

Possible sources are:

U. S. Small Business Administration
  Washington, DC 20416
U. S. Government Printing Office
  Washington, DC 20402
American Management Associations
  135 West 50th Street
  New York, NY 10020
SCORE (Service Corps of Retired Executives, volunteer business executive groups from local communities)
Community development agencies
University small business development centers
University incubator programs
University technology parks

SUMMARY

Owning a graphic arts business can be challenging and rewarding. It gives the entrepreneur potential for high earnings, control over his or her working conditions, and considerable flexibility. It will, however, require many daily hours of work along with the responsibilities of being the decision maker.

Success in a graphic arts business depends on many factors. Most can be controlled. Here are six ways to increase your business success: (1) Work hard to please your customers, (2) build and maintain a favorable business image, (3) encourage and develop teamwork among your employees, (4) plan well for today and tomorrow, (5) look for ways to increase profit volume while maintaining quality products and services, and (6) become involved in the community where your business is located.

UNIT 194 LEARNING EXPERIENCES: GRAPHIC ARTS CAREER OPPORTUNITIES

KEY TERMS

Unit 186
Apprenticeship   Journeyman

Unit 187
Compositor   Layout
Design   Production

Unit 188
Edition binding   Pamphlet binding

Unit 189
Motivation

Unit 191
Leadership

Unit 192
Entrepreneurship   Corporation
Sole proprietorship   Sub-chapter S Corporation
Partnership

DISCUSSION TOPICS

1. Why will there continue to be a need for graphic arts products?
2. How can a formal education help to qualify people to enter the graphic arts industry?
3. Why will it be necessary for people in type composition to take part constantly in training programs?
4. Why must a manager be good at the art of communication?
5. What are the opportunities in the paper industry for people who have an interest and competence in chemistry or law?
6. Identify ways to learn of graphic arts employment opportunities.

7. List the important points to consider in starting a business.
8. Identify the four main types of business ownership options.
9. List the three ways to become involved in a business as an owner.

ACTIVITIES

Units 186–189

1. Get career booklets describing opportunities within the graphic arts. These booklets are available from private industry as well as from local, state, and national graphic arts organizations. Talk with your school librarian and public librarian about materials available on careers in the manufacturing industries of which graphic arts is a part. Talk with your school vocational counselor, who should be knowledgeable about careers in several fields. One good source of information is the *Occupational Outlook Handbook* available from the U.S. Government Printing Office.
2. Visit a commercial graphic arts printing firm and talk with people in production, management, and sales about the opportunities in the graphic arts industry in your own geographical area. Talk with as many people as you can so that you build up representative sampling of ideas and opinions. Visit more than one commercial plant if possible. Prepare a detailed report of your visit and findings.

Units 186–190

3. Talk with your graphic arts teacher and other teachers about the opportunities and rewards of the teaching profession. Get information from the school vocational counselor, who should be able to

give you nationwide information on the teaching profession. Ask your graphic arts teacher what specific opportunities are available in the teaching of this technical area. Ask your teacher to let you try teaching by giving a short demonstration to fellow class members.

Unit 191

4. Visit a pulp and paper mill and talk with some of the production workers and management personnel. Get as much information as you can about the opportunities in the paper industry in your own geographical area as well as in the entire country. Watch all of the people on the job closely to see if the things that they are doing might interest you.

Units 186–189

5. After getting all of the information from the four previous activities, sit down and thoroughly analyze your findings. Ask yourself: What would I like to do? Am I interested in the graphic arts as a possible career? If so, what specific area might I be interested in? If at this time I cannot decide, where can I get more information?

Units 192–193

6. Interview someone who has started his or her own business. Ask that person what motivated them to start their business. Did they feel that they had the necessary information and resources at the time they started their business? In the time that they have been in business for themselves, have they found the satisfactions of entrepreneurship to outweigh the possible security of working for someone else. Ask them what advice they would offer to a beginning entrepreneur. Ask them to state that advice in two sentences.

GLOSSARY

Accelerators. Chemicals used to speed up the developing process of photographic film.

Acetic acid. A chemical commonly used in dilute solution with water as a stop bath for photographic film.

Additive plate. A pre-sensitized lithography printing plate usually coated with a diazo emulsion. Lacquer must be added to the surface to see the image.

Additives. Material added to prepared pulp to improve the quality of the paper.

Agitation. The act of moving the chemicals while processing photographic materials.

Airbrush. A compressed-air art tool for spraying ink or paint in a controlled manner.

Airbrush drawing. An illustration made with an airbrush.

Analine printing. The original name given to flexographic printing because alcohol-based analine dyes were used as the inks.

Analogous. A color harmony that results from using two colors next to each other on the color wheel.

Antihalation coating. A dye applied to the base of photographic film to absorb excess light.

Antihalation dye. A coating placed on film to prevent light from going through the film base.

Aperture. The part of the camera lens that adjusts to let more or less light through the lens. Aperture settings are called f-stops.

Aperture priority camera. A kind of camera on which the photographer sets the aperture and the camera automatically adjusts the shutter speed.

Apprenticeship. A specified period of time in which a person must work to learn the skills for a given technical trade. Also, the practice of learning a trade by working under the direction of a skilled worker.

Appropriateness. The measure of how well a typeface is suited for a specific printed product.

Artwork. A term sometimes used in place of the term *copy*.

ASA number. An outdated term. *See* ISO number.

Ascender. The top portion of a letter that extends above the main part of the letter, as in the letters *b, d,* and *h.*

Autoscreen film. A film that has a halftone screen built into the film emulsion.

Backbone. The back or binding edge of a case-bound book.

Backgage. The adjustable bar or fence on a hydraulic paper cutter that paper is positioned against to be cut at specific sizes.

Backing. Part of the case-binding method when the backbone is flared to receive the binder board covers.

Balance. The pleasing visual relationship of image elements on both sides of the vertical axis; can be formal or informal; a design principle of layout planning.

Base. In photographic and nonphotographic film, the material used to support the emulsion; also called support.

Basis weight. Refers to the standard used to specify the weight of paper, which generally refers to the paper thickness.

Bean cutter. A cutting tool designed to cut large circles in screen-printing film and stripping film.

Beating. Separating and modifying the wood fibers in the papermaking process so that the paper will be smooth and even.

Bellows. A light-tight area made of cloth or plastic material between the camera back and the camera lens. It permits the lens to be moved closer to or farther from the copyboard to focus the camera.

Binders board. A thick, gray colored, rigid paper board used in making a book case.

Binding. The process of fastening sheets of

paper together with wire, thread, adhesive, and other means, and covering them with hard material to form bound books.

Blackletter. A style of type that has a heavy and ornate face design; sometimes called Old English, and, in this book, text.

Blanket. A rubber-covered sheet used on the blanket cylinder of a lithographic or letter-set press that transfers the inked image from the plate to the paper (substrate).

Bleaching. Removing stains and other discoloring from the wood fibers in the paper-making process.

Blind embossing. The process of producing a raised (relief) image in paper (substrate) without using ink or hot stamp foil.

Block out. Liquid masking material used to cover the open areas of the screen printing fabric around the attached stencil.

Blotting. The process of removing excess water from screen-printing water-soluble film when adhering it to the screen fabric.

Body matter. The main blocks of typeset reading material on a page. Also called body copy.

Body type. Small face type in approximately the 7 to 12 point size range.

Bond paper. A category of printing paper generally used for printing letterheads, business forms, direct-mail advertising, etc.

Book paper. A category of printing paper generally used for printing books, pamphlets, catalogs, etc.

Book press. A special clamping device used to press books together in the hand case-binding method.

Bowl. The loop or rounded portion of a letter, such as in the letter *b*.

Bracket exposures. Making one or more exposures on both sides of the exposure calculated to be correct. This is done to be sure of obtaining one good exposure.

Bristol paper. A category of printing paper generally used for printing records, filing cards, self-mailers, file-folders, etc.

Buffers. Chemicals used in the developer to control the action of accelerators in photographic film processing.

Build-up. A flat piece of material, such as ¼-inch (6.35 mm) frosted glass, placed under the fabric when attaching a stencil to a screen printing unit.

Burnish. To rub dry transfer lettering with a smooth, blunt instrument or pen-like device in order to adhere it firmly to the base.

Calibrated gray scale. A piece of material with several shades of gray from white to black used in test exposures of photographic film. Each shade has been given a number value; also called Kodak Reflection Density Guide.

California job case. A compartmented drawer used for storage and retrieval of foundry type characters.

Camera back. The part of a process camera that holds photographic film in place with a vacuum while an exposure is made.

Camera body. Light-tight container that holds the film. The camera shutter is also located in the body of some cameras.

Camera lens. The part of a camera that passes light into the camera and focuses the photographic image.

Camera-ready. Typeset and artwork copy needing no preparation; ready to be photographed.

Capillary film. Used in screen printing for the printing stencil. *See* Presensitized direct film.

Carbon dioxide conditioning. One method of making a photopolymer plate very sensitive to ultraviolet light by displacing oxygen with carbon dioxide.

Caret marks. Cuts in the shape of inverted V's made in the packing of letterpress presses and used to align the makeready sheet with the typeform. *See* Platen dressing.

Carrier sheet. The material to which dry transfer lettering is attached.

Case binding. An expensive but durable type of binding in which a hard cover is placed on both sides of the bound sheets to form a useful book.

Casing-in. Part of the case-binding method in which the finished book bodies and book cases are united.

Casting box. A mechanical device used in the process of casting a stereotype plate from a paper matrix.

Casting. The process of pouring melted metal into a matrix, or mold, in order to make an impression; type is cast when molten typemetal is poured into matrixes to form the typeface.

Center mark. A small triangle cut made in a masking sheet to show the center of the masking sheet and to help identify the gripper edge of the plate.

Central impression flexographic press. A press that contains a large water-cooled central impression cylinder and has the printing units positioned around the outer edge.

Centricleaner. A special cleaner used in the papermaking process that separates unwanted materials from the prepared wood fibers.

Chalking. Ink that is smeared or easily removed from the printed sheet. The ink does not stick to the printed material.

Chase. Steel frame used for holding a letterpress typeform in a printing press.

Chaser lockup. A method of locking-up typeforms with dimensions of furniture that are not equal to standard furniture lengths.

Chipping. Reducing wood logs to small chips in the papermaking process.

Chokes. A photographic technique used to reduce the size of an image.

Chroma. The brightness or purity of a color. It is sometimes called the grayness of the color.

Chrome plating. The process of placing a thin coating of chrome over the surface of an engraved gravure cylinder to make it durable for long printing runs.

Circle cutter. A cutting tool designed to cut perfect circles in screen printing film and stripping film.

Clean floppy disc. A magnetic floppy or flexible disc containing error-free typeset copy.

Cleanup sheet. An absorbent, blotter-like sheet used on a lithographic duplicator to remove ink from the ink rollers.

Coding. Inserting special information in copy to be typeset. This information controls changes in the standard instructions, such as to insert subheadings, change to italic or boldface type, etc.

Cold type composition. Assembling alphabetical symbols by strike-on or hand mechanical methods. Some people include photographic and digital preparation of type in the 'cold' category.

Collate. To collect single sheets of paper in proper order. Collating is often done when making booklets.

Color correction. Adjustments made in the color separation process to bring the printed result as close as possible to the original photograph, despite the limitations of printing inks.

Color harmony. A pleasing combination of two or more colors used together in the same printed product.

Color printers. The negatives or positives resulting from the color separation process.

Color scanner. A computer-controlled machine used to make color separations by separating the four colors (yellow, magenta, cyan, and black) required to produce original color copy by one of the printing methods.

Color separation. The process of producing separate printing plates for each of the four colors in process printing.

Color wheel. A circular tool used by graphic designers that shows the primary, secondary, and intermediate colors.

Combinations. Both line copy and continuous-tone copy used together to prepare illustrations.

Commercial printing. The phase of the graphic arts industry that relies on piecework from a number of paying customers rather than from one customer only (as in inplant printshops) or one readership (as in newspaper, magazine, or book publishing).

Communication. The exchange of information among people using signs, symbols, gestures, sounds, or printed words.

Complementary. A color harmony that results from using two colors opposite each other on the color wheel.

Composing stick. A device (tool) in which foundry type is assembled into lines.

Compositor. The person who sets manuscript or handwritten copy into type in one of several typefaces; also called *typesetter*.

Comprehensive layout. A full-sized layout prepared by hand that shows the exact locations, colors, shapes, etc., of the image elements of a printed product—a master plan.

Coniferous. Cone-bearing, soft-wood trees that provide wood fibers used in the papermaking process.

Conservative typefaces. One group of the

novelty typeface classification. These typefaces have a novel or decorative appearance, but contain only minor alterations of standard typefaces.

Contact film. A type of photographic film used to make indirect contact exposures.

Contact print. A same size copy made with photographic materials in contact with a film negative or positive.

Contact printer. Equipment used to make photographic exposures with materials in contact. Same size reproductions result. Light passes through one material to strike another material that is in contact with it.

Contact screen. A type of screen used to produce halftone dots in high-contrast photographic film. It is placed in contact with the film during exposure.

Contemporary typefaces. A group of the novelty typeface classification. These typefaces have a novel or decorative appearance and are designed to echo as much as possible the thought or word that they convey.

Continuity. The look of belonging together; a design feature of typeface characters.

Continuous-tone color separations. Color separations that have not been screened to make halftones.

Continuous-tone copy. Copy that has various shades of gray plus black and white areas. A black and white photograph is an example of continuous-tone copy.

Contrast. The accenting of one or more elements in the total image elements of a page; a design principle in layout planning.

Cooper. Metal used in making a photoengraving; most often used when making half-tone photoengravings.

Copy. The original of an item to be printed. Copy is photographed to make an image carrier.

Copy cylinder. The cylinder of an electronic scanning or engraving machine on which the copy is placed.

Copy elements. Parts of a piece of copy; e.g., illustration, typeset or hand-lettered material, photographs. Common elements are line and continuous-tone copy.

Copy preparation. The pre-press phase during which type, illustrations, and photographs are assembled.

Copy support. Material (paper or board) on which copy is pasted up; also called the copy base.

Copyboard. The part of a process camera where copy is placed while the exposure is made.

Copyfitting. Preparing copy to fit a given space by choosing typesizes, leading, line length, etc.

Copyholder. A person who reads the original copy (manuscript) out loud to the proofreader.

Copying. Methods used to make prints directly from the original.

Copyright. The legal right of an author, artist, or composer to protect written and creative works against unauthorized copying by someone else.

Copyright infringment. Reproducing without permission a printed product protected by a registered copyright.

Copyright notice. The symbol or visual image that indicates that a publication has been copyrighted.

Copyright office. The facility located in the Library of Congress, Washington, D.C., where all copyright business is handled.

Counter. The central open area of letters where there is no image, as in the letter *o*.

Counter. The device on a printing press or other machine that counts and registers the number of sheets passing through it.

Counterfeiting. The process of imitating a sought-after product, such as paper money, designer clothes, or brand-name goods, with the intent to deceive the customer.

Cover paper. A category of printing paper generally used for printing booklet and manual covers, programs, announcements, etc.

Creasing. Placing an indention in paper in a narrow line to weaken the fibers so the paper will fold easily. *See* Scoring.

Cropping. Selecting the part of a photograph to be printed.

CRT. Cathode Ray Tube. The CRT is a vacuum tube that projects an electron beam on a fluorescent screen forming an image. In television, called a picture tube.

Cultural development. The process of improving the education and behavior of human beings; changes in the behavior, customs, and technology of human societies caused by education and the communication of ideas.

Culture. The knowledge, customs, arts, and tools of a human society transmitted to succeeding generations by means of education and permanent forms of communication.

Cursive script. The kind of script typeface where the letters do not touch but still look like handwritten or script letters. Also, see Non-joining script.

Cuts. Artwork converted to relief images for printing with letterpress presses.

Cutting stick. A wood or synthetic material used in a hydraulic paper cutter for the knife to strike at the end of its stroke.

Cyan. A color created with a combination of light from the primary light colors of blue and green. Used in process-color printing.

Cylinder press. A printing press design in which round and flat surfaces are used. Commonly used in letterpress and screen printing.

Cylinder cleaner. Special chemically formulated paste used to clean unwanted material from printing press cylinders.

Cylinder screen press. A screen printing press design using a flat rectangular frame for the fabric and stencil and a cylinder to hold the paper (substrate) while printing.

Cylinder system. A portion of a lithographic printing press that includes the plate, blanket, and impression cylinders.

Dampener. Refers to the various controls in the dampening system of a lithographic duplicator and press.

Dampening system. The dampening (water) rollers, fountain, and controls that regulate and apply dampening solution to the plate on a lithographic duplicator or press.

Dandy roll. The device used to produce a watermark in paper during its manufacture.

Darkroom. A room that can be darkened so light-sensitive materials can be processed.

Darkroom camera. A process camera in which the film can be loaded in the darkroom.

Daylight developing tank. A light-tight container that once loaded in a darkroom, can be used to process film in a lighted room.

Debarking. The bark-removing step in the papermaking process.

Deciduous. Hardwood trees that provide wood fibers used in the papermaking process.

Deep-etch plate. A lithography plate with the image slightly below the base material. The plates are used to print large numbers of copies.

Degreasing fabric. Removing the oily substance on the fabric to be used for screen printing.

Deletion fluid. A solution used to remove unwanted areas from pre-sensitized lithographic plates.

Delivery board. A wood board mounted at the front-center of a platen press and used to hold the printed sheets of paper.

Delivery system. A portion of a printing press designed to remove paper (substrate) from the press.

Densitometer. An electronic device used to measure the density of different materials.

Descender. The bottom portion of a letter that extends below the main part of the letter, as in the letters *p, q,* and *g.*

Design and layout. The production phase in which planning is done for a printed product.

Desktop composition. Assembling type, artwork, and halftones for printed products using special software and small (PC) computers.

Desktop publishing. *See* Desktop composition.

Developer. A chemical solution that changes exposed silver halide crystals on photographic film to black metallic silver; sometimes called a reducer.

Diaphragm. The part of a camera that controls the amount of light passing through the lens, measured in f-stops.

Diazo. A photo-sensitive emulsion usually coated on pre-sensitized lithographic plates.

Die cutting. The process of cutting special shapes into or from paper and other sheet materials.

Diffusion transfer. A photographic process used to make positive and negative reproductions directly from camera-ready copy using a process camera. This is done without the need for intermediate photographic steps.

Diffusion-transfer plate. A kind of lithographic plate made with a process camera without the need for negatives or flats.

Digital composition. A composition method in which the images, type, artwork, and halftone photographs are created with pixel images.

Digitizing. The process of converting visual images into many parts by electronic means, with each part being given a digital value.

Direct contact print. A photographic print that is the same size as the original.

Direct emulsion. A photosensitive liquid emulsion that is coated on both sides of a stretched screen in screen printing. When dry, the emulsion coating is exposed through a film positive and serves as the printing stencil. *See* Direct photoscreen.

Direct entry. Providing a typesetting machine with input data directly through a keyboard.

Direct photoscreen. A method of preparing a screen printing stencil by coating a light sensitive emulsion directly onto the screen fabric.

Direct-electrostatic copier. A kind of electrostatic copier on which the electrostatic charge is placed on a special coated paper.

Direct-image plates. Paper or plastic plates on which ink receptive (grease) images are typed or drawn.

Display type. Large face type approximately 18 to 144 points in size.

Doctor blade. A sharp steel blade that wipes ink from the non-image area of a gravure cylinder.

Dot etching. A hand color-correction technique done on color separation negatives.

DPI. Initials that stand for Dots Per Inch. Used to specify the fineness or coarseness of the images produced by computer laser printers and imagesetters.

Driers. Material added to printing ink to help it dry faster.

Dry point engraving. The process of producing images from hand-prepared intaglio plastic plates.

Dry transfer type. Alphabetical characters and illustrations pre-printed on the underside of special transparent carrier sheets.

When rubbed with a stylus, the images will transfer to another sheet, such as a paste-up.

Drying oven. A heated enclosure that holds portable drying racks to dry screen-printed products quickly.

Dual knife. A cutting tool with two knives that can be adjusted in width of separation and attached to a pen-shaped handle for use on screen printing film and stripping film.

Ductor roller. A printing-press roller that transfers ink or dampening solution from the fountain to the system of rollers.

Dummy layout. A folded representation of a booklet, pamphlet, or other multiple-page printed product, used to plan the location of pages in a signature.

Dumping. Removing foundry type from a composing stick.

Duotone. A two-color halftone reproduction of a single photograph.

Duplicate forms. Typeforms that are exactly alike. They are placed next to each other and printed on one large sheet. Later the large sheet is cut into the correct sizes.

Duplicating film. A type of photographic film used to make direct contact exposures: negatives from negatives and positives from positives.

Duplication. Methods of image transfer often used in offices. Duplication is usually less expensive than regular printing processes. Common methods are spirit duplication, mimeograph duplication, and lithography duplication.

Duplicator. A reproduction machine that generally requires less skill to operate and produces products of lower quality than a heavy-duty printing press.

Duplicator paper. A category of reproduction paper generally used when producing materials with the spirit duplicating process.

Easel. A device used to hold photographic paper in place while making projection prints with an enlarger.

Electrochemical. A process used in making an electrotype printing plate (*See* Electrolysis).

Electrolysis. The process of using electrical current to produce chemical changes needed when making an electrotype plate.

Electromechanical. Combining electronic

and mechanical principles and procedures to produce results, such as an imaged gravure cylinder, without using photographic film.

Electronic publishing. The systematic process of creating, assembling, editing, proofing, storing, retrieving, and preparing publications for printing and binding through the use of networking computers, printers, scanners, and imagesetters.

Electrostatic copier. An image-transfer machine where positively charged toner powder is attracted to a negatively charged image area and is heated until it fuses to create an imaged copy.

Electrostatic assist. A system designed to improve the ink transfer from a gravure cylinder to the substrate.

Electrostatic plate. A lithographic printing plate on which a printable image is placed with an electrostatic copier.

Electrotype. A duplicate, relief printing plate made mainly of copper and electrolytically formed from another relief image.

Elrod. A machine used to make leads and slugs for hot metal composition.

Em quad. Metal spacing material that is the square of a specific foundry type size. It is the basic spacing. In photographic typesetting, it is called the em space.

Em space. *See* Em quad.

Embossing. The process of producing a printed raised (relief) image in paper (substrate).

Emulsion. A thin coating that may or may not be light sensitive and that is applied to plastic or polyester sheets. Photographic film is a combination of light-sensitive emulsion and clear base material. Liquid, light-sensitive emulsion is applied to screen-printing fabric to make direct photoscreens.

Emulsion coating blade. A tool made of non-oxidizing metal used to apply light-sensitive liquid emulsion to the fabric of a screen printing frame.

En quad. Metal spacing material that is ½ the width of an em quad. In photographic typesetting, it is called the *en space*.

En space. *See* En quad.

Engraving. The process of removing material, such as in making the ink cells on a gravure cylinder. *See also* Intaglio.

Enlargement. Increasing the size of the copy photographically.

Enlarger. A machine used to make photographic projection prints (enlargements) of negatives.

Entrepreneurship. Being creative in the initiation of a business or product and having the knowledge and ability to be successful in the endeavor.

Enzyme. A product that causes a biochemical reaction to indirect photoscreen film, thus permitting it to be removed from screen printing fabric.

Etching. The removal of material, usually metal, by chemical action.

Extrusion. Method of making leads and slugs for hot metal composition; the metal is forced from the machine in strips.

F.P.M. Abbreviation for 'feet per minute.' F.P.M. is often used to designate the speed of a web printing press.

Fabric mesh. The fibers making up the screen fabric in screen printing; the fabric holds the stencil and permits ink to pass through.

Facsimile. A system of transmitting graphic images; the image is scanned and converted into electronic signals that can be sent by telephone or radio and used to make a copy of the original image at the receiving end.

Family. A group of specific typefaces having similar characteristics, e.g., Helios Lightface, Helios Bold, etc.

Fax. An abbreviation often used for the electronic image transmission system technically called facsimile machine.

Feed board. A wood board, mounted at the front-right of a platen press, used to hold the unprinted sheets of paper.

Feeding system. A part of a printing press designed to feed paper (substrate) into the press.

Ferrotype plate. A shiny and smooth sheet of metal on which photographic paper is dried.

Fiber-base paper. A kind of photographic paper consisting only of an emulsion coating on a high quality paper base.

Film knife. A cutting tool with a fixed blade attached to a pen-shaped handle. Often called an artist's knife.

Filmless engraving. The process of electronically engraving a gravure cylinder without using photographic film. A more accurate term to use would be *electronic engraving*.

Filter. Colored translucent material used in photography. Special filters are used on process cameras to make color separations.

Finishing. Includes the operations of folding, cutting, trimming, perforating, etc., to complete the manufacture of printed sheets.

Finishing and binding. The production phase in which printed materials are folded, cut, perforated, bound together, etc., to make a finished book or booklet.

First generation plate. A printing plate made directly from film negatives or by electronic scanning machines.

Fixer. A solution used to remove undeveloped silver halide crystals from photographic films and papers.

Flash exposure. An exposure used to give shadow detail to high-contrast, halftone negatives.

Flash lamp. A light used in photography for brief, intense exposures.

Flatbed screen press. A screen printing press design with the fabric and stencil attached to a flat rectangular wood or metal frame; the squeegee is pulled back and forth to force ink through the stencil to make printed copies.

Flexible letterpress plate. Thin relief plates that are attached to a printing cylinder.

Flexographic plate. A printing plate made of rubber or photopolymer that contains a relief image.

Flexography. A method of rotary letterpress printing that uses flexible rubber or photopolymer plates and fast-drying solvent-based fluid inks.

Floating on air. The condition created by blowing air into the top few sheets of paper in a press or other automatic feeding machine.

Flood stroke. In screen printing, to apply a coat of ink to the stencil immediately after raising the screen frame following printing.

Floppy disc. A plastic sheet that has been magnetically coated so that computer-generated data can be stored and retrieved. Often called a flexible disc.

Flush left or right. Type set to line up at the specified edge of the type area.

Focal length. The distance from the center of a camera lens to the focal plane when the lens is focused at infinity.

Focusing magnifier. A device used to help focus the enlarger when making projection prints.

Fogging. A weak, unwanted exposure on photographic film or paper.

Fold lines. Marks that are usually printed in the trim areas to show where press sheets are to be folded.

Folding bone. A flat stick-like device with smooth rounded edges used in hand-folding paper and in hand case-binding of books.

Folio. The page numbers on signature pages.

Font. An assortment of type of any one kind and style.

Form roller. A printing press ink or dampening roller that makes direct contact with the printing plate.

Forms duplicator. A specially designed web-fed lithographic duplicator used to print and produce multiple-part business forms.

Forwarding. A stage in case-binding when the book body is prepared to receive the case. It includes the specific operations of nipping, smashing, rounding, and backing.

Foundry type. Individual alphabetical characters that are cast in metal and are assembled by hand into lines ready to be used on a printing press.

Fountain solution. A solution of water, gum arabic, and other chemicals used in lithography to dampen the plate and keep nonprinting areas from accepting ink.

Fourdrinier. The endless wire belt on a papermaking machine. A name derived from the Fourdrinier brothers of England who built the first successful papermaking machine.

French curve. A drawing tool that serves as a pattern for producing curved lines.

Front case. The part of a process camera to which the lens and lens board are attached;

it moves in order to focus the camera.

Furniture. Wood and metal rectangular blocks placed between the typeform and chase to make a lockup.

Furniture-within-furniture lockup. A lockup method for letterpress typeforms with dimensions that are equal to standard furniture lengths.

f-stop. A numbered aperture opening on a camera lens; a ratio of the focal length of the lens.

Gallery camera. A process camera used in a lighted room.

Galley. A three-sided steel tray used for hot type storage and form make-up.

Galley proofs. Proofs made by one of several methods of columns of typeset material; used for proofreading.

Gathering. The assembly of printed signatures (sections) in preparation for binding.

Gauge pins. Special devices inserted into the tympan of the platen press dressing that hold the paper in place during printing.

Glass halftone screen. A precision screen placed between high-contrast photographic film and a camera lens to make halftone negatives.

Gloss inks. Inks that have a high gloss when printed.

Golden proportion. Created and used by the ancient Greek architects, the name given to a proportion in which the short part of a line has the same relationship to the long part as the long part has to the whole line (approximately 3 to 5). A page, type space, or illustration whose width and length are in the golden proportion are pleasing to the eye.

Goldenrod. The usual color of lithographic masking sheets.

Gothic type. A term inaccurately used to designate the sans-serif type classification. Because of its association with a style of architecture, it should be used to designate the Text typestyle.

Government Printing Office (GPO). The largest single printing plant in the world. Printed materials for the U.S. Congress and other government offices are produced there.

Graduate. A container used to measure quantities of liquids.

Grain. The silver halide crystals that become visible when photographic enlargement prints are made.

Grain focuser. A device used to produce sharp prints by focusing on the grain structure in a negative.

Grained plate. Lithographic printing plates on which the base material has been made rough to accept water better.

Graphic arts. The technical area of producing printed products. The term covers design and layout, copy preparation, photoconversion, image carriers, image transfer, and binding and finishing.

Graphic communications. The technology of communicating information through photographic, drawing, and printed means.

Gravure. An image transfer method in which an image is formed below the surface of the image carrier (plate) by photographic, chemical or electronic means. Ink is held in the recessed image area and then pressed onto a printing surface. *See also* Intaglio.

Gravure cylinder. The most common gravure image carrier, made of steel or copper, sometimes with a plastic or chromium coating, that contains the ink cells forming the printing image.

Gray scale. A strip of film or paper with a series of densities varying from clear (white) to black. Sometimes called platemaker's sensitivity guide.

Grid paper. Paper printed with light blue horizontal and vertical lines that are spaced at equal distances used for preparing layouts.

Gripper edge. The edge of the plate that fits into the plate cylinder clamps. Also, the edge of paper held by the press grippers when printed.

Gripper margin. A space marked on a masking sheet to show where the impression cylinder grippers will hold the press sheet.

Grippers. The finger-like devices on the impression cylinder and delivery units of a printing press that grasp and pull sheets of paper through the press.

Growth industry. An industry that grows at a greater rate than the economy as a whole.

Gum arabic. A liquid placed on pre-sensitized lithographic plates to prevent oxidation and minor scratches.

Gutter. The inner margin of a printed book or booklet; from type to binding.

Hair space. The narrowest space used for separating letters or numbers when setting type.

Halftone. A screened reproduction of continuous-tone copy such as a photograph.

Halftone exposure computer. A hand-held, nonelectronic device used to assist in determining halftone exposures.

Halftone-gravure. A special electromechanical process used in the preparation of gravure cylinders when printing magazine and catalog publications.

Hand mechanical type. Type composition prepared with template devices and by free-hand techniques using a technical inking pen.

Hand-cut film. Screen-printing stencil film that is hand cut with a knife.

Hard copy printer. An impact, laser, or thermal imaging machine that can be used to produce proofs of keyboarded copy for typesetting.

Hard copy proofs. Reading proofs made with impact, laser, or thermal printers, from copy that has been keyboarded on front-end typesetting machines.

Hard dots. Halftone dots that have fully formed. They appear as opaque dark dots in halftone film negatives.

Hardware. The equipment components of a computer system. *See also* Software.

Headbands. Colorful beads of thread used as decoration at the top and bottom of the backbone of a book.

Head margin. The white space at the top of a typed or printed page.

Heat sensitizing. One method of making a photopolymer plate very sensitive to ultraviolet light. Controlled heat is used to drive out the oxygen in the plate.

Heat sublimation ink. A special ink used in heat transfer. The ink turns to a vapor when heat and pressure are applied. The ink is most often used with textiles.

Heat transfer. A method used to place an image on another material by using heat and pressure. The process uses a special ink called heat sublimation ink or dye.

Heat-set ink. Ink that dries by using heat.

Hieroglyphics. A system of writing characters created by the Egyptian people using stylized pictures and symbols. Not an alphabet.

Highlights. The lightest areas on a positive print such as a photograph; the darkest areas on a film negative.

Hinge bar. The part on a hand-operated screen printing unit that serves as the hinge support for the frame.

Holland cloth. Material used as a protective covering for the ready-to-use rubber that is vulcanized into a rubber stamp.

Horizontal camera. A process camera in which the line of exposure is in a horizontal position.

Hot stamping. Placing images on various substrates by using relief type, heat, pressure and special imaging foil.

Hot type composition. Assembling alphabetical symbols prepared from molten metal.

Hue. Color, as in the color of printing ink.

Hydroquinone. In photography, the main developing agent; a chemical that turns exposed silver halides to black metallic silver.

Hypo. An abbreviation for sodium hyposulfite (sodium thiosulfate). *See* Fixer.

Ideogram. A picture or symbol used in a system of writing to represent a thing or an idea.

Illustrations. Photographs, drawings, and paintings used in printed matter.

Image breakdown. Loss of image in a lithographic plate while running on a press.

Image carrier. A device with a flat or round surface upon which an image has been etched, engraved, or photographically applied; used to reproduce printed copies.

Imagesetter. A composing machine in which laser light is used to expose type, line art, and halftones on phototypesetting paper and film. Images are produced at 2,450 dpi or higher.

Image transfer. The production phase in which images are printed on paper and other products.

Impact type composition. Alphabetical

characters formed directly on paper with an imaging machine; generally with a keyboard, a key containing the character, and carbon ribbon. *See* Strike-on composition.

Imposing stone. Now, a flat metal surface on which a letterpress lockup is made. Formerly, a limestone or marble surface was so used.

Imposing table. A table with a flat steel top and beveled edges on which foundry or hot type is handled and impositions made.

Imposition. The procedure of laying out pages so that they will be in the correct order when printed.

Impression. The act of transferring the image from the plate to the substrate during printing.

Impression cylinder. The cylinder on a printing press that provides a smooth, firm surface for the paper (substrate) during the printing action.

Impression lever. The part of a printing press used to control whether a print (impression) will be made.

In-plant shop. A printing or duplicating facility within a manufacturing company or business. This kind of shop does not do work outside of the parent company or business.

Incandescent light. Lights that use a hot wire in a vacuum to produce illumination; often used in photography because they are inexpensive but have the disadvantage of dimming with age.

Indirect contact print. A type of contact print in which a copy opposite from the original is produced.

Indirect photoscreen. The method of preparing a screen printing stencil by using a special light-sensitive film, which is attached to the screen fabric.

Infringer. A person who knowingly or unknowingly makes unauthorized copies of a work protected by a registered copyright.

Ink. A liquid or paste material used to produce an image on another material. Ink comes in different colors and forms to be used on different materials.

Ink brayer. Hand tool containing an ink roller and handle; used for spreading ink on the face of relief type forms prior to pulling a proof.

Ink cell. Minute dot-shaped areas engraved into a gravure cylinder.

Ink disk. The round plate-like device at the top of a platen press; used to distribute ink to the ink rollers.

Ink fountain. A special device designed to hold a supply of paste or liquid ink and to meter the ink to the ink rollers of a printing press.

Inking system. The ink rollers, fountain, and controls that apply and regulate ink to the plate on a printing press.

Inkjet printing. An imaging process in which tiny dots of ink are sprayed onto the receptor to form the images.

Inline flexographic press. A style of flexographic press that has one to several printing units positioned in a line so paper or other material can easily travel from one to another.

Input. Information given to a computer or computer-controlled machine so it can do its work.

Insoluble. The image parts of the photopolymer plate that have been hardened by the ultraviolet light and will not wash away.

Inspection light. Darkroom lights equipped with both ortho-safe and white lights; used to inspect film during and after processing.

Intaglio. Method of image transfer in which hand-prepared plates with below-the-surface images are inked and pressed on a printing surface. An example is engraving. *See also* Gravure.

Interface. Computer information connections.

Inermediate colors. Colors made by mixing a primary color with an equal amount of the secondary color next to it on the color wheel, e.g., yellow-green, red-orange, blue-violet.

Intertype. A brand of hot-type casting machine with a keyboard that casts a line of type in one piece.

ISO number. A number used to designate the light sensitivity or emulsion speed of photographic film. The initials ISO stand for International Standards Organization.

Italic. A typeface style that is slanted forward; used in small amounts to draw reader attention to parts of the printed matter that should be emphasized.

Joggers. Devices on a printing press that help to position sheets of paper in the delivery system.

Journalism. The occupation that includes writing, editing, and managing of publications that present information to a mass audience.

Journalist. A writer or editor for a periodical.

Journeyman. A person who has completed the apprenticeship requirements and who is a competent skilled worker in a technical trade.

Justify. To make all lines of type a certain length so that the right margin is even.

Kerning. Generally, the reduction of space between selected letter combinations like AW and TE. This improves the visual appearance of the line. Thus it results in good typography.

Key line. A copy-preparation method used when colors must butt or touch during printing.

Keyboard. Typewriter-like keys used to input information for computers or computer-controlled equipment.

Kick-leg. The support bar that keeps the screen printing frame up while a printed sheet is removed and a new sheet inserted.

Kodak Halftone Negative Computer. *See* Halftone exposure computer.

Kodak Reflection Density Guide. *See* Calibrated gray scale.

Lacquer. A liquid solution that is placed on additive pre-sensitized lithographic plates so the image can be seen.

Lacquer soluble film. Screen printing stencil film that is hand cut and whose emulsion will dissolve in lacquer.

Lacquer-base inks. Fast drying printing inks with a vehicle that can be thinned and dissolved in lacquer.

Laminating. The process of placing a thin layer of transparent film on both sides of a printed sheet.

Laser. An acronym formed from the phrase *Light Amplification by Stimulated Emission of Radiation.* A device using a single intense narrow light beam that can be perfectly controlled.

Laser printer. An image-producing device that is driven by input from a computer. Laser printers are capable of forming hundreds of type styles, line art, and halftones on uncoated bond papers.

Latent image. Film that has been exposed to a subject. The image becomes visible when processed in developing chemicals.

Layout. The combination of ideas presented in graphic form, used in planning and designing a product for printing.

Lead edge. The edge of a sheet that first goes into a printing press.

Leaders. Rows of dots or dashes used in tables to guide readers' eyes across open spaces to the next column.

Leading. Spacing between lines of type; also, the thin metal strips used to separate lines in hot metal composition.

Ledger paper. A category of printing paper generally used for printing bookkeeping record forms, statements, legal documents, etc.

Left cylinder end guard. A covering over the left end of the cylinder of a vertical cylinder letterpress that serves as a safety device during operation.

Legibility. The measure of how easily a type character or group of characters can be recognized and read.

Lens. A part of a camera made of glass, crystal, or clear plastic that bends light to focus an image on the film surface.

Lens collar. The ring on the outside of the lens barrel that turns in order to focus the lens.

Lensboard. The part of a process camera in which the camera lens is contained.

Lettering template. A device, usually made of plastic, containing letter and other image shapes that guide the technical inking pen when forming images.

Letterpress. An image-transfer method in which a raised image area is inked and then pressed to a printing surface; also called relief.

Letterset. A printing method that uses shallow flexible relief plates on an offset lithography press.

Letterspacing. Adjusting the space between

letters to improve the visual appearance or to assist in justifying a line of type.

Library corner. A special technique for folding book cloth around a corner of binders board when hand-binding a case-bound book.

Ligatures. Two or more letters tied together in design and cast in one piece of foundry type e.g., *ae, ff, ffi*.

Light meter. An electronic device used to measure the amount of light available for making an exposure on photographic film.

Light-sensitive emulsion. A liquid containing minute particles of light sensitive silver halides suspended in a gelatin solution.

Light table. A glass-top table with a light below the glass, used by strippers to prepare lithographic flats; also especially useful for tracing art and designing type.

Light trap. Two or more passages leading into a darkroom. By placing curtains within the passages, unwanted outside light is prevented from reaching the darkroom.

Light-safe (light-proof, light-tight). An area where light cannot enter and sensitive material such as coated direct photo-screen printing frames can be stored without being subjected to light.

Lignin. The natural glue-like material that bonds wood fibers together in trees.

Limestone. A porous rock, naturally formed from organic remains such as shells, used by Senefelder, the inventor of lithographic printing. It is still used today by artists to make lithograph prints.

Line copy. Copy that has only black and white image elements and no shades of gray. It is usually prepared by placing black images on a white background.

Line gauge. A measuring tool used to determine point and pica sizes, as well as inch measurements.

Line negative. A photographic film negative made from line copy. Clear areas correspond to black or red areas on the copy.

Linen tester. A type of magnifier used to inspect photographic film negatives and positives.

Lining. A stiff piece of paper placed over the backbone of a book body before the case is attached.

Linotype. A brand of hot type casting machine that produces lines of type by casting them all in one piece of metal.

Linseed oil varnish. A liquid material used as a vehicle to make printing ink.

Litho varnish. A vehicle or base used in lithographic printing ink.

Lithography. An image transfer method in which an oil-receptive image area accepts an oil-based ink, which is transferred to a rubber-covered cylinder and then transferred onto the printing surface; also called planographic printing or offset lithography (litho for short).

Living index. A measure of the quality of living of people in a given area or country.

Lockup. The procedure used to hold a letterpress typeform in a chase.

Loop knife. A cutting tool with a loop or circle shaped blade attached to a pen-shaped handle, used to cut screen printing film and stripping film.

Loose-leaf binding. The binding category that includes ring binding, post binding, base-and-prong binding, and friction binding.

Lowercase letters. The small letters of the English alphabet.

Ludlow. A brand of hot type casting machine without a keyboard; it casts a line of type in one piece.

Magazine. The storage case for matrixes (molds) in a slug typecasting machine. Also, a printed booklet with a regular publication schedule, containing a variety of topics.

Magenta. A color created with a combination of light from the primary light colors of blue and red; the color of one of the printers in four-color process printing.

Magnesium. Metal used in making a photoengraving.

Magnetic ink. Inks that have pigments sensitive to electronic devices. This kind of ink is used to print material such as numbers on bank checks.

Main exposure. An exposure used to produce highlight detail in a halftone negative. It is made through the lens with the copy in the copyboard of the process camera.

Makeready. Generally, all work done before running a printing press. In letterpress, the process of equalizing the impression of all parts of a typeform.

Makeready sheet. A piece of paper containing pieces of thin tissue paper in selected areas, used to equalize the impression of the type for letterpress printing.

Manuscript. The typewritten or handwritten copy from which type is set.

Margins. The area of white space at the four edges of a printed page.

Mask. In process-color photography, a negative with a weak image of the original color copy; used for color correction of copy.

Masking. Blocking out unwanted areas in and around an image being prepared for printing. Also, a technique used to obtain a multicolor print from a single piece of copy.

Masking sheet. The base material used to make a lithographic flat.

Mass communication. To communicate to large numbers of people. The mass media include radio, television, and daily and weekly newspapers.

Matrix. A pattern or mold used in casting metal; matrixes are used in casting hot metal type; a stereotype is cast from a specially prepared paper matrix.

Matrix board. A special fiber material used to create a sunken but right-reading mold for vulcanizing a rubber stamp.

Mechanical binding. The binding category that includes the specific methods known as spiral wire and plastic cylinder.

Mechanical fabric treatment. Scrubbing screen-printing fabric with a powdered cleanser and water to clean and roughen the fabric fibers.

Mechanical layout. An actual camera-ready paste-up of the image elements that serves as the last chance for a customer to make changes. Also called a *mechanical.*

Mechanical-color. Color copy separated for each color by hand rather than by electronic color separation methods.

Mercury vapor light. A kind of light that produces ultraviolet light for making printing plates.

Mesh count. A numerical system for identifying the fineness or courseness of screen printing fabric.

Metal halide light. An extremely bright light source used to expose printing plates.

Metallic ink. Ink containing metal powders as pigments. *See* Magnetic ink.

Microfiche. A sheet of film containing rows of microimages of printed page matter.

Microform. A generic term used for the several methods of storing images in extremely small spaces on light-sensitive film.

Microprocessor. A miniaturized version of the central processing unit of a standard computer.

Microstorage. The storage of data in extremely small form, generally on photographic film.

Middle tones. The gray areas of a photograph that are lighter than shadows and darker than highlights.

Mimeograph duplication. An imaging process of making printed copies from a stencil (image carrier). Ink passes through holes in the stencil. This method is sometimes called stencil duplicating.

Mimeograph paper. A category of printing paper generally used when producing materials with the mimeograph duplicating process.

Mitography. The artistic application of printed images through a stencil pattern and screen fabric. *See* Screen printing.

Modern type. A style of type with serifs that are generally straight, thin, and slightly rounded at the corners. The thin and thick strokes have extreme contrast. Generally considered part of the Roman typeface classification.

Moiré. An undesirable mottled pattern that results when two or more halftone images are printed on top of each other at the wrong angles.

Molleton. Absorbent thick cotton flannel-like material used as covering for lithographic dampening rollers.

Monochromatic. Having one hue or color.

Monofilament fabric. A type of synthetic material used for the fabric in screen printing that has only one filament or unit in each thread of the fabric.

Monotone. Having uniform lines; term used to describe the square-serif typeface because the letter strokes are often of the same width throughout the entire series of characters.

Motivation. The driving force that makes a person want to accomplish one or more tasks.

Mounting block. The specially shaped device, usually made of wood, to which a rubber stamp is fastened.

Multifilament fabric. A type of synthetic material used for the fabric in screen printing that has several threads twisted together to form each strand of the fabric.

Negative. An image that has densities opposite from those of the original subject. Generally refers to photographic film.

Newsprint. A category of printing paper generally used for printing newspapers, handbills, telephone directories, etc.

Nicked corner. A special technique for folding book cloth around a corner of binders board when hand-binding a case-bound book.

Nipping. Part of the case-binding method when the binding edges of the sewn signatures are pressed together with heat and pressure.

Obscenity. Material of low moral value, arousing disgust or erotic feeling in the viewers.

Occupational Safety and Health Act. Government legislation enacted to require employers to provide places of employment free from recognized hazards.

OCR. Initials which stand for Optical Character Recognition. An optical character reader scans typed material and converts it into electronic impulses that can be stored on tape or disk or fed into a computer typesetting system.

Off-contact. The technique used in screen printing when the stencil and screen frame do not touch the substrate except at the squeegee contact point.

Offset. The mechanical printing press principle of transferring ink from a plate to a blanket and then to paper (substrate).

Offset paper. A category of printing paper generally used for printing manuals, form letters, advertising, etc.

Offset letterpress. A printing method using flexible relief plates on an offset lithography press. (*See* Letterset).

Oil-base inks. Printing ink with a vehicle that can be thinned or dissolved with a petroleum solvent.

Old English. Another name for the Text typeface classification.

Oldstyle type. A style of type with rounded serifs and moderate contrast between the thin and thick letter strokes. Generally considered part of the Roman typeface classification.

Opaque. A material that does not permit light to pass through; A liquid material used to cover unwanted clear areas in a film negative.

Opaquing. Covering unwanted clear areas in film prior to making a lithographic plate exposure.

Optical center. The visual point or line in a space where the image elements will appear to be centered from top to bottom; located slightly above true center.

Optical disc. A high-density storage and retrieval device. *See* Videodisc.

Ortho-safe light. A light to be used during film processing that will not expose orthochromatic film. *See* Safelight.

Orthochromatic film. A category of photographic film that is blue and green light sensitive, but insensitive to red light.

Oscillator roller. A printing press ink or dampening roller that moves horizontally back and forth while turning, to help equally distribute ink or dampening solution.

Output. The results of the work produced by a computer or computer-controlled machine; e.g., the material produced by a typesetting machine.

Overexposure. Admitting too much light into a camera, resulting in an overly dense film negative.

Overlay. A sheet of paper attached to copy. The overlay is used to protect copy and to make notes. The copy for additional colors of a job is often placed on an overlay sheet.

Overlay sheet. A translucent (semi-transparent) sheet of paper placed over a comprehensive layout; used for listing specific instructions to art and copy preparation personnel.

Padding. A method of binding that uses liquid adhesive to fasten the single sheets of paper together.

Page description languages. Computer software programs that permit word processing and typesetting technologies to be brought together so data input can be transferred to one from another.

Page proportion. The size relationship of a page width to its height.

Pallet. A tool used for printing or gilding letters on book bindings. Also, a wooden platform to which bulky freight or cargo, such as bulk paper or folded and gathered sheets, is strapped for transport.

Panchromatic film. A category of photographic film that is sensitive to all three primary colors of light.

Pantograph. A tool or machine for quickly and accurately enlarging a smaller design; used to produce a matrix for foundry type.

Paper ribbon. A narrow web of paper either one or two book pages in width that is created by slitting (cutting) the wide web of printed paper in the finishing section of a web printing press.

Paper stencil. A stencil formed by cutting the image in a sheet of paper and attaching it to the fabric of a screen printing frame with ink.

Papyrus. A pre-paper product made by the Egyptians from papyrus reeds that grew along the Nile river.

Parallax. The term used to identify the error in the image difference from that seen in the camera viewfinder and that covered by the lens.

Paste-up. The procedure of attaching elements (type matter and illustrations) in the proper location to make a finished piece of camera-ready copy.

Percentage. The amount of enlargement or reduction of a piece of copy. Enlargements are shown as over 100%. Reductions are shown as less than 100%.

Perfect binding. The binding that uses adhesive to fasten the cut edges of individual sheets of paper together along the back.

Perforating. Cutting or punching a series of slits or holes in paper to facilitate tearing.

Phonogram. A symbol or character used to represent a word, sound, or syllable in a system of writing.

Photoconversion. The production phase in which camera-ready copy is converted to photographic film or paper.

Photoengraving. A relief printing plate made by photographic, chemical, and mechanical means.

Photograph. A picture made using a camera, processing equipment, photo paper, and chemicals. It is the most common kind of continuous-tone copy. *See* Photographic print.

Photographer's sensitivity guide. A strip of material with several shades of gray from white to black; often called a gray scale.

Photographic. Image-transfer method in which an image is made by means of a light source, a film negative, and light-sensitive paper. The image on the light-sensitive paper is made visible with developing chemicals.

Photographic print. A positive image made on photographic paper.

Photographic technician. The person who produces photographic film negatives and positives of imageset material from which printing plates are made.

Photolettering. The typesetting of display-sized letters, usually from 48 points to several hundred points in size.

Photopolymer. A plastic material used in the preparation of printing plates.

Photoprocessor. A machine for automatically processing photographic materials.

Photoresist. A light-sensitive liquid material used in making relief and intaglio printing plates.

Photosensitizing. One method of making a photopolymer plate very sensitive to ultraviolet light by exposing the plate to ultraviolet light through a special filter.

Phototypesetting. The method of producing alphabetical characters and other symbols by photographic means.

Pi. In printing, to drop or scramble hand-set foundry type.

Pica. A size value used to measure the length of lines of type. One pica is equal to 12 points; 6 picas equal approximately one inch.

Pictogram (Pictograph). An ancient or prehistoric drawing or painting done on a cave or rock wall.

Pigments. The material that gives color to ink and paint.

Pinholes. Small clear holes found in the black areas of a film negative; caused by dirt, contaminated developer, etc.

Pixel. A minute spot or space that makes up an electronic or photographic image.

Plain-paper copier. An electrostatic copier used to make copies on regular, untreated paper.

Planer block. A block of wood used to press all relief type down against the imposing table surface.

Planographic. *See* Lithography.

Plastic cylinder. A round, comb-like device used to bind a group of single sheets together.

Plastisol inks. A classification of screen-printing ink containing resin and plasticizer that will not air-dry on a screen or printed product. To dry (cure), the ink is subjected to intense, high heat such as that of infrared rays.

Plate bend. The part of the lithographic plate that is bent to fit into the clamp that holds the plate on the cylinder.

Platemaker. The person who prepares plates for printing on presses. The term is also used to identify the machine in which plates are exposed.

Platen. The flat plate-like area on a platen letterpress machine where the paper is positioned for printing. Commonly used in letterpress, screen, and intaglio printing.

Platen dressing. The sheets of paper used to cover the platen of a letterpress platen press; often called packing.

Platen press. A classification of a printing press on which the substrate (paper) and image carrier (type, plate, or stencil) are both in a flat or smooth position during the image-transfer (printing) operation.

Platen safety guard. A metal bar and attached heavy canvas that raises each time the platen press closes. Designed to keep hands from being caught between the platen and typeform.

Plates. *See* Image carriers.

PMT. Eastman Kodak's trademark label for materials used in the diffusion transfer process.

Point. A size value used to measure typefaces. Approximately 72 points equal one inch (2.54 cm).

Point source light. A device that produces light from a single spot or point.

Polarity. The condition of being electrically charged negative or positive. Electrostatic image transfer uses negative and positive charges to make the image.

Pornography. Printed material that is intended to cause sexual excitement.

Positive transparency. A processed orthochromatic film containing a right reading image.

Post binding. A method of binding in which two or more bolt type posts are used to fasten sheets of paper together.

PostScript.® A software language that was specially prepared for use with laser printers and imagesetters. The language makes it possible to produce hundreds of typestyles on these machines. Created and owned by Adobe System Incorporated.

Practicality. The measure of whether a typeface is available and economically suitable for a job.

Pre-layout planning. The thinking involved in answering some important questions before preparing a set of graphic layouts; usually summarized on a pre-layout planning form.

Presensitized direct film. Factory-manufactured, light-sensitive film that is attached to the fabric mesh of a stretched screen printing frame. It is exposed while on the screen fabric, washed out, and used as the printing stencil. Also, referred to as capillary direct film and capillary direct photostencil.

Presensitized indirect film. Factory-manufactured, light-sensitive film that is exposed, developed, and washed out before attaching to the fabric mesh of a stretched screen printing frame. Also, referred to as indirect photoscreen and indirect photostencil.

Presensitized plate. A lithographic plate that has a photosensitive emulsion coated on the surface of the metal, plastic, or paper base by the manufacturer.

Preservatives. Chemicals used to lengthen the usefulness of photographic developers.

Press. A precision piece of equipment that includes all controls and parts to produce high-quality printed products.

Press sheet. The cut paper size used to run through a printing press.

Pressing boards. Flat wooden boards with

a metal flange edge used in pressing hand-made case-bound books in the final binding stage.

Pressure sensitive. Material that has an adhesive coating that will stick to a surface when pressed lightly. A waxed carrier sheet holds the pressure sensitive material until needed.

Primary colors. The transmitted primary colors (light) are red, blue, and green. The reflective primary colors (pigment) are red, yellow, and blue.

Print dryer. A machine on which photographic prints are dried by using heat.

Printing belt. A strong but flexible belt used for mounting and printing thin flexible relief photopolymer plates on the Cameron Book Production System.

Printing side. The bottom side of a prepared screen printing frame, which is against the product being printed.

Process camera. A large camera used to photograph flat, two-dimensional copy. It is used to make enlargements, reductions, and same-size reproductions.

Process-color. The technique used to separate full-color copy into negatives or positives (usually three or four) that will faithfully reproduce the original.

Processing trays. Trays used to hold chemicals for developing, stopping, fixing, and washing photographic film; made of plastic, hard rubber, fiberglass, or stainless steel.

Projection print. An enlarged photograph made from the images on a negative.

Proof. A copy of an original that is made to check for errors before additional production work is done.

Proof press. A machine used to make copies (proofs) of relief typeset material so the type can be proofread.

Proof sheet. A photographic contact print made to obtain positive images of continuous-tone negatives.

Proofing. The process of making a copy of typeset material so it can be proofread for errors.

Proofreader. A person who carefully reads and reviews typeset copy for errors—spelling, spacing, positioning, etc.

Proofreaders' marks. Special symbols for marking errors or changes to be made in typeset copy.

Proofreading. The act of closely reading a proof of some typeset material to detect errors—spelling, spacing, positioning, etc.

Proportional scale. A device used to determine the percentage of enlargement or reduction of copy or to find the final dimensions for reproduction.

Public Law 94-553. The current copyright law.

Pulping. Processing the wood chips and logs to release the wood fibers from their lignin bonds during the papermaking process.

Pulsed xenon light. A bright light used in process photography and platemaking. Brighter than quartz light, pulsed xenon lights are used for both black-and-white and color work.

Punch-through. A condition, caused by too much press packing, in which the relief type presses too hard on the paper and makes a raised image on the back side.

Quartz light. A type of bright light that does not dim with age, used in black-and-white photography and platemaking.

Quick-set ink. Ink that dries rapidly on paper.

Quoins. Wedge-shaped devices used to tighten the furniture against the relief typeform and the chase. Quoin keys, or wrenches, are used to tighten the quoins.

Rangefinder. A part of a camera used to help the photographer focus a camera.

RC photographic paper. Light-sensitive paper with a special resin-coated surface.

Re-etching. A hand color correction technique done on color separation plates.

Readability. The measure of how efficiently a typeface can be read.

Reading proof. A copy (proof) of typeset material used in the proofreading process.

Receptors. The material on which the printing is done. Some receptors are paper, glass, wood, metal, plastic, cloth, and ceramic. Receptors are sometimes called substrate.

Recessed. A lowering or indentation of the image area from the non-image area. The intaglio and gravure image areas are recessed by mechanical or chemical means.

Reciprocity. The use of set combinations of apertures and shutter speeds to obtain a correct exposure.

Recycled paper. Paper manufactured in part from used paper.

Reduction. Making the size of copy smaller.

Refining. The papermaking step in which the wood fibers are cut and shortened to produce a more uniform pulp.

Reflection copy. Opaque copy that is photographed by reflecting light from the copy to the film. *See* Transmission copy.

Register. Correct positioning of images while printing on a substrate with other images.

Register marks. Cross-line marks used to help align images during stripping and printing.

Register pin. Devices placed in the holes made with a register punch. They are used to locate flats and plates accurately on the printing press.

Register punch. A punching machine used to make accurate round holes in masking sheets and plates for positioning copy during the pre-press stage and while printing.

Registration. The repeated printing of images in the correct position.

Reglets. Thin pieces of furniture used in making a letterpress lockup.

Rejustify. The process of making a line of foundry type the correct length after corrections have been made.

Relief. *See* letterpress.

Reproducibility. The measure of how well a typeface can be reproduced by using one or more of the printing processes.

Reproduction proof. Final proofs made on paper suitable for being photographed in order to make printing plates. Also called repro proof.

Resin-coated paper. A kind of photographic paper that has a resin coating on the paper base material. Abbreviation: RC.

Restrainers. Chemicals used in photo processing that slow up the speed of development.

Resumé. A brief written record of work experience, highlighting the job strengths of the applicant.

Reversal. A kind of line copy in which areas that normally would be white are made black; e.g., white lettering on a black background.

Rhythm. A design principle that gives a sense of order and movement in the page or visual content; an important factor in layout planning.

Right-reading film positive. A high-contrast photographic film positive with the emulsion on the right-reading side. For use when making photo stencils in screen printing.

Rotary press. A classification of printing press on which the substrate (paper) and image carrier (plate or stencil) are both wrapped around cylinders during the image transfer (printing) operation.

Rotary screen press. A screen printing press design with the fabric and stencil attached around a cylinder and the squeegee positioned in the center.

Rotogravure. Printing by the gravure method on a web-fed press.

Rough layout. A full-size layout that is a refinement of the image element arrangement in a thumbnail sketch.

Rounding. Part of the case-binding method in which the book body is given a convex shape on the backbone and a concave shape on the front edge.

Rubber stamp. A piece of vulcanized rubber containing a relief image, generally mounted on a special wood holder.

Rubbing-up. A name given to the procedure used to process a pre-sensitized lithographic plate.

Rules. Thin metal strips used to print borders and lines; the printed lines themselves.

Ruling pen. A pen made for drawing precise straight or curved lines. *See also* Technical pen.

Saddle. The center of a printed signature where it is stitched or stapled.

Saddle-wire stitching. A method of binding in which wire staples are placed through the folded edge of gathered signatures.

Safelight. A special colored light that will not expose certain categories of photographic materials. It is usually red, yellow, or green.

Same size. Making a print of equal size to the copy.

Sans-serif. A style of type without serifs (*sans* means without).

Scaling. Marking the finished size of copy or illustrations.

Scanner. An electronic-based machine designed to digitize graphic images and enter the data into computer memory for use in preparing pages of text, line art, and halftones.

Scoring. Placing a crease in paper in a narrow line to weaken the fibers so the paper will fold easily. *See* Creasing.

Scratch board. A piece of prepared drawing board coated with chalk. White lines are made in inked areas of the board by scratching through the chalked surface.

Screen base. Serves as the printing surface and the frame-hinging support for a hand-operated screen printing unit.

Screen fabric. The porous material that is tightly stretched over a screen printing frame and holds the stencil.

Screen frame. The rigid device, wood or metal, that holds the screen fabric tight.

Screen printing. The method of producing printed images by forcing ink through a hand or photographically prepared stencil that is attached to screen fabric.

Script. A typeface classification in which the letters look like handwriting; nonjoining letters are called cursive script.

Scroll. An early book form made from a roll of animal skins or crude paper.

Scumming. Ink printing in the non-image areas of a lithographic plate where it should not print.

Second generation plate. A duplicate printing plate made from a mold or pattern of an original plate.

Secondary colors. Colors made by mixing equal amounts of two primary (reflective) colors; they are orange, green, and violet.

Sensitivity guide. *See* Photographer's sensitivity guide.

Sensitization. Making the sensitive layer of a photopolymer plate very sensitive to ultraviolet light.

Sensitizer. Liquid powder, or crystal concentrate material, that is the light-sensitive agent mixed with the base emulsion to form the ready-to-use emulsion for direct photoscreen printing.

Series. The several sizes of mechanical type available in one kind and style.

Serif. A finishing stroke at the end of a main character stroke on many different styles of type. Originally, a finishing stroke added by stone cutters when carving inscriptions.

Set width. Width of a type character.

Setoff. Ink that transfers to the back of printed sheets while the ink is wet.

Sewing frame. A device used when sewing signatures together in hand case-binding.

Sewing tape. Nonadhesive strong fabric tape used to help hold the sewn signatures together in hand case-binding.

Sewn binding. A bookbinding method that uses thread to fasten sheets and signatures of paper together.

Shade. The degree of black in a color; grayness.

Shadows. The darkest areas on a positive print—the lightest areas on a photographic negative.

Sheetwise. A method of printing a signature. Half of the pages are printed on one side and the other half on the second side. This is sometimes called work-and-back.

Shutter. A part of the camera that controls how long light can enter the camera.

Shutter priority camera. A kind of camera on which the photographer sets the shutter speed and the camera computer automatically adjusts the aperture.

Side register guide. A guide on a printing press that must be accurately adjusted to obtain proper printing position.

Side-wire stitching. A method of binding in which staples are placed through the side or edge of single sheets of paper.

Signature. A group of pages of a book, booklet, or magazine printed on the same sheet. After printing, the sheet is folded so that the pages are in their correct places.

Silhouette method. A technique of preparing artwork for photosensitive screen printing.

Silk screen printing. An outdated term. *See* Screen printing.

Silver halide. The light-sensitive chemical used in many photographic emulsions.

Silverless film. A kind of film that uses an emulsion other than silver. The most common alternate emulsion is diazo.

Silverpoint drawing. A drawing done with a metal pencil on special paper.

Single-lens reflex camera. A category of camera that lets the photographer view the subject through the same lens that is used to take the picture.

Slitting. Cutting a web of paper with a sharp knifelike roller while the web passes through the finishing section of a printing press or paper folder.

Slug caster. Machine used for casting complete lines of relief type. *See* Intertype and Linotype.

Slugs. Lines of type made with hot type line casting machines. Also, strips of metal generally 6 points thick used to space and secure lines of foundry type.

Smashing. A step in the case-binding method in which the entire group of sewn signatures is pressed together to insure a consistent book thickness.

Sodium thiosulfate. Chemical used to fix the image on a photographic film after developing. *See* Fixer.

Soft dots. Halftone dots that have not fully formed. They appear to be brown on a halftone photographic negative.

Software. Programs written for computers and stored on a diskette. *See also* Hardware.

Space (two-dimensional). Area where words, artwork, and photographs are to be located and printed; a design element in layouts.

Specking. Small dots of ink that can be seen between halftone dots and in the clear areas of printed material.

Spell-check software. A computer program that individually compares words in a computer file with correctly spelled words in the computer dictionary.

Spirit duplication. An imaging method of making limited copies from a master (image carrier) with an analine dye image. The dye image is dissolved with an alcohol base solution so that it transfers when pressed against the paper to be printed on.

Spotting. A term sometimes used instead of *opaquing*.

Spreads. A photographic technique used to increase the size of an image.

Squeegee. A screen printing implement that contains a rubber or synthetic blade that is used to force ink through a stencil.

Squeegee side. The side of an attached screen printing stencil which the squeegee is rubbed against when making a printed image.

Stabilization. A special photographic process that requires only a two-chemical bath for processing phototypesetting paper and photographic prints.

Stack flexographic press. The original flexographic press design; it is similar to rotary letterpress and can contain one to six color printing stations.

Stencil. Material that serves as the image carrier in screen printing.

Step-wedge (test-strip). An exposure method to determine the best length of time to expose light-sensitive material.

Stereotype. A duplicate relief printing plate made mainly of lead and cast from a paper matrix.

Stock sheet. The large paper size generally purchased from the paper company and from which press sheets are cut.

Stop bath. A solution used in film processing to stop the action of the developer.

Strike-on type composition. *See* Impact type composition.

Strike-through. A problem of ink going through the sheet of paper. The ink can be seen on the back of the sheet of paper.

Stripper. A person who makes flats for preparing lithography plates.

Stripping. Process used to combine negatives and masking sheets into a flat that is used to expose a lithography plate.

Stripping blade. A pen-shaped tool with a rounded metal blade used to remove unwanted cut screen printing film and stripping film.

Stripping film. Non-photographic film made of two layers–the emulsion, usually red or orange, and the base–used to form visual images.

Stroke. A line that forms a letter or a part of a letter; e.g., the letter *t* has two strokes, *s* and *l* have one, and *B* has three (in hand block lettering).

Stylus. The smooth blunt instrument used to rub dry transfer type from the carrier page and adhere it firmly to the receptor.

Subheading. A less prominent heading used under a main heading or within a block of type matter.

Sublimable ink. Ink that is printed on paper and later transferred to cloth with heat and pressure.

Subtractive method. A technique used to eliminate primary colors from copy in the color separation process.

Subtractive plate. A pre-sensitized lithography plate with a diazo and lacquer surface. The lacquer is removed from the plate to form the non-image areas of the plate.

Super. Gauze-like fabric that is adhered to the backbone of a book with glue for the purpose of improved strength.

Surface plate. A lithography plate to which the image is applied by photochemical means.

Swivel-blade knife. A cutting tool with a rotating blade attached to a pen-shaped handle for use on screen printing film and stripping film.

Synthetic enamel inks. Printing ink that gives a glossy surface on decals, outdoor signs, and hard surfaces.

T-square. A drawing and drafting tool used to draw right angles and perpendicular lines.

Technical inking pen. A specially designed inking pen used to make precise lines and images. Pen points are available in different line widths.

Text paper. A category of printing paper generally used for printing booklets, brochures, menus, etc.

Thermographic copiers. A machine used to make copies by using heat reflected from the original.

Thermography. An imitation engraving process that produces raised printing by using a special powder and heat.

Three-em space (3 em). Metal spacing material used in foundry type composition that is $\frac{1}{3}$ the width of an em quad. It is the most common word spacing.

Three cylinder design. A lithographic duplicator or press containing the three standard cylinders–plate, blanket, and impression.

Thumbnail sketches. Small, simple idea sketches for a printed page, showing only rough outlines and no detail of pictures or words.

Timer. A kind of clock used to measure specific amounts of time.

Tint. A panel of color over which an illustration may be printed; various even-tone areas of a solid color.

Tonal range. The difference between the highlight density and the shadow density of a photograph as measured by a densitometer or calibrated gray scale.

Transfer-electrostatic copiers. A kind of electrostatic copier in which the electrostatic charge is placed on a photoconductive plate.

Transitional type. A style of type with serifs that are relatively long and contain smooth, rounded curves. Generally considered part of the Roman typeface classification.

Transmission copy. Copy which is photographed by passing light through the copy to the camera. Transparencies like 35mm slides are the most common kind of transmission copy.

Transparent. A material that light can pass through.

Triadic. A color harmony using any three colors at the points of an equilateral triangle on the color wheel; e.g., orange, violet, and green.

Trim lines. Marks printed on the press sheet to show where the sheet should be trimmed after printing.

Tusche. A liquid used to form the stencil image in the tusche and glue screen printing method. Also, a form of greasy ink used to repair holes in solid areas of a presensitized plate.

Twin-lens reflex camera. A category of camera with two lenses. One lens is used to view the subject and focus the image. The second lens is used to make the exposure. *See also* Parallax.

Two cylinder design. A lithographic duplicator containing two cylinders—the blanket and the combination cylinder—that includes the plate and impression areas.

Tympan. The special, smooth paper used as the packing sheet on platen and cylinder letterpress machines.

Type bank. A cabinet designed to hold

foundry type cases and line spacing material. It often has a sloping top where type cases can be placed during use.

Type casting. Molding movable metal (foundry) type; done by a line casting machine.

Type composition. Assembling alphabetical symbols into words, sentences, and entire pages.

Type matter. Letters used to form words.

Typecase. Cabinet used for storing type. See California type case.

Typeface. A particular style of letter, number, and punctuation marks with common design elements.

Typeform. A set of lines of metal type arranged into paragraphs or pages.

Typesetter. A composing machine in which negative film fonts or digitized CRT technology is used to expose high-quality type characters on phototypesetting paper or film.

Typesetting. The process of creating or assembling alphabetical symbols into words, sentences, etc., for the purpose of printed communication.

Typo. An error in typeset material; the abbreviation for the words *typographical error.*

Typographer. A person able to make typesetting decisions regarding kind of type, style, size, line lengths, line spacing, etc.

Ultraviolet curing ink. Ink that is dried by passing printed sheets under an ultraviolet light.

Ultraviolet. Light beyond the violet end of the visible spectrum that cannot be seen and that is used in making photopolymer printing plates.

Undercut (cylinder). The amount a printing press cylinder is made smaller to accept a thick plate or a blanket.

Underexposure. The condition of having too little light so that the image in the photographic material is thin and lacking in detail.

Unitized. To determine the quantity of space that type characters occupy when typeset.

Unity. The tying together of the image elements; a design principle in layout planning.

Uppercase letters. The large letters of the English alphabet; also called capitals.

UV inks. Printing ink used to print on most substrates that can be cured instantly by a high-output ultraviolet light source.

Vacuum frame. The part of a platemaker that causes tight contact between film and the plate.

Vacuum printing frame, vacuum camera back. Devices used to hold photographic material in tight contact by vacuum.

Value. The lightness or darkness of a color.

Vehicles. Liquids or pastes in which pigments are placed to make ink.

Vernier wheel. A small knurled wheel that is used to tighten the plate on the plate cylinder of a lithographic duplicator.

Vertical camera. A process camera with the line of exposure in a vertical position.

Videodisc. A high-density storage and retrieval device in which lasers are used to add and retrieve the information.

Vulcanized. The process of treating rubber or plastic material with chemicals or with heat to give the material useful properties such as elasticity, strength, and stability.

Wash drawing. An illustration made with ink mixed with water; water colors may also be used.

Washing out. Using running water to remove the image area of an exposed sheet of indirect photoscreen film and direct photographic stencils.

Washout screen. Similar to the tusche and glue method of preparing a screen printing stencil–painting in the image, blocking out the non-image area, then opening up (washing out) the image area.

Water mixer. A device attached to hot and cold water pipes to blend the water to a specific temperature.

Water soluble film. Screen printing stencil film that is hand cut and contains an emulsion that will dissolve in water.

Water-base inks. Printing ink with a vehicle that can be thinned and dissolved with water.

Watermark. An image placed in paper during manufacture without using ink.

Waxes. Material added to ink to prevent setoff.

Welding binding. A method of binding in which sheets of paper are bound together by ultrasonic radio waves.

Wetting agent. A solution used with continuous-tone photographic film to prevent water spots during processing.

Wetting down. Mixing pigments and vehicles together to make ink.

Whirler. A machine that contains a platform which turns and is used to evenly distribute light-sensitive coatings on printing plate material.

White space. Blank space on a page; an important design element.

Wicket dryer. An endless belt of lightweight metal racks that hold each screen-printed sheet during the drying travel distance.

Widow. A single word or part of a word that rests by itself on a line. Widows are not considered good typography.

Widow line. A very short last line of a paragraph that is used as a beginning for a new column or page. Widow lines are not considered good typography.

Window. A clear space in a high contrast line negative of copy into which a halftone negative will be inserted.

Wire staple binding. The binding category that includes the methods known as saddle-wire and side-wire.

Wood block. A relief image carrier or printing plate prepared from a block of wood with special cutting tools.

Wood cut. A relief printing plate. *See* Wood block.

Wood engraving. A relief printing plate. *See* Wood block.

Word processing. A method of typing on a computer-like machine in which the keyboarded material is seen on a video screen and recorded on magnetic media so that it can be manipulated before being printed out and stored for future correction and use. Word processed material can be input directly to computer typesetters for type composition without further keyboarding.

Word spacing. Adjusting the space between words to improve the visual appearance or to assist in justifying a line of type.

Work-and-tumble. A method used to print on both sides of a sheet of paper. Sheets are first printed on one side. The sheets are then turned end for end to print the second side.

Work-and-turn. A method of printing on both sides of a sheet of paper. The lead edge of the sheet remains the same when the sheet is printed on the second side. The lead edge is the edge that first goes into the press.

Wraparound plate. A flexible plate, generally of the letterpress type, that is wrapped around a printing cylinder and clamped in place before being used for printing purposes.

Yellow. In transmitted light, the combination of the primary colors of green and red. In reflected light, yellow is one of the primary colors and is one of the printers used in process color printing.

Zinc. Metal used in making a photoengraving, which is sometimes called a zinc cut.

INDEX

Solution for crossword puzzle on page 543